Southern Living®
Travel South

**by Rand McNally and
the Travel Editors of
Southern Living® Magazine**

Oxmoor House, Inc.
Birmingham, Alabama

Foreword

Travel South is the second edition of a vacation guide prepared for you by Rand McNally and the Travel Editors of *Southern Living* magazine.

In this guide you will find the most complete, up-to-date information available about travel in the South. To aid you in planning your vacation there are maps, descriptions of attractions throughout the South, and specific information, such as hours of operation and admission prices for each.

If you or any of your traveling companions are handicapped, telephone numbers for the various places of interest are included so that you can inquire about facilities available to make your visit convenient and comfortable. You may also telephone regarding the latest operation schedules and admissions, as these do change from season to season.

The best way to use the guide to plan a trip is first to consult the United States Map, which shows major roads. It appears on pages 10 and 11. The Driving-Time Map, on pages 12 and 13, shows distance and driving time between major cities. Since weather is important in planning when and where to go and what to wear, a Weather Chart for major Southern cities is on pages 14 and 15. Some Southern Vacations are described on pages 6 through 8, and pages 16 through 48 give pertinent information for 16 Southern states and Washington, D.C. and special vacation possibilities in each. Adjoining this information is the state map for each.

The greatest portion of the guide is devoted to Major Events and state Destinations, and these appear on pages 49 through 199. The places of interest found in Destinations are listed under cities and towns within each state. The text on page 50 explains how to use the section on Destinations.

Travel South is designed not only to give you information which will be valuable in planning your vacation, but to provide pleasurable reading material about the South and to show the beauty of the region in photographs and illustrations. We hope you find the guide both useful and enjoyable.

Library of Congress Catalog Card Number: 81-83639

Copyright © 1982 by Oxmoor House, Inc.

Book Division of Southern Progress Corporation

P.O. Box 2463, Birmingham, Alabama 35201

Southern Living® is a federally registered trademark of Southern Living, Inc.

ISBN: 0-8487-0534-3

Manufactured in the United States of America

Contents

Foreword   2
Southern Vacations   6-9
United States Map   10-11
Driving-Time Map   12-13
Weather Chart   14-15
State Introductions and Maps   16-48
State Destinations   49-199
Acknowledgments   200

INDEX TO THE STATES

ALABAMA
Introduction/Map   16-17
Major Events   51
Destinations   52-57
    Places of Interest
    Birmingham Map
    Special Features
Campgrounds   58

ARKANSAS
Introduction/Map   18-19
Major Events   59
Destinations   60-64
    Places of Interest
    Buffalo National River Map
    Special Features
Campgrounds   65-67

DELAWARE
Introduction/Map   20-21
Major Events   68
Destinations   69-72
    Places of Interest
    Special Features
Campgrounds   72

FLORIDA
Introduction/Map   22-23
Major Events   73
Destinations   74-81
    Places of Interest
    Tampa-St. Petersburg and
      Miami Maps
    Special Features
Campgrounds   81-82

GEORGIA
Introduction/Map   24-25
Major Events   83
Destinations   84-93
    Places of Interest
    Atlanta Map
    Special Features
Campgrounds   93-94

KENTUCKY
Introduction/Map   26, 28-29
Major Events   95
Destinations   96-102
    Places of Interest
    Louisville Map
    Special Features
Campgrounds   102-103

LOUISIANA
Introduction/Map   30-31
Major Events   104
Destinations   105-110
    Places of Interest
    New Orleans Map
    Special Features
Campgrounds   110

MARYLAND
Introduction/Map   20-21
Major Events   111
Destinations   112-119
    Places of Interest
    Baltimore Map
    Special Features
Campgrounds   119

MISSISSIPPI
Introduction/Map   32-33
Major Events   120
Destinations   121-125
    Places of Interest
    Natchez Trace Parkway
    Special Features
Campgrounds   125-126

NORTH CAROLINA
Introduction/Map   34, 36-37
Major Events   127
Destinations   128-134
    Places of Interest
    Charlotte Map
    Special Features
Campgrounds   135

OKLAHOMA
Introduction/Map   38-39
Major Events   136
Destinations   137-142
    Places of Interest
    Oklahoma City Map
    Special Features
Campgrounds   142-144

SOUTH CAROLINA
Introduction/Map   35-37
Major Events   145
Destinations   146-152
    Places of Interest
    Charleston Map
    Special Features
Campgrounds   152-153

TENNESSEE
Introduction/Map   27-29
Major Events   154
Destinations   155-160
    Places of Interest
    Nashville Map
    Special Features
Campgrounds   160-161

TEXAS
Introduction/Map   40-43
Major Events   162
Destinations   163-173
    Places of Interest
    Dallas-Fort Worth, Houston,
      and San Antonio Maps
    Special Features
Campgrounds   173-175

VIRGINIA
Introduction/Map 44, 46-47
Major Events 176
Destinations 177-184
    Places of Interest
    Richmond Map
    Special Features
Campgrounds 184-185

WASHINGTON, D.C.
Introduction/Map 48
Major Events 186
Destinations 186-191
    Places of Interest
    Washington, D.C. Street Map
    Special Features

WEST VIRGINIA
Introduction/Map 45-47
Major Events 192
Destinations 193-198
    Places of Interest
    Special Features
Campgrounds 198-199

Southern Vacations

Travel almost anywhere in the South, and you are always near water, whether it is the icy freshness of a mountain stream, the placid flatness of an island lake, or the salt spray of the ocean.

In the mountains, you find crystalline streams tumbling musically over and around rocks worn smooth through the eons. Waterfalls plunge powerfully over precipices into mountain gorges, their roar sometimes drowning out conversations between viewers. One of the states best known for its waterfalls is North Carolina. In the western part of the state are some 50 waterfalls, most of them along U.S. 64. There is Connestee Falls, named for an Indian princess who, so legend goes, threw herself from the top of the falls after being deserted by her English adventurer husband. Whitewater Falls is said to be the highest cascade in the region, its upper falls dropping some 411 feet. Bridal Veil Falls plummets right over a part of the highway, and Dry Falls allows you to walk underneath without getting wet.

Hidden in the folds of the South's foothills are the rivers and lakes, prime destinations for floating, fishing, sailing, and other water sports. For the adventuresome, there is the wild whitewater ride down the Gauley River in West Virginia. In contrast, the Chattahoochee River in Georgia offers a more sedate float trip.

One of the most popular lakes in the region is Greers Ferry in Arkansas. Formed by the impoundment of the Little Red River, it encompasses 276 miles of shoreline. In the middle of the lake rises Sugar Loaf Mountain, laced with hiking trails and topped by huge boulders favored by picnickers. Along its shores are resorts such as Indian Rock and Fairfield Bay. And tucked into the inlets, especially in early morning when the mist rises and paints the landscape with an opaque light, are the fishermen who seek their luck in the cool lake.

Elsewhere are lakes such as Guntersville and Eufaula in Alabama, Jackson and Okeechobee in Florida, Sidney Lanier in Georgia, Norman and Gaston in North Carolina, Norris and Watts Bar in Tennessee, and Ray Hubbard and Travis in Texas. All are popular, especially in summer.

Then there is the lure of the ocean, which draws vacationers like a magnet. Of the 16 Southern states, 11 claim coastlines on either the Atlantic Ocean or the Gulf of Mexico. Their beaches are as diverse as the states themselves, and the vacation experiences run the gamut, from the undeveloped beauty of nature under the stars to the luxury of resort and ocean rolled into one. Even the color and texture of the sand changes from one area of the South to another. Along the upper Atlantic Coast of the South, and again along the western Gulf Coast, the sand appears darker and is coarser to the touch. The most beautiful of all is the powdery sand of the Florida Panhandle, so brilliantly white the glare of the sun reflecting off the beach makes sunglasses a necessity.

The South's beachfront begins in Delaware, as the coastline slips around Cape Henlopen and out of Delaware Bay to face the Atlantic Ocean with what is known as the Delmarva Peninsula. Three states—Delaware, Maryland, and Virginia—share the peninsula. Along its shores are the older, established resort towns of Rehoboth Beach and Bethany Beach in Delaware, and Ocean City in Maryland. Chincoteague, Virginia, once a quiet fishing village, has in recent years become more crowded with summer visitors, mainly because of its proximity to Assateague Island. On the northern end of the island, which lies in Maryland, is the Assateague Island National Seashore. On the southern end, which lies in Virginia, across from Chincoteague and accessible by paved road, is the Chincoteague National Wildlife Refuge. The beach here stretches for miles and is excellent for sunbathing, strolling, and at times, surf fishing.

With a climate that ranges from temperate to sub-tropical and is pleasant year-round, the South holds a special appeal for people who like to spend their leisure time enjoying the outdoors. It really makes no difference what kind of outdoor activity you prefer; whatever it is, the South has it — especially water sports. Two-thirds of the Southern states border on either the Atlantic Ocean or the Gulf of Mexico; the others have more than their share of lakes, streams, and rivers. The photographs on these pages only hint at the vast number of possibilities: Sailing on a quiet lake; gathering seashells; building sand castles; angling for any one of dozens of species at an inland lake or stream on the ocean or gulf; jogging with wild horses, such as these on Cumberland Island National Seashore, off the Georgia coast; cruising in Florida waters on a paddle-wheeler; cooling off in the surf; or plowing the whitewaters of West Virginia in a rubber raft. It is only fair to add, however, that there is an abundance of things to do on dry land. Hikers, climbers, and backpackers revel in the hills and mountains of the Blue Ridge, Great Smokies, and Alleghenies, all part of the Appalachian chain. In other parts of the South, you can play on some of the world's finest golf courses, conjure up the romantic antebellum days in a visit to a Southern plantation, or recall the past in a visit to a historic battle site or the home of one of our early statesmen.

Some of the best surf fishing lies farther South. Below the resort area of Virginia Beach lies a stretch of barrier islands still relatively rustic and, in places, isolated. These are the Outer Banks of North Carolina. Fishing is good here most of the year, but it is best in fall, when anglers often haul in 15- and 16-pound bluefish during a run. The most popular fishing spot in the whole area is a spit of sand known as Cape Hatteras Point, within sight of the famous Cape Hatteras Lighthouse.

The small towns of the Outer Banks—Buxton, Hatteras, Rodanthe—contrast sharply to the resort areas that lie yet farther south, beginning with Myrtle Beach, South Carolina, and extending down into Florida.

Nicknamed the "Grand Strand," the 60-mile-beach area, including and lying to either side of Myrtle Beach, boasts numerous hotels, motels, resorts, fishing piers, and more than two dozen golf courses that bring visitors year-round. And this is only the beginning of the resort facilities to be found as you travel down the coast.

Kiawah, a short drive south of Charleston, South Carolina, is one of the best-planned and -executed developments along the Southern coast. It provides not only the luxury of a resort, but opportunities to appreciate the natural aspects of the island as well. Jeep safaris to explore the undeveloped areas of the island, available through the resort, are well worth the time and money involved. And if you walk along the beach at night, it's as if you're all alone with just the stars and the ocean, so cleverly have the resort facilities been placed behind the dunes.

Hilton Head in South Carolina sports excellent resort facilities, as do Seabrook and Fripp islands; and in Georgia, as do the islands off the coast near Brunswick. The famed Cloister on Sea Island is perhaps one of the most elegant of island resorts, almost an institution in the South. On Jekyll, smallest of the sea islands, some of the nation's wealthiest families built their winter homes and vacationed between 1886 and 1947. The names Gould, Rockefeller, and Vanderbilt are still spoken in reference to the magnificent homes along "millionaires' row" on the island.

Associated with Georgia's Cumberland Island is yet another name—Carnegie. Most of the island is now

Two particularly well-known places in the watery realm of the South are Sanibel Island in the Gulf of Mexico off Florida's west coast and Greers Ferry Lake in north-central Arkansas. Over 400 varieties of seashells wash onto the beaches at Sanibel and neighboring Captiva Island; the Greers Ferry Lake Water Festival in August includes water-ski shows, boat races, musical entertainment, and the hot-air balloon races.

under the jurisdiction of the National Park Service and is preserved as a national seashore. But descendants of Thomas Carnegie still live on the island and allow guests to stay overnight in one of the family homes. Greyfield Inn, reached only by private boat or ferry service from Fernandina Beach, Florida, provides a quiet, relaxed retreat very different from the bustle of other islands. One of the great joys of a visit to Cumberland is cycling or walking from the inn or from one of the campsites available through the park service to the beach, which is so deserted you often can walk for miles without encountering another person. Beachcombing and shelling are excellent here.

An even more relaxed atmosphere prevails on Little St. Simons Island, Georgia. Accommodations are rustic, and nature reigns supreme.

The coast of Florida seems to be almost solid beach, with natural areas mingling enticingly among the more developed stretches. Along the Atlantic, Canaveral National Seashore provides a natural anchor to popular places on either side, such as Daytona Beach, New Smyrna Beach, Cocoa Beach, and Vero Beach.

Among the special places along Florida's Gulf Coast are Sanibel and Captiva islands, where shellers have flocked year-round for as long as anyone can remember. St. Joseph Peninsula State Park, near Port St. Joe, is considered by many to be one of the most beautiful undeveloped stretches of beach anywhere in the region. And still as popular as ever are the resort areas of Panama City, Fort Walton Beach, Pensacola Beach, and Destin, where deep-sea fishing is the prime water sport.

Both Alabama and Mississippi briefly touch the Gulf of Mexico. Alabama takes advantage of its beachfront with Gulf State Park, a state resort park with excellent overnight and sports facilities, and Gulf Shores, a small resort town that has made a strong comeback from the destruction caused by Hurricane Frederick in 1979.

Mississippi spreads its Gulf Coast towns along U.S. 90. Biloxi is the largest, with a thin strip of beach right along the highway and easy access by boat to the unspoiled beauty of Ship Island out in the Gulf.

Alone among the South's coastal states, Louisiana has more marshland than beach along the Gulf. Its best-known beach, which seems better known to fisherman than to sunbathers, is on Grand Isle, almost due south of New Orleans. The route to Grand Isle is a long one, though, winding down St. 1 alongside beautiful Bayou Lafourche.

The Texas coast forms a crescent that offers a number of well-used beaches. The one at Sea Rim State Park, near Port Arthur, melts gently into marshland, so that a visit here offers not only a beach experience, but an opportunity to view the marsh either on foot via a boardwalk or on an airboat ride. Galveston has long been a popular resort area and is even more attractive now with the reopening of the old Galvez Hotel, which for years was just a remnant of earlier luxury.

The queen of Texas beaches, though, is Padre Island, which curves beside the coastline from Corpus Christi almost to the Mexican border, a distance of 110 miles. Padre Island National Seashore covers 81 of those miles. The northern tip of the island is undeveloped and provides an excellent day's outing. The southern tip is more developed, with a variety of hotels, condominiums, and marinas where you can charter a boat for fishing.

Summertime is the traditional season for a trip to the beach. But many of the South's beaches, particularly the southernmost ones, are being used in winter as well. When cooler weather approaches, the beaches are less crowded. Sunbathing isn't popular then, but in some places fishing is better then than at any other time, and so is shelling. According to conchologists, most shells are washed to shore in winter, when storms out in the Gulf and the Atlantic break them loose from their homes in deeper water and send them tumbling landward.

Whether traveling to the shore, to an inland lake, or to one of the many island resorts, *Travel South* includes aids for planning your trip. Among these are a United States Map, a Driving-Time Map, state maps, places of interest, major city maps, and campground locations and information.

State maps, on pages 16 through 48, show major roads and places. The Map Legend below explains the symbols, signs, and markings on the maps.

Major Events, places of interest under the heading Destinations, and Campgrounds appear on pages 51 through 199. The text on page 50 explains how to use this information.

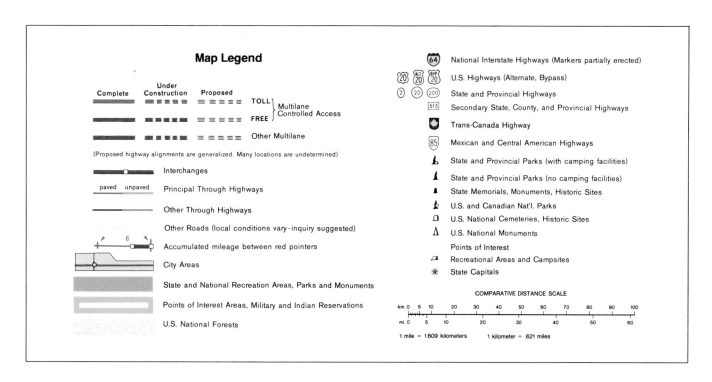

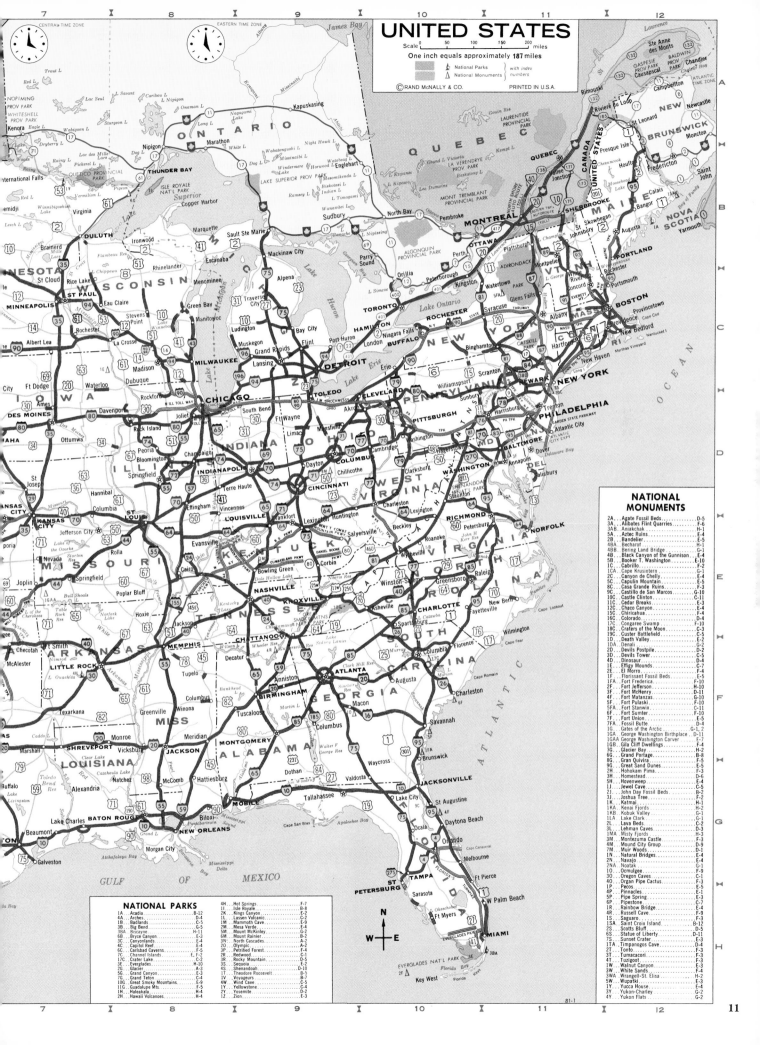

UNITED STATES

Scale
One inch equals approximately **187** miles

▲ National Parks
△ National Monuments

with index numbers

© RAND McNALLY & CO.   PRINTED IN U.S.A.

NATIONAL MONUMENTS

2A	Agate Fossil Beds	D-5
3A	Alibates Flint Quarries	F-6
3AB	Aniakchak	H-1
5A	Aztec Ruins	E-4
4B	Bandelier	E-4
4BA	Bechoraf	H-1
4BB	Bering Land Bridge	G-1
4B	Black Canyon of the Gunnison	E-4
5B	Booker T. Washington	E-10
1C	Cabrillo	F-2
1CA	Cape Krusenstern	G-1
2C	Canyon de Chelly	E-4
4C	Capulin Mountain	E-5
8C	Casa Grande Ruins	F-3
9C	Castillo de San Marcos	G-10
10C	Castle Clinton	C-11
11C	Cedar Breaks	E-3
12C	Chaco Canyon	E-4
15C	Chiricahua	F-4
16C	Colorado	D-4
17C	Congaree Swamp	F-10
18C	Craters of the Moon	C-3
19C	Custer Battlefield	C-5
1DA	Death Valley	E-2
2D	Devils Postpile	D-2
3D	Devils Tower	C-5
4D	Dinosaur	D-4
2E	Effigy Mounds	D-7
2E	El Morro	E-4
1F	Florissant Fossil Beds	E-5
2F	Fort Frederica	F-10
2F	Fort Jefferson	H-10
3F	Fort McHenry	D-11
4F	Fort Matanzas	G-10
5FA	Fort Stanwix	C-11
5F	Fort Pulaski	F-10
6F	Fort Sumter	F-10
7F	Fort Union	E-5
7FA	Fossil Butte	D-4
1G	Gates of the Arctic	G-1, 2
1GA	George Washington Birthplace	D-11
1GAA	George Washington Carver	E-7
1GB	Gila Cliff Dwellings	F-4
3G	Glacier Bay	H-2
6G	Grand Portage	B-8
8G	Gran Quivira	F-5
9G	Great Sand Dunes	E-5
1H	Honokam Pima	F-3
3H	Homestead	D-6
5H	Hovenweep	E-4
1J	Jewel Cave	C-5
2J	John Day Fossil Beds	B-2
3J	Joshua Tree	F-2
1K	Katmai	H-1
1KA	Kenai Fjords	H-2
1KB	Kobuk Valley	G-1
1LA	Lake Clark	G-1
2L	Lava Beds	C-2
3L	Lehman Caves	D-3
5L	Misty Fjords	H-3
3M	Montezuma Castle	E-3
4M	Mound City Group	D-9
7M	Muir Woods	D-1
2N	Natural Bridges	E-4
2N	Navajo	E-4
2NA	Noatak	G-1
1O	Ocmulgee	F-9
2O	Oregon Caves	C-2
3O	Organ Pipe Cactus	F-3
1P	Pecos	E-5
4P	Pinnacles	E-1
5P	Pipe Spring	E-3
6P	Pipestone	C-7
1R	Rainbow Bridge	E-4
4R	Russell Cave	E-8
1S	Saguaro	F-3
1SA	Saint Croix Island	B-12
6S	Scotts Bluff	D-5
6S	Statue of Liberty	D-11
7S	Sunset Crater	E-3
1TA	Timpanogos Cave	D-4
2T	Tonto	F-3
4T	Tuzigoot	F-3
1W	Walnut Canyon	E-3
5W	White Sands	F-5
3WA	Wrangell-St. Elisa	H-2
1W	Wupatki	E-3
3Y	Yucca House	E-4
3Y	Yukon-Charley	G-2
4Y	Yukon Flats	G-2

NATIONAL PARKS

1A	Acadia	B-12
4A	Arches	D-4
1B	Badlands	C-5
3B	Big Bend	G-5
3BA	Biscayne	H-11
6B	Bryce Canyon	E-3
3C	Canyonlands	E-4
4C	Capitol Reef	E-4
7C	Carlsbad Caverns	F-5
7C	Channel Islands	E, F-2
1E	Crater Lake	C-2
1E	Everglades	H-10
2G	Glacier	A-3
5G	Grand Canyon	E-3
5G	Grand Teton	C-4
10G	Great Smoky Mountains	E-9
11G	Guadalupe Mts.	F-5
1H	Haleakala	H-4
2H	Hawaii Volcanoes	H-4
4H	Hot Springs	F-7
1I	Isle Royale	B-8
2K	Kings Canyon	D-2
1L	Lassen Volcanic	C-2
1M	Mammoth Cave	E-9
2M	Mesa Verde	E-4
4M	Mount McKinley	G-2
5M	Mount Rainier	B-2
3N	North Cascades	A-2
2O	Olympic	B-1
3P	Petrified Forest	F-4
1R	Redwood	C-1
4R	Rocky Mountain	D-5
3S	Sequoia	E-2
4S	Shenandoah	D-10
1T	Theodore Roosevelt	B-5
1V	Voyageurs	B-7
4W	Wind Cave	C-5
1Y	Yellowstone	C-4
1Y	Yosemite	D-2
1Z	Zion	E-3

81-1

11

Driving-Time Map

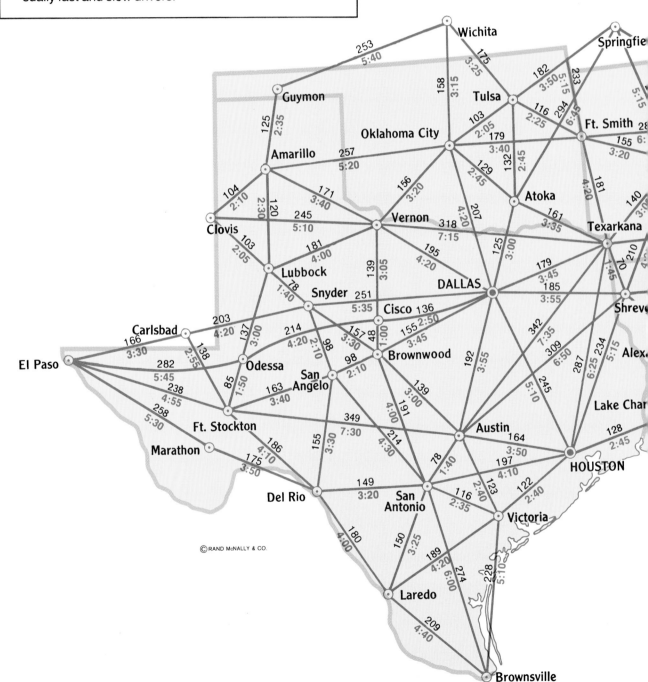

© RAND McNALLY & CO.

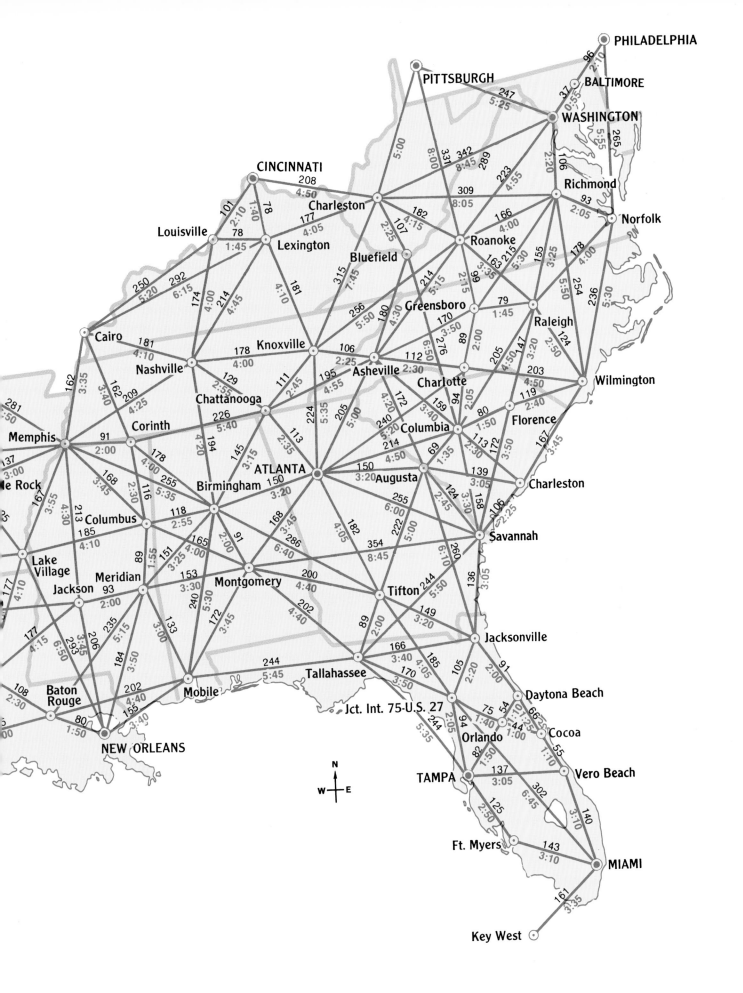

PHILADELPHIA

PITTSBURGH

BALTIMORE

WASHINGTON

247
5:25

96
2:10

37
0:55

106
2:20

265

CINCINNATI
208
4:50

5:00
8:00

331

342
8:45

289
4:55

223

Richmond

309
8:05

93
2:05

Norfolk

101
2:10

78
1:40

Charleston
177
4:05

182
4:15

166
4:00

178
4:00

Louisville
78
1:45

Lexington

107
2:25

Roanoke

155
3:25

254
5:50

236
5:30

Bluefield

315
7:45

214
5:15

99
2:75

163
3:35

215
5:30

250
5:20

292
6:15

174
4:00

214
4:45

181
4:10

256
5:50

180
4:30

Greensboro

79
1:45

Raleigh

124
2:50

Cairo
181
4:10

178
4:00

Knoxville

106
2:25

170
3:50

68
2:00

276
6:50

205
4:50

147
3:20

203
4:50

Wilmington

Nashville

112
2:30

Asheville

Charlotte

119
2:40

162
3:35

129
2:55

111
2:45

195
4:55

172
3:40

159

46
2:05

80
1:50

Florence

162
3:40

209
4:25

Chattanooga

226
5:40

224
2:35

205
5:35

205
5:00

240
5:20

Columbia

113
2:30

172
3:50

167
3:45

281
:50

91
2:00

113
3:15

145

214
4:50

69
1:35

139
3:05

Charleston

Memphis

137
3:00

Corinth

178
4:00

194
4:20

ATLANTA
150
3:20

Augusta

124
2:45

158

106
2:25

e Rock

168
3:45

255
5:35

Birmingham
150

255
6:00

222
5:00

260
6:10

Savannah

167
3:55

213
4:10

116
2:30

118
2:55

168
3:45

182
4:05

354
8:45

244
5:50

191
3:05

Columbus

68
1:55

151

91
2:00

286
6:40

Lake
Village

185
4:10

165
4:00

200
4:40

Tifton

149
3:20

136

177
4:10

Meridian

153
3:30

Montgomery

89
2:00

Jackson
93
2:00

240
5:30

172
3:45

202
4:40

244
5:45

Tallahassee

166
3:40

185
4:05

105
2:20

Jacksonville

91
2:00

177
4:15

206
3:45

235
5:15

133
3:00

170
3:50

Daytona Beach

293
6:50

184
3:50

202
4:40

Mobile

Jct. Int. 75-U.S. 27

75
1:40

54

66
1:10

44
1:00

Cocoa

108
2:30

Baton
Rouge

155
3:40

94

Orlando

55
1:10

Vero Beach

80
1:50

82
1:50

NEW ORLEANS

N
W   E

244
5:35

137
3:05

302
6:45

140
3:70

TAMPA

125
2:50

Ft. Myers

143
3:10

MIAMI

161
3:35

Key West

13

Weather Chart

	January Temp. High Low	January Precip.	February Temp. High Low	February Precip.	March Temp. High Low	March Precip.	April Temp. High Low	April Precip.	May Temp. High Low	May Precip.	June Temp. High Low	June Precip.
ALABAMA												
Birmingham	55 36	5	58 37	5	65 42	6	76 52	5	83 60	4	89 67	4
Mobile	61 41	5	64 44	5	69 49	7	78 58	6	85 64	5	90 71	6
Montgomery	58 37	4	61 40	4	68 45	6	77 54	4	84 61	3	89 69	4
ARKANSAS												
Little Rock	50 29	4	54 32	4	62 39	5	73 50	5	81 58	5	89 67	3
DELAWARE												
Wilmington	40 24	3	42 25	3	51 32	4	63 41	3	73 52	3	82 61	3
DIST. OF COLUMBIA												
Washington, D.C.	42 25	3	45 26	3	54 33	3	66 43	3	75 53	4	84 61	4
FLORIDA												
Jacksonville	65 44	3	67 46	4	72 50	4	79 57	3	85 64	3	88 70	6
Miami	76 59	2	77 59	2	79 63	2	83 67	4	85 71	6	88 74	9
Orlando	70 50	2	72 51	3	76 56	3	81 61	3	87 66	3	89 71	7
Tallahassee	64 41	4	66 43	5	72 48	6	80 56	4	87 63	4	90 70	7
Tampa	71 50	2	72 52	3	76 56	4	82 62	2	87 67	2	90 72	6
GEORGIA												
Atlanta	51 33	4	54 35	4	61 41	6	71 51	5	79 59	4	85 67	4
Savannah	61 39	3	64 40	3	69 46	4	78 54	3	85 62	4	89 69	6
KENTUCKY												
Louisville	42 24	4	45 26	3	54 34	5	66 45	4	76 54	4	84 63	4
LOUISIANA												
New Orleans	62 43	5	65 46	5	70 51	5	78 59	4	85 65	4	90 71	5
Shreveport	57 38	4	65 41	4	67 46	4	77 56	5	84 63	5	90 70	3
MARYLAND												
Baltimore	42 25	3	44 26	3	53 32	4	65 42	3	75 52	4	83 62	4
MISSISSIPPI												
Biloxi	61 43	5	63 46	5	69 51	5	76 60	5	83 67	4	89 72	5
Jackson	58 36	5	62 38	5	69 43	6	78 53	5	85 60	4	91 68	3
NORTH CAROLINA												
Charlotte	52 32	4	55 33	4	62 39	5	73 49	3	80 57	3	86 65	4
Raleigh	51 30	3	53 31	3	61 37	3	72 47	3	79 55	3	86 63	4
Wilmington	57 36	3	59 37	3	65 44	4	74 52	3	81 61	4	87 68	6
OKLAHOMA												
Oklahoma City	47 26	1	52 30	2	60 37	2	72 49	4	79 58	5	87 67	4
SOUTH CAROLINA												
Charleston	60 37	3	62 39	3	68 45	5	76 53	3	83 61	4	88 68	6
Columbia	57 34	3	60 35	4	66 42	5	77 51	4	84 60	3	90 67	4
Greenville	52 33	4	54 35	4	62 40	5	72 50	4	80 58	3	86 66	4
TENNESSEE												
Knoxville	49 32	5	52 33	5	60 39	5	72 49	4	80 57	3	86 65	4
Memphis	49 32	5	53 34	5	61 41	5	73 52	5	81 61	4	89 68	3
Nashville	48 29	5	51 31	4	59 38	5	71 49	4	80 57	4	87 66	3
TEXAS												
Dallas-Ft. Worth	56 34	2	60 38	2	67 43	3	76 54	4	83 62	4	91 70	3
El Paso	57 30	0	62 34	0	69 40	0	78 49	0	87 57	0	95 66	1
Houston	63 41	4	66 45	4	72 50	3	79 59	4	86 66	5	91 71	5
San Antonio	62 40	2	66 43	2	72 49	2	80 59	3	86 66	3	92 72	3
VIRGINIA												
Norfolk	49 32	3	50 33	3	57 39	3	68 48	3	76 57	3	83 65	4
Roanoke	46 27	3	48 28	3	56 34	3	68 44	3	76 53	4	83 60	4
WEST VIRGINIA												
Huntington	43 26	3	45 27	3	55 34	4	67 44	3	76 53	4	83 61	3

*Temp.: Temperature (°F); Precip.: Precipitation (inches)

	July Temp. High Low	July Precip.	August Temp. High Low	August Precip.	September Temp. High Low	September Precip.	October Temp. High Low	October Precip.	November Temp. High Low	November Precip.	December Temp. High Low	December Precip.
ALABAMA												
Birmingham	91 70	5	90 69	4	85 64	4	76 52	3	64 42	4	56 36	5
Mobile	90 73	9	91 72	7	86 58	7	80 58	3	69 47	3	63 43	6
Montgomery	90 71	5	91 71	3	86 65	4	78 53	2	67 43	3	59 38	5
ARKANSAS												
Little Rock	93 70	3	93 69	3	86 61	4	76 49	3	62 38	4	52 31	4
DELAWARE												
Wilmington	85 66	4	84 64	4	78 57	3	68 46	3	55 36	3	43 26	3
DIST. OF COLUMBIA												
Washington, D.C.	87 67	4	86 65	4	79 58	3	69 46	3	56 36	3	44 26	3
FLORIDA												
Jacksonville	90 72	7	90 72	8	86 70	8	79 62	5	71 51	2	66 45	3
Miami	89 75	7	90 76	7	88 75	9	85 71	8	80 64	3	77 60	2
Orlando	90 73	8	90 73	7	88 72	7	82 66	4	76 57	2	71 51	2
Tallahassee	91 72	9	90 72	7	87 69	7	81 58	3	71 46	3	65· 41	4
Tampa	90 74	8	90 74	8	89 65	6	84 65	3	77 56	2	72 51	2
GEORGIA												
Atlanta	86 69	5	86 69	4	81 63	3	72 52	2	62 41	3	53 34	4
Savannah	91 71	8	90 71	6	85 67	6	78 56	3	69 45	2	62 39	3
KENTUCKY												
Louisville	87 66	4	86 65	3	80 58	3	70 46	2	54 35	3	44 27	3
LOUISIANA												
New Orleans	90 73	7	91 73	5	87 70	6	80 60	2	70 50	4	64 45	5
Shreveport	93 73	3	94 72	3	88 67	3	79 56	3	67 45	4	59 39	4
MARYLAND												
Baltimore	87 66	4	85 65	4	79 58	3	68 46	3	56 36	3	44 27	3
MISSISSIPPI												
Biloxi	90 74	6	90 74	7	87 70	7	80 60	3	69 50	3	63 46	5
Jackson	93 71	4	93 70	4	88 64	3	80 51	2	68 42	4	60 37	5
NORTH CAROLINA												
Charlotte	88 69	5	87 68	4	82 62	3	73 50	3	62 40	3	52 32	3
Raleigh	88 67	5	87 66	5	81 60	4	72 48	3	62 38	3	52 30	3
Wilmington	89 72	8	88 71	7	83 66	6	75 55	3	67 44	3	58 37	3
OKLAHOMA												
Oklahoma City	93 71	3	93 70	3	85 61	4	75 51	3	61 38	2	50 29	1
SOUTH CAROLINA												
Charleston	89 71	8	89 71	6	84 66	5	77 55	3	68 44	2	61 38	3
Columbia	92 70	6	91 69	6	85 63	4	77 51	3	67 41	2	58 34	3
Greenville	88 69	4	87 68	4	81 62	4	72 51	3	62 40	3	52 33	4
TENNESSEE												
Knoxville	88 68	5	87 67	3	82 61	3	72 50	3	59 39	4	50 33	4
Memphis	92 71	4	91 70	3	84 63	3	75 51	3	61 40	4	52 34	5
Nashville	90 69	4	89 68	3	83 60	3	73 49	2	59 38	3	50 31	4
TEXAS												
Dallas-Ft. Worth	95 74	2	96 74	2	88 67	3	79 56	3	67 44	2	59 37	2
El Paso	95 70	2	93 68	1	87 61	1	78 49	1	66 37	0	58 31	0
Houston	94 73	4	94 72	4	90 68	5	83 58	4	73 49	4	66 43	4
San Antonio	96 74	2	96 73	2	90 69	4	82 59	3	71 48	2	65 42	2
VIRGINIA												
Norfolk	87 70	6	85 69	6	80 64	4	70 53	3	60 43	3	51 34	3
Roanoke	86 64	4	85 63	4	79 56	3	70 46	3	57 36	2	47 28	3
WEST VIRGINIA												
Huntington	86 65	4	85 63	3	79 56	3	69 45	2	55 36	3	45 27	3

Alabama

See also pages 51-58

The Yellowhammer State
Population: 3,890,061
Area: 51,609 square miles
   Land Area: 50,708 square miles
   Water Area: 901 square miles
Highest Point: Cheaha Mountain,
   2,407 feet
Capital: Montgomery
Statehood: December 14, 1819
State Motto: Audemus jura nostra
   defendere ("We dare defend our
   rights")
State Bird: Yellowhammer
State Flower: Camellia
State Tree: Southern Pine
Time Zone: Central

Mountains and Gulf Shores Are the Setting for Alabama Parks

Alabama's changing landscape surprises everyone—except Alabamians. After all, they daily scale its northern mountains, ply its meandering rivers and lakes, and wade in the mild tides of the Gulf shore. From the tallest peak to beach-ribboned coast, with an easy drive of major cities such as Birmingham, Huntsville, Mobile, and Montgomery, the state has taken advantage of its diversity with state parks well worthy of their resort surname. The parks boast a full complement of recreational facilities for the day, fine restaurants for dinner, and resort cottages and rooms for leisurely evenings. The real charm of these parks, however, stems first from their settings. Gulf State Park Resort lounges on 2½ miles of white sand, as tanned and relaxed as the people it attracts. Drawn by the combination of surf and sun, anglers try their luck at saltwater fishing, while sailors hoist multihued sails aloft, casting their fates to the steady winds and sun-freckled water.

Those same constant winds riffle the waters of Alabama's Lake Eufaula on the Georgia border. Here, tucked into the serpentine folds of shoreline, Lakepoint State Park Resort laments the bass that got away and boasts of the one that was caught. Those not lured by fishing can enjoy other freshwater sports, or explore the nearby national wildlife refuge, which is alive with waterfowl, especially in fall and winter. Fishing is a prime attraction, too, at Joe Wheeler State Park Resort, which dips its feet into the cool waters of the Tennessee River as it cuts its curling path through north Alabama's rolling terrain. Traveling southeast, that terrain reaches its true heights at Cheaha State Park Resort. Perched atop Cheaha Mountain, the state's tallest, this park towers grandly over the Talladega National Forest. Hiking trails vein its acres, and the overlooks are breathtakingly beautiful.

Alabama holds many other such sites, some perhaps not so dazzling, not so grand. Many cling to steep mountain land, while others nestle into river bends close upon water's edge. Together, they celebrate the best of a demure but distinctive countryside, an Alabama uncommon and unexpected.

The scenic richness of Alabama takes many forms and can be enjoyed several ways: An automobile ascending Cheaha Mountain, highest point in the state; a sailboat skimming across the waters of Lake Logan Martin; graceful DeSoto Falls plunging into a mountain lake. At top: Sea oats growing along the Gulf Coast send their roots to a depth of four feet, where they keep the sand dunes from eroding.

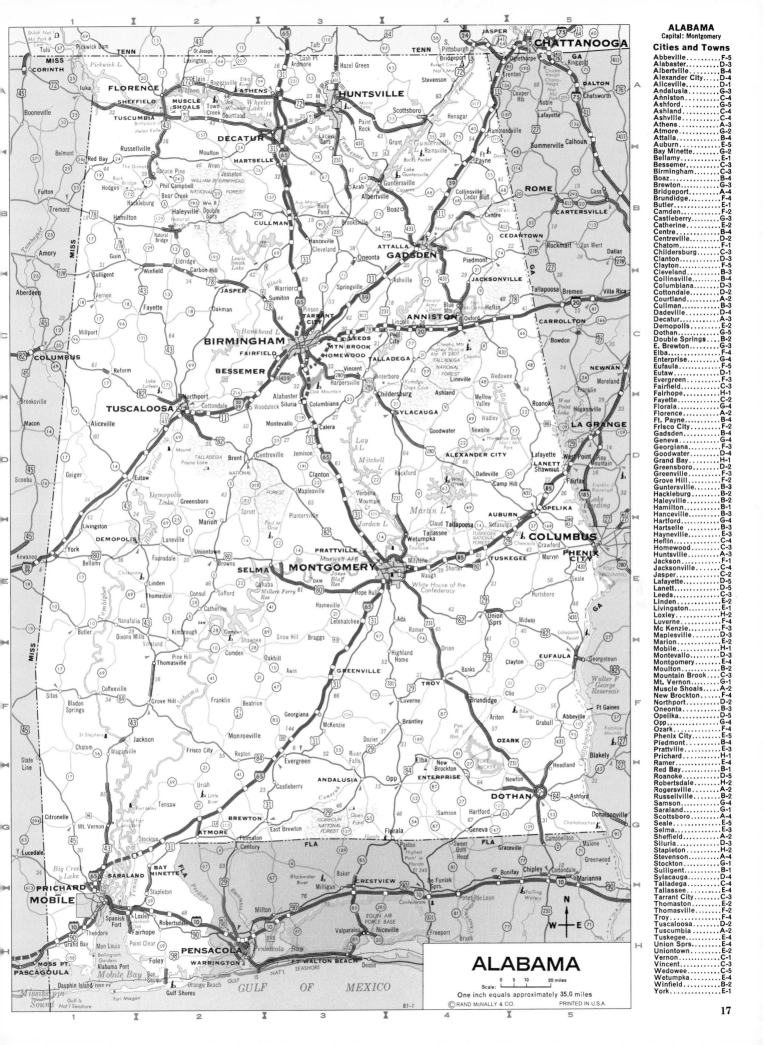

ALABAMA

Scale:
0 5 10   20 miles

One inch equals approximately 35.0 miles

© Rand McNally & Co.   PRINTED IN U.S.A.

81-1

ALABAMA

Capital: Montgomery

Cities and Towns

Abbeville	F-5
Alabaster	D-3
Albertville	B-4
Alexander City	D-4
Aliceville	D-1
Andalusia	G-3
Anniston	C-4
Ashford	G-5
Ashland	C-4
Ashville	B-4
Athens	A-3
Atmore	G-2
Attalla	B-4
Auburn	D-5
Bay Minette	G-2
Bellamy	E-1
Bessemer	C-3
Birmingham	C-3
Boaz	B-4
Brewton	G-3
Bridgeport	A-4
Brundidge	F-4
Butler	E-1
Camden	F-2
Castleberry	G-3
Catherine	E-2
Centre	B-4
Centreville	D-2
Chatom	F-1
Childersburg	C-3
Clanton	D-3
Clayton	F-5
Cleveland	B-3
Collinsville	B-4
Columbiana	D-3
Cottondale	D-2
Courtland	A-2
Cullman	B-3
Dadeville	D-4
Decatur	A-3
Demopolis	E-2
Dothan	G-5
Double Springs	B-2
E. Brewton	G-3
Elba	F-4
Enterprise	G-4
Eufaula	F-5
Eutaw	D-1
Evergreen	F-3
Fairfield	C-3
Fairhope	H-1
Fayette	G-2
Florala	G-4
Florence	A-2
Ft. Payne	B-4
Frisco City	F-2
Gadsden	B-4
Geneva	G-4
Georgiana	F-3
Goodwater	D-4
Grand Bay	H-1
Greensboro	D-2
Greenville	F-3
Grove Hill	F-2
Guntersville	B-3
Hackleburg	B-2
Haleyville	B-2
Hamilton	B-1
Hanceville	B-3
Hartford	G-4
Hartselle	B-3
Hayneville	C-2
Heflin	C-4
Homewood	C-3
Huntsville	A-3
Jackson	F-1
Jacksonville	C-2
Jasper	D-5
Lafayette	D-5
Lanett	D-5
Leeds	C-3
Linden	E-2
Livingston	E-1
Loxley	H-2
Luverne	F-3
Mc Kenzie	F-3
Maplesville	D-3
Marion	E-2
Mobile	H-1
Montevallo	D-3
Montgomery	E-4
Moulton	B-2
Mountain Brook	C-3
Mt. Vernon	G-1
Muscle Shoals	A-2
New Brockton	F-4
Northport	D-2
Oneonta	B-3
Opelika	D-5
Opp	G-4
Ozark	F-4
Phenix City	E-5
Piedmont	B-4
Prattville	E-3
Prichard	H-1
Ramer	E-4
Red Bay	B-1
Roanoke	D-5
Robertsdale	H-2
Rogersville	A-2
Russellville	B-2
Samson	G-4
Saraland	G-1
Scottsboro	A-4
Seale	E-5
Selma	E-3
Sheffield	A-2
Siluria	D-3
Stapleton	H-2
Stevenson	A-4
Stockton	G-1
Sulligent	B-1
Sylacauga	D-4
Talladega	C-4
Tallassee	E-4
Tarrant City	C-3
Thomaston	E-2
Thomasville	F-2
Troy	F-4
Tuscaloosa	D-2
Tuscumbia	A-2
Tuskegee	E-4
Union Sprs.	E-4
Uniontown	E-2
Vernon	C-1
Vincent	C-3
Wedowee	C-5
Wetumpka	E-4
Winfield	B-2
York	E-1

17

Arkansas

See also pages 59-67

The Land of Opportunity
Population: 2,285,513
Area: 53,104 square miles
    Land Area: 51,945 square miles
    Water Area: 1,159 square miles
Highest Point: Magazine Mountain,
    2,753 feet
Capital: Little Rock
Statehood: June 15, 1836
State Motto: Regnat Populus ("The
    People Rule")
State Bird: Mockingbird
State Flower: Apple Blossom
State Tree: Pine
Time Zone: Central

Arkansas Is Noted for Its Lakes, Rivers, and Springs

Landlocked though it is, Arkansas has become a popular vacation destination because of its water. From delta prairie to foothills and mountains, the state's rivers horseshoe through the country-side, while lakes wrap around miles of shoreline.

The Arkansas River, which splits the state in half, provided one of the first avenues for the state's settlement. Now, it steps down in locks from Fort Smith to the Mississippi River. Halfway along its course lies Little Rock, the capital, which honors the river each May with an event called Riverfest. South of Little Rock, the resort town of Hot Springs has been popular for its thermal waters since the sixteenth century, when Indians declared the springs sacred and neutral territory and came here to ease their rheumatic pains and battle-weary bodies in the warm mineral waters. Visitors still come to bathe in the spring waters. But nearby Lakes Ouachita, Hamilton, and Catherine also draw visitors who come to camp and enjoy a variety of water sports.

Elsewhere in the state, massive lakes have been scooped from Arkansas streams. In the high Ozark country, dams spread the shorelines of four major impoundments. On Beaver, Bull Shoals, Norfolk, and Greers Ferry lakes, skiers skim the expanses while fishermen haunt the inlets. Trout waver in the chilly waters below the dams. In streams like the White River below Bull Shoals and the Little Red River below Greers Ferry, the brown, rainbow, and speckled trout are prizes worth getting up early to catch.

Canoeists are also at home on the green, foaming mountain streams. You can float the Spring and the Kings, the Strawberry and the Mulberry, the White and the Little Red, the Ouachita and the Buffalo rivers. High limestone bluffs rise above the Buffalo River, where canoeists camp along the gravel banks. Spring-fed, the Buffalo's entire 148-mile course is now a national river.

Water also draws visitors to east Arkansas for a different kind of recreation. Here, the Mississippi River drains the prairie rice fields, and the rice fields feed migratory fowl. In fall and winter, around towns like Stuttgart, duck hunters crouch in the early morning to await their quarry. And every November, contestants from over the country come to participate in the annual World Championship Duck-Calling Contest.

A few of the many pleasures of Arkansas are folk music, aerial thrills, and the infinite bounty of nature. Left: Balloonists soar high above Greers Ferry Lake in north-central Arkansas during the annual mid-August Water Festival. Above: A fiddler tunes up before performing in the Ozark Folk Center; a monarch butterfly pauses for refreshment along the White River; backpackers pick their way across a rocky stream to rejoin with one of the state's many hiking trails.

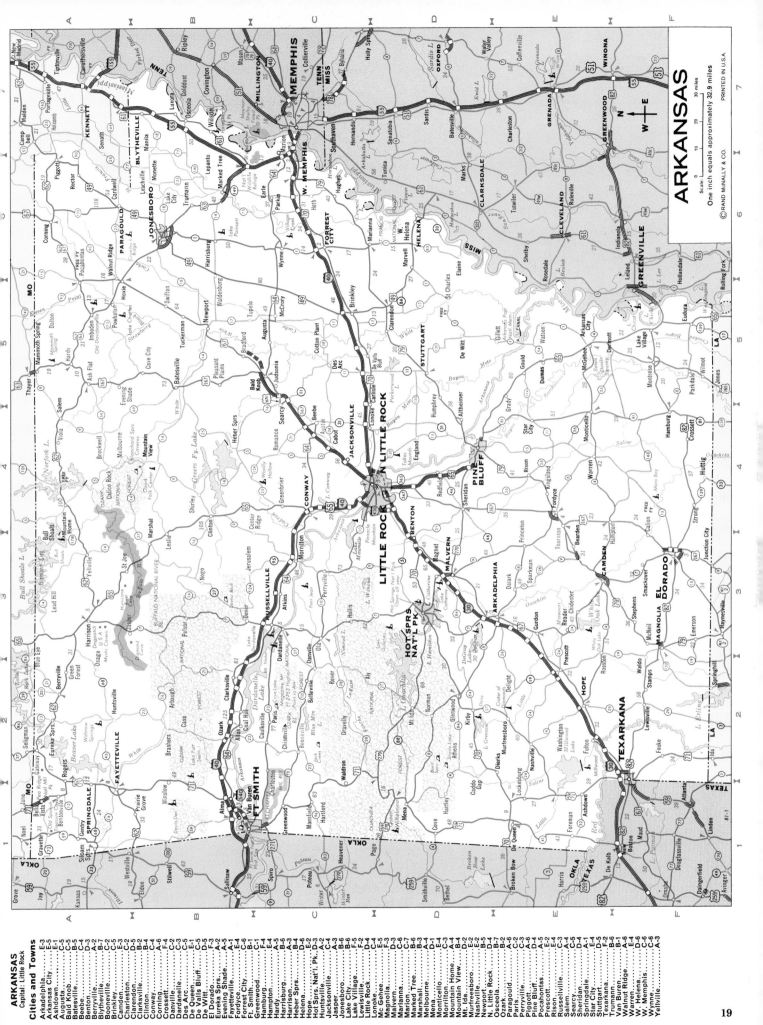

ARKANSAS

Capital: Little Rock

Scale:
0 10 20 30 miles

One inch equals approximately 32.9 miles

© RAND McNALLY & CO.

PRINTED IN U.S.A.

ARKANSAS

Capital: Little Rock

Cities and Towns

Arkadelphia	E-3
Arkansas City	E-5
Ashdown	E-1
Batesville	C-5
Bald Knob	B-5
Beebe	C-4
Benton	D-3
Berryville	B-7
Blytheville	A-7
Booneville	C-2
Brinkley	C-5
Camden	E-3
Clarendon	C-5
Charleston	C-2
Clarksville	B-4
Conway	C-4
Crossett	F-4
Danville	C-3
Dardanelle	C-3
Des Arc	C-5
De Queen	E-1
De Witt	D-5
El Dorado	F-3
Eureka Sprs.	A-2
Evening Shade	B-5
Fayetteville	B-1
Forrest City	C-6
Ft. Smith	C-1
Greenwood	C-1
Hampton	E-3
Hardy	B-5
Harrisburg	B-6
Harrison	A-3
Helena	D-6
Hope	E-2
Hot Sprs. Nat'l. Pk.	D-3
Huntsville	B-2
Jacksonville	C-4
Jasper	B-3
Jonesboro	B-6
Lake City	B-7
Lake Village	F-5
Lewisville	F-2
Little Rock	D-4
Lonoke	C-4
Magnolia	F-2
Malvern	D-3
Marianna	D-6
Marion	C-7
Marked Tree	B-6
Marshall	B-4
Mena	D-1
Monticello	E-4
Morrilton	C-3
Mountain Home	A-4
Mountain View	B-4
Mt. Ida	D-2
Murfreesboro	E-2
Nashville	E-2
Newport	B-5
N. Little Rock	D-4
Ozark	C-2
Osceola	A-7
Paris	C-2
Paragould	A-6
Perryville	C-3
Piggott	A-6
Pine Bluff	D-4
Pocahontas	A-5
Prescott	E-2
Rison	E-4
Russellville	C-3
Salem	A-5
Searcy	C-4
Sheridan	D-4
Springdale	A-1
Star City	E-4
Stuttgart	D-5
Texarkana	F-1
Trumann	B-6
Van Buren	B-1
Walnut Ridge	A-5
Warren	E-4
W. Helena	D-6
W. Memphis	C-7
Wynne	C-6
Yellville	A-3

19

Delaware

See also pages 68-72

The First State

Population: 595,225
Area: 2,057 square miles
 Land Area: 1,982 square miles
 Water Area: 75 square miles plus 350
  square miles of state-owned
  Delaware River and Bay
Highest Point: Unnamed, on Ebirght
 Road in Walton County, west of
 Claymont, 442 feet
Capital: Dover
Statehood: December 17, 1787
State Motto: Liberty and Independence
State Bird: Blue Hen
State Flower: Peach Blossom
State Tree: American Holly
Time Zone: Eastern

Rich History Contrasts Delaware's Diminuitive Size

What Delaware lacks in size, it makes up for in history. The first European settlers to land here, the Dutch, did so just 11 years after the English landed at Plymouth. The familiar log cabin of the pioneers was first introduced here by the Swedes, who settled what is now Wilmington. And Delaware was the first of the thirteen original states to ratify the Constitution of the United States, at a convention in Dover, now the capital of the state.

One place to indulge in the past is New Castle. Founded by the Dutch in 1651, the town is essentially the same as it appeared in the early 1800s, with fine architectural examples of the Dutch, Colonial, French, Georgian, Federal, and Empire periods. Another area rich in history lies along the Brandywine River, at such places as Eleutherian Mills, a du Pont residence overlooking the remains of the nineteenth-century powder mill. Nearby is Winterthur Museum and Gardens, another du Pont residence that houses an outstanding collection of early American decorative arts.

The emphasis on history doesn't preclude the natural attractions of the state, though. Resort towns such as Rehoboth Beach and Bethany Beach have long been favorite summertime haunts. Just as visitors flock to the beaches, so do waterfowl flock to the wildlife refuges of Bombay Hook and Prime Hook, providing excellent photographic opportunities in fall and winter.

Winterthur Museum, once the home of Henry Francis du Pont, has more than 200 rooms of furniture, antiques, and decorative items from the period of 1640 to 1840; the home was built in 1839.

Maryland

See also pages 111-119

Old Line State

Population: 4,216,446
Area: 10,577 square miles
 Land Area: 9,891 square miles
 Water Area: 686 square miles
Highest Point: Backbone Mountain,
 3,360 feet
Capital: Annapolis
Statehood: April 28, 1788
State Motto: Fatti Maschii, Parole
 Femine ("Manly Deeds, Womanly
 Words")
State Bird: Baltimore Oriole
State Flower: Black-eyed Susan
State Tree: White Oak
Time Zone: Eastern

Maritime Legacy and History Define the State of Maryland

Maryland wraps around the Chesapeake Bay, its cities and towns marked indelibly with a legacy of maritime history and industry.

Annapolis, the capital, is home of the U.S. Naval Academy and is one of the area's most picturesque ports for pleasure craft and working watermen. Baltimore, largest of the bay cities, has been undergoing redevelopment, making the city of today almost unrecognizable as the city of a decade ago. The difference is most obvious along the Inner Harbor, where the U.S. Frigate *Constellation*, the new National Aquarium, the Maryland Science Center, and Harbor Place, a mecca of shops and restaurants, are located.

Perhaps most enchanting are the smaller bay towns. Oxford, with picket fences, maples that flame in autumn, and a sprinkling of antique shops, also has the Robert Morris Inn, an overnight accommodation built by ships' carpenters and named for a signer of the Declaration of Independence. St. Michaels is known for its fine antique shops, but it also offers excellent seafood restaurants. Solomons is a sleepy fishing village, but makes the history of the Chesapeake come alive at its Calvert Marine Museum. And most unique of all are Ewell and Tylerton, on Smith Island in the middle of the bay. Quaint towns reached only by boat, where men still make their living on the water, they symbolize an almost legendary way of life.

Sailing easily ranks as one of the most popular outdoor activities in Maryland, a state that is bordered partially by the Atlantic Ocean on the east, by the Potomac River on the west, and is divided in two by Chesapeake Bay and its coves.

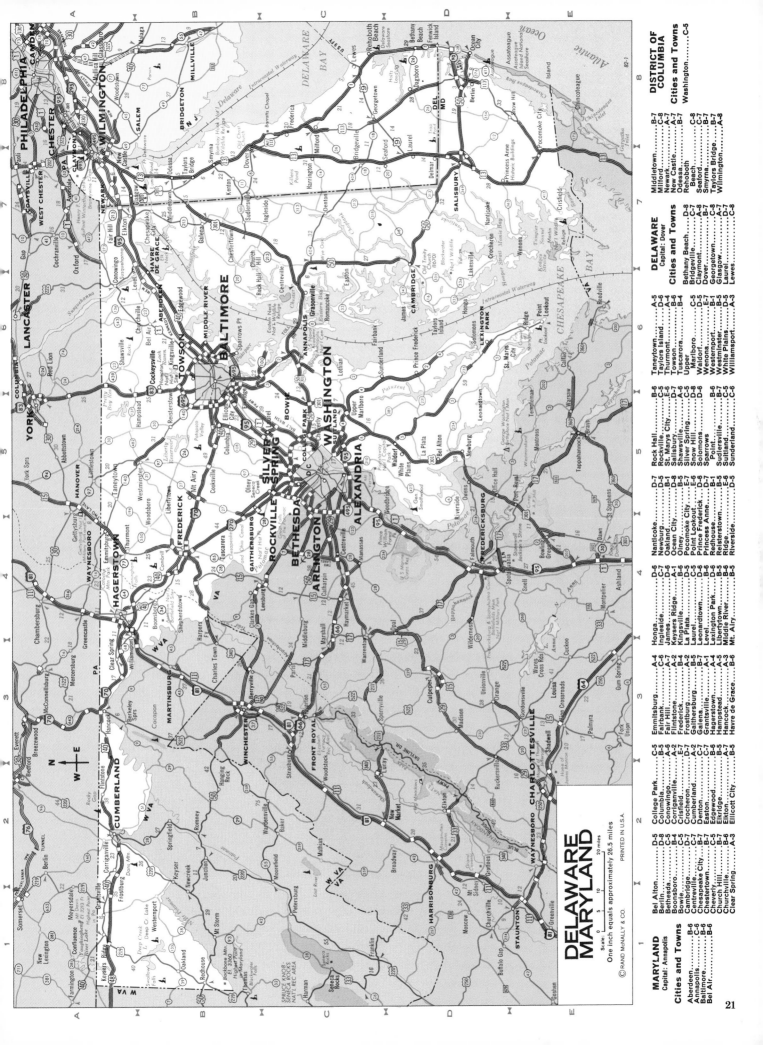

DELAWARE
MARYLAND

Scale: 0 5 10 20 miles
One inch equals approximately 26.5 miles

© RAND McNALLY & CO.   PRINTED IN U.S.A.

MARYLAND
Capital: Annapolis

Cities and Towns

Aberdeen	B-6
Annapolis	C-6
Baltimore	B-6
Bel Air	B-6
Bel Alton	D-5
Berlin	D-8
Bethesda	C-5
Boonsboro	B-4
Bowie	C-5
Cambridge	C-7
Centreville	C-6
Chesapeake City	B-7
Chestertown	B-7
Cheverly	B-6
Church Hill	B-7
Churchville	B-6
Clear Spring	B-4
College Park	C-5
Columbia	B-5
Conowingo	A-6
Corriganville	A-2
Crisfield	D-7
Crocheron	D-7
Cumberland	A-2
Denton	C-7
Dutton	C-7
Easton	C-7
Edgewood	B-6
Elkridge	B-6
Elkton	B-7
Ellicott City	B-5
Emmitsburg	A-4
Fairbank	C-6
Fair Hill	A-7
Flintstone	A-2
Frederick	B-4
Frostburg	A-2
Gaithersburg	B-5
Grantsville	A-1
Grasonville	C-7
Hagerstown	B-4
Hampstead	B-5
Hancock	A-3
Havre de Grace	B-6
Honga	D-6
Ingleside	C-7
James	A-7
Keysers Ridge	A-1
Kingsville	B-6
La Plata	D-5
Laurel	B-5
Lexington Park	D-6
Level	B-6
Leonardtown	D-6
Libertytown	B-5
Middle River	B-6
Mt. Airy	B-5
Nanticoke	D-7
Newburg	C-7
Oakland	B-1
Ocean City	D-8
Olney	B-5
Pocomoke City	D-7
Prince Frederick	C-6
Princess Anne	D-7
Redhouse	B-1
Reisterstown	B-5
Ridge	E-6
Riverside	D-5
Rock Hall	B-6
Rockville	B-5
St. Marys City	E-6
Salisbury	D-7
Shawsville	A-6
Silver Spring	C-5
Snow Hill	D-8
Solomons	D-6
Sparrows Point	B-6
Sudlersville	B-7
Sunderland	C-6
Taneytown	B-6
Taylors Island	C-5
Thurmont	A-4
Towson	B-6
Tuscarora	B-4
Upper Marlboro	C-5
Waldorf	C-5
Wenona	D-7
Westernport	A-2
Westminster	B-5
Westport	B-6
White Plains	C-5
Williamsport	A-3

DELAWARE
Capital: Dover

Cities and Towns

Bethany Beach	D-8
Bridgeville	C-7
Claymont	A-8
Dover	B-7
Georgetown	C-8
Glasgow	B-7
Laurel	D-7
Lewes	C-8
Middletown	B-7
Milford	C-8
New Castle	A-7
Newark	A-7
Odessa	B-7
Rehoboth	C-8
Seaford	C-7
Smyrna	B-7
Taylors Bridge	B-7
Wilmington	A-8

DISTRICT OF COLUMBIA

Cities and Towns

Washington	C-5

21

Florida

See also pages 73-82

Sunshine State
Population: 9,739,992
Area: 58,560 square miles
    Land Area: 54,090 square miles
    Water Area: 4,470 square miles
Highest Point: Unnamed, in Walton
    County, east of Paxton, 345 feet
Capital: Tallahassee
Statehood: March 3, 1845
State Motto: In God We Trust
State Bird: Mockingbird
State Flower: Orange Blossom
State Tree: Sabal Palmetto
Time Zones: Eastern (peninsula and
    part of western Florida); Central
    (western Florida west of Apalachicola
    River)

Miles of Beaches Define and Outline Florida's Diversity

The proverbial silver lining of Florida is its beaches, which highlight the state's shape and diversity. These beaches stretch for unbroken miles at places like Canaveral National Seashore near Titusville. Or they pepper the many convoluted harbors and bays that wind along the coast, at show places such as Sebastian Inlet, south of Melbourne, and Biscayne Bay, off the coast of Miami. These beaches distinguish the state, even as they define it. They cannot, however, overshadow the other Florida, the one that lies within a stone's throw of the ocean and Gulf.

In the north, Tallahassee holds capitol attractions, while to the west, near tiny Milton, spring-fed rivers like the Sweetwater and Blackwater snake southward, sweeping canoeists along their shallow course. To the east, the Stephen Foster Center plays the tunes and preserves the times of Florida's culture-rich heartland. University town Gainesville serves up a mix of diverse sights, from the marvels of the Florida State Museum to a miniature mountain forest inside a Florida sinkhole.

A short sprint south down the interstate, Ocala boasts a galloping thoroughbred business. Just to the east of that sprawls the Ocala National Forest, thick with pines, veined with trails, and pocked with lakes and gin-clear springs. Such icy springs boil up across the state. State parks are graced by some, like Ichetucknee, whose flow creates a crystalline river for tubing. Others, privately run, attract divers and swimmers to their chillsome depths.

Orlando performs a different kind of magic, combining wonder and wizardry. Here, Walt Disney World enchants, Sea World educates, and a host of other parks entertain. The roads roll on southward, stretching through Florida's citrus country and skimming past its inland lakes, magnets for skiers and anglers alike. Lake Okeechobee, granddaddy of them all, measures as one of the country's largest.

At land's end, Florida tapers into the vast marsh-grass river of the Everglades. It is a long way from Miami to the glades, with its fresh and saltwater areas, open Everglades prairies, and mangrove forests abundant with wildlife and colorful birds—the largest remaining subtropical wilderness in the conterminous United States. It is a distance of experience and not miles. This is the beauty of Florida. Its lazy-day beaches are only the shining silhouette of a truly complex personality.

Man-made attractions play a major role in Florida, where tourism leads all other industries, yet the state's natural attributes remain the significant part of its appeal. From top: Cinderella's Castle is a dominate feature at Walt Disney World's Magic Kingdom; fishermen stalk bonefish off the Florida Keys; a cormorant surveys its surroundings from a lofty perch; seashells beckon collectors on Sanibel Island; baskets of freshly caught shrimp wait to be picked up from a Captiva Island dock; a painter captures the lofty grandeur of a lighthouse.

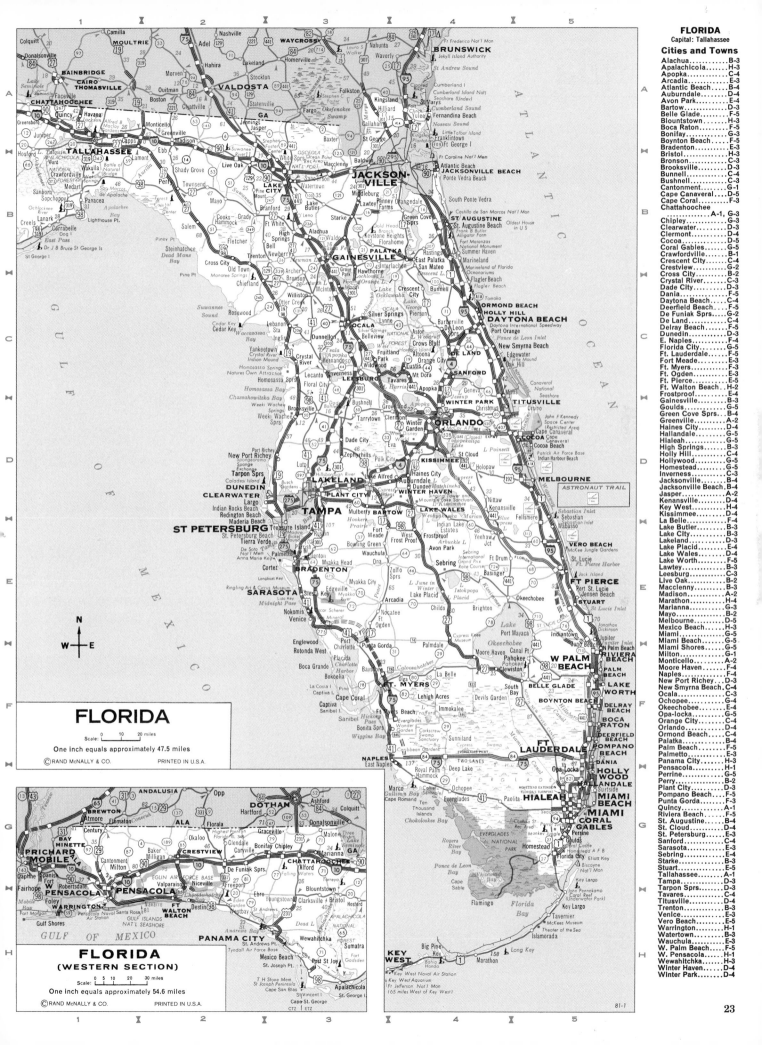

FLORIDA

Capital: Tallahassee

Cities and Towns

Alachua............B-3
Apalachicola.......H-3
Apopka............C-4
Arcadia............E-3
Atlantic Beach......B-4
Auburndale........D-4
Avon Park.........E-4
Bartow............D-3
Belle Glade........F-5
Blountstown........H-3
Boca Raton........F-5
Bonifay............G-3
Boynton Beach......F-5
Bradenton.........E-3
Bristol............H-3
Bronson...........C-3
Brooksville........D-3
Bunnell...........C-4
Bushnell..........C-3
Cantonment........G-1
Cape Canaveral.....D-5
Cape Coral.........F-3
Chattahoochee
.............A-1, G-3
Chipley...........G-3
Clearwater........D-3
Clermont..........D-4
Cocoa............D-5
Coral Gables.......G-5
Crawfordville......B-1
Crescent City......C-4
Crestview.........G-2
Cross City.........B-2
Crystal River......C-3
Dade City.........D-3
Dania............F-5
Daytona Beach......C-4
Deerfield Beach.....F-5
De Funiak Sprs.....G-2
De Land...........C-4
Delray Beach.......F-5
Dunedin...........D-3
E. Naples.........F-4
Florida City........G-5
Ft. Lauderdale......F-5
Fort Meade........E-3
Ft. Myers.........F-3
Ft. Ogden.........E-3
Ft. Pierce.........E-5
Ft. Walton Beach....H-2
Frostproof.........E-4
Gainesville........B-3
Goulds............G-5
Green Cove Sprs....B-4
Greenville.........A-2
Haines City........D-4
Hallandale.........G-5
Hialeah...........G-5
High Springs.......B-3
Holly Hill.........C-4
Hollywood.........G-5
Homestead.........G-5
Inverness.........C-3
Jacksonville.......B-4
Jacksonville Beach..B-4
Jasper............A-2
Kenansville........D-4
Key West..........H-4
Kissimmee.........D-4
La Belle..........F-4
Lake Butler........B-3
Lake City..........B-3
Lakeland..........D-3
Lake Placid........E-4
Lake Wales........D-4
Lake Worth........F-5
Lawtey............B-3
Leesburg..........C-3
Live Oak..........B-2
Macclenny.........B-3
Madison...........A-2
Marathon..........H-4
Marianna..........G-3
Mayo.............B-2
Melbourne.........D-5
Mexico Beach......H-3
Miami............G-5
Miami Beach.......G-5
Miami Shores.......G-5
Milton............G-1
Monticello.........A-2
Moore Haven.......F-4
Naples............F-4
New Port Richey....D-3
New Smyrna Beach..C-4
Ocala............C-3
Okeechobee........F-4
Opa-locka.........G-5
Orange City........C-4
Orlando...........D-4
Ormond Beach......C-4
Palatka...........B-4
Palm Beach........F-5
Palmetto..........E-3
Panama City.......H-2
Pensacola.........H-1
Perrine...........G-5
Perry............B-2
Plant City.........D-3
Pompano Beach.....F-5
Punta Gorda.......F-3
Quincy............A-1
Riviera Beach......F-5
St. Augustine......B-4
St. Cloud..........D-4
St. Petersburg......E-3
Sanford...........C-4
Sarasota..........E-3
Sebring...........E-4
Starke............B-3
Stuart............E-5
Tallahassee........A-1
Tampa............D-3
Tarpon Sprs.......D-3
Tavares...........C-4
Titusville..........D-4
Trenton...........B-3
Venice............E-3
Vero Beach........E-5
Warrington........H-1
Watertown.........B-3
Wauchula..........D-4
W. Palm Beach.....F-5
W. Pensacola......H-1
Wewahitchka.......H-3
Winter Haven......D-4
Winter Park........D-4

23

Georgia

See also pages 83-94

The Peach State
Population: 5,464,265
Area: 58,876 square miles
  Land Area: 58,073 square miles
  Water Area: 803 square miles
Highest Point: Brasstown Bald
  Mountain, 4,784 feet
Capital: Atlanta
Statehood: January 2, 1788
State Motto: Wisdom, Justice and
  Moderation
State Bird: Brown Thrasher
State Flower: Cherokee Rose
State Tree: Live Oak
Time Zone: Eastern

Georgia's Historic Renown Lives on in Its Small Towns

Atlanta's busy downtown is the heart of modern-day Georgia, but the quieter streets of its smaller cities and towns tell much of the state's past. In autumn, most roads rise north to the brilliantly colored mountains and to an area the Cherokees called *taulonica*, or *yellow metal*. Now known as Dahlonega, this was the site of the nation's first major gold rush in 1828. A museum and an old mine recall the days when the town housed a branch of the U.S. Mint.

While many are drawn to the coast in spring and summer, winter offers the serenity James Oglethorpe sensed when he claimed the wilderness as a colony. Downtown Savannah, a city he planned, still follows the original squares and parks. They are canopied with live oaks and are lovely for walking nearly any day of the year. Some of the islands off Georgia's coast have remained pristine, but others have become vacation spots. Jekyll Island has drawn visitors since the turn of the century when millionaires built extravagant winter homes there and as the place where the first transcontinental telephone call was made in 1915.

Spring is vibrant in middle Georgia, when azaleas color the streets of Piedmont towns. In Madison, they line the foundations of antebellum homes. Although Madison lay in Union General William T. Sherman's path during the Civil War, he chose not to burn it. Today, visitors to the town's spring pilgrimage see Madison much as it appeared in the mid-nineteenth century. In spring, peach blossoms frame highways that lead to towns such as Milledgeville, once the state capital, and Eatonton, hometown of Joel Chandler Harris, creator of the Uncle Remus stories. By summer, the harvest of those peaches fill roadside stands and city markets.

To slake the thirst of summer, you may turn to Columbus in west Georgia. Here, Confederates built ironclad gunboats, but soon after the Civil War, a doctor in his backyard laboratory concocted a formula that others would develop and call Coca-Cola.

Atlanta serves as headquarters for the industry today, just as it sets the pace for so much of the state. But many things that touched Georgia, the South, and the world came from the small cities and towns of the mountains, coast, and the Piedmont.

Atlantic Coast beaches and cosmopolitan Atlanta often head the list of attractions in Georgia, but the Peach State can boast of much more. Examples here include a stream tumbling through Cloudless Canyon; a golfer displaying his skill at the Masters Tournament in Augusta; and a pair of turtles sunning on a log in Okefenokee Swamp.

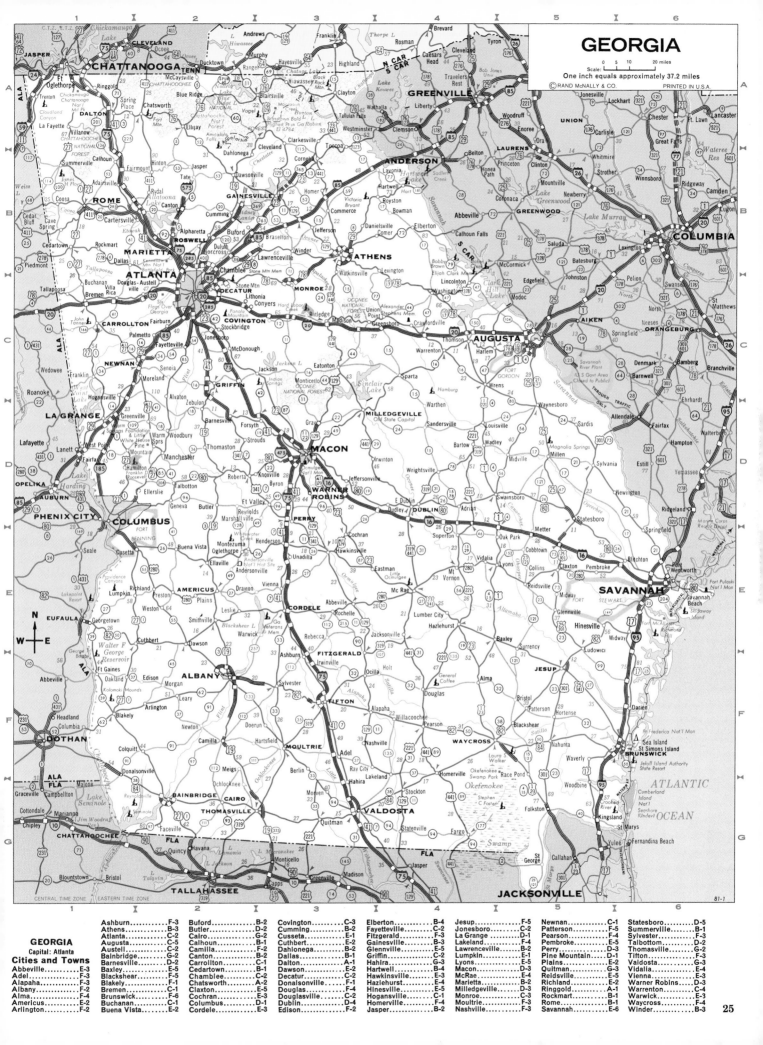

GEORGIA

Scale: 0 5 10   20 miles

One inch equals approximately 37.2 miles

© RAND McNALLY & CO.   PRINTED IN U.S.A.

GEORGIA

Capital: Atlanta

Cities and Towns

Abbeville......E-3	Buford......B-2	Covington......C-3	Elberton......B-4	Jesup......F-5	Newnan......C-1	Statesboro......D-5
Adel......F-3	Butler......D-2	Cumming......B-2	Fayetteville......C-2	Jonesboro......C-2	Patterson......F-5	Summerville......B-1
Alapaha......F-3	Cairo......G-2	Cusseta......E-1	Fitzgerald......F-3	La Grange......D-1	Pearson......F-4	Sylvester......F-3
Albany......F-2	Calhoun......B-1	Cuthbert......E-1	Gainesville......B-3	Lakeland......F-4	Pembroke......E-5	Talbotton......D-2
Alma......F-4	Camilla......F-2	Dahlonega......B-2	Glennville......E-5	Lawrenceville......B-2	Perry......D-3	Thomasville......G-2
Americus......E-2	Canton......B-2	Dallas......C-1	Griffin......C-2	Lumpkin......E-1	Pine Mountain......D-1	Tifton......F-3
Arlington......F-2	Carrollton......C-1	Dalton......A-1	Hahira......G-3	Lyons......E-5	Plains......E-2	Valdosta......G-3
Ashburn......F-3	Cedartown......B-1	Dawson......E-2	Hartwell......B-4	Macon......D-3	Quitman......G-3	Vidalia......E-4
Athens......B-3	Chamblee......C-2	Decatur......C-2	Hawkinsville......E-3	McRae......E-4	Reidsville......E-5	Vienna......E-3
Atlanta......C-2	Chatsworth......A-2	Donalsonville......F-1	Hazlehurst......E-4	Marietta......B-2	Richland......E-2	Warner Robins......D-3
Augusta......C-5	Claxton......E-5	Douglas......F-4	Hinesville......E-5	Milledgeville......D-3	Ringgold......A-1	Warrenton......C-4
Austell......C-2	Cochran......E-3	Douglasville......C-2	Hogansville......C-1	Monroe......C-3	Rockmart......B-1	Warwick......E-3
Bainbridge......G-2	Columbus......D-1	Dublin......D-4	Homerville......F-4	Moultrie......F-2	Rome......B-1	Waycross......F-4
Barnesville......D-2	Cordele......E-3	Edison......F-2	Jasper......B-2	Nashville......F-3	Savannah......E-6	Winder......B-3
Baxley......E-5						
Blackshear......F-5						
Blakely......F-1						
Bremen......C-1						
Brunswick......F-6						
Buchanan......C-1						
Buena Vista......E-2						

Kentucky

See also pages 95-103

Bluegrass State
Population: 3,661,433
Area: 40,395 square miles
    Land Area: 39,650 square miles
    Water Area: 745 square miles
Highest Point: Black Mountain,
    4,145 feet
Capital: Frankfort
Statehood: June 1, 1792
State Motto: United We Stand, Divided
    We Fall
State Bird: Kentucky Cardinal
State Flower: Goldenrod
State Tree: Kentucky Coffee Tree
Time Zones: Eastern (all eastern and
    most of central Kentucky); Central
    (part of central and all western
    Kentucky)

Kentucky Is the Land of Bluegrass and Thoroughbred Horses

Kentucky is the kingdom of the horse. From the famed Bluegrass to its river-marked western borders, the traditions and legends of its equine industry define the very land. The Bluegrass State begins in the Appalachian Mountains, which rise in its eastern boundaries. Here, places like Cumberland Gap and the Red River Gorge saddle the peaks and live with the legends of people like Daniel Boone.

Farther west, Lexington nourishes a different life, where tamer land invites a gentler style. Rich, rolling farmland surrounds the city, home to the champions that stride its famous tracks. Here, at the Kentucky Horse Park, the state pays tribute to the horse. White fences vein its land, and lush grass colors its fields. Park visitors can actually step behind the scenes to see how champions are raised and trained. The fruits of Lexington's love labors are easily visible. Fine-boned thoroughbreds race the track at Keeneland,

where afternoon crowds gather for a proper lunch and good-natured wagering. Standardbreds, too, pace and trot onto the scene, challenging each other at the famed Red Mile.

The roads connecting Lexington and Louisville pass regal horse farms where tall, private homes stand proudly behind handlaid fieldstone fences and miles of the traditional white wooden fences. Midway between lies Frankfort, with its stately homes and Old State Capitol. Louisville, also, boasts traditions. Perhaps the grandest is the Kentucky Derby. One of the nation's top thoroughbred contests, it draws the attention of millions each May when the best of the crop thunder down the historic track of Churchill Downs. Many visitors come even when there are no races, though, eager to tour Churchill Downs and glimpse the setting for one of racing's most honored standards.

Kentucky claims other legacies as well. Famous distilleries, home of the state's cherished bourbon and more, reside in picturesque towns such as Frankfort and Bardstown. And in the restored Shaker Village at Pleasant Hill, you can almost hear whispers of a culture that lived in the straightforward and unadorned setting. Yes, horses may rule Kentucky, but other traditions stand hard by, outlining a state as grand as it is proud.

Kentucky was the birthplace of Abraham Lincoln. The state is also known for bluegrass and for thoroughbred horses. You can see horses at such places as Kentucky Horse Park, northwest of Lexington (at top), and at Keeneland races and sales (below). Other attractions include buffalo at Land Between the Lakes; a portion of the 4,450-mile TransAmerica Bicycle Trail; and Cumberland Falls, one of the largest in the East. The falls is 120 feet wide and 70 feet high, but the most remarkable feature is the colored moonbow it produces on clear evenings when the moon is bright.

Tennessee

See also pages 154-161

Volunteer State
Population: 4,590,750
Area: 42,244 square miles
  Land Area: 41,328 square miles
  Water Area: 916 square miles
Highest Point: Clingmans Dome,
  6,643 feet
Capital: Nashville
Statehood: June 1, 1796
State Motto: Agriculture and Commerce
State Bird: Mockingbird
State Flower: Iris
State Tree: Tulip Poplar
Time Zones: Eastern (eastern
  Tennessee); Central (central and
  western Tennessee)

Tennessee Gateway City Knoxville Is 1982 World's Fair Host

Tennessee's four major cities, Knoxville, Chattanooga, Nashville, and Memphis, serve as gateways to the Volunteer State. All four are linked by interstate highways that thread you through the countryside. Each city is a destination in its own right. But as you travel from one to another, you can also take countless side trips to historical attractions, state parks, recreational areas, and natural areas that harbor a beauty unique to the region.

In the eastern end of the state, at Knoxville, is the gateway to the Great Smoky Mountains National Park. In 1982, however, Knoxville serves as the gateway to the world—from May until October, the city hosts the World's Fair. Traveling south to Chattanooga, you course through the rolling hills and valleys of the Appalachians. Chattanooga rests beside the Tennessee River, and towering high above it is magnificent Lookout Mountain. Hike the trails along its crest or make the short drive to Signal Point where the river carves an immense gorge through the Cumberland Plateau. Then you can top off your day with an evening of dining or browsing in the restaurants and shops at the Chattanooga Choo-Choo. There is even a hotel where you can spend the night in an old railroad car.

The road to Nashville is Interstate 24, which climbs to the lofty summit of the Cumberland Plateau. Detour to the secluded campus of the University of the South at Sewanee along the way or wind to the magnificent canyon of Savage Gulf State Natural Area. Nashville is just two hours away. Ryman Auditorium in the heart of Nashville is the birthplace of the Grand Ole Opry. Today, it is just a hall of memories but well worth a visit. A short distance away is

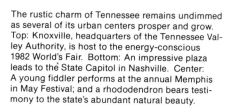

The rustic charm of Tennessee remains undimmed as several of its urban centers prosper and grow. Top: Knoxville, headquarters of the Tennessee Valley Authority, is host to the energy-conscious 1982 World's Fair. Bottom: An impressive plaza leads to the State Capitol in Nashville. Center: A young fiddler performs at the annual Memphis in May Festival; and a rhododendron bears testimony to the state's abundant natural beauty.

the new home of the Opry, the entertainment complex of Opryland.

Following Interstate 40 to Memphis, you leave behind the rolling hills of central Tennessee for the flat farmland of the west. In Memphis, tune your ear for a different kind of music—the Blues. The soul of the South sings on here while you sample one of the region's most succulent delicacies—barbecued ribs, Memphis style.

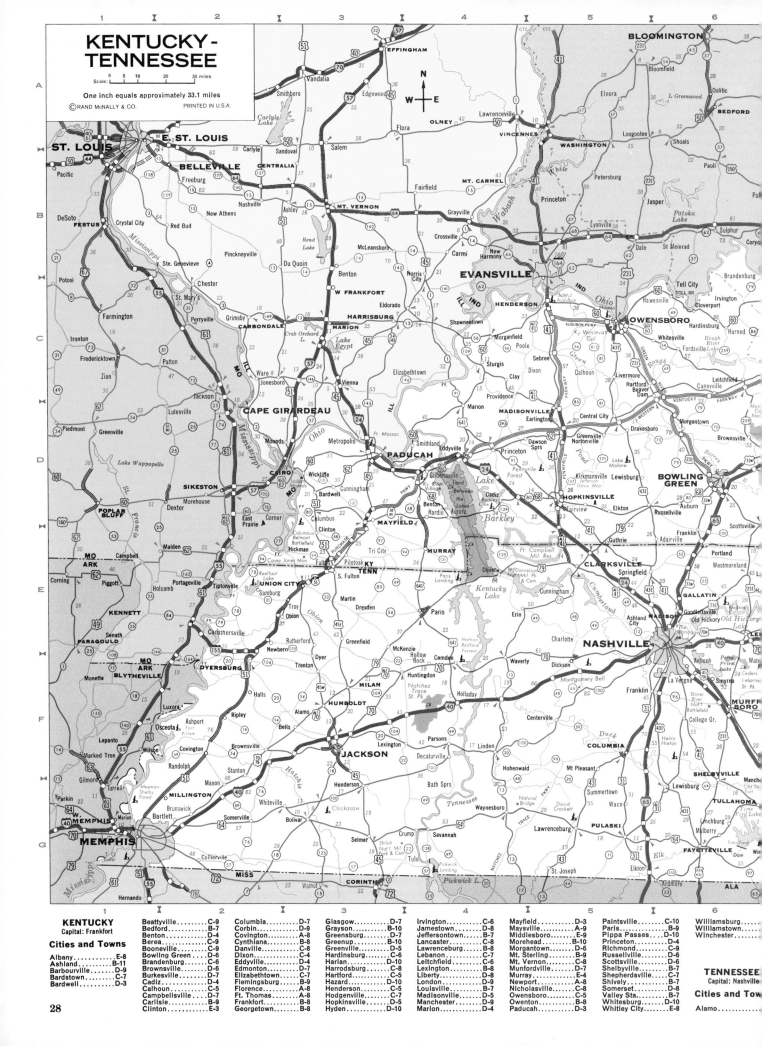

KENTUCKY-TENNESSEE

Scale
0 5 10   20   30 miles
One inch equals approximately 33.1 miles
© RAND McNALLY & CO.   PRINTED IN U.S.A.

KENTUCKY
Capital: Frankfort

Cities and Towns

Albany	E-8
Ashland	B-11
Barbourville	D-9
Bardstown	C-7
Bardwell	D-3
Beattyville	C-9
Bedford	B-7
Benton	D-4
Berea	C-9
Booneville	C-9
Bowling Green	D-6
Brandenburg	C-6
Brownsville	D-6
Burkesville	D-7
Cadiz	D-4
Calhoun	C-5
Campbellsville	D-7
Carlisle	B-9
Clinton	E-3
Columbia	D-7
Corbin	D-9
Covington	A-8
Cynthiana	B-8
Danville	C-8
Dixon	C-4
Eddyville	D-4
Edmonton	D-7
Elizabethtown	C-7
Flemingsburg	B-9
Florence	A-8
Ft. Thomas	A-8
Frankfort	B-8
Georgetown	B-8
Glasgow	D-7
Grayson	B-10
Greensburg	D-7
Greenup	B-10
Greenville	D-5
Hardinsburg	C-6
Harlan	D-10
Harrodsburg	C-8
Hartford	C-5
Hazard	D-10
Henderson	C-5
Hodgenville	C-7
Hopkinsville	D-5
Hyden	D-10
Irvington	C-6
Jamestown	D-8
Jeffersontown	B-7
Lancaster	C-8
Lawrenceburg	B-8
Lebanon	C-7
Leitchfield	C-6
Lexington	B-8
Liberty	C-8
London	D-9
Louisville	B-7
Madisonville	D-5
Manchester	D-9
Marion	D-4
Mayfield	D-3
Maysville	A-9
Middlesboro	E-9
Morehead	B-10
Morgantown	D-6
Mt. Sterling	B-9
Mt. Vernon	C-8
Munfordville	D-7
Murray	E-4
Newport	A-8
Nicholasville	C-8
Owensboro	C-5
Owenton	B-8
Paducah	D-3
Paintsville	C-10
Paris	B-9
Pippa Passes	D-10
Princeton	D-4
Richmond	C-9
Russellville	D-6
Scottsville	D-6
Shelbyville	B-7
Shepherdsville	C-7
Shively	B-7
Somerset	D-8
Valley Sta.	B-7
Whitesburg	D-10
Whitley City	E-8
Williamsburg	
Williamstown	
Winchester	

TENNESSEE
Capital: Nashville

Cities and Towns

Alamo	

28

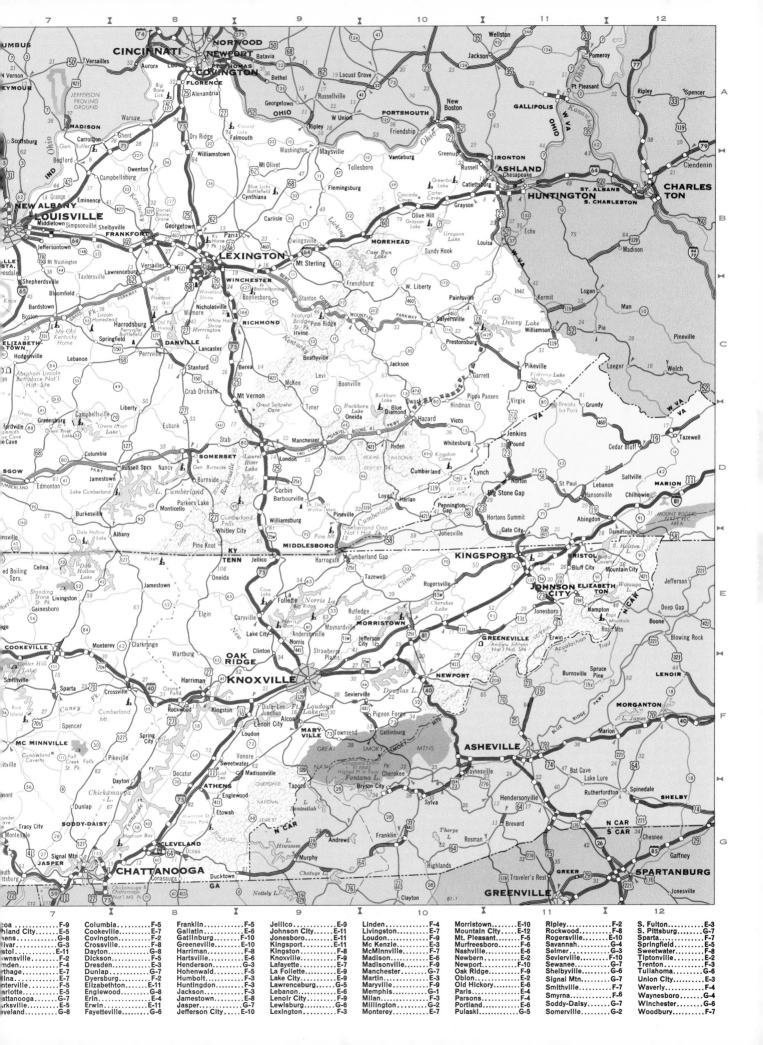

coa......7-9	Columbia......F-5	Franklin......F-5	Jellico......E-9	Linden......F-4	Morristown......E-10	Ripley......F-2	S. Fulton......E-3
hland City......E-5	Cookeville......E-7	Gallatin......E-6	Johnson City......E-11	Livingston......E-7	Rockwood......F-8	S. Pittsburg......G-7
ens......G-8	Covington......F-2	Gatlinburg......F-10	Jonesboro......E-11	Loudon......F-9	Mt. Pleasant......F-5	Rogersville......E-10	Sparta......F-7
lvar......G-3	Crossville......F-8	Greeneville......E-10	Kingsport......E-11	Mc Kenzie......E-3	Murfreesboro......F-6	Savannah......G-4	Springfield......E-5
stol......E-11	Dayton......G-8	Harriman......F-8	Kingston......F-8	McMinnville......F-7	Nashville......E-6	Selmer......G-3	Sweetwater......F-8
wnsville......F-2	Dickson......F-5	Hartsville......F-5	Knoxville......F-9	Madison......E-6	Newbern......F-2	Sevierville......F-10	Tiptonville......E-2
mden......F-4	Dresden......E-3	Henderson......G-3	Lafayette......E-6	Madisonville......F-9	Newport......F-10	Sewanee......G-7	Trenton......F-3
rthage......E-7	Dunlap......G-8	Hohenwald......F-5	La Follette......E-9	Manchester......F-7	Oak Ridge......F-9	Shelbyville......G-6	Tullahoma......G-6
lina......E-7	Dyersburg......F-2	Humbolt......F-3	Lake City......E-9	Martin......E-3	Oblon......E-2	Signal Mtn......G-7	Union City......E-3
nterville......F-5	Elizabethton......E-11	Huntingdon......F-4	Lawrenceburg......G-5	Maryville......F-9	Old Hickory......E-6	Smithville......F-7	Waverly......F-4
arlotte......E-5	Englewood......G-8	Jackson......F-3	Lebanon......E-6	Memphis......G-1	Paris......E-4	Smyrna......F-6	Waynesboro......G-4
attanooga......G-7	Erin......E-4	Jamestown......E-7	Lenoir City......F-9	Milan......F-3	Parsons......F-4	Soddy-Daisy......G-7	Winchester......G-6
arksville......E-5	Erwin......E-11	Jasper......G-7	Lewisburg......G-6	Millington......G-2	Portland......E-6	Somerville......G-2	Woodbury......F-7
veland......G-8	Fayetteville......G-6	Jefferson City......E-10	Lexington......F-3	Monterey......E-7	Pulaski......G-5		

Louisiana

See also pages 104-110

The Pelican State
Population: 4,203,972
Area: 48,523 square miles
  Land Area: 44,930 square miles
  Water Area: 3,593 square miles
Highest Point: Driskill Mountain,
  535 feet
Capital: Baton Rouge
Statehood: April 30, 1812
State Motto: Union, Justice, Confidence
State Bird: Eastern Brown Pelican
State Flower: Magnolia
State Tree: Bald Cypress
Time Zone: Central

Traditional Cuisines Are a Blend of Louisiana Cultures

Louisiana's blend of cultures has produced one of the nation's most exotic and varied cuisines. Here, you may literally taste the flavor of a state, and frequent visitors know that the best time to visit is at mealtime.

North Louisiana, with its rolling fields of cattle and cotton, was pioneered by settlers from the South. They brought their foods with them, and today tables in the homes and cafes of Ruston, Monroe, and Shreveport are set with catfish, cornbread, and collards. The first taste of French Louisiana comes in Natchitoches, the oldest town in the Louisiana Purchase. Here, the traditional food is the meat pie, a round of dough stuffed with ground beef, onions, and spices, and fried to a crispy crust. Natives eat it with red beans and rice; and they know you are from out of town if you eat meat pie with a fork instead of your fingers.

The foods of French Acadiana in southern Louisiana are found at almost every exit off Interstate 10. By travel-ing west to east from Texas to New Orleans, you will find a different taste at almost every stop. In Jennings, try boudin, a spiced sausage with mild and hot servings. Exit at Henderson for crawfish, and discover how the lowly crustacean has been lifted to haute cuisine. From Lafayette to Baton Rouge to New Orleans, Creole cookery reigns supreme. Seafoods are served with both French and Creole sauces, and nearly every restaurant offers the triumvirate of Louisiana cuisine—jambalaya, crawfish pie, and filé gumbo.

Throughout the year, Louisiana celebrates its food. You will find almost all of its flavors at New Orleans' food festival each July. Other towns in Louisiana pay homage to their own harvests from the land and the water: the sugarcane of New Iberia and the rice of Crowley; the strawberries of Ponchatoula and the pecans of Colfax; the shrimp of Morgan City, the oysters of Galliano, and the crawfish of Breaux Bridge. Not to be forgotten are the pastries so dear to the French Acadian's heart…golden croissants that seem to melt in your mouth, French butter cookies, custard-filled cream puffs, and light pastries topped with fresh fruit. In Louisiana, the palate counts its blessings, but never counts the calories.

Louisiana has preserved its storied past while striding purposefully into the future. This is particularly evident in New Orleans. In the top photograph, a skyscraper rises behind the colorful entrance to Piazza d'Italia, built as a tribute to the city's Italian inhabitants. Bottom: St. Louis Cathedral's steeples preside over the lively street scenes of Jackson Square, and visitors monitor Mississippi River traffic from a vantage point in a modern hotel. Right: Shrimp boats swing to their Bayou Lafourche moorings.

LOUISIANA

Capital: Baton Rouge

Cities and Towns

Abbeville	E-3
Alexandria	C-3
Amite	D-5
Arcadia	B-2
Bastrop	A-4
Baton Rouge	D-4
Benton	A-1
Bernice	A-2
Bogalusa	D-6
Bossier City	A-1
Bunkie	C-3
Campti	B-2
Chalmette	E-6
Clinton	D-5
Colfax	C-3
Columbia	B-3
Coushatta	B-2
Covington	D-6
Crowley	E-3
Denham Sprs	D-5
De Ridder	D-2
Donaldsonville	D-5
Edgard	D-5
Elizabeth	D-3
Eunice	D-3
Farmerville	A-3
Ferriday	C-4
Franklin	E-4
Franklinton	D-6
Gibsland	B-2
Glenmora	D-3
Golden Meadow	F-6
Grand Isle	F-6
Greensburg	D-5
Gretna	E-6
Hahnville	E-5
Hammond	D-5
Harrisonburg	B-3
Haynesville	A-2
Hodge	B-3
Homer	A-2
Houma	F-5
Jackson	D-4
Jeanerette	E-4
Jena	C-3
Jennings	E-3
Jonesboro	B-2
Kaplan	E-3
Lafayette	E-4
Lake Arthur	E-3
Lake Charles	E-2
Lake Providence	A-4
Laplace	D-5
Leesville	C-2
Many	C-2
Mansura	C-3
Marksville	C-3
Metairie	E-6
Minden	A-2
Monroe	A-3
Morgan City	E-5
Napoleonville	E-5
Natchitoches	C-2
New Iberia	E-4
New Orleans	E-6
New Roads	D-4
Newellton	B-4
Oakdale	D-3
Oak Grove	A-4
Oberlin	D-3
Opelousas	D-4
Pitkin	D-3
Plaquemine	D-4
Pointe a la Hache	F-6
Ponchatoula	D-5
Port Sulphur	F-6
Rayne	E-3
Rayville	A-4
Ruston	B-2
St. Francisville	D-4
St. Joseph	B-4
St. Martinville	E-4
Shreveport	A-1
Simmesport	C-3
Slidell	D-6
Sorrento	D-5
Springhill	A-2
Sulphur	E-2
Tallulah	B-4
Thibodaux	E-5
Vidalia	C-4
Ville Platte	D-3
Vivian	A-1
Washington	D-4
Waterproof	B-4
Welsh	E-2
W. Monroe	A-3
White Castle	D-4
Winnfield	B-3
Winnsboro	B-4

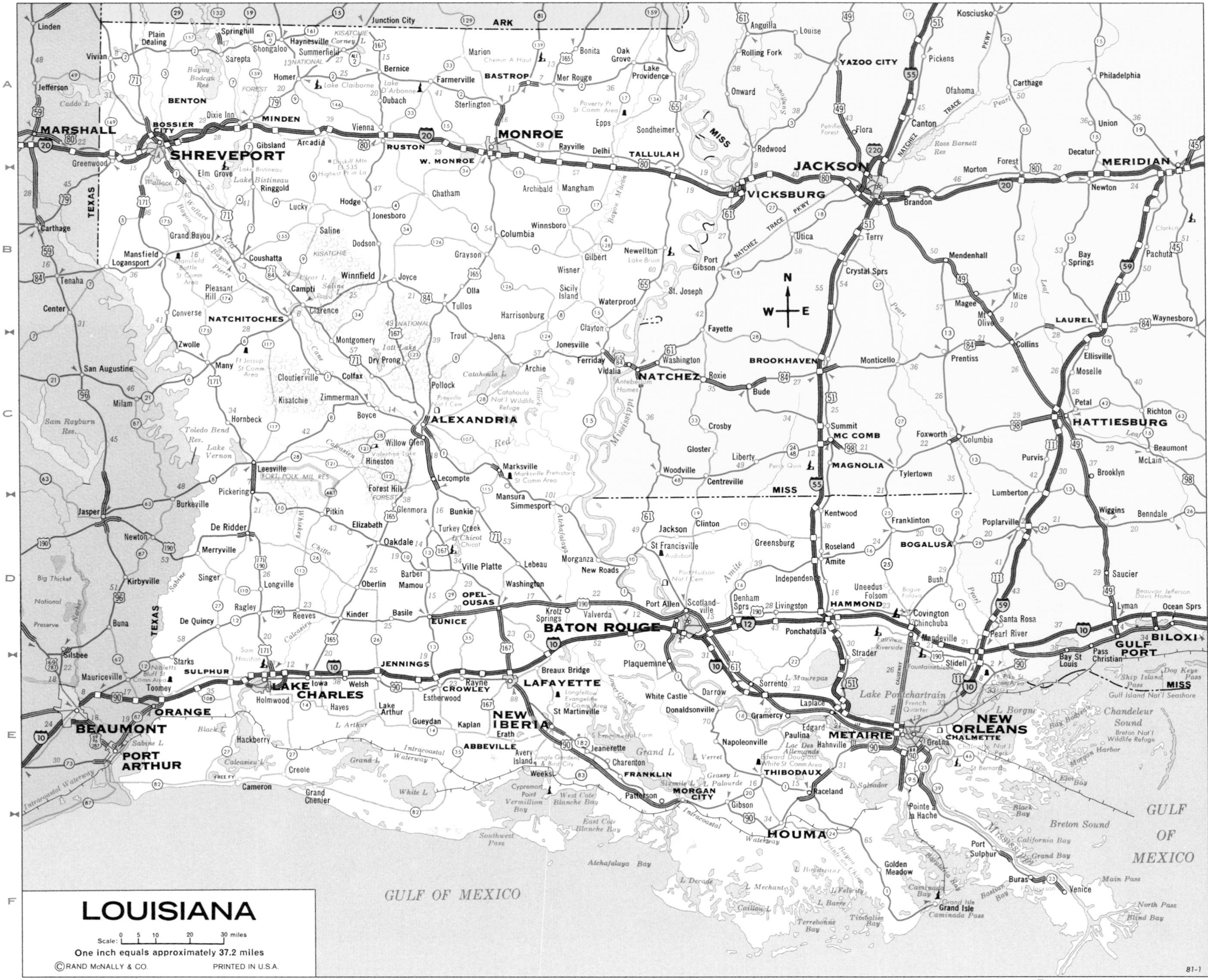

© RAND McNALLY & CO.   PRINTED IN U.S.A.

81-1

LOUISIANA

Scale
One inch equals approximately 37.2 miles

0   10   20   30 miles

31

Mississippi

See also pages 120-126

Magnolia State
Population: 2,520,638
Area: 47,716 square miles
  Land Area: 47,296 square miles
  Water Area: 420 square miles
Highest Point: Woodall Mountain,
  806 feet
Capital: Jackson
Statehood: December 10, 1817
State Motto: Virtute et Armis ("By Valor
  and Arms")
State Bird: Mockingbird
State Flower: Magnolia
State Tree: Magnolia
Time Zone: Central

Road to Mississippi History Is Its Namesake, the River

Mississippi's past is tied to the great wide river that forms its western boundary, nurtures the state's livelihood, and serves as a base of settlement. Much of Mississippi was pioneered west to east from the river, and you can discover the state the same way. Cross over at Greenville, and you will see how the river molded the character of the land. Mules and men carved cotton plantations from the delta wilderness; the antebellum Florewood River Plantation in Greenwood shows how the fiber has always rooted the lives and economy of the area. The river took the cotton to market; and as a Southern lifeline, it cradled the fortunes of the Confederacy. At Vicksburg, the national military park traces the struggle of the armies that fought for control of the waterway. Some of the houses that survived the seige and bombardment rise along Vicksburg streets. In one home, a gunboat cannonball is still embedded in a wall.

Mississippi is rightfully proud of its old homes, and each year many of its cities and towns, from Jackson, the state capital, to tiny Woodville, open their doors for pilgrimages. Few, however, can boast the architectural gems of Natchez, where lawns blush with azaleas during the spring pilgrimage. The French were among early Natchez settlers, but they waded ashore near Biloxi. Now, each spring and summer, Mississippians rediscover their coast, but they do not necessarily stop at the shore. Some steer their boats out to the sun-bleached beaches of the Gulf Islands National Seashore.

Mississippi is perhaps best expressed in song and story. Clarksdale's Delta Blues Museum houses music that was born in the delta. Meridian's Jimmie Rodgers Memorial and Museum tells the story of the singing brakeman who some call the father of country music. Much later, a Mississippian combined blues, country, and rock to capture audiences around the world. Elvis Presley's humble birthplace is preserved in Tupelo. William Faulkner tapped out his life's work on a typewriter in his Oxford home, Rowan Oak. The stories that won him the Nobel Prize for literature were set in his "postage stamp of soil," but they encompassed the universal terrain of the human heart, far beyond the boundary of the mud-brown Mississippi River.

Stately mansions and the great outdoors sum up much of what Mississippi is all about, as these photographs show. From left: A split-rail fence borders portions of the Natchez Trace Parkway; a yellow-crowned night heron ponders from a perch amid the flora; Stanton Hall, completed in 1857, evokes the antebellum charm of life in Natchez; fishermen cast their lines — and reflections — onto the smooth waters of a bayou near Pascagoula.

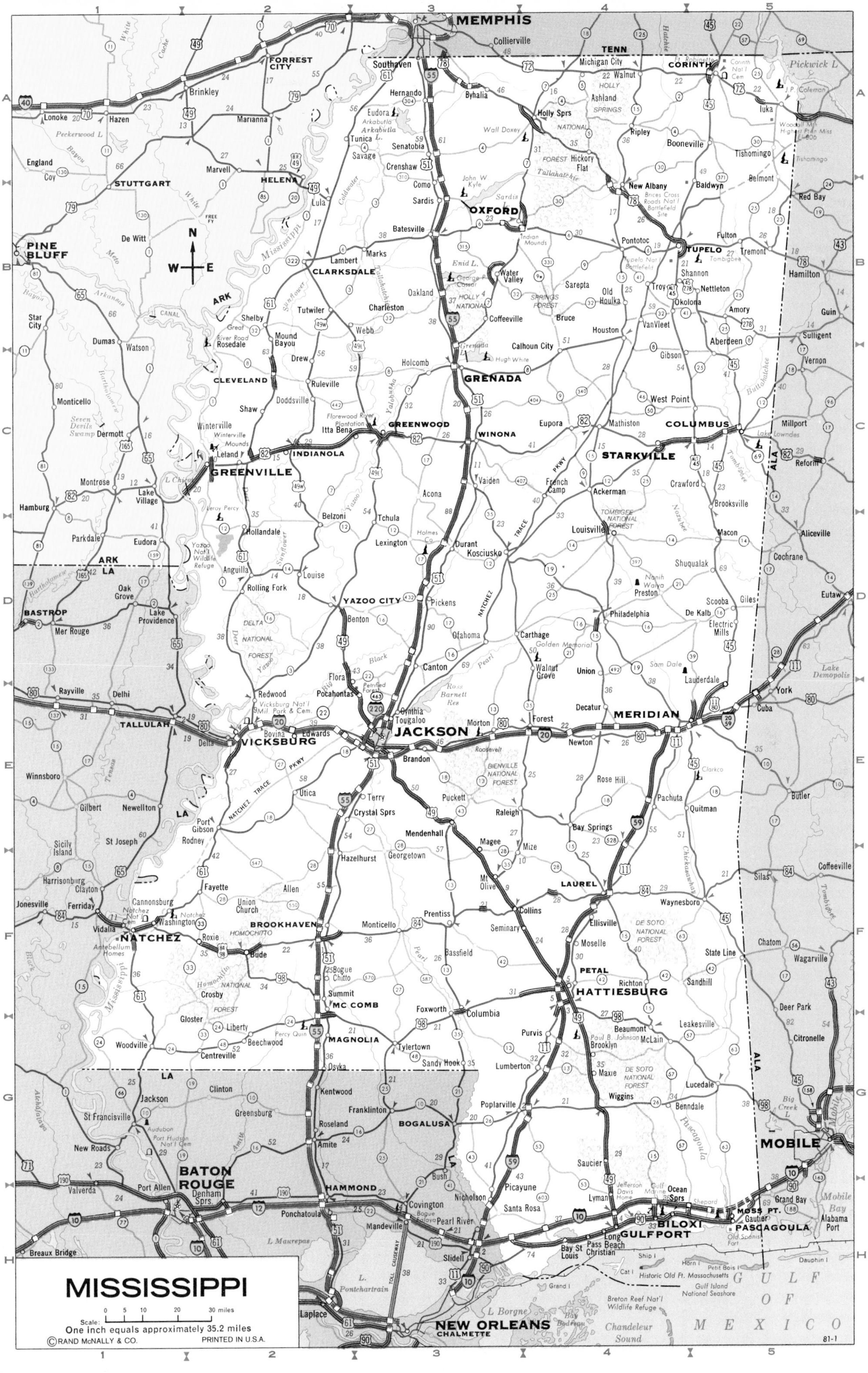

MISSISSIPPI

Scale:
0 5 10   20   30 miles
One inch equals approximately 35.2 miles

MISSISSIPPI
Capital: Jackson

Cities and Towns

Aberdeen..........C-5
Ackerman..........B-5
Amory..........D-2
Anguilla..........B-5
Baldwyn..........B-5
Batesville..........B-3
Bay St. Louis..........H-4
Bay Springs..........E-4
Beaumont..........G-4
Belmont..........B-5
Belzoni..........D-2
Biloxi..........H-4
Booneville..........A-5
Brandon..........E-3
Brookhaven..........F-2
Brooklyn..........G-4
Brooksville..........C-5
Bruce..........B-4
Bude..........F-2
Byhalia..........A-3
Calhoun City..........C-4
Canton..........D-3
Carthage..........D-3
Centerville..........G-2
Charleston..........B-3
Clarksdale..........B-2
Cleveland..........C-2
Coffeeville..........B-3
Collins..........F-3
Columbia..........F-3
Columbus..........C-5
Corinth..........A-5
Crosby..........F-2
Crystal Sprs...........E-2
Decatur..........E-4
De Kalb..........D-5
Drew..........C-2
Durant..........D-3
Edwards..........E-2
Ellisville..........F-4
Eupora..........C-4
Fayette..........F-2
Forest..........E-3
Foxworth..........F-3
Fulton..........B-5
Gloster..........G-2
Greenville..........C-2
Greenwood..........C-3
Grenada..........C-3
Gulfport..........H-4
Hattiesburg..........F-4
Hazlehurst..........F-2
Hernando..........A-3
Hollandale..........D-2
Holly Sprs...........A-4
Houston..........B-4
Indianola..........C-2
Itta Bena..........C-3
Iuka..........A-5
Jackson..........E-3
Kosclusko..........D-3
Lauderdale..........E-5
Laurel..........F-4
Leakesville..........G-5
Leland..........C-2
Lexington..........D-3
Liberty..........G-2
Long Beach..........H-4
Louisville..........D-4
Lucedale..........G-5
Lumberton..........G-4
McComb..........F-2
McLain..........F-4
Macon..........D-5
Magee..........F-3
Magnolia..........G-2
Marks..........B-3
Mathiston..........C-4
Mendenhall..........E-3
Meridian..........E-4
Mississippi City..........H-4
Monticello..........F-3
Morton..........E-3
Moselle..........F-4
Moss Pt...........H-5
Mt. Olive..........F-3
Natchez..........F-1
Nettleton..........B-5
New Albany..........B-4
Newton..........E-3
Nicholson..........H-3
Ocean Sprs...........H-4
Osyka..........G-2
Oxford..........B-3
Pascagoula..........H-5
Pass Christian..........H-4
Petal..........F-4
Philadelphia..........D-4
Picayune..........H-3
Pickens..........D-3
Pontotoc..........B-4
Poplarville..........G-3
Port Gibson..........E-2
Prentiss..........F-3
Purvis..........G-4
Quitman..........E-4
Raleigh..........E-3
Richton..........F-4
Ripley..........A-4
Rolling Fork..........D-2
Rosedale..........C-1
Roxie..........F-2
Ruleville..........B-3
Sardis..........B-3
Scooba..........D-5
Senatobia..........A-3
Shannon..........B-4
Shaw..........C-2
Shelby..........B-2
Starkville..........C-4
State Line..........F-5
Summit..........F-2
Tchula..........D-3
Terry..........E-3
Tunica..........A-3
Tupelo..........B-4
Tutwiler..........B-3
Tylertown..........G-3
Union..........D-4
Utica..........E-2
Vaiden..........C-3
Vicksburg..........E-2
Water Valley..........B-3
Waynesboro..........F-5
Webb..........B-3
West Point..........C-5
Wiggins..........G-4
Winona..........C-3
Woodville..........G-1
Yazoo City..........D-2

81-1

North Carolina

See also pages 127-135

The Tar Heel State
Population: 5,874,429
Area: 52,586 square miles
   Land Area: 48,798 square miles
   Water Area: 3,788 square miles
Highest Point: Mount Mitchell,
   6,684 feet
Capital: Raleigh
Statehood: November 21, 1789
State Motto: Esse Quam Videri ("To Be
   Rather Than To Seem")
State Bird: Cardinal
State Flower: Flowering Dogwood
State Tree: Pine
Time Zone: Eastern

Infinite Mountains and Historic Coast Prevail in North Carolina

If North Carolina evokes an image, it is a series of seemingly infinite mountains receding to the horizon. Nature pushed the western third of the state against the sky, wrapping the highest peaks in azure haze. Individual ranges, such as the Great Smokies, the Black, the Balsams, the Snowbirds, and the Brushy mountains, lure vacationers today as they have done for decades to see features only superlatives can describe—Mt. Mitchell, at 6,684 feet, the highest mountain in the East; Grandfather Mountain, one of the oldest mountains in the world; and Great Smoky Mountains National Park, one of the most visited parks in the country.

Where the slopes are steep, rhododendron and mountain laurel bloom profusely. In the deep shade of the cove forests, wildflowers peer above the humus. There are hundreds of miles of trails and thousands of acres of wilderness for the backpacker and surging rivers like the Nantahala and the Nolichucky for whitewater rafters. Small towns offer country stores and old inns, and country roads thread the highlands to bring you beautiful mountain scenery. Great Smoky Mountains National Park is the gem of the mountains, a 500,000-acre preserve spanning the border with Tennessee. Winding north and east from the park is the Blue Ridge Parkway, dancing along the eastern crest of the mountains until it passes into Virginia. Drive east from the parkway, and you leave the mountains behind to tour the rollercoaster hills of the Piedmont.

The state's largest cities are sprinkled through the Piedmont, as are some of the finest golf courses in the South. Spring is the season for golf, when the dogwood blooms hover cloudlike along the fairways. East of Raleigh, the capital, the land flattens to become the coastal plain, the agricultural heartland of the state. Furrowed fields spread to the horizon, sloped ever so slightly toward the coast.

The sandy coast is where the state's history began, at the Lost Colony on Roanoke Island. Along the wild reaches of the barrier islands known as the Outer Banks, man first took to the air at Kitty Hawk. Here also, guarding the miles of beaches, are the lighthouses, as much a symbol of the state as are the mountain ridges.

Like several of its sister states, North Carolina claims a share of the Appalachians, the Piedmont Plateau, and the Atlantic Coast. From top: Fall gently tinges mountain hardwoods; sunflowers grow in profusion along the Blue Ridge Parkway; fishermen test the surf at Cape Hatteras; thick stands of hardwood line the New River's banks.

South Carolina

See also pages 145-153

The Palmetto State
Population: 3,119,208
Area: 31,055 square miles
  Land Area: 30,225 square miles
  Water Area: 830 square miles
Highest Point: Sassafras Mountain,
  3,560 feet
Capital: Columbia
Statehood: May 23, 1788
State Motto: Animis Opibusque Parati
  ("Prepared in Mind and Resources")
  Dum Spiro Spero ("While I Breathe, I
  Hope")
State Bird: Carolina Wren
State Flower: Carolina Jessamine
State Tree: Palmetto
Time Zone: Eastern

South Carolina's Gentle Low Country Culture Spreads Inland

South Carolina enchants, charming its visitors with grace and poise, aristocracy and pride. From the Low Country to the state's high-mountain borders, South Carolina funneled early settlers inland, spreading a certain culture, cultivating that special style, as memorable and soft as the Low Country accent.

Charles Towne was the beginning. Here the English made their bid at settlement, founding a colony that spawned modern-day Charleston. A sense of the past still enfolds Charleston. Carriages roll along its streets, providing the best way to travel through its historic magic. Boats ferry visitors to Fort Sumter, where South Carolina blasted the Confederacy into actuality. North of the city stand mansions of the past, finely built ancestral homes surrounded by grounds lush with camellias, roses, azaleas, and stately moss-draped oaks.

Civilization spread out from Charleston, once the state capital, sending settlers north and south along the hundreds of coastal miles. Grand old homes of those settlers still line the streets of towns like Beaufort, facing east to the gentle ocean breezes. But life on the coast didn't stand still with the turning centuries. Today, resorts dot the string of sea islands. Savoring a relaxed Low Country style, they serve up natural beauty, ocean-side sports, and regional seafood delicacies, blending entertainment with a casual elegance.

Low Country legislators first moved north to Columbia in the 1700s, when that Piedmont city became the state capital. The grandness they brought survives in the old State House; the future they envisioned is symbolized by the state's university. Today, like spokes from a hub, modern interstates lead to other growing cities, such as Spartanburg, Greenville, and small but graceful Aiken, where polo and thoroughbreds stand as traditions.

Far to the north, where South Carolina cuts between its neighboring states, lofty mountains, as unexpected as they are beautiful, outline the state's border. This is a land a long way from the flatness of the Low Country, a landscape where mountains reach skyward and free-flowing waterfalls tumble toward the sea. It is a different South Carolina, to be sure, but it is one that charms just as surely as its sister coast enchants.

The Civil War began at Fort Sumter on Sullivans Island near Charleston, where reminders of the Old South, including Old Slave Market, have been preserved. Below: Camellias surround cypress knees in Magnolia Gardens, near Charleston, and a nest of turtle eggs on Fripp Island attest to the natural attributes of South Carolina.

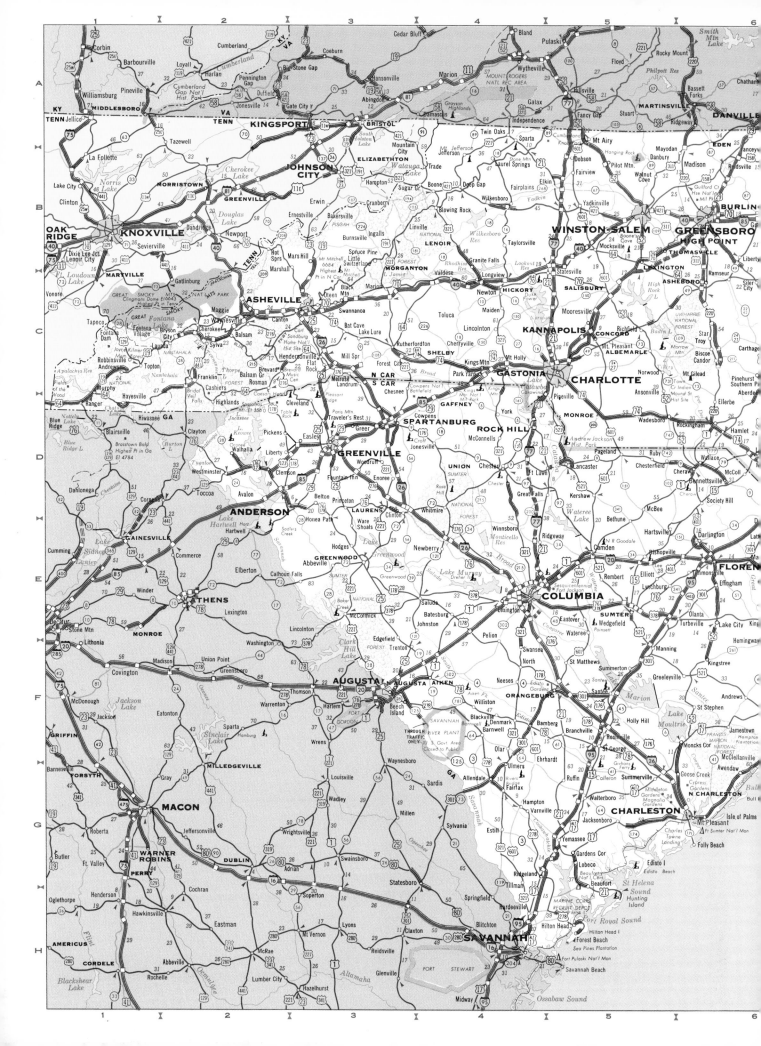

NORTH CAROLINA
Capital: Raleigh
Cities and Towns

Aberdeen	C-6
Ahoskie	B-9
Albemarle	C-5
Andrews	C-1
Apex	C-7
Asheboro	C-6
Asheville	C-3
Bakersville	B-3
Bayboro	C-9
Beaufort	D-9
Benson	C-7
Blowing Rock	B-4
Boone	B-4
Brevard	C-2
Bryson City	C-2
Burgaw	D-8
Burlington	B-6
Burnsville	B-3
Camden	C-2
Canton	C-2
Carthage	C-6
Cary	B-7
Chadbourn	E-7
Chapel Hill	B-6
Charlotte	C-5
Cherokee	C-2
Cherryville	C-4
Clayton	C-7
Clinton	D-7
Columbia	B-9
Columbus	D-2
Concord	C-5
Currituck	A-10
Danbury	B-5
Dobson	B-5
Dunn	C-7
Durham	B-7
Eden	A-6
Edenton	B-9
Elizabeth City	B-9
Elizabethtown	D-7
Enfield	B-8
Erwin	C-7
Farmville	C-8
Fayetteville	D-7
Flat Rock	C-3
Forest City	C-3
Franklin	C-2
Fuquay-Varina	C-7
Gastonia	C-4
Goldsboro	C-8
Graham	B-6
Granite Falls	B-4
Greensboro	B-6
Greenville	C-8
Halifax	B-8
Hamlet	D-6
Havelock	D-9
Hayesville	D-1
Henderson	B-7
Hendersonville	C-3
Hertford	B-9
Hickory	C-4
High Point	B-6
Hillsborough	B-6
Jackson	A-8
Jacksonville	D-8
Jefferson	B-4
Kannapolis	C-5
Kenansville	D-8
Kings Mtn.	C-4
Kinston	C-8
Lauada	C-2
Laurinburg	D-6
Lenoir	B-4
Lexington	C-5
Lillington	C-7
Lincolnton	C-4
Longview	C-4
Louisburg	B-7
Lumberton	D-7
Madison	B-6
Manteo	B-10
Marion	C-3
Marshall	B-3
Mars Hill	B-3
Maxton	D-6
Maysville	D-8
Mocksville	B-5
Monroe	D-5
Mooresville	C-5
Morganton	B-3
Mt. Airy	A-5
Mt. Gilead	C-6
Mt. Holly	C-4
Mt. Olive	C-7
Murphy	C-1
Nashville	B-8
New Bern	C-9
Newland	B-3
Newton	C-4
Norwood	C-5
Oteen	C-3
Oxford	B-7
Pilot Mtn.	B-5
Pinehurst	C-6
Pineville	D-5
Pittsboro	C-7
Plymouth	B-9
Raeford	D-6
Raleigh	B-7
Red Sprs.	D-6
Reidsville	B-6
Roanoke Rapids	A-8
Robbinsville	C-1
Rockingham	D-6
Rocky Mt.	B-8
Rose Hill	D-7
Rowland	D-6
Roxboro	B-6
Rutherfordton	C-3
St. Paul	D-6
Salisbury	C-5
Sanford	C-7
Scotland Neck	B-8
Shelby	C-4
Smithfield	C-7
Snow Hill	C-8
Southern Pines	C-6
Southport	E-8
Sparta	A-4
Spring Hope	B-7
Spruce Pine	B-3
Statesville	B-5
Swannanoa	C-3
Swanquarter	C-9
Swansboro	D-9
Sylva	C-2

Tabor City	E-7
Tarboro	B-8
Taylorsville	B-4
Thomasville	B-5
Trenton	C-8
Troy	C-6
Valdese	C-4
Vanceboro	C-8
Wadesboro	D-5
Wake Forest	B-7
Wallace	D-8
Walnut Cove	B-5
Warrenton	B-7
Warsaw	D-7
Washington	C-9
Waynesville	C-2
Wentworth	B-6
Whiteville	E-7
Wilkesboro	B-4
Williamston	B-8
Wilmington	E-8
Wilson	C-8
Windsor	B-9
Winston-Salem	B-5
Winton	A-9
Yanceyville	B-6

SOUTH CAROLINA
Capital: Columbia
Cities and Towns

Abbeville	E-3
Aiken	F-4
Allendale	G-4
Anderson	D-2
Andrews	F-6
Bamberg	F-4
Barnwell	F-4
Batesburg	E-4
Beaufort	G-5
Belton	D-3
Bennettsville	D-6
Bethune	D-5
Bishopville	E-5
Blackville	F-4
Branchville	F-5
Calhoun Falls	E-3
Camden	E-5
Charleston	G-6
Cheraw	D-6
Chester	D-4
Chesterfield	D-5
Clemson	D-2
Clinton	D-3
Columbia	E-4
Conway	F-6
Cowpens	D-4
Darlington	E-6
Denmark	F-4
Dillon	E-6
Easley	D-3
Edgefield	E-3
Elliott	E-5
Estill	G-4
Fairfax	G-4
Florence	E-6
Fountain Inn	D-3
Gaffney	D-4
Georgetown	F-6
Great Falls	D-4
Greeleyville	E-6
Greenville	D-3
Greenwood	E-3
Greer	D-3
Hampton	G-4
Hardeeville	H-4
Hartsville	E-5
Hemingway	E-6
Hodges	E-3
Holly Hill	F-5
Honea Path	D-3
Jacksonboro	G-5
Jamestown	F-6
Johnston	E-4
Jonesville	D-4
Kershaw	D-5
Kingstree	F-6
Lake City	E-6
Lancaster	D-5
Latta	E-6
Laurens	D-3
Lexington	E-4
Liberty	D-2
Loris	E-7
Lynchburg	E-5
McBee	D-5
McColl	D-6
McConnells	D-4
McCormick	E-3
Manning	F-5
Marion	E-6
Moncks Cor.	F-6
Mt. Pleasant	G-6
Murrells Inlet	F-6
Myrtle Beach	F-7
Newberry	E-4
Nichols	E-6
North	F-4
North Augusta	F-3
N. Charleston	G-6
Olanta	E-6
Orangeburg	F-5
Pageland	D-5
Pickens	D-2
Princeton	D-3
Rembert	E-5
Ridgeland	G-4
Rock Hill	D-4
St. George	F-5
St. Matthews	F-5
St. Stephen	F-6
Saluda	E-4
Society Hill	D-6
Spartanburg	D-3
Summerton	F-5
Summerville	G-5
Sumter	E-5
Swansea	F-4
Timmonsville	E-6
Traveler's Rest	D-3
Union	D-4
Varnville	G-4
Walhalla	D-2
Walterboro	G-5
Ware Shoals	E-3
Westminster	D-2
Whitmire	D-4
Williston	F-4
Winnsboro	E-4
Woodruff	D-3
York	D-4

NORTH-SOUTH CAROLINA
Scale:
One inch equals approximately 35.6 miles
© RAND McNALLY & CO.   PRINTED IN U.S.A.
81-1

CEDAR ISLAND—OCRACOKE FERRY
Reservations requested from the point of
departure within 30 days of departure.
Phone: Cedar Island (919) 225-3551
Ocracoke (919) 928-3841
Toll: Car and occupants—$5.00 one way

Oklahoma

See also pages 136-144

Sooner State
Population: 3,025,266
Area: 69,919 square miles
  Land Area: 68,782 square miles
  Water Area: 1,137 square miles
Highest Point: Black Mesa, 4,973 feet
Capital: Oklahoma City
Statehood: November 16, 1907
State Motto: Labor Conquers All Things
State Bird: Scissortailed Flycatcher
State Flower: Mistletoe
State Tree: Redbud
Time Zone: Central

Names and Places Reflect Oklahoma's Indian Heritage

The heritage of the American Indian is written across Oklahoma more than any other state. The cultures of the state's many tribes live on in art, festivals, dances, and tribal gatherings, and in the names of Oklahoma's places and people. The map of modern Oklahoma is liberally sprinkled with Indian names. Even the name Oklahoma comes from the Indian words for "home of the redman." Other Indian names like Muskogee and Okmulgee roll off the tongue as lyrically as music. Some are tricky. Will Rogers sometimes joked that he was reluctant to say he was from Oologah because "nobody but an Indian could pronounce Oologah."

Some 50,000 Indians of the Five Civilized Tribes, mostly from Southern states, were brought to Oklahoma after it was set aside as Indian Territory by the U.S. government in 1830. In Tahlequah in 1839, Creeks from North Carolina, Tennessee, Georgia, and Alabama established the Cherokee Nation. The Cherokees developed their own constitution and laws and built a capitol and supreme court building that still stand.

More Cherokee history comes to life at Tsa-La-Gi, the Cherokee Heritage Center, where there are reconstructions of early Cherokee villages and an outdoor theatre. The drama *Trail of Tears* is produced here each summer. The town of Sallisaw preserves the home of Sequoyah, the Indian scholar who invented the alphabet that gave the Cherokees a written language. In Muskogee, contemporary Indian art is showcased at the Five Civilized Tribes Museum. Tribal museums of the Osage, whose lands held huge oil deposits, are at Pawhuska; and Okmulgee, the capital of the Creek Indian Nation, has the Creek Council House Museum.

Another major center of Indian lore is Anadarko, where museums and the

reconstructed villages of Indian City trace the heritage of the seven Plains tribes. Each August, Anadarko visitors can sit in on one of the largest Indian gatherings in the nation at the American Indian Exposition. Traces of Oklahoma's Indian heritage linger in almost every part of the state, from old tribal towns to modern cities. Not far from its downtown skyscrapers, Tulsa preserves the Council Oak where Creek Indians

Oklahoma events range from ballet to roundups. Texas longhorns are rounded up annually at the Wichita Mountains National Wildlife Refuge. The Oklahoma Summer Institute ballet dancers perform at Quartz Mountain State Park, where phlox grow between the 536-million-year-old rocks.

renewed their council fire in a new home after journeying from Alabama. The name Tulsa is said to have come from the Creek word *tallasi*, which means town.

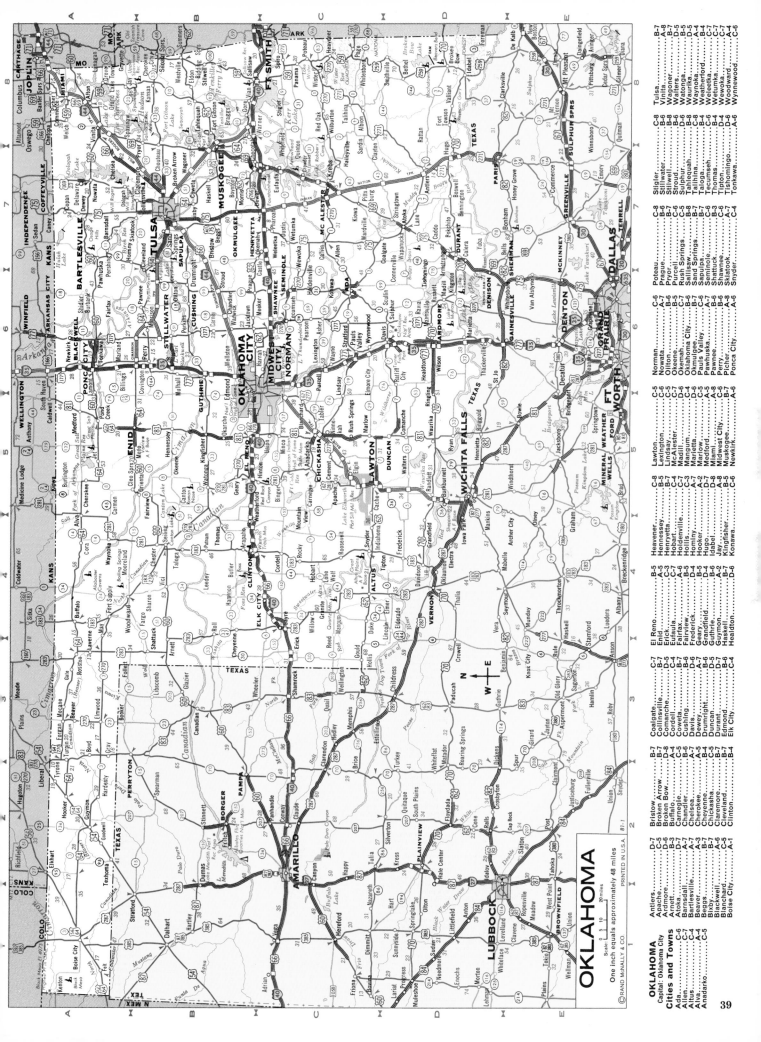

Texas

See also pages 162-175

The Lone Star State
Population: 14,228,383
Area: 267,338 square miles
   Land Area: 262,134 square miles
   Water Area: 5,204 square miles
Highest Point: Guadalupe Peak,
   8,749 feet
Capital: Austin
Statehood: December 29, 1845
State Motto: Friendship
State Bird: Mockingbird
State Flower: Bluebonnet
State Tree: Pecan
Time Zones: Central (all Texas except
   the westernmost area); Mountain (El
   Paso and Hudspeth counties)

The Big State of Texas with Its Big Ranches Has Big Cities

Just as vast ranches and wide-open spaces were once symbolic of Texas, the state is now just as recognized for its cities. More than half of the 14.2 million people in Texas live within the triangle formed by Houston, San Antonio, and Dallas-Fort Worth. In between, Austin perches on the rim of the Hill Country. And on the fringes, Corpus Christi sits on the coastal gateway to Padre Island; El Paso nestles in a desert pass beside the Rio Grande; and Amarillo rises on the Plains. Only a state as big as Texas could hold cities so diverse.

Houston is a city of brawn and brains—strong enough to load a thousand ships and delicate enough to transplant a heart. Almost as soon as the battle of San Jacinto gave Texas its independence, Texans rolled up their sleeves and started building Houston. And they are still at it. Houston has always tackled projects in grand style, from the Astrodome bringing football indoors to the Johnson Space Center helping put a man on the moon.

Meanwhile, the cities of Dallas and Fort Worth, ringed by more than 50 suburbs, literally reach from eastern Texas to western Texas in one long metropolitan center that holds almost three million people. Fort Worth is still thought of as one of the most western cities in the state. Downtown streets are paved with red bricks, and a rip-roaring stockyards district is reminiscent of the era when Fort Worth was a cow town on the cattle drives. Dallas, on the other hand, is thought of as a cosmopolitan center of fashion and finance. Newspaper columnist Damon Runyon once described the difference between Dallas and Fort Worth: "In Dallas, the women wear high heels. In Fort Worth, the men do." In San Antonio, the downtown River Walk winds back to the city's Spanish heritage that survives in landmarks like the Alamo, a trail of missions, and the Spanish Governor's Palace. San Antonio treats its past with as much gusto as some cities treat their future. Even the city's newest attraction, the San Antonio Museum of Art, is housed in a huge nineteenth-century brewery.

Austin is home to the state capitol, picturesque swimming holes, rolling hills, and country music. Corpus Christi is a sparkling coastal showplace. And El Paso is two cities in one, a thriving metropolis and a western outpost that shares culture and history with Juarez.

In a state as big as Texas, you expect plenty of variety, and the Lone Star State never disappoints you. Blooming cactus enliven an arid expanse of west Texas; cattle explore new surroundings at the Fort Worth stockyards; passengers pedal a boat along San Antonio's Paseo del Rio; horses get acquainted on a range near El Paso; Houston's ever-changing skyline and a gazebo cast their reflections on a park's pond; Lighthouse Rock acts as a sentry in Palo Duro Canyon State Park.

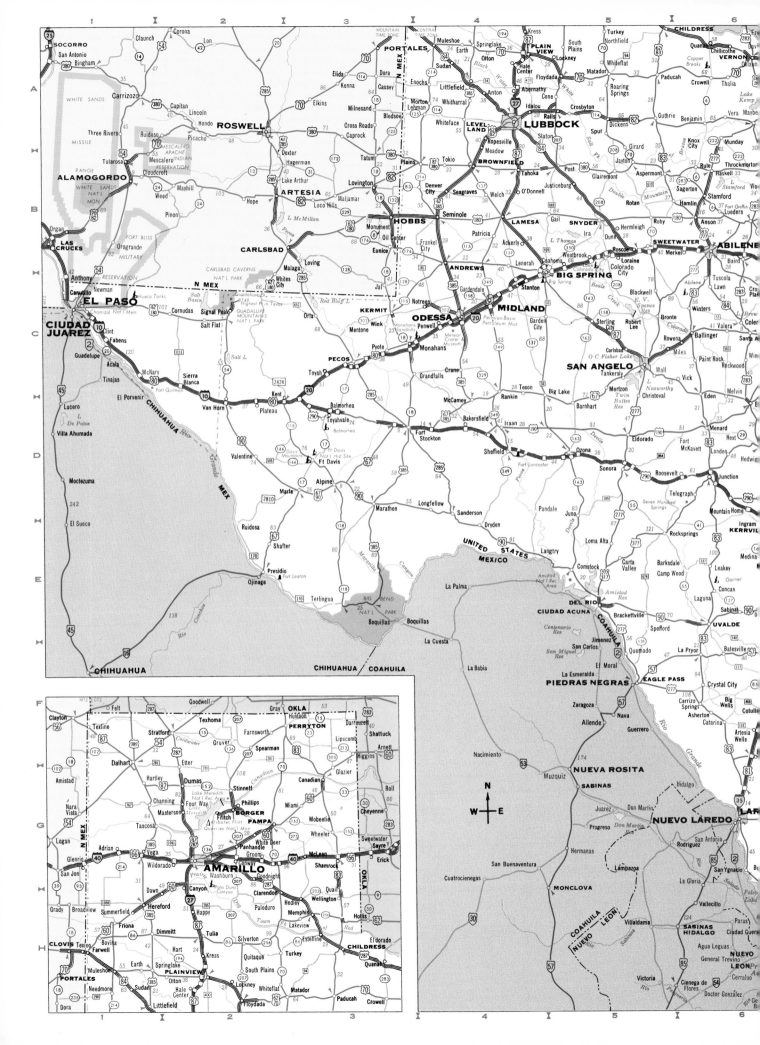

TEXAS
Capital: Austin

Cities and Towns

Abilene..........B-6
Albany..........B-6
Alice..........G-7
Alpine..........D-3
Amarillo..........G-2
Anahuac..........F-9
Anderson..........D-8
Andrews..........B-4
Angleton..........E-9
Anson..........B-6
Archer City..........A-7
Arlington..........B-7
Aspermont..........B-5
Athens..........C-8
Austin..........D-7
Baird..........B-6
Ballinger..........C-6
Balmorhea..........C-2
Bandera..........E-6
Bastrop..........D-7
Bay City..........E-8
Baytown..........E-9
Beaumont..........D-10
Beeville..........F-7
Bellville..........E-8
Belton..........D-7
Benjamin..........A-6
Big Lake..........C-5
Big Spring..........C-5
Boerne..........E-6
Bonham..........A-8
Borger..........G-2
Brackettville..........E-5
Brady..........D-6
Brazosport Area..........E-9
Breckenridge..........B-6
Brenham..........D-8
Brownfield..........B-4
Brownsville..........H-7
Brownwood..........C-6
Bryan..........D-8
Burnet..........D-7
Caldwell..........D-8
Cameron..........D-8
Canadian..........G-3
Canton..........B-8
Canyon..........G-2
Carrizo Springs..........F-6
Carthage..........B-9
Center..........C-10
Centerville..........C-8
Channing..........G-1
Childress..........A-5
Clarendon..........H-2
Clarksville..........A-9
Claude..........G-2
Cleburne..........B-7
Coldspring..........D-9
Coleman..........C-6
College
  Station..........D-8
Colorado City..........B-5
Columbus..........E-8
Comanche..........C-6
Conroe..........D-9
Cooper..........A-8
Corpus Christi..........G-7
Corsicana..........C-8
Cotulla..........F-6
Crane..........C-4
Crockett..........C-9
Crosbyton..........A-5
Crowell..........A-6
Crystal City..........F-6
Cuero..........B-9
Daingerfield..........B-9
Dalhart..........F-1
Dallas..........B-8
Decatur..........B-7
Del Rio..........E-5
Denison..........A-8
Denton..........B-7
Denver City..........B-4
Dickens..........A-5
Dimmitt..........H-1
Donna..........H-7
Dumas..........G-2
Eagle Pass..........F-5
Eastland..........B-6
Edinburg..........H-7
Edna..........E-8
Eldorado..........D-5
El Paso..........C-1
Emory..........B-8
Ennis..........C-8
Fairfield..........C-8
Falfurrias..........G-7
Farwell..........H-1
Floresville..........E-7
Floydada..........A-5
Ft. Davis..........D-3
Ft. Stockton..........D-3
Ft. Worth..........B-7
Franklin..........D-8
Fredericksburg..........D-6
Freeport..........E-9
Friona..........H-1
Gail..........B-5
Gainesville..........A-7
Galveston..........E-9
Garden City..........C-5
Gatesville..........C-7
Georgetown..........D-7
George West..........F-7
Giddings..........D-8
Gilmer..........B-9
Gladewater..........B-9
Glen Rose..........C-7
Goldthwaite..........C-6
Goliad..........F-7
Gonzales..........E-7
Graham..........B-6
Granbury..........B-7
Greenville..........B-8
Groesbeck..........D-9
Groveton..........D-9
Hallettsville..........E-8
Hamilton..........C-7
Harlingen..........H-7
Haskell..........B-6
Hebbronville..........G-6
Hemphill..........C-10
Hempstead..........D-8
Henderson..........C-9
Henrietta..........A-7
Hereford..........H-1
Hillsboro..........C-7
Hondo..........E-6
Houston..........E-9
Huntsville..........D-9
Jacksboro..........B-7
Jacksonville..........C-9

Jasper..........D-10
Jefferson..........B-9
Johnson City..........D-7
Jourdanton..........F-6
Junction..........D-6
Kamay..........A-7
Karnes City..........F-7
Kaufman..........B-8
Keltys..........C-9
Kermit..........C-3
Kerrville..........E-6
Kilgore..........B-9
Killeen..........D-7
Kingsville..........G-7
Kountze..........D-10
La Grange..........E-8
Lake Jackson..........E-9
Lamesa..........B-4
Lampasas..........D-7
Laredo..........G-6
Leakey..........E-6
Levelland..........A-4
Liberty..........D-9
Linden..........B-9
Lipscomb..........F-3
Littlefield..........A-4
Livingston..........D-9
Llano..........D-6
Lockhart..........E-7
Longview..........B-9
Lubbock..........A-4
Lufkin..........C-9
McAllen..........H-7
McKinney..........B-8
Madisonville..........D-8
Marathon..........D-3
Marfa..........D-3
Marlin..........C-8
Marshall..........B-9
Mason..........D-6
Matador..........A-5
Memphis..........H-3
Menard..........D-6
Mercedes..........H-7
Meridian..........C-7
Mertzon..........C-5
Miami..........G-3
Midland..........C-4
Mineral Wells..........B-7
Mission..........H-7
Monahans..........C-3
Montague..........A-7
Morton..........A-4
Mount Pleasant..........B-9
Mount Vernon..........B-9
Muleshoe..........A-4
Nacogdoches..........C-9
Nederland..........D-10
New Braunfels..........E-7
Newton..........D-10
Odessa..........C-4
Orange..........D-10
Orange Grove..........F-7
Ozona..........D-5
Paducah..........A-5
Paint Rock..........C-6
Palestine..........C-9
Palo Pinto..........B-7
Pampa..........G-2
Panhandle..........G-2
Paris..........A-9
Pearsall..........F-6
Pecos..........C-3
Perryton..........F-2
Pharr..........H-7
Pittsburg..........B-9
Plains..........B-4
Plainview..........A-4
Port Arthur..........E-10
Port Lavaca..........F-8
Post..........B-5
Quitman..........B-9
Rankin..........C-4
Raymondville..........H-7
Refugio..........F-7
Richmond..........E-9
Rio Grande City..........H-6
Robert Lee..........C-5
Robstown..........G-7
Roby..........B-5
Rockport..........F-8
Rocksprings..........E-5
Rockwall..........B-8
Rosenberg..........B-8
Rusk..........C-9
San Angelo..........C-5
San Antonio..........E-7
San Augustine..........C-10
San Benito..........H-7
Sanderson..........D-4
San Diego..........G-7
San Marcos..........E-7
San Saba..........D-6
Seguin..........E-7
Seminole..........B-4
Seymour..........A-6
Sherman..........A-8
Sierra Blanca..........C-2
Silverton..........H-2
Sinton..........F-7
Snyder..........B-5
Sonora..........D-5
Spearman..........F-2
Stamford..........B-6
Stephenville..........C-7
Sterling City..........C-5
Stinnett..........G-2
Stratford..........F-2
Sulphur Springs..........B-9
Sweetwater..........B-6
Tahoka..........B-4
Temple..........D-7
Terrell..........B-8
Texarkana..........A-10
Texas City..........E-9
Throckmorton..........B-6
Tilden..........F-7
Tulia..........H-2
Tyler..........B-9
Uvalde..........E-6
Van Horn..........D-2
Vega..........G-1
Vernon..........A-6
Victoria..........F-8
Waco..........C-7
Waxahachie..........B-8
Weatherford..........B-7
Wellington..........H-3
Weslaco..........H-7
Wharton..........E-8
Wheeler..........G-2
Wichita Falls..........A-7
Woodville..........D-10
Zapata..........G-6

43

Virginia

See also pages 176-185

Old Dominion State
Population: 5,346,279
Area: 40,817 square miles
  Land Area: 39,780 square miles
  Water Area: 1,037 square miles
Highest Point: Mount Rogers, 5,729 feet
Capital: Richmond
Statehood: June 25, 1788
State Motto: Sic Semper Tyrannis
  ("Thus Always to Tyrants")
State Bird: Cardinal
State Flower: Flowering Dogwood
State Tree: Dogwood
Time Zone: Eastern

Virginia Historic Homes Mark Birthplace of Nation's Leaders

Virginia is often referred to as the "Birthplace of the Nation." For it was here, at Jamestown, that the first permanent English settlement was founded in 1607. In the state also are the birthplaces and homes of many of the men who fought for freedom and who helped shape the fledgling United States of America.

George Washington was born about 38 miles east of Fredericksburg. Today the site is preserved as a national monument. In Winchester, the survey office he used during the erection of Ft. Loudoun now houses a museum. And just outside Washington, D.C. stands a reconstruction of the gristmill he operated on Dogue Run. The most famous site associated with the first president of the United States, though, is Mount Vernon, his plantation home just south of the nation's capital.

Another president, James Monroe, was born near Washington's birthsite. Only a roadside marker remains to note the fact. More tangible evidence of Monroe's life is found at the James Monroe Museum and Library in Fredericksburg, where he began his public career, and at Ash Lawn, his home that was designed by Thomas Jefferson and built on land adjacent to Jefferson's beautiful Monticello near Charlottesville.

Few homes can compare to Monti-cello, a living testament to the creativity and intelligence of Thomas Jefferson, who became the nation's third president. Another president, Woodrow Wilson, was born in Staunton, and his home there is open to visitors.

The traces of other famous men are scattered across the state. Scotchtown, in Ashland, was the home of Patrick Henry and the childhood home of Dolley Madison. Red Hill, near Brookneal, was the last home and burial site of Patrick Henry. George Rogers Clark, American Revolutionary frontier leader, was born near Charlottesville, and today a restored log cabin moved to the area marks the site. Stratford Hall, in Montross, is the birthplace of Robert E. Lee. His boyhood home is in Alexandria. And in Gloucester is the birthplace of Walter Reed, the army surgeon who discovered that a certain species of mosquito caused yellow fever.

There are also entire towns that wear the memory of a notable person. Lexington, home of Stonewall Jackson while he taught at Virginia Military Institute, is one. Both his restored house and a museum at VMI contain memorabilia of his life.

Handsome buildings and magnificent gardens are synonymous with Virginia. Left to right: Carter Grove is among the handsome homes on James River; the University of Virginia, planned by Thomas Jefferson, reflects the Palladian influence; Historic Garden Week includes jewellike gardens.

West Virginia

See also pages 192-199

The Mountain State
Population: 1,949,644
Area: 24,181 square miles
   Land Area: 24,070 square miles
   Water Area: 111 square miles
Highest Point: Spruce Knob, 4,862 feet
Capital: Charleston
Statehood: June 20, 1863
State Motto: Montani Semper Liberi
   ("Mountaineers Are Always Free")
State Bird: Cardinal
State Flower: Rhododendron
State Tree: Sugar Maple
Time Zone: Eastern

West Virginia Top-of-the-World Places Are Natural and Historic

All roads in West Virginia lead to the mountains. From cities and towns alike, they wind to the heavens, scaling the state's highest peaks, then drop into unexpectedly dazzling valleys, which are lush with vegetation and rich in legend and lore.

West Virginia's attractions, both natural and historic, are like fine gemstones—sometimes difficult to reach, but well worth the effort once attained. Among these is Helvetia, the tiny mountain community settled by Swiss families in the mid-1800s, which serves authentic Swiss food in a small restaurant and makes cheese unlike that made anywhere except in Switzerland. Another is the Cass Scenic Railroad, tucked into the Allegheny Mountains close to the Virginia border. The steam locomotive run to Whittaker Station is a fine experience, but the longer ride, over four hours round trip, to Bald Knob provides an unexcelled opportunity to picnic on what seems like the top of the world.

Another top-of-the-world spot is Dolly Sods Wilderness Area, a rugged bit of countryside known for its harsh winter winds; for the delicate blossoms of rhododendron and bush honeysuckle in season; and for the scattered spruce with branches growing longer on one side than on the other, like flags on a pole during strong winds. Then there are the rivers rushing swiftly through the valleys, exhilarating highways for rafters who come to seek the whitewater. But just as the state offers wild and natural areas virtually untouched, so does it have those with a bit of elegance.

At Snowshoe Ski Resort, skiers can sample some of the finest slopes in the South. And in White Sulphur Springs at the Greenbrier, one of the most sophisticated resort hotels in the country, golfers and tennis players find themselves surrounded by both tradition and superb facilities.

West Virginia's heart may be in the mountains, but its lifeblood is in the cities—in Charleston, the state capital; in Huntington; and in Wheeling. In some of those cities, such as Morgantown, New Martinsville, and Weston, the gem that is West Virginia glows in the form of brilliant molten glass. These are sites of the glass factories, where the tours are fascinating, but the shopping afterwards is the crowning touch.

West Virginia's rural charm manifests itself in a variety of ways. Left: A farm nestles below Seneca Rocks. Below: The rugged topography of Dolly Sods Wilderness covers more than 1,000 acres. Bottom: Old Stone Church, built in 1796 in Lewisburg, is one of the oldest churches in continuous use west of the Allegheny Mountains.

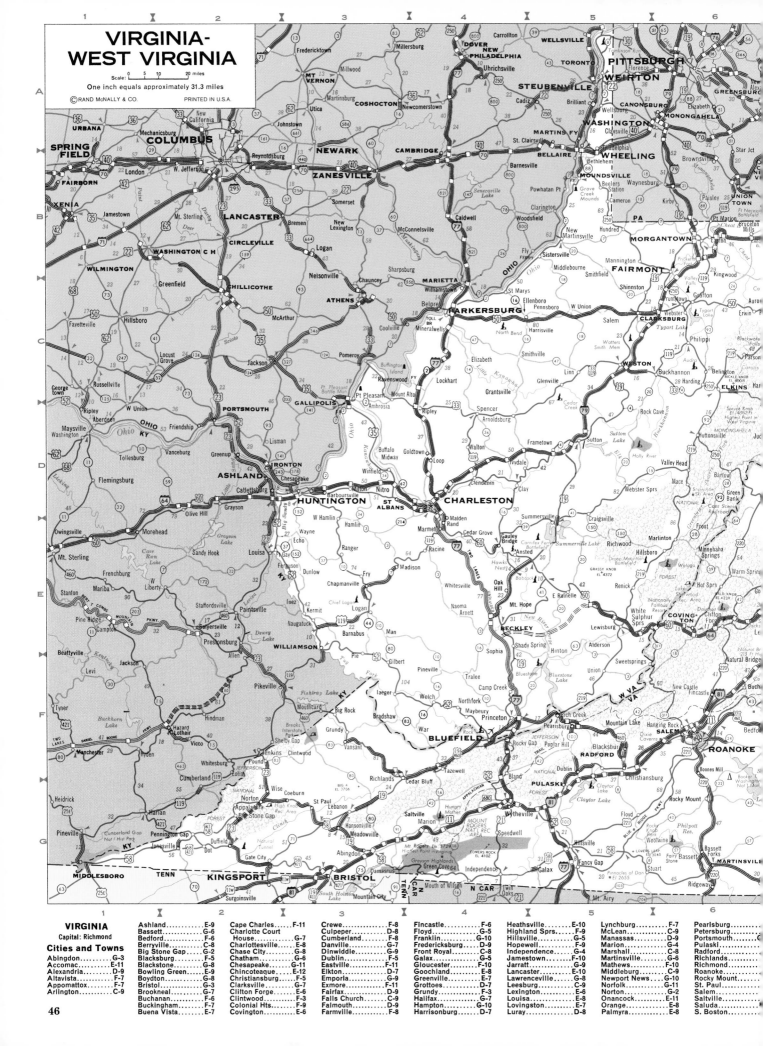

VIRGINIA-
WEST VIRGINIA

Scale: 0 5 10   20 miles

One inch equals approximately 31.3 miles

© RAND McNALLY & CO.   PRINTED IN U.S.A.

VIRGINIA

Capital: Richmond

Cities and Towns

Abingdon	G-3	Ashland	E-9
Accomac	E-11	Bassett	G-6
Alexandria	D-9	Bedford	F-6
Altavista	F-7	Berryville	C-8
Appomattox	F-7	Big Stone Gap	G-2
Arlington	C-9	Blacksburg	F-5
		Blackstone	G-8
		Bowling Green	E-9
		Boydton	G-8
		Bristol	G-3
		Brookneal	G-7
		Buchanan	F-6
		Buckingham	F-7
		Buena Vista	E-7

Cape Charles	F-11
Charlotte Court House	G-7
Charlottesville	E-8
Chase City	G-8
Chatham	G-7
Chesapeake	G-11
Chincoteague	E-12
Christiansburg	F-5
Clarksville	G-7
Clifton Forge	E-6
Clintwood	F-3
Colonial Hts.	F-9
Covington	E-6

Crewe	F-8
Culpeper	D-8
Cumberland	F-8
Danville	G-7
Dinwiddie	G-9
Dublin	F-5
Eastville	F-11
Elkton	D-7
Emporia	G-9
Exmore	F-11
Fairfax	D-9
Falls Church	D-9
Falmouth	D-9
Farmville	F-8

Fincastle	F-6
Floyd	G-5
Franklin	G-10
Fredericksburg	D-9
Front Royal	C-8
Galax	G-4
Gloucester	F-10
Goochland	E-8
Greenville	E-7
Grottoes	D-7
Grundy	F-3
Halifax	G-7
Hampton	G-10
Harrisonburg	D-7

Heathsville	E-10
Highland Sprs.	F-9
Hillsville	G-5
Hopewell	F-9
Independence	G-4
Jamestown	F-10
Jarratt	G-9
Lawrenceville	G-8
Leesburg	C-9
Lexington	E-6
Louisa	E-8
Lovingston	E-7
Luray	D-8

Lynchburg	F-7
McLean	C-9
Manassas	D-9
Marion	G-4
Marshall	C-8
Martinsville	F-6
Mathews	F-10
Middleburg	C-8
Newport News	G-10
Norfolk	G-11
Norton	G-2
Onancock	E-11
Orange	E-8
Palmyra	E-8

Pearisburg	F-5
Petersburg	F-9
Portsmouth	G-11
Pulaski	F-5
Radford	F-5
Richlands	F-4
Richmond	F-9
Roanoke	F-6
Rocky Mount	F-6
St. Paul	G-3
Salem	F-6
Saltville	G-4
Saluda	F-10
S. Boston	G-7

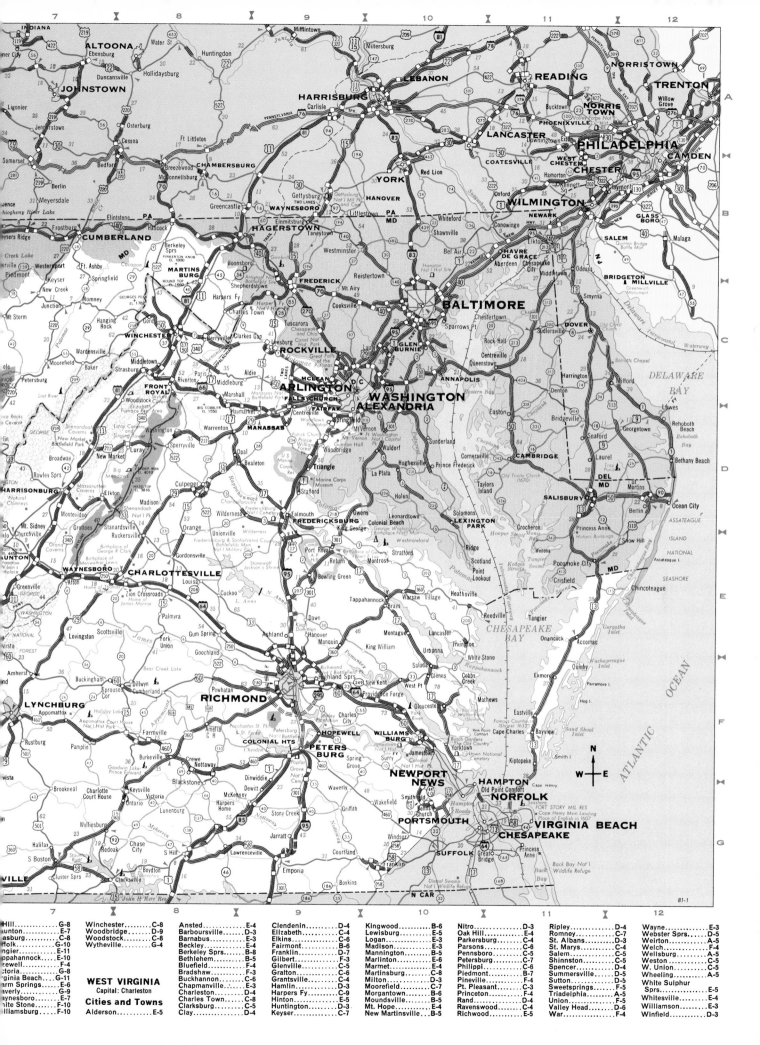

...Hill..........G-8   Winchester..........C-8   Ansted..........E-4   Clendenin..........D-4   Kingwood..........B-6   Nitro..........D-3   Ripley..........D-4   Wayne..........E-3
...nton..........E-7   Woodbridge..........D-9   Barboursville..........D-3   Elizabeth..........C-4   Lewisburg..........E-5   Oak Hill..........E-4   Romney..........C-7   Webster Sprs...... D-5
...sburg..........C-8   Woodstock..........C-8   Barnabus..........E-3   Elkins..........C-6   Logan..........E-3   Parkersburg..........C-4   St. Albans..........D-3   Weirton..........A-5
...folk..........G-10   Wytheville..........G-4   Beckley..........E-4   Fairmont..........B-6   Madison..........D-3   Parsons..........C-6   St. Marys..........C-4   Welch..........F-4
...ngier..........E-11   Berkeley Sprs..........B-8   Franklin..........D-7   Mannington..........B-5   Pennsboro..........C-5   Salem..........C-5   Wellsburg..........A-5
...appahannock...E-10   Bethlehem..........B-5   Gilbert..........F-3   Marlinton..........E-6   Petersburg..........C-7   Shinnston..........B-5   Weston..........C-5
...ewell..........F-4   Bluefield..........F-4   Glenville..........C-5   Marmet..........D-4   Philippi..........C-6   Spencer..........D-4   W. Union..........C-5
...ctoria..........G-8   WEST VIRGINIA   Bradshaw..........F-4   Grafton..........C-6   Martinsburg..........B-7   Piedmont..........B-7   Sutton..........D-5   Wheeling..........A-5
...rginia Beach...G-11   Capital: Charleston   Buckhannon..........C-6   Grantsville..........C-4   Milton..........D-3   Pineville..........F-4   Sweetsprings......F-5   White Sulphur
...arm Springs....E-6   Chapmanville..........D-3   Hamlin..........D-3   Moorefield..........C-7   Pt. Pleasant..........C-3   Triadelphia..........A-5   Sprs...........E-5
...averly..........G-9   Cities and Towns   Charleston..........D-4   Harpers Fy..........C-9   Morgantown..........B-6   Princeton..........F-4   Union..........F-5   Whitesville..........E-4
...ynesboro.......E-7   Charles Town..........C-8   Hinton..........E-5   Moundsville..........B-5   Rand..........D-4   Valley Head..........D-6   Williamson..........E-3
...ite Stone......F-10   Alderson..........E-5   Clarksburg..........C-5   Huntington..........D-3   Mt. Hope..........E-4   Ravenswood..........C-4   War..........F-4   Winfield..........D-3
...illiamsburg....F-10   Clay..........D-4   Keyser..........C-7   New Martinsville..........B-5   Richwood..........E-5

Washington, D.C.

See also pages 186-191

Capital of the United States
Population: 637,651
Site: Chosen by George Washington, for whom it was also named
Authorized: By Congressional Act, 1790; land granted by Maryland and Virginia in 1790-91; occupied by the United States government in 1800
City Plan: By Pierre Charles L'Enfant in 1791; merit of plan recognized in 1901; city developed accordingly
Motto: Justitia Omnibus ("Justice for All")
Bird: Wood Thrush
Flower: American Beauty Rose
Tree: Scarlet Oak

Government Buildings and Museums Line National Mall

Amid the processes of government, Washington, D.C. also offers rich cultural experiences. Whether it's space exploration, Postimpressionistic painting, African art, natural history, or American history, it lives in the museums of our nation's capital.

The Mall, lined with museums of the Smithsonian Institution and tipped at either end by the Capitol and the Washington Monument, is the most logical place to begin a visit. On the north side of the Mall, west from the Capitol, are the National Gallery of Art, Museum of Natural History, and Museum of American History. On the south side, east from Washington Monument, are the U.S. Department of Agriculture, Freer Gallery of Art, Smithsonian Castle, Arts and Industries Building, Hirschorn Museum, and National Air and Space Museum. From there, the city spreads out to encompass such special places as the National Cathedral, Ford's Theater, the C&O Canal, and Georgetown, with its many shops and restaurants. Even Metro, the subway system, offers exciting possibilities, whisking passengers from the center of the capital to fringe attractions such as the Pentagon and Arlington Cemetery.

American history is visible throughout the nation's capital. The Lincoln Memorial contains, in addition to a massive sculpture of the great president, his speeches engraved on its walls.

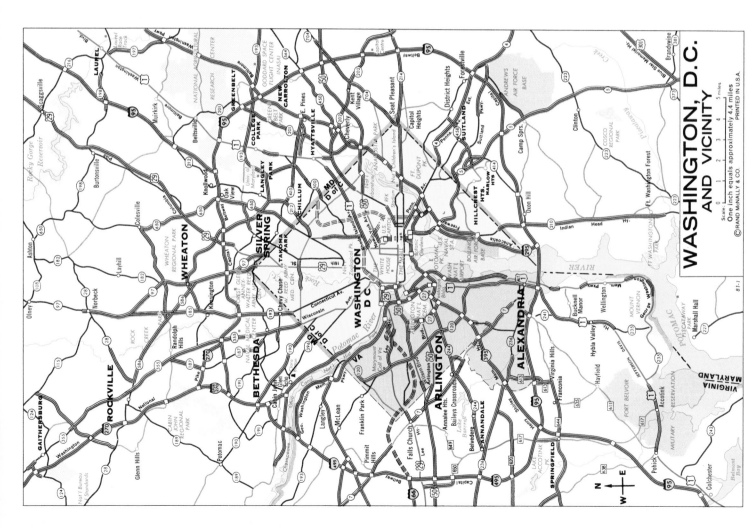

WASHINGTON, D.C. AND VICINITY

Scale
One inch equals approximately 4.4 miles
©RAND McNALLY & CO.
PRINTED IN U.S.A.

Southern Living®
Travel South
Major Events
Destinations
Campgrounds

Major Events
Destinations
Campgrounds

Major Events, Destinations, and Campgrounds for each of the 16 Southern states and Washington, D.C. are described on pages 51 through 199.

Major Events

Major Events are listed in chronological order and include the name of the event, the approximate date when it will be held, and where it will be held. Information also includes a brief description of the event, the admission, and the telephone number to call should you wish additional information.

Destinations

Places of interest are described under the city, town, or major park in which each is located. The names of the cities, towns, or major parks, which are in alphabetical order, are in boldface type. Following each city and town is its population; and following each city, town, and major park is a letter-number map reference key indicating its position on the state map.

Population

The population given for each city and town is the final 1980 census figure provided by the Bureau of the Census, U.S. Department of Commerce.

Letter-Number Map Reference Key

The letter-number map reference key for each city, town, or major park indicates its location on the state map, which appears with the state introduction on pages 16 through 48. This map reference key is determined by a grid system of squares formed by imaginary lines connecting the tick marks between the letters on the sides of the state map and the numbers at the top and bottom of the map. Therefore, a city, town, or park with a map reference key of H-2 is located in the square formed by the imaginary lines connecting the tick marks above and below H and those on either side of 2. A town not shown on the state maps is located to the nearest town or city shown on the map, with the letter-number map reference key of the nearest town or city given.

Highways and Roads

Highways and roads are identified in the text by the following abbreviations: Int., Interstate Highway; U.S., U.S. Highway; St., state highway; Co., county road. In Louisiana where counties are known as parishes, "county" roads are identified as parish roads. In Texas, some rural roads are known as ranch roads.

Months, Days, and Hours Open

The months, days, and hours when a place of interest is open to the public are given in that order. This varies, however, when the days and times a place is open differ by month and day. For example, if a place is open year-round but on different days in different months, the text style is as follows: May-Sept., Mon.-Fri., 9 A.M. to 5 P.M.; Sat.-Sun., 10 A.M. to 5 P.M.; other months, Mon.-Fri., noon to 4 P.M.; Sat.-Sun., 1 to 5 P.M. If a place of interest is open every day throughout the year but the hours vary by season, the text style is Daily, May-Sept., 9 A.M. to 5 P.M.; other months, 10 A.M. to 4 P.M.

Holidays

Most places are closed on major holidays (Thanksgiving, Christmas, and New Years days); however, this information is not included in the text. Before planning a visit to a place of interest on a major holiday, we suggest you call to be sure it is open.

Type Style

Places of interest within a city, town, or major park appear in boldface type. Places within the place of interest appear in boldface italics.

Facilities for the Handicapped

Most places of interest have special facilities for the convenience and comfort of handicapped persons; however, if you or any of your traveling companions are handicapped, you may wish to telephone about the availability of facilities for your particular needs. (A telephone number has been included for each place of interest which has one.)

Admission

The admission to a place of interest often changes from season to season. Therefore, you may wish to call for the admission charge at the time of your planned visit.

Campgrounds

Following each state's Destinations are tables listing the campgrounds at the state parks, recreation areas, and forests; and National Park Service, National Forest Service, and Corps of Engineers areas. For each campground area are a letter-number reference key indicating its location on the state map; the park name; road access to the park; acreage; tent spaces; trailer spaces; approximate fee; season open; facilities for fishing, swimming, and boating; playgrounds and other facilities; telephone number; and mail address.

Alabama

Major Events

Mardi Gras, mid- to late Feb., Mobile. There are parades, music, picnics, and other festivities to celebrate this pre-Lenten holiday. Free. 205/433-6951.

Azalea Trail Festival Official Opening, early Mar., Mobile. Opening ceremonies include an arts and crafts show, a footrace, and a parade through Mobile's historic section of Fort Condé Village. Free. 205/476-8828.

Historic Selma Pilgrimage, late Mar., Selma. Events include tours of homes, churches, and public buildings; an antique show; train rides; and a candlelight tour of Sturdivant Hall. Admission is charged for several events. 205/875-7241.

Birmingham Festival of the Arts, early Apr., Birmingham. Each year's festival salutes a foreign country with music and dance performances, art exhibitions, films, and various athletic events. Admission is charged for several events. 205/252-9825.

Dogwood Festival, all Apr., Birmingham. A parade heralds the opening of the dogwood trail, and throughout the month there are arts and crafts shows, a fashion show, a beauty pageant, an Easter egg hunt, and sporting events. Free. 205/979-6410.

Eufaula Pilgrimage, early Apr., Eufaula. Several homes are open to the public, and there is an antique show and sale as well as continuous musical entertainment. Admission is charged for several events. 205/687-3793.

NEACA Spring Craft Show, early Apr., Huntsville. Exhibitors primarily from the South demonstrate, exhibit, and sell their handcrafted items at the Parkway City Mall. Free. 205/533-1166.

Calico Fort Arts & Crafts Fair, mid-Apr., Fort Deposit. All types of original arts and crafts are on display and for sale at this event. Admission. 205/227-4331.

Easter Pageant, Easter, Mound State Park, south of Tuscaloosa. The final days of Christ's life on earth are depicted in music, narration, and drama atop the Indian mounds at the park. Free. 205/371-2641.

Annual 17 Springs Craft & Hobby Fair, early May, Millbrook, north of Montgomery. Craft demonstrations and exhibits, puppet shows, ballet, music, and refreshments are all featured. Admission. 205/265-7023.

Tuscaloosa Charity Horse Show, early May, Tuscaloosa. This is an all-breed show with a Western Show, a Hunter/Jumper Show, and Championship Night on the final evening. Admission. 205/553-4872.

Montgomery Jubilee, late May, Montgomery. The family entertainment at this event includes concerts, dances, riverboat rides, and a sunrise service on Sunday. Admission is charged for several events. 205/834-5206.

Alabama Jubilee, late May, Decatur. The highlight of the festivities is Alabama's only nationally sanctioned hot-air balloon rally, with entries from many different states participating. Free. 205/353-5312.

Atmore Mayfest, late May, Atmore. Tom Byrne Memorial Park is the site for arts and crafts, music, contests, an antique car show, and food. Free (except food). 205/368-3305.

International Folk Festival, early summer, Jasmine Hill Gardens, north of Montgomery. Folk dancers and musicians from a foreign country perform in the amphitheater, and food is served in the garden area. Admission. 205/265-2837.

Helen Keller Festival, late June, Tuscumbia. Tours of homes, arts and crafts, an art exhibit, and musical presentations are some of the festivities at this celebration. Admission is charged for several events. 205/383-4531.

Spirit of America Festival, July 4, Decatur. Held at Point Mallard Park, there are games, exhibits, displays, and food booths. Free (except food). 205/353-5312.

Alabama Deep-Sea Fishing Rodeo, mid-July, Dauphin Island, south of Mobile. This saltwater fishing tournament has many different categories of competition. Admission. 205/476-8828.

Blessing of the Fleet, late July, Bayou La Batre, southeast of Grand Bay. This event features a blessing of the fleet, a parade of decorated shrimp boats, an arts and crafts show, and seafood dinners. Free (except food). 205/824-2415.

Talladega 500, early Aug., Talladega. The Alabama International Motor Speedway is the site for this 500-mile NASCAR stock car race. Admission. 205/362-2261.

Lake Eufaula Summer Spectacular, late Aug., Eufaula. On the lake are championship motorboat races, and on the shore at Old Creek Town Park are various forms of entertainment and aerial exhibitions. Admission. 205/687-3879.

Festival in the Park, mid-Sept., Montgomery. Activities include arts and crafts; musical, dance, and dramatic performances; puppet shows; and children's activities. Free. 205/265-8593.

Racking Horse World Celebration, late Sept., Decatur. Ten championship events determine the Racking Horse World Champion. The racking horse is the official state horse of Alabama. Admission. 205/353-7225.

September Fest Arts and Crafts Fair, late Sept., DeSoto Caverns, near Childersburg. This two-day country-style celebration features arts and crafts, country music, square dance and clogging demonstrations, and a barbecue. Admission. 205/378-7252.

Barbara Mandrell's Benefit for Alabama Sheriffs Girls' and Boys' Ranches, early Oct., Montgomery. This is a long weekend of activities including tennis and golf tournaments, fishing contests, several footraces, and plenty of live entertainment, including a big concert on Saturday night at the Montgomery Civic Center featuring Barbara Mandrell and many other entertainers. Admission is charged for several events. 205/263-2217.

Alabama's Shrimp Festival, early Oct., Gulf Shores. The Gulf State Park Resort salutes the seafood industry with a beauty pageant, a waterskiing show, arts and crafts, street dances, and plenty of seafood. Free (except food). 205/968-7511.

Alabama State Fair, early to mid-Oct., Birmingham. Numerous agricultural exhibits and a large carnival midway with rides, games, and refreshments are just some of the attractions at the fair, which is held annually on the state fairgrounds. Admission. 205/787-2641.

National Peanut Festival and Fair, mid-Oct., Dothan. Most of the activities at this townwide event take place on the fairgrounds. There are parades, beauty contests, exhibits on peanut farming and other types of agriculture, a carnival, music, dances, and athletic activities. Admission is charged for several events. 205/793-4323.

Southern Championship Charity Horse Show, mid-Nov., Montgomery. There are events for Western, Arabian, Racking, and pleasure horses as well as competition in a variety of classes for Saddle and Walking horses. Admission. 205/262-8600.

Christmas on the River, early Dec., Demopolis. This festival begins with a children's parade, bands, and floats. In the early evening, a parade of lighted boats float along the Tombigbee River, set against a backdrop of fireworks. Free. 205/289-0270.

Christmas Candlelight Tour, late Dec., Decatur. Old Decatur has decorated streets, open houses, and musical entertainment, all in celebration of the holiday season. Admission. 205/353-5312.

The Hall of Fame College Bowl, late Dec., Birmingham. Two highly ranked NCAA teams play each other at Legion Field. There is an awards luncheon prior to the game for the recipients of scholarships which are awarded by the Bowl Committee. Admission. 205/252-5507.

Alabama Destinations

ANNISTON, 29,523, C-4. Settled in 1872 by the Tyler and Noble families, the city grew up around the iron works and textile mills. **State Theater of Alabama,** 1425 Woodstock Ave., is the site of the *Alabama Shakespeare Festival,* a summer repertory theater of note which tours the Southeast during the fall. Local performances: July and Aug., Tues.-Sat., 8 P.M.; Sun., 7 P.M.; Wed., Sat., and Sun., also 2 P.M. Adults $6-$8; students $5; persons under 16, $4. 205/237-2332 or 205/236-7503. **Anniston Museum of Natural History,** 4301 McClellan Blvd., in Lagarde Park, is one of the largest public-owned natural history museums in the Southeast. Facilities and activities include Werner Ornithology Hall, Lagarde African Hall, nature films, and art exhibits. Year-round, Mon.-Fri., 9 A.M. to 5 P.M.; Sat., 10 A.M. to 5 P.M.; Sun., 1 to 5 P.M. Free. 205/237-6766. **Women's Army Corps Museum,** at Fort McClellan, north of the city, has exhibits depicting the history of the Women's Army Corps. Year-round, Mon.-Fri., 8 A.M. to 4 P.M.; Sat.-Sun., noon to 4 P.M. Free. 205/238-3512 or 238-5559.

ATHENS, 14,558, A-3. **Altar of the New Testament,** in Founders Hall on the campus of Athens State College (1822), the oldest institution of higher learning in the state, has hand carvings by Eunice McDonald. Academic year, Mon.-Sat., 8 A.M. to 5 P.M. Free. 205/232-1802. **Browns Ferry Nuclear Plant,** south off U.S. 72, 15 miles west of Athens, grows plants and vegetables in an experimental greenhouse warmed by waste heat from the plant's cooling towers. Year-round, Mon.-Fri., 7:30 A.M. to 4:15 P.M. Free. 205/729-8316.

AUBURN, 28,471, E-5. This university city in the southern edge of the Piedmont Plateau is on the railroad line that connects Montgomery to Atlanta. **Auburn University,** whose main gate is at the southwest corner of Magnolia Ave. and College St., extends several blocks southwest and is the focal point of the city. *University Chapel,* on College St., was built in 1840 as the first Presbyterian Church in Auburn and is one of the oldest buildings on campus. It served as the campus theater from the late 1920s until 1970; it was restored into a house of worship in 1976. During the Civil War, it served as a Confederate hospital. Unusual features in this handsome building are the exposed ceiling beams which are joined at various points by large wooden pegs. Year-round, daily, 8 A.M. to 5 P.M. Free. *Langdon Hall,* on College St., was built in 1846 a few blocks away and moved on rolling logs to its present location in 1883. It is now a lecture hall. *Samford Hall,* next door, was built in 1888 and renovated in 1971. It not only stands on the site of Old Main, which burned in 1887, but also bore its name before it was designated Samford Hall. Ad-

ministrative offices are housed in this hall. *Katherine Cater Hall,* on West Thatch Ave., was built in 1915 as the home of the president. Now it is the Center of Student Affairs. The first floor of the house has been restored and furnished like the original house and is open to the public. Year-round, Mon.-Fri., 8 A.M. to 5 P.M. Free. The *Arboretum,* on S. College St., has 12 acres planted with 250 named plants and 150 trees native to Alabama. Always open. Arboretum pavilion, which offers guide service by a university instructor: Year-round, Mon.-Fri., 7:45 A.M. to 4:45 P.M. Free. Auburn University Information: 205/826-4000.

BESSEMER, 31,729, C-3. **Bessemer Hall of History Museum,** 1830 4th Ave. N, contains exhibits of prehistoric and later Indian artifacts, cases of pioneer tools, and objects from the Civil War and early days in Bessemer. Year-round, Tues.-Sat., 9 A.M. to 5 P.M. Free. 205/426-1633. **Tannehill Historical State Park,** east off Int. 59 southwest of Bessemer, has remains of Civil War-vintage iron furnaces, miles of hiking trails, and acres of piney woods. The *Alabama Iron and Steel Museum,* in the park, has artifacts from the times of the early Indians to the present. Year-round, daily, 8 A.M. to 4 P.M. Free. Park: Year-round, Sun.-Thurs., 7 A.M. to 9 P.M.; Fri.-Sat., 7 A.M. to 10 P.M. Admission $1. 205/477-6571.

BIRMINGHAM, 284,413, C-3. The accessibility of all the ingredients (iron ore, limestone, and coal) necessary for steel making attracted industrialists to the area

in the mid-1800s, and in 1871, Birmingham was incorporated and named for England's steel center. The development of a transportation artery soon followed. Today, the city is not only one of the major primary metal-producing areas in the United States, but it is also the home of one of the country's largest medical centers. **Vulcan Park,** off Valley Ave., overlooking the city, is the site of the 55-foot-tall statue of Vulcan, the mythological god of metallurgy. The cast-iron figure, which is mounted on a 124-foot-high pedestal, was constructed for Birmingham's display at the St. Louis Exposition in 1904. At the base of the pedestal is a museum and at the base of the statue is an observation deck, which offers an expansive view of the city and surrounding area. Year-round, daily, 8:30 A.M. to 10:30 P.M. Adults $1; children under 6, free. 205/254-2628. **Birmingham Botanical Gardens,** 2612 Lane Park Rd., has 2,000 rose bushes, a great variety of other blooming plants, a wildflower trail, and Japanese Gardens designed by Japanese landscape architect Buffy Murai. The conservatory is the largest in the Southeast. Year-round, daily, sunrise to sunset. Free. 205/879-1227. Adjacent is the **Birmingham Zoo,** 2630 Cahaba Rd., one of the youngest zoological gardens in the nation. It has 229 species of animals, a petting zoo for children, and a miniature train which takes passengers through the grounds. Year-round, daily, 9:30 A.M. to 5 P.M. Adults $2; persons 2-17, $1; under 2, free. 205/879-0408. **Arlington Historic House and Gardens,** 331 Cotton Ave. SW, is a Greek-

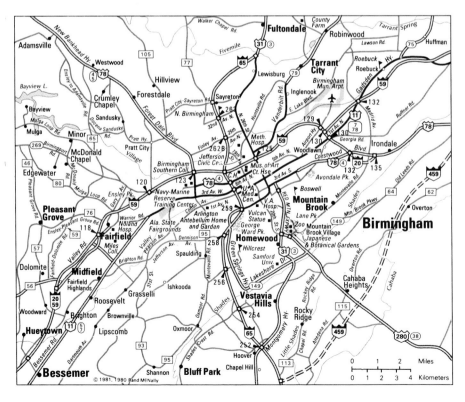

Revival home built in 1822 and enlarged to its present size in 1842. Union Gen. James H. Wilson commandeered *Arlington* toward the end of the Civil War and from here issued the orders to burn the University of Alabama and to destroy iron furnaces in the area. May-Nov., Tues.-Sat., 9 A.M. to 5 P.M.; other months, Tues.-Sat., 9 A.M. to 4:30 P.M. Year-round, Sun., 1 to 6 P.M. Adults $2; students 13-18, $1; children 4-12, 75¢. 205/780-5656. The **Birmingham-Jefferson Civic Center,** Number 1 Civic Center Plaza, is a complex comprising a concert hall, theater, exhibition hall, and coliseum. Organizations which perform here and events held here include the following: Alabama Symphony Orchestra, the Southern Regional Opera, ballet, theater, basketball tournaments, the Festival of Arts, the Festival of Sacred Music, Miss Alabama Beauty Pageant, the circus, and other major events. 205/328-8160. **Birmingham Museum of Art,** 2000 8th Ave. N, with the completion of its east wing, is one of the largest city museums in the Southeast. A Kress Collection, an extensive Wedgwood collection, and art of the Old West including many Remington bronzes alternate with traveling works. Year-round, Tues., Wed., Fri., 10 A.M. to 5 P.M.; Thurs., 10 A.M. to 9 P.M.; Sun., 2 to 6 P.M. Donations. 205/254-2565. **Red Mountain Museum,** 1425 22nd St. S, has a museum and a geological walkway carved into the cut made through the mountain for Birmingham's Red Mountain Expwy. Together they trace almost 190 million years of earth history and development. Geological data now visible along the 1,500-foot-long walkway is explained at some 20 marked stops. On display in the museum is a reconstructed skeleton of an 85-million-year-old mosasaur (a 14-foot-long fish-eating lizard), discovered in Alabama in recent years. Year-round, Tues.-Sat., 10 A.M. to 5 P.M.; Sun., noon to 5 P.M. Free. 205/254-2759. The **Robert R. Meyer Planetarium,** 800 8th Ave. on the Birmingham-Southern College campus, has seasonal sky shows. Year-round, monthly, 1st and 3rd Sun., 2 P.M.; 2nd and 4th Wed., 8 P.M.; every Thurs., 4 P.M. Adults $1.25, children 75¢. 205/328-5250.

BRIDGEPORT, A-4. *See* **Russell Cave National Monument.**

BRIERFIELD, 140, southwest of Montevallo, D-3. **Brierfield Ironworks Park** is on the site of one of Alabama's oldest industrial settlements. An outdoor summer drama, *Brighthope,* recalls the development of the iron industry. Year-round, sunrise to sunset. Free, except for special events. 205/665-1856.

CHILDERSBURG, 5,084, C-3. **DeSoto Caverns,** on St. 76, has onyx hangings more than 30 feet long. The main chamber of Kymulga Cave is larger than a football field and higher than a 12-story building. Apr.-Sept., Mon.-Sat., 9 A.M. to 6 P.M.; Sun., 12:30 to 6 P.M. Feb.-Mar. and Oct.-Nov.,

Sat., 9 A.M. to 6 P.M.; Sun., 12:30 to 6 P.M. Adults $4; children 5-11, $2.50; under 5, free. 205/378-7252. **Kymulga Gristmill,** off St. 76, is a water-activated, three-story gristmill dating from 1867. Corn grinding demonstrations: Year-round, Sat., 8 A.M. to noon. Gristmill: Apr.-Sept., Mon.-Sat., 9 A.M. to 5 P.M.; Sun., 12:30 to 5 P.M.; Feb.-Mar. and Oct.-Nov., Sat., 9 A.M. to 5 P.M.; Sun., 12:30 to 5 P.M. 205/378-5571.

CULLMAN, 13,084, B-3. Settled in 1873 along the newly laid railroad tracks by German immigrant Col. John G. Cullmann (he later dropped the last "n" off his name) and five other German families, Cullman grew with the influx of other settlers, primarily German. The **Cullman County Museum,** 211 Second Ave. NE, has documents and other items of county history. Year-round, Mon., Tues., Wed., Fri., 9 A.M. to noon, 1 to 4:30 P.M.; Thurs., 2 to 4:30 P.M.; Sat.-Sun., 1 to 4:30 P.M. Adults $1, children 50¢. 205/739-1258. **Ave Maria Grotto,** 1 mile east on U.S. 278, exhibits more than 150 miniature reproductions of famous churches, shrines, and buildings from all over the world. Year-round, daily, 7 A.M. to sunset. Adults $1.50; high school students 75¢; persons 6-15, 50¢. 205/734-4110. **Clarkson Covered Bridge,** 9 miles west off U.S. 278, is 275 feet long and 50 feet high. The largest such bridge in the state, it is supported by stone pyramids. Hiking trails, picnic facilities, and a gristmill are nearby on the site of the Battle of Hog Mountain (April, 1863). Year-round. Free. **Smith Lake Park,** 7 miles south of Int. 65 by way of the Good Hope interchange, is on 21,000-acre Smith Lake. Fishing, playing fields, carpet golf greens, and horseshoe courts. Camping and boating: Year-round. Some facilities: Mar.-Oct. Admission $1. 205/739-2916. **Hurricane Creek Park,** north on U.S. 31, is a natural area with unusual rock formations. A swinging bridge allows visitors to walk over a waterfall. Year-round, daily, sunrise to sunset. Adults $1.50; persons 3-18, $1; under 3, free. 205/734-2125.

DECATUR, 42,002, A-3. Named for naval hero Com. Stephen Decatur, the city was originally known as Rhodes Ferry. *Alabama Star* **Riverboat,** 720 Bank St. NE (office), a 100-foot-long, modern vessel patterned after the old paddle-wheel riverboats, takes cruises on the Tennessee River out of Decatur, Huntsville, and Joe Wheeler State Park. From Decatur Boat Harbor: Dinner cruise, year-round, Fri., 7 P.M. From Wheeler Lodge Marina, Joe Wheeler State Park, some 30 miles northwest off U.S. 72: Dinner cruise, year-round, Wed., 7 P.M. Dinner and cruise $20, gratuity and bar bill extra. 205/350-BOAT. (*See also* **Huntsville.**) **Cook's Natural Science Museum,** 412 13th St. SE, has displays of minerals, shells, coral, animals, and an extensive insect collection. Year-round, Mon.-Sat., 9 A.M. to noon, 1 to 5 P.M.; Sun., 2 to 5 P.M. Free. 205/350-9347. **Point Mallard,** Point

Mallard Dr., is a 749-acre park with beaches and two pools, one an Olympic-size pool used for outdoor diving championships and the other a wave pool (mechanically created waves). The park also offers ice skating as well as tennis, bike trails, and golf. Aquatic Center: Mid-May-Labor Day, Sun.-Wed., 10 A.M. to 7 P.M.; Thurs., 10 A.M. to 9 P.M.; Fri.-Sat., 10 A.M. to 8 P.M. Adults $3, children $1.50. Ice rink: Mid-Nov.-mid-Mar., Sun., 1 to 4 P.M., 6 to 9 P.M.; Mon., 6 to 9 P.M.; Tues., 10 A.M. to noon, 2 to 4 P.M., 6 to 9 P.M.; Wed., 6 to 9 P.M.; Fri., 3:30 to 6 P.M., 7 to 11 P.M.; Sat., 2 to 5 P.M., 7 to 11 P.M. Adults $2, children $1.50, skate rental $1. 205/350-3000. **Albany Heritage District,** north of Delano Park, was the residential section for a separate town from 1887 to 1927. Streets are named alternately for Confederate and Union soldiers. Many privately owned structures have been restored. **Old Decatur** and **Bank St.,** from U.S. 31 to Bank St., includes a commercial historic district with antique shops and art galleries, the restored 1833 Old State Bank, and private antebellum houses.

See also **Wheeler National Wildlife Refuge.**

DEMOPOLIS, 7,678, E-2. On the Tombigbee River, the area was originally settled by a French group who had been ruined by the downfall of Napoleon and came to Mobile in 1817. Among them were veterans who had served in close contact with Napoleon and had been granted four townships by the U.S. Government. **Bluff Hall,** 405 N. Commissioners Ave., is a plain brick Federal townhouse built in 1832 and altered by 1850 to reflect the Greek-Revival style. Year-round, Tues.-Sat., 10 A.M. to 5 P.M.; Sun., 2 to 5 P.M. Adults $2; students under 18, 50¢. **Gaineswood,** 805 S. Cedar St., was begun in 1821 by Gen. Nathan Bryan Whitfield, who continued to work on it until the Civil War. May-Oct., Mon.-Sat., 10 A.M. to 5 P.M.; Nov.-Apr., same days, 9 A.M. to 4 P.M.; year-round, Sat.-Sun., 1 to 4 P.M. Adults $2, students $1, children 50¢. 205/289-4846.

DOTHAN, 48,750, G-5. Site of the National Peanut Festival, Dothan is at the center of Alabama's "wiregrass" agricultural region. **Olympia Spa,** 5 miles south on U.S. 231, has a hot mineral spring and accompanying health facilities. Golf, tennis, swimming, accommodations. Always open. 205/677-3321. **Water World,** Westgate Park at the western end of Choctaw St., has a 180-foot-long wave pool, a three-flume water slide, and other recreational facilities on the grounds of a 12-acre landscaped park. Early May, Sat.-Sun., 10 A.M. to 7 P.M.; late May-Aug., Mon., Wed., Fri., Sat., 10 A.M. to 7 P.M.; Tues., Thurs., 10 A.M. to 9 P.M.; Sun., 1 to 7 P.M. Adults $3; persons 3-13, $1.50; over 54, $1. 205/793-0100.

ENTERPRISE, 18,033, G-4. **Boll Weevil Monument,** Main St., was erected in

1918 to honor the pest that destroyed the cotton crops, necessitating diversification of agricultural crops.

EUFAULA, 12,097, F-5. By 1823, when the first white settlers came down the Chattahoochee River, Eufaula was a well-established Indian (Creek and Eufaula) village. In 1832, the name Eufaula was changed to Irwinton to honor Gen. William Irwin, major landowner and in 1843, the name was changed back to Eufaula to avoid confusion with Irwinton, Georgia.

HISTORIC HOUSES AND DISTRICT: Fendall Hall, 917 W. Barbour St., is an antebellum (1854) Italianate home built by Edward B. Young and named for his wife, Ann Fendall Beale. The house was constructed of seasoned pine, and the dining room and drawing room walls were hand-stenciled. Open by appointment. Admission $2. Contact Eufaula Heritage Association, 340 N. Eufaula Ave., 205/687-3793. **Sheppard Cottage,** 504 E. Barbour St., is a raised Cape Cod cottage and the oldest known residence in the city. It houses the Chamber of Commerce. Year-round, daily, 8 A.M. to 5 P.M. 205/687-6664 or 205/687-3879. **Shorter Mansion,** 340 N. Eufaula Ave., was built by Eli Sims Shorter and Wileyna Lamar Shorter, heiress to the SSS Tonic business, in 1906. The Greek-Revival home houses the Eufaula Historical Museum, which has antique furnishings, Confederate relics, and memorabilia of six Alabama governors from Barbour County. Year-round, Mon.-Sat., 10 A.M. to 4 P.M.; Sun., 1 to 4 P.M. Adults $2; persons 65 and over, $1.50; children 50¢. 205/687-3793. **The Tavern,** 105 Front St., was the first permanent structure (1836) built in early Irwinton. An inn, it served as a steamboat stop and later as a Confederate hospital. It now houses a commercial business. Visitors welcome. Year-round, Mon., Tues., Thurs., Fri., 9 A.M. to 5 P.M. 205/687-4451. **Wellborn House,** 680 E. Broad St., was the first example (1839) of Greek-Revival architecture in Eufaula. Purchased in 1971 and moved from Livington St. by the Eufaula Arts Council, it houses a permanent art collection. Year-round, Mon.-Fri., 8 A.M. to 5 P.M. Donations. 205/687-9755 (Historic Chattahoochee Commission). **Seth Lore Historic District,** Livingston and Orange Sts. and Randolph and Eufaula Aves., was named for Lore, who laid out plans for the city. It has 75 structures listed in the National Register of Historic Places; several are in the annual Eufaula Pilgrimage in April. Driving-tour maps are available through the Chamber of Commerce. 205/687-3879 or 205/687-6664.

HISTORIC CHURCHES: First Presbyterian Church, N. Randolph St., remains much the same as it was on completion in 1869, with the original Tiffany stained-glass windows, pulpit Bible, pews, folding blinds, and gaslight fixtures. Year-round, daily. **St. James Episcopal Church,** (1905), N. Eufaula Ave., has a hand-carved altar and rose window. Year-round, daily.

AQUARIUM: Tom Mann's Fish World, 6 miles north of Eufaula on U.S. 431, has one 38,000-gallon aquarium and ten 1,400-gallon aquariums which display 29 species of game fish; also Indian portraits and relics. Year-round, daily, 9 A.M. to 5 P.M. Adults $1.50; children 4-12, 50¢; under 4, free. 205/687-6695.

WILDLIFE REFUGE: Eufaula National Wildlife Refuge, off St. 165 ten miles north of Eufaula, was created on the Walter F. George Reservoir (now known as Lake Eufaula) by the U.S. Army Corps of Engineers to provide a feeding and resting area for migratory waterfowl. In the refuge are an observation tower, photography blind, and hiking trails. Year-round, daily, daylight hours. Guided tours by request. Free. 205/687-4065.

FLORENCE, 37,029, A-2. Originally a trading post (1779), the settlement was later chosen by river traders as a base for a flatboat fleet. Other settlers followed, and in 1818, the Cypress Land Company, which bought the property Florence stands on now, was formed by such notables as Gen. John Coffee, surveyor-general of Alabama, and John McKinley, who later became a U.S. Supreme Court Justice. **Indian Mound and Museum,** S. Court St., preserves the area where Indians of the Stone Age Mississippian Culture built a 43-foot-high quadrilateral mound and fortified it with a semicircular wall. The museum contains artifacts of the mound builders dating back 10,000 years. Year-round, Tues.-Sat., 9 A.M. to noon, 1 to 4 P.M. Adults $1; students, kindergarten through high school, 25¢. 205/766-6742. **Pope's Tavern,** 203 Hermitage Dr., the oldest building in Florence, was built in 1811 as a stagecoach stop. Among the furnishings are those formerly exhibited at the Susan K. Vaughn Museum, the University of North Alabama. Year-round, Tues.-Sat., 9 A.M. to noon, 1 to 4 P.M. Adults $1, children 25¢. 205/766-2662. **W. C. Handy Home and Museum,** 620 W. College St., is in the log cabin where the "Father of the Blues" was born in 1873. The son of a Methodist minister, Handy won fame and fortune as the composer of "St. Louis Blues," "Memphis Blues," and other popular songs. In the museum are many of Handy's manuscripts, instruments, and other mementoes. Year-round, Tues.-Sat., 9 A.M. to noon, 1 to 4 P.M. Adults $1, children 25¢. 205/766-7410.

FORT PAYNE, 11,485, B-4. **Little River Canyon,** southeast on St. 35, then south on St. 275, is the deepest (600 feet) canyon east of the Mississippi River. A 20-mile paved scenic drive runs along the west rim of the canyon. **Sequoyah Caverns,** about 16 miles northwest off Int. 59, is called the Looking Glass Caverns because of the mirrorlike reflective pools and formations. Daily, Memorial Day-Labor Day, 8 A.M. to 7 P.M.; other months, 8:30 A.M. to 5 P.M.

Vulcan statue atop Red Mountain in the city of Birmingham is the largest iron figure ever cast. The giant work of art is 55 feet high and weighs 120,000 pounds. If its own size weren't impressive enough, it stands atop a 124-foot-high pedestal, which has an observation deck overlooking the city (while the city can easily look up and see the statue). Vulcan was the Roman god of fire, and with good reason he became the chosen symbol of Birmingham, a city long renowned as a major producer of iron and steel. The statue was designed by Italian sculptor Guiseppe Moretti for the Birmingham District exhibit at the 1904 Louisiana Purchase Exposition in St. Louis. It was made of Birmingham iron; and because of its weight, it was cast in several sections. Each foot weighs about 10,000 pounds. The massive head alone is made of over six tons of iron. The statue and pedestal, which also include an exhibit area, are surrounded by a beautifully landscaped park with a fountain.

Adults $3.75; children 6-11, $1.75; under 6, free. 205/635-6423. *DeSoto Falls,* 16 miles northeast via St. 35, Co. 80, and DeSoto Pkwy., is in **DeSoto State Park.** The 100-foot waterfall plus a mountain lake for swimming, fishing, and boating are in the park, which is also noted for its rhododendrons, azaleas, and mountain laurel.

FORT RUCKER, F-4. The **U.S. Army Aviation Museum** near the fort entrance, north off U.S. 84 at the intersection of St. 85, St. 248, and St. 249, traces the history of army aviation from World War II to the present. More than 100 aircraft are on display. Year-round, Mon.-Fri., 10 A.M. to 5

P.M.; Sat.-Sun., 1 to 5 P.M. Free. 205/255-4507.

GADSDEN, 47,565, B-4. **Gadsden Museum of Art,** 856 Chestnut St., has an assorted collection of paintings and other visual arts. Year-round, Mon.-Fri., 8 A.M. to 5 P.M.; Sat., 9 A.M. to 5 P.M.; Sun., 1 to 5 P.M. Free. 205/546-7365. **Emma Sansom Monument,** in a small park at Broad and First Sts., honors the 15-year-old girl who reputedly helped guide Confederate troops under the command of General Forrest through a ford in Black Creek, thus avoiding encounter with Union troops commanded by Colonel Streight. **Noccalula Falls Park,** off Int. 59 at Exit 188, combines the natural beauty of the 90-foot falls and surrounding area with a village of split-log buildings, botanical gardens, and Pioneer Museum. Year-round, 8 A.M. to sunset. Adults $1.50, children 50¢. 205/543-7412.

GULF SHORES, 1,000, H-2. This resort area on a 32-mile-long man-made island is undergoing a beautification program in its recovery from the damage rent by Hurricane Frederick. **Gulf State Park,** also on the island, has frontage (white sand beach) on the Gulf and on three freshwater lakes. Facilities include a golf course, an 825-foot pier, cottages, campgrounds, and a convention center. Always open. 205/968-7544. **Fort Morgan,** St. 180W at Mobile Point, served as a garrison and with Fort Gaines, at the eastern end of Daulphin Island, stood guard at the entrance to Mobile Bay, which was blockaded in the Civil War. With orders to capture both forts, Union Comdr. David G. Farragut forced entrance through the heavily mined blockade which inspired his command "Damn the torpedoes, full speed ahead." The Confederate fleet was dispersed and the forts eventually surrendered. The museum has Union and Confederate mementoes. Fort: Year-round, daily, 8 A.M. to sunset. Museum: Year-round, daily, 8 A.M. to 5 P.M. Fort and museum: Adults $1; persons under 17, free. 205/540-7125.

HODGES, 250, B-1. **Rock Bridge Canyon,** 2 miles northwest of Hodges on Co. 45 off St. 172, has a 100-foot-high natural rock bridge with walkway, cold spring waterfalls, and the state's largest rock, rising 285 feet above the canyon floor. Year-round, daily, 8 A.M. to 6 P.M. Adults $2; children under 6, free. 205/935-3750.

HUNTSVILLE, 142,513, A-3. Originally called Twickenham when the city was incorporated in 1811, it was renamed for John Hunt, a Virginian who settled here in 1805. The growth of space-age technology in conjunction with the Marshall Space Flight Center has made Huntsville a center of science, industry, medicine, and the arts. **Alabama Space and Rocket Center,** on Governor's Dr., west of the city, is a "hands-on" exhibit of space exploration and research. Its extensive exhibits include such spacecraft as the Apollo 16 and a mockup of

Skylab. Space simulation rides and experiences include a flight to the moon, a space shuttle flight, and the machine in which astronauts learned to exist in an atmosphere of weightlessness. Also living at the center is Miss Baker, the first primate to travel in space, and her companion. Daily, June-Aug., 8 A.M. to 7 P.M.; Sept.-May, 9 A.M. to 6 P.M. Adults: Space Center $4, NASA bus tour $3.25, both $6. Persons 65 and over and military: Space Center $2.25, NASA bus tour $1.50, both $3.25. Children 6-12: Space Center $2.25, NASA bus tour $1.50, both $3. 205/837-3400. **Burritt Museum,** on Monte Sano Mountain, is built in the shape of a Maltese cross. Exhibits pertain to Huntsville, along with the Pioneer Village, which includes log cabins, a blacksmith shop, smokehouse, and formal gardens. Apr.-Oct., Tues.-Sun., noon to 6 P.M.; other months, same days, noon to 5 P.M. Donations. 205/536-2882. **Huntsville Museum of Art,** 700 Monroe St. SW in the Von Braun Civic Center, features works of national, regional, and local artists. Year-round, Tues.-Sat., 10 A.M. to 5 P.M.; Thurs., also 7 to 9 P.M.; Sun., 1 to 5 P.M. Free. 205/534-4566. In **Old Town,** east and north of Courthouse Sq., are many 19th- and 20th-century houses. **Twickenham Historic Preservation District,** south and east of Courthouse Sq., has 60 restored antebellum structures (privately owned homes) spanning 160 years of building styles. Tours may be arranged through the Huntsville Heritage Tours, Huntsville Chamber of Commerce, 205/533-0125.

LINEVILLE, 2,257, C-4. Cheaha State Park, 17 miles north of Lineville on St. 49, encompasses 2,407-foot-high Cheaha Mountain, highest point in the state, and Cheaha Lake. In the park are lodging and campground facilities and a lookout tower at the top of the mountain. Year-round, daily, 8 A.M. to 9 P.M. 205/488-5111.

MOBILE, 200,452, H-1. Port city for the state, Mobile was founded by the French in 1711 and served under England, Spain, and the Confederacy. The first **Mardi Gras** celebration in the United States was held in

Mobile and continues to be held annually, the week before Lent.

GARDENS: Bellingrath Gardens and Home. *See* **Theodore.**

HISTORIC HOUSES AND SITES: Oakleigh, 350 Oakleigh Pl., was built from handmade bricks and hand-hewn timbers by Mobile merchant James W. Roper. Acting as his own architect and builder, Roper incorporated unusual designs, such as windows that converted into doors. Year-round, Mon.-Sat., 10 A.M. to 3:30 P.M.; Sun., 2 to 3:30 P.M. Adults $2; persons 65 and over, $1.50; 12-18, $1; 6-11, 50¢; under 6, free. 205/432-1281. **Carlen House,** 54 Carlen St., is a Creole cottage-style structure with furnishings typical of its period (c. 1842). Year-round, Tues.-Sat., 10 A.M. to 5 P.M.; Sun., 1 to 5 P.M. Free. 205/438-7569. **Fort Condé,** 150 S. Royal St., is a reconstructed French fort built 1724-35. Year-round, daily, 9 A.M. to 5 P.M. Adults $2, children $1. 205/438-7304. **Charlotte House,** 104 Theatre St., was built between the south bastions of Fort Condé as the city's first official jail (1822-24); it was converted to a residence about 1850. Each room reflects a period and nationality in Mobile's past. Year-round, Tues.-Sat., 10 A.M. to 4 P.M. Adults $1.50, children 50¢. 205/432-4722.

MUSEUMS: Battleship USS *Alabama*, Battleship Pkwy., on U.S. 90/98, served in both the Atlantic and Pacific fleets in World War II, earning nine battle stars. It is on exhibit with fleet-type submarine USS *Drum* and other military equipment in Battleship Park. Year-round, daily, 8 A.M. to sunset. Adults $2.50, children $1. 205/433-2703. **Fine Arts Museum of the South at Mobile,** Museum Dr. in Langan Park, has varied exhibits of paintings, art objects, and furniture. Year-round, Wed.-Sat., 10 A.M. to 5 P.M.; Sun., noon to 5 P.M. Free. 205/342-4642. **Museum of the City of Mobile,** 355 Government St., in Bernstein-Bush house (1872), features historical displays of Mobile and the Gulf Coast area since 1702 and a large Boehm porcelain collection. Year-round, Tues.-Sat., 10 A.M. to 5 P.M. Free. 205/438-7569. **Phoenix Fire Museum,** 203 S. Claiborne St., is the museum of the history of fire fighting in Mobile since 1819. Year-round, Tues.-Sat., 10 A.M. to 5 P.M.; Sun., 1 to 5 P.M. Free. 205/433-5343.

RIVERBOAT: *Magnolia Blossom* Riverboat is an authentic stern-wheeler plying the waters of Mobile Bay. Cruise (1½ hours long) departure time: June-Aug., daily, 1 P.M.; Fri., also 7:30 P.M.; Sept.-May, Sat., 1 P.M.; Sun., 3 P.M. Adults $4, children $2. 205/433-BOAT.

MONTEVALLO, D-3. *See* **Brierfield.**

MONTGOMERY, 178,157, E-4. Located on a bend of the Alabama River, Alabama's capital city (since 1846) was also the capital of the Confederacy. It was named for Maj. Lemuel Montgomery, who was killed at the Battle of Horseshoe Bend while serving with Andrew Jackson in the Creek War.

GOVERNMENT BUILDINGS: State Capitol, at the apex of Dexter Ave., is a white-domed, Greek-Revival structure which looks down over the city from Goat Hill. A brass star on the west portico marks the spot where Jefferson Davis stood to take the oath of office as the first President of the Confederacy. Year-round, daily, 8 A.M. to 5 P.M. Free. 205/832-3550. **Executive Mansion,** 1142 S. Perry St., is of Greek-Revival architecture, with Alabama-made reproductions of Victorian furnishings. Year-round, Tues., Thurs., 2 to 4 P.M.; 10:30 A.M. to 12:30 P.M. by appointment. Free. 205/834-3022. **Alabama Department of Archives and History,** 640 Washington Ave., exhibits Alabama artifacts and provides research facilities for the study of Alabama history. Year-round, Mon.-Fri., 8 A.M. to 5 P.M.; Sat.-Sun., 8 A.M. to noon, 1 to 5 P.M. Free. 205/832-6510.

HISTORIC BUILDINGS: First White House of the Confederacy, 644 Washington Ave., was occupied by Confederate Pres. Jefferson Davis before the Confederacy capital was moved to Richmond. It contains memorabilia of President Davis. Year-round, Mon.-Fri., 8 A.M. to 5 P.M.; Sat.-Sun., 8 A.M. to noon, 1 to 5 P.M. Free. 205/832-5269. **Old North Hull Historic District,** 310 N. Hull St., is a "hands-on" experience of Southern history. Featured are a tavern, church, log cabin, grange hall, doctor's office, and townhouse. Year-round, Mon.-Sat., 9:30 A.M. to 4 P.M.; Sun., 1:30 to 4 P.M. Adults $2.50; students 6-18, $1; children under 6, free. 205/263-4355.

MUSEUMS: Lurleen B. Wallace Museum, 725 Monroe St., has an audio-video tape on the life of Alabama's first woman governor and a collection of her personal objects. Year-round, 8 A.M. to 5 P.M. Free. 205/832-6615. **Montgomery Museum of Fine Arts,** 440 S. McDonough St., displays a permanent collection of 19th- and 20th-century paintings and graphics; also regional contemporary works. Year-round, Tues.-Sat., 10 A.M. to 5 P.M.; Thurs., 10 A.M. to 9 P.M.; Sun., 1 to 6 P.M. Free. 205/834-3490. **Tumbling Waters Museum of Flags, Inc.,** 131 S. Perry St., has permanent and changing

exhibits which show flags. Year-round, Mon.-Fri., 10 A.M. to 4 P.M.; other times, by appointment. Free. 205/262-5535.

GARDEN: Jasmine Hill, Jasmine Hill Rd. off U.S. 231N. Scattered among the flowers, which bloom year-round, are marble and bronze replicas of works of Greek sculptors and reproductions of Greek temple ruins. Mar.-Nov., Tues.-Sun., 9 A.M. to 5 P.M. Adults $2.50; children 6-12, 50¢; under 6, free. 205/263-1440.

PLANETARIUM: W. A. Gayle Planetarium, 1010 Forest Ave. in Oak Park, has seasonal shows and special events depicting space travel and other subjects. Year-round, Sat.-Sun., 2 and 3 P.M. Adults $1.50, students 75¢. 205/265-6225.

RIVERBOAT: *General Richard Montgomery,* Riverfront Park, at the foot of Commerce St., cruises on the Alabama River. Year-round, Wed.-Sun., 1:30 P.M. boarding for 2 to 3:15 P.M. cruise; Sat.-Sun., also 3:30 P.M. boarding for 4 to 5:15 P.M. cruise. Adults $3; persons 65 and over, $2.50; children 4-12, $1.50; under 4, free. 205/834-9862.

ZOO: Montgomery Zoo, 329 Vandiver Blvd. More than 600 birds, mammals, and reptiles make up the population of this 8-acre zoo. Daily, Apr.-Oct., 9:30 A.M. to 5 P.M.; other months, 9:30 A.M. to 4:30 P.M. Adults 75¢; children 2-12, 25¢. 205/265-3536.

MOUNDVILLE, 1,310, south of Tuscaloosa off St. 69, D-2. **Mound State Monument,** a major site of the prehistoric Mississippian Indians, has an archaeological museum, reconstructed temple, and village. Year-round, daily, 9 A.M. to 5 P.M. Museum: Adults $2, children $1. 205/348-7550.

MUSCLE SHOALS, 8,911, A-2. **Wilson Dam,** at the **Tennessee Valley Authority National Fertilizer Development Center** on the Tennessee River, has one of the world's largest single-lift locks in which the water level is raised and lowered 100 feet to permit the passage of barges and other craft on the river. Tours from the Visitors Center, off St. 133 on the south side of the dam, take visitors to see the 21 hydroelectric generators which produce electricity to operate the dam and gates. Year-round, daily, 9 A.M. to 5 P.M. Free. 205/386-2444. Lock: 205/764-5223.

See also **Sheffield.**

NATURAL BRIDGE, B-2. This two-span sandstone formation off U.S. 278 was an early landmark and Indian meeting ground. The main arch of this natural bridge is 148 feet long, 60 feet high, and 33 feet wide, with a cavernous overhang. Year-round, daily, 8 A.M. to sunset. Adults $2; children $1; under 6, free. 205/486-5330.

PHIL CAMPBELL, 1,549, B-2. **Dismals,** on U.S. 43, was once ceremonial land of the Chickasaws. Canyons, falls, grottoes, and caves are connected by hiking trails bordered by a variety of flora. Among spe-

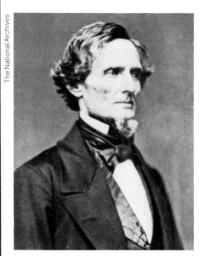

Jefferson Davis, the only president of the Confederacy and one of the South's greatest heroes, was born in 1808 in southwestern Kentucky and died in 1889 in New Orleans. Davis was inaugurated president of the Confederacy on two occasions — once on February 18, 1861, in Montgomery, Alabama, where, today, the First White House of the Confederacy displays mementoes of his occupancy. The other occasion was on February 22, 1862, in Richmond, Virginia. He also distinguished himself as a military officer, a U.S. representative, a U.S. senator, and as the secretary of war in President Franklin Pierce's cabinet.

cial features are the mysterious fissures which wind through the rocks of Witches Cave. Year-round, daily, 8 A.M. to sunset. Adults $2; children and persons 65 and over, $1. 205/993-5537.

POINT CLEAR, 750, H-1. This point of land which juts out into Mobile Bay was first settled in 1820. Soon after this, the Point Clear Hotel was built. After it was demolished in 1940, it was replaced by the world-famous Grand Hotel.

RUSSELL CAVE NATIONAL MONUMENT, A-4. Eight miles northwest of Bridgeport off U.S. 72, the park preserves an unusual archaeological area. Excavations reveal human habitation here from at least 7000 B.C. to about A.D. 1650. During this time, Russell Cave was used only intermittently as a shelter. Studies also reveal that plant and animal life remained virtually unchanged for thousands of years, until European settlers felled the trees for lumber and opened the area to farming. Visitors Center has displays. The 310-acre park also has nature trails. Year-round, daily, 8 A.M. to 5 P.M. Free. 205/495-2672.

SELMA, 26,684, E-3. Like many Southern cities, Selma is a mixture of the historic and the new. One of the earliest visitors to the vicinity was Hernando de Soto in 1540. During the Civil War, Selma was the site of

a Confederate navy yard, naval foundry, and an arsenal; and during World War II, Craig Air Force Base was established here. **Sturdivant Hall,** 713 Mabry St., is an antebellum house and museum. Built in 1853 by Thomas Helm Lee, a cousin of Robert E. Lee, it is a neoclassical-style house with a front and back portico with columns, lacy ironwork, and a spiral staircase. Year-round, Tues.-Sat., 9 A.M. to 4 P.M.; Sun., 2 to 4 P.M. Adults $2; students $1; children, free. 205/872-5626. **Joseph T. Smitherman Building,** 109 Union St., is a museum and civic center with displays of Civil War relics and Indian artifacts. Year-round, Mon.-Fri., 9 A.M. to 4 P.M.; Sun., 2 to 4 P.M. Free. 205/872-8713. **Water Avenue Historic District,** a five-block area on the riverfront, has been restored with new sidewalks, new streetlights, shops, and restaurants. **Cahaba,** 9 miles west on St. 22 then 4 miles south on a county road, is the site of Alabama's first capital (1819-26). At the confluence of the Alabama and Cahaba rivers, it was subject to floods, which eventually caused its demise. Some streets have been identified. Among the ruins are circular brick columns of one of Alabama's most elegant early houses. Year-round, daily, sunrise to sunset. Free. 205/875-7241.

SHEFFIELD, 11,903, A-2. This recording studio center claims five major studios, including Muscle Shoals Sound Studio, one of the world's largest recording complexes under one roof. (The town of Muscle Shoals is across the highway.) **Muscle Shoals Music Association,** 1307 Broadway, conducts tours of the studios. 205/381-1442.

TALLADEGA, 19,128, C-4. **Alabama International Motor Speedway,** 1 mile south of Int. 20, is a tri-oval track with 50-foot-high, 33-degree banked turns. Events include NASCAR (National Association for Stock Car Auto Racing) racing, featuring the **Winston 500** in May and the **Talladega 500** in August. Bus tours (available when races and time trials are not being held): Year-round, daily, 9 A.M. to 5 P.M. Adults 50¢, children free. 205/362-2261.

THEODORE, 1,200, H-1. **Bellingrath Gardens** and **Home,** on St. 163 off Int. 10 and U.S. 90, are one of the world's most beautiful gardens and home. On a bluff overlooking the Isle-aux-Oies River, the 800-acre estate has extensive gardens; the *Bellingrath Gallery of Boehm Porcelains,* which•contains the world's largest display of porcelain sculpture of birds and flowers by Edward Marshall Boehm; a wildlife refuge; and the *Bellingrath Home,* which remains as it was when occupied by the late Walter D. and Bessie Bellingrath, who established the nonprofit Bellingrath Morse Foundation to administer the gardens and home for the public to enjoy. The gardens have seasonal plantings of flowering shrubs and bedding plants which bloom as follows: Jan., camellias; Feb.-Mar., azaleas and tulips; Apr.-Sept., perennials; Apr.-Dec., roses;

Oct.-Dec., chrysanthemums. The wildlife refuge harbors flamingos, swans, migratory birds, and other fauna. Year-round, daily, sunrise to sunset. Gardens: Adults $3; children 6-11 and military, $1.50; under 6, free. Home: Adults $3.75. 205/973-2217.

TROY, 12,587, F-4. **Pike Pioneer Museum,** U.S. 231N, shows the rural life-style of southeast Alabama from the 1870s to about 1930. Year-round, Mon.-Sat., 10 A.M. to 5 P.M.; Sun., 1 to 5 P.M. Adults $1, children 50¢. 205/566-6158.

TUSCALOOSA, 75,143, D-2. On the Black Warrior River, the city got its name from the same source. After floods forced removal of the state capital from Cahaba, Tuscaloosa became the seat of state government in 1826 and served in this capacity until 1846, when the capital was moved to Montgomery. **University of Alabama,** on University Blvd. in the eastern part of the city, was chartered in 1819 and opened its doors to students in 1831. During the Civil War much of the campus was destroyed by fire; only four buildings survived. These were Gorgas House, the Little Round House, the Old Observatory, and the president's mansion. *Gorgas House,* which was built in 1829 as the college dining hall, today houses a collection of Spanish colonial silver. Year-round, Tues.-Fri., 10 A.M. to noon, 1 to 4 P.M.; Mon.-Sat., 2 to 5 P.M.; Sun., 3 to 5 P.M. Free. 205/348-5906. *University of Alabama Museum of Natural History,* in Smith Hall, has geological, malacological, and historic exhibits. Year-round, Mon.-Fri., 8 A.M. to 4:45 P.M. Free. 205/348-7550. *Garland Hall Art Gallery,* on campus, has art in all mediums and frequently changing student exhibits. Year-round, Mon.-Fri., 8 A.M. to noon, 1 to 4 P.M.; Sun., 2 to 5 P.M. Free. 205/348-5967. **Battle-Friedman House,** 1010 Greensboro Ave., was built in 1835 by wealthy planter Alfred Battle and bequeathed to the city by its last owners, the Friedman family. Year-round, Tues.-Fri., 10 A.M. to noon, 1 to 4 P.M.; Sat.-Sun., 1 to 4 P.M. Adults $1, chil-

dren 50¢. 205/758-6138. The **Old Tavern,** 28th Ave. and University Blvd., was built by William Dunton in 1827 as an inn and stagecoach stop. It contains memorabilia from Tuscaloosa's capital period. Year-round, Tues.-Fri., 10 A.M. to noon, 1 to 4 P.M.; Sat.-Sun., 1 to 4 P.M. Adults $1; children 6-12, 50¢; under 6, free. 205/758-8163.

TUSCUMBIA, 9,137, A-2. **Ivy Green,** 300 W. North Common St., is the birthplace of Helen Keller, the deaf and blind woman who inspired the world with her ability to overcome her handicaps. *The Miracle Worker,* a story of her life, is staged on the grounds each summer. Ivy Green: Year-round, Mon.-Sat., 8:30 A.M. to 4:30 P.M.; Sun., 1 to 4:30 P.M. Adults $1.50; children 6-11, 50¢; under 6, free. 205/383-4066.

TUSKEGEE, 12,716, E-4. **Tuskegee Institute National Historic Site** honors the college for black Americans founded in 1881 by Booker T. Washington. Preserved here are the student-made brick buildings, Washington's home, and George Washington Carver Museum. Year-round, daily, 9 A.M. to 5 P.M. Free. 205/727-6390.

WETUMPKA, 4,341, E-4. **Fort Toulouse-Jackson Park,** 3 miles south off U.S. 231, is the site of two forts—Toulouse, built by the French in 1717, and Jackson, built by Gen. Andrew Jackson during the Creek Indian War of 1813-14. On bluffs overlooking three rivers, the park also has picnic and boating facilities and displays. Daily, Apr.-Oct., 6 A.M. to 9 P.M.; Nov.-Mar., 8 A.M. to 5 P.M. Free. 205/567-3002.

WHEELER NATIONAL WILDLIFE REFUGE, A-3. The **Wildlife Interpretive Center,** off St. 67 southeast of Decatur, displays exhibits of 48 species of mammals, 23 of fish, 277 species of birds, including 51 of waterfowl, and many reptiles. Also included are exhibits relating to amphibians and cave dwellers. Interpretive Center and Waterfowl Observation Building: Year-round, Wed.-Sun., 10 A.M. to 5 P.M. Free. 205/353-7243.

Information Sources

Alabama Bureau of
Publicity and Information
532 S. Perry St.
Montgomery, AL 36130
205/832-5510

Alabama Mountain
Lakes Association
Box 1075
Decatur, AL 35601
205/350-3500

Alabama Travel Council
660 Adams Ave.
Suite 254
Montgomery, AL 36104
205/263-3407

Greater Birmingham Convention
and Visitors' Bureau
2027 First Ave. N
Birmingham, AL 35203
205/252-9825

Cherokee County
Tourist Association
Box 518
Cedar Bluff, AL 35959
205/779-6680

Decatur Tourism Bureau
Box 2003
Decatur, AL 35602
205/353-5312

DeKalb County
Tourist Association
205 Gault Ave. S
Box 125
Fort Payne, AL 35967
205/845-2741

Gulf Shores Tourist Association
P.O. Drawer 457
Gulf Shores, AL 36542
205/968-7511

Historic Chattahoochee Commission
630 E. Broad St.
Box 33
Eufaula, AL 36027
205/687-9755, or 687-6631

Huntsville Convention
and Visitors' Center
700 Monroe St. SW
Huntsville, AL 35801
205/533-0125

Mobile Area Chamber of Commerce
351 Government St.
Box 2187
Mobile, AL 36602
205/433-6951

Montgomery Chamber of Commerce
41 Commerce St., Box 79
Montgomery, AL 36101
205/834-5200

Alabama Campgrounds

FEES REFLECT MINIMUM RATE FOR 2 ADULTS AND ARE SUBJECT TO INCREASE OR SEASONAL CHANGES

• – at the campground
○ – within one mile of campground
$ – extra charge
** – limited facilities during winter months
A – adults only
B – 10,000 acres or more
C – contribution

E – tents rented
F – entrance fee or premit required
N – no specific number, limited by size of area only
P – primitive
R – reservation required
S – self-contained units only

U – unlimited
V – trailers rented
Z – reservations accepted
LD – Labor Day
MD – Memorial Day
UC – under construction
d – boat dock

g – public golf course within 5 miles
h – horseback riding
j – whitewater running craft only
k – snow skiing within 25 miles
l – boat launch
m – area north of map
n – no drinking water

p – motor bikes prohibited
r – boat rental
s – stream, lake or creek water only
t – tennis
u – snowmobile trails
w – open certain off-season weekends
y – drinking water must be boiled

Map Reference	Park Name	Access	Acres	Tent Spaces	Trailer Spaces	Approximate Fee	Season	Swimming Pool	Other Swimming Pool	Fishing Boating	Playground	Other	Telephone Number	Mail Address
	STATE PARKS													
B4	Desoto	Fr Ft Payne, 8 mi NE on Co 89	4869	31	47	6.00	All year	•	•		•	g	205/845-0051	Rt 1 Box 210, Ft Payne 35967
E2	Roland Cooper	Fr Camden, 6 mi NW on Hwy 41	200	8	41	6.00	All year	•	•	l		g	205/682-4838	PO Box 130, Camden 36726
H2	Gulf	Fr Foley, 10 mi S on Hwy 59, at Gulf Shores	6000	300	300	6.50	All year	•	•	dlr		gt	205/968-6353	SR Box 9, Gulf Shores 36542
C4	Cheaha	Fr Lineville, 17 mi N on Hwy 49	2719	73	73	6.00	All year	•	•			g	205/488-5111	Lineville 36266
C3	Oak Mountain	Fr Birmingham, 15 S on I-65	9940	90	50	F6.00	All year	$		dlr	•	gt	205/663-6771	PO Box 278, Pelham 35124
B4	Lake Guntersville	Fr Guntersville, 6 mi NE on Hwy 227	5559	322	322	6.00	All year	•	•	dlr	•	t	205/582-8418	SR Box 52, Guntersville 35976
F5	Blue Springs	Fr Clio, 6 mi SE on Hwy 10	103	50	50	5.00	All year	•	•		•		205/397-4875	Rt 1, Clio 36017
C3	Rickwood Caverns	Fr Warrior, 7 mi N on I-65, Hayden Corner ext, 4 mi to CG	380	55	50	2.00	All year	•	•		•		205/647-9692	Rt 3, Box 68-C, Warrior 35180
C2	Lake Lurleen	Fr Tuscaloosa, 12 mi NW on US 82	1625	86	86	6.00	All year	•	•	dlr	•	g	205/339-1558	Rt 1, Box 479, Coker 35452
E5	Lakepoint Resort	Fr Eufaula, 7 mi N on Hwy 431	1220	110	190	6.00	All year	•	•	dlr	•	gt	205/687-6676	Rt 2 Box 94,Eufaula 36027
A2	Joe Wheeler	Fr Athens, 12 mi N on US 72	2550	110	110	6.00	All year	$	•	dlr	•		205/247-1184	Rt 2, Town Creek 35672
B4	Buck's Pocket	Fr Groveoak, 2 mi N	2000	15	58	6.00	All year				•	p	205/659-2000	Rt 1, Box 24, Groveoak 35975
D3	Tannehill	Fr Bessemer, 11 mi W on I-59, Bucksville ext, 4-1/2 mi E	1000	50	75	6.00	All year	•	•			gp	205/477-6571	Rt 1, Box 124, McCalla 35111
D3	Brierfield Ironworks Pk	Fr Montevallo, 8 mi S on St Hwy 25, fol signs		30	25	2.00	All year	•	•				205/665-1856	Rt 1 Bx 123A,Brierfield 35035
	STATE AREAS													
D2	Mound State Monument	Fr Tuscaloosa, 13 mi S on Hwy 69; in Moundville	320	20	18	F4.00	All year	○		l		p	205/371-2572	Mound St Mmt,Moundville 35474
	NATIONAL FORESTS													
	Talladega NF(Oak Mulgee)													
D2	Payne Lake East Side	Fr Greensboro, 16 mi NE on Hwy 25	49	37	37	2.00	3/15-9/30	1	•	dl				Greensboro
D2	Payne Lake Spillway	Fr Greensboro, 16 mi NE on Hwy 25	3	14	14	2.00	2/15-11/15		•	dl				Greensboro
D2	Payne Lake West Side	Fr Greensboro, 16 mi NE on Hwy 25	10	33	33	2.00	5/15-9/30		•	dl				Greensboro
	Talladega NF (Talladega)													
C4	Pine Glen	Fr Heflin, 2.5 mi W on US 78, 8 mi N on FR 500	5	31	31	2.00	3/20-12/31	•	•	d				Heflin
C4	Lake Chinnabee	Fr Talladega, 6.8 mi NE on Hwy 21, 12 mi E on Co 96, 1.3 mi SW on FR 646	2	14	14	2.00	All year	•	•	d				Talladega
C4	Coleman Lake	Fr Heflin, 8 mi N on US 78, 2.5 mi NW on Co 61, 4.6 mi NW on FR 553, 1.5 mi NE on FR 5004	15	39	39	2.00	4/29-11/15	•	•	dl	h			Heflin
	William B Bankhead NF													
B2	Corinth	Fr Double Springs, 4 mi E on US 278, 3 mi S on FR 113	29	70	70	2.00	4/1-10/31	•	•	dlr				Double Springs
B2	Brushy Lake	Fr Moulton, 15 mi S on Hwy 33, 5 mi E on FR 245	3	13	13	None	All year	•	•	dl				Moulton
	Conecuh NF													
G3	Open Pond	Fr Andalusia, 10 mi SW on US 29, 5 mi S on Hwy 137, .5 mi E on Co 24, 1 mi SE on FR 336	3	28	26	2.00	All year	1	•	dl				Andalusia
	CORPS OF ENGINEERS													
	Walter F George Lake	For additional CG information, see Georgia											912/768-2462	Box 281, Ft Gaines GA 31751
F5	White Oak Creel Pk	Fr Eufaula, 10 mi S on Hwy 95	170	49	49	2.00	All year			l			205/289-3540	Ft Gaines, GA 31751
	Demopolis Lake														PO Box 520, Demopolis 36732
E2	Forkland	Fr Demopolis, 10 mi N on Hwy 43	98	14	14	2.00	All year	•	•	l				Demopolis
E2	Lock 5	Fr Demopolis, 9 mi NE on Co 13	55	12	12	2.00	All year	•	•	l				Demopolis
E1	Damsite, Lower Pool	Fr Demopolis, 5 mi W off Hwy 80	24	9	9	None	All year	○	•	l				Demopolis
E1	Runaway Branch PUA #2	Fr Demopolis, 5 mi W on US 43	40	5	5	2.00	All year		•					Demopolis
E1	Foscue Creek	Fr Demopolis, 5 mi W on US 80	99	40	40	2.00	All year	•	•	l			205/682-4244	Rt 1, Box 43-H, Camden 36726
	"Bob" Woodruff Lake														
E3	Prairie Creek PUA	Fr Montgomery, 35 mi W on Hwy 80 to Benton ext, fol signs	50		34	None	All year	•	•	l			205/289-3540	Box 520,Demopolis 36732
	Warrior Lake														
D2	Lock 8 PUA	Fr Akron, 4 mi W on Co 36	24	10	10	2.00	All year	•	•	l				Akron
D2	Lock 7 PUA E	Fr Eutaw, 8 mi SE on Hwy 14	20	11	11	2.00	All year	○	○	l				Eutaw
D2	Jennings Ferry	Fr Eutaw, 8 mi SE on Hwy 14	30	13	13	2.00	All year	•	•	l				Eutaw
D2	Lock 7 PUA (West)	Fr Eutaw, 8 mi SE on Hwy 14	48	9	9	None	All year	•	•	l			912/768-2462	Demopolis
	George W Andrews Lake														Box 281, Ft Gaines 31751
F5	Coheelee Creek PUA	Fr Columbia, 10 mi N on Co		7	7	None	All year	○	○					Ft Gaines, GA
F5	Abbie Creek	Fr Columbia, 22 mi N on Co		5	5	None	All year	○	○					Ft Gaines, GA
D5	Amity Pk	Fr I-85, Lanett ext, N on US 29 to State Line Rd N on State Line to park sign	418	92	92	4.00	4/1-9/30	•		l	•	p	404/645-2937	Bx 574 West Point 31833
	Coffeeville Lake													205/289-3540	Box 520, Demopolis 36732
F1	Okatuppa Creek	Fr Barrytown, 3 mi E on Co	21	8	8	None	All year	○	○	l				Barrytown
E1	Lock 3 (R Bank)	Fr Demopolis, 12 mi S on Co 21		7	7	None	All year	○	○	l				Demopolis
F1	Service	Fr Coffeeville, 4 mi W on US 84	100		19	2.00	All year							Demopolis
E1	Lock 2 (R Bank)	Fr Nanafalia, approx 5-1/2 mi W on Hwy 10, N on Co 114	40		10	2.00	All year	•	•	l			205/289-3540	Demopolis
	Holt Lake														Box 520, Demopolis 36732
C2	Rocky Branch	Fr Tuscaloosa, 7 mi E on Hwy 116	340	25	25	2.00	All year	○	○	l				Tuscaloosa
C2	Deerlick Creek	Fr Tuscaloosa, 8 mi NE on Hwy 47	300	39	39	2.00	All year	○	○	l				Tuscaloosa
C2	Blue Creek	Fr Tuscaloosa, 25 mi NE on Hwy 47	172	18	18	None	All year	○	○	l			205/682-4244	Tuscaloosa
	Bill Dannelly Reservoir														Rt 1 Box 43-H Camden 36726
F2	Bridgeport Pk	Fr Camden, 4 mi NE on Hwy 41, ext for Reservoir	300	20	20	2.00	All year	•	•	l		g		Camden
E2	Chilatchee	Fr Catherine, 8 mi E on Hwys 5 & 29	500	14	14	2.00	All year	•	•	l			205/289-3540	Camden
	Claiborne Lake														
F2	Bells Landing Pk	Fr Hwy 41, 3 mi S of Hybert	340	6	S6	None	All year	•		r				Rt 1 Box 43H, Camden 36726
F2	Silver Creek Pk	Fr Grove Hill, 6 mi E on Co 12, 1 1/2 mi N on Co, 4 mi E on gravel road	45	6	S6	None	All year	•		l				Camden 36726
F2	Haines Island Pk	Fr Hwy 41, W on Hwy 17, 2 mi on gravel rd, fol signs	390	11	S11	None	All year	•	•	l		p	205/682-4244	Rt 1, Bx 43-H, Camden 36726
E2	East Bank Access Area	Fr Miller's Ferry, 2 mi W on Hwy 28	45	6	56	None	All year	•	•	dl			205/682-4244	Rt 1 Bx 43-H, Camden 36726

Arkansas

Major Events

See state map, page 19

DeGray State Park Eagle Watch, late Jan., DeGray State Park, northwest of Arkadelphia. This event is designed to make participants more knowledgeable of the bald eagle, and it features guest lecturers, live animals, films, and field observations. Free. 501/865-4501.

Jonquil Festival, mid-Mar., Old Washington State Park, south of Nashville. Blooming jonquils, crafts demonstrations, bluegrass music, and tours of the restored 19th-century town are featured. Admission. 501/983-2684.

Arkansas Folk Festival, mid- to late Apr., Ozark Folk Center, Mountain View. There are craft demonstrations, live music, folk dancing, a rodeo, and a parade. Admission. 501/269-3851.

Ozark Foothills Handicraft Guild Spring Show & Sale, mid-Apr., Mountain View. Held at the Guilds Fairgrounds, this event has numerous craftspersons displaying and selling their work as well as demonstrating their crafts skills. Admission. 501/269-3896.

Spring Tour of Historic Houses, late Apr., Eureka Springs. Several homes are open to the public for tours. Admission. 501/253-8737.

The Great Passion Play, May through Oct., Eureka Springs. A cast of 300 performers portray the events of the last week of Christ's life in a large outdoor amphitheater. Admission. 501/253-8781.

Festival of Two Rivers, early May, Arkadelphia. This event features an antique show, arts and crafts, food booths, bluegrass music, and sporting contests. Free (except food). 501/246-5542.

Old Fort River Festival, early May, Fort Smith. This celebration of the arts is held on Fort Smith's riverfront. There is continuous musical entertainment, ranging from bluegrass music to symphony performances. Arts and crafts, sporting events, and ethnic foods are also featured. Free (except food). 501/783-6118.

Riverfest, late May, Little Rock. The visual and performing arts are celebrated at this event held in both the downtown and riverfront areas. Free. 501/376-4781.

Old Fort Days & Arkansas-Oklahoma Rodeo, late May to early June, Fort Smith. The onetime frontier town holds its rodeo at Harpers Stadium. Other festivities include a parade, food, and a carnival. Admission. 501/783-6118.

Arkansas Fun Festival, early to mid-June, Hot Springs. This event features activities for the entire family. A parade of boats, gospel singing, a turkey shoot, and an antique show and sale are only a few of the events. Free. 501/321-1700.

Pink Tomato Festival, mid-June, Warren. The tomato harvest is celebrated with a parade, an all-tomato lunch, a beauty pageant, and a tomato-eating contest. Free. 501/226-5225.

Johnson County Peach Festival, late June, Clarksville. One of the oldest annual events in the state, it includes a parade, street dance, flea markets, crowning of a queen, and a country music concert. Admission for pageant. 501/754-8785.

Rodeo of the Ozarks, early July, Springdale. The rodeo is held at Parsons Rodeo Arena. There is a parade, and food stands serve refreshments. Admission. 501/751-4694.

Libertyfest, July 4, Petit Jean State Park, northwest of Perryville. Fireworks, entertainment, and an air show at the nearby airport are part of the celebration. Free. 501/727-5435.

White River Water Carnival, early Aug., Batesville. A parade, arts and crafts, a beauty pageant, and a catfish dinner are featured along with a hot-air balloon race. Free (except food). 501/793-2378.

Greers Ferry Lake Water Festival, mid-Aug., Greers Ferry Lake. Many private resorts and attractions join the local tourist association in hosting a variety of events including hot-air balloon races, water skiing shows, boat races, and musical shows. Free. 501/362-2892.

Watermelon Festival, mid-Aug., Hope. The watermelon harvest is celebrated with the judging of prize melons, a watermelon-eating contest, and music and dancing. Free. 501/777-3640.

Arkansas Old-Time Fiddlers State Championship, late Sept., Mountain View. The Ozark Folk Center is the site for this statewide competition which will determine the state champion fiddler. Admission. 501/269-3851.

Arkansas Apple Festival, early Oct., Lincoln, southwest of Fayetteville. This festival features a street dance, the Apple Harvest Queen Contest, an arts and crafts show, and a parade. Free. 501/824-3305.

Arkansas State Fair and Livestock Show, early Oct., Little Rock. This event features champion livestock exhibits, live entertainment, a rodeo, youth talent competition, and two beauty contests. Admission. 501/372-8341.

Ozark Frontier Trail Festival and Craft Show, early Oct., Heber Springs. Highlights of this annual fall festival include a craft exhibition and sale, a pioneer parade, an antique show, folk music, and a muzzle-loading shoot. Admission is charged for several events. 501/362-2444.

Arkansas Rice Festival, early Oct., Weiner. This festival celebrates and promotes the rice industry in Arkansas and features tractor-pulling contests, a rice buffet with over 400 different rice dishes, and exhibits on Arkansas' rice industry. Free (except food). 501/684-2284.

National Wild Turkey–Calling Contest and Turkey Trot Festival, early Oct., Yellville. In addition to the contest, the festival includes entertainment on the town square, arts and crafts show, a carnival, parade, dances, queen's contest, and dinners. Admission is charged for several events. 501/449-4676.

Arkansas Oktoberfest, mid-Oct., Hot Springs. German food, music, and dancing are featured at this traditional German celebration of autumn. Admission is charged for several events. 501/321-1700.

Ozarks Arts & Crafts Fair, mid-Oct., War Eagle Mills Farm, near Eureka Springs. Craftsmen from four states are selected for the quality and originality of their work; they display and demonstrate their crafts and skills at this three-day fair. Admission. 501/789-5398.

Ozark Folk Festival, early Nov., Eureka Springs. Square dances, arts and crafts, a festival queen contest, and a parade are featured at the oldest festival in the hills. Admission is charged for several events. 501/253-8737.

National Fiddlers Convention & Championships, early Nov., Mountain View. The Ozark Folk Center is the site of this national championship for bluegrass fiddlers. Admission. 501/269-3851.

Frontier Days, early Nov., Old Washington State Park, south of Nashville. Various 19th-century pioneer activities enliven the setting at the restored town of Old Washington. Knife making, butter making, and lard making are just some of the demonstrations given. Free. 501/983-2684.

Arkansas Arts, Crafts, and Design Fair, late Nov., Little Rock. Some 100 artists are invited to this juried invitational exhibition and sale of artwork. The four-day event is held at the Convention Center Exhibit Hall. Admission is charged for several events. 501/224-7300.

World Championship Duck-Calling Contest, late Nov., Stuttgart. Contestants from the U.S. and Canada compete for awards in duck calling; there is a carnival on Main St. and an arts and crafts fair. Free. 501/673-1602.

Ozark Christmas, early Dec., Mountain View. An old-fashioned Ozark Christmas is held throughout the town as well as at the Ozark Folk Center. Crafts, music, and food are all part of the Yuletime festivities. Free (except food). 501/269-3851.

Arkansas Destinations

ARKADELPHIA, 10,005, E-3. Founded in 1839, Arkadelphia became the Clark County seat four years later and was an important river port during the steamboat days. It is the gateway to the 13,400-acre DeGray Lake and DeGray Lake State Park, 8 miles north off Int. 30.

ARKANSAS POST NATIONAL MEMORIAL, E-5. On St. 169, 7 miles south of Gillett, the post, often called the Birthplace of Arkansas, was the site of French and Spanish forts and trading stations, a territorial capital, a river port, and a Civil War battleground. Today, the park is a memorial to those who traveled the river, met, fought, mixed, and settled the frontier. Few historic structures are visible; however, the natural setting, the exhibits, and an audiovisual program at the Visitors Center help re-create the history. The park is also a wildlife sanctuary, harboring many species of birds. Year-round, daily, 8 A.M. to 5 P.M. Free. 501/548-2432.

BUFFALO NATIONAL RIVER, B-3. Declared a national river on March 1, 1972, exactly 100 years after Yellowstone was authorized the first national park, the Buffalo River is one of the few remaining unpolluted, free-flowing rivers in the conterminous United States. In its 148-mile course (132 miles are in the national river unit), it flows through bluffs and past caves and springs in a half-wilderness area, yet it is never more than 10 miles from a road, and often closer. Here are some statistics related to the river: Its bluffs are 500 feet high; more than 13 clear-water fish species and 43 mammal species have been identified here; 800 to 1,000 different kinds of plants bloom along the way; the river tumbles down 1,900 feet over its course, ending up 400 feet above sea level, where it joins the White River; Hemmed-in Hollow, one of the side canyons, has a waterfall which drops 200 feet. Topographic maps, which are available at the river headquarters and district ranger stations along the river, are recommended for those planning to canoe on the river. Buffalo National River Headquarters, New Federal Building, Walnut and Erie Sts., Harrison. 501/741-5443. Year-round, Mon.-Fri., 8 A.M. to 4:45 P.M. Ranger Stations: On St. 7, 15 miles south of Harrison where the bridge crosses the river, mid-Mar.-Labor Day, daily, 8 A.M. to 5 P.M., intermittently other months. On U.S. 65, south of St. Joe, intermittently year-round. Off St. 14 on St. 268, south of Yellville, year-round, daily, 8 A.M. to 5 P.M.

CLINTON, 1,284, B-4. **Watergate Museum,** south at the intersection of St. 9 and U.S. 65, is a replica of a turn-of-the-century town, with a doctor's office, church, soda parlor, saloon, and jail. Mar.-Dec., daily, 9 A.M. to 5 P.M. Adults $2.50, children $1.50. 501/745-2602.

CRATER OF DIAMONDS STATE PARK, E-2. In 1906 John M. Huddleston, who owned a farm northeast of Murfreesboro, was puzzled because part of the land would not yield crops. Walking through the barren area one day, he found two crystals, which he had inspected by jewelers in Little Rock and St. Louis. Much to his and the jewelers' surprise, the crystals were identified as diamonds. Geologists examined the land and determined that the area in which the diamonds were found was the peridotite of an ancient volcano, which had been noted as early as 1842; however, Huddleston was the first to discover diamonds here. The crater was commercially mined between 1908 and 1924, and though less than successful, record diamonds were found. Among them was the 40.23-carat "Uncle Sam," claimed to be the largest diamond found in North America. In 1942, the area was opened to the public. Now it is a state park where visitors may search for diamonds and keep what they find, regardless of their value. Mining tools can be rented or purchased at the park and officials will examine suspect diamonds to determine their authenticity. Daily, Mar.-Dec., 8 A.M. to 5 P.M.; Jan.-Feb., 8 A.M. to 4:30 P.M. Adults $3; persons 6-15, $1. 501/285-3113.

EUREKA SPRINGS, 1,989, A-2. One of the oldest resorts in the state, its 63 springs made it a popular health resort as early as the 1800s. This mountaintop community has streets which plunge and twist over the Ozark hills, and houses cling to the steep slopes. Each of the floors of the seven-story-high Basin Park Hotel Museum can be reached from ground level, while the St. Elizabeth Church grounds are entered through the bell tower. **Eureka Springs Historical Museum,** 95 S. Main St., relates the town's history. Apr.-Nov., Tues.-Sat., 9:30 A.M. to 4 P.M. Adults $1, children 75¢. 501/253-9417. **Carry Nation's Hatchet Hall,** 35 Steele St., was the last home of the temperance crusader of the early 1900s. Apr.-Oct., daily, 9 A.M. to 5 P.M. Adults $2; persons 65 and over, $1.75; students $1.50; under 6, free. 501/253-7324. **Elva Smith Foundation,** U.S. 62, includes a Bible Museum, Christ Only Art Gallery, and presents *The Great Passion Play.* Bible Museum and Art Gallery: May-Oct., daily, 8 A.M. to 8 P.M.; Mon., Thurs., 8 A.M. to 5:30 P.M.; other months, Sat.-Sun., 9 A.M. to 4 P.M. Museum: Adults $1.50; children 6-12, 50¢. Art Gallery: Adults $2; children 6-14, 50¢; both, under 6, free. *The Great Passion Play:* May-Oct., nightly except Mon. and Thurs., 8:30 P.M.; after Labor Day, 7:30 P.M. General admission $4.50, children $1. Reserved seats $5.50, $6.50, $7.50. 501/253-8781. **Miles Musical Museum,** U.S. 62 west, has musical instruments, music boxes, nickelodeons, clocks, miniature circus; many are antique and rare. May-Oct., daily, 9 A.M. to 5 P.M. Adults $3; persons 6-15, $1.50; under 6, free. 501/253-8961. **Pine Mountain Jamboree,** east on U.S. 62, presents live country music and comedy by local musicians. Apr., Sat.; May, Mon., Wed., Thurs., Sat.; June-Aug., Mon.-Sat.; Sept., Mon., Wed., Thurs., Sat.; Oct., Mon.-Sat. Performance 8 P.M. Adults $4.50, children $2. 501/253-9156. **Blue Springs,** largest springs in northwest Arkansas, is west on U.S. 62. A historical theater describes the history and terrain. Apr.-Oct., daily, 8 A.M. to 7:30 P.M. Adults, $2.50; children 6-11, $1.50. 501/253-9244. **Onyx Cave Park,** east off U.S. 62,

Thorncrown Chapel rises triumphantly amid its wooded surroundings off U.S. 62, west of Eureka. Built primarily of wood and glass, the nondenominational chapel has won several architectural awards for its designer, E. Fay Jones, who once studied under Frank Lloyd Wright. The chapel is 60 feet long, 24 feet wide, and 48 feet high. To avoid marring the natural beauty of the site, heavy equipment was banned during construction of the chapel. As a result, all materials had to be carried in by hand.

has unusual geological formations. Year-round, daily, 8 A.M. to 8 P.M. Adults $2.50; persons 4-13, $1; under 4, free. 501/253-9321.

FAYETTEVILLE, 36,604, A-1. The **University of Arkansas Museum,** in Hotz Hall, Garland and Cleveland Sts., has four major areas of exhibits: geology, zoology, anthropology, and history. Year-round, Mon.-Sat., 9 A.M. to 5 P.M.; Sun., 1 to 5 P.M. Free. 501/575-3555. Engraved in the university's **Senior Walk,** instituted in 1905, are the names of graduates since that time.

FORT SMITH, 71,384, B-1. At **Fort Smith National Historic Site,** Rogers Ave. between Second and Third Sts., a fort was established in 1817 to stop the confrontation between the Cherokee, Osage, and some white settlers. While soldiers under the command of Bvt. Maj. William Bradford struggled to build the fort, they also struggled to keep peace on the frontier. Although peace was achieved, bands of horse thieves, bandits, and fugitives from justice rode the territory, and a handful of U.S. deputy marshals and the tribal Light Horse attempted to keep order. In 1875, Judge Isaac C. Parker arrived. During his 21 years on the bench, he tried more than 13,000 cases, and more than 9,000 were convicted. Of these, 344 were tried for capital offenses and 151 were sentenced to be hanged; and although only about half met their demise through this punishment, Parker was referred to as the "hanging judge." He responded that he did not hang them, the law did. Judge Parker's courtroom is in the Old Barracks Building, now a Visitors Center. Year-round, daily, 9 A.M. to 5 P.M. Free. 501/783-3961.

HARRISON, 9,567, A-3. **Dogpatch U.S.A.,** 9 miles south on St. 7, is a theme park based on the characters in Al Capp's "Lil' Abner" comic strip. The park has live and puppet shows, a trout farm and trout fishing, and rides for all ages. Late Apr.-mid-May, weekends; late May-late Aug., daily; Sept., weekends; all 9 A.M. to 6 P.M. Adults $7.50; persons 4-12 and 65 and over, $6.50; 3 and under, free. Admission covers all except Antique Road ride. 501/743-1111. *See* also **Buffalo National River.**

HOT SPRINGS, 35,166, D-3. This city, with a backdrop of the Ouachita Mountains and Ouachita National Forest, is famous for its medicinal waters, resulting in its main attraction—Hot Springs National Park. Hernando de Soto and his followers are believed to have explored the region in 1541. The Indians were here many years before. According to legend, they considered the springs to be sacred and made them neutral territory. As a result, warriors from hostile tribes came here and together eased their rheumatic pains in the medicinal waters. **Hot Springs National Park** is surrounded by the city, and together the park and city have some 17 bathing establishments using thermal water from the 47 springs here. Each day about one million gallons of 144° F. water flow into the park from the springs, is collected, cooled, and piped to central reservoirs for bathhouse and thermal use. Several drinking fountains on Reserve Ave., along the Promenade, and on Bathhouse Row provide hot thermal water, and there are jug fountains on Reserve Ave. for those who wish to take the water with them. The park terrain covers five mountains (Hot Springs, North, West, Sugar Loaf, and Indian) and oak-hickory forests abundant also with shortleaf pine, flowering trees (dogwood and magnolia), and wildflowers. The Visitors Center, Central and Reserve Aves., has exhibits explaining the natural history of the springs. Exhibits also relate the history of the bathing industry and medicinal bathing, which was traditional in ancient times. The springs became a national park on March 4, 1921. Visitors Center: Daily, Memorial Day-Labor Day, 8 A.M. to 7 P.M.; other months, 8 A.M. to 5 P.M. Free. 501/624-3383. (Cost for bathhouse use charged by individual concessions.) *Josephine Tussaud Wax Museum,* 250 Central Ave., has over 100 life-size figures of famous persons. Daily, Apr.-Labor Day, 9 A.M. to 10 P.M.; other months, 9:30 A.M. to 5 P.M. Adults $3.50, children $2. 501/623-5836. **Magic Springs Family Fun Park,** east on U.S. 70, has rides, live entertainment, and craft centers in three sections—County Fair, Mill Town, and River Town. Memorial Day-Labor Day, daily; Apr., May, Sept., Oct., weekends, all 10 A.M. to 8 P.M. Admission $7.50 (covers everything except food and beverage). 501/624-5411. **Mid-America Center Museum,** 400 Mid-America Blvd., 6½ miles west off U.S. 270W on St. 227, has exhibits on life, energy, perception, matter, and Arkansas. In an outdoor setting of trees, the museum has exhibits arranged for "hands on"—for the visitor to explore, as well as view, and a freshwater aquarium. "Lands Alive!" demonstrates the forces that shape the earth; the "Gravity Tower" illustrates gravity, pneumatics, acceleration, and resonance. Year-round, Tues.-Sun., 10 A.M. to 5 P.M. Adults $3.50; persons 6-17 and 65 and over, $2.50. 501/767-3461.

JONESBORO, 31,530, B-6. The **Arkansas State University Museum,** in the Learning Resources Bldg., Caraway and Aggie Rds., has Indian and pioneer artifacts, exhibits on fossil and natural history, and a research library covering these subjects. Year-round, Mon., Wed., Fri., 1 to 4 P.M.; Tues. and Thurs., 9 A.M. to noon, 1 to 4 P.M. Free. 501/972-2074.

LITTLE ROCK, 158,461, D-4. The state capital of Arkansas, Little Rock got its name from the large moss-covered rock jutting out from the south bank of the Arkansas River near the Arkansas Territorial Restoration. This rock, which marks the transition from the plains to the highlands, was a landmark for the Indians and early explorers and marked a practical ford across the river for settlers coming down the Mississippi River.

GOVERNMENT BUILDINGS: State Capitol, Woodland Blvd., facing Capitol Ave. Designed by Cass Gilbert, it has two wings extending from a classic portico, with a tall dome circled with Ionic columns and capped by a minaret of similar columns. In the lower level are exhibits relating the state's early exploration, steamboat travel, and plantation life. Year-round, Mon.-Fri., 7:30 A.M. to 6 P.M.; Sat.-Sun., 1 to 5 P.M. Free. Tours available during these hours. Special musical events are also held during the Christmas season. For a schedule, call the Secretary of State's office, 501/371-1010. Information services, 501/370-5159. **The Old State House,** 300 W. Markham St., now has Arkansas history exhibits, including six period rooms and inaugural gowns worn by Arkansas governors' wives. Year-round, Mon.-Sat., 9 A.M. to 5 P.M.; Sun., 1 to 5 P.M. Free. 501/371-1749. **Pulaski County Courthouse,** W. Markham and Spring Sts., is a four-story building, with balustrades and arches in Italian Renaissance design. The rotunda has a stained-glass dome. Year-round, Mon.-Fri., 8:30 A.M. to 4:30 P.M. Free. Tours available from Room 100, County Judge's Office. 501/378-7993.

MUSEUMS AND ARTS CENTER: Arkansas Arts Center, MacArthur Park, is noted for its graphic and applied arts. The Center has five exhibit galleries, a small theater, classrooms, and a sculpture court. Year-round, Mon.-Sat., 10 A.M. to 5 P.M.; Sun., noon to 5 P.M. Free. 501/372-4000. **Arkansas Territorial Restoration,** Third and Scott Sts., includes 13 original, authentically furnished structures dating from 1820-40. A recent addition is a reconstructed dogtrot log house (two one-room buildings set side by side and connected by a wide hall open at both ends) from a plantation east of Little Rock. Also on the grounds are the first print shop of the *Arkansas Gazette,* oldest newspaper west of the Mississippi River, and 200-year-old boxwood hedges grown from Mt. Vernon cuttings. The Arkansas Herb Society maintains the kitchen garden in a manner typical of the period. The Visitors Center has an exhibit gallery displaying works of local artists and a shop featuring Arkansas crafts. Year-round,

Mon.-Sat., 9 A.M. to 5 P.M.; Sun., 1 to 5 P.M. Adults $1; persons under 16 and 65 and over, 25¢. 501/371-2348. **Museum of Science and History,** 500 E. Grant St., MacArthur Park, occupies the Tower Building of the original Little Rock Arsenal. Built between 1836-40, the structure was the birthplace of Gen. Douglas MacArthur, whose father served as post commandant at the time. The museum, now undergoing restoration, has extensive three-dimensional exhibits based on the theme "Arkansas . . . Its Land and People." Year-round, Mon.-Sat., 9 A.M. to 5 P.M.; Sun., 1 to 5 P.M. Free. 501/376-4321. **Trapnall Hall,** 423 E. Capitol Ave., was built in 1843 and restored

in 1963 by the Junior League as a pilot project for restoration of the Quapaw Quarter. Year-round, Mon.-Fri., 9 A.M. to 1 P.M. Free. 501/372-4791. **Villa Marre,** 1321 Scott St., is an Italianate Victorian authentically furnished home built in 1881. Year-round, Tues.-Fri., noon to 4 P.M.; Sun., 1 to 4 P.M. Adults $1, students 50¢. 501/371-0075.

HISTORIC AREA: Quapaw Quarter, where Little Rock was first settled, extends from the Arkansas River on the north, to Roosevelt Rd. on the south, and from Little Rock Regional Airport on the east, to the Capitol grounds on the west. In the area are antebellum and Victorian homes.

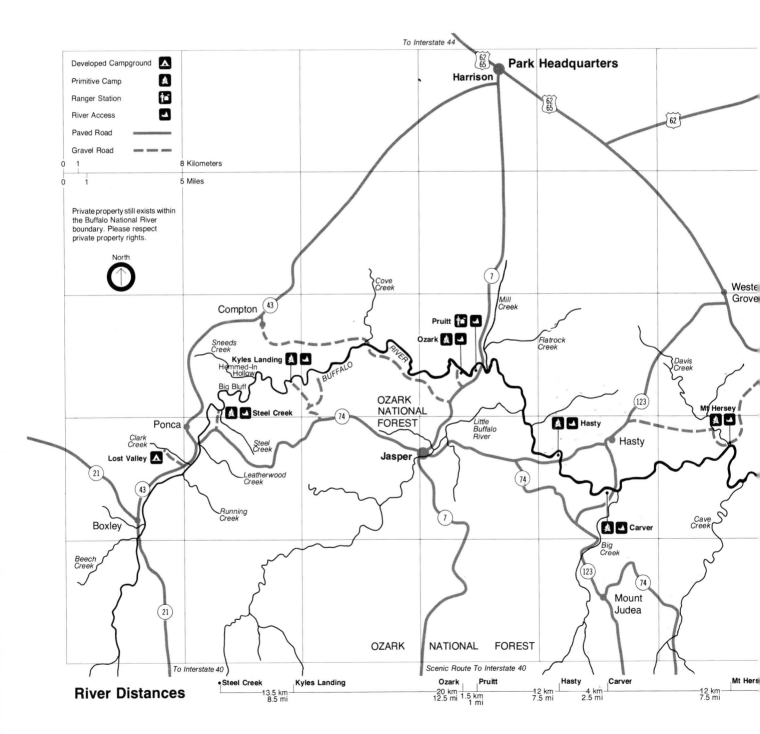

PARKS: Burns Park, Int. 40 in North Little Rock, has an indoor-outdoor tennis center, a 27-hole golf course, picnic areas, zoo for children, archery range, nature trails, launching ramps for fishing and boating on the Arkansas River, and 10 miles of scenic roads. **Murray Park,** Rebsamen Park Rd., east of Murray Lock and Dam on the Arkansas River, has picnic areas and boating ramps. **War Memorial Park,** between W. Markham St. and W. 12th St. at Fair Park Blvd., includes Ray Winder Field; War Memorial Stadium, where the University of Arkansas Razorbacks play; an 18-hole golf course; Olympic-size swimming pool; small park for children; Robert Walker Tennis Center; archery range; miniature golf course; and zoo. Other parks are **Boyle Park,** 3101 Boyle Park Rd., with picnicking areas and jogging trails; **Hindman Park and Golf Course and Raymond Rebsamen Tennis Center,** 1501 Leisure Pl.; **MacArthur Park,** E. 9th St.; and **Rebsamen Park and Golf Course,** next to Murray Park.

SHOPPING: MetroCenter Mall, Main St. between Third and Seventh Sts. in downtown Little Rock, is a paved mall with plantings, fountains, and a $185,000 Henry Moore sculpture.

ZOO: Zoo of Arkansas, War Memorial Park, includes over 600 exhibits. Recent additions are a rain forest and monkey island. There are also a Petting Zoo and miniature sight-seeing train. Year-round, daily, 9:30 A.M. to 5:30 P.M. Free. 501/663-4733.

MAMMOTH SPRING STATE PARK, A-5. This large natural spring spurts nine million gallons of cool water per hour. Also in the park are an 18-acre lake formed by the spring at the headwaters of the Spring River and a restored depot. Year-round, daily, 8 A.M. to 5 P.M. Free. 501/625-7364.

MORRILTON, 6,814, C-3. **Winrock International Livestock Research and**

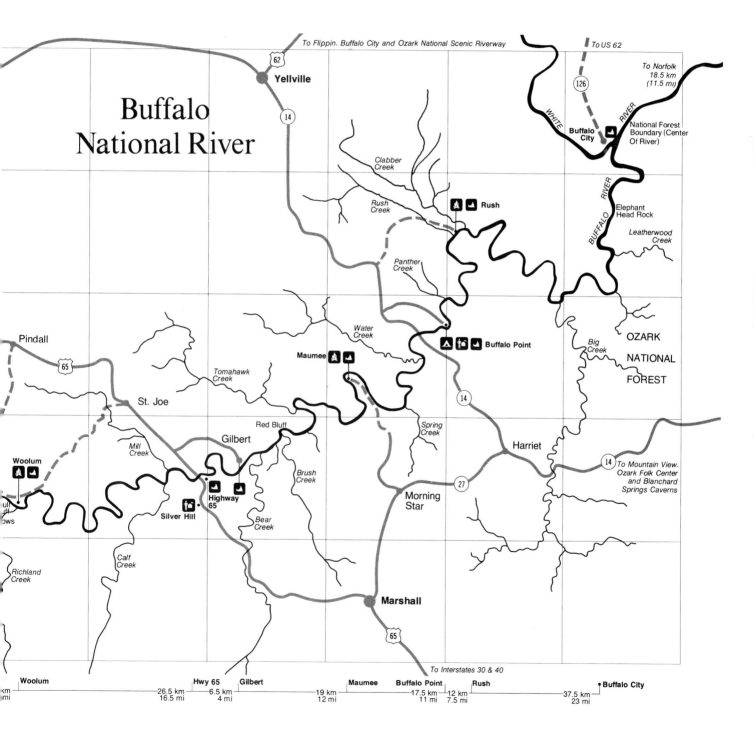

Training Center, 20 miles west off St. 154, was established by the late Gov. Winthrop Rockefeller, who built the ranch, where he lived, and the adjoining conference center. **Winrock Farm,** a purebred Santa Gertrudis breeding station, is nearby. The entire facility is at the top of Petit Jean Mountain. Visitors Center: Year-round, daily, 8 A.M. to 6 P.M. Free. 501/727-5435. **Petit Jean State Park** is 15 miles southwest of Morrilton on St. 154, west off St. 9. This scenic area has towering bluffs, unusual rock formations, Cedar Falls, overlooks onto the Arkansas River Valley, and a large network of nature trails. Park: Year-round, daily, 8 A.M. to 10 P.M. Visitors Center: Memorial Day-Labor Day, daily, 8 A.M. to 8 P.M. Free. 501/727-5441. **Museum of Automobiles,** 15 miles southwest of Morrilton on St. 154, founded by Governor Rockefeller in 1964, has over 50 antique cars. Year-round, daily, 10 A.M. to 5 P.M. Adults $2.50; persons 6-16, $1. 501/727-5427.

MOUNTAIN HOME, 7,447, A-4. This vacation center is located between Bull Shoals and Norfork lakes. **Norfork National Fish Hatchery,** 12 miles southeast on St. 5, then east on St. 177, is the largest federal trout hatchery in the country. It annually distributes more than 1.5 million rainbow trout. Year-round, daily, 7:30 A.M. to 3:30 P.M. Free. 501/499-5255.

MOUNTAIN VIEW, 2,147, B-4. **Blanchard Springs Caverns,** north off St. 69 in Ozark National Forest, is operated by the U.S. Forest Service. The cave was first explored in the early 1930s by a Forest Service recreation planner; five years of exploration began in 1955; and the first public tours were given in 1973. Now, two tours are conducted from the Visitors Center, which has audiovisual programs and exhibits. The *Dripstone Trail* goes through two major rooms—*Cathedral Room*, large enough to hold three football fields and more, and *Coral Room*, with large formations of pure calcite. The *Discovery Trail* takes the routes of early explorers and includes the area with the natural entrance through which they dangled from ropes and also includes the stream which comes from Blanchard Springs. Visitors Center: Year-round, daily, 9 A.M. to 6 P.M. Dripstone Trail tour: Year-round, every half hour, 9:30 A.M. to 4:30 P.M. Discovery Trail tour: Memorial Day-Labor Day, same time. Each tour: Adults $3.50; children 6-12, $1.50; under 6, free. 501/757-2211.

OZARK FOLK CENTER, B-4. This 915-acre hillside state park, 1 mile north of Mountain View off St. 5, St. 9, and St. 14, was established to preserve the cultural traditions of the area and share them with others. In the **Crafts Forum,** located in numerous buildings and areas, local artisans demonstrate quilt making, spinning, wood carving, basketry, broom caning, and primitive furniture and doll making. Classes are

also available in some of the craft areas and in folk music. At night, Stone County musicians perform in the 1,043-seat auditorium. They jig, square dance, sing, and play the ancient ballads of the hills on traditional instruments (dulcimer, autoharp, banjo, pickin' bow, and fiddle), which many have made themselves. In the Visitors Center is a **Folklore Research Library**. The park also has lodging and restaurant facilities. Park: May, Sept., Wed.-Sun.; June-Labor Day, daily; Oct., Tues.-Sun. Craft Forum: 10 A.M. to 6 P.M. park-open days. Park entrance: Adults $2.50; children 6-15, $1.50; under 6, free. Evening musical program, Memorial Day-Labor Day, Mon.-Sat., 8 P.M.; other months, same days as park. Adults $2.50; children 6-12, $1.50; under 6, free. 501/269-3851.

PEA RIDGE NATIONAL MILITARY PARK, A-2. Ten miles northeast of Rogers on U.S. 62/71, the park is the site of the battle which brought to an end the March 7-8, 1862, a campaign that began on Christmas Day, 1861. Also in the park is **Old Telegraph Road** over which the Butterfield Overland Mail Company routed its stagecoaches to Fort Smith and then westward to California in 1858. The park Visitors Center has exhibits and audiovisual programs. Daily, June-Aug., 8 A.M. to 6 P.M.; other months, 8 A.M. to 5 P.M. Free. 501/451-8122.

PINE BLUFF, 56,576, D-4. On **West Barraque St.,** in this noted cotton market city, are many antebellum homes built by the early planters. Local folks claim that the first shot fired in the Civil War was the warning from the musket discharged from the riverbank in April, 1861, when Jefferson Guards, a Pine Bluff militia unit, halted several Federal boats transporting supplies up the Arkansas River to Fort Smith and Fort Gibson. The only Civil War battle fought in Pine Bluff took place on October 25, 1863; bales of cotton were used as barricades by those defending the town against Confederate troops, which later withdrew. **Southeast Arkansas Arts and Science Center,** 200 E. 8th St., has paintings, sculpture, changing exhibits, two major galleries, a junior gallery, and theater. Year-round, Mon.-Fri., 10 A.M. to 5 P.M., Sat., 10 A.M. to 4 P.M. Free. 501/536-3375. **Martha Mitchell's Home,** W. 4th Ave. and Elm St., is the home of the late wife of the U.S. Attorney General during the Nixon Administration. Year-round, daily, by appointment. Free. 501/535-4973.

STUTTGART, 10,941, D-5. In the midst of one of the most productive rice-growing areas in the country, this is a stopover for ducks and geese traveling the Mississippi flyway. The largest number of these transients are here from November to March, when they stop off and feed in the rice fields, rivers, and reservoirs. The **Arkansas County Agricultural Museum,** 921 E. 4th St., covers 75 years of farming history (hay,

cattle, and rice industries) in the Stuttgart area. Year-round, Tues.-Sat., 10 A.M. to noon, 1 to 4 P.M.; Sun., 1:30 to 4:30 P.M. Donations. 501/673-7001. A **Fish Farming Experimental Station,** operated by the U.S. Fish and Wildlife Service, is 9 miles east on St. 130 (which extends east of St. 11). The station has tanks, aquariums, and ponds of catfish, minnows, and a hybrid of the grass carp. Year-round, Mon.-Fri., 7:30 A.M. to 4 P.M. Free. 501/673-8761.

WASHINGTON, 265, E-2. **Old Washington Historic State Park** is a living museum of historic places in this early Arkansas community which served as the state capital from 1863-65. Buildings and houses, which are a part of the park, are the *Blacksmith's Shop* where, according to legend, James Black, a silversmith who came West from Philadelphia, forged the first Bowie knife; *Old Tavern,* a reconstruction of the building where Bowie and Davy Crockett supposedly stayed en route to the Alamo (they were both killed in that fateful battle); the *Confederate State Capitol,* the seat of government for Arkansas while Union troops occupied Little Rock; *Old Washington Gun Museum,* which has more than 600 firearms from several countries and Bowie knives; *Pioneer Cemetery;* and historic homes and churches. Park: Adults $2; persons 6-16, $1; under 6, free. Tours: Year-round, Mon., Wed., Thurs., Fri., Sat., 9 A.M. to 4 P.M.; Sun., 1 to 5 P.M. Free. 501/983-2684.

Arkansas Campgrounds

FEES REFLECT MINIMUM RATE FOR 2 ADULTS AND ARE SUBJECT TO INCREASE OR SEASONAL CHANGES

•	at the campground	E	tents rented	U	unlimited	g	public golf course within 5 miles	p	motor bikes prohibited
○	within one mile of campground	F	entrance fee or permit required	V	trailers rented	h	horseback riding	r	boat rental
$	extra charge	N	no specific number, limited by size of area only	Z	reservations accepted	j	whitewater running craft only	s	stream, lake or creek water only
**	limited facilities during winter months	P	primitive	LD	Labor Day	k	snow skiing within 25 miles	t	tennis
A	adults only	R	reservation required	MD	Memorial Day	l	boat launch	u	snowmobile trails
B	10,000 acres or more	S	self-contained units only	UC	under construction	m	area north of map	w	open certain off-season weekends
C	contribution			d	boat dock	n	no drinking water	y	drinking water must be boiled

Map Reference	Park Name	Access	Acres	Tent Spaces	Trailer Spaces	Approximate Fee	Season	Swimming Pool/Other Swimming	Fishing	Boating	Playground	Other	Telephone Number	Mail Address
	STATE PARKS													
B6	Lake Poinsett	Fr Harrisburg, 1 mi E on Hwy 14, 2 mi S on Hwy 163	80	25	25	5.00	All year		•	l •	p		501/578-2064	Harrisburg 72432
C6	Village Creek	Fr I-40 at Forrest City, 12 mi N on Hwy 284	7000	104	104	5.00	All year	•	•	dlr	p		501/238-9406	Rt 3 Bx 49B, Wynne 72396
A6	Crowley's Ridge	Fr Paragould, 10 mi W on Hwy 25, 2 mi S on Hwy 141	270	18	18	5.00	All year	• •		r	p		501/573-6751	PO Box 97, Walcott 72474
B1	Devils Den	Fr Fayetteville, 7 mi S on US 71, 18 mi SW on Hwy 170	2280	24	72	4.50	All year	•	•	r •	hp		501/761-3325	Westfork 72774
A3	Bull Shoals	Fr Mountain Home, 6 mi NW on Hwy 5, 6 mi W on Hwy 178	725	20	85	5.00	All year		•	dlr •	p		501/431-5521	Bx 205, Bull Shoals 72619
C3	Petit Jean	Fr Morrilton, 8 mi S on Hwy 9, 12 mi W on Hwy 154	3700	127	127	5.00	All year	•	•	rl •	hp		501/727-5441	Rt 3, Morrilton 72110
C3	Mount Nebo	Fr Dardanelle, 7 mi W on Hwy 155	3400	30	30	4.00	All year	•		•	p		501/229-3655	Rt 2 Bx160-A Dardanelle 72834
D3	Lake Catherine	Fr Malvern, 2 mi N on US 270, 12 mi NW on Hwy 171	2180	70	70	5.00	All year	•	•	dlr •	p		501/844-4176	Rt 19 Bx 360, Hot Sprgs 71901
D2	Daisy	Fr US 70 in Daisy, 1 mi S to pk rd entr	272	21	89	5.00	All year		•	l •	p		501/398-4487	Daisy Rt Bx 66 Kirby 71950
D3	Lake Ouachita	Fr Hot Springs, 3 mi W on US 270, 15 mi N on Hwy 227	370	25	77	5.00	All year		•	dlr •	p		501/767-9366	Star Route, Mt Pine 71956
F5	Lake Chicot	Fr Lake Village, 8 mi N on Hwy 144	128	127	127	5.00	All year	•	•	dlr •	p		501/265-5480	Rt 1 Bx 648,Lk Village 71653
D1	Queen Wilhelmina	Fr Mena, 13 mi NW on Hwy 88	640	42	42	4.00	All year	•			p		501/394-2863	Mena 71953
A2	Withrow Springs	Fr Huntsville, 6 mi N on Hwy 23	790	25	25	5.00	All year	• ○ ○		r	jp		501/559-2593	Route 3, Huntsville 72740
A5	Old Davidsonville	Fr Pocahontas, 9 mi SW on US 62, 9 mi S on Hwy 166	160	10	25	5.00	All year		•	l •	p		501/892-4708	Rt 2, Pocahontas 72455
A5	Lake Charles	Fr Hoxie, 8 mi NW on US 63, 2 mi S on Hwy 25	116	10	120	5.00	All year		•	lr •	p		501/878-6595	Star Rt, Powhatan 72458
	Lake Dardanelle		294										501/967-5516	Rt 5 Bx 527,Russellville 72801
B3	Dardanelle Area	Fr Dardanelle, 3 mi NW on Hwy 22		18	18	5.00	All year		•	dlr	p			
B3	Russellville Area	Fr Russellville, 2 mi W on Hwy 326		65	65	5.00	All year		•	dlr	p			
B3	Ouita Area	Fr Russellville, 3/4 mi N on US 64		15	15	4.50	All year		•	l	p			
E3	White Oak	Fr Prescott, 20 mi E on Hwy 24, 2 mi S on Hwy 387	610	4	42	5.00	All year		•	dlr •	p		501/685-2748	Star Rt, Bluff City 71722
B1	Lake Ft Smith	Fr Mountainburg, N on US 71 to access rd, 1 mi E	126	12	12	5.00	All year	•	•	dlr •	p		501/369-2469	Mountainburg 72946
F4	Moro Bay	Fr El Dorado, 20 mi NE on Hwy 15	110	20	20	5.00	All year		•	dlr •	p		501/463-8555	Star Route, Jersey 71651
D3	De Gray	Fr Arkadelphia, 10 mi N on Hwy 7	915	34	113	5.00	All year		•	dlr •	gp		501/865-4695	Rt 1 Bx 144, Bismark 71929
E2	Millwood	Fr Texarkana, 16 mi N on US 71, 8 mi E on Hwy 32	825	114	114	5.00	All year		•	dlr •	p		501/898-2800	Rt 1 Bx 37AB, Ashdown 71822
C4	Woolly Hollow	Fr Conway, 12 mi N on US 65, 6 mi E on Hwy 285	400	17	17	3.50	All year		•	lr •	p		501/679-2098	Rt 1 Bx 374, Greenbriar 72058
E2	Crater of Diamonds	Fr Murfreesboro, 2 mi SW on Hwy 301	888	60	60	5.00	All year				p		501/285-3113	R 1 Bx 364,Murfreesboro 71958
	NATIONAL PARKS													
A3	Buffalo National River		B										501/449-4311	Rt A Bx 214, Yellville 72687
A2	Buffalo Point	Fr Yellville, 17 mi S on Hwy 14, 3 mi E on Hwy 268	2020	23	95	3.00	All year			l	p			Yellville 72687
	Lost Valley	Fr Harrison, 30 mi S on Hwy 43	200	15	S10	None	All year	•			p			
D3	Hot Springs NP												501/741-5443	Bx 1173 Harrison, Ar 72601
	Gulpha Gorge CG	Fr center of Hot Springs, 2 mi NE on US 70B		47	47	3.00	All year				g		501/624-3383	Box 1860, Hot Springs 71901
	NATIONAL FORESTS													
	Ouachita NF													
C1	Little Pines	Fr Waldron, 5.2 mi W on Hwy 248, 6.2 mi SW on CO 247	10	15	15	3.00	3/15-10/31	• •		dl				Waldron
D2	Charlton	Fr Hot Springs, 13 mi W on US 270	3	57	57	3.00	4/4-9/30	• •		dlr				Hot Springs
C3	Lake Sylvia	Fr Perryville, 9 mi S on Hwy 9, 4 mi SW on Co 324	10	19	19	3.00	4/4-11/24	• •		dl				Perryville
D2	Bard Springs	Fr Athens, 2 mi NW on Co 246, 6 mi N on FR 38, .5 mi E on FR 106	4	7	7	None	All year	• •			h			Athens
D2	Shady Lake	Fr Athens, 2 mi NW on Co 246, 2 mi N on FR 38	21	97	97	3.00	All year	• •		dr				Athens
D2	Mazarn	Fr Pearcy, 2 mi NW on Co 730	3	7	7	2.00	5/19-9/30	• •						Pearcy
D2	Big Brushy	Fr Pencil Bluff, 6 mi NW on US 270	3	11	11	None	3/1-11/17	• •						Pencil Bluff
D2	Mill Creek	Fr Waldron, 20 mi SE on US 270	8	24	24	2.00	4/4-9/15	• •						Waldron
C2	Knoppers Ford	Fr Boonville, 3 mi S on Hwy 23, 1 mi E on Hwy 116, 7 mi SE on FR 19	2	6	6	None	All year	• •						Boonville
C2	Jack Creek	Fr Boonville, 3 mi S on Hwy 23, 1 mi E on Hwy 116, 5 mi SE on FR 19, 1 mi E on FR 141	1	5	5	None	4/14-12/1	• •						Boonville
D2	Albert Pike	Fr Langley, 2 mi N on Hwy 369, 4 mi NW on FR 73	14	22	22	3.00	4/3-9/30	• •		d				Langley
D2	Crystal	Fr Norman, 1 mi N on Hwy 27, 3 mi NE on FR 177	4	9	9	None	All year	• •						Norman
D2	Rocky Shoals	Fr Mount Ida, 5.4 mi NW on US 270	4	7	7	None	All year	• •		dl				Mount Ida
D2	River Bluff	Fr Mount Ida, 3 mi NW on US 270, 6 mi NE on Hwy 27, 3.7 mi N on CO 59, 2.8 mi N on FR 138	2	7	7	None	All year	• •		dl				Mount Ida
D2	Dragover	Fr Sims, 3 mi E on Hwy 88, 1 mi S on FR 138A	4	7	7	None	All year	• •		dl				Sims
D2	Fulton Branch	Fr Mount Ida, 4.4 mi NW on US 270, 4 mi N on Hwy 298, 1.6 mi NE on CO 621, 3 mi N on FR 7437	3	7	7	None	All year	• •		dl				Mount Ida
D2	Shirley Creek	Fr Pencil Bluff, 6.5 mi W on Hwy 88, .5 mi SE on CO 7991	5	7	7	None	All year	• •		d				Pencil Bluff
	Ozark St. Francis NF													
B2	Redding	Fr Ozark, 1 mi W on US 64, 16 mi N on Hwy 23, 2 mi E on FR 1003	13	26	26	2.00	All year		•	dlr				Ozark
A1	Lake Wedington CG	Fr Fayetteville, 12 mi W on Hwy 16	6	18	18	2.00	4/18-9/15	1 •		dlr				Fayetteville
B4	North Sylamore	Fr Fifty Six, 1.5 mi E on Hwy 14, 3.5 mi N on FR 1110	16	30	30	3.00	All year		•	dlr	h			Fifty Six
B4	Gunner Pool	Fr Fifty Six, 1.5 mi NW on Hwy 14, 3 mi N on FR 1102	1	22	19	2.00	All year		•	d				Fifty Six
B3	Upper Brock Creek	Fr Jerusalem, 5.9 mi N on FR 1305, 1 mi NE on FR 1331	2	7	7	None	All year			d				Jerusalem
A4	Matney	Fr Norfork, 4 mi NW by boat	5	8		None	All year		•	dlr				Norfork
B2	White Rock	Fr Mulberry, 15 mi N on Hwy 215, 8 mi N on FR 1505	2	8		2.00	4/18-11/15			n				Mulberry
B2	Shores Lake	Fr Mulberry, 16 mi N on Hwy 215, 1 mi N on FR 1505	6	19	19	3.00	All year	1 •		d				Mulberry
B2	Horsehead Lake	Fr Clarksville, 7.6 mi NW on Hwy 103, 3.8 mi W on Hwy 164, 2.8 mi NW on FR 1408	4	10	10	3.00	All year		•	dl				Clarksville
B2	Wolf Pen	Fr Clarksville, 20 mi NW on Hwy 103, .3 mi W on Hwy 215	4	6	6	None	All year			n				Clarksville
B2	Ozone	Fr Ozone, 2.8 mi N on Hwy 21	8	8	8	None	All year			n				Ozone
B3	Long Pool	Fr Dover, 5.4 mi N on Hwy 7, 3.6 mi NW on Hwy 164, 2.7 mi NE on FR 1801, 2.1 mi NW on FR 1804	26	19	19	3.00	All year		•	d				Dover
B3	Haw Creek Falls	Fr Pelsor, 12.9 mi N on Hwy 123, .4 mi SE on FR 1837	3	8	8	None	All year		•	d				Pelsor
B3	Fairview	Fr Pelsor, 1.5 mi N on Hwy 7	4	11	11	None	All year							Pelsor
B3	Bayou Bluff	Fr Hector, 3.1 mi N on Hwy 27, 2.4 mi NE on FR 1303	6	5	2	None	All year		5	n				Hector
C2	Cameron Bluff	Fr Paris, 1.1 mi S on Hwy 109, 12.2 mi SE on Hwy 309, 1.9 mi W on FR 1606	8	16	16	None	All year			n				Paris
C2	Cove Lake	Fr Paris, 1.1 mi S on Hwy 109, 7.5 mi SE on Hwy 309, .6 mi SE on FR 1608	18	30	30	3.00	All year		•	dl				Paris
C2	Spring Lake	Fr Belleville, 4.1 mi N on Hwy 307, 2.9 mi NE on FR 1602, 1.2 mi SE on FR 1602A	7	13	13	3.00	4/18-11/26		•	dl				Belleville
D6	Beech Point	Fr Marianna, 7 mi SE on Hwy 44	2	8	6	3.00	All year	1 •		dlr				Marianna
D6	Lone Pine	Fr Marianna, 7.4 mi SE on Hwy 44, .5 mi NE on FR 1915, .5 mi N on FR 1913, .8 mi SW on FR 1913C	3	14	14	3.00	4/15-11/30	2 •		dlr				Marianna

Map Reference	Park Name	Access	Acres	Tent Spaces	Trailer Spaces	Approximate Fee	Season	Other Swimming	Swimming Pool	Fishing	Boating	Playground	Other	Telephone Number	Mail Address
D6	Maple Flat	Fr Marianna, 7.4 mi SE on Hwy 44, .5 mi NE on FR 1915, .4 mi S on FR 1913	5	10	10	3.00	4/15-11/30	1	1		dlr				Marianna
D6	Storm Creek Lake	Fr West Helena, 2 mi N on Hwy 242, 4.4 mi E on FR 1900	9	14	14	2.00	All year	1	1		dl		n		West Helena
	CORPS OF ENGINEERS														
	Lock & Dam 3														
D4	Rising Star	Fr Pine Bluff, 11 mi E on US 65, 3-1/2 mi NE at Linwood	91	22	22	3.00	All year			•	lr •	p			Pine Bluff
D4	Trulock Bend	Fr Pine Bluff, 8-1/2 mi E on US 65, 3 mi N at Noble Lk	41	15	15	None	All year			•	lr •	p			Pine Bluff
E5	Huffs Island	Fr Grady, 8 mi N on Hwy 11	40	8	8	None	All year			•					Grady
	Lock & Dam 5														
D4	Tar Camp	Fr Redfield, 6 mi E on access rd	100	41	41	4.00	All year			•	lr •	p			Redfield
D4	Wrightsville	Fr Woodson, 4 mi NE on US 365	50	9	9	None	All year			•	lr				Woodson
	Toad Suck Ferry Lock													501/968-5008	Russellville 72801
C4	Toad Suck Park	Fr Conway, 5 mi W on US 63		31	31	4.00	All year			•	l •	p			
C3	Point Remove	Fr Morrilton, 2 mi SW		21	21	2.00	All year			•	l •	p			
C3	Cypress Creek	Fr Houston, 2 mi N		9	9	None	All year			•	l •	p			
	Lock & Dam 9													501/968-5008	Russellville 72801
C3	Sweeden Island	Fr Atkins, 10 mi SW		53	53	3.00	All year			•	l	p			
C3	Cherokee	Fr Morrilton, 3 mi SW	20	26	26	4.00	All year			•	lr •	p			Morrilton
C3	Sequoya	Fr Oppelo, 2 mi NW	20	14	14	None	All year			•		p			Oppelo
	Bull Shoals Lake	(See Missouri for additional Campgrounds)													
A3	Tucker Hollow	Fr Lead Hill, 9 mi NW on Hwy 14	16	30	30	3.00	All year	•		•	dlr •	p			Lead Hill
A3	Lead Hill	Fr Lead Hill, 4 mi N on Hwy 7	55	77	77	3.00	All year	•		•	dlr •	p			Lead Hill
A3	Highway 125	Fr Yellville, 17 mi NW on Hwy 14, 12-1/2 mi N on Hwy 125	25	42	42	3.00	All year	•		•	dlr •	p			Peel
A3	Buck Creek	Fr Protem, Mo, 5 mi SE on Hwy 125	48	33	33	3.00	All year	•		•	dlr •	p			Protem, MO
A3	Oakland	Fr Mountain Home, 30 mi NW on Hwys 5 & 202	76	34	34	3.00	All year	•		•	dlr •	p			Oakland
A3	Ozark Isle	Fr Mountain Home, 30 mi NW on Hwys 5 & 202, W of Oakland CG	190	118	118	3.00	All year	•		•	lr •	p			Oakland
A3	Bull Shoals	Fr Flippin, 9 mi N on Hwy 178	9	12	12	2.00	All year	•		•	lr	p			Bull Shoals
A3	Lakeview	Fr Mountain Home 6 mi NW on Hwy 5, 7 mi N on Hwy 178	54	81	81	3.00	All year	•		•	dlr •	p			Lake View
A3	Point Return	Fr Flippin, 9 mi N on Hwy 178, 1/2 mi N of Bull Shoals CG	38	22	22	3.00	All year	•		•	lr	p			Bull Shoals
A3	Dam Site 2	Fr Flippin, 9 mi N on Hwy 178	10	35	35	3.00	All year	•		•		p			Bull Shoals
	Lock & Dam 2														
E5	Merrisach Lake	Fr DeWitt, S on Hwy 1, 5 mi E on Hwy 44, 10 mi S at Tichnor	102	46	43	3.00	All year			•	lr •	p			Tichnor
E5	Morgan Point	Fr Dumas, 16 mi E on Hwy 54	137	16	16	None	All year			•	lr •	p			Dumas
E5	Notrebes Bend	Fr Dewitt, S on Hwy 1, 5 mi E on Hwy 44, 15 mi S at Tichnor		25	25	3.00	All year			•	l •	p			
D5	Little Bayou Meto	Fr Reydel, 2 mi S	12	8	8	None	All year			•	lr	p			
E5	Pendleton Bend	Fr Dumas, 12 mi NE		10	10	None	All year			•	l	p			
	Beaver Lake														
A2	Dam Site	Fr Eureka Springs, 9 mi NW on US 62, 2-1/2 mi S on paved rd	93	78	78	3.00	All year	•		•	lr	p			Springdale
A2	Lost Bridge	Fr Gateway, S on US 62 to Garfield, 6 mi SE on Hwy 127	29	94	94	3.00	All year	•		•	dlr	p			Garfield
A2	Starkey	Fr Eureka Springs, 4 mi NW on US 62, 8-1/2 mi SW on Hwy 187	17	32	32	3.00	All year	•		•	dlr	p			Eureka Springs
A2	Indian Creek	Fr Gateway, 1 mi E on US 62, 5 mi S on gravel rd	20	42	42	None	All year	•		•		p			Gateway
A2	Prairie Creek	Fr Rogers, 4 mi E on Hwy 12	118	119	119	3.00	All year	•		•	dlr	p			Rogers
A2	Rocky Branch	Fr Rogers, 11 mi E on Hwy 12, 4-1/2 mi E on access rd	39	50	50	3.00	All year	•		•	dlr	p			War Eagle
A2	Horseshoe Bend	Fr Rogers, 6 mi E on Hwy 94	166	103	103	3.00	All year	•		•	dlr	p			Rogers
A2	Hickory Creek	Fr Springdale, N on US 71 to Vogel, 6-1/2 mi E on Hwy 264	90	38	38	3.00	All year	•		•	dlr	p			Springdale
A2	War Eagle	Fr Springdale, 12 mi NE on Hwy 68 to Nob, 3 mi NW	29	22	22	3.00	All year	•		•	lr	p			Springdale
A2	Blue Springs	Fr Springdale, 8 mi E on Hwy 68	33	17	17	2.00	All year	•		•	lr	p			Springdale
	Blue Mountain Lake														
	Hise Hill	Fr Booneville, 7 mi E on Hwy 10 to Magazine, 6 mi S to Sugar Grove, 2 mi E	22	9	9	None	All year			•	lr	p			Sugar Grove
C2	Outlet Area	Fr Booneville, 20 mi E on Hwy 10 to Waveland, 2 mi S	6	25	25	3.00	All year			•	r	p			Outlet Area
C2	Lick Creek	Fr Booneville, 20 mi E on Hwy 10 to Waveland, 6 mi SW		7	7	None	All year			•	l	p			Waveland
C2	Waveland Park	Fr Booneville, 20 mi E on Hwy 10 to Waveland, 1 mi S, 1 mi W	18	44	44	3.00	All year			•	l	p			Waveland
C2	Ashley Creek	Fr Booneville, 15 mi E on Hwy 10 to Blue Mtn, 2 mi S	8	10	10	None	All year			•	dlr	p			Blue Mtn
	Murray Lock & Dam													501/968-5008	Russellville 72801
D4	Maumelle	Fr Little Rock, 3 mi E on Hwy 130		44	44	4.00	All year			•	l •	p			
	David D Terry Lake														
D4	Willow Beach	Fr Scott, 5 mi W on Hwy 130		21	21	3.00	All year			•	lr	p			
	Lock & Dam 13													501/968-5008	Russellville 72801
C1	Lee Creek	Fr Van Buren, 1 mi W		10	10	None	All year			•		p			
C1	Dam Site South	Fr Barling, 2 mi N	10	49	49	3.00	All year			•		p			Barling
	Lake Dardanelle														
B2	Cane Creek	Fr Paris, 5.5 mi E on Hwy 22, NE on Hwy 109, to Scranton, 3 mi E, 2 mi N	48	8	8	None	All year			•	lr	p			Scranton
B2	Horsehead	Fr Clarksville, 5-1/2 mi SW on US 64, 3-1/2 mi S	107	10	10	None	All year			•	lr	p			Hartman
B2	Spadra	Fr Russellville, W on I-40 to Hwy 103, 3-1/2 mi S	82	31	31	4.00	All year			•	dlr	p			Clarksville
B2	Flat Rock	Fr Russellville, W on US 64 to Piney	59	15	15	2.00	All year			•	lr	p			Piney
B2	Piney Bay	Fr Russellville, W on I-40 to Piney, 3 mi N on Hwy 359	118	39	39	3.00	All year			•	lr	p			Piney
B2	Cabin Creek	Fr Russellville, W on I-40 to Knoxville, 2 mi W on gravel rd	54	5	5	None	All year			•	lr	p			Knoxville
C2	Shoal Bay	Fr Dardanelle, 12 mi W on Hwy 22, 1-1/2 mi N on Hwy 197	93	60	60	3.00	All year			•	dlr	p			New Blaine
C3	Delaware	Fr Dardanelle, 6 mi W on Hwy 22, 2-1/2 mi NE on Hwy 393	140	15	15	2.00	All year			•	lr	p			Delaware
C3	Dam Site West	1 mi N of Dardanelle	73	22	22	2.00	All year			•		p			Dardanelle
C3	Old Post Road	Fr Russellville, 3 mi SW on Hwy 7		16	16	3.00	All year			•	l •	p			
	Greers Ferry Lake														
B4	Choctaw	Fr Choctaw, 4 mi E on Hwy 330	63	146	146	3.00	All year			•	dlr •	p			Clinton
B4	South Fork	Fr Clinton, 3 mi E on Hwy 16, 7 mi SE on access rd	15	13	13	None	All year			•	lr	p			Clinton
B4	Van Buren	Fr Hwy 16 in Shirley, 7 mi S on Hwy 330	44	65	65	3.00	All year			•	dlr	p			Shirley
B4	Sugar Loaf	Fr jct Hwy 92 & US 65, 11 mi NE, 3 mi W on Hwy 337	55	96	96	3.00	All year			•	dlr	p			Heber Springs
B4	Mill Creek	Fr jct Hwy 92 & US 65, 13 mi NE, N on access rd	30	27	27	3.00	All year			•	dlr	p			Heber Springs
B4	Hill Creek	Fr Prim, 7 mi SW on gravel rd	38	40	40	None	All year			•	lr	p			Heber Springs
B4	Narrows	Fr Shirley, 15 mi SE on Hwy 16	50	60	60	3.00	All year			•	dlr	p			Heber Springs
B4	Devil's Fork	Fr Shirley, 10 mi E on Hwy 16	30	55	55	3.00	All year			•	lr	p			Heber Springs
B4	Cherokee	Fr Drasco, 5 mi SW on Hwy 92, S on gravel rd	20	33	33	None	All year			•	lr	p			Heber Springs
B4	Shiloh	Fr Shirley, 11 mi SE on Hwy 16, 3 mi S on Hwy 110	72	116	116	3.00	All year			•	lr	p			Heber Springs
B4	Cove Creek	Fr Hwy 25, NW on Hwy 16, NE on access rd	35	67	67	2.00	All year			•	lr	p			Heber Springs
B4	Old Highway 25	Fr Heber Spgs, 9 mi N on Hwy 25	47	100	100	3.00	All year			•	lr	p			Heber Springs
B4	Dam Site	Fr Heber Spgs, 3 mi NE on Hwy 25	110	321	321	4.00	All year	•		•	dlr •	p			Heber Springs
B4	Heber Springs	Fr Heber Springs, 3 mi W on Hwy 110	61	146	146	4.00	All year	•		•	dlr •	p			Heber Springs
B4	John F Kennedy	Fr Heber Springs, 3 mi NE on Hwy 25	10	52	52	4.00	All year			•	lr	p			Heber Springs
	Millwood Lake		807											501/898-3343	Rt 1 Box 37A, Ashdown 71822
E2	White Cliffs	Fr Ashdown, 10 mi N on Hwy 71, 5 mi E on Hwy 27, 6 mi S on Hwy 317	58	18	18	None	All year	•		•	l	p			Ashdown 71822
E2	River Run East	Fr Ashdown, 10 mi E on Hwy 32, 1/2 mi E on access	20	13	13	None	All year	o		•	l	p			Ashdown 71822
E2	Beard's Lake	Fr Ashdown, 9 1/2 mi N on Hwy 32, 1/2 mi S on access	20	5	5	1.00	All year	o		•	l	p			Ashdown 71822
E2	Cottonshed Landing	Fr Saratoga, 5 mi N on Hwy 355, 4 mi W on Co, 3 mi S on Co	30	50	50	2.00	All year	•		•	lr	p			Ashdown 71822
E2	Beard's Bluff	Fr Ashdown, 10 mi E on Hwy 32, N on access	50	33	33	1.00	All year	•		•	l •	p			Ashdown 71822

Map Reference	Park Name	Access	Acres	Tent Spaces	Trailer Spaces	Approximate Fee	Season	Swimming	Fishing	Boating	Playground	Other	Telephone Number	Mail Address
E2	Ashley's Camp	Fr Ashdown, 10 mi N on Hwy 71, 2 mi SE on Old Hwy 71	1	7	7	None	All year		•	l	p			Ashdown 71822
E2	Saratoga Landing	Fr Ashdown, 12 mi E on Hwy 32, 1/2 mi N on Co	200	35	35	None	All year		•	lr	p			Ashdown 71822
E2	Paraloma Landing	Fr Paraloma, 1/2 mi S on Co	100	68	68	2.00	All year		•	lr	p			Paraloma
E2	Millwood St Pk	Fr Ashdown, 8 mi E on Hwy 32		123	123	5.00	All year	•	•	dlr				Ashdown 71822
E2	River Run West	Fr Ashdown, 9 mi E on Hwy 32	4	4	4	1.00	All year		•		p			Ashdown 71822
D1	Cassatot Reefs PUA	Fr Gillham, 6 mi W on Co, 1/2 mi S on Gov Rd	110	30		3.00	All year		•	l				
D1	Oak Grove PUA	Fr DeQueen, 4 mi N on Hwy 71, 6 mi W on Co, 1/4 mi N on Co	432	20	18	3.00	All year		•	l •			501/386-2141	Rt 3, Box 184, Gillham 71841
D1	Pine Ridge PUA	Fr DeQueen, 4 mi N on Hwy 71, 6 mi W on Co, 1-1/2 mi N on Co	480	55		3.00	All year		•	l			501/386-2141	Rt 3, Box 184, Gillham 71841
D1	Bellah Mine PUA	Fr DeQueen, 8 mi N on Hwy 71, 5 mi W on Co	130	20			All year		•	l			501/386-2141	Rt 3, Box 184, Gillham 71841
	Lake Greeson	Lake Greeson												
D1	Coon Creek Pub Use Area	Fr Gillham, 6 mi W on Co, 2 mi N on Gov Rd	860	11	10	None	All year		•	l			501/386-2141	Rt 3, Box 184, Gillham 71841
D2	Kirby Landing	Fr Kirby, 3 mi W on US 70, 2 mi SW	230	81	81	4.00	All year		•	lr				Murfreesboro
D2	Laurel Creek	Fr Murfreesboro, 10 mi N on Hwy 27, 4 mi W on unpaved rds	230	18	18	None	All year		•	l				Murfreesboro
D2	Self Creek	Fr Murfreesboro, 7 mi W on US 70	103	105	105	3.00	All year		•	lr •				Murfreesboro
D2	Arrowhead Point	Fr Kirby, 9 mi W on US 70, 1/4 mi N	36	24	24	None	All year		•	•				Murfreesboro
D2	Bear Creek	Fr Kirby, 1/2 mi S on Hwy 27, 1 mi W	125	10	10	None	All year		•	•				Murfreesboro
D2	Star of the West	Fr Daisy, 6 mi W on US 70; 12 mi W of Kirby	36	12	12	None	All year		•	•				Murfreesboro
D2	Pikeville	Fr Murfreesboro, 6 mi N on Hwy 19 to Narrows Dam, 5 mi NW on unpaved rds	129	10	10	None	All year		•	•				Murfreesboro
D2	Narrows Dam Area	Fr Murfreesboro, 6 mi N on Hwy 19, NW on access	230	35	35	4.00	All year		•	lr				Murfreesboro
D2	Parker Creek	Fr Murfreesboro, 6 mi N on Hwy 19, 4 mi W & NE on unpaved rds	229	30	30	None	All year		•	•				Murfreesboro
D2	Cowhide Cove	Fr Murfreesboro, 9 mi N on Hwy 27, 2 mi W on unpaved rds	170	52	52	4.00	All year		•	•				Murfreesboro
	Lk Ouachita (Blakely Mt)	Lk Ouachita (Blakely Mt)												
D2	Crystal Springs	Fr Hot Springs, 19 mi W on US 270 to Crystal Spgs, 2 mi N, fol signs	120	62	62	4.00	All year		•	lr				Hot Springs
D2	Joplin (Mtn Harbor)	Fr Mt Ida, 15 mi E on US 270 to Joplin, 2 mi N, fol signs	128	60	60	4.00	All year		•	lr				Mount Ida
D2	Tompkins Bend	Fr Mt Ida, 13 mi E on US 270, 3 mi N, fol signs	149	77	77	4.00	All year		•	lr				Mount Ida
D2	Denby Pt-Gap Creek	Fr Mt Ida, 12 mi E on US 270, 1 mi N, fol signs	97	68	58	4.00	All year		•	lr				Mount Ida
D2	Twin Creek	Fr Mt Ida, 11 mi E on US 270, 1 mi N, fol signs	5	6	6	None	All year		•	l				Mount Ida
D2	Little Fir	Fr Mt Ida, 7 mi N on Hwy 27, 9 mi NE on Hwy 188; fol signs	68	15	15	None	All year		•	lr				Mount Ida
D2	Big Fir	Fr Mt Ida, 7 mi N on Hwy 27, 12 mi E on Hwy 188 & gravel rd; fol signs	144	10	10	None	All year		•	l				Mount Ida
D2	Hwy 27 Landing	Fr Mt Ida, 1 mi NW & 9 mi NE on Hwy 27, fol signs	17	6	6	None	All year		•	l				Mount Ida
D3	Ouachita St Pk	Fr Hot Springs, 13.9 mi NW on Hwy 227, 3.3 mi W on paved rd	88	72	72	5.00	All year		•	lr				Hot Springs
D3	Stephen's Pk	Fr Hot Springs, 10.8 mi NW on Hwy 227, 2 mi W on paved rd to dam	60	9	9	None	All year		•	lr				Hot Springs
D3	Brady Mountain	Fr Hot Springs, 12 mi W on US 270, 6.5 mi N, fol signs	119	64	64	4.00	All year		•	lr				Hot Springs
D3	Lena Landing	Fr Hwy 7, 12.5 mi W on Hwy 298, 1 mi S	74	6	6	None	All year		•	lr				Blue Springs
	DeGray Lake	DeGray Lake												
D3	DeGray St Pk	Fr Arkadelphia, 9 mi N on Hwy 7, 2 mi W on paved rd	870	82	82	5.00	All year		•	•				Arkadelphia
D3	Edgewood	Fr Arkadelphia, 10 mi N on Hwy 7, 5 mi W on gravel rd	55	38	S47	4.00	All year		•	•			501/246-5501	30 Circle, Arkadelphia 71923
D3	Ozan Point	Fr Arkadelphia, 21 mi W on Hwy 8, 12 mi E	50	50			All year		•			g	501/246-5501	30 Circle, Arkadelphia 71923
D3	De Roche Ridge	Fr Arkadelphia, 10 mi N on Hwy 7	88	10	31	4.50	All year		•	l				Arkadelphia
D3	Brushy Creek	Fr Arkadelphia, 21 mi W on Hwy 8, 7 mi E	325	53	S53	2.00	All year		•	l				30 Circle, Arkadelphia 71923
D3	Alpine Ridge	Fr Arkadelphia, 21 mi W on Hwy 8, 10 mi E	70	49	49	4.00	All year		•	l •			501/246-5501	30 Circle, Arkadelphia 71923
D3	Arlie Moore	Fr Arkadelphia, 13 mi N on Hwy 7, 3 mi W on paved rd	161	44	89	4.00	All year		•	l				Arkadelphia
D3	Cox Creek	Fr Arkadelphia, 15 mi N on Hwy 7, 15 mi W on Hwy 84, 2 mi N on Hwy 346, 2 mi E	140	53	S53	2.00	All year		•	l			501/246-5501	Rt 2, Bx 472, Arkadelphia 71923
D3	Point Cedar	Fr Arkadelphia, 15 mi N on Hwy 7, 8 mi W on Hwy 84, 3 mi S	140	62	S62	2.00	All year		•	l			501/246-5501	30 Circle, Arkadelphia 71923
D3	Iron Mt	Fr Arkadelphia, 7 mi N on Hwy 7, 3 mi W, 1 mi N	240	22	69	4.00	All year		•	l				Arkadelphia
D3	Lenox Marcus	Fr Arkadelphia, 17 mi N on Hwy 7, 3 mi W on Hwy 84, 4 mi S on gravel rd	230	N		None	All year		•	l			501/246-5501	30 Circle, Arkadelphia 71923
D3	Shouse Ford	Fr Arkadelphia, 15 mi N on Hwy 7, 8 mi W on Hwy 84, 3 mi S at Pt Cedar	125	35	100	4.00	All year		•	l				Arkadelphia
D3	Caddo Drive	Fr Arkadelphia, 10 mi N on Hwy 7, 5 mi W on gravel rd	60	72	45	4.00	All year		•	l •			501/246-5501	Arkadelphia
	Nimrod Lake													
C3	Carden Point	Fr Plainview, 6 mi SE on Hwy 60	10	9	9	None	All year		•	lr	p			Plainview
C3	County Line	Fr Plainview 6 mi SE on Hwy 60	17	20	20	3.00	All year	•	•	dlr	p			Plainview
C3	Quarry Cove	Fr Plainview, 8 mi SE on Hwy 60	30	31	31	3.00	All year		•	lr	p			Plainview
C3	River Road	Fr Plainview, 8.5 mi SE on Hwy 60, 1/2 mi on Hwy 7	15	15	15	3.00	All year	•	•	dlr	p			Plainview
C3	Sunlight Bay	Fr Plainview, 1.5 mi SE on Hwy 60, 2 mi SW on Sunlight rd	17	28	28	3.00	All year		•	lr	p			Plainview
C3	Project Point	Fr Plainview, 8.5 mi SE on Hwy 60	10	6	6	3.00	All year		•	lr	p			Plainview
C3	Carter Cove	Fr Plainview, 4 mi SE on Hwy 60	14	16	16	2.00	All year		•	lr	p			Plainview
	Ozark Lake													
B2	River Ridge	Fr Lavaca (at Hwy 96) 13 mi NE on Co	120	14	14	None	All year		•	l	p			Lavaca
B2	Citadel Bluff	Fr Cecil, 1 mi N on Co	175	36	36	2.00	All year		•	l	p			Cecil
B2	Dam Site South	Fr Ozark, 4 mi SE on Co	249	24	24	2.00	All year		•	l	p			Ozark
B2	White Oak	Fr Mulberry (at US 64), 5 mi E on Co	85	7	7	None	All year		•	l	p			Mulberry
B2	Vine Prarie	Fr Mulberry, 2 mi S on Co	185	47	47	3.00	All year		•	l	p			Mulberry
B2	Clear Creek	Fr Kibler, 4 mi E on Co	147	36	36	4.00	All year		•	l	p			Kibler
B2	Vache Grasse	Fr Lavaca (at Hwy 255), 4 mi W on Co	230	24	24	None	All year		•	l	p			Lavaca
	Norfork Lake	(See Missouri for additional campgrounds)												Mountain Home
A4	Red Bank	Fr Gamaliel, 3 mi SW on Hwy 101 & access rd	8	12	12	2.00	All year		•	lr	p			Mountain Home
A4	Cranfield	Fr Mountain Home, 7 mi NE on US 62 & access rd	78	74	74	3.00	All year	•	•	dlr •	p			Mountain Home
A4	Gamaliel	Fr Gamaliel, 3 mi SW on Hwy 101 & access rd	20	28	28	3.00	All year		•	dlr	p			Gamaliel
A4	Howard Cove	Fr Gamaliel, 5 mi S on Hwy 101	13	14	14	2.00	All year		•	dlr	p			Gamaliel
A4	Pigeon Creek	Fr Mountain Home, 5 mi N on Hwy 201	12	5	5	None	All year		•	•	p			Mountain Home
A4	Henderson	Fr Mountain Home, 10 mi NE on US 62	18	38	38	3.00	All year		•	dlr	p			Henderson
A4	Panther Bay	Fr Mountain Home, 9 mi NE on US 62	52	28	28	3.00	All year		•	dlr	p			Mountain Home
A4	Bidwell Point	Fr Gamaliel, 6 mi S on Hwy 101	34	48	48	3.00	All year		•	dlr	p			Gamaliel
A4	Robinson Point	Fr Mountain Home, 10 mi NE on US 62, S on access rd	48	102	102	3.00	All year		•	lr •	p			Mountain Home
A4	Jordan	Fr Mountain Home, 17 mi SE on Hwy 5, 10 mi N on gravel rd	27	33	33	3.00	All year		•	dlr	p			Jordan
A4	Dam-Quarry	Fr Mtn Home, 11 mi SE on Hwy 5, 2 mi N on Hwy 177	124	59	59	3.00	All year		•	dlr	p			Norfork
A4	Woods Point	Fr Mtn Home, 12-1/2 mi NE on US 62, S on Hand Rd	10	11	11	None	All year		•	dlr	p			Henderson
A4	Tracy	Fr Mountain Home, 8 mi SE on Hwy 5 & Tracy's Ferry Rd	10	7	7	None	All year		•	dlr	p			Mountain Home
A4	Georges Cove	Fr Mountain Home, 6 mi S on Hwy 5, 5 mi E on Hwy 342	20	12	12	None	All year		•	lr	p			Mountain Home
	Table Rock Lake	(See Missouri for additional campgrounds)												
A2	Beaver	Fr Eureka Springs, 7 mi NW on Hwy 23, 3 mi W	16	25	25	None	All year		•	lr	p			Beaver
A3	Cricket Creek	Fr Omaha, N on US 65 to Hwy 14, 5 mi W	57	48	48	3.00	All year		•	dlr	p			Omaha
	Dierks Lake													
D1	Jefferson Ridge	Fr Dierks, 2 mi W on Hwy 701, 3 mi N on Co, 3 mi W on Co	375	84	84	3.00	All year		•	l			501/286-2346	Dierks Lake
D1	Blue Ridge PUA	Fr Dierks, 3 mi N on Hwy 70, 4 mi NW on Hwy 4, 4 mi W on Co (Weyh)	125		S21	None	All year		•	l			501/286-2346	Dierks Lake
	NATIONAL WILDLIFE REFUGE White Riv Wildlife Ref													
E5	Jacks Bay Landing	Fr Dewitt, 10 mi S on Hwy 1, 9 mi E on Hwy 44, E on Co	10	N		None	3/1-10/31		•	l	p			Box 308, Dewitt 72042

Delaware

See state map, page 21

Major Events

Old Dover Days, early May, Dover. There is a self-guided driving and walking tour of over 30 historic homes and buildings. Also featured are a parade, arts and crafts, and a concert which opens the festival. Admission is charged for the house tour. 302/678-0892.

Winterthur Point-to-Point Races, early May, Winterthur, northwest of Wilmington. This event features an afternoon of steeplechase racing over a three-mile course. Spectators bring picnics, and they are also treated to a parade of antique carriages. Admission. 302/656-8591.

Mason Dixon 500, mid-May, Dover. NASCAR and Winston Cup Series drivers race at Dover Downs International Speedway. Admission. 302/674-4600.

A Day in Old New Castle, mid-May, New Castle. Tours of houses and museums are conducted along with militia drilling, food booths, and a maypole. Admission is charged for several events. 302/571-3059.

World Weakfish Championship Tournament, mid-May, Milford. Anglers may try their luck at catching Delaware's state fish in Delaware Bay. Other festivities include boat parades, dinners, and awards ceremonies. Admission. 302/422-3300.

Greek Festival, late May to early June, Wilmington. Each night a different Greek dinner is served along with wine and hors d'oeuvres. Greek crafts and dancing are also featured. Admission. 302/654-4446.

Scottish Games and Sheep Dog Trials, early June, Newark. There are a series of competitive events in highland dancing, bagpiping, fiddling, and sheep dog activities. Many different Scottish clans are represented, and Scottish food is served. Admission. 302/731-5100.

Italian Festival, early to mid-June, Wilmington. The Feast of St. Anthony is celebrated with food, music, crafts, and fireworks. Free (except food). 302/421-3747.

Delaware State Fair, late July, Harrington, west of Milford. The State Fairgrounds has displays, a carnival, stage shows, agricultural exhibits, and arts and crafts. Admission. 302/398-3269.

CRC Chemicals 500, mid-Sept., Dover. NASCAR drivers compete at Dover Downs International Speedway. Admission. 302/674-4600.

Nanticoke Indian Pow Wow, mid-Sept., Millsboro, southeast of Georgetown. Traditional dancing is performed, and foods and crafts are displayed. Donations accepted. 302/945-3111.

Winterthur Fall Festival, late Sept., Winterthur, northwest of Wilmington. This all-day event features museum tours, colonial craft demonstrations, children's rides, entertainment, hot-air balloon races, food, and antique cars. Admission. 302/656-8591.

Delaware Agricultural Museum Fall Harvest Festival, late Oct., Dover. A Delaware community of the late 19th century is re-created with a mill, a blacksmith, food booths, steam engines, music, and crafts. Admission. 302/734-1618.

Port Penn Marshland Festival, early Nov., Port Penn, northeast of Odessa. This townwide event features a craft show, food, music, the state duck-calling contest, and snapping turtle races. Admission is charged for several events. 302/834-7519.

Christmas in New Castle, mid-Dec., New Castle. Houses are decorated for the Christmas season, and tours of these homes are conducted. Admission. 302/571-3059.

Delaware Destinations

BETHANY BEACH, 300, D-8. This beach resort was settled by the Christian Church or Disciples of Christ in 1901 and used as a retreat for summer camp meetings. The town was named through a nationwide contest; the winner received an oceanfront lot. Swimming, surfing, boating, sunbathing, crabbing and clamming, and ocean (bay and inlet) fishing are available along Bethany's shore. The boardwalk is the site of the annual **Boardwalk Arts Festival,** which is held here each summer. Small shops and restaurants are near the beach. Just south of Bethany Beach is **Fenwick Island,** noted for the 82½-foot-high lighthouse, which was built in 1857. Fenwick was the focus of a long-standing feud between William Penn and Lord Baltimore because the area appeared as Cape Henlopen in some documents, thus making Penn's land grant farther south than Baltimore believed it should be. In 1751, the dispute was resolved, and the first marker indicating the official east-west boundary between Delaware and Maryland was erected at Fenwick. Bethany and Fenwick, along with other beaches south of the Indian River Inlet, are billed as the "Quiet Resorts" because they offer rest and relaxation. Bethany Beach-Fenwick Island Chamber of Commerce: 302/539-8129.

BOWERS, 198, northeast of Frederica, C-8. The **Island Field Archaeological Site and Museum,** at South Bowers Beach (from Alt. U.S. 113 by way of St. 19 or St. 20—there is no bridge from Bowers to South Bowers), reflects the history of the first Delaware inhabitants, the Indians, who used the land between the Murderkill and Mispillion rivers for their hunting grounds. Residents of nearby Milford Neck collected shells along the beach for trading purposes. Excavations of the Island Field burial site, which dates from A.D. 600 to 700, have uncovered some of the Indians' possessions and revealed their burial practices. Archaeological collections and a regional prehistory library are in the museum. Mar.-Nov., Tues.-Sat., 10 A.M. to 4:30 P.M.; Sun., 1:30 to 4:30 P.M. Free. 302/335-5395.

DOVER, 23,512, B-7. Believed to have been named by William Penn for Dover, England, the city was planned by Penn in 1683 and laid out in 1717. Dover became the chief business center for Kent County, and many fine homes and buildings were constructed. At the time of the American Revolution, Caesar Rodney, a member of the three-man Delaware delegation to the 1776 Continental Congress, was summoned from Dover to Philadelphia to cast his vote, breaking a tie and assuring the state's adoption of the Declaration of Independence. Dover became the state capital in 1777, and it served as a rallying place for the citizens as the new nation emerged after the Declaration of Independence was adopted. On December 7, 1787, Delaware ratified the U.S. Constitution, the first state to do so, thus earning its nickname "First State." Southern fugitives found protection here on their way to the North in the pre-Civil War period. Some of Delaware's most prominent families were reputed to have aided runaway slaves, making their homes stations on the Underground Railroad. Harriet Tubman, the "Moses of her people," traveled through Dover several times, leading escaped slaves to freedom in the North. **GOVERNMENT BUILDINGS:** The **Old State House,** east end of The Green, was built between 1787 and 1792 and was shared by Kent County and state government until 1873 when the county moved out. The second oldest seat of government in continuous use in the United States, Delaware's State House has been restored and is furnished with period pieces and reproductions. Although government business now is conducted in **Legislative Hall,** the Old State House remains Delaware's Capitol and contains the governor's ceremonial office. Year-round, Tues.-Sat., 10 A.M. to 4:30 P.M.; Sun., 1:30 to 4:30 P.M. Free. 302/736-4266. The **Supreme Court Building** is next door to the Old State House. A highlight of the building is the carved Coat of Arms. Year-round, Mon.-Fri., 8 A.M. to 4:30 P.M. Free. 302/736-4155. **Legislative Hall,** between Legislative Ave. and C St., was built in 1933, the first Georgian-revival capitol in the country. It serves the General Assembly of Delaware, and the governor's official office is here. Portraits of Delaware's governors and World War II heroes are on display. Year-round, Mon.-Fri., 8 A.M. to 4:30 P.M. Free. 302/736-4869. The **Hall of Records,** Duke of York St. and Legislative Ave., is the repository of Delaware's historical documents dating from 1650. Hall of Records: Year-round, Mon.-Fri., 8:30 A.M. to 4:30 P.M. Library: Mon.-Fri., 8:30 A.M. to noon, 1 to 4:30 P.M.; Sat., 8 A.M. to 12:30 P.M., 1 to 3:45 P.M. Free. 302/736-5314.

HISTORIC CHURCH: Christ Church, State and Water Sts., is the burial site of Caesar Rodney, one of the signers of the Declaration of Independence. The church was constructed between 1734 and 1747, but its congregation was formed in 1703. Year-round, Mon.-Fri., 9 A.M. to 5 P.M. Free. 302/734-5731.

HISTORIC HOMES: John Dickinson Mansion, 6 miles south on U.S. 113 to Kitts Hammock Rd., was built about 1740 by Samuel Dickinson and is an example of Delaware plantation architecture. It was the boyhood home of John Dickinson, who was called the "Penman of the Revolution" because of his eloquently written support of events leading up to the Revolution. Year-round, Tues.-Sat., 10 A.M. to 4:30 P.M.; Sun., 1:30 to 4:30 P.M. Free. 302/736-4266. **Woodburn,** Kings Hwy., south of Division St., is the official residence of the governor of Delaware. The Georgian mansion, built about 1790, was believed to have been a station on the Underground Railroad. Of particular note are Dutch doors, a 12-pane fanlight window, and paneling carved in the Chippendale manner. Mar.-June, Sept.-Dec., Sat., 2:30 to 4:30 P.M. Free. 302/736-5656.

HISTORIC AREA: The Green, State St., is a small park which served as the center of activity in the capital. In 1776, Delaware's Continental Regiment was assembled for duty on The Green, and the Declaration of Independence was read to the people here in the marketplace. Many of the oldest homes in Dover border The Green; today, the park is the site of the festivities of **Old Dover Days** in May.

MUSEUMS: Delaware State Museum, 316 S. Governors Ave., not only contains artifacts representing life in Delaware from the 17th century to the present, but the buildings themselves also are of historic interest. The main building, constructed in 1790, is the restored, historic Presbyterian church where John Dickinson and his committee drafted the Delaware Constitution in 1792. There are a restored log house, typical of those built by the Swedes about 1700, and exhibits on Delaware's Indians, natural resources, industry, agriculture, commerce, transportation, furniture, silver, clothing, and tools. Also in the museum complex is the *Johnson Memorial* which contains records, recording equipment, and phonographs of Eldridge R. Johnson, who founded the Victor Talking Machine Company, now RCA. Of particular interest are the large collection of Caruso recordings and the oil painting of *Nipper,* the dog listening to "His Master's Voice," RCA's trademark for many years. Year-round, Tues.-Sat., 10 A.M. to 4:30 P.M.; Sun., 1:30 to 4:30 P.M. Free. 302/736-4266. **Octagonal Schoolhouse,** east on St. 8 from U.S. 13 to St. 9 between Little Creek and Leipsic, has been restored to its 1836 appearance. Built shortly after the passage of the Free School Act, the school served as District No. 12 School in Kent County until 1930. It contains a collection of 1800-1920 textbooks. Year-round, Sat.-Sun., 1:30 to 4:30 P.M. Free. 302/736-4266. **Delaware Agricultural Museum,** 866 N. Du Pont Hwy., is a farm-life museum which depicts agricultural life—past, present, and future—on the Delmarva Peninsula. A tour of the seven-building complex begins with a slide show which sets the stage for a visit to a 1750 Swedish cabin, one-room schoolhouse, grist- and sawmills, blacksmith-wheelwright shop, and typical farmhouse and outbuildings. Collections of wagons, tractors, and other farm equipment also are displayed. Special events are held which focus on seasonal work, life-style, and recreation in the agricultural community. The museum features a gift shop with locally produced crafts, books, and foodstuffs. Apr.-Nov., Tues.-Sat., 10 A.M. to 4 P.M.; Sun., 1 to 4 P.M. Adults $3; persons between 10 and 16 and 65 and over, $2; under 10, free. 302/734-1618.

FREDERICA, 864, C-8. **Barratt's Chapel,** known as the "Cradle of Methodism in America," was the site of the meeting where plans were made to establish the Methodist-Episcopal Church in this country, thus separating it from the Church of England. The two-story chapel was built in 1780. An old cemetery is near the chapel. Year-round, Tues.-Sat., 9:30 A.M. to 4:30 P.M.; Sun., 1 to 5 P.M. Sun. services in summer, 7:30 P.M. Free. 302/335-5544.
See also **Bowers.**

LEWES, 2,197, C-8. Settled as a whaling colony in the spring of 1631 by some 30 immigrants from Hoorn, Holland, Lewes is

Delaware's State House, second oldest state house in active use in the United States, was built between 1787 and 1792. A late-Georgian-colonial structure, it has a Palladian window and an octagonal tower and cupola with a captain's walk.

known as the "Birthplace of the First State." Buildings which date from the 18th and 19th centuries are scattered around the city, off whose shore pirates once sailed. Lewes, near the confluence of Delaware Bay and the Atlantic Ocean, historically has been associated with the sea and shipping. Swimming, boating, fishing, and driftwood and shell collecting are among its major recreational activities.

MUSEUMS: Zwaanendael Museum, Kings Hwy. and Savannah Rd., is an ornate replica of the Town Hall in Hoorn, Holland. Built in 1931 to commemorate the 300th anniversary of the first Dutch settlement in Delaware, its peaked facade is topped with a statue of Capt. David Pietersen de Vries who sponsored the first colony which was called Zwaanendael, or "Valley of the Swans." The museum contains artifacts of 17th-century Dutch inhabitants and collections that reflect the early history of Lewes, the War of 1812, and the arts of the 18th and 19th centuries. Year-round, Tues.-Sat., 10 A.M. to 4:30 P.M.; Sun., 1:30 to 4:30 P.M. Free. 302/645-9418. **Joshua Fisher House,** (circa 1728), behind the Zwaanendael Museum at Kings Hwy. and Savannah Rd., was owned by the gentleman whose name it bears. A wealthy merchant, farmer, navigator, and chartmaker, Fisher is credited with charting the first accurate map of Delaware Bay. The building now serves as a Visitors Center. Memorial Day-Labor Day, Thurs.-Mon., 10 A.M. to 4 P.M. Free. 302/645-8073. **Cannonball House and Marine Museum,** Front and Bank Sts., was given its name after being struck by a cannonball in the War of 1812 when Lewes was bombarded by the British. The cypress-shingled building (circa 1797) has been restored and features nautical equipment, documents, and ship models. Memorial Day-Labor Day, Tues.-Sat., 10 A.M. to 4 P.M. Admission 50¢.

302/645-8740. **Historic Complex,** Shipcarpenter and 3rd Sts., is a compound of several buildings of historic interest which have been restored and moved to the compound from other locations. *Burton-Ingram House* has cellar walls of ship ballast and brick, and the main section of the house is constructed of handhewn timbers and cypress shingles. Built in the early 1800s, the house is typical of those owned by well-to-do Lewes families. *Rabbit's Ferry House* is a part of an early 18th-century one-room farmhouse, with a sleeping loft. Its cypress shingles and brick nogging walls are original; a mid-18th-century addition still has its original doors, window trim, mantle, and paneling. The *Thompson Country Store,* built about 1800 and operated by the Thompson family from 1888 to 1962, is stocked much as it was when it served as a general store. Its counters and cabinets are believed to be original furnishings. The *Early Plank House,* some experts believe, may be the oldest building in the area. It has a wooden floor and handcarved clothes pegs and appears to be of early Swedish construction. Historic complex buildings: Memorial Day-Labor Day, Tues.-Sat., 10 A.M. to 4 P.M. Admission $2. 302/645-8740. *Lightship Overfalls,* Rehoboth Canal off Pilottown Rd., now a museum, was one of the last lightships to operate on the East Coast. When the 114-foot ship was brought to her permanent berth in Lewes, she was rechristened *Overfalls* for the lightship which patrolled the entrance to Delaware Bay from 1892 to 1961. Memorial Day-Labor Day, Tues.-Sat., 10 A.M. to 4 P.M. Admission 75¢. 302/645-8740.

NEW CASTLE, 4,907, A-7. With its cobblestoned streets and well-preserved buildings, New Castle has retained its early flavor and charm. Flags of the Netherlands, Sweden, Great Britain, and the United States have flown over New Castle since it was founded by the Dutch in 1651. Taken on Trinity Sunday in 1654, the Swedes changed the city's name from Fort Casimir to Fort Trefalldigheet, meaning Fort Trinity. Recaptured by Pieter Stuyvesant in 1655, it became New Amstel, the Dutch capital. After the British took possession in 1664, the city was christened New Castle, and later it became a part of William Penn's land grant from the Duke of York. It served as the seat of government of "the three lower counties" of Pennsylvania from 1704 to 1776 and as the state capital from 1776 to 1777. Handsome old homes and buildings filled with fine colonial furniture are a lasting tribute to the vision of the owners and the craftsmanship of the builders.

HISTORIC BUILDINGS: New Castle Court House, Delaware St., built in 1732 on the site of a courthouse of the 1680s, was Delaware's colonial capitol. The spire of the cupola is the center of the 12-mile arc, (surveyed by Mason and Dixon) which forms the boundary between Delaware and Pennsylvania. Based on a drawing by Benjamin Henry Latrobe, the Court House has been restored to its 1804 appearance and is still used by community groups and local businesses. Year-round, Tues.-Sat., 10 A.M. to 4:30 P.M.; Sun., 1:30 to 4:30 P.M. Free. 302/571-3059. The **Old Town Hall,** 220 Delaware St., was built in 1823 with an unusual arch through the middle of the structure, allowing passage from Delaware St. to Market St. Once the firehouse and later a Federal court building, it now houses town offices. Year-round, Mon.-Fri., 9 A.M. to 5 P.M. 302/328-4804.

HISTORIC CHURCHES: Immanuel Episcopal Church, Market and Harmony Sts., founded in 1689, was the first Church of England parish in Delaware. Destroyed by fire in February 1980, the church is being rebuilt. George Read, one of the signers of the Declaration of Independence, is buried in the church's graveyard. 302/328-2413. **New Castle Presbyterian Church,** 25 Second St., was built in 1707 and has been restored to its appearance during the time of the British occupation when churches had boxed pews and high pulpits. The church's congregation was one of the charter members of the official Presbytery in this country. Year-round, daily, 9 A.M. to sunset. Free. 302/328-3279.

HISTORIC HOME: George Read II House, 42 The Strand, is a Georgian mansion completed in 1804 by the son of a signer of the Declaration of Independence. Outstanding features in the high-ceilinged entrance hall are the four graduated arches, the Palladian window, the intricate punch and gouge work on the mantels and trim, the hotwater system, and the wall of iron bells in the kitchen which summoned servants to individual rooms. Special bedroom door locks, operated by a pulley, allowed a person in bed to unlatch the door without rising. The formal garden was laid out in 1847. Mar.-Dec., Tues.-Sat., 10 A.M. to 4 P.M.; Sun., noon to 4 P.M. Adults $2, children and students $1. 302/322-8411.

HISTORIC AREAS: The Battery, now a park and playground along the waterfront off Delaware St., once was fortified to protect the city from naval attacks. **The Strand,** a fashionable thoroughfare in the early days of the city, is lined with trees and fine old houses. Many of the houses were inns which served travelers going to Boston, New York, Philadelphia, Baltimore, and Washington. In 1824 a fire destroyed much of the east side of The Strand. **Packet Alley,** where packet boats (those carrying mail and passengers) docked, leads from the riverfront to The Strand.

MUSEUMS: Old Dutch House Museum, (1700) 3rd St. between Delaware and Harmony Sts., is still in its original form. Furnished with Dutch-Colonial antiques, it is believed to be the oldest brick house in Delaware. Apr.-Oct., Tues.-Sat., 11 A.M. to 4 P.M.; Sun., noon to 4 P.M. Admission 50¢. 302/322-9168. **Amstel House Museum,** 4th and Delaware Sts., was built about 1730 with an older structure incorporated into it. In 1784, George Washington was a wedding guest here. Today, the house contains antique furnishings, an impressive collection of china, and a colonial kitchen. Apr.-Nov., Wed.-Sat., 11 A.M. to 4 P.M.; Sun., 1 to 4 P.M. Admission $1. 302/322-2794.

ODESSA, 384, B-7. A small town between Wilmington and Dover, Odessa is a trove of 18th- and 19th-century architecture. Settled by the Dutch and Swedes, the town first was called Appoquinimink for the nearby creek, and later, Cantwell's Bridge. Until the mid-19th century, it was a leading commercial center for this agricultural area, with granaries and docks dotting the waterway. The Henry Francis du Pont Winterthur Museum, in Wilmington, administers the Corbit-Sharp House, the Wilson-Warner House, and the Brick Hotel Gallery of American Art in the town. The **Corbit-Sharp House,** Main St., is of Georgian style, built between 1772 and 1774 by William Corbit, a wealthy tanner. Original furnishings include Chippendale chairs, a mahogany secretary, and Duncan Beard clocks. The **Wilson-Warner House,** adjacent to the Corbit-Sharp House, has one portion dating from 1740; the main part was constructed in 1769. It was built by David Wilson, Corbit's brother-in-law. Many of the furnishings are family pieces. The **Brick Hotel Gallery of American Art,** Main St., was built in 1822 by William Polk, onetime owner of the Wilson-Warner House, and became Cantwell's Bridge Hotel in 1823. In 1966, Winterthur acquired the house and restored it for use as an art gallery, principally for the Sewell C. Biggs Collection of paintings, furniture, and silver. Paintings by Bierstadt, Inness, Peale, and Cole, 18th- to early 20th-century American artists, are displayed here. Year-round, Tues.-Sat., 10 A.M. to 4:30 P.M.; Sun., 1 to 4:30 P.M. Adults $2 per building, $5 for all three; students and persons over 12 and 65 and over, $1.50 per building, $3.75 for all three; children under 12, free. 302/378-4069.

REHOBOTH BEACH, 1,730, C-8. Settled over a century ago by the Methodist Episcopal church, which sought a place where a "resort with religious influences" could be established, the town was named for the biblical word meaning "room enough." In 1873, a town was laid out and the first hotel and boardwalk were built. Swimming, surf fishing, clamming and crabbing, boating, surfing, golfing, tennis, roller skating, and cycling are available at the beach, where there are also restaurants, shops, special entertainment, and events, including the **Annual Rehoboth Beach Sand Castle Contest.**

SMYRNA, 4,750, B-7. **Bombay Hook National Wildlife Refuge,** southeast off St. 9, is a nesting and feeding spot for thousands of migratory birds. Within its more than 15,000 acres are bike and hiking trails, observatowers, auto routes, and a boardwalk. Year-round, daily, sunrise to sunset. Free. Office: Mon.-Fri., 8 A.M. to 4:30 P.M. 302/653-9345. *Allee House,* in the wildlife refuge, is an example of 18th-century rural Delaware architecture. Furnishings follow a 1775 family estate inventory. Year-round, Sat., Sun., 2 to 5 P.M. Free. 392/736-4266.

WILMINGTON, 70,195, A-8. One of the world's major chemical centers, Wilmington was founded in 1638 by the Swedes, who called it Fort Christina in honor of their Swedish queen. In 1731, the area became known as Willingtown, named for an English landholder; it was renamed Wilmington when William Shipley, a wealthy Quaker, was elected chief burgess of the borough. Wilmington soon became an important industrial, railroad, and port center. Wilmington is indelibly linked with E. I. du Pont de Nemours, who came from France and settled in the area. The production of gunpowder was the first of many successful business ventures by the du Pont family.

HISTORIC BUILDINGS: Old Town Hall, 512 Market St., once was the center of the city's political life. Built in the late 18th century, the Georgian Federal-style building now serves as the Historical Society of Delaware Museum and contains artifacts of the colonial and Revolutionary War eras. Delaware history is documented in the museum through pictures, maps, and newspapers. Among its many pieces are a wooden statue of Washington, locally crafted silver services, and an elaborately furnished miniature model house of the mid-1800s. Year-round, Tues.-Fri., noon to 4 P.M.; Sat., 10 A.M. to 4 P.M. Free. 302/655-7161. **Grand Opera House,** 818 Market St. Mall, is a Victorian structure with an ornate cast-iron facade. Built in 1871, the historic building has been restored to its former grandeur and now serves as Delaware's Center for the Performing Arts. Year-round, Mon.-Fri., 9 A.M. to 5 P.M.; open house and short tours every Thurs., 11:30 A.M. to 2:30 P.M. Free. 302/658-7897.

HISTORIC CHURCH: Holy Trinity (Old Swedes) **Church,** 606 Church St., is believed to be the oldest Protestant church (1698) in North America still standing as originally built and regularly used as a place of worship. In the building are a black walnut pulpit, the oldest in this country; a model of the settlers' ship *Kalmar Nyckel;* and an altar cloth embroidered by the king of Sweden. Year-round, Mon.-Sat., noon to 4 P.M. Free. 302/652-5629.

HISTORIC HOMES: Nemours, Rockland Rd. between St. 141 and U.S. 202, was once the 300-acre estate of Alfred I. du Pont. Filled with antiques, family furnishings, heirlooms, tapestries, and priceless collections from around the world, the 77-room modified Louis XVI French château and gardens still exude the aura of the du Ponts, who had many interests and hobbies. Built in 1909-10, the estate was opened to

Fort Delaware, a Civil War bastion and museum on Pea Patch Island, was built between 1850 and 1860 to protect Philadelphia and Wilmington harbors. Open summer weekends, the fort and island are accessible by boat from Delaware City.

the public in 1977 and remains as it was when the du Pont family lived here. On the grounds are a one- and-one-half-acre cutting garden; a greenhouse complex; ten lakes; sunken gardens; a 30-bell carillon; and massive fountains and sculptures, including the Colonnade and Temple of Love. One set of gates to the estate was constructed in 1488 for Wimbledon Manor in England; another set was made for Catherine the Great's palace outside St. Petersburg, Russia. On the grounds of the estate is the Alfred I. du Pont Institute, a children's hospital. The mansion tour takes an hour and a half and the gardens, two hours. Reservations recommended. May-Nov., Tues.-Sat., tours at 9 and 11 A.M., 1 and 3 P.M.; Sun., 11 A.M., 1 and 3 P.M. Admission $4, persons under 16 not admitted. 302/573-3333. **Henry Francis du Pont Winterthur Museum,** 6 miles northwest on St. 52, unfolds the evolution of American architecture and furnishings from 1640 to 1840. Furniture, silver, needlework, paintings, crystal and china, household implements, and crafts are arranged in the 196-room museum as they might have been in the homes of well-to-do families of the times. Many rooms, including walls, woodwork, ceilings, and windows, were moved nearly intact from the buildings in which they were found. Named for a city in Switzerland, the estate, built in 1839, was the home of Henry Francis du Pont, who combed the country for the exquisite, quality pieces which represent the 17th century, William and Mary, Queen Anne, Chippendale, Federal, and Empire periods. The mansion,

originally 28 rooms, had to be enlarged to accommodate his collection, which eventually numbered 50,000 pieces. In 1951, du Pont built another house nearby where he lived until his death in 1969. In the museum are rooms taken from homes in each of the 13 original colonies. A complete tour of the house takes two hours; an abbreviated, unreserved tour through the Washington Wing provides visitors with an American Sampler Tour of 18 exhibit areas and takes 45 minutes. Special interest tours (silver, needlework, textiles, period furniture, paintings, etc.) also are available. The 200-acre gardens on the 900-acre estate may be toured independently; a Visitors Center, cafeteria, and gift shop are on the premises. Bus transportation through the grounds is available throughout the day. Unreserved tours: Year-round, Tues.-Sat., 10 A.M. to 4 P.M.; Sun., noon to 4 P.M. Admission $2. Reserved tours: Year-round, Tues.-Sat., 10 and 10:30 A.M., 1 and 1:30 P.M.; Sun., 1 and 1:30 P.M. Adults $6; persons 12 to 16, $3; children under 12 not admitted. Gardens only: Admission $2. 302/654-1548. **Rockwood,** the Shipley-Bringhurst-Hargraves Museum, 610 Shipley Rd., was built between 1851 and 1857 by Joseph Shipley, great-grandson of William Shipley, the first chief burgess of Wilmington. Of rural-Gothic architecture, the estate comprises a mansion, several outbuildings, and gardens. The mansion, featuring furnishings from the William and Mary period through the Victorian era, documents the life-style of five generations of Delawareans. Year-round, Tues.-Sat., 11

A.M. to 4 P.M. Adults $2; persons 65 and over, $1; family $4 (spouse and children under 18); optional tour of grounds and gardens $1. 302/571-7776.

HISTORIC SITES: Fort Christina Monument, at the foot of E. 7th St. on the banks of the Christina River, marks the site where the Swedes landed in 1638. They named the settlement, the first permanent one in Delaware, for the queen of Sweden. The monument, by sculptor Carl Milles, represents the settlers' flagship and was given to Delaware by the people of Sweden in 1937 at the 300th anniversary of the founding of Fort Christina. The site is now a small park. Year-round, Tues.-Sat., 10:30 A.M. to 4:30 P.M.; Sun., 1:30 to 4:30 P.M. Free. 302/736-5314.

HISTORIC AREA: Willingtown Square, Market St. Mall between 5th and 6th Sts., is a quiet plaza surrounded by six 18th- and 19th-century houses, moved here from other locations. The exteriors of the houses have been restored as authentically as possible. *Zachariah Ferris House,* of Swedish design, is the oldest house in the Square, probably dating from 1718. Two of the houses, which are identical, were built by Thomas Coxe in 1801 for his daughters (descendants of the Coxe family lived in these houses until 1957). The adjoining *Dingee Houses,* built by brothers Obadiah and Jacob Dingee, reflect the Quaker influence in the 1770s. The **Dr. Simms House,** sixth house in the historic complex, probably was built in the late 1700s or the early 1800s by William Cook. Dr. Simms, who purchased the house in 1840, prepared his own medicines in the cellar and is thought to have used part of the dwelling as an apothecary shop. Willington Square: Always open. Free. 302/655-7161.

MUSEUMS: The **Delaware Museum of Natural History,** 5 miles northwest on St. 52, displays nature in a simulated setting. Year-round, Tues.-Sat., 10 A.M. to 5 P.M.; Sun., noon to 5 P.M. Adults $2; persons 65 and over, $1.50; students $1; under 6, free. 302/652-7600 or 302/658-9111. **Hagley Museum,** on the bank of the Brandywine River, 3 miles north on St. 52 and ½ mile east on St. 141, introduces visitors to life in a 19th-century industrial community. The museum is the site of the black powder works begun by E. I. du Pont in 1802. Self-guided tour maps and information on the museum complex can be obtained at the Visitors Center. In the museum are miniature working exhibits which graphically trace every step of industrial development along the Brandywine, from the early days of manufacturing to the present, including the tanning, textile, paper, iron and steel, gunpowder, and flour industries. The daily life of the workers is interpreted through three original buildings, the 1817 *Brandywine Manufacturers Sunday School* (a school begun for the workers' children), a powder foreman's house, and the millwright shop where all machinery is operated as it was in 1875. Jitneys with recorded tours transport visitors through the 200-acre grounds from Hagley Mills to *Eleutherian Mills* (1803), du Pont's Georgian-style home on a little hill overlooking the black powder works. Even though there was great danger from explosions at the mill, du Pont believed that the director of a factory should live near his workers. In 1923, Henry A. du Pont purchased the ancestral home for his daughter, Mrs. Louise du Pont Crowninshield. Few of the original owners' furnishings remained, but Mrs. Crowninshield furnished it with pieces which reflect the tastes of the five generations of du Ponts who lived in the house. Near the house stands a small building which served as an office for the business. This unpretentious building was the birthplace of the du Pont Company. Hagley Mills and Eleutherian Mills: Year-round, Tues.-Sat., 9:30 A.M. to 4:30 P.M.; Sun., 1 to 5 P.M. Adults $2.50; persons 65 and over, $1.25; students $1; children under 14, free. 302/658-2400.

Delaware Art Museum, 2301 Kentmere Pkwy., is a memorial to Howard Pyle, an American illustrator who founded the Brandywine School of Art. The museum, which was begun about 1912 with the collection of Pyle works, also contains works by Winslow Homer, Thomas Eakins, John Sloan, N. C. Wyeth, Andrew Wyeth, Frank Schoonover, Edward Hopper, and others. Museum: Year-round, Mon.-Sat., 10 A.M. to 5 P.M.; Sun., 1 to 5 P.M. Research library: Year-round, Mon.-Fri., 10 A.M. to 4:30 P.M. Donations. 302/571-9590.

Information Sources

Delaware Travel
630 State College Rd.
Dover, DE 19901
302/736-4254

Delaware State
Chamber of Commerce
1102 West St.
Wilmington, DE 19801
302/655-7221

Greater Wilmington
Convention &
Visitors Bureau
P.O. Box 111
Willingtown Square
Wilmington, DE 19899
302/571-4088

Bethany-Fenwick
Chamber of Commerce
P.O. Box 502
Bethany Beach, DE 19930
302/539-8129

Central Delaware Chamber
of Commerce
Treadway Towers
Loockerman St.
Dover, DE 19901
302/678-0892

Visitors Center
Margaret O'Neill Building
Court and Federal St.
Dover, DE 19901
302/736-4266

Lewes Chamber
of Commerce
Box 1
Lewes, DE 19958
302/645-8073

Greater Milford
Chamber of Commerce
Front St.
Milford, DE 19963
302/422-3300

Rehoboth Beach
Chamber of Commerce
Convention Hall
Rehoboth Beach,
DE 19971
302/227-2233

Delaware Campgrounds

FEES REFLECT MINIMUM RATE FOR 2 ADULTS AND ARE SUBJECT TO INCREASE OR SEASONAL CHANGES

- • – at the campground
- ○ – within one mile of campground
- $ – extra charge
- •• – limited facilities during winter months
- A – adults only
- B – 10,000 acres or more
- C – contribution
- E – tents rented
- F – entrance fee or permit required
- N – no specific number, limited by size of area only
- P – primitive
- R – reservation required
- S – self-contained units only
- U – unlimited
- V – trailers rented
- Z – reservations accepted
- LD – Labor Day
- MD – Memorial Day
- UC – under construction
- d – boat dock
- g – public golf course within 5 miles
- h – horseback riding
- j – whitewater running craft only
- k – snow skiing within 25 miles
- l – boat launch
- m – area north of map
- n – no drinking water
- p – motor bikes prohibited
- r – boat rental
- s – stream, lake or creek water only
- t – tennis
- u – snowmobile trails
- w – open certain off-season weekends
- y – drinking water must be boiled

Map Reference	Park Name	Access	Acres	Tent Spaces	Trailer Spaces	Approximate Fee	Season	Other Swimming Swimming Pool	Fishing Boating	Other Playground	Telephone Number	Mail Address
	STATE PARKS											
D8	Trap Pond	Fr Laurel, 5 mi SE on Hwy 24	968	72	72	7.00	4/1-10/31	• •	lr		302/875-5153	Laurel
C8	Cape Henlopen	Adj to Lewes Terminal of Cape May-Lewes Ferry	2761	80	80	7.00	4/1-10/31	• •	lr		302/645-8983	Lewes
D8	Delaware Seashore	Fr Rehoboth Beach, 6 mi S on Hwy 14	2020	154	141	10.00	All year	• •	lr		302/227-2800	Rehoboth
B7	Lums Pond	Fr Kirkwood, 1-1/2 mi S on US 71	908	32	S32	5.00	4/1-10/31	• •	l	hp	302/368-1050	Kirkwood
C8	Killens Pond SP	Fr Felton, 1 mi SE	582		60	7.00	4/1-10/31	•	lr		302/284-4526	RD 1, Box 198, Felton 19901
	STATE FORESTS											
B7	Blackbird	Fr Smyrna, 5 mi N on US 13, 2 mi W on Co 471	1800	P8		None	All year			hp		Smyrna
C8	Redden	Fr Georgetown, 3 mi N on US 113, 1/2 mi E on Co 565	4600	P20		None	All year			hp		Georgetown

Florida

Major Events

See state map, page 23

Greek Epiphany Day, Jan. 6, Tarpon Springs. The old-world observance honoring the baptism of Christ is celebrated with a procession and an informal fiesta with Greek food, music, and dancing. Free. 813/937-3540.

Speed Weeks, late Jan. to early Feb., Daytona Beach. Two weeks of racing at Daytona International Speedway include several small races and the Daytona 500. Admission. 904/255-5301.

Old Island Days, early Feb. to mid-Mar., Key West. The city's past is recalled with Old Key West house tours, a sidewalk art show, a conch shell-blowing contest, and a blessing of the fishing fleet. Admission is charged for the house tours. 305/294-9501.

Gasparilla Pirate Invasion, early Feb., Tampa. An authentic pirate ship sails into Tampa Bay with 500 costumed pirates who capture the keys to the city and take over for a day of fun and festivity. Special activities also take place in Ybor City. Free. 813/228-7338.

Medieval Fair, mid-Mar., Sarasota. The Ringling Museums complex is the site for this re-created medieval city square. Activities include a living chess match, with costumed participants acting as the chess pieces; a sheep-shearing contest; musical concerts; medieval morality plays; and various sporting events from the Middle Ages. Admission. 813/355-5101.

Festival of States, late Mar. to early Apr., St. Petersburg. High school bands from Florida and throughout the nation gather to compete in musical and marching contests. Concerts, sports events, and the coronation of Mr. Sun and Miss Sungoddess are among other attractions. Admission is charged for several events. 813/898-3654.

Springtime Tallahassee, early Apr., Tallahassee. Florida's capital city pays tribute to its founding with a parade, a jubilee, cultural events at local universities, plantation tours, and sports events. Free. 904/224-5012.

Indian River Festival, late Apr., Titusville. This event features an arts and crafts show; a carnival; food booths; and several water sports activities, including the Great Indian River Raft Race. Free (except food). 305/267-3036.

Fiesta of Five Flags, mid- to late May, Pensacola. The city commemorates its history under five different nations with a week of activities, including a reenactment of the 1559 landing of Spanish colonists, a treasure hunt, a parade, art exhibits, concerts, and sports events. Free. 904/433-3065.

Florida Folk Festival, late May, White Springs, northwest of Lake City. Folk music is performed and crafts are exhibited on the banks of the Suwannee River at the Stephen Foster Center. Florida foods are served, and dancing and folk tales are performed by local artists. Admission. 904/397-2192.

Billy Bowlegs Festival, late May to early June, Fort Walton Beach. Pirates take over the city for a week of festivities, including a pirate invasion, a boat parade, treasure hunts, and a yacht race. Free. 904/244-8191.

New College Music Festival, late May to mid-June, Sarasota. Internationally known musicians, gathered for intensive workshops, perform six major public concerts. Admission. 813/355-2116.

***Cross and Sword* Outdoor Drama,** mid-June to late Aug., St. Augustine. Florida's official state play, an outdoor drama written by Paul Green, is based on the founding of St. Augustine. It depicts the struggle between Spanish explorers and the Indians and French. Performances are nightly, except Sundays, in the amphitheater located on Anastasia Island. Admission. 904/471-1965.

Jefferson County Watermelon Festival, mid- to late June, Monticello. Watermelon-eating and seed-spitting contests are just part of the festivities at this event honoring the watermelon harvest. Of particular interest is the canoe race, where canoes loaded with watermelons are raced across a lake. Admission is charged for beauty pageant. 904/997-5552.

Silver Spurs Rodeo, early July, Kissimmee. Cowboys compete for thousands of dollars and national points in bull riding, bronc riding, calf roping, and steer wrestling. Admission. 305/847-5000.

Florida State Championship Belly-flop Contest, July 4, Trenton. This celebration features hayrides, tug-of-war contests, country-and-western music, and a large fireworks display. The highlight of the event is the belly-flopping competition, which goes on all day. Admission. 904/463-2696.

Annual Celebration of the Launch of Apollo 11, July 16, Cape Canaveral. Man's historic first walk on the moon is commemorated with a day of activities, including prominent guest speakers, at the Kennedy Space Center. Free. 305/452-2121.

Wausau Fun Day and Possum Festival, early Aug., Wausau. This old-fashioned celebration includes contests in corn pone baking, greased pole climbing, and hog calling. Live entertainment consists of gospel, country, and bluegrass music; but the highlight of the day's activities is a possum auction. Free. 904/638-1017.

International Worm-Fiddling Contest, early Sept., Caryville. The brief contest features worm fiddlers who drive wooden stakes into the ground and drag metal bars across the stakes. This creates a vibration that brings the worms to the surface where they are bagged and used for bait. A fishing contest follows, as well as a fish fry, a horseshoe-pitching contest, and other activities. Free. 904/548-5116.

Seafood Festival, mid-Sept., Pensacola. Land and water activities offer entertainment both in town and on Pensacola Beach, including a blessing of the fleet, boat parade, water-ski show, seafood-cooking contests, and food booths that feature many different types of seafood dishes. Free (except food). 904/433-3065.

World's Chicken-Pluckin' Championship, early Oct., Spring Hill. Teams compete in chicken-plucking contests at one of the nation's leading poultry centers north of New Port Richey. Other activities include dance performances and the Miss Drumstick contest. Free. 904/796-2420.

Seafood Festival, mid-Oct., Cedar Key. This celebration offers mullet dinners and other types of seafood dishes. Other activities include a fishing contest and a parade. Free (except food). 904/543-5510.

Swamp Buggy Races, late Oct., Naples. Vehicles designed to traverse the Everglades race on a six-foot-deep track of mud. Other activities include a parade of swamp buggies and the traditional dunking of the Mud Dutchess. Admission. 813/774-2701.

Birthplace of Speed Antique Car Meet, late Nov., Ormond Beach. This turn-of-the-century celebration features a gaslight parade of horseless carriages, a costume contest, and a re-enactment of early races on the sand beach. Free. 904/677-3386.

Christmas Night Watch, early Dec., St. Augustine. The city's colonial history is commemorated with period clothing and British military procedures, which used to require that the city be secured at sunset and the citizens be made to carry lighted lanterns in the streets after dark. Free. 904/829-9792.

Orange Bowl Festival, mid-Dec. to mid-Jan., Miami. The highlight of this festival is the parade on New Year's Eve and the football game on New Year's night. Other activities include sports events, fireworks, and a large dance. Admission is charged for several events. 305/642-5211. The Junior Orange Bowl Festival in Coral Gables is held in late December, and it features several different types of sports tournaments and a parade. 305/445-7920.

Florida Destinations

BIG PINE KEY, 600, H-4. **National Key Deer Refuge**, U.S. 1, protects about 400 key deer and endangered species. Visitors Center: Year-round, Mon.-Fri., 8 A.M. to 5 P.M. Free. 305/872-2239.

BISCAYNE NATIONAL PARK, G-5. The new **Biscayne National Park** adds 7,000 acres to the former national monument's 104,000 acres of prime coastal waters, keys, and coral reefs, which support a diversity of tropical plant and animal life. Campgrounds on Elliott Key are accessible by private boat only. 305/247-2044.

BRADENTON, 30,170, E-3. **De Soto National Memorial**, 5 miles west of Bradenton on St. 64, commemorates Hernando de Soto's landing in Florida in May, 1539. Year-round, daily, 8 A.M. to 5 P.M. Free. 813/792-0458. **Gamble Plantation State Historic Site**, east of Bradenton on U.S. 301 in Ellenton, features the mid-19th-century tabby mansion built by Maj. Robert Gamble as headquarters for his sugar plantation. Year-round, daily. Site: 8 A.M. to dusk. Mansion: By tour only, hourly from 9 A.M. to 4 P.M. Admission 50¢; children under 6, free. 813/722-1017. **South Florida Museum and Bishop Planetarium**, 201 10th St. W, exhibits artifacts of Florida history. Planetarium shows: Tues.-Sun., 3 P.M.; Fri.-Sat., also 7:30 P.M. Year-round, Tues.-Fri., 10 A.M. to 5 P.M.; Sat.-Sun., 1 to 5 P.M. Museum or planetarium: Adults $1.50; persons 6-18, $1; children under 6, free. Combined admission: Adults $2.50; persons 6-18, $1.50; under 6, free. 813/746-4131.

BROOKSVILLE, 5,582, D-3. **Florida's Weeki Wachee Spring**, U.S. 19 and St. 50, is best known for its mermaid show, which is viewed through a glass-walled, underwater theater. The park also displays birds of prey and exotic birds and features a river cruise. Year-round, daily, 9 A.M. to sunset. Adults $5.50; children 3-11, $3.95; under 3, free. 905/596-2062.

CANAVERAL NATIONAL SEASHORE, C-5. Located within **Merritt Island National Wildlife Refuge**, Canaveral National Seashore extends over 25 miles of shoreline between Mosquito Lagoon and the Atlantic Ocean. Facilities along the unspoiled beaches invite swimming, boating, water-skiing, surfing, and fishing. Access is via Playalinda Beach, at the southern end, and New Smyrna Beach, at the northern end. Year-round, daily, sunrise to sunset. (Closed for special launch operations at the Kennedy Space Center.) 305/867-4675.

CAPE CANAVERAL, 5,733, D-5. **Kennedy Space Center** is the major launch base of the National Aeronautics and Space Administration (NASA). The Visitors Center, 6 miles east of U.S. 1 on St. 405, has exhibits covering the exploration of space.

A chronology in the "Hall of History" places all the separate pieces of the space drama in technological perspective. Year-round, daily, 8 A.M. to sunset. Free. 305/452-2121. Kennedy Space Center tours leave from the East Wing. Daily, 8 A.M. to two hours before sunset. Adults $3; persons 13-18, $1.75; children 3-12, $1. 305/452-2121. For information regarding space launches which may be viewed, call 1-800-432-2153 (Florida only).

CORAL GABLES, 43,241, G-5. **Fairchild Tropical Garden**, 10901 Old Cutler Rd., covers 83 acres and includes a rare plant house, library, and palm products museum. Year-round, daily, 10 A.M. to 4:30 P.M. Adults $3; children under 13, free. 305/667-1651. **Lowe Art Museum**, 1301 Stanford Dr., on the University of Miami campus, houses changing exhibits and a Kress collection. Year-round, Tues.-Fri., noon to 5 P.M.; Sat., 10 A.M. to 5 P.M.; Sun., 2 to 5 P.M. Free. 305/284-3535. **Venetian Pool**, 2701 DeSoto Blvd., offers swimming in a lagoon setting carved from coral rock. Sept.-May, daily, 10 A.M. to 4:45 P.M.; June-Aug., Mon.-Fri., 10:30 A.M. to 7:45 P.M.; Sat.-Sun., 10 A.M. to 4:45 P.M. 305/442-6483.

DAYTONA BEACH, 54,176, C-4. Focal point of the 70-mile-long stretch of beach that extends from St. Augustine to New Smyrna, Daytona invites thousands of visitors each year. **Daytona International Speedway**, 1801 Volusia Ave., is open for tours when no events are scheduled. Visitors can tour the track and pit area. Tours: Year-round, daily, 9 A.M. to 5 P.M. Admission 50¢. 904/253-6711. **Museum of Arts and Sciences**, 1040 Museum Blvd., has a permanent exhibit of Cuban art bequeathed by General Batista. Planetarium shows: Year-round, Sat., 2:30 P.M.; Wed., 7:30 P.M. Museum: Year-round, Tues.-Fri., 9 A.M. to 5 P.M.; Sat., noon to 5 P.M.; Sun., 1 to 5 P.M. Adults $1, children 50¢ (includes planetarium show). 904/255-0285.

See also **Ponce Inlet.**

DE LAND, 15,354, C-4. **De Land Mu-**

seum, 449 E. New York Ave., has permanent exhibits of Indian artifacts, antique dolls, and a habitat of Florida wildlife. Jan.-July, Sept.-Dec., Mon.-Fri., 9 A.M. to 5 P.M.; Sun., 2 to 4 P.M. Free. 904/734-4371. **Hontoon Island State Park**, off Hontoon Rd., is accessible by free park service ferry from a parking lot in De Land. The 1,550-acre park has an 80-foot-high observation tower, a nature trail, picnic areas, tent sites, and rustic cabins. Year-round, daily 9 A.M. to sunset. Park: Free. 904/734-7158.

DELRAY BEACH, 34,325, F-5. The **Morikami Museum of Japanese Culture**, 4000 Morikami Park Rd., is housed in a Japanese-style modern building set in a Japanese-style garden. Year-round, Tues.-Sun., 10 A.M. to 5 P.M. Free. 305/499-0631.

DESTIN, 3,600, H-2. **Edens State Gardens**, 30 miles east off U.S. 98, are 10½-acre gardens surrounding a restored 1895 mansion furnished with authentic Louis XVI furniture. Park: Year-round, daily, sunrise to sunset. Free. Mansion: Early-May-mid-Sept., 15, daily, 9 A.M. to 5 P.M.; mid-Sept.-late Apr. Fri.-Tues., 9 A.M. to 5 P.M. Admission 50¢. 904/231-4214.

EVERGLADES NATIONAL PARK, G-4. A six-inch-deep, 50-mile-wide river that inclines imperceptibly toward Florida Bay, the Everglades encompass eight distinct types of ecosystems, ranging in landscape from freshwater sloughs and marsh prairie to mangrove trees and saltwater estuaries. Write to P.O. Box 279, Homestead, FL 33030 for monthly schedules of guided activities such as lectures, swamp tramps, and canoe trips. Visitors Center, Park Headquarters, 15 miles southwest of Homestead on St. 27, has maps, brochures, and other information. Park: Always open. Admission $2 per car. 305/247-6211. Royal Palm Visitors Center, 2 miles south of the park entrance, is the starting point of Anhinga and Gumbo Limbo trails. Flamingo, 38 miles southwest of the park entrance, has concessions, overnight accommodations, canoe and houseboat rentals, and sightseeing trips. 305/253-2241 or 813/695-3101. Shark Valley, off U.S. 41, offers a 17-mile guided tram trip. Schedules vary; reservations are recommended. Adults $2; persons under 15 and over 62, $1. 305/221-8445. Everglades City, western gateway to the park, has a boat tour and canoe rental concession. 813/695-2591.

FERNANDINA BEACH, 7,224, A-4. This is the major community of Amelia Island and the self-billed birthplace of Florida's modern shrimping industry. **Centre Street Historic District,** a 30-block downtown area, calls itself the birthplace of America's shrimp fleet and features many 19th-century Victorian buildings. Visitors can obtain a walking- or driving-tour map of the district at the Fernandina Beach Chamber of Commerce, 102 Centre St. **Fort Clinch State Park,** St. A1A, covers more than a thousand acres of the northern tip of Amelia Island. Focal point is *Fort Clinch,* a brick fortification begun in 1847 and never completed. White sand beaches and thick hammock growth around the fort invite visitors to use camping, picnic, and fishing facilities. Always open. Fort: Year-round, daily, 9 A.M. to 5 P.M. Admission 50¢ for fort during summer months. 904-/261-4212.

FORT LAUDERDALE, 153,256, F-5. Discovery Center Museum, 231 S.W. 2nd Ave., is a "hands-on" museum of art, science, and history, with a sponge room, computer rooms, laser shows, an insect zoo, and changing exhibits. The planetarium has hourly shows. The adjacent *King Cromartie* house, built around 1900, displays period antiques in a two-story, ten-room cracker-type wood structure. Jan.-Aug., Oct.-Dec., Sat., 10 A.M. to 5 P.M.; Sun., 1 to 5 P.M. Admission $1, King Cromartie house tours 50¢. 305/462-8803. **Gold Coast Railroad Museum,** S.W. 9th Ave., has two locomotives dating from 1913 and 1922 and the armour-plated presidential car used by Presidents Franklin Roosevelt, Truman, and Eisenhower. Year-round, Sun., 1 to 5 P.M. Adults $3; children 3-12, $1.50; under 3, free. 305/524-5339. **Flamingo Gardens/Floyd L. Wray Memorial,** Flamingo Rd., have 30 acres of gardens, citrus groves, a petting zoo, a transportation museum, and an Everglades museum. Jan.-Aug., Oct.-Dec., daily, 9 A.M. to 5:30 P.M. Adults $3, children $1.50. 305/473-0064.

FORT MATANZAS NATIONAL MONUMENT, B-4. Fourteen miles south of St. Augustine on St. A1A, Fort Matanzas, initiated in 1740, is a coquina structure located in a 298-acre park that covers the tip of Anastasia Island and all of Rattlesnake Island. The Visitors Center is on Anastasia Island. The National Park Service provides ferry service every 15 minutes to the fort on Rattlesnake Island. Daily, early May to late Oct., 8:30 A.M. to 5:30 P.M.; other months, 9 A.M. to 6 P.M. Ferry service: June-Labor Day, daily, 9 A.M. to 4:45 P.M.; other months,

Library of Congress

Inventor Thomas Edison (1847-1931), who lived and did much of his research in New Jersey, spent some 35 winters at his Fort Myers estate at 2350 McGregor Blvd. He drew the plans for the estate's main and guest houses in 1885, and had the wood precut to size in Fairfield, Maine, and shipped by schooner to Florida in 1886. He also had a swimming pool built of cement processed in a kiln he invented. During the winters at Fort Myers, Edison worked in his laboratory, where he developed rubber from the goldenrod plant. Today, the estate with its two homes, a honeymoon cottage, chemical laboratory, an office, and a museum displaying one of the largest collections of his inventions (he held 1,097 U.S. patents), is open to the public year-round.

Thurs.-Mon., 9 A.M. to 4:45 P.M. Free. 904/471-0116 or 904/829-6506.

FORT MYERS, 36,638, F-3. **Corkscrew Swamp Sanctuary,** 20 miles southeast on Co. 846, features the largest stand of virgin bald cypress trees and the largest nesting rookery of wood storks in the United States. Always open. Visitors Center: 9 A.M. to 5 P.M. Boardwalk: 9 A.M. to sunset. Adults $3; students $1; under 12, free. 813/657-3771. **Thomas A. Edison Winter Home and Museum,** MacGregor Blvd., offers guided tours every 30 minutes through Edison's home and botanical gardens and a museum of his inventions. Year-round, Mon.-Sat., 9 A.M. to 4 P.M.; Sun., 12:30 to 4 P.M. Adults $3; persons 6-17, $1; under 6, free. 813/334-3614. **Koreshan State Historic Site,** 10 miles south on U.S. 41, preserves the remains of a settlement founded by religious visionary Cyrus Reed Teed in 1894. Year-round, daily, 8 A.M. to sunset. Admission 50¢, guided tours 50¢.

FORT PIERCE, 33,802, E-5. **St. Lucie State Museum,** St. A1A in Pepper Park, has artifacts from Fort Pierce and the Ais Indians. Year-round, Wed.-Sun., 9 A.M. to 5 P.M. Admission 50¢; children under 12, free. 305/461-1570.

FORT WALTON BEACH, 20,829, H-2. **Indian Temple Mound Museum,** Miracle Strip, traces 10,000 years of local Indian history with artifacts, burial mound relics, and displays of tools and pottery. Museum: Year-round, Tues.-Sat., 11 A.M. to 4 P.M.; Sun., 1 to 4 P.M. Admission 50¢; children under 10, free. 904/243-6521. **Gulfarium,** U.S. 98E, has marine-life shows. Daily, June-Aug., 9 A.M. to 6 P.M.; other months, 9 A.M. to 4 P.M. Adults $5; children 4-11, $2.50; under 4, free. 904/244-5169. **Historical Society Museum,** 12 miles north in Valparaiso, 115 Westview Ave., displays

household implements, tools, and crafts from western Florida's pioneer era. Year-round, Tues.-Sat., 11 A.M. to 4 P.M. Free. 904/678-2615.

GAINESVILLE, 81,371, B-3. **William Reuben Thomas Center for the Arts,** 306 N.E. 6th Ave., known for its Renaissance-style architecture, now houses the Department of Cultural Affairs. Year-round, Mon.-Fri., 8:30 A.M. to 5 P.M. Free. Special programs on weekends. 904/374-2197. **University Art Gallery,** S.W. 13th St. and 4th Ave., University of Florida, features ten exhibits a year, ranging in subject from pre-Columbian American to modern Chinese art. Year-round, Mon.-Fri., 9 A.M. to 5 P.M.; Sun., 1 to 5 P.M. Closed school holidays and between exhibits. Free. 904/392-0201. **Florida State Museum,** off St. 441 on Museum Rd., provides visitors with the experience of being in a reconstructed cave, in a forest with a Timucuan Indian village of 500 years ago, in the area of a fossil dig, and in a 900-year-old Mayan temple. Year-round, Mon.-Sat., 9 A.M. to 5 P.M.; Sun., 1 to 5 P.M. Free. 904/392-1721. **Morningside Nature Center,** 3540 E. University Ave., is a 280-acre wildlife sanctuary and a restored 1880s farm. Farm programs in household arts and crafts are held Sun., 1:30 to 3 P.M. Natural history programs: Sat., 9:30 to 11 A.M. Nature Center: Year-round, Tues.-Sat., 8 A.M. to 6 P.M.; Sun., noon to 6 P.M. Free. 904/374-2170. **Devil's Millhopper State Geological Site,** 4732 N.W. 53rd Ave., has a 117-foot-deep sinkhole with a stairway to the bottom. Year-round, daily, 9 A.M. to sunset. Free. 904/377-5935. **Paynes Prairie State Preserve,** 1 mile north of Micanopy, off U.S. 441, is the major wintering ground for the eastern population of the sandhill crane. Indian artifacts found on the site date to at least 7,000 B.C. Boating, fishing, and swimming are permitted at Lake

Wauberg, in the preserve. Year-round, daily, 8 A.M. to sunset. Admission 50¢. 904/466-3397. **Marjorie Kinnan Rawlings State Historical Site,** 21 miles south of Gainesville in Cross Creek, was the home of the Pulitzer prize-winning author of *The Yearling* and *Cross Creek* from 1928 until her death in 1953. Year-round, daily, 9 A.M. to 5 P.M. Admission 50¢; children under 6, free. 904/466-3672.

HAINES CITY, 10,578, D-4. **Ringling Brothers and Barnum & Bailey Circus World,** Int. 4 and U.S. 27, offers a day at the circus in many dimensions: an actual circus, an "illusion circus" magic show, sideshows, a lion and tiger display, an elephant research area, rides, and an opportunity for the visitor to perform. Year-round, daily, 9 A.M. to 6:30 P.M. Adults $9.50; children 3-11, $7.95; under 3, free. 305/422-0643.

HOMESTEAD, 20,668, G-5. The **Orchid Jungle,** 26715 S.W. 157 Ave., breeds orchids and has about 90,000 types. Self-guided tours take visitors through a 25-acre hammock planted with exotic foliage and into the orchid research laboratory. Year-round, daily, 8:30 A.M. to 5:30 P.M. Adults $2.50; persons 10-14, $1; under 10, free. 305/247-4824.

See also **Everglades National Park.**

HOMOSASSA SPRINGS, 900, C-3. **Homosassa Springs,** U.S. 19, allows visitors to descend into an underwater observatory for a look at the freshwater and saltwater fish. A boat ride to a nature park, alligator and hippopotamus feedings, petting animals, and displays of waterfowl and manatees are also featured. Year-round, daily, 9:30 A.M. to 5:30 P.M. Adults $4.75; children 5-15, $2.50; under 5, free. 904/628-2311.

JACKSONVILLE, 540,898, B-4. Jacksonville covers more than 800 square miles, making it the country's largest mainland city in area. From its first settlement as an Indian village on the St. Johns River, Jacksonville has mushroomed into a major commercial center. **Cummer Gallery of Art,** 829 Riverside Ave., stands on the site of the former Cummer family home amidst formal English and Italian gardens. The museum's ten galleries houses 14th- through 17th-century European paintings and a rare collection of early Meissen porcelain. Year-round, Tues.-Fri., 10 A.M. to 4 P.M.; Sat., noon to 5 P.M.; Sun., 2 to 5 P.M. Donation. 904/356-6857. **Jacksonville Art Museum,** 4160 Boulevard Center Dr., has a permanent collection of Oriental porcelain, a sculpture garden, and changing exhibits. Jan.-July, Sept.-Dec., Tues., Wed., Fri., 10 A.M. to 5 P.M.; Thurs., 10 A.M. to 10 P.M.; Sat.-Sun., 1 to 5 P.M. Free. 904/398-8336. **Jacksonville Museum of Arts and Sciences,** 1025 Gulf Life Dr., offers matinees on science themes and planetarium shows. Oct.-Aug., Tues.-Fri., 9 A.M. to 5 P.M.; Sat.,

11 A.M. to 5 P.M.; Sun., 1 to 5 P.M. Planetarium shows: Tues.-Fri., 5 P.M.; Sat., noon, 2, and 5 P.M.; Sun., 2 and 4 P.M. Adults $2; persons 4-18, $1; under 4, free. 904/396-7062. **Jacksonville Zoological Park,** 8605 Zoo Rd., is laid out with naturalistic settings for more than 800 animals on 61 acres. Year-round, daily, 9 A.M. to 4:45 P.M. Adults $2.50; children 4-12, 75¢; under 4, free. 904/757-4463. **Jacksonville University,** N. University Blvd., offers campus visitors two points of interest. *Delius House,* the restored home of the British composer, is open daily by appointment, 8:30 A.M. to 4 P.M. Free. 904/744-3950. *Alexander Brest Museum,* in the Phillips Fine Arts Building, has collections of pre-Columbian artifacts and Steuben glass as well as changing exhibits. Sept.-May, Mon.-Fri., 9 A.M. to 4 P.M. Free. 904/744-3950. **Kingsley Plantation,** Fort George Island, St. 105, is the site of the oldest plantation house in Florida. Year-round, daily, 8 A.M. to 5 P.M. Adults 50¢; children under 6, free. Tours: 9:30 and 11 A.M., 1:30 and 3 P.M. 904/251-3122. **Fort Caroline National Memorial,** 12713 Fort Caroline Rd., 10 miles east of Jacksonville via St. 10, commemorates the Huguenot Colony founded along the St. Johns River in 1564. The sod and timber walls of the fort have been reconstructed; a museum adds historical background. Year-round, daily, 9 A.M. to 5 P.M. Free. 904/641-7111.

KEY BISCAYNE, 6,337, south of Miami, G-5. **Bill Baggs Cape Florida State Recreation Area,** 1200 S. Crandon Blvd., offers guided tours of Cape Florida Lighthouse. Park admission 50¢; lighthouse tours, 50¢ extra. Year-round, daily, 8 A.M. to sunset. 305/361-5811. **Planet Ocean,** 3979 Rickenbacker Causeway, is an oceanographic museum with exhibits of the planets and their environments. Year-round, daily, 10 A.M. to 6 P.M. Adults $4; children $2.25; under 6, free. 305/361-5786. **Miami Seaquarium,** 4400 Rickenbacker Causeway, is a marine attraction and research institute. Year-round, daily, 9 A.M. to 6:30 P.M. Adults $7; children $3.50; under 5, free. 305/361-5705.

KEY LARGO, 2,866, H-5. **John Pennekamp Coral Reef State Park,** off U.S. 1, is the country's first underwater state park. It surrounds an area of reef and has concession facilities for snorkeling, scuba diving, sailing, boat rentals, and glass-bottom boat rides. The Visitors Center has an aquarium, walking trails, and observation towers. Year-round, daily, 8 A.M. to sunset. Admission 50¢. 305/451-1621.

KEY WEST, 24,292, H-4. First sighted by Spanish explorers in the 18th century, Key West served mostly as a base for pirates during its early years. In the first part of the 1800s, salvaging became the city's major industry, followed by cigar making. Today, Key West still draws on that century-old flavor, with its many restored buildings and slow-paced ways. Old Mallory Square

and Duvall Street provide the tone and set the scene for a relaxed day of shopping and dining, while the surrounding blue waters beckon the more adventuresome to try their luck at fishing, diving, and snorkeling. **Ernest Hemingway Home and Museum,** 907 Whitehead St., built in 1851, was the home of the author from 1931 to 1961. Year-round, daily, 9 A.M. to 5 P.M. Adults $2, children $1. 305/294-1575. **Audubon House,** 205 Whitehead St., memorializes a visit paid by John J. Audubon in 1832. The Double Elephant folio *Birds of America,* other Audubon artwork, and antique furnishings are on display. Year-round, daily, 9 A.M. to noon, 1 to 5 P.M. Adults $1.50, children 50¢. 305/294-2116. **Lighthouse and Military Museum,** 938 Whitehead St., has war artifacts, including a small Japanese submarine. Year-round, daily, 9:30 A.M. to 5 P.M. Adults $1.75, children 50¢. 305/294-0012. **Municipal Aquarium,** Whitehead St., showcases marine life of the Florida keys. Year-round, daily, 10 A.M. to 6 P.M. Adults $4; students and persons over 55, $3; children 6-12, $1; under 6, free. 305/296-2051. **Fort Jefferson National Monument,** 60 miles off the coast and accessible by amphibious aircraft or private boat, attracts birdwatchers, history buffs, and swimmers and snorkelers to the warm waters and coral reef around the seven Dry Tortuga Islands. Year-round, daily, sunrise to sunset. Free. Inquire about seaplane service at the Key West Chamber of Commerce, 402 Wall St. 305/294-2587. **Conch Tour Trains** leave on the hour from these three depots for one-and-one-half-hour tours of Key West: N. Roosevelt Blvd., Angela and Duval Sts., Mallory Square. Year-round, daily, 9 A.M. to 4 P.M. Adults $5, children and military $2.50. 305/294-5161. **Flipper's Sea School,** 2407 N. Roosevelt Blvd., offers trained dolphin shows as well as opportunities to see dolphins in the ocean rather than in tanks. Year-round, daily, (weather permitting), 10 A.M. to 5 P.M. Adults $4; children 4-12, $2.25; under 4, free. 305/294-8827.

KISSIMMEE, 15,487, D-4. **Gatorland Zoo,** U.S. 441, claims to have the largest alligator in captivity in addition to hundreds of other inhabitants. Year-round, daily, 8 A.M. to 6 P.M. Adults $3; children 3-12, $2; under 3, free. 305/855-5496. **Ringling Brothers and Barnum & Bailey Circus World.** *See* **Haines City.**

LAKE BUENA VISTA, 1,290, west of Orlando, D-4. **Walt Disney World,** off U.S. 192, covers 43 square miles of central Florida with amusements and resort facilities. The Magic Kingdom is the primary attraction, with its six theme parks and 40 Disney-style diversions. Travel on a monorail or ferryboat to the Magic Kingdom entrance, where Mickey Mouse welcomes visitors to Main Street, U.S.A.; Adventureland; Frontierland; Liberty Square; Fantasyland; and Tomorrowland. Shows, rides, shops, and restaurants provide entertainment. Daily, June-Labor Day, 9 A.M. to 1 A.M.; Sept.-May, 9 A.M. to 6 P.M. Adults $13; persons 12-17, $12; 3-11, $11; under 3, free. 305/824-4321. **EPCOT** (Environmental Prototype Community of Tomorrow), with permanent world showcases and pavilions, opens October 1982. 305/824-4321.

LAKELAND, 47,406, D-3. **Florida Southern College,** Johnson and Lake Hollingsworth Aves., grew into a unique showcase of Frank Lloyd Wright architecture during Wright's 22-year association with the college. *Annie Pfeiffer Chapel, Danforth Chapel,* and the administration, seminar, classroom, and science buildings are open to visitors. Year-round, daily, 8 A.M. to 5 P.M. 813/683-5521.

LAKE WALES, 8,466, D-4. **Bok Tower Gardens,** off U.S. 27A, offers carillon music every half hour, with a 45-minute recital every day at 3 P.M. On Tuesday, Wednesday, Saturday, and Sunday the recitals are live; others are recorded. The 53-bell carillon is housed in a 205-foot-high marble and cochina tower. Tours: Year-round, Mon.-Sat., 11 A.M. and 2 P.M.; Sun., 2 P.M. Gardens: Year-round, daily, 8 A.M. to 5:30 P.M. Admission $2 per car. 813/676-1408.

MIAMI, 346,931, G-5. Miami, Florida's Big Orange, traces its origins to the 1800s, but its primary ambience is purely metropolitan. Miami serves as a destination for American and foreign visitors, offering topflight entertainment, myriad restaurants of all specialties, and cosmopolitan shopping at a variety of malls and stores. **Vizcaya,** 3251 S. Miami Ave., was completed in 1920 as the Italian Baroque dream home of industrialist James Deering. Now a museum, it has 30 rooms open to the public and Italian formal gardens. Year-round, daily, 10 A.M. to 5 P.M. Adults $3.75; children 6-11, $2; under 6, free. Gardens: $2. "Sound and Light" Show, Fri.-Sat., 8 P.M. Admission $5. 305/579-2708. The **Cloisters of the Monastery of St. Bernard de Clairvaux,** 16711 W. Dixie Hwy., is technically the oldest building in the United States. It was built as a Cistercian Monastery in Sacramenia, Spain, in 1141. William Randolph Hearst purchased the Romanesque structure in 1925. Left in storage for decades, the monastery was then bought and reassembled in Miami; it is now owned by the local Episcopal Diocese, which maintains its formal landscaped gardens. Year-round, Mon.-Sat., 10 A.M. to 5 P.M.; Sun., noon to 5 P.M. Admission $3; persons 65 and older, $2; children 6-12, 75¢; under 6, free. 305/945-1461. **Historical Museum of Southern Florida,** 3280 S. Miami Ave., is designed as a maze that allows visitors to walk through history from Indian habitation to the Space Age. Year-round, Mon.-Sat., 9 A.M. to 5 P.M.; Sun., noon to 5 P.M. Free. 305-854-3289. **Museum of Science and Space Transit Planetarium,** 3280 S. Miami Ave., specializes in "hands-on" scientific exhibits. Plane-

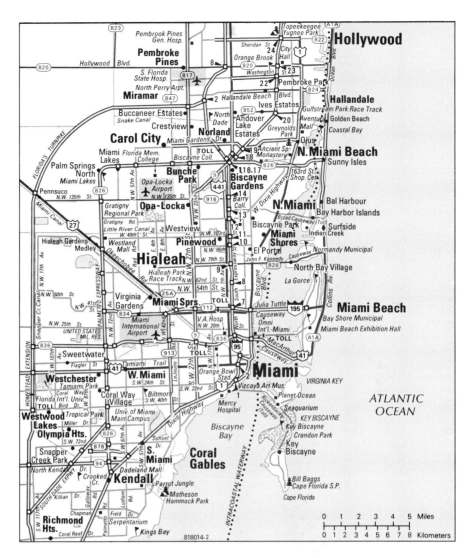

tarium shows have varying themes; call 305/854-2222 for schedules and prices. Year-round, Mon.-Fri., 9 A.M. to 5 P.M., 7 to 10 P.M.; Sat., 9 A.M. to 10 P.M.; Sun., 11 A.M. to 10 P.M. Free. 305/854-4242. **Metrozoo,** 12400 S.W. 152nd St., a 740-acre cageless zoo, is under construction. Visitors can see completed habitats of Eurasian animals, including Bengal tigers, Siberian ibex, and white-bearded gnus. Year-round, daily, 10 A.M. to 4:30 P.M. Adults $3; children 2-12, $1.50; under 2, free. 305/251-0402. **Parrot Jungle,** 11000 S.W. 57th Ave., has shows of performing parrots and flamingos on parade as well as 1,200 parrots at home in 12 acres of gardens. Year-round, daily, 9:30 A.M. to 5 P.M. Adults $5; children 6-12, $2.50; under 6, free. 305/666-7834.
See also **Key Biscayne.**

MIAMI BEACH, 96,298, G-5. **Bass Museum of Art,** 2100 Collins Ave., includes Rubens' "Holy Family" among its permanent collection of paintings and sculpture. Year-round, Tues.-Sat., 10 A.M. to 5 P.M.; Sun., 1 to 5 P.M. Adults $1, children 50¢. Free on Tuesdays. 305/673-7530. **Art Deco National Historic District** is a mile-square section of south Miami Beach con-

taining a large concentration of 1930s Art Deco design style. Miami Beach Design Preservation League, on Euclid Ave., distributes maps and organizes events. 305/672-2014.

NAPLES, 17,581, F-4. **Collier County Museum and Archives,** 3301 Tamiami Trail E., has changing displays and permanent exhibits on the Seminole and Calusa Indians; Barron C. Collier, the major land developer of the area; historic ranch enterprises; and local taxidermy. Year-round, Mon.-Fri., 8 A.M. to 5 P.M. Free. 813/774-8477. **Old Marine Market Place** is a collection of boutiques, waterfront pubs, and craftsmen in renovated tin-roofed harbor warehouses. Free. Year-round, daily, 8 A.M. to 5 P.M.

OCALA, 37,170, C-3. Central Florida's Horse Farms are scattered around Ocala, where thoroughbred breeding and training is a thriving business. The Ocala Marion County Chamber of Commerce offers a tour list of 29 farms that can be visited. Free. 904/629-8051. Florida's **Silver Springs,** St. 40, is an amusement park operated around the natural spectacle of Silver Springs.

Year-round, daily, 9 A.M. to 5:30 P.M. Adults $6.95; children 3-11, $4.95; under 3, free. 904/236-2121. **Six Gun Territory,** St. 40, offers scenes from an Old West Town, with over 20 old-fashioned shops, can-can shows, and a train ride. Daily, June-Labor Day, 9:30 A.M. to 6:30 P.M.; other months, 10 A.M. to 5:30 P.M. Adults $4.50; children 4-12, $3.75; under 4, free. Amusement and train rides, 25¢ and 50¢. 904/236-2211. **Wild Waters,** 1 mile east on St. 40, is a water-theme park with flume rides and wave pool. Mar. to late Sept., daily, 10 A.M. to 9 P.M. Adults $5.25; children 3-11, $4.25; under 3, free. 904/236-2043.

ORLANDO, 128,394, D-4. The hub of Florida's citrus country, Orlando is dotted by lakes and green, open parks, where swimming, water-skiing, and sunning are the modus operandi. Located within a short distance of a variety of attractions, the city serves as a prime gateway for central Florida's theme-park playground—Walt Disney World, Sea World, and more. **Loch Haven Art Center,** 2416 N. Mills Ave., exhibits a permanent collection of 350 pieces of pre-Columbian art dated from 2000 B.C. to A.D. 1500.Year-round, Tues.-Fri., 10 A.M. to 5 P.M.; Sat., noon to 5 P.M.; Sun., 2 to 5 P.M. Free; admission may be charged for special exhibits. 305/896-4231. **John Young Science Center,** 810 E. Rollins St., invites children to play with exhibits in the Discovery Room. A Foucault pendulum illustrates the earth's rotation, and telescopes allow skywatching sessions every Friday at 9 P.M., weather permitting. The planetarium has a 40-foot domed screen and a star projector. Shows: Year-round, Mon.-Thurs., 2:30 P.M.; Fri., 2:30 and 8 P.M.; Sat.-Sun., 2:30 and 3:30 P.M. Museum and Planetarium: Year-round, Mon.-Thurs., 9 A.M. to 5 P.M.; Fri.-Sat., 9 A.M. to 9 P.M.; Sun., noon to 5 P.M. Adults $1.75; persons 4-17 and over 55, $1.25; under 4, free; family rate, $4. 305/896-7151. **Orange County Historical Museum,** 812 E. Rollins St., traces the history of the county. Year-round, Tues.-Fri., 10 A.M. to 4 P.M.; Sat.-Sun., 2 to 5 P.M. Free. 305/898-8320. **Harry P. Leu Botanical Gardens,** 1730 N. Forest Ave., include a formal rose garden among ten landscapes laid out on 55 acres. Year-round, daily, 9 A.M. to 5 P.M. Admission 50¢. 305/894-6021. **Central Florida Zoological Society Park,** north of Orlando on St. 17/92 in Sanford, has over 200 animals. Youngsters can get an eye-level look at animals in the Children's Zoo. Year-round, daily, 9 A.M. to 5 P.M. Adults $3, children $1. 305/323-4450. **Sea World of Florida,** Int. 4 and Beeline Expwy., is a marine-life theme park with whale, dolphin, and seal shows; a shark habitat; a water-ski shows; an aquarium; walrus exhibit; a Japanese village with pearl-diving exhibits; an Hawaiian village with daily luaus; and a water and light show. Daily, June-Aug., 8:30 A.M. to 8 P.M.; other months, 9 A.M. to 7 P.M. Adults $9.50; children 3-11, $8.50; under 3, free. 305/351-

0021. **Wings and Wheels,** 8989 Florida Rd. South, houses milestones in the history of transportation. Year-round, daily, 9:30 A.M. to 6 P.M. Adults $5.50; children 6-12, $2.75; under 6, free. 305/859-9600. **Stars Hall of Fame,** 6825 Starway Dr., has more than 200 wax figures of movie, TV, and recording stars. Year-round, daily, 10 A.M. to 5 P.M. school days; other days, 10 A.M. to 10 P.M. Adults $6.75, children free. 305/351-2628. **Walt Disney World.** *See* **Lake Buena Vista.**

ORMOND BEACH, 21,378, C-4. **Ormond Beach Memorial Art Gallery Museum and Gardens,** 78 E. Granada St., feature a setting of three acres of tropical flora, paths, ponds, and a museum which has religious paintings. Oct.-Aug., Mon.-Tues., Thurs.-Sun., noon to 5 P.M. Free. 904/677-1857.

PALATKA, 10,175, B-4. **Ravine State Gardens,** off St. 20, are situated around a natural ravine with several artesian springs. Year-round, daily, 8 A.M. to sunset. Free. 904/328-4366.

PALM BEACH, 9,729, F-5. The **Henry Morrison Flagler Museum,** 1 Whitehall Way, was built in 1901 by Henry Flagler. Thirty rooms display original furnishings, a ballroom copied from Versailles, works of art, and period costumes. Year-round, Tues.-Sat., 10 A.M. to 5 P.M.; Sun., noon to 5 P.M. Adults $3; children 6-12, $1. 305/655-2833. **Worth Avenue** is lined with shops distinguished by their merchandise and Spanish-style architecture.

PANAMA CITY, 33,346, H-2. Panama City Beach attracts summer visitors with its stretch of white beaches. **Miracle Strip Amusement Park,** 12001 W. U.S. 98, features a beachside carnival midway, a water-theme park, and a sightseeing tower. Year-round, daily. Admission individually priced. 904/234-3333. **Shell Island** is a barrier island with white, secluded beaches, accessible only by boat. **Capt. Anderson's,** Thomas Dr., offers round-trip island excursions twice daily, 9 A.M. and 1:15 P.M. Adults $3.50; children under 12, $1.75. 904/234-3435.

PENSACOLA, 57,619, H-1. **Gulf Islands National Seashore** extends over barrier islands strung around the Gulf from Mississippi to Florida. Historical sites on Florida's mainland portion recall America's coastal defense system from before the Civil War through World War II. Points of interest include *Fort Pickens* (1834); a museum of historical artifacts; and *The Sandbox,* an aquarium with shell displays. Park: Year-round, daily, 9 A.M. to 5 P.M. Park entrance, $1. 904/932-5307. The **West Florida Museum of History** maintains several buildings in the **Seville Square Historic District.** The *Hispanic Building,* 200 E. Zaragoza St., is a late 19th-century warehouse with exhibits depicting local history.

Year-round, Tues.-Sat., 10 A.M. to 5 P.M. 904/432-6717. The *Transportation Building,* 201 E. Zaragoza St., is a late 19th-century warehouse with displays of transportation history and a re-created 19th-century street scene. Year-round, Mon.-Sat., 10 A.M. to 4:30 P.M.; Sun., 1 to 4:30 P.M. Donation. 904/434-1042. *Piney Woods Sawmill,* Barracks and Main Sts., is a turn-of-the-century operation which typifies the region's industry. Year-round, daily, 8 A.M. to 5 P.M. Free. *Dorr House,* 311 S. Adams St., is a Victorian residence built in 1891 and furnished to show the life-style of a middle-class family during the 19th-century lumber boom. Year-round, Mon.-Sat., 10 A.M. to 2 P.M.; Sun., 1 to 2 P.M. Donation. *Pensacola Historical Museum,* 405 S. Adams St., is housed in Old Christ Church (1832). Year-round, Mon.-Sat., 9 A.M. to 4:30 P.M. Free. 904/433-1559. Also in the Seville Square Historic District are *Walton House,* 221 E. Zaragoza St. and *Quina House,* 204 S. Alcaniz St., two 1810 structures with period furnishings. Walton House: Mid-May-mid-Oct., Tues.-Sun., 1 to 4 P.M. Adults 50¢; children under 12, free. Quina House: Mid-May-mid-Oct., daily, 1 to 4 P.M. Donations. 904/434-1042. The **Naval Aviation Museum,** on the Pensacola Naval Air Station, is the U.S. Navy's only aviation museum. Year-round, daily, 9 A.M. to 5 P.M. Free. 904/452-3604.

PONCE INLET, 966, south of Daytona Beach, C-4. **Ponce de Leon Inlet Lighthouse,** 4931 S. Peninsula Dr., built in 1886, stands 175 feet high. The lighthouse keeper's home has been restored with its original 19th-century furnishings. The museum has lighthouse artifacts. Year-round, daily, 10 A.M. to 5 P.M. Adults $1, children 25¢. 904/761-1821.

PORT ST. JOE, 4,027, H-3. **Constitution Convention State Museum,** 200 Allen Memorial Way, recalls the history of the town where Florida's first state constitution was drawn up. Year-round, Mon.-Sat., 9 A.M. to 5 P.M.; Sun., 1 to 5 P.M. Admission 25¢; children under 6, free. 904/229-8029.

ST. AUGUSTINE, 11,985, B-4. The first permanent European settlement in what became the United States, St. Augustine was founded by Spanish Adm. Pedro Menéndez de Avilés in 1565. The city was under Spanish rule until 1763, when Florida was ceded to Great Britain. Spain regained St. Augustine and east Florida in 1784 and held the territory until it was transferred to the United States in 1821. **HISTORIC SITES: St. Augustine Antiguo** is a restored area of 18th-century St. Augustine developed and maintained by the Historic St. Augustine Preservation Board. Walking tours are conducted by guides in period clothing. In addition to the *Blacksmith Shop,* the 19th-century *Benet Store,* and the remains of the DeMesa/Sanchez and DeHita/Gonzalez sites, the tour includes: the *Peso de Burgo-Pellicer House,* a

British-period duplex that holds an exhibit of antique Spanish furnishings; the *Gallegos House,* a two-room tabby structure of the First Spanish Period; *Sanchez de Ortigosa House,* a two-room coquina home from the First Spanish Period; the *Arrivas House,* which reflects both 18th- and 19th-century architecture; and the *Ribera House,* which has a formal garden with fruit trees and an arbor. Year-round, daily, 9 A.M. to 5:15 P.M. Adults $2; persons 8-18, 75¢; under 8, free; family, $5. 904/824-3355.

Castillo de San Marcos National Monument, off Castillo Dr. overlooking Matanzas Bay, is a gray coquina moated fort begun in 1672, but not completed until 1756. The 12-foot-thick outer walls of Castillo San Marcos stymied attacks by Carolina colonists in 1702 and the fort defied a British siege in 1740. Daily, May-late Oct., 9 A.M. to 5:45 P.M.; other months, 8:30 A.M. to 5:15 P.M. Adults 50¢; persons under 16 and over 65, free. 904/829-6506. **Mission of Nombre de Dios,** San Marcos Ave. at Old Mission Ave., was the founding site of St. Augustine; the first mass in the United States was celebrated here in 1565. The 208-foot-high cross was set up in 1965 to commemorate the 400th anniversary of the Spaniards' landing. Year-round, daily, 7 A.M. to sunset. Donation. 904/829-5696 or 904/824-6734.

HISTORIC HOUSES: Oldest House, 14 St. Francis St., is the oldest documented house of the Spanish settlement. Built in the early 1700s, it was constructed of coquina and then enlarged with a wooden second story. Admission provides entry to the adjacent *Toval House,* where museum exhibits illustrate techniques used in the historic house. Year-round, daily, 9 A.M. to 5:40 P.M. Adults $1.25; children 6-8, 50¢; under 6, free. 904/829-5514. **Oldest Wooden Schoolhouse,** 14 St. George St., is a brick-floored cedar building constructed as a home during the First Spanish Period and later used as a school. Structural highlights include hand-hewn planks and an encircling chain designed to keep the building from blowing away during hurricanes. Year-round, daily, 9 A.M. to 5 P.M. Adults $1; persons 6-11, 50¢; under 6, free. 904/829-3621. **Dr. Peck House,** 143 St. George St., was built as early as 1687, but most of the coquina and clapboard structures date to 1837, when Dr. Seth S. Peck moved his family here from Connecticut. Year-round, Tues.-Fri., 10 A.M. to 4 P.M. Adults $1, children 50¢. 904/829-5064. **Zorayda Castle,** 83 King St., was built in 1883 by Franklin Smith as a 1:10-scale replica of one wing of the Alhambra. Abraham Mussallem purchased the castle in 1913 to house his collection of Oriental teakwood, ivory, and mother-of-pearl furnishings. Daily, June-late Aug., 9 A.M. to 9 P.M.; other months, 9 A.M. to 5:30 P.M. Adults $2; children 6-12, $1.50; under 6, free. 904/824-3097.

MUSEUMS: Lightner Museum, King St., is housed in the former Alcazar Hotel built in 1888 by Henry M. Flagler. The building was

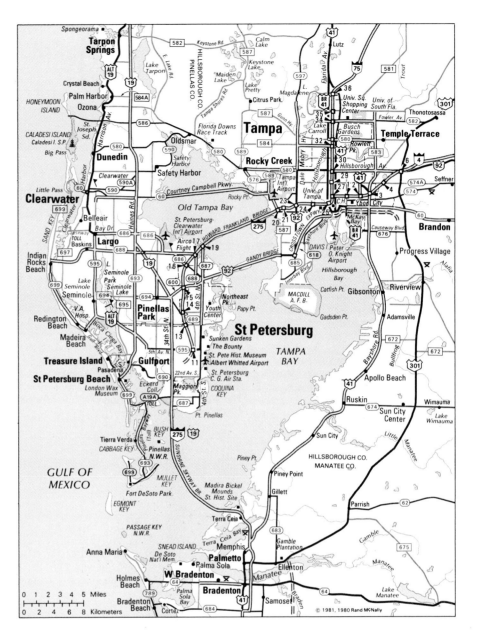

purchased in 1947 by Otto C. Lightner, who transferred his extensive hobby collections to the three-floor hotel. Year-round, daily, 9 A.M. to 5 P.M. Adults $2; persons 12-18, 75¢; under 12, free. 904/829-9677. **Oldest Store Museum,** 4 Artillery Lane, boasts the world's largest collection of country store merchandise. Year-round, daily, 9 A.M. to 5 P.M. Adults $1.75; children 6-12, $1; under 6, free. 904/829-9729.

VISITORS SERVICES: The **St. Augustine Visitors Information Center,** 10 Castillo Dr., offers free maps and a movie twice each hour on the half hours. Year-round, daily, 8 A.M. to 5:30 P.M. 904/829-5681. **St. Augustine Sightseeing Trains, Inc.,** 3 Cordova St., offers train tours every 15 minutes. Daily, June-Aug., 8:30 A.M. to 8 P.M.; other months, 8:30 A.M. to 5 P.M. 24-hour ticket: Adults $4; children 6-12, $2; under 6, free. Trains can be boarded at city stations or at tour headquarters. 904/829-6545. **St. Augustine Transfer Co.,** Bay Front near the

entrance to Castillo de San Marcos, offers horse-drawn carriage tours. Year-round, daily, 8:30 A.M. to 5 P.M. Adults $3; children 6-12, $1; under 6, free. 904/829-2818. **Scenic Cruise Tours** offer tours aboard *Victory II,* which leave from City Yacht Pier. Adults $4, children $1.50. 904/824-1806.

NEARBY: Marineland of Florida, St. A1A, 20 miles south of St. Augustine, attracts audiences with porpoise feedings and trained dolphin shows as well as exhibits of other sea creatures, shells, and birds. Year-round, daily, 8 A.M. to 6:30 P.M. Adults $5; children 6-11, $2.50; under 6, free. 904/471-1111. **Washington Oaks State Gardens,** south on St. A1A, is an exotic garden located in a 340-acre hammock of hardwood trees between the ocean and the intracoastal waterway. Displays at the Visitors Center portray the gardens' citrus groves and wildlife. Picnicking and fishing are permitted. Year-round, daily, 8 A.M. to sunset. Admission 50¢, 904/445-3161.

ST. PETERSBURG, 236,893, E-3. St. Petersburg bases its reputation on its unlimited sunshine, and that is one of the main reasons the city has become a major winter vacation resort. Miles of beaches stretch from south of St. Petersburg, north to Tarpon Springs, inviting sun worshippers and boat lovers. Nearby Tampa has a decidedly different flavor, drawn from its ethnic roots in Ybor City, home of the city's original Cuban settlers. Here visitors can still see cigars rolled by hand or dine at any number of authentic Cuban restaurants. **St. Petersburg Historical Museum,** 335 2nd Ave. NE, has a variety of exhibits including an Egyptian mummy, American Indian artifacts, an Oriental collection, and old-fashioned toys for children. Year-round, Mon.-Sat., 11 A.M. to 5 P.M.; Sun., 1 to 5 P.M. Adults 75¢; children 6-15, 25¢; under 6, free. 813/894-1052. **Haas Museum,** 3511 2nd Ave. S, affiliated with the Historical Museum, includes the 19th-century *Grace Turner House,* the 1850 *Lowe House,* a 1926 train caboose, an old dentist's office, and a barber shop. Oct.-Aug., Tues.-Sun., 1 to 5 P.M. Adults $1, children 25¢. 813/894-1401. **Science Center of Pinellas County,** 7701 22nd Ave. N, features a mosaic walkway that celebrates the 50 states in the *Starley White Gardens.* Year-round, Mon.-Fri., 9 A.M. to 4 P.M. Free. 813/384-0027. **Museum of Fine Arts,** 255 Beach Dr. NE, has two completely furnished English rooms from the Georgian and Jacobean periods, French Impressionist paintings, and an Oriental gallery. Year-round, Tues.-Sat., 10 A.M. to 5 P.M.; Sun., 1 to 5 P.M. Donations. 813/896-2667. **Florida's Sunken Gardens,** 1825 4th St. N, began as a sinkhole and now blooms with 7,000 tropical plants, 50,000 annuals, and an orchid arbor. Year-round, daily, 9 A.M. to 5:30 P.M. Adults $4.50; children 6-12, $2.50; under 6, free. 813/896-3186. **Metro-Goldwyn-Mayer Bounty Exhibit,** 345 2nd Ave. NE, allows visitors to see the square-rigger used in the movie *Mutiny on the Bounty.* Year-round, daily, 9 A.M. to 10 P.M. Adults $3.25; children 4-12, $1.75; under 4, free. 813/896-3117.

SANIBEL, 3,363, F-3. **J. N. "Ding" Darling National Wildlife Refuge,** Sanibel-Captiva Rd., is a 5,000-acre protected home for migratory birds, shore birds, and waterfowl. Walking trails begin on Tarpon Bay Rd. Canoe trails and rentals are at the Tarpon Bay Marina. Year-round, daily, sunrise to sunset. Free. 813/472-1100.

SARASOTA, 48,868, E-3. The **Ringling Museums,** north on U.S. 41, are a complex of four historic and cultural landmarks on the 68-acre former estate of circus entrepreneur John Ringling. The *John and Mable Ringling Museum of Art,* styled after a 15th-century Florentine villa, houses Ringling's collection of more than 500 paintings. *Ca'd'Zan,* the Ringlings' 32-room residence, was patterned after the Doge's Palace in Venice and elaborately furnished with mar-

ble bathrooms, a 4,000-pipe organ, tapestries, and art. *Museum of the Circus* houses circus artifacts. *Asolo Theatre,* an 18th-century theater, was imported from Asolo, Italy, and installed on the Ringling property for public performances. Year-round, Mon.-Fri., 9 A.M. to 10 P.M.; Sat., 9 A.M. to 5 P.M.; Sun., 11 A.M. to 6 P.M.. All museums: Adults $3.50; children under 12, free. 813/355-5101. **Bellm's Cars and Music of Yesterday,** 5500 N. Tamiami Trail, has 170 antique and special-interest cars, 1,500 mechanical music-makers, and a turn-of-the-century arcade. Year-round, Mon.-Sat., 8:30 A.M. to 6 P.M.; Sun., 9:30 A.M. to 6 P.M. Adults $4.50; persons 6-16, $2; under 6, free. 813/355-6228. **Marie Selby Botanical Gardens,** 800 South Palm Ave., is an epiphytic garden, featuring 10,000 air plants. Year-round, daily, 10 A.M. to 5 P.M. Adults $3; persons under 16, with adult, free. 813/366-5730. **Sarasota Jungle Gardens,** 3701 Bay Shore Rd., has 16 acres of botanical gardens, bird shows, reptile shows, a petting zoo, a shell museum, and a butterfly museum. Highlights include the *Gardens of Christ,* over 350,000 plant varieties, and 100 types of tropical birds. Year-round, daily, 9 A.M. to 5 P.M. Adults $4.50; persons 6-16, $2.50; under 6, free. 813/355-5305.

STUART, 9,467, E-5. **Gilbert's Bar House of Refuge,** 301 S.E. MacArthur Blvd., built in 1875, is the only survivor of a string of ten lifesaving stations along Florida's east coast. Nov.-May, Tues.-Sun., 1 to 5 P.M.; other months, daily, 1 to 5 P.M. Adults 50¢; children 6-13, 25¢; under 6, free. 305/225-1875. **Elliott Museum,** 825 N.E. Ocean Blvd., is housed in the former winter residence of Sterling Elliott, the inventor of the kingpin mechanism that paved the way for the invention of the steam automobile. Year-round, daily, 1 to 5 P.M. Adults $1; children 6-13, 50¢; under 6, free. 305/225-1961.

TALLAHASSEE, 81,548, A-1. The Florida **State Capitol,** Duval St., located on the highest hill in Tallahassee, is topped by an observation deck. Guided tours of the 22-story building include legislative areas and the chapel. Tours: Mon.-Fri., 8:30 A.M. to 4:30 P.M. Sat.-Sun., 11 A.M. to 4 P.M. Year-round, Free. 904/488-6167. **Museum of Florida History,** Pensacola and Bronough Sts., represents Florida chronology with a historical slide series and exhibits of Indian, Spanish, and 19th- and 20th-century American artifacts. Year-round, Mon.-Fri., 10 A.M. to 4:30 P.M.; Sat., 9 A.M. to 4:30 P.M. Free. 904/488-1484. **Tallahassee Junior Museum,** 3945 Museum Dr., has nature trails that lead through 52 acres of wildlife habitats. Year-round, Tues.-Sat., 9 A.M. to 5 P.M.; Sun., 2 to 5 P.M. Adults $2; persons 4-18, $1; under 4, free. 904/576-1636. **Alfred B. Maclay State Gardens,** north on U.S. 319, has 28 acres in bloom from January to April. Year-round, daily, 8 A.M. to 5 P.M. Jan.-Apr.: Adults $1.50, children 75¢. May-

Dec.: Admission 50¢. 904/894-4232. **Wakulla Springs,** 14 miles south on St. 61, is one of the world's largest and deepest springs. Glass-bottom-boat trips showcase the clarity of the 185-foot-deep pool and the marine life in it. Daily, May-Sept., 9:30 A.M. to 6:30 P.M.; other months, 9:30 A.M. to 5:30 P.M. Single tours: Adults $3; children over 6, $1.80; under 6, free. Both tours: Adults $5; children over 6, $3; under 6, free. 904/640-7011.

TAMPA, 271,523, D-3. **Ybor City,** a historic district within Tampa, recalls the cigar industry that began here in 1886 and the Cuban community that grew up with it. **Ybor Square,** 13th St. and 8th Ave., is a group of shops housed in one of the oldest cigar factories; cigars are still hand rolled in a shop on the second floor. Year-round, daily, 10 A.M. to 5 P.M. Free. **Ybor City State Museum,** 1818 9th Ave., displays artifacts of early cigar factories in the area's oldest bakery. Year-round, daily, 9 A.M. to noon, 1 to 5 P.M. 813/247-6323. Admission 25¢; children under 6, free. **University of Tampa,** 401 W. Kennedy Blvd., was opened as a lavish hotel by Henry B. Plant in 1892 and converted to educational use in 1933. The five-story Moorish-style landmark exhibits furnishings from the hotel period in the *Henry B. Plant Museum.* Guided tours leave from the lobby of Plant Hall, Sept.-May, Tues. and Thurs., 1:30 P.M. Free. Building: Year-round, daily, 8 A.M. to 5:30 P.M. 813/253-8861. The **Tampa Museum,** 601 Doyle Carlton Dr., has two galleries of changing exhibits. Year-round, Tues., Thurs., Fri., 9 A.M. to 6 P.M.; Wed., 10 A.M. to 9 P.M.; Sat., 10 A.M. to 5 P.M.; Sun., 1 to 5 P.M. Free. 813/223-8128. **The Dark Continent, Busch Gardens,** 3000 Busch Blvd., is a 300-acre African theme park, with a Moroccan bazaar, elephant and safari rides, exotic birds at the Busch gardens, other areas of African geography, and a new water-raft ride. Daily, mid-June-Labor Day, 9:30 A.M. to 8 P.M.; other months, 9:30 A.M. to 6 P.M. Admission $10.50 includes all rides, shows, and attractions; under 4, free. Parking $1. 813/988-5171. **Adventure Island,** 4545 Bougainvillea Ave., is a seven-acre theme park with four major areas and swimming facilities. Apr.-May, daily, 10 A.M. to 6 P.M.; June-Aug., daily, 10 A.M. to 10 P.M.; Sept.-Oct., Sat.-Sun., 10 A.M. to 6 P.M. Adults $6.75; children under 4, free. 813/977-6606.

See also **St. Petersburg.**

TARPON SPRINGS, 13,251, D-3. **Spongeorama,** on the Sponge Docks, celebrates the historic local sponge diving industry and Greek community. It includes museum displays, a representation of a 1910 Greek sponge-diving village, a working sponge factory, and specialty shops. Adults $1; children 4-11, 50¢; under 4, free. Year-round, daily, 10 A.M. to 6 P.M. Free. 813/937-4111. **St. Nicholas Greek Orthodox Cathedral,** Orange St. and U.S. 19A, was built in 1943 as a replica of St. Sophia Church in Constantinople. Year-round, daily, 9 A.M. to 5 P.M. Free. 813/937-8540.

TITUSVILLE, 31,910, D-4. **Merritt Island National Wildlife Refuge**, on St. 401 west off U.S. 1 about 5 miles east of Titusville, is a 220-square-mile reserve which is host to more endangered wildlife species than any other refuge in the country, as well as to more than 285 species of nesting birds. U.S. Fish and Wildlife Service Office, St. 402, 7 miles east of Titusville. Refuge: Year-round, daily, sunrise to sunset. Office: Year-round, Mon.-Fri., 8 A.M. to 4:30 P.M. Free. 305/867-4820.

See also **Canaveral National Seashore.**

WEST PALM BEACH, 62,530, F-5. **Norton Gallery and School of Art,** 1451 S. Olive Ave., has collections of French Impressionist and Postimpressionist paintings; American 20th-century art; and Chinese jades, bronzes, and ceramics. Year-round, Tues.-Fri., 10 A.M. to 5 P.M.; Sat.-Sun., 1 to 5 P.M. Donations. 305/832-5194. **Dreher Park Science Museum and Planetarium of Palm Beach County,** 4801 N. Dreher Trail, includes whale and mastodon skeletons and a discovery room with live animals. Planetarium shows: Tues.-Sun., 3 P.M.; Fri., also 8 P.M. Adults $1; children and persons 65 and over, 75¢. Museum: Year-round, Tues.-Sat., 10 A.M. to 5 P.M.; Fri., also 6:30 to 10:30 P.M.; Sun., 1 to 5 P.M. Adults 50¢; children 5-15, 25¢. 305/832-1998. **Lion Country Safari,** west on St. 80, allows visitors to drive through a 320-acre preserve where African and Asian wildlife roam. Year-round, daily, 9:30 A.M. to 4:30 P.M. Admission $7.50 includes rides and tours; children under 3,

free. 305/793-1084. *Island Queen,* a Mississippi paddle-wheeler, departs four times daily from Phil Foster Park for an 80-minute cruise tour along the Intracoastal Waterway. Year-round, Tues.-Sun., 1, 3, 5, and 7 P.M. Adults $3, children $2. 305/793-7575.

WINTER HAVEN, 21,119, D-4. **Florida Cypress Gardens**, St. 540, features Gardens of the World, divided into sections of Oriental, Hawaiian, All-American Rose, English courtyard, and other plantings. The gardens encompass theaters, rides, a nature center, and an aviary, as well as wooded areas, canals, and rustic paths. There are electric boat tours of the canals and cruises on the lake. Aquarama, an underwater stage, invites photographers to snap underwater scenes through 80 feet of picture windows. Water-skiing shows: Year-round, daily, 10 A.M., noon, 2 and 4 P.M. Gardens: Year-round, daily, 8 A.M. to 6 P.M. Adults

$6.95; children 6-11, $3.95; under 6, free. 813/324-2111. **Slocum Water Gardens,** 1101 Cypress Gardens Rd., is an aquatic nursery where garden-pool plants flourish in greenhouses and outdoor ponds are stocked with colorful fish. Year-round, Mon.-Sat., 8 A.M. to noon, 1 to 4 P.M.; Sat., 8 A.M. to noon. Free. 813/293-7151.

WINTER PARK, 22,314, D-4. **Morse Gallery of Art,** 133 E. Welbourne Ave., features a unique collection of the works of Louis Comfort Tiffany. Stained-glass windows rescued from the artist's fire-razed home highlight the small gallery. Year-round, Tues.-Sat., 9:30 A.M. to 4 P.M.; Sun., 1 to 4 P.M. Adults $1.50, children $1. 305/645-5311. **Beal Maltbie Shell Museum,** Holt Ave. on Rollins College campus, displays examples of 100,000 known shell species. Year-round, Mon.-Fri., 10 A.M. to 5 P.M. Adults $1, children 50¢. 305/646-2364.

Information Sources

State of Florida
Department of Natural
Resources
Office of Education
and Information
Room 321, Crown Building
Tallahassee, FL 32304
904/488-7326

Florida Department
of Commerce
Division of Tourism
Van Buren St.
Tallahassee, FL 32304
904/488-1462

Florida
Attractions Association
P.O. Box 833
Silver Springs, FL 32688
904/694-5444

National Forests
in Florida
P.O. Box 13549
Tallahassee, FL 32308
904/878-1131

Jacksonville Convention
& Visitors Bureau
206 N. Hogan St.
Jacksonville, FL 32202
904/353-9736

Office of Information
& Visitors Bureau
City of Miami
150 S.E. 2nd Ave.
Suite 1250
Miami, FL 33131
305/579-6327

Orlando Chamber
of Commerce
P.O. Box 1234
Orlando, FL 32802
305/425-1234

Panama City Resort Council
P.O. Box 9473
Panama City Beach, FL 32601
904/234-6575

Pensacola Escambia
Development Commission
803 N. Palafox St.
Pensacola, FL 32501
904/433-3065

Pinellas Suncoast
Tourist Council
Clearwater/St. Petersburg Airport
Clearwater, FL 33520
813/877-8200

St. Augustine Visitors
Information Center
10 Castillo Dr.
St. Augustine, FL 32084
904/829-5681

Tallahassee Convention
& Tourism Division
Tallahassee Greater
Chamber of Commerce
P.O. Box 1639
Tallahassee, FL 32301
904/224-8116

Greater Tampa Convention
& Visitors Bureau
Chamber of Commerce
P.O. Box 420
Tampa, FL 33601
813/228-7777

Florida Campgrounds

FEES REFLECT MINIMUM RATE FOR 2 ADULTS AND ARE SUBJECT TO INCREASE OR SEASONAL CHANGES

- • – at the campground
- ○ – within one mile of campground
- $ – extra charge
- ** – limited facilities during winter months
- A – adults only
- B – 10,000 acres or more
- C – contribution

- E – tents rented
- F – entrance fee or premit required
- N – no specific number, limited by size of area only
- P – primitive
- R – reservation required
- S – self-contained units only

- U – unlimited
- V – trailers rented
- Z – reservations accepted
- LD – Labor Day
- MD – Memorial Day
- UC – under construction
- d – boat dock

- g – public golf course within 5 miles
- h – horseback riding
- j – whitewater running craft only
- k – snow skiing within 25 miles
- l – boat launch
- m – area north of map
- n – no drinking water

- p – motor bikes prohibited
- r – boat rental
- s – stream, lake or creek water only
- t – tennis
- u – snowmobile trails
- w – open certain off-season weekends
- y – drinking water must be boiled

Map Reference	Park Name	Access	Acres	Tent Spaces	Trailer Spaces	Approximate Fee	Season	Swimming Pool	Other Swimming	Fishing	Boating	Playground	Other	Telephone Number	Mail Address
	STATE PARKS														
G4	Collier Seminole	Fr Naples, 17 mi SE on US 41	6423	130	130	4.00	All year		•		dl	•		813/394-3397	Gen Del, Marco 33937
A4	Fort Clinch	Fr Fernandina Bch, 3 mi N on Hwy A1A	1085	62	62	4.00	All year		• •		dl	•		904/261-4212	2601 AtlanticAve,FernadinaBch
C4	Blue Spring SRA	Fr Deland, 4 mi S on Hwy 17	945		44	4.00	All year		•		dlr	•		904/775-3663	Star Rt 3 Orange City 32763
G3	Florida Caverns	Fr Marianna, 3 mi N on Hwy 167	1784		32	4.00	All year		• •		l	•	g	904/482-3632	2701 Caverns Rd,Marianna32446
B3	Mike Roess Gold Head	Fr Keystone Heights, 6 mi NE on Hwy 21	1481	107	107	4.00	All year		• •		dlr	•		904/473-4701	Rt 1,Box 545,Keystone Hghts
E4	Highlands Hammock	Fr Sebring, 6 mi W on US 27 & 98 and Hwy 634	3800		136	4.00	All year		• •			•		813/385-0011	Rt 1 Box 310, Sebring 33870
D3	Hillsborough River	Fr Zephyrhills, 6 mi SW on US 301	2964	118	118	4.00	All year		•		lr	•	g	813/986-1020	Rt 4 Bx 250L, Zephyrhill33599
E5	Jonathan Dickinson	Fr Stuart, 13 mi S on US 1	B	135	135	4.00	All year		• •		dlr	•	gh	305/546-2771	14800 SE Fed Hwy, Hobe Sound
C2	Manatee Springs	Fr US 19/98 ext in Chiefland, 6 mi W on Hwy 320	2074	100	74	4.00	All year		• •		dlr	•		904/493-4288	Rt 2 Box 362,Chiefland 32626
E3	Myakka River	Fr Sarasota, 17 mi E on Hwy 72	B	76	76	4.00	All year		•		lr	•		813/924-1027	Rt 1 Box 72, Sarasota 33577

Map Reference	Park Name	Access	Acres	Tent Spaces	Trailer Spaces	Approximate Fee	Season	Other Swimming / Swimming Pool	Fishing	Boating	Playground	Other	Telephone Number	Mail Address
B3	O'Leno	Fr Lake City, 20 mi S on US 41	5898		64	4.00	All year	• •		dlr	•		904/454-1853	Rt 2 Bx 307, High Spgs 32643
H2	St Andrews SRA	Fr Panama City Bch, 3 mi E on Hwy 392	1062		179	4.00	All year	• •		dlr	•		904/234-2522	4415 Thomas Dr,PanamaCty32407
A2	Suwannee River	Fr Madison, 14 mi E on US 90	1831	32	32	4.00	All year	•		l	•		904/362-2746	Rt 8 Bx 297, Live Oak 32060
C4	Tomoka	Fr Ormond Bch, 2 mi N on N Beach St	914	100	100	4.00	All year	•		dlr	•		904/677-3931	Bx 695, Ormand Bch 32074
C4	Flagler Beach SRA	Fr Flagler Beach, 2 mi S on US A1A	145	34	34	4.00	All year	•		l	•		904/439-2474	Bx 717, Flagler Bch 32036
G3	Torreya	Fr Bristol, 13 mi NE on Hwy 12	1063	35	35	4.00	All year	•			•		904/643-2674	Star Rt,Bristol 32321
G3	Three Rivers SRA	Fr Sneads, 1 mi N on US 90	834	65	65	4.00	All year	•		dl	•		904/593-6565	Rt 1 Box 15-A, Sneads 32460
H5	Pennekamp Coral Reef	Fr Key Largo, N on US 1	2289		47	5.00	All year	• •		dlr	•		305/451-1202	PO Box 487, Key Largo 33037
C3	Lake Griffin SRA	Fr Leesburg, 2 mi N on US 27-441, at Fruitland Pk	415	47	47	4.00	All year	•		dlr	•		904/787-7402	Box 608,Fruitland Pk 32731
H4	Bahia Honda SRA	Fr Marathon, 12 mi S on US 1 to Bahia Honda Key	276		69	5.00	All year	• •		dlr	•		305/872-2681	R 1 Bx 782, Big Pine Key33043
B4	Anastasia SRA	At St Augustine Beach, on Hwy A1A	888		139	4.00	All year	• •		l	•		904/829-2668	Bx 167, St Augustine 32084
G3	Falling Waters SRA	Fr Chipley, 3 mi S on Hwy 77A	154	24	24	4.00	All year	•			•		904/638-4030	Rt 5 Box 660, Chipley 32428
F3	Koreshan SRA	Fr Fort Myers, 13 mi S on US 41, at Estero	156	60	60	4.00	All year	•		l	•		813/992-2771	PO Box 7, Estero 33928
A4	Little Talbot	Fr Jacksonville, 17 mi NE on Hwys 105 & A1A	2500	40	59	4.00	5/15-10/1**	• •		l	•		904/251-3231	PO Box 246, Ft George 32226
G2	Fred Gannon Rocky Bayou	Fr Niceville, 3 mi E on Hwy 20	632	50	50	4.00	All year	•		dl	•		904/897-3222	PO Box 597, Niceville 32578
H2	Grayton Beach SRA	Fr Ft Walton Bch, S on US 98 to Hwy 30A	356	36	36	4.00	All year	• •		l	•		904/231-4210	Box 25,Santa Rosa Bch 32458
F5	Pahokee SRA	In Pahokee on US 441	30	40	40	4.00	All year	• •		dl	•		305/924-7832	Drawer 719, Pahokee 33476
B1	Ochlockonee River	Fr Sopchoppy, 4 mi S on Hwy 319	392	30	30	4.00	All year	•		dl	•		904/962-2771	PO Box 5, Sopchoppy 32358
H3	T H Stone Memorial	Fr Port St Joe, 10 mi S on Hwys 98 & 30	2516	115	115	4.00	All year	• •		dlr	•		904/227-1327	Box 909, Port St Joe, 32456
G2	Basin Bayou SRA	Fr Freeport, 7 mi W on Hwy 20	287	20	20	4.00	All year	•		l	•		904/835-2633	Rt 1 Box 68-V,Freeport 32439
B4	Faver-Dykes	Fr St Augustine, 15 mi S to US 1-I-95 jct; E to Park Rd	752	30	30	4.00	All year	•		dl	•		904/794-0997	Rt 4 Box 213 J-1,St Aug 32084
G2	Blackwater River	Fr Milton, 15 mi E on US 90, 3 mi N of Harold	360	18	18	4.00	All year	•		l	•		904/623-2363	Rt 1 Bx 47-C,Holt 32564
H3	Dead Lakes	Fr Wewahitchka, 4 mi N on Hwy 71, E on park road	41	30	30	4.00	All year	•		l	•		904/639-2702	PO Box 989,Wewahitchka 32465
H4	Long Key SRA	At Long Key on US 1	849	60	60	5.00	All year	•		l	•		305/664-4815	Box 776, Long Key 33001
E3	Oscar Sherer SRA	Fr Osprey, 2 mi S on US 41	462	104	104	4.00	All year	• •		r	•		813/966-3154	Bx 398 S Trail, Osprey 33559
D5	Sebastian Inlet SRA	At Sebastian on US 1	578	90	90	4.00	All year	• •		dl	•		305/589-3754	PO Box 728, Wabasso 32970
G5	Chekika SRA	Fr Homestead, 11 mi NW, SW 237th St & Grossman Dr	640	30	20	5.00	All year	• •			•		305/253-0950	Box 1313, Homestead 33030
	South Fla Water Mgmt Dis	South Fla Water Mgmt Dist												PO Box V, W Palm Beach 33402
E4	Okee-Tantie Rec Area	Fr Okeechobee, 3 mi S on US 441 to Hwy 78, 4-1/2 mi W	130	250	215	5.50	All year				p		813/763-2622	Rt 4 Box 644 Okeechobee 33472
D4	Southport Pk	Fr Kissimmee, SW on US 17/92, 7 mi S on rd 531, 6 mi E on Southport Rd	30	41	41	5.50	All year	•		dlr	•	p	305/348-5822	2001 Southpt, Kissimmee 32741
	STATE FORESTS													
H2	Pine Log	Fr Ebro, 1 mi S on Hwy 79	6911		20	None	All year	• •		l		p		715 W 15th,Panama City 32401
B1	Newport Fire Tower	In Newport, on US 98, on St Marks River	10	13	13	4.16	All year			l		p		Tallahassee
G4	Copeland Fire Tower	Fr jct US 41 & Hwy 29, 3 mi N on Hwy 29	7	9	9	4.16	All year	•				p		Tice
E5	Donald McDonald Pk	Fr Vero Bch, 15 mi N, 1 mi W on Co 505	37	30	30	4.16	All year			dl	•	p		Okeechobee
G2	Blackwater River	Fr jct Hwys 191 & 4, 1 mi E, 1 mi N on paved rd	B	58	58	4.16	All year	• •		d		hp	904/957-4111	Rt 1 Bx 77, Milton 32570
D3	Withlacoochee	Fr Brooksville, approx 11 mi N on US 98, 4 mi N on Croom Rd	B	120	120	4.16	All year	•		l			904/796-4958	7255 US 41N, Brooksville 33512
C4	Orange City Fire Tower	Fr Orange City, 1 mi N on US 17/92	10	14	14	4.16	All year					p		Bunnell
	NATIONAL PARKS													
	Everglades	(For additional CGs, see 'Backpack or Boat Access Areas')	B										305/247-6211	PO Box 279 Homestead 33030
G5	Long Pine Key	Fr Homestead, 16 mi SW on Hwy 27		107	107	F3.00	All year							Homestead 33030
H4	Flamingo	Fr Homestead, 50 mi SW on Hwy 27		308	170	F3.00	All year	o		dlr				Flamingo 33030
	Biscayne													
	NATIONAL MONUMENTS													
	Ft Jefferson NM													
	NATIONAL SEASHORES													
	Gulf Islands		B										904/932-3192	PO Box 100 Gulf Breeze 32561
H1	Fort Pickens CG	Fr Pensacola, E on US 98, S on Hwy 399		84	81	F4.00	All year	• •					904/932-5018	Gulf Breeze 32561
	NATIONAL FORESTS													
	Apalichicola NF													
B1	Whitehead Lake	Fr Bristol, 11.4 mi E on Hwy 20, 3.2 mi S on Hwy 65, 15.1 mi SE on Hwy 67, 3.2 mi E on FR 111	2	4	2	None	All year			•				Bristol
B1	Hitchcock Lake	Fr Bristol, 11.4 mi E on Hwy 20, 3.2 mi S on Hwy 65, 22.8 mi SE on Hwy 67, 1.5 mi E on FR 125B	3	6	4	None	All year			dl				Bristol
H3	Wright Lake	Fr Bristol, 12.8 mi S on Hwy 12, 22 mi S on Hwy 379, 2 mi S on Hwy 65, 2 mi W on FR 101	8	21	6	None	All year	•		dl				Bristol
H3	Hickory Landing	Fr Bristol, 12.8 mi S on Hwy 12, 22 mi S on Hwy 379, 2 mi S on Hwy 65, 1.8 mi SW on FR 101	2	6		None	All year	1		dl				Bristol
H3	Cotton Landing	Fr Bristol, 12 mi S on Hwy 12, 16.2 mi S on Hwy 379, 2.8 mi SW on FR 123, .7 mi E on FR 123B	7	6	6	None	All year	•		dl				Bristol
H3	Camel Lake	Fr Bristol, 12.1 mi S on Hwy 12, 2 mi E on FR 105	4	6	5	None	All year	•		dl				Bristol
B1	Buckhorn	Fr Crawfordv'le, 6.4 mi N on US 319, 12 mi NW on Hwy 267, 2 mi S on FR 350	8	10		None	11/1-1/31					n		Crawfordville
B1	Silver Lake	Fr Tallahassee, 4.1 mi W on US 90, 5.2 mi SW on Hwy 20, 3 mi S on Co 260	7	15	30	3.00	All year	• •						Tallahassee
B1	Mack Landing	Fr Sopchoppy, 10.1 mi W on Hwy 375, .9 mi W on FR 375D	3	3	2	None	All year	• •		dl				Sopchoppy
	Osceola NF													
B3	Ocean Pond	Fr Lake City, 13.7 mi E on US 90, 2.2 mi N on FR 250A, .6 mi W on Hwy 263	25	12	39	2.00	All year	• •		dl				Lake City
	Ocala NF													
C4	Juniper Springs	Fr Ocala, 28 mi E on Hwy 40	47	79	79	2.00	All year	• 2		dr				Ocala
C4	Mill Dam	Fr Ocala, 19 mi E on Hwy 40, 1.3 mi N on FR 79	4	10	3	2.00	All year	• •		dlr				Ocala
C4	Hopkins Prairie	Fr Ocala, 24.2 mi E on Hwy 40, 6.3 mi N on FR 88, 4.6 mi E on FR 86, .6 mi N on FR 51	5	6		None	All year							Ocala
C3	Lake Eaton	Fr Silver Spgs, 17.2 mi E on Hwy 40, 4.2 mi N on Co 314A, .4 mi E on FR 79A, 1 mi N on FR 96	2	6	6	None	All year			d				Silver Spgs
C4	Salt Springs	Fr Ocala, 10.9 mi E on Hwy 40, 18.4 mi NE on Hwy 314, .8 mi N on Hwy 19	86	455	402	5.50	All year	• •		dlr				Ocala
C3	Johnson Field	Fr Palatka, 17.2 mi SW on Hwy 19, .3 mi W on FR 77	5	15	3	2.00	All year	1		dl				Palatka
C3	Grassy Pond	Fr Ocala, 11 mi E on Hwy 40, 19.8 mi NE on Hwy 314, 5.2 mi NW on Hwy 316, .6 mi N on FR 88E	2	6		None	All year							Ocala
C3	Lake Delancy	Fr Ocala, 11 mi E on Hwy 40, 19.8 mi NE on Hwy 314, 5.7 mi N on Hwy 19, 2 mi NW on FR 75	4			None	All year	•		dlr				Ocala
C3	Fore Lake	Fr Ocala, 11 mi E on Hwy 40, 6 mi NE on Hwy 314	10	20	7	2.00	All year	•		dl				Ocala
C4	Lake Dorr	Fr Unatilla, 5.6 mi N on Hwy 19	10	15	15	2.00	All year	• •		dl				Unatilla
C4	Clearwater Lake	Fr Umatilla, 2.6 mi W on Hwy 19, 6.2 mi E on Hwy 42	8	7	35	3.00	All year	• •		dl				Umatilla
C4	Big Scrub	Fr Altoona, 6.2 mi N on Hwy 19, 7 mi W on FR 73	9	33	33	None	All year	3		d		n		Altoona
C4	Alexander Springs	Fr Umatilla, 7.8 mi N on Hwy 19, 5.2 mi NE on Hwy 445	30	67	67	3.00	All year	• •		dlr				Umatilla
	CORPS OF ENGINEERS													
	Lake Seminole	(See Georgia for additional CGS)												
G3	East Bank Area	Fr Chattahoochee, 2 mi N on Jim Woodruff Dam Rd	158	25	10	3.00	All year	o		dl	g		912/662-2814	Bx 96,Chattahoochee 32324
G3	River Junction	Fr Chattahoochee, 4 mi No on Jim Woodruff Dam Rd	160	11	11	3.00	All year			dl	g		912/662-2814	Bx 96,Chattahoochee 32324
G3	Neal's Landing	Fr Donalsonville Ga, 12 mi W	121	15	15	3.00	All year	•		l			912/662-2865	Bx 96, Chattahoochee, 32324
	Okeechobee Lake													
E5	St Lucie Lock & Dam	Fr Stuart, 6 mi S on Hwy 76	15	10	10	None	All year	•		l			305/287-2665	Bx 1327, Clewiston, 33440
F4	Ortona Lock	Fr La Belle, 8 mi S on Hwy 78	5	10	10	None	All year	•		l			813/675-0616	Bx 1327, Clewiston, 33440
F4	W P Franklin Lock & Dam	Fr Jct of Hwys 31 & 78, 5 mi E on Hwy 78	2	12	S12	None	All year	•		l		p	813/694-2582	Box 1327, Clewiston, 33440

Georgia

Major Events

See state map, page 25

Antiques at the Crossroads, early Feb., Perry. The National Guard Armory is the site for this show where 30 dealers sell items such as furniture, cut glass, silver, and jewelry. Admission. 912/987-1234.

Hawkinsville Harness Festival, mid-Mar., Hawkinsville. Harness racing, arts and crafts, a beauty pageant, and musical entertainment are all part of the festivities. Admission. 912/783-1717.

St. Patrick's Day Festival, Mar. 17, Savannah. This citywide celebration features Irish food and entertainment and a 500-float parade. Free. 912/233-3067.

Tour of Homes and Gardens, late Mar., St. Simons Island. Contemporary homes, slave cabins, and churches may be viewed during this all-day driving tour. Admission. 912/638-2274.

Tour of Homes and Gardens, late Mar., Savannah. Thirty-three homes dating from the mid- to late 19th century may be toured in Savannah's Historic District. Reservations are advised, and dinner is available. Admission. 912/234-8054.

Georgia Steam and Gas Show, early Apr., Tifton. The Georgia Agrirama, home of the State Museum of Agriculture, hosts this display of tractors and antique steam engines. Admission. 912/386-3344.

Dogwood Festival, early Apr., Atlanta. Georgia's state capital celebrates spring with dancing, music, crafts demonstrations, and other events. A queen presides over the parade and party festivities. Free. 404/521-0845.

Masters Golf Tournament, early Apr., Augusta. The best in the United States Professional Golf Association tee off here to compete for this prestigious title. Gallery admission. 404/738-7761.

Easter Sunrise Service, Easter, Pine Mountain. This nondenominational service is conducted as the sun rises over Robin Lake Beach in Callaway Gardens. Easter brunch is available afterwards at the Callaway Gardens Inn. Service: Free. Brunch: Admission. 404/663-2281.

Rose Festival, late Apr., Thomasville. In addition to the rose displays, some of the activities scheduled are a rose-patch country fair, plantation tours, a golf tournament, and a children's rosebud parade. Admission is charged for several events. 912/226-9600.

"Night in Old Savannah," late Apr., Savannah. This international festival features ethnic foods, costumes, dances, and music from all over the world. Admission. 912/233-6651.

Georgia Mountain Jubilee, late Apr. to early May, Gainesville. The Georgia Mountain Center hosts paratroopers, stunt men, and live bands at this festival. Free. 404/534-1100.

Prater's Mill Festival, early May, Dalton. An arts and crafts show is held in the atmosphere of an 1890s country fair at Prater's Mill. Cloggers and bluegrass musicians provide the entertainment. Admission. 404/278-7373.

Piedmont Park Arts Festival, mid-May, Atlanta. Children's activities and the visual and performing arts are highlighted. On display are crafts by approximately 175 artists, with an exhibition by and for the handicapped. Free. 404/885-1125.

Winterville Marigold Festival, late June, Winterville. Thousands of blooming marigolds are the highlight of the festival which also offers a country breakfast, a footrace, a parade, crafts, clogging, and live entertainment. Free. 404/742-8600.

Peachtree Road Race, July 4, Atlanta. Twenty-five thousand runners compete in one of the largest footraces in the country on July 4th. Winners' trophies are original stained-glass artworks. Prior to the race is a runner's film festival and exposition. Free. 404/231-9064.

Masters Water Ski Tournament, early to mid-July, Pine Mountain. Robin Lake at Callaway Gardens is the setting for this international event in waterskiing. Admission to lake area. Tournament: Free. 404/663-2281.

Georgia Mountain Fair, early to mid-Aug., Hiawassee. Located in an authentically re-created mountain town of the 1800s, this fair features demonstrations in mountain cookery and moonshine making; live entertainment; and a clogger's convention. Admission. 404/896-2256.

Mountain "Do" Festival, late Aug., Buford. The Lake Lanier Islands are the setting for this country-oriented festival with music, dancing, crafts, and lots of food. Free (except food). 404/945-6701.

1896 County Fair, early Sept., Tifton. The Georgia Agrirama hosts this fair with old-time entertainment. Exhibitions include baked and canned goods, and different types of contests for adults and children are held. Admission. 912/386-3344.

Power's Crossroads Fair, early Sept., Newnan. An arts and crafts festival with 300 exhibitors is the focus of this event. Music and dancing are held on an 18th-century plantation southwest of Newnan via St. 34. Admission. 404/253-2011.

Oktoberfest, weekends from mid-Sept. to early Oct., Helen. This German festival features plenty of food, beer, and dancing. Admission. 404/878-2521.

Yellow Daisy Festival, mid-Sept., Stone Mountain. A rare species of yellow daisy that grows here at Stone Mountain Park is the basis for a celebration that includes a flower show, arts and crafts, field events, and the state fiddling championship. Admission. 404/469-9831.

National Pecan Festival, mid-Sept., Albany. Pecans are honored at this festival with a pecan-cooking sweepstakes, the "Arts in a Nutshell" crafts show, and the 10,000-meter Nut Run. Free. 912/883-6900.

Heritage Holidays Festival, early to mid-Oct., Rome. A celebration of Rome's heritage, the festival offers an arts and crafts show, live entertainment, and a re-enactment of one man's 67-mile ride to warn the townspeople of oncoming Union troops during the Civil War. Admission is charged for several events. 404/295-5576.

Prater's Mill Country Fair, mid-Oct., Dalton. Over 180 artists display arts and crafts at this 19th-century mill. Live entertainment is also featured. Admission. 404/278-7373.

Gold Rush Days, mid-Oct., Dahlonega. The gold rush that took place here in 1828 is reenacted during this festival. The town square is the location for dancing, children's wagon races, a greased pig race, and many craft displays. Free. 404/864-2531.

Scottish Festival and Highland Games, mid-Oct., Stone Mountain. Stone Mountain Park is the setting for this celebration featuring highland games and a bagpipe competition. Food may be purchased from a number of booths. Admission. 404/469-9831.

Fair of 1850, late Oct. to early Nov., Lumpkin. In the re-created 1850s village of Westville, demonstrations of fall activities are performed. Cane grinding, syrup making, open-hearth cooking and a mule-powered cotton gin may be observed. Admission. 912/838-6310.

Cane-Grinding Parties, late Nov. to early Dec., Tifton. The Georgia Agrirama hosts these special evenings of family fun. Candy pulling, cane grinding, syrup making, wagon rides, and musical entertainment are all part of the festivities. Admission. 912/386-3344.

Yuletide Season, mid- to late Dec., Lumpkin. This Christmas celebration in the restored 1850s village of Westville features carollers, a Yule log ceremony, and the traditional German custom of lighting the tree. Admission. 912/838-6310.

Christmas Activities and Living Nativity Pageant, mid- to late Dec., Stone Mountain. Christmas is celebrated throughout the park with special concerts, children's story hours, and a re-creation of the first Christmas performed nightly on the lawn. Admission. 404/469-9831.

Georgia Destinations

ALBANY, 73,934, F-2. **Chehaw Wild Animal Park,** in Chehaw Park on St. 91, is a 100-acre wildlife preserve for buffalo, fox, coyote, deer, and elephants. There are protected trails and elevated walkways for visitors. Year-round, daily, 9 A.M. to 6 P.M. Free. 912/432-2371. **Thronateeska Heritage Museum,** 100 Roosevelt Rd., has the McIntosh collection of Indian arrowheads and artifacts and a model railroad exhibit. Adjacent **Heritage Plaza** includes an 1857 train depot; the frame *Jerrad House* built in the mid-1800s; and the *Hilman Kitchen,* one of the finest examples of 19th-century kitchen architecture. Year-round, Tues.-Sun., 2 to 5 P.M. Free. 912/432-6955. **Radium Springs,** St. 3, offers swimming at Georgia's largest natural springs, which pump 70,000 gallons per minute at 68°F. June-Aug., daily, 10 A.M. to 6 P.M. Adults $1.75; children under 10, $1.25. 912/883-7072.

ANDERSONVILLE NATIONAL HISTORIC SITE, E-2. Andersonville, or Camp Sumter as it was known officially, was the largest of several Confederate military prisons established during the Civil War. Today the 470-acre **Andersonville National Historic Site** consists of the prison site and *Andersonville National Cemetery,* where funerals for U.S. military veterans are still held. Historical information is available at the Visitors Center; and there are commemorative monuments erected by various states around the Visitors Center. Daily, June-Aug., 8:30 A.M. to 7 P.M.; other months, 8:30 A.M. to 5 P.M. Free. 912/924-0343.

ATHENS, 42,549, B-3. "Athens of Old" tours begin at 280 E. Dougherty St. in an 1820 Federal-style building believed to be the oldest surviving residence in Athens. Known as the **Church-Waddell-Brumby House,** the fully restored structure was the home of two former presidents of the University of Georgia and now serves as the Athens Welcome Center. The do-it-yourself tours, researched by the **Athens-Clarke Heritage Foundation,** showcase over 50 of the city's historic sites, including the University of Georgia. Year-round, Mon.-Sat., 9 A.M. to 5 P.M.; Sun., 2 to 5 P.M. Free. 404/546-1805. The **Georgia Museum of Art,** on the University of Georgia campus, houses 5,000 paintings and prints in its permanent collections and traveling exhibits that are changed frequently. Sept.-July, Mon.-Fri., 8 A.M. to 5 P.M.; Sat., 8 A.M. to noon. Free. 404/542-3254. In the **University of Georgia Chapel** hangs the 135-year-old "Interior of St. Peter's," a 17-by-23½-foot painting by American artist George Cooke, of St. Peter's Cathedral in Rome. Year-round, Mon.-Fri., 8 A.M. to 4:30 P.M. Free. The **University of Georgia Botanical Garden,** 1000 W. Whitehall Rd., conserves native plants of the Georgia Piedmont and small populations of wildlife on nearly 300 acres. Seven color-coded trails wind through the garden for a total of five miles. Year-round, daily, 8:30 A.M. to sunset. Free. 404/542-1244. **Founders Memorial Garden and Museum House,** 325 S. Lumpkin St., is the state headquarters of the Garden Club of Georgia. The 1847 brick house was built as a residence for University of Georgia professors and is filled with 18th- and 19th-century antiques. The 2½-acre series of gardens surrounding the house include a formal boxwood garden, two courtyards, and an arboretum. Year-round, Mon.-Fri., 9 A.M. to noon, 1 to 4 P.M. Free. 404/542-3631. The **Taylor-Grady House,** 634 Prince Ave., was built by Gen. Robert Taylor in 1845 and later became the residence of *Atlanta Constitution* editor Henry W. Grady. Year-round, Mon., Wed., Fri., 10 A.M. to 2 P.M.; Sun., 2 to 5 P.M. Admission $1. 404/549-8688. **Fire Station Number Two,** 489 Prince Ave., was built in 1901 as a fire station. The two-story brick building, in the shape of a truncated triangle, is now a house museum and headquarters of the Athens-Clarke Heritage Foundation. Year-round, Mon.-Fri., 9 A.M. to 4 P.M. Free. 404/543-8930. The **Double-Barreled Cannon,** corner of Hancock and College Aves., is a unique piece of artillery. John Gilleland devised it in 1863 to help the war effort but failed to get the two barrels to fire simultaneously. The **Tree That Owns Itself,** corner of Finley and Dearing Sts., is a white oak tree that was deeded a plot of land, eight feet in radius from its trunk, by its former owner, Col. William H. Jackson, a professor at the University of Georgia.

ATLANTA, 425,022, C-2. Transportation has played a major role in Atlanta's history. The site of a Creek Indian settlement called Standing Peachtree was designated the southern terminus of the Western & Atlantic Railroad in 1837; after the railroad was completed in 1845, its major nexus was incorporated as the city of Atlanta—a name coined from that of the railroad. In the Civil War, about 400 of Atlanta's 4,500 houses and commercial buildings were destroyed. In 1866, Atlanta became the sectional headquarters for federal reconstruction, and the wrecked railroads were subsequently repaired and expanded. At a state constitutional convention held by the reconstruction government in 1867, Atlanta representatives proposed that the state capital be moved from the small town of Milledgeville to their rapidly growing city. The proposal was accepted in 1868 and confirmed by statewide vote in 1877. Atlanta remains both the capital of Georgia and the center of transportation for the southeastern United States, with the huge new transfer hub at Hartsfield Atlanta International Airport.

GOVERNMENT BUILDINGS: The Georgia State Capitol, Capitol Square, was completed in 1889, its dome sheeted with gold leaf mined around Dahlonega in the northeast Georgia mountains. In addition to state offices, the Capitol houses the *Georgia State Museum of Science and Industry;* the *Hall of Flags;* and the *Hall of Fame,* which has busts of famous Georgians and an oil portrait of the late Dr. Martin Luther King, Jr. Year-round, Mon.-Fri., 8 A.M. to 5 P.M. Free. 404/656-2884. The **Governor's Mansion,** 319 W. Paces Ferry Rd. NW, is Greek Revival in style and furnished with a fine collection of Federal-period antiques. Tours: Year-round, Tues., Wed., Thurs., 10 to 11:45 A.M. Free. 404/261-1776.

HISTORIC BUILDINGS AND PLACES: Atlanta Historical Society, 3099 Andrews Dr. NW has three adjoining major structures—McElreath Hall, Swan House, and Tullie Smith House. *McElreath Hall* houses the administrative offices, a museum, and the *Margaret Mitchell Memorial Library.* In 1966, the historical society purchased *Swan House,* a 1928 Anglo-Palladian-style mansion furnished with 18th-century and period antiques. *Tullie Smith House,* built about 1840, exemplifies mid-19th-century "plantation plain" architecture and displays the simple furniture and crafts of its original owner, a yeoman farmer. Year-round, Tues.-Sat., 10:30 A.M. to 4:30 P.M.; Sun., 2 to 4:30 P.M. Margaret Mitchell Memorial Library: Year-round, Mon.-Fri., 9 A.M. to 5 P.M. McElreath House and grounds: Free. Swan and Tullie Smith houses (each): Adults $2, students $1. Both houses: Adults $3, students $1.75; children under 6, free. 404/261-1837. **Fort Peachtree,** 2630 Ridgewood Rd. NW, was built as a defense against the Indians during the War of 1812 and later became an Indian trading post. The old log cabin has been reconstructed and has ancient Indian pottery, arrowheads, and other historical artifacts. Year-round, Mon.-Fri., 10 A.M. to 4 P.M. Free. 404/355-8229. **Wren's Nest,** 1050 Gordon St. SW, was the home from 1880 to 1908 of Joel Chandler Harris, author of the Uncle Remus stories. It contains the original furniture and the mailbox where wrens nested for many years, giving the house its name. Year-round, Mon.-Sat., 9:30 A.M. to 5 P.M.; Sun., 2 to 5 P.M. Adults $2, teenagers $1, children 50¢. 404/753-8535.

MUSEUMS AND MEMORIALS: The **Atlanta Memorial Arts Center,** 1280 Peachtree St. NE, stands as a memorial to the 122 members of the Atlanta Arts Alliance who died in a 1962 plane crash outside Paris. It is the home of the *Atlanta Symphony Orchestra,* the *Alliance Theatre,* the *Children's Theatre,* the *Atlanta College of Art,* and the *High Museum of Art.* The museum has permanent collections of 19th- and 20th-century European paintings, prints and decorative arts; a junior gallery for chil-

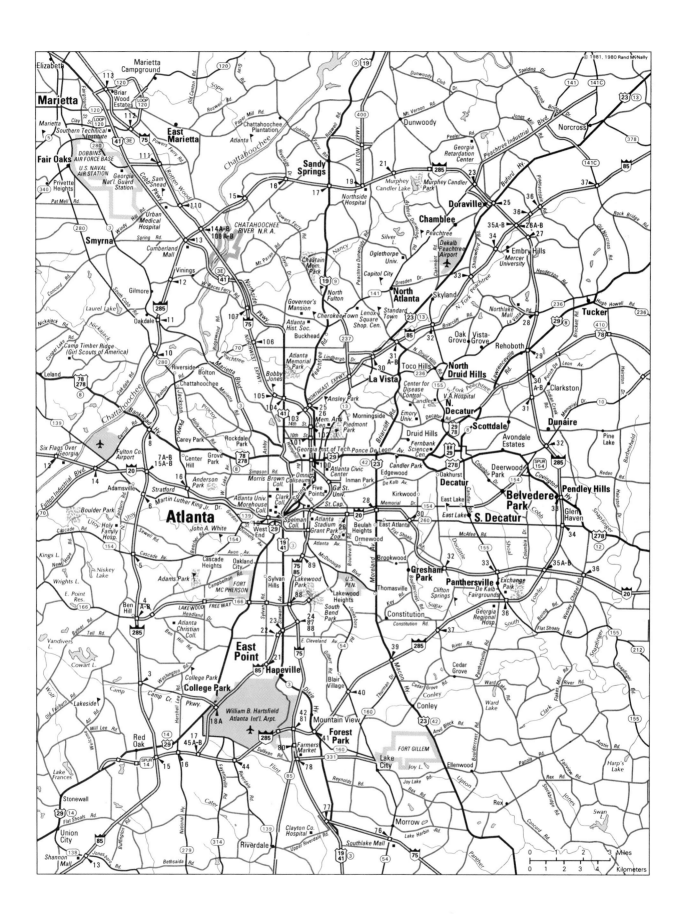

dren; and visiting exhibits. Year-round, Tues.-Sat., 10 A.M. to 5 P.M.; Sun., noon to 5 P.M. Free. 404/892-3600. **Fernbank Science Center,** 156 Heaton Park Dr., has six major and many smaller resource areas devoted to scientific awareness and education. Among these are a forest with walking trails, an experimental garden, and a Braille-marked trail; a science reference library; an observatory with a 36-inch reflecting telescope; and an electron microscope laboratory. It also has the third largest planetarium in the United States. Planetarium shows: Year-round, Tues.-Fri., 8 P.M.; Sat., 11 A.M. and 3 P.M.; Sun., 3 P.M. Adults $1.50; students 75¢; children under 6, not admitted. Admission to other areas is free. Exhibit Center: Year-round, Tues.-Fri., 8:30 A.M. to 10 P.M.; Sat., Mon., 8:30 A.M. to 5 P.M.; Sun., 1:30 to 5 P.M. Nature Trail: Year-round, Mon.-Fri., 2 to 5 P.M.; Sat., 10 A.M. to 5 P.M. 404/378-4311. **Martin Luther King, Jr. Historic District,** 449 Auburn Ave. NE, includes the civil rights leader's birthplace and grave and his pastorate, Ebenezer Baptist Church. Information Center: Year-round, Mon.-Fri., 9:30 A.M. to 5:30 P.M.; Sat.-Sun., 9:30 A.M. Tours: Mon.-Sat., 10 A.M. to 4 P.M. Adults $1, children 50¢. 404/524-1956. **Toy Museum of Atlanta,** 2800 Peachtree Rd. NE, has an international collection of some 100,000 toys dating from the mid-1800s to the present. Year-round, Mon.-Sat., 10 A.M. to 5 P.M.; Sun., 2 to 5 P.M. Adults $2; children 6-12, $1.50; under 6, free. 404/266-8697.

PARKS AND ZOO: Atlanta Botanical Garden, Piedmont Rd. at the Prado NE, is a 5-acre-tract of Japanese, rose, and vegetable gardens with nature trails; a conservatory; and Visitors Center, all in Piedmont Park. Year-round, Mon.-Fri., 9 A.M. to 4 P.M.; Sat., 9 A.M. to noon; Sun., 1 to 4 P.M. Free. 404/876-5858. **Atlanta Zoo,** Georgia and Cherokee Aves. SE, has one of the world's largest reptile collections, and it has big cats, monkeys, apes, elephants, other animals, and a petting zoo for children. Year-round, daily, 10 A.M. to 5 P.M. Adults $2; children 4-11, $1; under 4, free. 404/658-7059. **Stone Mountain Park,** St. 78, surrounds the world's largest granite mass, which has carved on its steep, north side figures of Gen. Robert E. Lee, Gen. Stonewall Jackson, and Confederate Pres. Jefferson Davis. One of the sculptors was Gutzon Borglum, also sculptor of the four U.S. presidents carved on Mt. Rushmore in South Dakota. The 3,200-acre park features a Swiss skylift to the top of the 825-foot-high mountain, a steam locomotive ride around the base of the mountain, a game and wildlife ranch, an antebellum plantation, hiking trails, picnic areas, tennis courts, roller skating, a beach, golf course, and lodging accommodations. Daily, June-Aug., 10 A.M. to 9 P.M.; Sept.-May, 10 A.M. to 5:30 P.M. Park entrance: $2.50 per car, separate fees for other attractions. 404/469-9831.

SHOPPING: Atlanta State Farmer's Mar-

ket, 16 Forest Pkwy., Forest Park, serves as a retail outlet for Georgia farmers and a distribution center for wholesalers. With 146 acres of fresh produce, it is one of the largest farmers' markets in the world. Always open. 404/366-6910.

SPORTS: Atlanta-Fulton County Stadium, 521 Capitol Ave. SW, is the home of the Atlanta Braves baseball team (404/577-9100), the Atlanta Falcons football team (404/588-1111), and the Atlanta Chiefs soccer team (404/577-5425). The **Omni Coliseum,** 100 Techwood Dr. NW, is the site of the Atlanta Hawks basketball team home games (404/681-2100).

THEME PARK: Six Flags Over Georgia, west of Atlanta on Int. 20 at Six Flags Dr., offers dozens of rides and shows in a 331-acre family entertainment park. Featured attractions are the first triple roller coaster, a whitewater raft ride, and a 225-foot parachute jump ride. Mid-May-Labor Day, daily, 10 A.M. to 10 P.M.; Sept.-Oct., early Mar.-mid-May, Sat., 10 A.M. to 10 P.M.; Sun., 10 A.M. to 6 P.M.; Nov., Sat.-Sun., 10 A.M. to 6 P.M. Admission $11.50; children under 2, free. Admission covers all rides and shows. 404/948-9290.

AUGUSTA, 47,532, C-5. Founded by James Oglethorpe in 1736, Augusta is Georgia's second oldest city and intermittently, between 1783 and 1795, served as the state capital. At **St. Paul's Episcopal Church,** 605 Reynolds St., a Celtic cross marks the site of Fort Augusta, Oglethorpe's original settlement. The church is the fourth one built on the site; its Baptismal Fount dates from 1750, when the first church was established.

HISTORIC SITES: Signer's Monument, Greene St. at Monument St., honors Georgia's signers of the Declaration of Independence: Lyman Hall, George Walton, and Button Gwinnett. Hall and Walton are buried beneath the 50-foot obelisk, which was dedicated July 4, 1848. **Confederate Monument,** 7th and 8th Sts. at Broad St., is a 76-foot shaft of Carrara marble carved with life-size figures of Gen. Robert E. Lee, Gen. Stonewall Jackson, and two native Georgian commanders; at the top of the shaft is a statue of a Confederate private. An obelisk chimney, 176 feet tall, is all that remains of the **Confederate Powder Works,** 1717 Goodrich St., which once manufactured more than two million pounds of gunpowder. The chimney stands in front of the **Sibley Mill,** built in 1880, and beside the **Augusta Canal,** built in 1847. **Old Slave Market Column,** 5th St. at Broad St., is the only column remaining from the Old Augusta Market Place. The **Old Richmond Academy Building,** 504 Telfair St., was built in 1802 as a new headquarters for the first boys' public high school in the country. It houses the *Augusta Museum,* which features history, art, military, archaeology, and natural science collections. Year-round, Tues.-Sat., 10 A.M., to 5 P.M.; Sun., 2 to 5 P.M. Free. 404/722-8454.

HISTORIC HOMES: Meadow Garden, 1320 Nelson St., built from 1792 to 1804, was the home of George Walton, a signer of the Declaration of Independence and a Georgia governor. Year-round, Tues.-Sat., 10 A.M. to 4 P.M. Adults $1, children 50¢. 404/724-4174. The **Nicholas Ware Mansion,** 506 Telfair St., is better known as "Ware's Folly," because Mr. Ware spent what was considered the exorbitant sum of $40,000 to construct it in 1818. The late-Federal-style structure is noted for its three-tiered porch, horseshoe staircase outside, and four-story spiral staircase inside. It now houses the *Gertrude Herbert Memorial Institute of Art.* Year-round, Tues.-Fri., 10 A.M. to noon, 1 to 4 P.M.; Sat., 4 to 6 P.M. Free. 404/722-5495. The **Woodrow Wilson Home,** 7th and Telfair Sts., was built as a manse for the First Presbyterian Church in 1860, while Woodrow Wilson's father was the church's minister. President Wilson spent his boyhood here. Year-round, Mon.-Fri., 9 A.M. to 5 P.M. Admission $5. 404/722-4556. **Augusta Heritage Trust,** 629 Greene St., has free brochures that map walking tours of historic sites in Augusta. Year-round, Mon.-Fri., 9 A.M. to 4:30 P.M. 404/724-2324.

BAXLEY, 3,586, E-5. The **Edwin I. Hatch Visitors Center,** U.S. 1, illustrates nuclear power with animated exhibits, films, and special effects. Year-round, Mon.-Fri., 9 A.M. to 5 P.M.; Sun., 1 to 5 P.M. Free. 912/367-3668.

BLAIRSVILLE, 530, A-3. **Brasstown Bald** (4,784 ft.), St. 66, is the highest mountain in Georgia. The Visitors Center at the top offers a commanding view of *Chattahoochee National Forest.* Take a minibus from the parking lot or climb the 930-yard trail. May-Oct., daily, 10 A.M. to 5:30 P.M.; mid-Mar.-Apr., Nov., Sat.-Sun., 10 A.M. to 5:30 P.M. Free. 404/896-2556. **Richard B. Russell Scenic Highway** (designated St. 348), off St. 66, goes through the Chattahoochee National Forest between Neel's Gap and Helen, offering one of the most beautiful mountain drives in Georgia.

BLAKELY, 5,880, F-1. On the courthouse square is claimed to be the last remaining Confederate flagpole still standing. **Kolomoki Mounds State Park,** north of Blakely, preserves an area in which are located seven Indian mounds dating from the 12th and 13th centuries. An interpretive museum relates the history of these mounds, which have been designated a National Historic Landmark. Year-round, Tues.-Sat., 9 A.M. to 5 P.M.; Sun., 2 to 5:30 P.M. Free. 912/723-5296.

BRUNSWICK, 17,605, F-6. Although Brunswick is best known as a point of access to Georgia's Golden Isles, the Old Town section of the city features English street names unchanged since before the American Revolution and much Victorian architecture. Brunswick-Golden Isles Visitors Bureau, 777 Gloucester St.: Year-round, daily, 8:30 A.M. to 5 P.M. 912/265-0620. **Marshes of Glynn Overlook Park,** U.S. 17, offers an unobstructed view of the largest salt marshes on the East Coast and picnic facilities. Always open. Free. At the **Coastal Exhibit Room,** U.S. 17S, the marine exhibits include aquariums representing marine communities, seashell collections, and petting aquariums for children. Year-round, Mon.-Fri., 8 A.M. to 5 P.M. Free. 912/264-7218. Welcome Centers: Int. 95 between Exits 8 and 9, 912/264-0202; and Glynn Ave. on U.S. 17, 912/264-5337. Year-round, daily, 9 A.M. to 5 P.M.

ST. SIMONS ISLAND: During the 1560s, Spain established a claim on the Golden Isles by building missions in the area. After these were abandoned, James Oglethorpe, founder of Georgia, staked a claim for England and built **Fort Frederica** in 1736. The brick and tabby ruins of the fort, including some cannons, are now a national monument. Exhibits at the Visitors Center tell the story of the fortifications' early inhabitants. Daily, June-Sept., 8 A.M. to 5:30 P.M.; Oct.-May, 8 A.M. to 5 P.M. Free. 912/638-3639. **Christ Church,** Frederica Rd., has served a Congregation continuously since 1734 when the first church building was erected. The first two priests were Charles and John Wesley, respectively. Year-round, daily, 2 to 5 P.M. during Daylight Saving Time, 1 to 4 P.M., during Standard Time. Free. 912-638-8441. **Bloody Marsh Battle Site,** Frederica Rd., marks the decisive battle of 1742 in which British soldiers turned back Spanish invaders. The **Museum of Coastal History,** Beachview Dr., was built in 1869 as a lighthouse keeper's cottage adjacent to the 104-foot-high lighthouse. The museum has displays from the 18th-century Hofwyl Rice Plantation and John Couper's Cannon Point Plantation. Memorial Day-Labor Day, Tues.-Sat., 10 A.M. to 5 P.M.; Sun., 1:30 to 4 P.M.; other months, Tues.-Sat., 1 to 4 P.M.; Sun., 1:30 to 4 P.M. Free. 912/638-4666.

JEKYLL ISLAND: Now a resort area run by the state of Georgia, the island has a fishing pier, picnic areas, a large indoor swimming pool, golf courses, and ten miles of white sand beach. Admission to the beach is free. From the beginning of the Jekyll Island Club in 1886 until the beginning of World War II, Jekyll Island was an exclusive winter retreat for Rockefellers, Morgans, Vanderbilts, and other wealthy families. **Millionaire's Village** is a partial restoration of some of their homes, as well as the interfaith chapel they built which has a stained-glass window designed, installed, and signed by Louis Comfort Tiffany. Most of the interiors can be viewed only on the guided tours that leave from Macy Cottage, Riverview Dr. Year-round, daily, 11 A.M., 1 and 3 P.M. Adults $3; students 6-17, $2; children under 6, $1. 912/·635-2727.

SEA ISLAND: Privately owned, **Sea Island** is the site of the luxurious *Cloister Hotel.* The island's elegant homes can be seen from Sea Island Drive.

BUFORD, 6,697, B-2. **Lake Lanier Islands** is a 1,200-acre recreation resort built on land that was meant to be flooded by the overflow from Buford Dam. A mathematical miscalculation resulted in four green islands—the tops of foothills that were not completely submerged. Lake Lanier is one of the South's major inland lakes for sailing. The resort area has boat rentals, fishing, trout ponds, riding stables, beaches and bathhouses, a 430-foot water slide, an amphitheater, and camping and lodging facilities. Always open. The $2.50 per car parking fee includes shuttle bus. Islands Welcome Center: 404/945-6701.

CALHOUN, 5,335, B-1. **New Echota,** off Int. 75, was the capital of the Cherokee Indian Nation from 1825 to 1838. The 191-acre restoration includes *Worcestor House,* originally owned by a missionary who supported the Cherokee cause; replicas of the supreme court building and the print shop where the *Cherokee Phoenix* newspaper was produced; and a museum that features artifacts dug from the site. Year-round, Tues.-Sat., 9 A.M. to 5 P.M.; Sun., 2 to 5:30 P.M. Guided tours: Tues.-Sat., 9:30 and 11 A.M., 1:30 and 3 P.M.; Sun., 2:30 P.M. Free. 404/629-8151.

CARTERSVILLE, 9,508, B-2. **Etowah Indian Mounds,** off St. 61, were built by inhabitants of the Etowah Valley between A.D. 1000 and 1500. Mounds were the center of the religious and political life of the corn-farming culture; a museum at the historic site houses examples of native aboriginal art. Year-round, Tues.-Sat., 9 to 5 P.M.; Sun., 2 to 5:30 P.M. Free. 404/382-2704.

CHATSWORTH, 2,493, A-2. **Vann House,** U.S. 76, was built in 1804 by James Vann, a prominent member of the Cherokee nation. The interior is noted for its hanging stairway and balcony and elaborate carvings in the Cherokee Rose motif. Year-round, Tues.-Sat., 9 A.M. to 5 P.M.; Sun., 2 to 5:30 P.M. Free. 404/695-2598. **Fort Mountain State Park,** U.S. 76, takes its name from a prehistoric fortification, of which only a 1500-foot-long stone wall remains. A lake offers fishing and swimming; hiking trails go through acres of woodland. Year-round, daily, 7 A.M. to 10 P.M. Free. 404/695-2621. **Cohutta Wilderness,** north of Chatsworth on U.S. 411 in Chattahoochee National Forest, is ideal for backpackers (U.S. Forest Service Ranger, Box M, Chatsworth 30705).

CHICKAMAUGA, 2,323, north of La Fayette, A-1. *Chickamauga Battlefield,* one of several separate units within **Chickamauga and Chattanooga National Military Park,** U.S. 27, was the site of the last major Confederate victory in the Civil War. On September 18, 1863, Union forces led by

Gen. William S. Rosecrans met Gen. Braxton Bragg's Confederate army near Reeds Bridge, in the vicinity of what is now U.S. 27. During the following three days of fighting, General Rosecrans and half of his army were driven from the field. Gen. George H. Thomas, who became known as "The Rock of Chickamauga," took command and held his ground under heavy attack before being forced to withdraw. The battle took a toll of 16,000 Confederate and 18,000 Union casualties. The Visitors Center features a slide/film presentation and a 355-weapon collection of military shoulder arms. Daily, early May-mid-Oct., 8 A.M. to 5:45 P.M.; other months, 8 A.M. to 4:45 P.M. Free. 404/866-9241. **Historic Chickamauga** is a village of frontier and Victorian buildings. The Visitors Center, 101 Thomas Ave., offers a 30-minute slide show and 12-passenger limousine tours of the town by appointment. Year-round, Mon.-Sat., 8:30 A.M. to 6 P.M. Free. 404/866-9241.

CLAYTON, A-3. *See* **Dillard.**

CLEVELAND, 1,583, A-3. The **Old White County Courthouse,** Cleveland Sq., was built in 1857-59 and used until 1965. It houses the White County Historical Society and is open by appointment. 404/865-3225.

See also **Helen.**

COLUMBUS, 169,441, D-1. **Chattahoochee Promenade,** a park along the river, links several points of interest, including the Confederate Naval and National Infantry museums. The **Confederate Naval Museum,** 101 4th St., includes among its collection of Confederate Navy relics the hull of the iron-clad gunboat *Muscogee,* which lay at the bottom of the Chattahoochee River for 98 years before being salvaged. Year-round, Tues.-Sat., 10 A.M. to 5 P.M.; Sun., 2 to 5 P.M. Free. 404/327-9798. The **National Infantry Museum,** on Baltzell Ave. in the Main Post area of Fort Benning, U.S. 27, has an extensive collection of military small arms. Exhibits trace the evolution of the infantry from the French and Indian War to the present. Year-round, Tues.-Fri., 10 A.M. to 4:30 P.M.; Sat.-Sun., 12:30 to 4:30 P.M. Free. 404/545-2958. The **Heritage Tour** meets at the Georgia Visitors Center, 1000 Victory Dr. A two-hour tour includes: *Pemberton House,* 11 7th St., the home of Dr. John Pemberton from 1855 to 1860, when he originated the formula for Coca-Cola; *Walker-Peters-Langdon House,* 716 Broadway, a Federal-style cottage built in 1826 and the oldest house in Columbus; *Rankin House,* 1440 2nd Ave., a restored French Empire home with cast-iron trim, constructed between 1850 and 1870; *Springer Opera House,* 103 10th St., a restored Victorian theater built around 1871; and the headquarters of the *Historic Columbus Foundation,* 700 Broadway, a two-story brick Victorian-style townhouse built around 1870 and furnished with period antiques. Year-round, Wed., Sat., 10 A.M. Adults $5, students and military $2.50. 404/322-0756.

CONYERS, 6,567, C-2. The **Monastery of the Holy Spirit,** southwest of Conyers via St. 138 and St. 212, was founded in 1944 by Cistercian monks whose practice of self-sufficiency includes operating their own shops (bakery, stained-glass, etc.), in which they make products sold in Atlanta and

other areas. Tours: Mon.-Sat., by appointment. Also on the grounds are a greenhouse and gift shop. Greenhouse: Year-round, Thurs.-Fri., 10 A.M. to noon, 2:30 to 4:30 P.M.; Sat., 10 A.M. to 4:30 P.M. Gift Shop: Year-round, Mon.-Sat., 8:30 A.M. to 5:15 P.M. 404/483-8705.

CRAWFORDVILLE, 594, C-4. The

Alexander H. Stephens Memorial State Park, St. 22, pays tribute to the vice president of the Confederacy, who also served as governor of Georgia and a U.S. congressman. Stephens' home, *Liberty Hall,* built in 1875, has been restored with many of its original furnishings. An adjacent museum contains one of the finest collections of Confederate memorabilia in Georgia. Year-

From *The American Soldier in the Civil War.* Copyright 1895, by Stanley-Bradley Publishing Co., New York

General William Tecumseh Sherman's march, which ravaged the countryside, is shown on this map. Sherman's troops — 63,000 men — left Atlanta on November 16, after setting fire to it, and headed to the sea, following the rail line. They traveled over a swath of 30 miles on either side of the rail line, pilfering the land. Their aim was to destroy General Lee's food supply and to break the will of the people. They took food, livestock, vehicles of various kinds, and other objects from plantations and small farms along the way. Among the cities and towns they passed through were Milledgeville, Sandersville, Louisville, and Millen. They reached Savannah, their destination, on December 21. Sherman's Atlanta Headquarters is shown as drawn in 1863.

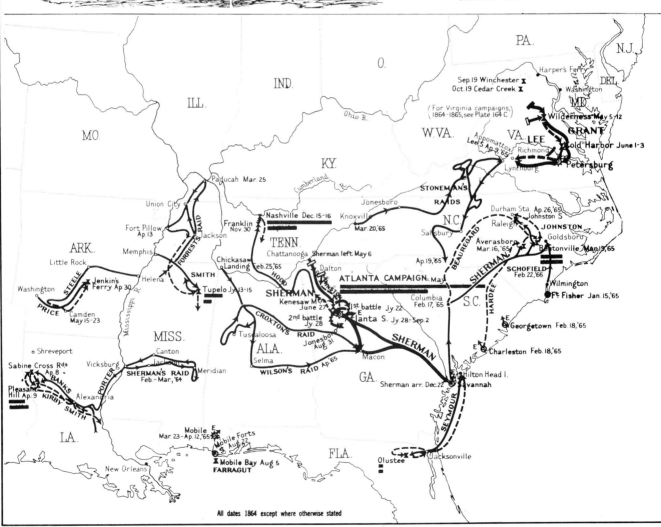

round, Tues.-Sat., 9 A.M. to noon, 1 to 6 P.M.; Sun., 1 to 6 P.M. Adults $1; persons 12-17, 50¢; under 12, free. 404/456-2221.

DAHLONEGA, 2,844, B-2. The name of this town was derived from the Cherokee word *taulonica,* meaning "yellow metal," and signifies the area's main attraction— gold. The **Dahlonega Courthouse Gold Museum,** on the town square, commemorates the nation's first major gold rush, which took place here in 1828, and recounts the operation of a branch of the U.S. Mint here from 1837 to 1861. Year-round, Tues.-Sat., 9 A.M. to 5 P.M.; Sun., 2 to 5:30 P.M. Adults $1; persons 12-17, 50¢; under 12, free. 404/864-2257. **Crisson's Gold Mine,** an active gold mine on Wimpy Mill Rd., offers visitors a chance to pan for gold. Early Apr.-early Nov., daily, 10 A.M. to 6 P.M. Adults $1.25, children $1. 404/864-6363.

DALTON 20,743, A-1. The **Creative Arts Guild,** Old Firehouse, Pentz St., a community center for the visual and performing arts, holds regularly scheduled gallery exhibits and the annual *Firehouse Festival of Arts and Crafts* in late September. Year-round, Mon.-Fri., 9 A.M. to 5 P.M.; Sat., 11 A.M. to 2 P.M. Free. 404/278-0168. **Crown Gardens and Archives,** 715 Chattanooga Ave., houses exhibits that show the development of the handtufted bedspread industry, which originated in Dalton homes in the late 1800s. Year-round, Tues.-Sat., 9 A.M. to 5 P.M. Free. 404/278-0217. **Prater's Mill,** 101 Timberland Dr., is a working gristmill built in 1859 and powered by underwater turbines in Coahulla Creek. Drive by anytime or visit when it is open for the *Prater's Mill Country Fair,* on Mother's Day and Columbus Day weekends. Sat.-Sun., 10 A.M. to 6 P.M. Adults $2, children free. 404/259-5765.

DARIEN, 1,731, F-6. Built below Altamaha Bluff in 1721 to protect the British colonies from French and Spanish expansion, **Fort King George,** off U.S. 17, is now marked by a graveyard and a museum. Year-round, Tues.-Sat., 9 A.M. to 5 P.M.; Sun., 2 to 5:30 P.M. Free. 912/437-4770. **Hofwyl-Broadfield Plantation,** 7 miles south of Darien on U.S. 17, is a typical rice plantation of the 1800s. The house, which has the original furnishings, was built around 1851. A museum relates the rice culture activities of the region; and a walking trail goes into the freshwater marsh where rice once was grown. Year-round, Tues.-Sat., 9 A.M. to 5 P.M.; Sun., 2 to 5:30 P.M. Adults $1; persons 12-17, 50¢; under 12, free. 912/264-9263. *See also* **Meridian.**

DILLARD, 238, north of Clayton, A-3. **Andy's Trout Farm and Square Dance Resort,** Betty's Creek Rd., offers rainbow trout fishing that doesn't require a license, western square dance programs, camping facilities, and lodging. Fishing: Mid-Mar.-mid-Nov., Mon.-Sat., 9 A.M. to 6 P.M.; Sun., noon to 6 P.M. Square Dancing: Apr.-Oct.,

reservations required; call 404/746-2134. **Sky Valley Resort,** on St. 106 north of Dillard, is a year-round resort with golf course, swimming pool, and other summer facilities; ski slopes for beginners, intermediates, and experts in winter; and a lodge and rental cottages. Always open. 404/483-8705.

EATONTON, 4,833, C-3. The **Uncle Remus Museum,** U.S. 441, is housed in a log cabin fashioned from two former slave cabins to represent the home of Uncle Remus, the fictional character created by Joel Chandler Harris. The museum has carved wooden figures from the Uncle Remus stories and first editions of Harris' works. June-Aug., Mon.-Sat., 10 A.M. to noon, 1 to 5 P.M.; Sun., 2 to 5 P.M.; other months, closed Tues. Adults 50¢, children 25¢. 404/485-6856. **Rock Eagle Effigy,** U.S. 129/441, is a 101-by-120-foot milky quartz rock formation in the form of an eagle. It is believed to be over 5,000 years old. Observation tower open year-round, sunrise to sunset. Free.

FARGO, G-4. *See* **Okefenokee National Wildlife Refuge.**

FITZGERALD, 10,187, F-3. The **Blue and Gray Museum,** Municipal Building, contains Civil War relics from both the Union and Confederate armies. Ironically, Fitzgerald was founded by Union veterans in 1895. Apr.-Sept., Mon.-Fri., 2 to 5 P.M.; Oct.-Mar. by appointment. Adults 50¢, children 25¢. 912/423-3337.

FOLKSTON, G-5. *See* **Okefenokee National Wildlife Refuge.**

GAINESVILLE, 15,280, B-3. The **Quinlan Art Center,** 514 Green St. NE, features traveling exhibits by regional and national artists. Year-round, Mon.-Fri., 10 A.M. to noon, 1 to 4 P.M.; Sun., 2 to 4 P.M. Free. 404/536-2575. **Road Atlanta,** Braselton, southeast of Gainesville on St. 53, is the home of the *Sports Car Club of America National Championship Race* as well as a racing and sports car museum. Year-round, Mon.-Fri., 9 A.M. to 6 P.M. Museum: Free. Races: Admission varies. 404/967-6143.

HELEN, 265, northeast of Cleveland, A-3. Remodeled as a Bavarian-style village with cobblestone plazas, flower boxes, a glockenspiel, and Bavarian shops and restaurants, Helen celebrates **Oktoberfest** through September and early October, **Fasching Karnival** in late January and February, and the **Helen-to-Atlantic Balloon Race** in June. Call 404/878-2521 for dates. The **Old Sautee Store,** St. 17 and 255, houses a museum collection of general store merchandise from the 19th and 20th centuries in a 107-year-old country store. Year-round, Mon.-Sat., 9:30 A.M. to 5:30 P.M.; Sun., 1 to 6 P.M. Free. 404/878-2281. **Anna Ruby Falls,** a 1,600-acre scenic area 1½ miles north of **Unicoi State Park** (take main road through park), features 50- and 153-foot-high twin waterfalls, with an observa-

tion platform. Park: Always open. Free. 404/878-2201.

HINESVILLE, 11,309, E-5. **The 24th Infantry Museum and Fort Stewart,** corner of Wilson Ave. and Utility St., has weapons, uniforms, flags, and equipment dating from the Civil War to the present. Year-round, Mon.-Fri., 1 to 5 P.M.; Sat.-Sun., 2 to 6 P.M. Free. 912/767-4891.

JEFFERSON, 1,802, B-3. The **Crawford W. Long Museum,** College St., is located at the site of the office where, on March 30, 1842, Dr. Long performed the first operation using ether. Displays include the doctor's personal possessions, photographs, and a story of the development of anesthesia. Year-round, Tues.-Sat., 9 A.M. to noon, 1 to 5 P.M.; Sun., 1:30 to 4 P.M. Free. 404/367-5307.

JEKYLL ISLAND, F-6. *See* **Brunswick.**

JULIETTE, 300, northwest of Macon, D-3. The **Jarrell Plantation,** 15 miles east of Int. 75, Juliette Rd. exit, is administered by the Georgia Department of Natural Resources as a 7.5-acre working farm with over 20 historic structures from the 1840s to the 1940s. Year-round, Tues.-Sat., 9 A.M. to 5 P.M.; Sun., 2 to 5:30 P.M. Free. 912/986-5172.

KENNESAW, 5,095, northwest of Marietta, B-2. **Big Shanty Museum,** St. 293, houses *The General,* a vintage locomotive that won lasting fame on April 12, 1862, when Union soldiers seized it at the Big Shanty (now Kennesaw) depot while the train's conductor, William Fuller, was eating breakfast at a nearby hotel. The event, recounted at the museum, became known as the "Great Locomotive Chase." Year-round, daily, 9:30 A.M. to 6 P.M. Adults $1; children over 10, $1; under 10, free. 404/427-2117.

LA FAYETTE, A-1. *See* **Chickamauga** and **Lookout Mountain.**

LA GRANGE, 24,204, D-1. **Bellevue,** 204 Ben Hill St., was built in 1861-62 by Benjamin H. Hill, a Georgia legislator and U.S. senator who entertained Jefferson Davis and other members of the Confederate government in the white frame house. The Greek-Revival structure is distinguished by its Ionic columns and massive carved mantels within. Year-round, Tues.-Sat., 10 A.M. to noon, 2 to 6 P.M.; Sun., 2 to 6 P.M. Admission $1; under school age, free. 404/884-4726. The **Callaway Memorial Tower,** Truitt and 4th Aves., was built in 1929 as a tribute to textile magnate Fuller E. Callaway. **Lafayette Fountain,** erected on the town square, salutes the Revolutionary War hero with a replica of the Lafayette statue in LePuy, France.

LOOKOUT MOUNTAIN, 1,505, north of La Fayette, A-1. Located atop Lookout Mountain, **Rock City** is a huge, natural rock formation with panoramic views of the

Appalachians, garden trails, Fairy Land Caverns, and, for children, Mother Goose Village. Year-round, daily, 8:30 A.M. to sunset. Adults $4.75; children 6-12, $2.75; under 6, free. 404/820-2531.
See also **Chattanooga** in Tennessee.

LUMPKIN, 1,335, E-1. **Museums on the Square,** Lumpkin town square, include the restored 1836 *Bedingfield Inn,* which was both a family residence and a stagecoach stop; and the *Drugstore Museum,* which was the town's apothecary from 1875 to 1950. June-Aug., daily, 1 to 5 P.M.; other months, Sat.-Sun., 1 to 5 P.M. Adults $1, children 50¢. 912/838-4201. **Westville,** off U.S. 27, is a living-history village of the 1850s that was assembled from authentic buildings moved in from the surrounding area and restored. Year-round, Mon.-Sat., 10 A.M. to 5 P.M.; Sun., 1 to 5 P.M. Adults $3; college students and persons 65 and over, $2; other students $1; preschoolers free. 912/838-6310. **Providence Canyon State Park,** 7 miles west of Lumpkin on St. 39, has been called the "Little Grand Canyon" because of its colorful sand formations. The canyon area has nature trails and an interpretive center. Park: Year-round, daily, 7 A.M. until sunset. Center: Year-round, Mon.-Sat., 8 A.M. to 5 P.M.; Sun., 1 to 6 P.M. Free. 912/838-6202.

MACON, 116,860, D-3. **Ocmulgee National Monument,** U.S. 80, is the site of the largest archaeological excavation and restoration of ancient Indian civilization in the East. The main theme of the area is the Mississippi site, dated A.D. 900 to 1100; but mounds along a walking trail and exhibits of artifacts illustrate the life-styles of six groups of Indians who occupied the land from 8000 B.C. to A.D. 1717. The Visitors Center houses an archaeological museum and offers tours of the **Earthlodge,** a restored ceremonial building with its original 1000-year-old floor intact. Year-round, daily, 9 A.M. to 5 P.M. Free. 912/742-0447. The **Museum of Arts and Sciences** and the **Mark Smith Planetarium,** 4182 Forsyth Road., feature a walk-through limestone cave, nature trails, art and science exhibits, and planetarium shows. Museum: Year-round, Mon.-Fri., 9 A.M. to 5 P.M.; Fri., 7 to 9 P.M.; Sat., 11 A.M. to 5 P.M.; Sun., 2 to 5 P.M. Admission 50¢; Sat. and Mon., free. Planetarium shows: Year-round, Fri., 7:30 P.M.; Sat., 2 P.M.; Sun., 3 P.M. Adults $1.50, children $1. 912/477-3232. **Cannonball House,** 856 Mulberry St., survived attack in 1864 when a cannonball bounced off one of its white columns, smashed through a front window, and landed in the main hallway. Built in 1853, the restored mansion still has the cannonball and a museum in the old servants' quarters. Year-round, Tues.-Fri., 10:30 A.M. to 1 P.M., 2:30 to 5 P.M.; Sat.-Sun., 1:30 to 4:30 P.M. Adults $1, children 50¢. 912/745-5982. **Hay House,** 934 Georgia Ave., is a finely crafted and elaborately furnished 1855 Italian Renais-

sance Revival-style mansion filled with antiques from around the world. Year-round, Tues.-Sat., 10:30 A.M. to 4:30 P.M.; Sun., 2 to 4 P.M. Adults $3; students $1.50; children under 12, $1. 912/742-8155. The **Grand Opera House,** 651 Mulberry St., was built in 1884 and restored in 1970. Now in use as an arts center, it is open by appointment. 912/745-7925. **Fort Benjamin Hawkins,** U.S. 80E., has a reconstructed blockhouse resembling that of 1806 when the fort was established. Apr.-Oct., Sun., 2 to 6 P.M.; other times by appointment. Free. 912/742-2627. *See also* **Juliette.**

MADISON, 2,954, C-3. The **Madison-Morgan Cultural Center,** 434 S. Main St., has exhibits of local history, art galleries, and a schoolroom museum, all housed in a restored 1895 school building. Year-round, Mon.-Fri., 10 A.M. to 4:30 P.M.; Sat.-Sun., 2 to 4 P.M. Adults $1.50; students 75¢; under 5, free. 404/342-4743. The **Presbyterian Church,** 382 S. Main St., built in 1840, is still in use and known for its Tiffany windows and silver communion service, which was stolen during the Civil War and later returned by order of Union General Slocum. Referred to as the "town Sherman refused to burn," Madison has many antebellum homes, over half of which are listed on the National Register of Historic Places. Interiors can be seen during the city's **Tour of Homes** events held in May and December. Call Madison-Morgan Cultural Center for tour information: 404/342-4743.

MARIETTA, 30,805, B-2. **Kennesaw Mountain National Battlefield Park,** off U.S. 41, is the site of the major Civil War battle that anticipated the siege and fall of Atlanta. Gen. Joseph E. Johnston's Confederate Army of about 50,000 held Kennesaw Mountain against two coordinated attacks by Gen. William T. Sherman's troops on June 27, 1864. The Visitors Center and exhibits along park routes through the battlefield depict the Atlanta campaign. Daily, May-Aug., 8:30 A.M. to 7 P.M.; other months, 8:30 A.M. to 5:30 P.M. Free. 404/432-8011. *See also* **Kennesaw.**

MARSHALLVILLE, 1,540, D-3. The **Camellia Gardens,** off St. 49 south of Fort Valley, bloom with nine acres of camellias from November to March. The headquarters of the American Camellia Society also has a gallery of 140 porcelain bird sculptures by Edward Marshall Boehm. Gardens: Year-round, daily, 8:30 A.M. to 4:30 P.M. Gallery: Year-round, Mon.-Fri., 8:30 A.M. to 4 P.M. Free. 912/967-2358.

MERIDIAN, 150, northeast of Darien, F-6. Meridian offers access by boat to **Sapelo Island,** the 9,250-acre unspoiled estaurine sanctuary that was once the exclusive preserve of millionaire R. J. Reynolds. Now the coastal island preserves the natural beauty and is a wildlife haven. Tours: Wed., Sat., by the Department of Natural Resources. Boat fee: $2 per person; children under 6,

free. Reservations: 912/264-7330.

MIDWAY, 457, E-6. **Midway Church,** U.S. 17, built in 1792, was the main meeting house of the midway society, a congregation that included two signers of the Declaration of Independence and two Revolutionary War generals as well as grandparents and parents of Supreme Court Justice Oliver Wendell Holmes, inventor Samuel Morse, and Pres. Theodore Roosevelt. The museum next to the church has furniture, artifacts, and documents from the early 18th to mid-19th centuries. Year-round, Tues.-Sat., 10 A.M. to 4 P.M.; Sun., 2 to 4 P.M. Free. 912/884-5837.
See also **Richmond Hill.**

MILLEDGEVILLE, 12,176, D-3. The **Old State Capitol,** 201 E. Green St., marks Milledgeville's place in history as the capital of Georgia from 1805 to 1867. The building is now used for educational purposes and houses a museum of local memorabilia. Year-round, Mon.-Fri., 8 A.M. to 5 P.M. Free. 912/453-3481. The **Old Governor's Mansion,** 120 S. Clark St., was built in 1838 in the Greek-Revival style and housed ten Georgia governors. Year-round, Tues.-Sat., 9 A.M. to 5 P.M.; Sun., 2 to 5 P.M. Adults $1, students 50¢. 912/453-4545. Driving tour maps of the city and area are available at the Chamber of Commerce, 130 S. Jefferson St. Tours of historic Milledgeville, departing from Chamber of Commerce: Year-round, daily, 2 to 4 P.M. Adults $5; children 12 and under, $3. 912/452-4687.

MILLEN, 3,988, D-5. The **National Fish Hatchery,** U.S. 25, has a 26-tank aquarium displaying fish raised by the hatchery and a variety of other species. Year-round, daily, 9 A.M. to 5 P.M. Free. 912/982-4168.

OKEFENOKEE NATIONAL WILD-LIFE REFUGE, G-4. Most of the Okefenokee Swamp has been designated a national wildlife refuge to protect this 681 square miles of wilderness in southeastern Georgia. Okefenokee Swamp is mislabeled, since the water is neither still nor stagnant but in continuous motion as part of a huge watershed that feeds the St. Marys and Suwanee rivers; and the bottom is not mud but firm, white sand. Visitors navigate the swamp boat, passing among both floating and solid islands to view cypress trees, herbs and shrubs, alligators, turtles, lizards, snakes, deer, black bears, bobcats, raccoons, aquatic birds, and fish. The wildlife refuge has three entrances. **Okefenokee Swamp Park,** 10 miles south of Waycross west off U.S. 1/23, has guided boat trips, an observation tower, ecology and swamp life exhibits, and interpretive displays. Regularly scheduled 25-minute and two-hour guided trips daily, depending on the water level; all-day excursions by appointment. Daily, June-Labor Day, 9 A.M. to 6:30 P.M.; other months, 9 A.M. to 5:30 P.M. Admission includes short boat trip. Adults $5; children 6-11, $3; under 6, free. 912/283-0583. The

Suwanee Canal Recreation Area, 12 miles northwest of Folkston west off U.S. 1/23, features guided boat tours, fishing, a 4,000-foot boardwalk, and an observation tower. Daily, Mar.-mid-Sept., 7 A.M. to 7 P.M.; other months, 8 A.M. to 6 P.M. Free. **Stephen C. Foster State Park,** 17 miles northeast of Fargo, east off U.S. 441, has guided boat tours, fishing, canoeing, camping, and cottage facilities. Daily, Mar.-Sept. 14, 6:30 A.M. to 8:30 P.M.; mid-Sept.-early Feb., 7 A.M. to 7 P.M. Park entrance free. 912/637-5274. Okefenokee National Wildlife Refuge Headquarters: 912/283-2580.

PINE MOUNTAIN, 984, D-1. **Callaway Gardens,** U.S. 27, a 2,500-acre family resort, offers walking trails, display greenhouses, 63 holes of golf, tennis, a 175-acre fishing lake, horseback riding, quail hunting in season, skeet and trap shooting, beaches, and overnight accommodations. The resort features native plants and wild flowers as well as special sections of ornamental plants from other regions of the United States and foreign countries. The gardens are noted for 600 varieties of azaleas, 100 varieties of chrysanthemums, 475 species of holly, and 80 kinds of rhododendron as well as a 7½-acre vegetable garden. **Robin Lake Beach** is open for swimming from April to September; children's rides, canoeing, water-skiing shows, and Florida State University Flying High Circus Shows are summer attractions. Beach: Late Apr.-early June, Sat.-Sun., 8 A.M. to 7 P.M. Adults $4.25; children 6-11, $2.50; under 6, free. June-Aug., daily, 8 A.M. to 8 P.M. Adults $6.50; children 6-11, $4; under 6, free. Admission also includes gardens and all activities except tennis. 404/633-2281.

RICHMOND HILL, 1,177, east of Midway, E-6. **Fort McAllister,** St. 144, an earthwork fortification built by the Confederacy in 1861 on the south bank of the Great Ogeechee River, was the key to Savannah's defense during the Civil War. It withstood nine naval attacks before falling to Gen. William B. Hazen in December, 1864, in the defeat that marked the end of Gen. William T. Sherman's March to the Sea. Year-round, Tues.-Sat., 9 A.M. to 5 P.M.; Sun., 2 to 5:30 P.M. Adults $1; persons 12-17, 50¢; under 12, free. 912/727-2339.

RINGGOLD, A-1. *See* **Rossville.**

ROME, 29,654, B-1. Founded in 1834 and built, like ancient Rome, on seven hills, Rome, Georgia, displays a bronze replica of the Capitoline statue, *Romulus and Remus.* It was presented to the city by the governor of Rome, Italy, in 1929 and is located at the Municipal Building on Broad St. The **Chieftains,** 80 Chatillion Rd., was once the home of Cherokee leader Major Ridge. The structure now holds a museum of local history, including Indian artifacts and exhibits of 19th-century life-styles and industry. Year-round, Tues.-Fri., 10 A.M. to 2 P.M.; Sun., 1 to 5 P.M. Free. 404/291-9494. **Oak**

Hill and the **Martha Berry Museum and Art Gallery,** U.S. 27 N., across from Berry College, are part of the legacy of pioneer educator Martha Berry (1866-1942). Year-round, Tues.-Sat., 10 A.M. to 5 P.M.; Sun., 1 to 5 P.M. Free. 404/291-1883.

ROSSVILLE, 3,749, northwest of Ringgold, A-1. **John Ross House,** off U.S. 27, a two-story log cabin, was the home of John Ross, chief of the Cherokee nation from 1828 to 1866. Built in 1797, the cabin has a mysterious secret room that originally had no door or other entry. Daily, June-Labor Day, 2 to 6 P.M.; Apr.-May, Sept.-Oct., Sat.-Sun., 2 to 6 P.M. Free. 404/861-2375.

ROSWELL, 23,337, B-2. Founded in 1838 by a group of affluent Georgia coast families led by Roswell King, the city today features 15 structures that survived the Civil War. **Bulloch Hall,** built in 1840, was the scene of Martha Bulloch's marriage to Theodore Roosevelt, Sr. in 1853. Year-round, Wed., 10 A.M. to 3 P.M. Admission 50¢. 404/992-1731. The **Roswell Historical Society** is located on Bulloch Ave. Year-round, Mon.-Fri., 10 A.M. to 3 P.M. 404/992-1665. **Chattahoochie Nature Center,** 9135 Willeo Rd., with over 40 acres, has a museum, nature trails, a boardwalk into the marshes of the Chattahoochie River, and an aviary for hawks and owls. The center cares for injured and orphaned wild animals, has educational programs, and sponsors several special events. Year-round, Mon.-Sat., 9 A.M. to 5 P.M.; Sun., 1 to 5 P.M. Donations. 404/992-2055.

ST. MARYS, 3,596, G-6. **Cumberland Island National Seashore,** 16 miles long and 3 miles wide, is separated from the mainland by a salt marsh and estuary that supports mosquito fish, ducks, fiddler crabs, herons, egrets, and other wildlife. The central part of the island has forests of live oaks laced with woody vines and Spanish moss, magnolia, holly, and pines, as well as ponds that support alligators, mink, and otter. The white beaches and sand dunes are a refuge for terns, pelicans, and loggerhead turtles. Ruins of the *Dungeness Mansion* recall the island's history: Gen. Nathanael Greene bought the site in 1783; Gen. Light-Horse Harry Lee, a friend of the Greene family, died here in 1818; and Thomas Carnegie purchased the property and began building the landmark mansion in 1881. Island Visitors Centers are located at Sea Camp Dock and Dungeness Dock. A National Park Service 45-minute passenger-ferry ride provides access to Cumberland Island. Year-round, Mon., Thurs., Fri., Sat., Sun., 9:15 A.M. and 1:45 P.M. (daily during peak summer season). Adults $2; persons under 16 and over 62, $1. Call for reservations at least one week in advance. 912/882-4335.

ST. SIMONS ISLAND, F-6. *See* **Brunswick.**

SAVANNAH, 141,634, E-6. Led by James

E. Oglethorpe, Georgia's first settlers landed at Savannah on February 12, 1733. When Georgia was made a Royal Province in 1754, Savannah became its seat of government and remained the colonial capital until 1782. When clipper ships and steamers came into port to pick up cargoes, they deposited their ballast of stones, which were used to pave streets and build warehouses along the Savannah River. The activities of cotton brokers, called factors, dominated the waterfront.

HISTORIC SITES: Savannah's **National Historical Landmark District** includes more than 1,100 restored buildings and 25 original squares in a 2½-square-mile area. The Visitors Center is in a restored 1860 railroad station at 301 W. Broad St. Year-round, Mon.-Fri., 8:30 A.M. to 5 P.M.; Sat.-Sun., 9 A.M. to 5 P.M. 912/233-3067. Among points of interest in the district are: *Emmett Park,* Bay and E. Broad Sts., named for Irish patriot Robert Emmett and site of the *Old Harbor Light,* a cast-iron beacon erected in 1852 to guide ships into the harbor; *Forsyth Park,* Gaston St. and Park Ave., a fragrance garden for the blind; *Johnson Square,* the first square finished, at Bull, Bay, and Congress Sts., and marked by the *Nathanael Greene Monument,* where the Revolutionary War hero is buried, and surrounded by the sites of the first inn, public mill, and general store in Georgia. *Trustees Garden Site,* E. Broad St. near Bay St., was established by General Oglethorpe as America's first public experimental garden. *Factors Walk,* Bay St., was the center of Savannah's cotton commerce. Ornate iron bridgeways connect the red brick buildings that once held cotton factors' offices. Landmarks include the *City Exchange Bell;* the *Old Cotton Exchange; Washington Guns;* and *Oglethorpe Bench,* which marks the site of the first landing of English colonists in Savannah. *Riverfront Plaza,* River St., is a nine-block waterfront promenade with a view of the freighters in the harbor and access to the parks, galleries, restaurants, and boutiques now housed in the cotton warehouses.

CHURCHES: Cathedral of St. John the Baptist, 222 E. Harris St., is the oldest Roman Catholic Church in Georgia; **Christ Episcopal,** 28 Bull St., was the first church in Georgia, where John Wesley founded what is believed to be the world's first Sunday School; **First African Baptist,** 403 W. Bryan St., was organized in 1788 as the first Afro-American church in the United States; **Mickve Israel Temple,** 20 E. Gordon St., founded 1733, is the oldest congregation of Reform Judaism in the United States; and **St. John's Church,** 14 W. Macon St., is known for its stained-glass windows, chimes, and Parish House (also known as the Green-Meldrim House), where General Sherman made his headquarters during the Federal occupation of 1864.

FORTS: Fort Jackson (1808-76), U.S. 80

E., the oldest remaining brickwork fort in the states, has exhibits, artifacts, and special weekend programs from April through November. Year-round, Tues.-Sun., 9 A.M. to 5 P.M. Admission 1.50; students, military, and persons 65 and over, 75¢; preschoolers free. 912/232-3945. **Fort Pulaski,** U.S. 80 E, built 1829-47, was Robert E. Lee's first engineering assignment after graduation from West Point. The fort houses a museum of Civil War artifacts and relics. Daily, Memorial Day-Labor Day, 8:30 A.M. to 7 P.M.; other months, 8:30 A.M. to 5:30 P.M. Free in winter; $1 per carload in June-Aug. 912/786-5787. **Fort Screven,** U.S. 80E on Tybee Island at Savannah Beach, was completed in 1897 and manned during the Spanish-American War and both World Wars. *Tybee Museum,* in one of the fort's batteries, has displays of Georgia history dating to precolonial times. Early May-late Sept., daily, 10 A.M. to 6 P.M.; Oct.-Apr., daily, 1 to 5 P.M. Adults $1; children under 13, free. 912/786-4077.

HISTORIC HOUSES: Davenport House (1815-20), 324 E. State St., is one of Savannah's best examples of late Georgian architecture. Year-round, daily, 10 A.M. to 4:30 P.M. Adults $2; students 75¢; children under 10, free. 912/236-8087. **Juliette Gordon Low Girl Scout National Center,** Bull St. and Oglethorpe Ave., was the birthplace of Juliette Gordon Low, who founded the Girl Scouts in 1912. The house (circa 1819) has been restored to the period of Mrs. Low's childhood. Year-round, Mon.-Tues., Thurs.-Sat., 10 A.M. to 4 P.M.; Feb.-Nov., Sun., 1:30 to 4:30 P.M. Adults $2; persons under 18, $1; under 6, free; reduced admissions for Girl Scouts. 912/233-4501. **Andrew Low House,** 329 Abercorn St., was built 1845-48 by Andrew Low, a cotton factor and the father-in-law of Juliette Gordon Low. Year-round, daily, 10:30 A.M. to 4:30 P.M. Adults $1.75; persons 13-18, $1; Girl Scouts and children 75¢. 912/233-6854. **Owens-Thomas House,** 124 Abercorn St., built in 1816-19, is praised as Savannah's finest example of English Regency architecture. Jan.-Aug., Oct.-Dec., Tues.-Sat., 10 A.M. to 4:30 P.M.; Sun.-Mon., 2 to 4:30 P.M. Adults $2; students $1; children 6-12, 50¢; under 6, free. 912/233-9743. The **William Scarborough House,** 41 W. Broad St., was built 1818-19 and now houses Historic Savannah Foundation offices and exhibits on the restoration of Savannah. Year-round, Mon.-Sat., 10 A.M. to 4 P.M. Adults $1.50, children 75¢. 912/233-7787.

MUSEUMS: Telfair Mansion and Art Museum, 121 Barnard St., is housed in a stucco Regency mansion built in 1818. Exhibits include Impressionist paintings and sculpture. Year-round, Tues.-Sat., 10 A.M. to 5 P.M.; Sun., 2 to 5 P.M. Adults $1.75; other admission charges vary. 912/232-1177. **Ships of the Sea,** 503 E. River St., features collections of ship models, scrimshaw, figureheads, and ships in bottles. Year-round, daily, 10 A.M. to 5 P.M. Adults $2; military

and persons 65 and over, $1; children 75¢. 912/232-1511. **Science Museum,** 4405 Paulsen St., has displays of the natural and physical sciences. Year-round, Tues.-Sat., 10 A.M. to 5 P.M.; Sun., 2 to 5 P.M. Adults $1, children 50¢. 912/355-6705. **Evans Antique Cars,** 313 W. River St., has 1904-41 period autos, including a 1920 gold- and silver-plated Pierce Arrow. Memorial Day-Labor Day, Mon.-Sat., 9 A.M. to 6 P.M.; Sun., 1 to 6 P.M.; other months, Mon.-Sat., 10 A.M. to 5 P.M. Adults $2, children $1. 912-233-3525. **Oatland Island Education Center,** off Islands Expwy., showcases wildlife in natural habitats, with aviaries, a nature trail, and a barnyard. The center also has an 1850s log cabin, a cane mill, and handicraft programs. Year-round, Mon.-Fri., 8:30 A.M. to 5 P.M. Free. Canned dog food donations for the animals welcomed. 912/897-3773.

TALLULAH FALLS, 162, A-3. **Tallulah Gorge,** U.S. 441 and St. 23, is one of the oldest in North America. It is 1½ miles long, 2,000 feet deep, and has three waterfalls. **Terrora Park,** across from the gorge, has nature trails, lighted tennis courts, fishing piers (with facilities for handicapped), campgrounds, and a Visitors Center. June-Labor Day, daily, 10 A.M. to 7 P.M.; Apr., Sept.-Oct., Sat.-Sun., 10 A.M. to 5 P.M. Free. 404/754-6036.

THOMASVILLE, 18,463, G-2. At the **Rose Test Gardens,** 1840 Smith Ave., over 2,000 rose bushes bloom from mid-April to mid-November. The garden is devoted to testing new varieties for All-American Rose Selections. The **Rose Festival,** held in Thomasville the last weekend in April, salutes the local industry. Year-round, daily, daylight hours. Free. 912/226-5568. **Lapham-Patterson House,** 626 Dawson St., an 1884 vacation "cottage" of elaborate Victorian design, has been named a National Historic Landmark. Year-round, Tues.-Sat., 9 A.M. to 5 P.M.; Sun., 2 to 5:30 P.M. Adults $1; persons 12-17, 50¢; under 12, free. 912/226-0405. The city's oldest landmark is a 300-year-old oak tree at the corner of E. Monroe and E. Crawford Sts.

TIFTON, 13,749, F-3. **Georgia Agrirama,** Int. 75 and 8th St., re-creates a rural Georgia community of the late 1800s. Among the facilities are a working farm, gristmill, turpentine still, village newspaper, cotton gin and warehouse, chapel, train depot, craft areas, country store, and special events. Memorial Day-Labor Day, daily, 9 A.M. to 6 P.M.; other months, Mon.-Sat., 9 A.M. to 5 P.M.; Sun., 12:30 to 5 P.M. Adults $3; persons 6-16, $1.50; under 6, free. 912/386-3344.

TOCCOA, 9,104, A-3. **Traveler's Rest,** off U.S. 123, was built in 1815 and in 1830 (in two sections) by James Rutherford and purchased by Deveraux Jarrett in 1838; thus, the clapboard structure, flanked by stone and brick chimneys, came to be

known as Jarrett Manor. Year-round, Tues.-Sat., 9 A.M. to 5 P.M.; Sun., 2 to 5:30 P.M. Adults $1; persons 12-18, 50¢; under 12, free. 404/886-2256.

VALDOSTA, 37,596, G-3. **Crescent House,** 904 N. Patterson St., is named for its semicircular, white-pillared portico, which its builder, Col. William S. West, is alleged to have first traced on the land with his walking stick. Year-round, Fri., 2 to 5 P.M. Free. 912/242-2740.

WARM SPRINGS, 425, D-2. **Franklin D. Roosevelt's Little White House and Museum,** St. 85W, is a memorial to President Roosevelt, who first came to Warm Springs in 1924 for treatment of paralysis caused by poliomyelitis. The warm stream that flows from the base of Pine Mountain had been considered therapeutic by Indians and later by white settlers. Roosevelt came here frequently after he became president of the United States. The house has been left exactly as it was at the time of his death here on April 12, 1945. The museum of Roosevelt memorabilia, a half block from the Little White House, was the home of a neighbor who bequeathed it to the agency that oversees the property. June-Aug., Mon.-Fri., 9 A.M. to 4:30 P.M.; Sat.-Sun., 9 A.M. to 5:30 P.M.; other months, daily, 9 A.M. to 4:30 P.M. Adults $3; children 6-12, $1.50; under 6, free. 404/655-3511.

WASHINGTON, 4,662, C-4. Laid out in 1780, Washington claims to be the first town in America to be incorporated in the name of George Washington. More than 40 white-columned antebellum mansions still exist. A free map-keyed brochure of these homes and other historic sites can be obtained from the Wilkes Chamber of Commerce, 25 East Square. Year-round, Mon.-Tues., Thurs.-Fri., 8:30 A.M. to 4:30 P.M.; Wed., 8:30 A.M. to noon. 404/678-2013. The **Washington Wilkes Historical Museum,** an 1835 dwelling at 308 E. Robert Toombs St., contains busts of famous Georgians, a Confederate gun collection, Indian artifacts, and Ku Klux Klan robes. Year-round, Tues.-Sat., 9 A.M. to 1 P.M., 2 to 5 P.M.; Sun., 2 to 5:30 P.M. Free. 404/678-2105. The **Mary Willis Library,** Liberty and Jefferson Sts., was built in 1888. One of the oldest privately endowed public libraries in the state, it is noted for its detailed Victorian architecture and stained-glass windows. A Confederate chest, on exhibit, was believed to have been used to bring Confederate gold from Richmond. Year-round, Mon., Wed., Thurs.-Fri., 8:30 A.M. to 5:30 P.M.; Tues., 8:30 A.M. to 9 P.M.; Sat., 10 A.M. to 4 P.M. Free. 404/678-7736. A complex of early American dwellings, **Callaway Plantation,** U.S. 78, includes a 1785 hewn-log kitchen, a 1790 Federal plain-style house, and an 1869 Greek-Revival mansion. Mid-Apr.-mid-Oct., Mon.-Sat., 10 A.M. to 5 P.M.; Sun., 2 to 5 P.M. Free. 404/678-7060.

WATKINSVILLE, 1,240, B-3. **Eagle Tavern,** on U.S. 441, was built in the late

1700s and opened as a tavern and stage-coach stop in 1801. Authentically restored, the structure is furnished with pre-Civil War furniture, crockery, English pewter and china, and handmade housewares. Year-round, Mon.-Fri., 9 A.M. to 5 P.M. Free. 404/769-5197.

WAYCROSS, F-4. **Okefenokee Swamp,** 10 miles south of Waycross, abounds with wildlife. Nearby lakes and the Suwanee River are popular fishing areas. *See* **Okefenokee National Wildlife Refuge.**

Information Sources

Georgia Department
of Industry & Trade
1400 N. Omni International
P.O. Box 1776
Atlanta, GA 30301
404/656-3553

Georgia Department
of Natural Resources
270 Washington St. SW
Atlanta, GA 30334
404/656-3530

Southeast Regional Office
National Park Service
1895 Phoenix Blvd.
Atlanta, GA 30349
404/221-5187

Atlanta Convention
& Visitors Bureau
Suite 200
Peachtree Harris Building
233 Peachtree St. NE
Atlanta, GA 30043
404/659-4270

Greater Augusta
Chamber of Commerce
P.O. Box 657
Augusta, GA 30903
404/722-0421

Brunswick-Golden Isles
Chamber of Commerce
Tourist & Convention Council
P.O. Box 250
Brunswick, GA 31521
912/265-0620

Columbus Convention
& Visitors Bureau
P.O. Box 2768
Columbus, GA 31902
404/322-1613

Macon Convention
& Visitors Bureau
P.O. Box 169
Macon, GA 31298
912/743-3401

Rome Tourist
& Convention Commission
Rome, GA 30161
404/295-5576

Savannah Convention
& Visitors Bureau
301 W. Broad St.
Savannah, GA 31499
912/233-3067

Georgia Campgrounds

FEES REFLECT MINIMUM RATE FOR 2 ADULTS AND ARE SUBJECT TO INCREASE OR SEASONAL CHANGES

- • — at the campground
- ○ — within one mile of campground
- $ — extra charge
- ** — limited facilities during winter months
- A — adults only
- B — 10,000 acres or more
- C — contribution

- E — tents rented
- F — entrance fee or premit required
- N — no specific number, limited by size of area only
- P — primitive
- R — reservation required
- S — self-contained units only

- U — unlimited
- V — trailers rented
- Z — reservations accepted
- LD — Labor Day
- MD — Memorial Day
- UC — under construction
- d — boat dock

- g — public golf course within 5 miles
- h — horseback riding
- j — whitewater running craft only
- k — snow skiing within 25 miles
- l — boat launch
- m — area north of map
- n — no drinking water

- p — motor bikes prohibited
- r — boat rental
- s — stream, lake or creek water only
- t — tennis
- u — snowmobile trails
- w — open certain off-season weekends
- y — drinking water must be boiled

Map Reference	Park Name	Access	Acres	Tent Spaces	Trailer Spaces	Approximate Fee	Season	Other Swimming Pool	Swimming	Fishing	Boating	Other Playground	Other	Telephone Number	Mail Address
	STATE PARKS														
E1	George T Bagby	Fr Ft Gaines, 15 mi N on Hwy 39	289	50	S50	4.00	All year			•		l	p	912/768-2660	Georgetown 31754
A2	Amicalola Falls	Fr Dawsonville, 3 mi W on Hwy 53, 13 mi NW on Hwys 183 & 52	263	24	24	4.00	All year							404/265-2885	
B3	Ft Yargo	Fr Winder, 2 mi S on Hwy 81	1680	34	34	4.00	All year		•	•		dlr	•	404/867-3489	Winder 30680
A3	Black Rock Mtn	Fr Clayton, 3 mi N on US 23/441	1182	75	75	4.00	All year			•		•		404/746-2141	Mountain City 30562
B4	Bobby Brown	Fr Elberton, 18 mi SE on Hwy 79	664	80	80	4.00	All year	$	•	•		dl		404/238-3313	Rt 7, Elberton 30635
B4	Elijah Clark	Fr Lincolnton, 7 mi NE on US 378	447	251	251	4.00	All year		•	•		dlr	•	404/359-4461	Lincolnton 30817
B4	Watson Mill Bridge	Fr Comer, 1-1/4 mi S on Hwy 22	140	25	25	4.00	All year			•				404/783-5349	Comer 30629
A1	Cloudland	Fr LaFayette, 20 mi NW on US 27 & Hwy 143	1699	50	50	4.00	All year			○		•		404/657-4050	Rising Fawn 30738
G6	Crooked River	Fr Kingsland, 10 mi NE on Hwy 40 & access rd	500	62	62	4.00	All year	$	•	•		dl		912/882-5256	Kingsland 31548
E6	Skidaway Island	Adj. to Skidaway Narrows Causeway	480	100	100	4.00	All year		•			•	p	912/352-8599	Savannah 31406
A2	Ft Mountain	Fr Chatsworth, 5 mi SE on US 76/Hwy 52	1897	114	114	4.00	All year		•	•		r		404/864-3789	Chatsworth 30705
D2	F D Roosevelt	Fr Pine Mtn, 5 mi SE on US 27	4980	175	175	4.00	All year	$	•	•		dr	•	404/633-4146	Pine Mountain 31822
E3	Georgia Veterans Mem	Fr Cordele, 7 mi W on US 280/Hwy 30	1307	85	85	4.00	All year	$	•	•		dl		912/273-2190	Cordele 31015
C3	Hard Labor Creek	Fr Rutledge, 2 mi N	5804	125	125	4.00	All year			•		lr	•	404/557-2863	Rutledge 30663
C2	Indian Springs	Fr Jackson, 5 mi SE on US 23	510	130	130	4.00	All year		•	•		dlr	•	404/775-7241	Indian Springs 30231
C2	High Falls	Fr Jackson, 9 mi SW on Hwy 36	969	140	140	4.00	All year		•	•		dlr		912/994-5080	Jackson 30233
B4	Hart	Fr Hartwell, 1 mi NE on US 29, 1 mi N on Hwy 8	147	100	100	4.00	All year		•	•		dl			Hartwell
F1	Kolomoki Mounds	Fr Blakely, 6 mi N on US 27 & access rd	1293	35	35	4.00	All year		•	•		lr		912/723-5296	Blakely 31723
F5	Laura S. Walker	Fr Waycross, 10 mi SE on US 84	306	106	106	4.00	All year	$	•	•		dl	•	912/283-4424	Waycross 31501
E4	Little Ocmulgee	Fr McRae, 1 mi NE on US 280, 1 mi N on US 319/441	948	50	50	4.00	All year	$	•	•		l	g	912/982-1660	McRae 31055
D5	Magnolia Springs	Fr Millen, 7 mi N on US 25/Hwy 21	1162	118	118	4.00	All year	$	•	•		dlr	•	912/982-1660	Millen 30442
F4	General Coffee	Fr Douglas, off US 441, 5 mi E on Hwy 32	1495	50	50	4.00	All year		•	•					Nicholls
B2	Red Top Mtn	Fr Cartersville, 6 mi SE on US 41 & access rd	1246	270	270	4.00	All year		•	•		dl	•	404/974-5182	Cartersville 30120
C4	Hamburg	Fr Sandersville, 8 mi E on Hwy 24, 16 mi N on Hwy 248	740	30	30	4.00	All year			•		dlr		912/552-5846	Rt 2 Box 135, Mitchell 30820
G1	Seminole	Fr Donalsonville, 16 mi S on Hwy 39	343	50	50	4.00	All year		•	•		dl	•	912/496-7509	Donalsonville 31745
G5	Stephen C. Foster	Fr Fargo, 18 mi NE on Hwy 177	80	70	70	4.00	All year			•		dl		912/496-7509	Fargo 31631
C1	John Tanner	Fr Carrollton, 6 mi W on Hwy 166	139	70	70	4.00	All year	$	•	•		dlr		404/832-7545	Rt 4, Carrollton 30117
B3	Victoria Bryant	Fr Royston, 3 mi W on US 29, N on Hwy 327	381	25	25	4.00	All year	$			•		g	404/245-6270	Royston 30662
A3	Vogel	Fr Blairsville, 9-1/2 mi S on US 129	221	85	85	4.00	All year		•	•		•	h	404/475-2628	Blairsville 30512
E6	Richmond Hill	Fr Savannah, 12 mi SW on US 17, S on Hwy 67 & 67 Spur to terminus	190	75	75	4.00	All year			•		dl			Richmond Hill
C4	Mistletoe	Fr Appling, 10 mi N on Hwy 47	1920	100	100	4.00	All year	$	•	•		dl		404/595-1416	Appling 30802
C4	A H Stephens Mem	In Crawfordville	1161	44	44	4.00	All year					lr		404/456-2221	Crawfordville 30631
B4	Tugaloo	Fr Lavonia, 6 mi N on Hwy 328	393	138	138	4.00	All year		•	•		dlr	•	404/356-3377	Rt 1, Lavonia 30553
A3	Moccasin Creek	Fr Clarkesville, 20 mi N on Hwy 197	31	56	56	4.00	All year			•		l		404/947-3194	Clarkesville 30523
F3	Reed Bingham	Fr Adel, 8 mi W on Hwy 37	1605	85	85	4.00	All year			•		l	•	912/896-7788	Box 459, Adel 31620
A3	Unicoi	Fr Helen, 1 mi NW on Hwy 356	1000	30	50	4.00	All year		•	•		r	•	404/878-2201	Helen 30545
	STATE AREAS														
B2	Stone Mtn Pk Fmly CG	Fr I-285, Stone Mtn-Athens ext, 7-1/2 mi NE to pk,fol signs	3200	65	393	F7.50	All year		•	•		lr	gt	404/469-9831	Stone Mountain 30086
	NATIONAL FORESTS														
	Chattahoochee-Oconee														
A3	Lake Chatuge	Fr Hiawassee, 2.6 mi W on US 76, .8 mi S on Hwy 288	12	32	18	2.00	4/11-10/27		•	•		dlr			Hiawassee
A2	Deep Hole	Fr Dahlonega, 26.9 mi N on Hwy 60, .2 mi SW on FR 293	2	8		2.00	4/1-12/10		•						Dahlonega
A2	Cooper Creek	Fr Dahlonega, 23.6 mi N on Hwy 60, 3.4 mi N on FR 236	7	17	17	2.00	4/1-12/10		•						Dahlonega
A2	Frank Gross	Fr Dahlonega, 27.1 mi N on Hwy 60, 5.1 mi SW on FR 69	1	11		2.00	4/1-12/10		•						Dahlonega
A2	Mulky	Fr Dahlonega, 25.6 mi N on Hwy 60, 4.7 mi NE on FR 4	8	10		2.00	4/1-12/10		•						Dahlonega
A2	Lake Winfield Scott	Fr Blairsville, 10.3 mi S on US 19, 6.5 mi W on Hwy 180	27	37	14	2.00	4/11-6/2		•	•		d			Blairsville
A3	Andrews Cove	Fr Helen, 6 mi N on Hwy 75	3	11		2.00	4/26-10/31		•						Helen
A3	Desoto Falls	Fr Cleveland, 14.7 mi NW on US 129	13	30	24	2.00	5/24-10/31								Cleveland
A3	Waters Creek	Fr Dahlonega, 12.3 mi NE on US 19, .9 mi NW on FR 34	2	10	10	None	All year		•	•					Dahlonega
A3	Dockery Lake	Fr Dahlonega, 11.5 mi N on Hwy 60, .7 mi NE on FR 654	4	11	11	2.00	3/29-10/31			•		d			Dahlonega
A2	Morganton Point	Fr Morganton, 1.2 mi W on Hwy 1234	12	38		3.00	4/15-11/15		•	•		dlr			Blue Ridge
A2	Lake Blueridge	Fr Blue Ridge, 1.7 mi E on US 76, 2.1 mi S on FR 605	15	48	48	3.00	5/24-9/10		•	•		dlr			Blue Ridge
A3	Rabun Beach	Fr Clayton, 6.6 mi S on US 441, .1 mi W on Co 10, 1.7 mi S on Hwy 15, 4.7 mi W on Co 10	70	44		3.00	All year		•	•		dlr			Clayton

Map Reference	Park Name	Access	Acres	Tent Spaces	Trailer Spaces	Approximate Fee	Season	Fishing / Other Swimming / Swimming Pool	Boating / Playground / Other	Telephone Number	Mail Address
B3	Lake Russell	Fr Mt Airy, .4 mi E on US 123, 2.8 mi SW on FR 59	30	36	30	3.00	5/18-9/30	• •	dl		Cornelia
A3	Tallulah River	Fr Clayton, 8 mi SW on US 76, 4.3 mi N on Co 70, 1.3 mi NW on FR 70	4	16	16	2.00	All year	•			Clayton
A3	Tate Branch	Fr Clayton, 8.9 mi NW on US 76, 4.3 mi N on Co 70, 3.9 mi NW on FR 70	5	11	11	2.00	3/26-11/3	•			Clayton
A2	Lake Conasauga	Fr Chatsworth, 14.1 mi E on US 76, 3 mi NW on FR 18, 10.1 mi N on FR 68	6	21	21	2.00	4/4-10/27	• •	d		Chatsworth
B1	The Pocket	Fr Lafayette, 12.8 mi E on Hwy 143, 7.1 mi S on FR 203	8	22	22	2.00	5/1-11/10	1			Lafayette
B1	Hidden Creek	Fr Calhoun, 7.8 mi W on Hwy 156, 1.9 mi NW on FR 231, 3.3 mi N on FR 228, .9 mi N on FR 955	9	16		None	5/24-9/2				Calhoun
C3	Oconee River	Fr Greensboro, 12.3 mi NW on Hwy 15	4	7		None	All year	•	d		Greensboro
C3	Lake Sinclair	Fr Eatonton, 10 mi S on US 129, 1 mi SE on Hwy 212, 1 mi E on Co 1062, .3 mi N on FR 1105	22	10	15	3.00	5/30-9/30	• •	dl		Eatonton
	CORPS OF ENGINEERS										
	Walter F George Lake	For additional CG information, see Alabama									Bx 2288,Mobile,36628
F1	Sandy Creek PUA	Fr Ft Gaines, 4 mi N on Hwy 39	48	30	S8	None	All year	•	l		Bx 2288, Mobile, 36628
F1	George T Bagby	Fr Ft Gaines, 12 mi N off Hwy 39 on Pataula Creek	289	36	S8	None	All year	• •	l	912/768-2660	Bx 2288, Mobile,AL 36628
F1	Cotton Hill PUA	Fr Ft Gaines, 6 mi N on Hwy 39	270	47	25	2.00	All year	• •	l p		Bx 2288, Mobile,AL 36628
	Clark Hill Reservoir	(See S C and 'Backpack or Boat Access Areas' for additional CG's)								404/722-3770	Clarks Hill, SC 29821
B4	Broad River	Fr Lincolnton, 14 mi NW on Hwy 79 to Broad Riv Bridge	31	13	13	2.00	3/30-9/30	• •	l		Clarks Hill, SC
B4	Hesters Ferry	Fr Lincolnton, 9 mi N on Hwy 79, 3 mi NE on dirt rd	213	26	26	3.00	3/30-9/30	• •	l p		Clarks Hill, SC
C5	Old Petersburg Rd	Fr Pollards Corner, 3 mi NE on US 221, 1.5 mi N on dirt rd	50	20	20	3.00	3/30-9/30	• •	l p		Clarks Hill, SC
C5	Ridge Road	Fr Pollards Cor, 6 mi NW on Hwy 104 to Leah, 4.5 mi E on Ridge Rd	59	50	50	3.50	3/1-12/1	• •	l		Clarks Hill, SC
C4	Clay Hill	Fr Amity, 1 mi E on Hwy 220, 2 mi S on paved rd	65	19	19	2.00	3/30-9/30	• •	l		Clarks Hill, SC
C4	Winfield	Fr Hwy 150 in Winfield, 2 mi N on paved rd, 1 mi W on dirt rd	99	22	22	2.00	3/30-9/30	• •	l		Clarks Hill, SC
C4	Big Hart Creek	Fr Thomson, 12 mi N on US 78, 2.5 mi E on dirt rd	451	15	15	2.00	3/30-9/30	• •	l		Clarks Hill, SC
C4	Raysville Bridge	Fr Thomson, 10 mi N on Hwy 43	101	28	28	3.50	3/30-9/30	• •	l		Clarks Hill, SC
C5	Mosely Creek	Fr Double Branches, SE on access rd	137	15	15	2.00	3/30-9/30	• •	l		Clarks Hill, SC
B4	Murry Creek	Fr Lincolnton, 5 mi NE on US 378, 3 mi NW on paved rd, 2 mi N	47	17	17	2.00	3/30-9/30	• •	l		Clarks Hill, SC
B4	Murry Creek Pk	Fr Lincolnton, 8 mi NW on Hwy 79, 1 mi E on pk access rd	631	15	15	None	3/30-9/30	• •	l		Clarks Hill, SC
	Allatoona Lake									404/382-4700	Box 487, Cartersville 30120
B2	Glade Farm PUA	Fr I-75, ext 121, 3 mi N on Co Glade R, 1 mi W on Co	32	38	N	2.00	All year	• •	l p		Bx 487, Cartersville 30120
B2	Clark Creek S PUA	Fr I-75, ext 121, 2 mi N on Co Glade Rd	30	40	32	4.00	4/1-12/1	• •	l p		Bx 487, Cartersville 30120
B2	Clark Creek N PUA	Fr I-75, ext 121, 2 1/4 mi N on Co Glade Rd	12	24	10	3.00	4/1-12/1	• •	l p		Bx 487, Cartersville 30120
B2	Old Hwy 41 No 1	Fr Acworth, 2 mi NW on Hwy 293	15	8		None	All year	• •	l p		Bx 487,Cartersville 30120
B2	Old Hwy 41 No 3	Fr Acworth, 2-1/2 mi NW on Hwy 293, 1/4 mi N on paved rd	35	50	20	3.00	4/1-12/1	• •	l p		Bx 487,Cartersville 30120
B2	McKinney	Fr I-75 ext 121,3 mi N on Co Glade Rd, 1 mi W on Co, 1/4 mi SW on paved rd	200	74	74	2.00	All year	• •	l p		Bx 487,Cartersville 30120
B2	Allatoona Pass	Fr I-75 ext 122, 1 mi SE on Co, 3/4 mi NE on Co gravel rd	10	11	N	None	All year	• •	p		Bx 487, Cartersville 30120
B2	McKaskey Creek PUA	Fr I-75, ext 125, 1/10 mi E on Hwy 20, 1-1/2 mi S on Hwy 294 N, 1-1/2 mi E on Co rd	34	50	40	4.00	All year	• •	l p		Bx 487, Cartersville 30120
B2	Macedonia CG	Fr I-75, ext 125, 8-1/2 mi E on Hwy 20, 4-1/2 mi S on Co gravel rd	35	26	N	2.00	All year	• •	l p		Bx 487, Cartersville 30120
B2	Upper Stamp Creek PUA	Fr I-75, ext 125, 6-1/2 mi E on Hwy 20, 1-1/2 mi S & 1 mi E on Co gravel rd	23	9	N	None	4/1-12/1	• •	l p		Bx 487, Cartesville, 30120
B2	Payne	Fr I-75, ext 120, 1 mi N on Hwy 92, 3.5 mi N & E on old Hwy 92	40	50	N	3.00	4/1-12/1	• •	p		Bx 487, Cartersville, 30120
B2	Victoria	Fr I-75, ext 118, 2 mi N on Co Wade Green Rd, 1/2 mi E on Hwy 92, 4 mi N on Hwy 205, 2.2 mi W on Co	30	10	N	2.00	All year	• •	l p		Bx 487, Cartersville, 30120
B2	Sweetwater Creek	Fr Jct Hwys 5 & 20, 5-1/2 mi W on Hwy 20, 2 mi S on Co	67	70	70	2.00	All year	• •	l • p		Bx 487, Cartersville, 30120
	Lake Seminole	(See Florida for additional campgrounds)								912/662-2814	Box 96,Chattahoochee FL 32324
G1	Henry Cummings	Fr Donalsonville, 18 mi S on Hwy 39	57	25	10	3.00	All year	• •	dl		Bx 96, Chattahoochee,32324
G1	River Junction	Fr Bainbridge, 20 mi SW on Hwy 253	160	20	10	3.00	All year	• •	dl g		Bx 96, Chattahoochee, 32324
G1	Ray's Lake	Fr Bainbridge, 20 mi SW on Hwy 253, N at sign for Sealy Pt	40	6	6	None	All year	• •	dl		Bx 96, Chattahoochee, 32324
G1	Sealy Point	Fr Bainbridge, 20 mi SW on Hwy 25, S at sign	172	14	14	3.00	All year	• •	dl		Bx 96, Chattahoochee, 32324
G2	Hale's Landing	Fr Bainbridge, SW on Hwy 253, S on Co	88	10			All year	•	dl		Bx 96, Chattahoochee, 32324
G2	Faceville Landing	Fr Bainbridge, 10 mi SW on Hwy 97	125	18	18	None	All year	• •	dl		Bx 96, Chattahoochee, 32324
	Lk Sidney Lanier(Buford)									404 945-9531	Bx 267, Buford, 30518
B2	Bald Ridge Creek	Fr, Cumming, 6 mi E on Co Rd	42	30	S30	2.00	3/20-9/15	• •	l p		Box 267, Buford
B2	Two Mile Creek	Fr US 19, 8 mi E on Hwy 369, 2 mi S on Co Rd.	28	38	35	2.00	3/20-10/27	•	l p		Bx 267, Buford, 30518
B2	Bethel Pk	Fr Cumming, N on US 19, 8 mi E on Hwy 369, 1-1/2 mi S on Co	74	20	S20	2.00	All year	• •	l gp		PO Bx 267, Buford 30518
B2	Shady Grove Pk	Fr Cumming 6 mi N on US 19 & Hwy 141, 4 mi S on Co	102	44	33	2.00	3/6-9/15	• •	l p		Cumming
B2	Six Mile Creek	Fr Cumming 6 mi NE on US 19 & Hwy 141	5	P14	S14	2.00	All year	• •	l p		Box 267, Buford, 30518
B2	Sawnee	Fr Cumming 4 mi E on Co; 1/2 mi NW of Buford Dam	37	50	S20	3.00	3/6-11/27	• •	l • p		Box 267, Buford, 30518
B2	Shoal Creek	Fr Buford 2.5 mi NW on Shadburn Ferry Rd	154	113	95	3.00	3/6-10/27	• •	l • p		Box 267, Buford, 30518
B2	Burton Mill	Fr Buford, 4 mi N on US 23, 2 mi W on Co	43	20		2.00	All year	• •	l p		Box 267, Buford, 30518
B2	Van Pugh Pk	Fr Buford 4 mi N on US 23, 4 mi W on Co	104	57	57	3.00	3/20-10/27	• •	l • p		Box 267, Buford,GA 30518
B2	Chestnut Ridge	Fr Buford 4 mi N on Hwy 23, 2 mi W on Co	114	70	63	3.00	3/20-10/27	• •	l • p		Box 267, Buford, GA 30518
B2	Old Federal Road Pk	Fr Flavery Branch, 1 mi N on Hwy 23, 2 mi NW on Co	87	80	80	3.00	3/20-9/15	• •	l • p		Box 267, Buford, GA 30518
B2	Duckett Mill	Fr Gainesville, 7 mi NW on Hwy 53, 2 mi SW on Co rd	96	54	23	2.00	3/20-9/15	• •	l p		Box 267, Buford, GA 30518
B2	Keith Bridge	Fr Gainesville, 9 mi NW on Hwy 53, 2 mi SE on Hwy 306	25	P10	P10	2.00	All year	• •	l p		Box 267, Buford, GA 30518
B2	Little Hall Pk	Fr Gainesville, 7 mi W on Hwy 53 to Bolling Bridge	43	44	22	2.00	3/20-9/15	• •	l p		Box 267, Buford, GA 30518
B2	Toto Creek	Fr Gainesville, 12 mi NW on Hwys 60 & 136	64	P10	S10	None	All year	•	l p		Box 267, Buford, GA 30518
B2	Bolling Mill	Fr Gainesville, 8 mi NW on Hwys 53 & 226, 1 mi S	68	P14	S14	None	All year	•	l p		Box 267, Buford, GA 30518
B2	War Hill Pk	Fr Gainesville 12 mi NW on Hwy 53, 4 mi E on Co	84	P19	S19	2.00	All year	•	l p		Box 267, Buford, GA 30518
B2	Robinson Pk	Fr Gainesville, 5 mi NW on Hwy 53, 1 mi S on Co	46	24		None	All year	•	l p		Box 267, Buford, GA 30518
B3	Little River	Fr Gainesville 5 mi N on Hwy 129, 1/2 mi W on Co	16	P18	S18	2.00	All year	•	l p		Box 267, Buford, GA 30518
	Carter Lake									404/334-2248	PO Bx 42, Oakman 30732
A2	Doll Mountain	Fr Ellijay, 13 mi S on Airport Rd, 1/2 mi on Pk access rd		55	12	2.50	4/1-10/1	• •	l		PO Box 42, Oakman, 30732
A2	Oak Hill	Fr Ellijay, 11 mi SW on Airport Rd, 2-1/2 mi on Pk Access Rd		7		2.00	4/1-10/1	• •			PO Box 42, Oakman, 30732
A2	Harris Branch	Fr Ellijay, 16 mi SW on Airport Rd, 2 mi on Pk Access Rd		14		None	4/1-10/1	• •			PO Box 42, Oakman, 30732
A2	Damsite Area	Fr Fairmont, 13 mi N on Hwy 411, 4 mi E on Hwy 136, 2 mi N on Pk Access Rd		40		None	4/1-10/1	• •	l •		PO Box 42, Oakman, 30732
A2	Ridgeway	Fr Ellijay, 4 mi W on Hwy 282, 3-1/2 mi S on pk access rd		17		2.00	4/1-10/1	• •	l		PO Box 42, Oakman, 30732
A2	Woodring Branch	Fr Ellijay, 8 mi W on Hwy 282, 4 mi S on pk access rd		39	7	2.00	4/1-10/1	• •	l		PO Box 42, Oakman, 30732
	West Point District										
D1	State Line Pk	Fr West Point, 18 mi N on West Point Lake Rd	591	130	S130	4.00	5/15-9/30	• •	dl • t	404/645-2937	Box 574, West Point 31833
	Hartwell Reservoir	(See South Carolina for additional campgrounds)								404/376-4788	Hartwell 30643
B4	Paynes Creek Pk	Fr Reed Creek Crossing, 3 mi NW	399	97	97	2.00	4/1-9/30	• •	l p		Hartwell 30643
B4	Milltown	Fr Reed Creek, SE on access rd	29	39	39	3.00	4/1-9/30	• •	l		Hartwell 30643
B4	Chandlers Ferry	Fr Reed Creek, N & W on access rds	48	68	68	3.00	4/1-9/30	• •	l		Hartwell 30643
B4	Watsadler's	Fr Hartwell, 4 mi E on US 29	34	35	25	3.00	All year	• •	l		Hartwell 30643
B4	Hartwell Group Camp	Fr Hartwell Dam, 3 mi W on US 29	22	16	16	2.00	4/1-9/30	• •	l p		Hartwell 30643
B4	Gum Branch	Fr Hartwell, E on US 29, 3.5 mi NE on Co 8	19	20	20	2.00	4/1-9/30	• •	l		Hartwell 30643
B4	River	Fr Hartwell, 5 mi N on US 29	10	15	S8	2.00	4/1-9/30	•	p	404/376-4788	Hartwell 30643

Kentucky

Major Events

See state map, pages 28-29

Sue Bennett Folk Festival, late Mar. to early Apr., London. Craftsmen, storytellers, musicians, dancers, singers, and authors join together at Sue Bennett College for five days of celebrations devoted to Appalachian culture. Free. 606/864-7670.

Tater Day, early Apr., Benton. Benton City Park comes alive with a beauty contest, a flea market, horse pulls, a parade, an antique car show, a swapping ring, arts and crafts, and a road race. Admission is charged for several events. 502/527-7665.

Painted Stone Festival, late Apr., Shelbyville. Arts and crafts, pioneer displays, games, food booths, and a health fair are all featured on the grounds of West Middle School. Free (except food). 502/633-1636.

Kentucky Derby Festival, late Apr. to early May, Louisville. There are more than 60 events taking place at this 10-day festival. The most important happening is the running of the Kentucky Derby, which attracts the finest three-year-old thoroughbred horses in the world. Other top events include the Pegasus Parade, the Great Steamboat Race, the Great Balloon Race, and the Philip Morris Festival of Stars. Admission is charged for several events. 502/584-6383.

Maifest, early May, Covington. Main Strasse Village hosts a spring festival with bands, dancers, arts and crafts, rides, and food. Free (except food). 606/261-4677.

Kentucky Guild of Artists and Craftsmen's Fairs, mid-May and late Sept., Berea. Numerous exhibits and demonstrations of arts and crafts are at the Indian Fort Theater, along with music, dance, and regional food. Admission. 606/986-3192.

Kentucky Mountain Laurel Festival, late May, Pineville, north of Middlesboro. A queen contest, a parade, a ball, art exhibits, fireworks, a golf tournament, and crafts exhibits are highlights of this festival. Admission. 606/337-6103.

Kentucky Fiddlers Contest, late May, Elizabethtown. Along with the fiddling contest, there are other musical contests and old-time music. Prizes are awarded to the winners. Admission. 502/737-3836.

Kentucky Horse Trials, late May, Lexington. The Kentucky Horse Park welcomes riders from around the world in all different types of competition at this three-day event. Admission. 606/233-2362.

Capital Expo, early June, Frankfort. Capital Plaza comes alive for three days with arts and crafts, ethnic foods, a balloon race, a film festival, puppet shows, and an antique car auction. Free (except food). 502/223-5329.

Bluegrass National Open Sheep Dog Trials, mid-June, Lexington. This two-day event features more than 60 sheep dogs competing in several different types of contests. Admission. 606/233-1483.

Legend of Daniel Boone **Outdoor Drama,** mid-June to late Aug., Harrodsburg. The Old Fort Harrod State Park Amphitheater has performances nightly (except Sunday) of this story depicting the life of Kentucky's great frontiersman. Admission. 606/734-3346.

The Stephen Foster Story **Outdoor Drama,** mid-June to early Sept., Bardstown. My Old Kentucky Home State Park stages this musical, nightly except Monday, that includes the story of Stephen Foster's life as well as many of his most famous songs like "Camptown Races" and "My Old Kentucky Home." Admission. 502/348-5971.

Appalachian Celebration, mid- to late June, Morehead. Appalachian culture is celebrated at the Morehead University campus with several events, including arts and crafts, live music, storytelling, and Appalachian foods. Admission is charged for several events. 606/783-4731.

Founders Festival, early July, Richmond. The founding fathers of Richmond are honored, and the Fourth of July is celebrated with activities which include live entertainment, contests, and a flea market. Free. 606/623-1720.

Shaker Festival, early July, South Union, southwest of Bowling Green. This old Shaker town comes to life for 10 days with tours of the town's museum, a play which is presented nightly, and a buffet dinner. Admission. 502/542-4167.

Founders Day Weekend, mid-July, Hodgenville. Rail-splitting, pioneer crafts, art displays, and tours of Lincoln's birthplace are featured at the nearby Abraham Lincoln Birthplace National Historic Site. Free. 502/358-3874.

International Banana Festival, mid-Aug., Fulton, southeast of Clinton. The nation's banana capital of yesteryear goes back to the days when it used to be a large distribution point for the South American fruit. A one-ton banana pudding is served to visitors on Saturday, and there are free bananas, parades, and entertainment at Fulton City Park. Free. 502/472-2975.

Great Ohio River Flatboat Race, mid-Aug., Owensboro to Henderson. The days of the flatboat are brought back with this race down the Ohio River. The riverfront at Second St. in Henderson is the finish line; and there are arts and crafts, contests, a street dance, food booths, and fireworks at the end of the race. Free (except food). 502/826-4000.

Shaker Heritage Weekends, three weekends in Sept., Pleasant Hill, northeast of Harrodsburg. Shaker music and dances are performed, craftsmen demonstrate their skills, exhibits are on display, and wagon rides are offered. Admission is charged for several events. 606/734-5411.

Great Dulcimer Convention, late Sept., Pineville, north of Middlesboro. Pine Mountain State Resort Park hosts this series of events centered around the dulcimer. Performances, dulcimer lessons, workshops in dulcimer building, and arts and crafts demonstrations are some of the activities. Admission. 606/337-3066.

Apple Festival and Fair, late Sept., Liberty. Festivities at Courthouse Square include live music, apple peeling, the "world's largest apple pie," arts and crafts, and contests. Free. 502/564-4930.

Kentucky Apple Festival of Johnson County, early Oct., Paintsville. The apple harvest is celebrated with a parade, a band festival, an antique car show, a horse show, the Miss Apple Blossom Pageant, arts and crafts, a footrace, and a country music show. Admission is charged for several events. 606/789-3187.

Big River Arts and Crafts Festival, early Oct., Henderson. Area artists display their works and demonstrate their crafts at John James Audubon State Park. Free. 502/826-2247.

Butchertown Oktoberfest, early Oct., Louisville. This German celebration of autumn features German beer, foods, and music. Free (except food). 502/587-8365.

Logan County Tobacco Festival, early Oct., Russellville. The harvesting and auctioning of the tobacco crop is celebrated with a pageant, tobacco judging, historic home tours, athletic events, and a parade which is followed by a marching band contest. Admission is charged for several events. 502/726-2206.

Daniel Boone Festival, early Oct., Barbourville. Daniel Boone's search for a route through the mountains into Kentucky is commemorated at this festival with a beauty contest, horse shows, a barbecue, antique displays, and townspeople wearing coonskin caps. Admission is charged for several events. 606/546-4300.

Sorghum Festival and Flea Market, mid-Oct., Springfield, north of Lebanon. Sorghum making, arts and crafts, a flea market, and home-baked goods are highlights of this festival. Free (except food). 606/336-3810.

October Court Days, mid-Oct., Mount Sterling. The downtown area of Mount Sterling becomes a gathering place for hundreds of people who buy, sell, and swap antiques and other goods. Live music is also provided. Free. 606/498-5343.

Kentucky Destinations

BARDSTOWN, 6,115, C-7. The site of **Federal Hill,** an estate made famous by Stephen Foster's song "My Old Kentucky Home, Good Night," Bardstown was settled in 1775. The state's second oldest town, it has come to represent Kentucky's traditional charm. Foster wrote his song after visiting his uncle's estate in 1852. The Georgian-Federal mansion is now part of **My Old Kentucky Home State Park,** on U.S. 150. Mar.-Nov., daily, 9 A.M. to 5 P.M.; other months, Tues.-Sun., same time. Free. Home tours: Adults $1.50, children 75¢. 502/348-3502. *The Stephen Foster Story,* a two-hour outdoor drama featuring the songs of Stephen Foster, is performed in the park during the summer. Mid-June-Labor Day, Tues.-Sun., 8:30 P.M.; also Sat., 2:30 P.M. Adults $7; children under 13, half price. 502/348-5971. **Wickland Mansion,** U.S. 62, completed in 1817, is said to be one of the finest examples of Georgian architecture in the United States. Two governors of Kentucky and one of Louisiana, all members of the same family, lived in the home at various times. Memorial Day-Labor Day, daily, 9 A.M. to 7 P.M.; other months, by appointment. Adults $1.50; persons high-school age and 65 and older, $1; grade-school age, 50¢; under school age, free. 502/348-5428. **St. Joseph's Proto-Cathedral,** 310 W. Stephen Foster St., the first Roman Catholic cathedral west of the Allegheny Mountains, was completed in 1819. Apr.-Nov., Mon.-Fri., 9 A.M. to 5 P.M.; Sat., 9 A.M. to 2:30 P.M.; Sun., 1 to 5:30 P.M. Freewill offering. 502/348-3126. **Talbott Tavern,** 107 W. Stephen Foster St., began as a stagecoach stop in 1779 and has been in continuous operation since. Year-round, daily. 502/348-3494. **Spalding Hall,** Fifth and Flaget Sts., built in 1839, served as a Civil War hospital, an orphanage, and a boys' preparatory school. It now houses the *Spalding Hall Museum,* which displays Indian relics, a hat of the outlaw Jesse James, and the stole worn by Pope John XXIII during his coronation. Memorial Day-Labor Day, Mon.-Fri., 10:30 A.M. to 5:30 P.M.; Sun., 1:30 to 5:30 P.M.; other months, by appointment. Adults 50¢, children 25¢. 502/348-6402. The **Barton Museum of Whiskey History,** U.S. 31E, depicts the 200-year history of the distilling industry in the United States. Displays include bottles, licenses, and advertising posters. Year-round, daily, 8 A.M. to noon, 1 to 4 P.M. Free. 502/348-3991. **Bernheim Forest,** 15 miles northwest on St. 245, is a 10,000-acre area with a wildlife sanctuary, lakes, nature center, and hiking trails. Mid-Mar.-mid-Nov., daily, 9 A.M. to one-half hour before dusk. Free. 502/543-2451.

BEREA, 8,226, C-9. In the early 1850s, Kentucky statesman Cassius Marcellus Clay urged abolitionist minister John

Daniel and Rebecca Boone and other pioneers are portrayed as they crossed the Cumberland Gap in the Cumberland Mountains (in the Appalachians) en route to Kentucky in 1775. Cumberland Gap, on the Kentucky-Virginia border, had long been used to cross the Appalachian Mountains, which offered security to the colonists, but kept them entrapped on the eastern seaboard. Boone, more than anyone else, helped open the way westward. He spent two years exploring the area, and with 30 men marked the Wilderness Trail from the Gap into Kentucky. The trail followed the path used by the buffalo and Indians and later by French hunters and trappers. Cumberland Gap, now a national historical park, contains over 20,000 acres in Kentucky, Tennessee, and Virginia. It can be reached by U.S. 25E in Kentucky and Tennessee and by U.S. 58 in Virginia.

Gregg Fee to begin a school that would serve needy Appalachian students and other persons, regardless of race. **Berea College** was founded in 1855 and continues for the same purpose to this day. Students from throughout the world work in a unique labor program in exchange for full scholarships. Campus tours offered. Academic year, Mon.-Fri., 9 A.M. and 2 P.M.; Sat., 9 A.M.; other months, Mon.-Sat., 9 and 10:30 A.M.; 1:30 and 3 P.M. Free. 606/986-9341. **The Appalachian Museum,** Jackson St., features farm tools, furniture, and an exhibit of Appalachian photographs taken in 1930-31 by Doris Ulmann, a New York photographer. Year-round, June-Aug., Mon.-Sat., 9 A.M. to 9 P.M.; Sun., 1 to 6 P.M.; other months, Mon.-Sat., 9 A.M. to 6 P.M.; Sun., 1 to 6 P.M. Adults $1, children 50¢. 606/986-9341. **Churchill Weavers,** Lor-raine Ct., was begun in 1922 by David Churchill, who designed and patented his handlooms, brought them to this Appalachian area, and established an industry to boost its economy. A gift shop adjoins the loomhouse. Tours of the loomhouse permitted. Year-round, Mon.-Fri., 9 A.M. to noon, 1 to 4 P.M. Free. 606/986-3126.

BOWLING GREEN, 40,450, D-6. **Beech Bend Park,** 3 miles west of Bowling Green off U.S. 31W, is a 1,000-acre amusement park that features several campgrounds, various rides, a miniature golf course, and drag racing. Late May-late Aug., Tues.-Thurs., noon to 9 P.M.; Fri., noon to 10 P.M.; Sat.-Sun., 10 A.M. to 10 P.M.; other months, Sat.-Sun., 10 A.M. to 10 P.M. Admission 10¢ (rides extra). Campgrounds: Year-round, daily. 502/842-8101. **The Kentucky Mu-**

seum and Library, both in the Kentucky Building on the Western Kentucky University campus, feature antique furniture, traditional tools and implements, photographs, and paintings in the museum and a noncirculating collection of primary research material, rare books, original manuscripts, and geneological records in the library. Year-round, Tues.-Sat., 9:30 A.M. to 4 P.M.; Sun., 1 to 4 P.M. Free. 502/745-2592. **Riverview**, 736 Sherwood Dr., is a three-story antebellum home built by Col. Atwood Hobson and used as a munitions storehouse during the Civil War. The Italianate mansion features frescoed walls and ceilings painted by French artist Fritz Leiber. Year-round, Tues.-Sun., 2 to 5 P.M.; other times, by appointment. Adults $1; children 8-14, 50¢; under 8, free. 502/842-6932.

CORBIN, 7,317, D-9. At **Cumberland Falls State Resort Park,** in Daniel Boone National Forest 20 miles west of Corbin on St. 90, one of two known moonbows (the other is at Victoria Falls, in Africa) in the world can be seen at times over the falls during a full moon. One of the largest in the East, the waterfall measures 120 feet across, 70 feet high, and produces a colored bow in its mist on clear evenings when the moon is bright. Always open. Free. 606/528-4121. Whitewater rafting is offered on the Cumberland River below the falls. No experience necessary. May-early June, Labor Day-Nov., weekends; June-Labor Day, daily. Trips leave at 10 A.M. Adults $24; persons under 16, $18. 606/523-0629.

COVINGTON, 49,013, A-8. Just across the Ohio River from Cincinnati, Ohio, Covington is the major city in an urban area referred to as Northern Kentucky. The **Cathedral Basilica of the Assumption,** 9 E. 12th St., was modeled after Notre Dame Cathedral in Paris, France, and claims one of the largest stained-glass windows in the world. Year-round, daily, 7:30 A.M. to 6 P.M. Guided tours: June-Aug., Sun., 2 P.M. Free. 606/431-2060. **Riverboat cruises** of varying lengths are available by reservation in Covington, with a regular sightseeing cruise sailing every afternoon. Mar.-Dec., daily. From $2.50 to $15.95. 606/261-8500. **Monte Cassino,** one of the world's smallest churches, may be seen on the Thomas More College campus, Turkey Foot Rd., in nearby Fort Mitchell. Built by Benedictine monks in 1901, it has an interior measurement of 6 by 9 feet. Year-round, daylight hours only. Free. 606/341-5800. **Main Strasse** is a development with quaint German shops. *Carroll Chimes,* at the head of the Main Strasse, 6th and Philadelphia Sts., is a 100-foot-high bell tower built with small mechanical figures which act out the story of the *Pied Piper of Hamelin* with chime accompaniment. Apr.-Nov. (except during snow), daily, 10 A.M. to 6 P.M. on the hour. Free. 606/261-4677. **Mother of God Church,** 119 Sixth St., was built in 1871 and displays five murals by Johann Schmitt. Year-round, daily, 8

A.M. to 6 P.M. Free. 606/431-0614. **Latonia Race Course,** U.S. 25 near Florence, features fall, winter, and spring thoroughbred racing and summer harness racing. Jan.-Apr., Tues.-Fri., post time 7:30 P.M.; Sat., post time 1:30 P.M.; May-mid-Aug., Tues.-Sat., 7:30 P.M. Admission $1.50, clubhouse $2.50 extra. 606/371-0200.

CUMBERLAND GAP NATIONAL HISTORICAL PARK, off U.S. 25E north of Middlesboro, D-9. In 1750, Dr. Thomas Walker entered Kentucky through a natural passage in the rugged Appalachian Mountains. About two decades later, Daniel Boone followed, bringing a party of frontiersmen who cleared Cumberland Gap, which became the major overland route from Virginia to the West. **Cumberland Gap National Historical Park** includes over 20,000 acres and runs for 34 miles across the top of the Cumberland Mountains. One of the features in the park is *Hensley Settlement,* a living history restoration of a family settlement (early 1900s) on Brush Mountain. An isolated, self-sufficient farm community, it can be reached only on foot. The Visitors Center has exhibits and a living history program. Daily, June-Aug., 8 A.M. to 7 P.M.; Sept.-May, 8 A.M. to 5 P.M. Free. 606/248-2817.

DANVILLE, 12,942, C-8. In 1792, Kentucky became the 15th state in the Union. Its first constitution was drawn up in the town square in Danville, now the site of a state shrine. Year-round, daily, 9 A.M. to 5 P.M. Free. 606/236-5089. **Dr. Ephraim McDowell's Office,** 125 S. Second St., is where, in 1809, Dr. McDowell successfully removed an ovarian tumor and, as a result, became noted as having been the first surgeon to perform this operation with success. His office has been restored. Apr.-Oct., Mon.-Sat., 10 A.M. to noon, 1 to 4 P.M.; Sun., 2 to 4 P.M.; Nov.-Mar., Tues.-Sun., same hours as other months. Adults $1.50, children 50¢. 606/236-2804.

ELIZABETHTOWN, 15,380, C-7. The **Lincoln Heritage House,** just off U.S. 31W, was begun in 1789 and completed in 1807. Abraham Lincoln's father, a carpenter, built the stairways and mantelpieces. June-Sept., Tues.-Sat., 10 A.M. to 6 P.M.; Sun., 1 to 6 P.M. Adults 50¢; persons 6-12 and 65 and over, 25¢. 502/769-9077. The **Brown-Pusey House,** 128 N. Main St., was built in 1825 as a stagecoach inn, and is where Gen. George Custer lived during the two years he was stationed in Elizabethtown. Year-round, Mon.-Sat., 10 A.M. to 4 P.M. Free. 502/765-2515. The **Coca-Cola Museum,** U.S. 31W, features memorabilia of the soft-drink company from the 1880s through the 1960s. Year-round, Mon.-Fri., 9 A.M. to 4 P.M. Free. 502/769-3323.

FAIRVIEW, 198, D-5. The **Jefferson Davis Monument,** on U.S. 68 in Fairview, marks the site of the birthplace of Jefferson Davis, President of the Confederate States

John James Audubon (1785-1851), artist and ornithologist, was born in Santo Domingo, spent his childhood in France, returned to America, and spent several years in the South. He lived 14 of these years in Louisville and Henderson, where he and a partner had a general store and other enterprises. He began painting birds in France and continued painting them in America. In the museum at John James Audubon State Park, east of Henderson, are 126 of the original paintings from his book, *Birds of America,* which was published in England in 1838. About 200 copies were printed of the first edition, a four-volume set, which sold for $1,000 a set.

of America during the Civil War. The monument, one of the tallest concrete obelisks in the country, is part of a state shrine commemorating the birth of President Davis on June 3, 1808. Year-round, daily, 8 A.M. to 10 P.M. Free. 502/886-1765.

FORT BOONESBOROUGH STATE PARK, on St. 388, just off St. 627 between Richmond and Winchester, C-9. This restoration of the fort built over 200 years ago by Daniel Boone is near the village of **Boonesboro.** Here pioneer crafts from the 18th century are demonstrated by Kentuckians using equipment of the frontier days. Apr.-Labor Day, daily, 10 A.M. to 6:30 P.M.; other months, Wed., Sun., 10 A.M. to 6:30 P.M. Adults $2; children 6-12, $1; under 6, free. A sternwheel excursion boat, the *Dixie Belle,* operates one-hour excursions, which leave from the Fort Boonesborough boat dock. May-Labor Day, daily, 11 A.M. to 7 P.M., hourly. Adults $3, children $1.75. 606/527-3328.

FRANKFORT, 25,973, B-8. Kentucky's capital, Frankfort is a small city that straddles the Kentucky River. Several governmental structures highlight the town's architecture, and in its oldest sections are 19th-century homes, many of which are open to the public. Daniel Boone and his wife, Rebecca, are buried in Frankfort Cemetery, high above the river.

GOVERNMENT BUILDINGS: The **State Capitol,** on Capitol Ave., built with marble from Italy and the United States, features 70 Ionic columns outside and 36 in its nave. The *State Reception Room* is a replica of

Marie Antoinette's drawing room. A 34-foot floral clock is on the grounds of the nearby Capitol Annex. Year-round, Mon.-Fri., 8 A.M. to 4:30 P.M. Free tours. 502/564-3449. The **Governor's Mansion**, Capitol Ave., was built to resemble the Petit Trianon, Marie Antoinette's villa near the Palace of Versailles. It overlooks the Kentucky River and features eight Ionic columns, an oval garden, and historic furnishings. 502/564-3449. The **Old State Capitol Building**, St. Clair St. and Broadway, was designed by Kentuckian Gideon Shryock when he was 24 years old. Completed in 1830, the Greek-Revival structure was built of hand-quarried marble from Frankfort and features circular stairs that are supported only by their own weight. Year-round, Mon.-Sat., 9 A.M. to 4 P.M.; Sun., 1 to 5 P.M. Free. 502/564-3016. **Old Governor's Mansion**, 420 High St., was begun in 1797 and served as the original mansion for Kentucky's governors. Now the Georgian home is the resi-

dence of the state's lieutenant governor. Among guests at the home have been seven Presidents, the Marquis de Lafayette, and Henry Clay. Year-round, Tues. and Thurs., 10 A.M. to 4 P.M.; other days, by appointment. Free tours. 502/564-5500.

HISTORIC HOMES: Liberty Hall, 218 Wilkinson St., was built in 1796-1800 by Sen. John Brown. Among the guests here were Pres. James Monroe and Gen. Andrew Jackson and Maj. Zachary Taylor, both of whom later became President of the United States. Year-round, Tues.-Sat., 10 A.M. to 5 P.M.; Sun., 2 to 5 P.M. Adults $1.50; children and students, 50¢. 502/227-2560. The **Orlando Brown House,** 202 Wilkinson St., was designed by Gideon Shryock and built in 1835-36. It was the home of Orlando Brown, who served as Commissioner of Indian Affairs under his friend Pres. Zachary Taylor. Year-round, Tues.-Sat., 10 A.M. to 4 P.M.; Sun., 2 to 4 P.M. Adults $1.50, children 50¢. Both Liberty Hall and Orlando Brown House: Adults $2.50, children 75¢. 502/875-4952.

DISTILLERIES AND MUSEUMS: Ancient Age Distillery, U.S. 421, was built on the site of Leestown, a settlement founded by Gen. George Rogers Clark in 1773. Year-round, Mon.-Fri., 10 A.M. to 1 P.M. Free tours. 502/223-3338. **Old Grand-Dad Distillery,** U.S. 460. Year-round, Mon.-Fri., 8:30 A.M. to 3:30 P.M. Free. 502/223-8251. **Old Taylor Distillery,** south of Frankfort on Glenns Creek Rd., 4 miles off U.S. 60, features a castlelike structure built in 1887 as a distillery, and the *Old Taylor Hall of Fame Museum,* a collection of memorabilia depicting the history of bourbon whiskey in America. Year-round, Mon.-Fri., 8:30 A.M. to 3:30 P.M. Free. 502/223-8251. The **Kentucky Military History Museum,** U.S. 60 at Capitol Ave., exhibits weapons, uniforms, flags, and equipment from pioneer times through the Vietnam era. An extensive collection of automatic weapons is included. Year-round, Mon.-Sat., 9 A.M. to 4 P.M.; Sun., 1 to 5 P.M. Free. 502/564-3265.

HARRODSBURG, 7,265, C-8. The oldest town in Kentucky, Harrodsburg was established as a fort in 1774 by James Harrod and his company of settlers. **Old Fort Harrod State Park,** U.S. 68/127, is a reproduction of the fort. May-Nov., daily, 9 A.M. to 5 P.M. Adults $1; children 6-12, 50¢. 606/734-3314. *The Legend of Daniel Boone,* an outdoor drama depicting pioneer life, is performed nightly in the park's amphitheater. Mid-June-Aug., 8:30 P.M. Adults $6, children $3.50. 606/734-3346. **Beaumont Inn,** 638 Beaumont Dr., was built in 1845 as a girls' preparatory school. It now operates as a restaurant and inn. Mar.-Nov., daily. 606/734-3381.

See also **Shaker Village at Pleasant Hill.**

HENDERSON, 24,834, C-5. Noted artist and ornithologist John James Audubon lived in this small river town from 1810 to 1820. Here he spent many hours observing

in the forest, which is a point on the migratory route of many species of birds. Paintings of his observations were later published as *The Birds of America.* **John James Audubon State Park,** on U.S. 41N, today protects the forest, which is a part of the park. In the park museum are many paintings by Audubon and his sons and 126 first-edition prints of his paintings. Museum: Apr.-Oct., daily, 9 A.M. to 5 P.M.; Nov.-Mar., Sat.-Sun., 9 A.M. to 5 P.M. Adults $1, children 50¢. 502/827-1893. **James C. Ellis Park,** U.S. 41, features thoroughbred racing. July-Labor Day, Mon.-Sat., post time 2 P.M. Admission $1.75, clubhouse $1 extra, reserved seat $2 extra. 502/683-0266. **Audubon Raceway,** U.S. 41, has two standardbred meets a year. Late Apr.-late June, Tues.-Sat.; mid-Sept.-Nov., Wed.-Fri.; post time 7:30 P.M. 502/827-5641.

HODGENVILLE, 2,459, C-7. **Abraham Lincoln Birthplace National Historic Site,** U.S. 31E, commemorates the location of Sinking Spring farm, where Abraham Lincoln was born. The remains of a tremendous oak tree known to Lincoln as the "boundary oak," which marked the family's property line, are still here. The original farm cabin is enclosed in an impressive granite and marble memorial shrine. Daily, June-Aug., 8 A.M. to 6:45 P.M.; Sept.-May, 8 A.M. to 4:45 P.M. Free. 502/358-9474.

KENTUCKY HORSE PARK, B-8. The 1,032-acre park, east off Int. 75 on Iron Works Pike, was designed to illustrate the Kentucky thoroughbred industry and honor horses of every type. Once the site of Walnut Hall, a historic Kentucky horse farm, it is now an educational and recreational complex. A statue of **Man o' War** stands at the entrance of the park, which also has a Visitors Center, an **International Museum of the Horse,** two cinemas, equestrian-event courses, racetrack, polo grounds, clubhouse restaurant, and campgrounds. Activities include numerous national and international

United States Department of Agriculture

Kentucky bluegrass (sometimes called junegrass) is used principally for lawn and turf purposes, but it is also used extensively for pasture. The definite date of its introduction into the United States is not known; however, agriculturalists believe early colonists brought seed of Kentucky bluegrass to this country in mixtures with the other grasses. It is believed to be a native of the Old World, as it occurs over much of Europe and Asia. Kentucky bluegrass grows 18 to 24 inches tall, under exceptionally favorable conditions reaches 36 inches, and is easily identified by its boat-shaped leaf tip. It is a long-lived perennial.

events, horse-drawn tours, horseback riding, pony riding, and walking farm tours to see grooming, training, shoeing, harness-making, and several breeds of horses. Daily, May-Labor Day, 9 A.M. to 7 P.M.; other months, times, and days vary. Park: Adults $1.50, children $1. Additional charges for museum, film, carriage rides, and special events. 606/233-4303.

LAND BETWEEN THE LAKES, D-4. Developed by the federal government as a national demonstration in outdoor recreation and environmental education, **Land Between the Lakes,** U.S. 62/641, U.S. 68 and St. 80, just south of Int. 24, is a 170,000-acre area separating Kentucky's two largest man-made lakes—Kentucky Lake and Lake Barkley, which also extend into Tennessee. The preserve has several camping areas; no commercial development is allowed. *The Homeplace-1850* is a living-history farm built with original structures dating to the mid-19th century. Year-round (some facilities close mid-Dec.-mid-Feb.), daily. Demonstrations and facilities: Mar.-Nov., Wed.-Sun., 9 A.M. to 5 P.M. Free. 502/924-5602.

LEBANON, C-7. *See* **Loretto.**

LEXINGTON, 204,165, B-8. Center of Kentucky's thoroughbred horse industry, largest burley tobacco market in the world, and home of the University of Kentucky, Lexington is the heart of the celebrated Bluegrass Region. The state's second-largest city, Lexington was settled in 1779.

HISTORIC HOMES AND BUILDINGS: Ashland, Richmond Rd. (U.S. 25/421 south), southeast Lexington, was the home of Henry Clay, Kentucky congressman, senator, and secretary of state under John Quincy Adams. Year-round, daily, 9:30 A.M. to 4:30 P.M. Adults $2, children 50¢. 606/266-8581. **Hunt-Morgan House,** 201 N. Mill St., built in 1814 by John Wesley Hunt, was later the home of Confederate Gen. John Hunt Morgan, "Thunderbolt of the Confederacy." Kentucky's first Nobel Prize winner, Thomas Hunt Morgan, was born in this Federal-style home. Year-round, Tues.-Sat., 10 A.M. to 4 P.M.; Sun., 2 to 5 P.M. Adults $2, children 50¢. 606/253-0362. **Mary Todd Lincoln House,** 511 W. Short St., built as an inn in 1803-06, was the home of Abraham Lincoln's wife-to-be, Mary Todd, when she was a young woman. Lincoln was a guest in the house three times. *Parker Place,* also at 511 W. Short St., is the site of the home of Mary Todd's grandmother, Elizabeth Parker, who helped raise six-year-old Mary following her mother's death. Mary Todd Home and Parker Place: Year-round, Tues.-Sat., 10 A.M. to 4 P.M. Adults $3, children $1. 606/233-9999. **Waveland,** south of Lexington off U.S. 27, is a Greek-Revival mansion built in 1847 by Joseph Bryan, grandnephew of Daniel Boone. The home now contains displays of Kentucky furniture and silver, Civil War relics, and other historic items.

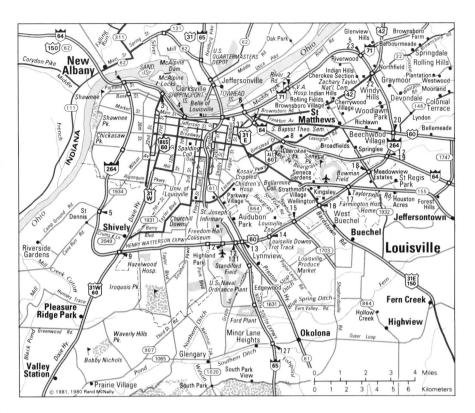

Year-round, Tues.-Sat., 9 A.M. to 4 P.M.; Sun., 1:30 to 4:30 P.M. Adults $1; high school and college students, 50¢; grade-school students, 25¢. 606/272-3611. **Lexington Opera House,** 401 W. Short St., has been restored to its original elegance, with crystal chandeliers, red velvet upholstering, and flocked wallpaper, after serving a number of roles over the years. It was built in 1886. Weekend performances, mid-Sept.-mid-June. 606/233-3565.

HORSE INDUSTRY: Keeneland Race Course, U.S. 60, features thoroughbred racing on land for which the original deed was signed by Patrick Henry. Apr. (two weeks), Oct., (two weeks) Tues.-Sat., post time 1:30 P.M. Admission $1.25, reserved seats $1.75 extra. 606/254-3412. The **Red Mile,** 847 S. Broadway, was established in 1875 and is claimed to be the fastest standardbred (trotters and pacers) track in the world. Spring Meet: Apr.-June, post time 7:30 P.M. Grand Circuit Meet: Sept.-Oct., post time 1:15 P.M. Fall Meet: Nov., post time 7:30 P.M. Admission $1, clubhouse $2. 606/255-0752. The **Kentucky Horse Center,** 3380 Paris Pike, a facility for training and selling horses, opened in 1978. Visitors may see a multimedia program depicting the history of the thoroughbred. Year-round, Mon.-Sat., one tour, 10 A.M.; multimedia program, 11 A.M. Tour and film: $2. 606/299-5212.

MUSEUM: The Headley-Whitney Museum, 6 miles west of Lexington on Old Frankfort Pike (St. 1681), features jeweled bibelots, a shell grotto, and a collection of Oriental art. Year-round, Wed.-Sun., 10 A.M. to 5 P.M. Adults $2; students $1; children free. 606/255-6653.

LORETTO, 954, northwest of Lebanon, C-7. **Star Hill Farm,** St. 52, just off U.S. 68, is the home of Maker's Mark Distillery, a National Historic Landmark founded in 1840. Tours: Year-round, Mon.-Fri., 10:30 A.M. to 3:30 P.M.; Sat., by appointment. Free. 502/865-2881.

LOUISVILLE, 298,451, B-7. Kentucky's largest city and home of the Kentucky Derby, Louisville was founded in 1781 by Gen. George Rogers Clark. Situated by the falls of the Ohio River, the city quickly became a major portage for inland shipping and remains one of the busiest river ports in the United States.

HISTORIC BUILDINGS: The American Printing House for the Blind, 1839 Frankfort Ave., is the world's largest publishing house for the blind. Tours: Year-round, Mon.-Fri., 9 to 10:45 A.M., 1 to 2:45 P.M. Free. 502/895-2405. **Bakery Square,** 1324 E. Washington St., is a 19th-century bakery which has been converted into specialty shops and restaurants in this old German community of Butchertown. Year-round, Mon.-Sat., 10 A.M. to 5 P.M.; Sun., 12:30 to 5 P.M. Free. 502/584-7425. **Brennan House,** 631 S. Fifth St., is a late 19th-century Victorian home filled with furnishings gathered from throughout the world. Year-round, Wed., 10 A.M. to 2 P.M. Adults $2, children free. 502/582-3727. **Farmington,** Bardstown Rd., just off Int. 264, was built by John Speed in 1810 from a design by Thomas Jefferson. The home was visited by Abraham Lincoln when he was a young man and a friend of Speed's son. Year-round, Mon.-Sat., 10 A.M. to 4:30 P.M.; Sun., 1:30 to 4:30 P.M. Adults $2; students $1; children under 6, free. 502/452-9920. **Locust Grove** (circa 1790), 561 Blankenbaker Lane, was built by George Rogers Clark's sister and her husband. Clark lived here from 1809 until his death. Year-round, Mon.-Sat., 10 A.M. to 4:30 P.M.; Sun., 1:30 to 4:30 P.M. Adults $2; students $1; children under 6, free. 502/897-9845. **Thomas Alva Edison Home,** 729 E. Washington St., near Bakery Square, is where Edison lived in 1886. Year-round, Sat.-Sun., 2 to 4 P.M. Free. 502/893-7767. **Actors Theatre,** 316 W. Main St., the State Theater of Kentucky, is a nationally acclaimed resident professional company that performs in a complex whose lobby was originally part of a Greek-Revival bank built in 1837. Oct.-May, Tues.-Sun., 8 P.M. curtain time. Tickets: $3.15-$9.35. 502/584-1205.

MUSEUMS AND PLANETARIUM: The American Saddle Horse Museum, 730 W. Main St., features saddlebred horse paintings, photographs, and horse-drawn vehicles. Year-round, Mon.-Sat., 10 A.M. to 4 P.M.; Sun., 1 to 5 P.M. Adults $1; servicemen, students, and persons 65 and over, 75¢; persons under student age 50¢. 502/585-1342. **J. B. Speed Art Museum,** S. Third St., houses collections of European and American paintings, medieval tapestries, and contemporary art. Year-round, Tues.-Sat., 10 A.M. to 4 P.M.; Sun., 2 to 6 P.M. Free. 502/636-2893. The **Filson Club,** 118 Breckinridge St., houses collections of early Kentucky costumes, maps, books, photographs, and prints. Year-round, Mon.-Fri., 9 A.M. to 5 P.M.; Oct.-June, Sat., 9 A.M. to noon. Free. 502/778-5531. The **Museum of Natural History and Science,** 727 W. Main St., features "touch and feel" as well as traditional "look and see" exhibits. Year-round, Mon.-Sat., 9 A.M. to 5 P.M.; Sun., 1 to 5 P.M. Adults $1; servicemen, students, and persons 65 and over, 75¢; children 5-12, 50¢. Free. 502/587-3137. **Rauch Memorial Planetarium,** on the University of Louisville's Belknap campus, on Third St., offers regular and special shows. Regular shows: Year-round, Fri., 8 P.M.; Sun., 3 and 5 P.M. Children's show: Year-round, Sat., 2 P.M. Adults $1, children 50¢. 502/588-6664.

CEMETERY: Zachary Taylor National Cemetery, 4701 Brownsboro Rd., includes the grave of Zachary Taylor, 12th president of the United States. Year-round, daily, 8 A.M. to 5 P.M. Free. 502/893-3852.

DISTILLERIES: Brown-Forman Distillers Corp., 850 Dixie Hwy., is Kentucky's largest distilling company. Tours: Year-round, Mon.-Fri., 9 A.M. to 4 P.M. Free. 502/778-5531. **Old Fitzgerald Distillery,** Fitzgerald Rd., is an old-fashioned distiller, using no chemicals or air-conditioned warehouses. Tours: Year-round, Mon.-Fri., by appointment. Free. 502/448-2860.

RACETRACKS: Churchill Downs, 700 Central Ave., is the home of the celebrated *Kentucky Derby*, one of the world's most famous horse races, which is held each year on the first Saturday in May. *Derby Mu-*

Shaker Georgian is how the style of architecture of Shaker Village at Pleasant Hill, Kentucky, is often described. Its simplicity is so elegant, it causes visitors to stand in awe as they look up at this spiral staircase, which rises three floors and ends in the dome of the Trustees' House, built in 1839. The twin staircases (another is across the hall) rise seemingly unsupported and are framed with three-inch-thick white oak members. The balustrades are of cherry wood. According to religious custom, the Meeting House (the most important structure) was painted white; other buildings were yellow or dark red. The religious revival of 1799-1805 spawned the westward movement of the Shakers. Pleasant Hill was built in 1809, and by 1850, there were at least 260 structures on the 5,000 acres of Shaker land. When restoration began in 1961, 27 buildings remained to be restored. Today, dining and overnight lodging are offered at the authentically restored village, which also has craft-making demonstrations by local villagers and tours.

seum is at the track. Other racing is scheduled about 80 days a year. Year-round, daily, 9:30 A.M. to 4:30 P.M.; during racing season, 9 to 11 A.M. Guided tours: May-Sept. Free. Races (excluding Derby): Admission $1.50, reserved seats $2 extra, clubhouse $3 extra. Museum: 502/634-3261. Track: 502/589-3561. **Louisville Downs,** Poplar Level Rd., offers nighttime harness racing. Spring Meet, Feb.-Apr.; Fall Meet, July-Sept.; post time 7:30 P.M. Admission $1, clubhouse $2.50 extra. 502/964-6415.

RIVERBOAT: The *Belle of Louisville* is one of America's few remaining authentic sternwheel riverboats. Built in 1914, the triple-deck vessel has been cruising on the Ohio River since 1932. Departures are from the wharf at Fourth and River Sts. Day cruises: Memorial Day-Labor Day, Tues.-Sun., boarding time 1 P.M. Adults $3.50, children $1. Dance cruises: Year-round, Sat., boarding time 7:30 P.M. Adults $7.50. 502/582-2547 or 502/778-6651.

ZOO: The Louisville Zoo, 1100 Trevilian Way, is nationally known for its authentic habitats; it has no cages or glass walls. June-Aug., Mon.-Sat., 10 A.M. to 6 P.M.; Sun. and holidays, 10 A.M. to 7 P.M.; Sept.-May, Tues.-Fri., 10 A.M. to 5 P.M.; Sat.-Sun., 10 A.M. to 6 P.M.; Oct.-Apr., Tues.-Sun., 10 A.M. to 5 P.M. Adults $2; persons 4-12 and 65 and over, 75¢. 502/459-2181.

SPECIAL TOUR: Philip Morris Inc., 1930 Maple St., manufacturer of tobacco products, offers tours that show cigarettes being made. Year-round, Mon.-Fri., 8 A.M. to 4 P.M. Free. 502/566-1234.

MAMMOTH CAVE NATIONAL PARK, D-6. In south-central Kentucky, the main entrance is on St. 70, west of Park City. This national park preserves Mammoth Cave, which has more than 200 miles of caverns, making it one of the largest cave systems in the world. Early Indians lighted their way through the caves with torches; oil lamps were used by miners searching for nitrate to be used in gunpowder during the War of 1812. Today, electricity lights most of the tours; however, one cave expedition requires crawling and sliding with no light other than mining-type helmets and hand-held lanterns. Above ground, the park includes over 50,000 acres of wooded hills, valleys, and long hiking trails. Park: Always open. Free. Visitors Center: Daily, mid-Apr.-mid-June, 8 A.M. to 5:20 P.M.; mid-June-early Sept., 7:30 A.M. to 7 P.M.; early Sept.-early Nov., 8 A.M. to 5:20 P.M.; early Nov.-mid-Apr., 8 A.M. to 5 P.M. Cave tours start from the Visitors Center: Adults $1.50 to $4.20; persons under 16, 75¢ to $2. 502/758-2328.

MAYSVILLE, 7,983, A-9. This small city is the heart of Kentucky's historic northeastern river town area. Nearby Washington and Augusta may be added to form a triangle of communities whose 18th- and 19th-century heritage is displayed at every turn. The **Mason County Museum,** 215 Sutton St., contains a historical and genealogical library and an art gallery. Year-round, Tues.-Sat., 10 A.M. to 4 P.M.; May-Labor Day, Sun., 2 to 4 P.M. Adults $1, children 50¢. 606/564-5865. **Washington,** 4 miles southwest of Maysville at the junction of U.S. 62 and U.S. 68, was settled in 1786 and named for Pres. George Washington. The town is still laid out according to its original plan, with flagstone streets and various 18th-century log structures. Tours: May-mid-Aug., Mon.-Sat., noon to 4 P.M.; Sun., 1 to 4 P.M.; mid-Aug.-first weekend of Dec., Mon.-Fri., by appointment; Sat., noon to 4 P.M.; Sun., 1 to 4 P.M. Adults $2, students 50¢. 606/759-7843 or 606/759-7814. **Augusta,** 17 miles west of Maysville on St. 8, was a busy port for traders and settlers in the 18th and 19th centuries. This community was cast as early 19th-century St. Louis in the television mini-series *Centennial.* Tours daily. 606/756-2261.

MIDDLESBORO, E-9. *See* **Cumberland Gap National Historical Park.**

MIDWAY, 1,445, north of Versailles, B-8. A small community halfway between Lexington and Frankfort on U.S. 62, Midway is one of Kentucky's best-known specialty shopping areas. Many of Midway's older buildings, most of which line a railroad track that bisects the town, have been renovated to house antique shops, boutiques, clothing stores, and restaurants. Year-round, Mon.-Sat., 10 A.M. to 5 P.M.

MOREHEAD, 7,789, B-10. **Cave Run Lake,** 8,270 acres just south of Morehead on U.S. 60, is unique among Kentucky's other major impoundments because of the forested Appalachian foothills that surround it. Cave Run Lake is in the northern portion of 660,000-acre **Daniel Boone National Forest,** which stretches north-south through much of eastern Kentucky. The U.S. Forest Service has built campgrounds, a large beach area, and boat ramps for visitors' use. Muskie, bass, bluegill, catfish, and crappie may all be caught at Cave Run. Houseboats and other watercraft can be rented at either of two marinas. Year-round, daily. 606/784-5624 or 606/784-6264.

NATURAL BRIDGE STATE RESORT PARK, east of Stanton on St. 11, C-9. An unusual feature in this mountain environment in **Daniel Boone National Forest** is a natural sandstone bridge that spans 80 feet at a height of 65 feet. Park accommodations include a lodge on a ledge overlooking a deep valley, cottages, camping sites, and nature center. Always open. 606/663-2214.

The Filson Club, Louisville, Kentucky

Fort Boonesborough, now restored as a state park, is where in September, 1775, the Boones arrived. The fort included a few rough cabins, a few cornfields, and surrounding forests. Some of the first settlers soon left, joining other expeditions or returning to Virginia. But the Boones stayed on until the fort closed after it had withstood a ten-day siege in September, 1778. Daniel and Rebecca Boone are buried in Frankfort, where their hilltop graves overlook the state's capital.

OWENSBORO, 54,450, C-5. Kentucky's third-largest city, Owensboro is a major tobacco market and Ohio River port. **Glenmore's Little Museum,** Hardinsburg Rd. at U.S. 60E, contains collections of miniature bottles, old whiskey jugs, a moonshine still, and old whiskey advertisements. Museum: Year-round, daily, sunrise to sunset. Free. 502/926-1110. **Owensboro Museum of Fine Arts,** 901 Frederica St., has a permanent collection of 18th- to 20th-century art, an art reference library, and monthly exhibits. Year-round, Mon.-Fri., 10 A.M. to 4 P.M.; Sun., 1 to 4 P.M. Free. 502/685-2182. The **Owensboro Area Museum,** 2829 S. Griffith Ave., has art galleries and natural science and historic displays. Year-round, Mon.-Fri., 8 A.M. to 4 P.M.; Sat.-Sun., 1 to 4 P.M. 502/683-0296.

PADUCAH, 29,315, D-3. Kentucky's westernmost metropolitan center, Paducah is the commercial hub for the state's most popular recreation area, its western lakes region. The **Market House,** Broadway at Second St., once the city's busy produce market, is now the home of Paducah's art gallery, museum, and theater. Paducah Art Guild Gallery: May-Aug., Tues.-Sat., 10 A.M. to 4 P.M.; other months, Sun., 1 to 5 P.M. Free. Museum: Year-round, Tues.-Sat., noon to 4 P.M.; Sun., 1 to 5 P.M. Admission 50¢; under 6, free. 502/442-0015. The **Alben Barkley Museum,** Madison at Sixth St., houses memorabilia of Vice President (under Truman) Alben W. Barkley and his family. Year-round, Sat.-Sun., 1 to 4 P.M.; other times by appointment. Adults 50¢, children 25¢. 502/554-9690.
See also **Land Between the Lakes**

PARK CITY, C-6. *See* **Mammoth Cave National Park.**

RED RIVER GORGE GEOLOGICAL AREA, west of Stanton, C-9. This area, about 50 miles southeast of Lexington off the Bert T. Combs Mountain Pkwy., is a 26,000-acre preserve noted for its natural stone arches, sheer cliff faces, and diverse plant life. One arch, **Sky Bridge,** is 30 feet high and 90 feet long. The area features over 500 types of vascular plants, dozens of species of animals, and numerous kinds of fish. There are two dozen hiking trails, from only a few hundred yards to more than eight miles in length, and several camping areas. The **Red River** is a popular canoeing stream. Always open. Free. 606/663-2852.

RENFRO VALLEY, 50, north of Mt. Vernon off U.S. 25, C-8. In the 1930s, radio personality John Lair decided to leave Chicago, come back to his native state, and start a center for country music. He bought a valley in south-central Kentucky, built a small country music empire, and broadcast his *Saturday Night Barn Dance* across much of America, introducing some country music stars in the process. The *Barn Dance,* the *Sunday Mornin' Gatherin',* and John Lair are still going strong. Mar.-Dec., Sat., 7:30 and 9:30 P.M. Admission $5. Sun., 8:30 A.M. Free. 606/256-2664.

RICHMOND, C-9. *See* **Fort Boonesborough State Park.**

SHAKER VILLAGE AT PLEASANT HILL, C-8. Seven miles northeast of Harrodsburg on U.S. 68, this Shaker restoration contains 27 historic buildings and over 2,000 acres of rolling countryside. The Shakers, a religious sect noted for their architecture and furniture, began this settlement in 1805. Dining and overnight lodging are offered in authentic Shaker buildings. Craft making is demonstrated by villagers; interpreters assist during self-guided tours. Daily, mid-Mar.-late Nov., 9 A.M. to 5 P.M.; other months, 9 A.M. to 4:30 P.M. Adults $4; persons 12-18, $1.75; 6-11, $1; under 6, free. Shaker Village: Always open. 606/734-5411.

STANTON, C-9. *See* **Natural Bridge State Resort Park** and **Red River Gorge Geological Area.**

VERSAILLES, B-8. *See* **Midway.**

Kentucky Campgrounds

FEES REFLECT MINIMUM RATE FOR 2 ADULTS AND ARE SUBJECT TO INCREASE OR SEASONAL CHANGES

- • – at the campground
- ○ – within one mile of campground
- $ – extra charge
- ** – limited facilities during winter months
- A – adults only
- B – 10,000 acres or more
- C – contribution

- E – tents rented
- F – entrance fee or permit required
- N – no specific number, limited by size of area only
- P – primitive
- R – reservation required
- S – self-contained units only

- U – unlimited
- V – trailers rented
- Z – reservations accepted
- LD – Labor Day
- MD – Memorial Day
- UC – under construction
- d – boat dock

- g – public golf course within 5 miles
- h – horseback riding
- j – whitewater running craft only
- k – snow skiing within 25 miles
- l – boat launch
- m – area north of map
- n – no drinking water

- p – motor bikes prohibited
- r – boat rental
- s – stream, lake or creek water only
- t – tennis
- u – snowmobile trails
- w – open certain off-season weekends
- y – drinking water must be boiled

Map Reference	Park Name	Access	Acres	Tent Spaces	Trailer Spaces	Approximate Fee	Season	Other Swimming Swimming Pool	Fishing	Boating	Playground	Other	Telephone Number	Mail Address
	STATE PARKS													
D4	Kentucky Dam Village	Fr Paducah, 20 mi SE on Hwy 62	1200	225	225	5.00	All year	○	○	dlr	●	gh	502/362-4271	Gilbertsville 42044
A7	General Butler	Fr US 42 in Carrollton, 2 mi S on Hwy 227	809	135	135	5.00	All year	○	○	r	●	g	502/732-4384	Carrollton 41008
C9	Natural Bridge	Fr Winchester, 35 mi SE on Mt Pkwy to Slade, 5 mi S on Hwy 11	1337	95	95	5.00	4/1-10/31	●	○	○	dr	●	h	606/663-2214	Slade 40376
D9	Levi Jackson	Fr I-75 in London, 3 mi SE on US 25	815	200	200	5.00	4/1-10/31	●				●	h	606/878-8000	London 40741
D9	Cumberland Falls	Fr I-75, Corbin/Williamsburg exit, 8 mi S on US 25, 8 mi W on Hwy 90	1720	70	70	5.00	4/1-10/31	○	○			●	h	606/528-4121	Corbin 40701
D8	Lake Cumberland	Fr Jamestown, 14 mi S on US 127, 5 mi E on Hwy 1370	2791	150	150	5.00	All year	●	○	●	dlr	●	gh	502/343-3111	Jamestown 42629
B10	Carter Caves	Fr Olive Hill, 5 mi E on US 60, 3 mi N on Hwy 182	1000	86	86	5.00	4/1-10/31	●	○	○	dr	●	gh	606/286-4411	Olive Hill 41164
C11	Jenny Wiley	Fr Prestonburg, 3 mi N on US 23	1700	126	126	5.00	All year	●	●	dlr	●	ghp	606/886-2711	Prestonburg 41653
D9	Pine Mountain	Fr Pineville, 1 mi S on US 25E	2500	36	36	5.00	4/1-10/31	○	○			●	gh	606/337-3066	Pineville 40977
E4	Kenlake	Fr Murray, 15 mi NW on Hwy 94	1800	92	92	5.00	4/1-10/31	●	○	○	dlr	●	gh	502/474-2211	Hardin 42048
B10	Greenbo Lake	Fr Greenup, 8 mi SE on Hwy 1	3330	65	65	5.00	4/1-10/31	○	○	dlr			606/473-7324	Greenup 41144
D3	Columbus Belmont	Fr Columbus, 2 mi W on Hwy 80	177	38	38	5.00	4/1-10/31	●					502/677-2327	Columbus 42032
D5	Pennyrile Forest	Fr Dawson Springs, 5 mi S on Hwy 109	B	68	68	5.00	4/1-10/31	○	○	dlr	●	gh	502/797-3421	Dawson Springs 42408
C5	Audubon	Fr Henderson, 3 mi N on US 41	590	64	64	5.00	4/1-10/31	○		r	●	g	502/826-2247	Henderson 42420
A9	Kincaid Lake	Fr US 27 in Falmouth, 3 mi NE on Hwy 159	700	84	84	5.00	4/1-10/31	○	○	dlr	●		606/654-3531	Falmouth 41040
D8	General Burnside	Fr Burnside, 1 mi S on US 27	400	129	129	5.00	4/1-10/31	●		l	●		606/561-4104	Burnside 42519
C6	Rough River Dam	Fr Leitchfield, 11 mi NW on Hwy 54, 7 mi N on Hwy 79	9234	70	70	5.00	4/1-10/31	●	○	dlr	●	h	502/257-2311	Falls of Rough 40119
C7	My Old Kentucky Home	In Bardstown, on Hwy 49	75	40	40	5.00	4/1-10/31					●	g	502/348-3502	Bardstown 40004
C9	Ft. Boonesboro	Fr Boonesboro, 1 mi N on Hwy 338	90	187	187	5.00	All year	○	○	dlr	●		606/527-3328	Rt 5, Richmond 40475
D7	Barren River Lake	Fr Glasgow, 13 mi S on US 31E	1800	99	99	5.00	4/1-10/31	●	●	dlr	●	g	502/646-2151	Lucas 42156
A8	Big Bone Lick	Fr Cincinnati, 18 mi S on I-75 to Richwood, W on Hwy 338	248	62	62	5.00	4/1-10/31	●			●		606/384-3522	Union 41091
B9	Blue Licks Battlefield	Fr Mt Olivet, 15 mi S on Hwy 165	100	51	51	5.00	4/1-10/31	●			●	h	606/289-5507	Mt Olivet 41094
D10	Buckhorn Lake	Fr Buckhorn, 5 mi S on Old Hwy 28	865	72	72	5.00	4/1-10/31			dlr			606/398-7510	Buckhorn 41721
B10	Grayson Lake	Fr Grayson, 10 mi S on Hwy 7		71	71	5.00	4/1-10/31			dlr			606/474-9727	Grayson 41143
D7	Green River Lake	Fr Campbellsville, 7 mi S on Hwy 55		90	90	5.00	4/1-10/31			dlr			502/465-8255	Campbellsville 42718
E7	Dale Hollow Lake	Fr Hwy 90, S on Hwy 449	3497	144		5.00	4/1-10/31			d			502/433-7431	Bow 42714
D4	Lake Barkley	Fr Cadiz, 7 mi W on US 80, N on Hwy 1489	3500	80	80	5.00	4/1-10/31	●	○	dlr	●	gh	502/924-1171	Cadiz 42211
D5	Lake Malone	Fr Dunmor, 2 mi W on Hwy 973	338	24	24	5.00	4/1-10/31	●		dl	●	g	502/657-2111	Dunmor 42339
88	Kentucky Horse Pk CG	Fr I-75, ext 115, N on Newton Pike to Iron Works Rd	1032	260	260	8.00	All year				●	hpt	606/233-4303	Rt 6, Iron Works Rd Lexington 4051
	NATIONAL PARKS													
	Mammoth Cave		B										502/758-2251	Box 68, Mammoth Cave 42259
D6	Headquarters	Fr Bowling Green, 20 mi NE on I-65, 10 mi W on Hwy 255		60	51	3.00	All year		○			l			Box 68, Mammoth Cave 42259
D6	Houchin's Ferry	Fr Brownsville, 3 mi NE on Houchins Ferry Rd		P12			All year		●			l			Box 68, Mammoth Cave 42259
	NATIONAL FORESTS													
	Daniel Boone NF													

Map Reference	Park Name	Access	Acres	Tent Spaces	Trailer Spaces	Approximate Fee	Season	Other Swimming / Swimming Pool	Fishing	Boating	Playground	Other	Telephone Number	Mail Address
B9	Claylick Boat-In CG	Fr Morehead, .5 mi W on US 60, 7 mi S on Hwy 519, .6 mi W on Hwy 801, 1 mi S on Hwy 1274	42	20		None	All year	1	•			dlr		Morehead
C9	Turkey Foot	Fr McKee, 3 mi N on Hwy 89, 1.5 mi E on Co, 1.8 mi E on FR 4, .2 mi N on DE 482	10	15	15	5.00	4/1-11/1		•					McKee
C9	Koomer Ridge	Fr Slade, 3.4 mi SE on Hwy 15.	45	54	40	3.00	4/1-11/1					hn		Slade
C9	S Tree	Fr Mckee, 3.8 mi SW on Hwy 89, 1.3 mi W on FR 43, 17 mi S on FR 20	3	7	7	None	All year					n		McKee
D9	White Oak	Fr London, 17 mi W on Hwy 192, 2 mi S on FR 772, .6 mi S.	145	39		None	All year		•	•				London
D9	Bee Rock	Fr Somerset, 1.5 mi NE on Hwy 80, 17.2 mi SE on Hwy 192, .5 mi SE on FR 623.	10	18	17	None	4/1-11/1		•					Somerset
D9	Rockcastle RA	Fr London, 16 mi W on Hwy 192, 6 mi S on Hwy 1193, .1 mi NE on FR 626.	15	25	29	2.00	4/1-10/31		•			dlr		London
D9	Craigs Creek	Fr London, 15 mi W on Hwy 192, 2 mi S on FR 62.	12	45	45	None	4/1-10/31	1	•			dlr		London
D9	Sawyer Lake	Fr Sawyer, 1.6 mi NE on Hwy 896, 1.7 mi N on FR 1609	8	19		None	4/1-11/1		•			dl		Sawyer
D8	Alum Ford	Fr Whitley City, 2 mi N on US 27, 5 mi W on Hwy 700.	2	7		None	4/1-11/1		•					Whitley City
B10	Rodburn RA	Fr Morehead, 2 mi NE on US60, 1 mi NW on FR 13.	3	11	11	None	4/4-11/1	2 1				dlr / dl		Morehead
B9	Twin Knobs	Fr Morehead, 8.5 mi SW on US 60, 5.5 mi SE on Hwy 801, 7.5 mi W on FR 1017.	480	121	121	4.00	4/4-11/1	1	•			dl		Morehead
B9	Clear Creek	Fr Salt Lick, 3.6 mi S on Hwy 211, 1 mi E on Co 1118, 1.5 mi SE on FR129.	10	24	24	None	4/4-1/2	5				r		Salt Lick
E8	Great Meadow	Fr Stearns, 6 mi W on Hwy 92, 12 mi SW on Hwy 1363, 5 mi SW on FR 137.	2	8		None	4/1-11/1		•			dlr		Stearns
	CORPS OF ENGINEERS													
	Buckhorn Lake	Fr Hazard, 10 mi W on Hwy 15, 18 mi W on Hwy 28 to Buckhorn										dlr		Buckhorn 41721
D10	Dam Site 9		25	29	S29	2.00	MD-LD**	o	•	•		l	606/398-7251	Buckhorn 41721
D10	Trace Branch	Fr Hyden, 15 mi N on Hwy 257 to Dry Hill Brdg, 5 mi W on gravel & dirt rds	25	30	30	None	MD-LD**		•	•		l	606/398-7251	Buckhorn 41721
	Nolin River Lake												502/286-4813	Leitchfield 42754
D6	Brier Creek	Fr Leitchfield, 17 mi S on Hwy 259, E on Co 728, fol signs	144	50	50	None	All year		•	•	p	dl		Leitchfield 42754
D6	Moutardier	Fr Leitchfield, 15 mi S on Hwy 259, 2 mi SE on Moutardier Rd	35	167	147	4.00	3/15-12/15		•	•	p	dlr		Leitchfield 42754
D6	Dog Creek	Fr Leichtfield, 4 mi E on US 62, 12 mi SE on Hwy 88, fol signs	98	50	50	None	3/15-12/15*		•	•	p	dl		Leitchfield 42754
D6	Wax	Fr Wax, 4 mi E on US 62, 9 mi S on Hwy 88	193	100	100	4.00	3/15-12/15		•	•	p	dlr		Leitchfield 42754
	Fishtrap Lake	(For additional CGs, see 'Backpack or Boat Access Areas')												Pikeville 41501
C11	Grapevine CA	Fr Pikeville, 25 mi S on Hwy 460, 5 mi N on Hwy 1499, 7 mi N on Hwy 194	47		S28	None	5/1-9/15		•		p	l	606/437-7496	Phyllis 41554
	Lake Cumberland												606/679-6337	Somerset 42501
D8	Wolf Creek	Fr Russell Spgs, 3 mi E on Hwy 80, 8 mi SE on Hwy 76	5	17	17	3.50	4/1-11/1		•	•		l		Somerset 42501
D8	Fall Creek	Fr Monticello, 5 mi N on Hwy 1275	18	10	10	None	4/1-11/1		•			l		Somerset 42501
D8	Waitsboro RA	Fr Somerset, 4 mi SW on US 27	23	20	20	3.50	4/1-11/1		•	•		l		Somerset 42501
D8	Fishing Creek	Fr Somerset, 5 mi W on Hwy 80, 3 mi W on Hwy 1248	19	44	44	5.00	4/1-11/1		•	•		l		Somerset 42501
D8	Kendall	Fr Russell Spgs, 12 mi S on US 127	10	41	41	5.00	4/1-11/1		•	•		l		Somerset 42501
D8	Grider Hill RA	Fr Albany, 8 mi N on Hwy 734	20	10	10	None	4/1-11/1		•	•		l		Somerset 42501
D8	Cave Creek	Fr Somerset, 14 mi S on US 27, 8 mi E on Blue John	6	10	10	None	4/1-11/1		•			l		Somerset 42501
D8	Omega RA	Fr Somerset, 8 mi SE on Hwy 769, 5 mi W on Co	35	12	12	None	4/1-11/1		•	•		l		Somerset 42501
D8	Cumberland Pt	Fr Somerset, 4 mi W on Hwy 80, 1 mi S on Hwy 235, 10 mi S on Hwy 761	20	30	30	4.00	4/1-11/1		•	•		l		Somerset 42501
	Lake Barkley	(see Tenn for additional CGs)											502/362-4236	Box 218, Grand Rivers 42045
D4	Hurricane Creek RA	Fr Eddyville, 6 mi S on Hwy 93, 5 mi S on Hwy 274	35	51	51	5.00	4/1-11/1		•	•		l	502/522-8821	Bx 218, Grand Rivers 42045
D4	Prizer Pt RA & Marina	Fr Cadiz, 12 mi NW on Hwy 276	50	20	29	None	All year					dlr	502/522-3762	Bx 218, Grand Rivers 42045
D4	Eddy Creek RA	Fr Eddyville, 5 mi S on Hwy 93	30	35	35	None	4/1-11/1		•			lr		Bx 218, Grand Rivers 42045
D4	Grand Rivers RA	Fr Grand Rivers, 1-1/4 mi S on Hwy 453	50	44	44	None	4/1-11/1		•		g	lr		Bx 218, Grand Rivers 42045
D4	Boyds Landing RA	Fr Kuttawa, 1 mi W on US 641, 8 mi S on Hwy 810	25	P20	P20	None	4/1-11/1		•			l		Bx 218, Grand Rivers 42045
D4	Eureka RA	Fr Kuttawa, 1 mi W on US 641, 3 mi S on Hwy 1271; fol signs	50	35	35	None	4/1-11/1		•			l		Bx 218, Grand Rivers 42045
D4	Canal RA	Fr Grand Rivers, 1 mi S on Hwy 453/The Trace	60	89	89	5.00	4/1-11/1		•	•	g	l		Bx 218, Grand Rivers 42045
D4	Devils Elbow RA	In Canton off US-68	30	21	0	None	4/1-11/1		•			l	502/362-4236	Box 218, Grand Rivers 42045
	Barren River Lake		1248										502/646-2055	Leitchfield 42754
D7	Austin	Fr Glasgow, 13 mi S on US-31 E, 7 mi SE on Hwy 87	64	10			All year		•	•	p	dl		Leitchfield 42754
D6	Bailey's Pt	Fr Scottsville, N on US 31E, 1 mi W on Hwy 252, 2 mi N on Hwy 517		177	225	4.00	4/1-12/31		•	•	p	dl		Leitchfield 42754
D6	Brown's Ford	Fr Scottsville, E on Hwy 98, fol signs	47	6			All year		•	•	p	dl		Leitchfild 42754
D6	Walnut Creek	Fr Scottsville, 6 mi N on US 31E to KY Hwy 252, to Hwy 1855	147	118	32	2.50	All year		•	•	p	dlr		115 E Market, Leitchfld 42754
D6	The Narrows	Fr Glasgow, 12 mi SE on US 31E, 6 mi W on Hwy 1318	8	29	54	4.00	All year		•	•	p	dl		Leitchfield 42754
D6	Beaver Creek	Fr Glasgow, 6 mi N on US 31E, 3 mi W on Hwy 252, fol signs	57	35	35		All year		•	•	p	dlr		Leitchfield 42754
D6	Tailwater	Fr Glasgow, 5 mi S on US 31E, W on Hwy 252	110	48	48	3.00	All year		•	•	p	dl		Leitchfield 42754
	Green River Lake												502/465-4463	Leitchfield 42754
D7	Holmes Bend	Fr Columbia, 4 mi N on Holmes Bend Rd	531	125	125	4.00	4/15-10/31		•	•	p	dlr		Leitchfield 42754
D7	Pike's Ridge	Fr Campbellsville, 3 mi E on Hwy 70, 3 mi SE on Hwy 76, S at sign	2525	100	100	None	All year		•		p	l		Leitchfield 42754
	Rough River Lake												502/257-2061	Leitchfield 42754
C6	Axtel	Fr Roff, 2 mi S on Hwy 259, 1 mi W on Hwy 79	77	133	158	4.00	5/1-10/1		•	•	gp	dlr	502/257-2584	Leitchfield 42754
C6	Cave Creek	Fr Rough Riv Dam SRA, 2 mi S on Hwy 79	121	26	100	None	All year		•	•	gp	dl		Leitchfield 42754
C6	Laurel Branch	Fr Roff, 3 mi S on Hwy 259, 1 mi W on Hwy 110	10	72	72	3.00	All year		•		p	dl	502/257-8839	Leitchfield 42754
C6	Peter Cave	Fr Leichtfield, 10 m NW on Hwy 737, fol signs	40	30	S30	None	All year		•		p	dl		Leitchfield 42754
C6	North Fork	Fr Roff, 1.5 mi S on Hwy 259	20	125	108	4.00	All year		•	•	p	dlr	502/257-8823	Leitchfield 42754
	TENNESSEE VALLEY AUTHORITY													
	Land Between The Lakes	See Tennessee for additional campgrounds											502/924-5602	Golden Pond, 42231
D4	Hillman Ferry CG	Fr Grand Rivs, 4 mi SE on Hwy 453, 1 mi W	400	130	260	4.00	All year		•	•		l		Golden Pond, 42231
	Lake Barkley Access Areas												502/924-5602	Golden Pond, 42231
D4	Eddyville Ferry	Fr Grand Rivs, 7.5 mi SE on Hwy 453, 6 mi NE		N	N	None	All year		•		p	l		
D4	Devils Elbow	On Lk Barkley Shoreline, US 68		PN	PN	None	All year		•			l		
D4	Bacon Creek	Fr Fenton, 4 mi E on US 68, 6 mi S on unpaved rd	15		S15	None	All year		•		p			
D4	Cravens Bay	Fr Grand Rivs, 7.5 mi S on The Trace (Hwy 453), 4 mi E	12		S12	None	All year		•		p			
D4	Demumbers Bay	Fr Grand Rivs, 4 mi S on The Trace (Hwy 453), 2 mi E	5		S5	None	All year		•		p			
D4	Kuttawa Landing	Fr Grand Rivs, 7.5 mi S on The Trace (Hwy 453), 7 mi E	6		S6	None	All year		•			l		
D4	Nickell Branch	Fr Grand Rivers, 1 mi S on The Trace (Hwy 453), 1 mi E	11		S11	None	All year		•			l		
D4	Taylor Bay	Fr Grand Rivs, 13 mis S on The Trace (Hwy 453), 5 mi E on Mulberry Flat Rd	13		13	None	All year		•			l		
	Kentucky Lake Access Area												502/924-5602	Golden Pond, 42231
D4	Twin Lakes	Fr Grand Rivs, 3.5 mi S on The Trace (Hwy 453), 2 mi W	15		S15	None	All year		•		gp	l		
D4	Fenton	On Kentucky Lk Shoreline, US 68		PN	PN	None	All year		•			l		
D4	Sugar Bay	Fr Grand Rivs, 16 mi S on The Trace (Hwy 453)	16		S16	None	All year		•			l		
D4	Redd Hollow	Fr Golden Pond, 4 mi S on The Trace (Hwy 453), W on Redd Hollow Rd	14		S14	None	All year		•		p			
D4	Pisgah Pt	Fr Grand Rivers, 6 mi S on The Trace (Hwy 453), 2 mi W	6		S6	None	All year		•		p			
D4	Birmingham Ferry	Fr Grand Rivs, 8.5 mi SE on The Trace (Hwy 453), 3 mi W	24		S10	None	All year		•		p			
D4	Turkey Bay	Fr Golden Pond, 4 mi W on US 68, 1 mi S on The Trace (Hwy 453)	10		S10	None	All year		•			l		
D4	Smith Bay	Fr Grand Rivs Canal, 9 mi S on The Trace (Hwy 453), 4 mi E on Old Ferry Rd	40		S40	None	All year		•	•	p	l		

Louisiana

See state map, page 31

Major Events

The Sugar Bowl Classic, Jan. 1, New Orleans. Aside from the well-known football game between two top-notch NCAA football teams in the Superdome on New Year's Day, there are several other sporting events taking place in other parts of the city at the same time, such as the Sugar Bowl Tennis Classic tournament for junior players in City Park and a large sailing regatta on Lake Pontchartrain. Admission is charged for several events. 504/522-8772.

Mardi Gras in New Orleans, mid- to late Feb., New Orleans. Street parades and cultural events throughout the city lead up to the culmination of the Mardi Gras season, which is Mardi Gras Day, otherwise known as Fat Tuesday (the day before Ash Wednesday). Canal St. is the parade ground on Mardi Gras Day, and most of the largest and best-known parades may be seen here. Other Mardi Gras activities include costume contests, athletic events, dances, lots of musical entertainment, and food and spirits at many different locations. Admission is charged for several events; the street parades are free. 504/566-5011.

Mardi Gras Day, late Feb., Lafayette. Downtown Lafayette is the setting for a large parade, a street dance, a cookout, and live music. Free. 318/235-1072.

Audubon Pilgrimage, mid-Mar., St. Francisville. A tour of several private homes is conducted, and there are art shows, live music, and a candlelight tour. Admission is charged for the house tour. 504/635-6330.

Spring Home & Garden Tour, late Mar., Covington. Private residences and gardens are open to the public for guided tours. Admission. 504/892-3216.

Strawberry Festival, early Apr., Ponchatoula. The strawberry-picking season is celebrated with a strawberry ball, a parade, a strawberry-eating contest, and a street dance. Free. 504/386-2403.

Easter Sunrise Services, Easter, Hodges Gardens, south of Many. A dramatization of the story of Christ's final days on earth is told in narration and music at an outdoor service. Free. 318/586-3523.

Holiday-In-Dixie, mid- to late Apr., Shreveport. Festivities are held in different locations in the city. There are contests, races, a carnival, live entertainment, a parade, an air show, art and flower shows, and a queen pageant. Admission is charged for several events. 318/222-9347.

New Orleans Spring Fiesta, mid-Apr. to early May, New Orleans. There are 19 days and nights of plantation tours, and tours of homes and buildings in the French Quarter, the Garden District, and other parts of the city. Admission. 504/581-1367.

Contraband Days, late Apr. to early May, Lake Charles. This event features shows, carnivals, boat races, a square dance, live entertainment, a beauty pageant, and other activities honoring local heritage. A parade and a fireworks display are also part of the festivities. Admission is charged for several events. 318/436-5508.

New Orleans Jazz and Heritage Festival, late Apr. to early May, New Orleans. The Fair Grounds Race Track is the site of live music indigenous to Louisiana. Jazz, blues, gospel, Cajun, and country music are all featured on several different stages simultaneously. Food booths serving local cuisine, crafts booths with items handcrafted by artisans throughout the state, and open-air theater performances are some of the other major events. Several concerts on Mississippi River steamboats are also featured. Admission. 504/522-4786.

Breaux Bridge Crawfish Festival, early May, Breaux Bridge, northeast of Lafayette. This biennial event takes place during even-numbered years and features crawfish-eating and -peeling contests, a parade, a fais-dodo, and plenty of boiled crawfish and crawfish dishes. Admission is charged for several events. 318/332-2171.

Fest-For-All Summer Arts Festival, late May, Baton Rouge. Nearly 200 artists and craftsmen come to Baton Rouge from all over the country to display and sell their works. There are many live performances of music and dance, including ballets, folk dances, and operas. Free. 504/344-8558.

Jambalaya Festival, mid-June, Gonzalez, northwest of Sorrento. This festival honors Louisiana's famous rice dish with a jambalaya-cooking contest, an arts and crafts show, live music, and plenty of jambalaya. Free (except food). 504/644-3652.

La Fête de la Nouvelle Orleans, late June to mid-July, New Orleans. There are actually 10 separate festivals going on at the same time at various locations throughout the city. The most famous of these is the New Orleans Food Festival. Food-tasting booths and special dinners and banquets reflect the unique cuisine of the city. There is a celebration of Bastille Day with fireworks and many activities. Admission is charged for several events. 504/525-4143.

Louisiana Oyster Festival, mid-July, Galliano, north of Golden Meadow. The oyster is honored at this event which features a coronation, an oyster-eating contest, an art show, musical entertainment by Cajun bands, and lots of oysters. Admission is charged for the coronation. 504/693-7788.

Louisiana Shrimp & Petroleum Festival, early Sept., Morgan City. A shrimp boat parade follows the blessing of the fleet, and street parades, a bass tournament, petroleum exhibits, arts and crafts, boat races, and street dances are some of the other activities. Free. 504/385-0703.

Festivals Acadiens, late Sept., Lafayette. This is a weekend of activities commemorating the French Acadian heritage of the Cajuns of southern Louisiana. There are several festivals occurring simultaneously, including the Bayou Food Festival, the Cajun Music Festival, the Louisiana Native Crafts Festival, and the Acadiana Fair and Trade Show. Admission is charged for several events. 318/232-3808.

Louisiana Sugarcane Festival & Fair, late Sept., New Iberia. The Louisiana sugarcane crop and sugarcane products are highlighted with a parade, a coronation, and a carnival. Free. 318/364-1836.

Red River Revel, early Oct., Shreveport. This event is a celebration of the arts. Over 100 artists display and sell their works and demonstrate their crafts. Food booths serve local cuisine and foods from many different countries. Live entertainment in the form of music and dance are also featured. Free (except food). 318/424-4000.

Louisiana Cotton Festival, early Oct., Ville Platte. Cotton exhibits, the coronation of the Cotton Queen, a parade, and dances are highlights of this harvest-time festival. Free. 318/363-1878.

Natchitoches Tour of Homes, early Oct., Natchitoches. The tours feature town homes, antebellum homes, and large plantation houses in the Natchitoches area. Admission. 318/352-8072.

International Rice Festival, mid-Oct., Crowley. The town of Crowley celebrates the local rice crop with a rice-eating contest, a livestock show, a children's parade and carnival, musical competition, and a rodeo. Free. 318/783-3067.

Louisiana State Fair, late Oct., Shreveport. The State Fairgrounds come alive for 10 days with agricultural exhibits, parades, a carnival midway, many athletic events, family entertainment, and exhibits from all facets of Louisiana's culture and economy. Admission. 318/635-1361.

Baton Rouge Fall Crafts Festival, late Oct., Baton Rouge. Over 50 artisans come to the Old State Capitol to display and sell their handcrafted items. Folk craft demonstrations are also given during the two-day show. Free. 504/344-8558.

Natchitoches Christmas Festival, early Dec., Natchitoches. Fireworks, parades, live entertainment, and Christmas lights displays welcome the Christmas season to Louisiana's oldest town. Free. 318/352-8072.

Louisiana Destinations

ALEXANDRIA, 51,565, C-3. Located near the geographical center of the state, Alexandria has been a trade center, a lumber town, a large base for training troops in World War II, and is now the industrial and agricultural capital for central Louisiana. The **Alexandria Museum,** 933 Main St., contains a permanent collection of art as well as special exhibits which are changed frequently. Year-round, Tues.-Fri., 9 A.M. to 5 P.M.; Sat., 10 A.M. to 2 P.M. Free. 318/443-3458. The **City Zoo,** off Masonic Dr., is one of the largest zoos in the state. Adjacent is an amusement area for children. Daily, March-Oct., 9 A.M. to 6:30 P.M.; other months, 9 A.M. to 5 P.M. Free. 318/473-1387. **Hot Wells State Resort,** 18 miles west on St. 121 via St. 496, is a state-owned and operated curative mineral resort. There are baths, masseurs, accommodations, and a swimming pool. Year-round, daily, 9 A.M. to 5 P.M.. Park: Free. 318/793-2116. The **Kent House State Commemorative Area,** on St. 496, was built in the early 1800s and is the oldest house of its type in central Louisiana. The house and grounds have been restored to the period of the early 19th century. Year-round, Mon.-Sat., 9 A.M. to 5 P.M.; Sun., 1 to 5 P.M. Adults $1; children 6-12, 50¢; under 6, free. 318/445-5611.

BATON ROUGE, 219,486, D-4. Translated into English, Baton Rouge means "Red Stick." The city derived its name from a huge red post which was used to mark an ancient boundary line separating the hunting grounds of two Indian tribes. The post has long since disappeared, and the hunting grounds it separated have grown into Louisiana's capital and educational center as well as a large inland shipping port and base for the state's petrochemical industry. **GOVERNMENT BUILDINGS: The Louisiana State Capitol,** on State Capitol Dr., was completed in 1932. Rising 34 stories, it is the tallest state capitol in the nation. Massive bronze entrance doors nearly 50 feet in height lead to the building's interior. The first two floors contain the *House and Senate Chambers and Memorial Hall,* a large room with murals and statuary depicting the history of Louisiana. There is an observation deck on the 27th floor from which much of Baton Rouge may be seen. Directly in the center of a sunken garden facing the Capitol, a 12-foot bronze statue marks the grave of Huey P. Long, colorful governor and U.S. Senator of Louisiana who was responsible for the construction of the Capitol. In 1935, he was shot down in one of its hallways. Year-round, daily, 8 A.M. to 4 P.M. Free. 504/342-7317. The **Governor's Mansion,** 1001 Baton Rouge Expwy., was completed in 1963 and is an example of the columnar style developed in the plantation houses of the 19th century. Tours: Year-round, Mon.-Fri., 9 to 11 A.M., 2 to 4 P.M. Free. 504/342-5855.

MUSEUMS AND GALLERIES: Louisiana Arts and Science Center, Riverside, River Rd. at North Blvd., is housed in a restored railroad depot originally built in 1925. Exhibits include paintings, history and wildlife displays, and a three dimensional model of the changing Mississippi River channel. Adjacent is a 1918 steam engine and several vintage train cars containing a small museum of railroad memorabilia. Year-round, Tues.-Sat., 10 A.M. to 5 P.M.; Sun., 1 to 5 P.M. Free. 504/344-9463. The **Anglo-American Art Museum,** in the Memorial Tower on the campus of Louisiana State University, is divided into English and American wings. Each wing has furniture and sculpture of various periods, ranging from the 17th century to the present. Changing art exhibits are also on display. Year-round, Mon.-Fri., 8 A.M. to 4:30 P.M.; Sat., 9 A.M. to noon, 1 to 4:30 P.M.; Sun., 1 to 4:30 P.M. Free. 504/388-4003. **Louisiana State University Rural Life Museum,** 6200 Burden Lane, Essen Lane exit at Int. 10, occupies a five-acre plot on the Burden Research Plantation and contains artifacts related to early rural life in the state. Tools, household utensils, and farming implements are displayed in restored barns, slave cabins, blacksmith's shop, sugar house, and other buildings. Year-round, Mon.-Fri., 8:30 A.M. to 4 P.M. Closed university holidays. Donations. 504/766-8241.

PARKS AND GARDENS: Greater Baton Rouge Zoo, on Thomas Rd., 1 mile east of St. 19, has more than 500 animals from six continents. A tram runs periodically through the park. Year-round, Mon.-Fri., 10 A.M. to 5 P.M.; Sat.-Sun., 9 A.M. to 6 P.M. Adults 50¢; children, 25¢; 12 and under, free. Tram: 35¢. Elephant ride: $1 per person. 504/775-3877. **Cohn Memorial Arboretum,** 12056 Foster Rd., is a 16-acre tract of rolling terrain with more than 120 varieties of native and adaptable trees and shrubs, many labeled for identification. A greenhouse contains many rare and exotic plants. Year-round, Mon.-Fri., 8 A.M. to 4:30 P.M.; Sat.-Sun., 9 A.M. to 5 P.M. Free. 504/775-1006.

BOSSIER CITY, 49,969, A-1. The **Louisiana Hayride,** 7 miles north on St. 3, is the home of the old radio-stage show that at one time rivaled the Grand Ole Opry in popularity. Hank Williams, Elvis Presley, and other famous performers launched their careers here. Year-round, Sat., 7:45 to 9:45 P.M., followed by a dance at 10 P.M. ($2 per person). Adults $3.75; children 12 and under, $1.50. Show and dance: $5 per person. 318/742-7803.

BURNSIDE, northwest of Laplace, E-5. **Houmas House,** on St. 942 off Burnside Exit, Int. 10, represents two periods. The rear portion of the house was built in the

---

Louisiana Lexicon

Bayou: A sluggish stream or natural canal.

Cajun: A popular name for a descendant of Acadian settlers.

Chicory: A carrotlike root that is ground and blended with coffee.

Fais-dodo: A country dance, popular in southern Louisiana; also, a get-together where people eat, drink, and dance.

Filé: A powder prepared from sassafras leaves, an important ingredient of gumbo.

Gumbo: A thick soup prepared with okra or filé and chicken or seafood.

Jambalaya: A rice dish cooked with shrimp, sausage, chicken, or other ingredients.

Lagniappe: A "little something extra" from a merchant to a customer that is thrown in with a purchase.

Parish: A term synonymous with "county" in other states.

Poor Boy: A long sandwich made with French bread.

Roux: Flour browned in butter or lard; the basis of many Louisiana dishes, particularly gumbo and jambalaya.

1700s. The main part, a Greek-Revival structure with Doric columns, was built in 1840. The estate, which also includes gardens and statuary, has been the setting for several Hollywood films. Daily, during standard time, 10 A.M. to 5 P.M.; other months, 10 A.M. to 4 P.M. 504/277-8186.

CHALMETTE NATIONAL HISTORICAL PARK, E-6. The park, on St. 46 (St. Bernard Hwy.), preserves the site of the Battle of New Orleans, which was fought on the Chalmette plantation during the War of 1812. A 100-foot-tall monument stands in the park. The **Beauregard Home,** a 19th-century plantation house, has been restored and now serves as the Visitors Center. Sections of the American line of defense have been rebuilt and may be visited. A national cemetery is also within the park limits. Year-round, daily, 8 A.M. to 5 P.M. Free. 504/277-8186.

FRANKLIN, 9,584, E-4. **Oaklawn Manor Plantation,** 5 miles on Irish Bend Rd., was built in 1837. Set in the midst of formal gardens and a large grove of live oaks, this brick mansion with marble floors contains many European antiques. Daily, Mar.-Sept., 9:30 A.M. to 5:30 P.M.; other months, 9:30 A.M. to 4:30 P.M. Adults $3.50; students, $2; children, $1.50; under 7, free. 318/828-0434.

HAMMOND, 15,043, D-5. This town is in the heart of one of the nation's largest strawberry-growing regions. **Zemurray Gardens,** 10 miles northeast on St. 40 off

U.S. 51, contains 150 acres of flowers and plants, including azaleas, camellias, and dogwoods. Paths also lead around a small lake on the premises. Mar.-June, daily, 10 A.M. to 6 P.M. Adults $1; persons under 12 and over 65, 50¢. 504/878-9777.

JEANERETTE, 6,511, E-4. **Albania,** on St. 182, was built in 1837 on the Bayou Teche. The mansion contains a large collection of Louisiana antiques and a collection of old and rare dolls. Accommodations are available in an adjacent slave cabin, which is furnished with antiques. Feb.-Dec., Tues.-Sat., 10 A.M. to 3:30 P.M.; Sun., 2 to 4 P.M. Adults $3; children under 12, $1.50. 318/276-4816.

JENNINGS, 12,401, E-3. **Zigler Museum,** 411 Clara St., is an art museum in a colonial-style structure. It contains the work of artists from the United States and Europe. Also included are dioramas of southwestern Louisiana wildlife. Year-round, Tues.-Fri., 10 A.M. to noon, 2 to 4:30 P.M.; Sat.-Sun., 2 to 4:30 P.M. Free. 318/824-0114.

LAFAYETTE, 81,961, E-3. The majority of 18th-century refugees from Acadia settled in the Lafayette region and grew rice and sugarcane and raised cattle. The Cajun culture grew and flourished here, and many traditions and customs still remain. Most of the city's population still speak French or patois, and the food and music that made Acadiana famous still may be found in many locations. Since 1950, Lafayette has nearly tripled in size, largely because of the rich offshore oil and natural gas fields of Vermilion Parish. **Acadian Village and Gardens,** on Mouton Rd. south of St. 342, contain a number of 19th-century Acadian dwellings and other buildings that have been brought together to represent an early Cajun bayou village. Year-round, daily, 10 A.M. to 5 P.M. Adults $3; persons 6-18 and over 62, $1.50; under 6, free. 318/981-2364. The **Art Center for Southwest Louisiana,** 105 Girard Park Dr., contains an exhibit of 19th-century paintings and changing exhibits of paintings done by Louisiana artists. These collections are housed in a replica of an Acadian-style plantation house. Year-round, Mon.-Fri., 10 A.M. to 5 P.M.; Sun., 2 to 5 P.M. Free. 318/232-1169. **Lafayette Natural History Museum, Planetarium, and Nature Station,** 637 Girard Park Dr., features changing exhibits relating to southern Louisiana and natural history. The planetarium has star shows and telescopic observation of the heavens. The nature station, 5 miles north in Acadiana Park, is an interpretive center for the 3.5-mile nature trail which runs through the 120-acre park. Museum: Year-round, Mon., Wed., Fri., 9 A.M. to 5 P.M.; Tues., Thurs., 9 A.M. to 9 P.M.; Sat.-Sun., 1 to 5 P.M. Free. Planetarium: Year-round, Tues., 7:30 P.M.; Sun., 2 and 3:30 P.M. Free. Nature Station: Year-round, Mon.-Fri., 9 A.M. to 5 P.M.; Sat.-Sun., 1 to 5 P.M. Free. 318/261-8350.

LAKE CHARLES, 75,051, E-2. Lumber, sulphur, rice, shipping, and the petrochemical industry have aided in making Lake Charles the industrial mecca of southwestern Louisiana. Just off Int. 10 is a large, white sand beach, bathhouses, and parking area. **Imperial Calcasieu Museum,** 204 W. Sallier St., contains many items pertaining to local history. Several rooms have been furnished with antiques and other items from various periods in the town's history. Year-round, Mon.-Fri., 10 A.M. to noon, 2 to 5 P.M.; Sat., 10 A.M. to noon; Sun., 2 to 5 P.M. Donation. 318/439-3797. **Creole Nature Trail** begins at Lake Charles and follows St. 27 south to the Gulf.

MANSFIELD BATTLE STATE COMMEMORATIVE AREA, B-1. The 44-acre park preserves the site of the April 8, 1864 battle in which Confederate troops under the command of Gen. Dick Taylor defeated Union troops commanded by Gen. N. P. Banks. The Confederate victory climaxed the Red River Campaign. The park museum has artifacts of the campaign and other Civil War encounters and an audiovisual room where events are recalled. The event is also recalled at a two-day re-enactment celebration held every five years (the next will be in 1985). Park and museum: Year-round, Mon.-Sat., 9 A.M. to 5 P.M.; Sun., 1 to 5 P.M. Adults $1; students 50¢; persons under 6, free. 318/872-1471.

MANY, 3,988, C-2. **Hodges Gardens,** 12 miles south on U.S. 171, is a 4,700-acre tract of land covered with forests, gardens, lakes, and streams. Flowers bloom year-round, and numerous drives and trails lead through the grounds. Elk, deer, and other forms of wildlife roam about and may easily be seen. Resort facilities are available on the premises. Year-round, daily, 8 A.M. to sunset. Adults $5; children under 14, free. 318/586-3523.

MARKSVILLE STATE COMMEMORATIVE AREA, C-3. Here on the site of a prehistoric village are six Indian mounds, which have been excavated by archaeologists from the Smithsonian Institution. Some of the relics that have been found from this 2,000-year-old Indian culture are on display in an adjacent museum. Year-round, daily, 7 A.M. to sunset. Park: Free. Museum: Year-round, Mon.-Fri., 9 A.M. to 5 P.M.; Sat.-Sun., 1 to 5 P.M. Adults $1; children 12 and under, 50¢. 318/253-9546.

MONROE, 57,597, A-3. Located on the banks of the Ouachita River, Monroe was settled in 1785 by Jean Baptiste Filhiol. Fort Miro was constructed on the site in 1790 to ward off Indian attacks, and the little settlement grew slowly until the arrival of the first steamboat in 1819. The steamboat era aided in Monroe's growth as a cotton and shipping hub of northeastern Louisiana. The discovery of a huge natural gas field nearby in 1916 also brought about

an industrial boom. Today, Monroe is still highly industrialized, with numerous paper and chemical plants in the area. The **Masur Museum of Art,** 1400 S. Grand St., has a permanent collection of paintings and special art exhibits that are changed every month. Year-round, Tues.-Thurs., 10 A.M. to 6 P.M.; Fri.-Sun., 2 to 5 P.M. Free. 318/329-2237. The **Bible Research Center and Elsong Gardens,** 2004 Riverside Dr., is a nonsectarian, nondenominational foundation whose purpose is "to allow all to discover enlightened understanding through research into the little known facts of the Bible." There is a research library, a rare book room, and a reading solarium. Numerous rare Bibles, biblical maps, and illuminated manuscripts are on display. There are antique furnishings in the house and formal gardens on the grounds outside. Sept.-July, Mon.-Thurs., 9 A.M. to noon, 1 to 4:30 P.M.; also by appointment. Free. 318/387-5281. **Louisiana Purchase Gardens and Zoo,** off U.S. 165 on Tichelli Rd., is a 100-acre complex that contains formal gardens and more than 750 animals from all over the world. Many rides and other forms of entertainment for children are also in the park. Year-round, daily, 10 A.M. to 5 P.M. Zoo: Adults $1.25; children 8-12, $1; children 3-7, 60¢; under 3 and over 65, free. Rides: 45¢ each. 318/329-2400.

MORGAN CITY, 16,114, E-4. **Swamp Gardens,** north of U.S. 90 on Myrtle St., features a three-and-one-half-acre natural swamp area with raised pathways for guided walking tours. There are life-size dioramas depicting Atchafalaya Swamp history and an 800-year-old cypress tree. Alligators and other swamp wildlife may be seen at a small zoo adjacent to the gardens. Tours: Year-round, Tues.-Sat., 10:30 A.M. to 3:30 P.M.; Sun., 1:30 to 3:30 P.M. Adults $1; students 6-22, 50¢; under 5, free. 504/384-3343.

NAPOLEONVILLE, 829, E-5. **Madewood Plantation,** on St. 308, has fluted Ionic columns lining the upper and lower galleries. The interior features antiques, detailed woodwork and plasterwork, the original kitchen, and a ballroom. Recently moved to the grounds was a restored riverboat captain's house. Year-round, daily, 10 A.M. to 5 P.M. Adults $3; children 5-10, $2; under 5, free. 504/369-7151.

NATCHITOCHES, 16,664, B-2. Founded in 1714, Natchitoches is the oldest town in the state as well as the oldest in the vast territory once known as the Louisiana Purchase. The town grew in the 18th century as an outpost on America's western frontier and as the eastern terminus of El Camino Real, a trade route leading to Mexico City. In the early 1800s, Natchitoches also served as a cotton port on the Red River until the river changed its course in 1832 and left the town high and dry. The Civil War brought economic hardship to Natchitoches, but no

Towering wooden bonfire structures begin to appear along the Mississippi River in St. James Parish shortly after Thanksgiving. On Christmas Eve they are set afire as people gather on the riverfront to celebrate the holiday season. This tradition dates back to the early settlers of the region, and many legends explain the purpose of the bonfires. One popular Cajun legend claims that the bonfires aid Pere Noel (Santa Claus) to guide his pirogue (canoe) down the river while it is being pulled by eight alligators, so that he may bring presents to all the Cajun girls and boys. If a drive along River Road on Christmas Eve is inconvenient, Oak Alley Plantation, on St. 18 between St. James and Vacherie, lights their bonfire at a Christmas open house held in mid-December. Admission. 504/265-2151.

combat took place in the town, so there are still many fine antebellum structures to be seen. **Roque House,** on River Bank Dr., is a rustic plantation building constructed in the early 1800s. It is of bousillage construction, which is a mixture of moss and mud packed between cypress beams. Year-round, Mon.-Sat., 9 A.M. to 5 P.M. Free. 318/357-1714. **Melrose Plantation,** 13 miles southeast on St. 493 via St. 1, is a complex of plantation structures including the *Melrose Manor House* (1833), *Yucca* (the original home, 1796), and a structure that appears to be of African influence. Four 19th-century log cabins from the surrounding Cane River region have been moved to the plantation grounds and restored to resemble their original appearance. Year-round, Tues., Thurs.-Sun., 2 to 4:30 P.M. Adults $3; persons 13-18, $1.50; children 6-12, $1; under 6, free. 318/379-0055. **Lemee House,** 310 Jefferson St., was built in 1830 and contains furniture from the mid-19th century. The house also has a cellar, a rarity in 19th-century Louisiana structures. Daily by appointment. Adults $1, children 50¢. 318/

NEW IBERIA, 32,766, E-4. **Shadows on the Teche,** Maine and Center Sts. by the Bayou Teche, was built in the 1830s and is a fine representation of Classical/Revival architecture in Louisiana. The most typical Louisiana architectural feature is the outside staircase on the west end of the house. The woodwork and plaster detail inside the house have been preserved. Three acres of grounds surrounding the house contain live oaks with Spanish moss and a formal garden. Tours: Year-round, daily, 9 A.M. to 4:30 P.M. Adults $2; students and persons 65 and over, $1. 318/369-6446. **Jungle Gardens and Bird Sanctuary,** 10 miles southwest via St. 329 on Avery Island, consist of 200 landscaped acres around the home of the late Edward Avery McIlhenny. Different types of flowering plants and other vegetation have been brought here from around the world. Egrets and herons are among the many species of birds that inhabit the sanctuary. Avery Island is on top of a huge salt dome, and thousands of tons of salt are mined here annually. Also on the island is the **McIlhenny Tabasco Factory** where Tabasco sauce is manufactured. One-half-hour guided tours. Gardens: Year-round, daily, 9 A.M. to 5 P.M. Adults $2.50; children 6-12, $1.50; under 6, free. 318/365-8173. Tabasco factory: Year-round, Mon.-Fri., 9 to 11:45 A.M., 1 to 4:15 P.M.; Sat., 9 A.M. to noon. Free. 318/365-8173.

NEW ORLEANS, 557,482, E-6. The city of Dixieland jazz and Creole cooking began as a military outpost on the Mississippi River in 1718. The settlement was named in honor of the Duc D'Orleans, Regent of France. During the mid-18th-century administration of the Marquis de Vaudreuil, New Orleans developed into one of the early social centers of the South. The citizenry copied the Marquis' elegant manners and his fondness for festivity. Since that time, New Orleans has been noted for its unique culture and for the socially exclusive Creoles, descendants of the original French and Spanish settlers. The city came under Spanish rule in 1763, much to the dislike of the independent-minded citizens. Two fires destroyed most of the city in 1788 and 1794. France regained control on November 30, 1803; but 20 days later, New Orleans was bought by the United States in the Louisiana Purchase. The city developed rapidly during the first half of the 19th century. The first steamboat was put into service between New Orleans and Natchez in 1812, and the city quickly became an international port and market for cotton, slaves, and sugar. New Orleans also became the cultural center of the South. The city reveled in balls and receptions, horse and steamboat racing, dueling, and gambling. During the Civil War, New Orleans surrendered without resistance in April, 1862, and it was held by Union Gen. Benjamin F. Butler for the duration of the war. Commerce was halted, and the city stagnated for 17 years. Following reconstruction, New Orleans slowly rebuilt. The Port of New Orleans grew, railroads sprang up along the docks, and the channel at the mouth of the river was made deeper. The port is now the nation's second largest. Despite the large amount of industrial activity now in the area, New Orleans has carefully preserved many buildings and past customs.

FRENCH QUARTER: Bounded by Canal and Esplanade Sts. and N. Rampart St. and the Mississippi River, the French Quarter is the oldest section of the city and the site of the original settlement. Iron-latticed balconies, narrow streets, and walkways leading to courtyards behind many of the buildings characterize the French and Spanish influence in the area. **Jackson Square,** bounded by Chartres, St. Peter, St. Ann, and Decatur Sts., was originally a parade ground for soldiers. The square was landscaped in the mid-1800s, and a 10-ton bronze statue of Andrew Jackson was erected in its center. The square is also surrounded by a wrought iron fence, and many local artists display and sell their work on the surrounding sidewalks. **St. Louis Cathedral,** on Chartres St. facing Jackson Square, was built in 1793 on the site where two other churches had stood. The church, substantially enlarged in 1851, has three steeples. Year-round, Mon.-Sat., 9 A.M. to 5 P.M.; Sun., 1 to 5 P.M. Free. Behind the church is the *St. Anthony's Garden,* with several flower beds and a marble monument. The **Pontalba Buildings,** both facing Jackson Square on St. Peter St. and on St. Ann St., were completed in 1849 and used as apartment buildings and shops. The two rowhouse structures have elaborate wrought iron balconies which face the square. **French Market,** on Decatur St., faces the remaining side of the square. Several buildings along Decatur and St. Peter Sts. make up the market, where there are shops, restaurants, and produce stands. The *Café du Monde* is also here, serving café au lait and beignets (powdered doughnuts) 24 hours a day. **Beauregard-Keyes House,** 1113 Chartres St., is a raised cottage of Federal design. Built in 1827, it was the birthplace of Paul Morphy, famous chess champion. Gen. Pierre Gustave Toutant Beauregard also lived here for several years after returning from the Civil War. Author Frances Parkinson Keyes bought the house in 1944, renovated it, and for many years used it as her winter quarters, where she did much of her writing. Tours: Year-round,

Mon.-Sat., 10 A.M. to 3 P.M. Adults $2.50; students and persons 65 and over, $1.75; children under 12, 75¢. 504/523-7257. The **Gallier House,** 1118-32 Royal St., was designed and built by the noted 19th-century architect James Gallier, Jr. The house is decorated and furnished in the style of the mid-1800s. An adjoining building contains changing exhibits on 19th-century New Orleans. Year-round, Mon.-Sat., 10 A.M. to 4:30 P.M. Adults $2.50; children 5-11, $1; 65 and over, $2; under 5, free. 504/523-6722. The **Louisiana State Museum** is housed in several historic buildings in the French Quarter. The Cabildo and the Presbytère, adjacent to and on either side of St. Louis Cathedral on Jackson Square, are two Spanish structures built in the late 18th century. The *Cabildo* housed the Spanish governing council; the formal signing of the Louisiana Purchase in 1803 took place in a second floor room here. The building now houses the death mask of Napoleon Bonaparte and historical and art collections from around the state. The *Presbytère* was originally designed to be a priest's residence but was never used for that purpose. Similar in design to the Cabildo, this building contains historical exhibits and artwork. The *1850 House,* located in a portion of the Lower Pontalba Building at 523 St. Ann St., is a restored rowhouse reflective of life in mid-19th-century New Orleans. The *Louisiana State Museum Library* is also housed in the Lower Pontalba Building. *Madame John's Legacy,* 632 Dumaine St., was built in 1789 and is an example of colonial Creole architecture. Here are a collection of colonial Louisiana furniture and special exhibition galleries with changing exhibits on the history and life of Louisiana. Museum, Cabildo, Presbytère, 1850 House, Museum Library, Madame John's Legacy: Year-round, Tues.-Sun., 9 A.M. to 5 P.M. Adults $1; students 50¢; children under 12, free. *Jackson House* and the *State Arsenal,* 619 St. Peter St., are recently renovated 19th-century buildings, which contain exhibitions of Louisiana's folk and native art. Year-round, Tues.-Sun., 9 A.M. to 5 P.M. Admission for each building: Adults $1; persons 12-18, 50¢; under 12, free. 504/568-6968. The **Historic New Orleans Collection,** 533 Royal St., is a complex of buildings with public exhibition galleries, two historic houses, and a research center. Of particular interest are the paintings and photographs depicting the history of the city. Year-round, Tues.-Sat., 10 A.M. to 5 P.M. Royal St. gallery (downstairs): Free. House and ten upstairs galleries: Tours, adults $1, children 50¢. 504/523-7146.

GARDEN DISTRICT: The Garden District is a residential section extending from Jackson Ave. to Louisiana Ave. and from St. Charles Ave. to Magazine St. When Americans began moving to the city, they settled in this area and built many mansions with large gardens and lawns. The **St. Charles Streetcar Line,** one of the last in the country, is listed on the National Register of Historic Places and runs up St. Charles Ave. from Canal St. and passes by the Garden District and through Uptown, where many turn-of-the-century mansions are located. Fare: 40¢. The **Streetcar Store,** 111 St. Charles Ave., (downtown) has information on the streetcar line and its history and sells a guide of all the sights along the way. Year-round, daily, 9 A.M. to 6 P.M. 504/524-2626. The **Women's Guild Garden District Home,** 2504 Prytania St., is an antebellum mansion of Greek-Revival and Italianate architecture. It is furnished with early 19th-century and Victorian pieces and contains paintings and other pieces of art. Sept.-mid-July, Mon.-Fri., 1 to 4 P.M. Donation: $2. 504/899-1945.

CITY PARK AREA: City Park, City Park Ave. at Marconi Dr., contains the New Orleans Museum of Art, lagoons for boating and fishing, horseback riding, tennis courts, four 18-hole golf courses, a miniature train, and an amusement park for children. Of the many live oaks in the park, the most interesting are the Dueling Oak, where battles of honor were once fought, and Suicide Oak. Year-round, daily, sunrise to 11 P.M. Park: Free. 504/482-4888. The **New Orleans Museum of Art,** on Lelong Ave. in City Park, has permanent collections of art from the Western world, dating from the pre-Christian era to the present. African, Far Eastern, and pre-Columbian exhibits are also on permanent display. Changing exhibits include collections of artwork from major museums throughout the world. Year-round, Tues.-Sun., 10 A.M. to 5 P.M. Adults $2; persons 3-17 and 65 and over, $1; under 3, free. Thurs., free. 504/488-2631. The **Pitot House,** 1440 Moss St., is a restored 18th-century plantation on Bayou St. John. Once the residence of James Pitot, the first mayor of the city, it is furnished with Federal-period antiques. Year-round, Thurs., 11 A.M. to 4 P.M. Admission $1.50. 504/482-0312.

MODERN STRUCTURES: The **Louisiana Superdome,** 1500 Poydras St., is one of the world's largest indoor sports arenas. Held here are many different events, including amateur and professional sports, circuses,

© 1981, 1980 Rand McNally

Walking Tour of New Orleans

New Orleans' French Quarter is so compact it's best to explore it on foot. Guided walking tours are conducted free by the National Park Service from Jackson Square (offices at 400 Royal Street, Room 200), and for a fee by The Friends of The Cabildo (701 Chartres Street). Or, you can explore on your own. Begin at the tourist office, 334 Rue Royal, which offers free maps and guides to local attractions. Then stroll down Royal to the many antique shops, boutiques, art galleries, and restaurants such as Brennan's and Court of Two Sisters. To one side of Royal lies Bourbon Street. On the other side is Chartres Street, which invites browsing in its many antique shops and, if you're in the mood for fine pastries, stop by La Marquise, a small bakery at 625 Rue Chartres. St. Peter Street intersects Chartres and leads to St. Louis Cathedral and Jackson Square, stage for fence artists at work and wandering musicians. Across Decatur Street sits the French Market and Cafe du Monde, popular for beignets and coffee. Beyond that lies the Mississippi River, accessible via the Moon Walk. Nearby, riverboats depart for cruises on the river. Walking back to the edge of the Quarter, across Canal Street to St. Charles Avenue, you can board the St. Charles Streetcar for a ride to the Garden District.

concerts, and parades. Numerous restaurants, lounges, and shops are also located inside the building. Tours: Year-round, daily, 9:30 A.M. to 3:30 P.M. (except during certain events). Adults $3; children 5-12, $1.50; under 5, free. 504/587-3663. The **Lake Pontchartrain Causeway,** Causeway Blvd. at Lake Pontchartrain, is the world's longest bridge. Nearly 24 miles in length, it crosses Lake Pontchartrain to Covington. Always open. Toll: $1.

PARKS AND GARDENS: Audubon Park and Zoological Gardens, St. Charles Ave. across from Tulane University, stretches from St. Charles Ave. to the Mississippi River. The park has a golf course, tennis courts, live oaks, a miniature train, and 40 acres of land overlooking the river. The 58-acre zoological gardens contain many species of wildlife from several continents, a sea lion aquarium, elephant house, and a children's zoo. Park: Year-round, daily, sunrise to 11 P.M. Free. Zoo: Year-round, Mon.-Fri., 9:30 A.M. to 5 P.M.; Sat.-Sun., 9:30 A.M. to 6 P.M. Adults $2.50; children 3-15, $1.25; under 3 and 65 and over, free. 504/861-2537. **Longue Vue House and Gardens,** 7 Bamboo Rd., is a 20th-century home built in the classical tradition, with gardens influenced by those in England and Spain. There are gallery exhibitions in the house, which is also furnished with 18th- and 19th-century pieces. The gardens are highlighted by seasonal blooms and sculptured fountains. Year-round, Tues.-Fri., 10 A.M. to 4:30 P.M.; Sat.-Sun., 1 to 5 P.M. House and gardens: Adults $5, students $3. Gardens: Adults $2, students $1. 504/488-5488. The **Moon Walk,** a linear park across from Jackson Square and bordering on the Mississippi River, is a popular place to sit and watch the river traffic.

See also **CITY PARK AREA.**

CRUISES: Several riverboats cruise the Mississippi River and adjacent waterways on tours of the city. Among them are the *Natchez,* the *Cotton Blossom,* the S.S. *President,* and the *Mark Twain,* 504/586-8777; and the *Voyageur,* 504/523-5555.

POVERTY POINT STATE COMMEMORATIVE AREA, A-4. Located on St. 577, **Poverty Point** is the site of one of the earliest aboriginal culture groups yet discovered in the Lower Mississippi Valley. The mounds here date from 1700 to 700 B.C. The bird-shaped effigy mound is of particular interest. Trails, tram cars, an observation tower, and a museum are also on the grounds. Daily, May-Aug., 8 A.M. to 7 P.M.; other months, 8 A.M. to 5 P.M. Park: Free. Museum: Admission. 318/926-5492.

ST. FRANCISVILLE, 1,471, D-4. During the steamboat era, St. Francisville was one of the largest ports between Natchez and New Orleans; however, the advent of the railroads and the end of river trade during the Civil War brought about the decline of the town. Despite shelling by Union gunboats during the war, many antebellum

structures still remain. The **Audubon State Commemorative Area,** 4 miles east of U.S. 61 on St. 965, is a 100-acre woodland park which includes the *Oakley Plantation House.* John James Audubon lived here for a while, during which time he created many of his bird paintings. The house has been restored as a museum containing Audubon memorabilia and is furnished as it was when he lived here. Within the park are nature trails and a formal garden. Park: Apr.-Sept., daily, 8 A.M. to 7 P.M.; other months, 8 A.M. to 4:45 P.M. Admission: $1 per carload up to four people, 25¢ for each additional person. House: Year-round, Mon.-Sat., 9 A.M. to 4:15 P.M.; Sun., 1 to 4:15 P.M. Free with paid admission to the park. 504/635-3739. The **Audubon Art Gallery,** located in the Holiday Inn on U.S. 61 at St. 10, contains a complete collection of Audubon's 435 life-size bird portraits. Year-round, daily. Always open. 504/635-3821. **Rosedown Plantation and Gardens,** on St. 10 at U.S. 61, was built in 1835. The white-columned house on this 2,400-acre working plantation contains paintings and many pieces of Victorian, Federal, and Empire furniture. In the gardens are 140-year-old plants and shrubs as well as gazebos and statuary. An oak alley leads to the mansion's front door. Daily, Mar.-Oct., 9 A.M. to 5 P.M.; other months, 10 A.M. to 4 P.M. Adults: House and garden $5, garden $3. Children: House $2, garden free. 504/635-3110. The **Myrtles,** 1 mile north of St. 10 on U.S. 61, has a 110-foot-long front gallery with iron grillwork, intricate interior plasterwork, antique furnishings, and landscaped grounds. Overnight accommodations are available. Year-round, daily, 9 A.M. to 5 P.M. Adults $3.50, children $2. 504/635-6277. **Afton Villa Gardens,** U.S. 61, are beautifully terraced gardens surrounding the ruins of a 40-room mansion that burned in 1963. The grounds, which were laid out by a French landscape artist, are planted in seasonal flowers. Year-round, daily, 9 A.M. to 4:30 P.M. Admission $1.50. 504/635-6773. **Catalpa Plantation,** U.S. 61, 5 miles north, is one of the oldest Louisiana homesites still owned and lived in by descendants of the original owners. Feb.-Nov., daily, 9 A.M. to 5 P.M.; other months, by appointment. Admission $3.50. 504/635-3372. The **Cottage Plantation,** U.S. 61, 5 miles north, is an antebellum plantation on which the first portion of the house was built in 1795. The second section was added in 1810 and the wing in 1850. Surrounding the house are gardens dating to the 18th century. Lodging and breakfast are available. Tours: Year-round, daily, 9 A.M. to 5 P.M. Adults $3.50; children 6-12, $1; under 6, free. Cost for overnight lodging includes a tour of the house and gardens. 504/635-3674.

ST. MARTINVILLE, 7,965, E-4. The town is perhaps best known as the setting for part of Henry Wadsworth Longfellow's poem "Evangeline"; various landmarks involved in the poem have been preserved. St. Martinville is the center of a rich sugar-

cane-, rice-, and cotton-growing area. **Longfellow-Evangeline State Commemorative Area,** on St. 31, is located just north of town on the Bayou Teche. The park centers around a late 18th-century Acadian house built of handhewn cypress timbers fastened with wooden pegs. The outdoor kitchen of the house has been restored and equipped with utensils. The *Acadian Craft Shop,* housed in an accurate wood and mud replica of an old Acadian cottage, has displays of Acadian handiwork; some items are for sale. Park: Year-round, daily, 8 A.M. to 7 P.M. House: Year-round, Mon.-Sat., 9 A.M. to 5 P.M.; Sun., 1 to 5 P.M. Admission: $1 per carload up to four people, 25¢ for each additional person. 318/394-3754. The **Evangeline Oak,** at E. Port St. and the Bayou Teche, marks the landing place of the Acadians upon their arrival in this region. It is believed that the spot was also the meeting place of Emmeline Labiché and Louis Arceneaux—the Evangeline and Gabriel of Longfellow's poem. Year-round, daily, always open. The **Statue of Evangeline,** beside St. Martins Church on Main St., was donated by a movie crew who filmed a version of the poem here in 1929 and marks the grave of Emmeline Labiché. Year-round daily, always open.

SHREVEPORT, 205,815, A-1. In 1833, Henry Miller Shreve broke through the Great Raft, an almost solid jam of driftwood on the Red River, and reached the small settlement of Bennett and Cane's Bluff. Several years later, Shreve and other investors bought the land at Bennett and Cane's Bluff and laid out the streets and sold plots of land for what was then called "Shreve Town." In 1839, the town was officially incorporated as Shreveport. Navigability of the river made Shreveport a shipping and marketing center for the large cotton plantations of northwest Louisiana. The discovery of oil northwest of town in 1906 brought new prosperity to Shreveport. Today, the city still drills for petroleum and natural gas, and has become the industrial center of northwest Louisiana as well as one of the largest cities in the state.

HISTORIC SITE: Old Shreve Square, the 100 block of Texas St., contains many restored Victorian buildings that date back to the 1890s. Many are now occupied by restaurants, shops, and nightclubs. Always open.

MUSEUMS AND GALLERIES: The **State Exhibit Museum,** 3015 Greenwood Rd. adjacent to the Louisiana State Fairgrounds, features a marble rotunda one-eighth mile in circumference. Inside, there are murals, paintings, and historic relics. The museum also contains a series of dioramas depicting the industries, wildlife, natural resources, and recreational facilities of Louisiana. Year-round, Mon.-Sat., 9 A.M. to 5 P.M.; Sun., 1 to 5 P.M. Free. 318/635-2323. The **R. W. Norton Art Gallery,** 4747 Creswell Ave., contains American and European paintings, sculptures, and decorative arts spanning nearly four centuries in its 13 exhibition galleries. American paintings include a large collection of those by Frederic Remington and Charles M. Russell. Year-round, Tues.-Sun., 1 to 5 P.M. Free. 318/865-4201.

PARKS AND GARDENS: The **American Rose Center,** north of U.S. 79/80 on Jefferson-Paige Rd., is the headquarters of the American Rose Society. On the 118-acre grounds are nearly 10,000 rose bushes planted in 30 separate gardens. There are numerous other blooming plants, all set amidst a forest of virgin pine. A carillon tower provides chime music daily. An information center is in the headquarters building. April-Oct. or Nov., Mon.-Fri., 8:30 A.M. to 6:30 P.M.; Sat.-Sun., noon to 6 P.M.; other months, daily, 8:30 A.M. to 4:30 P.M. Adults $1.50; children under 12, free. 318/938-5402. **R. S. Barnwell Memorial Garden and Art Center,** 501 Clyde Fant Pkwy., has a large domed botanical conservatory with many native and tropical flowers and plants. Changing art exhibits are featured in the gallery. Year-round, Mon.-Fri., 9 A.M. to 4:30 P.M.; Sat.-Sun., 1 to 5 P.M. Free. 318/226-6495. **Jacobs Nature Park,** 12 miles northwest via Blanchard-Furrh Rd., is a 160-acre preserve with hardwood bottom lands and other forms of plant and animal

life. Many trees and plants are labeled for identification. Nature trails and an interpretive building are also on the grounds. Year-round, Wed.-Sat., 8 A.M. to 5 P.M.; Sun., 1 to 5 P.M. Free. 318/929-2806.

THIBODAUX, 15,810, E-5. The **Edward Douglass White State Commemorative Area,** 5 miles north on St. 1, includes the 130-year-old homestead of the former statesman and Chief Justice of the U.S. Supreme Court. The white frame raised cottage has been restored and furnished in the period of 1830 to 1890. Year-round, Tues.-Sat., 9 A.M. to 5 P.M.; Sun., 1 to 5 P.M. Adults $1; persons 7-12, 50¢; under 7 and 65 and over, free. 504/447-3473. **Laurel Valley Plantation,** on Parish 33, east of St. 308, has more than 75 structures still standing and is one of the largest surviving 19th-century sugar plantation complexes in the country. By appointment, year-round, Mon.-Fri., 9 A.M. to 5 P.M. Donation: $1.50. 504/447-7352.

VILLE PLATTE, 9,201, D-3. The **Louisiana State Arboretum,** 6 miles north on St. 3042, is located in Chicot State Park. Some 300 acres of the park have been set aside as a living, natural exhibition of over 100 species of plant life native to Louisiana.

Nature trails lead through the arboretum, and many plant specimens are labeled for identification. Year-round, daily, 8 A.M. to 6 P.M. Free. 318/363-2403.

Information Sources

Louisiana Office
of Tourism
Department of Culture,
Recreation & Tourism
P.O. Box 44291
Baton Rouge, LA 70804
504/925-3860

Alexandria-Pineville
Convention and Tourist
Commission
Box 992
Alexandria, LA 71301
318/442-6671

Baton Rouge Area
Convention and
Visitors Bureau
P.O. Box 3202
Baton Rouge, LA 70821
504/383-1835

Greater New Orleans
Tourist and
Convention Commission
334 Royal St.
New Orleans, LA 70130
504/566-5011

Iberia Parish
Tourist Commission
P.O. Box 970
New Iberia, LA 70560
318/365-1540

Lafayette Parish
Convention and
Visitors Commission
P.O. Box 52066
Lafayette, LA 70505
318/232-3808

Lake Charles/
Calcasieu Parish
Convention & Tourist
Commission
P.O. Box 1912
Lake Charles, LA 70601
318/436-9588

Monroe/West Monroe
Convention &
Visitors Bureau
141 DeSiard St., Suite 114
Monroe, LA 71201
318/387-5691

Natchitoches Parish
Tourist Commission
Box 411
Natchitoches, LA 71457
318/352-8072

Shreveport-Bossier
Convention and
Tourist Bureau
P.O. Box 1761
Shreveport, LA 71166
318/222-9391

Louisiana Campgrounds

FEES REFLECT MINIMUM RATE FOR 2 ADULTS AND ARE SUBJECT TO INCREASE OR SEASONAL CHANGES

- • — at the campground
- ○ — within one mile of campground
- $ — extra charge
- ** — limited facilities during winter months
- A — adults only
- B — 10,000 acres or more
- C — contribution

- E — tents rented
- F — entrance fee or premit required
- N — no specific number, limited by size of area only
- P — primitive
- R — reservation required
- S — self-contained units only

- U — unlimited
- V — trailers rented
- Z — reservations accepted
- LD — Labor Day
- MD — Memorial Day
- UC — under construction
- d — boat dock

- g — public golf course within 5 miles
- h — horseback riding
- j — whitewater running craft only
- k — snow skiing within 25 miles
- l — boat launch
- m — area north of map
- n — no drinking water

- p — motor bikes prohibited
- r — boat rental
- s — stream, lake or creek water only
- t — tennis
- u — snowmobile trails
- w — open certain off-season weekends
- y — drinking water must be boiled

Map Reference	Park Name	Access	Acres	Tent Spaces	Trailer Spaces	Approximate Fee	Season	Other Swimming Swimming Pool	Fishing	Boating	Other Playground	Telephone Number	Mail Address
	STATE PARKS												
A4	Chemin-A-Haut	Fr Bastrop, 10 mi N on Hwy 139	355	50	24	5.00	All year	$	•	•	r	318/281-5805	Rt 5 Box 617, Bastrop 71220
D3	Chicot	Fr Ville Platte, 6 mi N on Hwy 3042	6480	60	36	5.00	All year		•	•	dlr	318/363-2403	Rt 3 Box 494, Ville Platte
D6	Fontainbleau	Fr Mandeville, 3 mi E on US 190	2755	100	80	5.00	All year	$	•	•		504/626-8052	Box 152, Mandeville 70448
A2	Lake Bistineau	Fr Minden, 20 mi SW on Hwy 163	950	50	35	5.00	All year		•	•	lr	318/745-3526	Box 607-A, Doyline 71023
E6	St Bernard	Fr Chalmette, 8 mi E on Hwy 47, 1 mi S on Hwy 39	300	50	50	5.00	All year			•	d	504/682-2101	P O Box 534, Violet 70092
E2	Sam Houston Jones	Fr Lk Charles, 12 mi N on Hwy 378	1068	35	70	5.00	All year		•	•	lr	318/855-7371	Rt 4 Box 212, Lk Charles 7060
B4	Lake Bruin	Fr St Joseph, 4 mi N on US 604	54	112	112	5.00	All year		•	•	lr	318/766-3530	Rt 1 Box 183, St Joseph 71366
D6	Fairview Riverside	Fr Madisonville, 2-1/2 mi E on Hwy 22	100	60	80	5.00	All year		•	•	lr	504/845-3318	Box 97, Madisonville 70447
A2	Lake Claiborne	Fr Homer, 7 mi SE on Hwy 146	97	N	N	3.50	All year		•	•	dlr	318/927-2976	PO Box 246, Homer 71040
F6	Grand Isle	Fr Hwy 1, S to E end of Island	140	100	100	2.50	All year		•	•	lr	504/787-2559	PO Box 741, Grand Isle 70358
	STATE FORESTS												
	Alexander St Forest		8000										
C3	Indian Creek RA	Fr Alexandria, 10 mi S on US 165 to Woodworth, 1/4 mi E, 3.2 mi S	100	71	71	7.00	All year		•	•	dl • p	318/445-2933	Woodworth 71485
	NATIONAL FORESTS												
	Kisatchie NF												
C2	Dogwood	Fr Kisatchie, 5.5 mi N on Hwy 117.	6	10	10	None	All year				n		Kisatchie
D2	Fullerton Lake	Fr Pitkin, 6 mi W on Hwy 10, 3.5 mi NE on Hwy 399.	3	8	8	None	All year		•		d		Pitkin
C3	Valentine Lk North Shor	Fr Alexandria, 16.8 mi W on Hwy 28, .2 mi SW on Hwy 121.	6	13	13	2.00	All year	1	•		d		Alexandria
A2	Upper Caney	Fr Minden, 5 mi N on Hwy 159, 2 mi W on Co 809.	10	28	28	3.00	All year	1	•		dl		Minden
B2	Cloud Crossing	Fr Dodson, 15 mi W on Hwy 126, 2.5 mi S on Hwy 1233, 1 mi W on FR 513.	7	13	13	None	All year		•		dl		Dodson
C3	Stuart Lake	Fr Pollock, 1.5 mi W on Hwy 8, 1 mi S on FR 144.	3	7	7	2.00	All year		•	•			Pollock
B3	Gum Springs	Fr Winnfield, 8 mi W on US 84.	1	13	13	None	All year				n		Winnfield
	CORPS OF ENGINEERS												
A2	South Abutment East	Fr Shreveport, 13 mi NE on 79/80, 8 mi N on Hwy 157 to Bellevue, 2 mi NE to damsite	10	10	S10	None	All year		•		l	318/326-4190	PO Drawer 546, Plain Dealings

Maryland

Major Events

See state map, page 21

NASA Goddard Space Flight Center Model Rocket Launching, 1st and 3rd Sunday of each month, weather permitting, at the Goddard Space Flight Visitors Center, Greenbelt. Free. 301/344-8101.

Winterfest, mid-Mar., McHenry, north of Oakland. The Wisp Ski Area celebrates the winter season with skiing, snowmobiling, sleigh rides, races, contests, and a banquet and show. Admission. 301/334-3888.

Maple Syrup Demonstrations, mid-Mar., Cunningham Falls State Park, Thurmont. Tree tapping, sap boiling, and an interpretation are performed by a park ranger. Maryland-made maple syrup products are for sale also. Free. 301/271-7574.

Maryland Day Celebration, late Mar., St. Mary's City. Activities center around a gathering of the Maryland General Assembly in the State House of 1676. A parade and craft demonstrations are held on the State House grounds. Free. 301/994-0779.

Sugarloaf's Spring Crafts Fair, mid-Apr., Gaithersburg. Professional craftsmen display and sell pottery, stained glass, woodwork, jewelry, quilts, and scrimshaw. Food and live music are also featured. Admission. 301/831-9191.

Ward Foundation World Championship Wildfowl Carving Competition, late Apr., Ocean City. The Convention Hall in Ocean City is filled with more than 2,000 entries in 150 different categories of competition for wildfowl and feather carving and painting. A workshop is held on the first day. Admission. 301/742-4988.

Maryland House and Garden Pilgrimage, early May, Calvert County, south of Annapolis. There is a tour of stately tidewater plantation homes. Admission. 301/832-6933.

Montpelier Spring Festival, early May, Laurel. The Montpelier Mansion and grounds and the Montpelier Cultural Arts Center are the setting for an arts and crafts show and sale, concerts, and children's entertainment. Free. 301/953-9595.

Preakness Festival and Race, early to mid-May, Baltimore. Festivities are held throughout the city, including the Preakness Parade, the Inner Harbor regatta, ethnic festivals, art shows, concerts, and house and garden tours. The running of the Preakness, second jewel in the Triple Crown of thoroughbred racing, takes place on a Saturday at the Pimlico Race Course. Admission is charged for several events. 301/685-8689.

Cavalier Days in Calvert County, mid-May, Prince Frederick. A fair of 1780 is re-created at the County Fairgrounds. Many participants wear colonial costumes of the 17th and 18th centuries. Music, playlets, medieval combat, and a colonial militia rally are presented. Admission. 301/535-0144.

DELMARVA Chicken Festival, mid-June, Princess Anne. The campus of the University of Maryland/Eastern Shore is the site of this event, which features a chicken-cooking contest, a beauty contest, flea markets, arts and crafts, and a parade. Free. 302/856-6050.

Heritage Days Festival, mid-June, Cumberland. This event is held in the Washington Street Historic District with arts and crafts, an antique show, children's entertainment, and tours of historic buildings. Free. 301/777-5905.

Annapolis Arts Festival, mid-June, Annapolis. The City Dock is the scene for this outdoor arts and crafts exhibition. Live entertainment supplements the many arts and crafts displays under circus tents overlooking Annapolis Harbor. Admission. 301/267-7922.

Military Field Days, late July, Big Pool, southwest of Clear Spring. Military units of the French and Indian War, the American Revolution, and the Civil War set up camps and engage in tactical demonstrations. Crafts demonstrations, food, and live music are other features of this annual event held in Fort Frederick State Park. Admission. 301/842-2155.

Jonathan Hager Frontier Crafts Day, early Aug., Hagerstown. This festival features demonstrations and sales of frontier crafts on the lawn of Hager House in City Park. Free. 301/791-3130.

Calvert County Jousting Tournament, late Aug., Port Republic, south of Prince Frederick. Costumed medieval knights engage in mock battle. Jousting is the official state sport of Maryland. Admission. 301/586-0565.

Maryland State Fair, late Aug. to early Sept., Timonium, north of Towson. The 100-acre State Fairgrounds is the site for Maryland's annual fair. Numerous agricultural exhibits, including 4,000 head of livestock, are featured along with thoroughbred horse racing, arts and crafts displays, an antique auto show, and a carnival midway. Admission. 301/252-0200.

National Hard Crab Derby & Fair, early Sept., Crisfield. This seafood center presents a unique crab race with entries from many states, a Miss Crustacean contest, Maryland seafood delicacies, parades, and entertainment at the Crisfield Marina. Admission. 301/968-2682.

The Maryland Seafood Festival, early to mid-Sept., Sandy Point State Park, northeast of Annapolis. The state park hosts three days of live entertainment, arts and crafts, Chesapeake Bay heritage exhibits, and plenty of seafood. Admission. 301/268-7676.

Defender's Day Ceremony, mid-Sept., Baltimore. This event commemorates the defense of Fort McHenry and the writing of "The Star Spangled Banner." Patriotic music, precision marching and drill, and a mock bombardment and defense of the fort are highlights of the festivities. The singing of "The Star Spangled Banner" and a fireworks display cap off the day's events. Free. 301/539-3678.

Sunfest, mid- to late Sept., Ocean City. The beach at Ocean City comes alive with arts and crafts, surf-fishing contests, seafood booths, and live music. Many events are held under a big-top tent. Free. 301/289-8221.

Baltimore City Fair, mid- to late Sept., Baltimore. Held at Baltimore's Inner Harbor, there are a myriad of Maryland and ethnic foods, a giant midway, entertainment, an international village, and the main focus of the fair—exhibits from many of Baltimore's neighborhoods. Admission. 301/547-0015.

Autumn Glory Festival, early Oct., Oakland. This townwide event features fall foliage tours, an Oktoberfest, banjo and fiddler championships, and a parade. Free. 301/334-3888.

Columbus Day Parade, mid-Oct., Baltimore. This is one of the largest Columbus Day parades in the country. There are over 40 marching bands, many drum and bugle corps, and numerous veterans and civic groups. Free. 301/396-8933.

Maryland Crafts Festival, mid-Oct., Timonium, north of Towson. The State Fairgrounds hosts 250 artists and craftsmen displaying and selling their original creations. Food booths, crafts demonstrations, and live music are also featured. Admission. 301/831-9191.

Chesapeake Appreciation Days, late Oct. to early Nov., Sandy Point State Park, northeast of Annapolis. Maryland's oyster-dredging skipjacks, last working sailing fleet in North America, compete for "Top Skipjack" title on Chesapeake Bay. Many maritime-oriented exhibits and other activities are also featured. Seafood booths offer oysters served in a variety of styles. Admission. 301/267-7100.

Holiday Arts & Crafts Show, early Dec., Gaithersburg. Some 60 local artisans exhibit stained glass, macrame, jewelry, woodwork, dolls, candy, and homemade gifts, all geared toward the Christmas season, at the Gaithersburg Community Center. Free. 301/840-1862.

Maryland Destinations

ABERDEEN, 11,533, B-6. **U.S. Army Ordnance Museum,** Aberdeen Proving Ground, has weapons from the American Revolution to the present. Included are tanks, missiles, artillery, guns of every type, and uniforms. Year-round, Tues.-Fri., noon to 5 P.M.; Sat.-Sun., 10 A.M. to 5 P.M. Free. 301/278-3602.

ANNAPOLIS, 31,740, C-6. By 1694, the need for a capital more accessible by land caused the archives and provincial government of the colony of Maryland to be moved from St. Mary's City to Anne Arundel Town. This former Puritan settlement of Providence was soon to be renamed Annapolis for Princess Anne, later Queen Anne of England. Sir Francis Nicholson, second governor of the colony of Maryland, was instrumental in laying out the town. Streets were designed to radiate from State Circle, where the capitol was to be built.

GOVERNMENT BUILDINGS: Maryland State House (1772-79), State Circle, is the oldest state house in continuous legislative use in the country. *Old Senate Chamber,* in the State House, is where the new Congress of the United States met from November 16, 1783, to June 3, 1784; where, on December 23, 1783, George Washington resigned as commander in chief; and where, on January 14, 1783, Congress ratified the Treaty of Paris to end the American Revolution. Year-round, daily, 9 A.M. to 5 P.M. Tours available 9 A.M. to 4:30 P.M. every hour on the hour in the morning and every hour on the half hour in the afternoon. Slide presentations at the Visitors Center. 301/269-3400. **Hall of Records,** College Ave., historical agency for the state of Maryland, has documents, maps, and other official records. Public Research Room is open Mon.-Sat., 8:30 A.M. to 4:30 P.M.; closed on state holidays. **Government House** (1869), State Circle, is the residence of the governor of Maryland. Mid-Sept.-mid-June, Tues., Thurs., 10:30 A.M. to 3:30 P.M. Tours, by appointment only. 301/267-8606.

HISTORIC BUILDINGS: Old Treasury Building (1735), on the grounds of the State House, was first used as a chamber council and later (1837-1903) as a treasury, which accounts for the iron doors and massive locks and hinges. It is also the starting point for walking tours offered by Historic Annapolis, Inc. Oct.-May, Mon.-Fri., 9 A.M. to 4 P.M.; other months, daily, same time. 301/267-8149. **Anne Arundel County Court House** (1824), Church Circle, contains circuit courts, a law library, and tax records. Year-round, Mon.-Fri., 9 A.M. to 5 P.M. Free.

HISTORIC HOMES: Chase-Lloyd House, 22 Maryland Ave., was begun by Samuel Chase, one of the signers of the Declaration of Independence, and was sold in 1771 to Col. Edward Lloyd, a delegate to the Continental Congress, and completed in 1774. A special feature of this Georgian-style house is the cantilevered stairway, illuminated on the middle level by a large Palladian window. Year-round, Mon.-Tues., Thurs.-Sat., 10 A.M. to noon, 2 to 4 P.M. Admission 75¢. 301/263-2723. **Hammond-Harwood House,** 19 Maryland Ave., was built in 1770-74 by Matthias Hammond, a close friend of Colonel Lloyd. One of the most magnificent Georgian residences in America, it was designed and ornamented by William Buckland, 18th-century architect, who did the interior of the Chase-Lloyd House. Apr.-Oct., Tues.-Sat., 10 A.M. to 5 P.M.; Sun., 2 to 5 P.M.; other months, Tues.-Sat., 10 A.M. to 4 P.M.; Sun., 1 to 4 P.M. Adults $2; students $1; under 12, 50¢. 301/269-1714. **London Town Publik House and Gardens** (c. 1744-50), 839 Londontown Rd., off St. 253, 8 miles southeast of Annapolis, is the only remaining building of the town of London, where early travelers from Philadelphia and Williamsburg crossed the South River by ferryboat. Adjoining Publik House, a two-story inn, are a series of natural woodland gardens. House and gardens: Mar.-Dec., Tues.-Sat., 10 A.M. to 4 P.M.; Sun., noon to 4 P.M. Adults $1.50; persons 6-12 and 65 and over, 50¢; under 6, free. 301/956-4900. **William Paca House and Gardens,** 186 Prince George St., is an accurate restoration of the 1765 Georgian mansion of Gov. William Paca, a signer of the Declaration of Independence. The gardens, 1 Martin St., are a restoration of the original gardens of the Paca mansion. The Visitors Center has interpretive exhibits. House and gardens: Year-round, Mon.-Sat., 10 A.M. to 4 P.M.; Sun., noon to 4 P.M. Adults $3.50; students $2; under 6, free. House: Adults $2.50; students $1.50; under 6, free. 301/263-5553. Gardens: Adults $1.50; students 75¢; under 6, free. 301/267-6656. **Shiplap House** (1723), 18 Pinkney St., has been restored into offices by Historic Annapolis, Inc. The name "Shiplap" refers to the house's wooden siding, which was put on with the traditional wooden boat siding technique. Year-round, Mon.-Fri., 9 A.M. to 5 P.M. Free. 301/267-7619.

ACADEMY AND COLLEGE: The United States Naval Academy, bordered by King George St. (visitor's gate entrance on this street) and the Severin River, was opened at Fort Severin on October 10, 1845, and has been in use here as the Naval Academy continuously, with the exception of the Civil War years. At that time, the academy was transferred to Newport, Rhode Island, and the Annapolis facility became a military hospital and camp. In the *Naval Academy Chapel* is the crypt containing the bronze and marble sarcophagus of John Paul Jones. *Bancroft Hall,* the midshipmen's dormitory, has a sample room open for inspection. The *U.S.N.A. Museum,* in Preble Hall, has ship models, paintings of naval heroes, and naval memorabilia. The Visitors Center, in Ricketts Hall, is open year-round, Mon.-Sat., 9 A.M. to 5 P.M.; Sun., noon to 5 P.M. 301/267-3363. Guided walking tours depart from Ricketts Hall, Mar.-May, Sept.-Nov., every hour between 10 A.M. and 4 P.M.; June-Aug., every half hour between 9:30 A.M. and 4 P.M. Adults $1.50; children under 12, 75¢. For tour information, call 301/263-6933. **St. John's College,** College Ave., traces its beginning to King William's School, which was established in the late 1600s. Its patrons included the Maryland signers of the Declaration of Independence. *McDowell Hall* was started in the middle 1700s as a residence for the governor of Maryland, but not completed until 40 years later when it was taken over by the college.

MARKET AREA: Market House, restoration of an 1885 building near the city dock, features seafood fresh from Chesapeake Bay, produce from the surrounding areas, and other specialties. Year-round, Mon., Wed., Thurs., 9 A.M. to 6 P.M.; Fri.-Sat., 9 A.M. to 7:30 P.M.; Sun., 10 A.M. to 6 P.M. *See also* **Kent Island.**

ANTIETAM NATIONAL BATTLEFIELD SITE, B-4. The battle of Antie-

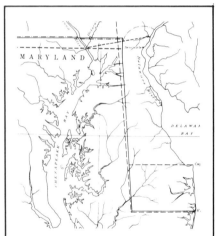

Mason and Dixon were two English surveyors. The line they created is still used to describe the dividing point between the North and the South. Actually, the Mason-Dixon Line was the final result of several highly involved colonial and state boundary disputes which began in 1632. Had all of Maryland's claims been acknowledged, Philadelphia would be in Maryland; had all of Pennsylvania's claims been acknowledged, Baltimore would be in Pennsylvania and Maryland would be a narrow strip of land. Charles Mason and Jeremiah Dixon completed their survey in 1767 and established the Pennsylvania-Maryland border at 39° 43'17.6" north latitude. In 1784, the border was extended westward.

tam, on September 17, 1862, altered the course of the Civil War. It began at dawn with 41,000 Confederates under the command of Gen. Robert E. Lee pitted against 87,000 Federals under Gen. George B. McClellan, was fought on a 12-mile-square area, and ended at dusk. Losses on both sides were staggering. Wounded or killed were 12,410 Federal troops and 10,700 Confederates. Neither side gained, but General Lee was turned back into Virginia. Daily, June-Aug., 8 A.M. to 6 P.M.; other months, 8:30 A.M. to 5 P.M. Free. 301/432-5124.

ASSATEAGUE ISLAND NATIONAL SEASHORE, E-8.

Assateague Island was formerly the southern end of a peninsula originating in southeastern Delaware and extending unbroken to the present tip of the island; but in 1933, a hurricane cut an inlet just below Ocean City, Maryland, creating a separate island. This 37-mile-long island includes a national seashore, state park, and national wildlife refuge, where visitors can watch birds and wildlife. Large flocks of ducks, geese, swans, and other birds nest in the wildlife refuge, which is also home of the Chincoteague ponies, who roam wild, living off marsh grass and bayberry leaves. Legend attributes the origin of these ponies to horses that swam ashore from a wrecked galleon, but historians now suggest that horses imported to the mainland by eastern shore planters in the mid-17th century were set loose on the island to graze and some were never recovered. Two bridges connect the island with the mainland, one from Maryland on St. 611, the other from Virginia on St. 175. Visitors Center for the national seashore is at the northern end of the island on St. 611, 6 miles off U.S. 50. Mar.-Dec., daily, 8:30 A.M. to 5 P.M.; Jan.-Feb., weekends, same hours. 301/641-1441.

BALTIMORE, 786,775, B-6.

Numerous tracts of land were patented, exchanged, broken up, and repatented before the present site of Baltimore was finally determined. In 1696, Charles and Daniel Carroll resurveyed and patented a thousand acres on the west side of Jones Falls; several years later other landholders united with the Carrolls to form a town, and on August 8, 1729, the General Assembly passed a bill establishing Baltimore Town. Over the years, Baltimore has become one of the country's major ports, declining and rising in this position. It endured the hardships of the War of 1812 and the Civil War, and was ravaged by fire in February, 1904, but soon rehabilitated itself.

HISTORIC HOUSES: Carroll Mansion, 800 E. Lombard St., was built in 1823 on land Charles Carroll, of Carrollton, a signer of the Declaration of Independence, deeded to his daughter Mary and her husband, Richard Caton. Now a museum, Carroll Mansion is one of the finer remaining 18th-century townhouses in Baltimore. Year-round, Tues.-Sun., 10 A.M. to 4 P.M.

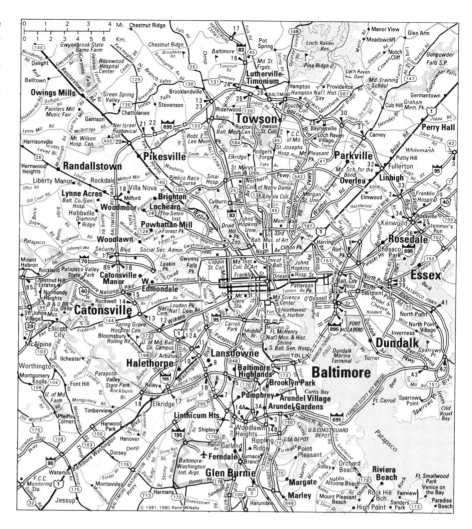

Free. 301/396-4980. **Edgar Allan Poe House,** 203 Amity St., is where the famous poet lived in a garret chamber from 1832 to 1835. Year-round, Wed.-Sun., noon to 4 P.M. Adults $1, children 75¢. 301/525-1274 or 301/396-7932. **Mount Clare Mansion,** Monroe St. and Washington Blvd., was built in 1754 by Charles Carroll, the barrister and a distant cousin of Charles Carroll, who signed the Declaration of Independence. The only remaining pre-Revolutionary house in the city, the mansion contains many of Carroll's furnishings. Year-round, Tues.-Sat., 11 A.M. to 3:15 P.M.; Sun., 1 to 3:15 P.M. Adults $1.50, children 25¢. 301/837-3262. **Star-Spangled Banner Flag House,** 844 E. Pratt St., is the home of Mary Pickersgill, who made the flag honored in the famous song. Year-round, Tues.-Sat., 10 A.M. to 4 P.M.; Sun., 2 to 4:30 P.M. Adults $1; persons 12-18, 50¢; under 12, free. 301/837-1793.

HISTORIC SITES: Fort McHenry National Monument and Historic Shrine, east end of Fort Ave., south Baltimore, is the fort where the successful defense of September 13 and 14, 1814, inspired Francis Scott Key to write the poem which was to become our national anthem. Daily, Memorial Day-Labor Day, 9 A.M. to 8 P.M.; other months, 9 A.M. to 5 P.M. Free. 301/962-4290.

Shot Tower, Fayette and Front Sts., was built in 1828, and used until 1892 for making shot. Year-round, daily, 10 A.M. to 4 P.M. Free. 301/539-8209. **Washington Monument,** 700 block N. Charles St., was the first monument to George Washington to be begun, and except for the rough stone tower near Boonsboro, was the first of importance to be completed. It was designed by Robert Mills, who designed the Washington (D.C.) Monument. Visitors may climb to the top for a view of the city and harbor. Year-round, Fri.-Tues., 10:30 A.M. to 4:30 P.M. Free. Observation tower 25¢. 301/752-9103. **Battle Monument,** Calvert and Fayette Sts., was dedicated to those slain in the 1815 Battle of Baltimore (War of 1812).

HISTORIC AREAS: Fells Point, an old seaport area of Baltimore, has residences of American Federal architecture, many of which are being restored. **2600 Block of Wilkens Ave.** is the longest, unbroken block of rowhouses, with their white marble steps, in Baltimore. **Mount Vernon Place,** Charles and Monument Sts., forms a cross radiating from the base of Washington Monument. Laid out in 1872, it became the center of a favored residential section. Here are civic monuments, fountains, townhouses, and cultural institutions, including the Peabody Conservatory of Music. **Union**

Square, bounded by Hollins, Lombard, Stricker, and Gilmour Sts., has a refurbished square, rowhouses, and the residence of editor and satirist H. L. Mencken (1880-1956). Owned by the University of Maryland, the Mencken residence is open on special occasions. 301/528-6102.

MUSEUMS AND GALLERIES: Babe Ruth Birthplace Shrine and Museum, 216 Emory St., is the house in which George Herman Ruth, Jr., was born on February 6, 1895. He lived here until he was five and played his first organized baseball at the old St. Mary's Industrial School. In the shrine are a life-size wax figure of Ruth, oil paintings and photographs, memorabilia, and a film which traces his life from childhood through his illustrious baseball career. Year-round, Wed.-Sun., 10:30 A.M. to 4 P.M. Adults $1; persons 12-17, 50¢; under 12, free. 301/727-1539. **The Baltimore Museum of Art,** Art Museum Dr. off Charles and 32nd Sts., has American paintings and decorative arts, Antioch mosaics from the second to the sixth century, English sporting art, modern paintings and sculpture, old master paintings, Oriental art, over 80,000 prints and drawings, and tribal arts. Year-round, Tues.-Sat., 11 A.M. to 5 P.M.; 1st and 3rd Thurs., Sun., 1 to 5 P.M.; Sept.-May, also 7 to 10 P.M. Free. 301/396-7101. **B & O Railroad Museum,** Pratt and Poppleton Sts., takes visitors on a round trip through history. Reminders of the past are original tracks and wooden turntable, and a collection of original engines, including the Old War Horse (1848). Year-round, Wed.-Sun., 10 A.M. to 4 P.M. Adults $2, children $1. 301/237-2387. **Baltimore Streetcar Museum,** 1901 Falls Rd., is designed to reflect streetcar terminals of the past. The carhouse has over a dozen vehicles, from the oldest horse cars to the last car on the streets of Baltimore in 1963. Visitors may also ride in one of the cars on a mile-long track. Year-round, Sun., noon to 5 P.M.; Thurs., 7 to 9 P.M.; Sat., noon to 4 P.M. Free. Streetcar rides: Adults $1; children 4-11, 50¢; under 4, free. 301/547-0264. The *Pride of Baltimore* is berthed on the west shore of Baltimore in the Inner Harbor when in port. A living museum, it is an authentically reproduced 1812 Baltimore clipper schooner (it was handcrafted as a Bicentennial project in 1976) and is the first Baltimore clipper to sail in more than a century. When in port, she usually can be visited daily, noon to 6 P.M. **Museum and Library of Maryland History,** 201 W. Monument St., has period rooms and exhibits relating Maryland's history. Among the museum's treasures are 8,800 letters, 325 paintings and drawings, and 14 diaries by Benjamin Henry Latrobe, architect for the U.S. Capitol and many other famous buildings, including the Basilica of the Assumption in Baltimore. Museum: Year-round, Tues.-Sat., 11 A.M. to 4 P.M.; Sun., 1 to 5 P.M. Library: Year-round, Tues.-Sat., 9 A.M. to 4:30 P.M. Nonmembers: Library admission, $2.50 per day; museum,

These decorative pintail decoys look more like real ducks than carvings. The pair, however, was carved by Tan Brunet of Galliano, Louisiana, and awarded top prize in the decorative decoy pair category of the world championship carving contest held each spring in Maryland. The 1981 contest, which was held in Ocean City Convention Hall, included over 2,000 carvings by about 600 carvers who came not only to exhibit their carvings but to learn from other carvers. The world championship carving then becomes a permanent part of the exhibit at the National Wildfowl Museum of Art in Halloway Hall at Salisbury State College, Salisbury, Maryland. The museum has over 2,300 carvings relating the story of decoy and wildlife carving and is open every day from 1 to 5 P.M., year-round. Mr. Brunet, a regular contributor to the contest, has won three world championships. He claims he has had a lot of practice (his carvings prove he has a lot of talent, persistence, and research skills).

He has been carving wildfowl for over 30 years; he began as a teen-ager, and to date, has done over 300 carvings. This pair of pintails was carved from the trunk of a tupelo gum tree and took about six months working time (three to four hours a day, five to six days a week). Before carving the pintails, Mr. Brunet did extensive research on them. He studied live pintails and mounted pintails, and their feather patterns, dimensions, and floating capacity. He then selected the tree trunk, cut it to block size with a chain saw, and traced the pattern of the duck on the block. He did the carving first with a hatchet and then with a knife made of a straight razor. He used a rasp and sandpaper to create its outer form and texture. Then he hollowed out the bird and inserted a weight (a method he devised in 1976) so that it would float like the real pintail. He created the feathers with burning tools and the color with oils. This championship decorative decoy pair is now on display at the National Wildfowl Museum of Art.

adults $1.50; persons 65 and over, $1; children 75¢. Members: Library and museum, free. 301/685-3750. **Maryland Institute, College of Art,** 1300 Mount Royal Ave., is a late 19th-century Roman Revival-style building which houses the college of art and design. Two galleries are open to the public. Year-round, Mon.-Tues., Fri.-Sat., 10 A.M. to 5 P.M.; Wed.-Thurs., 10 A.M. to 9 P.M. 301/669-9200. **Maryland Science Center & Planetarium,** 601 Light St., on the Inner Harbor, is the home of the Maryland Academy of Sciences, founded in 1797 in Baltimore. The museum has interpretive exhibits on different scientific subjects. *Davis Planetarium,* on the second floor, has constellation programs. *Boyd Theatre,* on the third floor, has science shows and lectures. There is also a Keys into the Discovery of Science Room (K.I.D.S.), where preschoolers can learn about science. July-Labor Day, daily, 10 A.M. to 10 P.M.; Sept.-June, Tues.-Thurs., 10 A.M. to 5 P.M.; Fri.-Sat., 10 A.M. to 10 P.M.; Sun., noon to 6 P.M. Adults $2.50; stu-

dents, military, and 65 and over, $1.50; 6-12, $1; under 6, free. 301/685-5225. The **National Aquarium in Baltimore,** 501 E. Pratt St., Pier 3, of the Inner Harbor, houses 8,000 specimens of over 600 different species of mammals, fish, birds, reptiles, amphibians, and invertebrates. The aquarium holds over one-and-a-half million gallons of fresh and salt water and features reproductions of a Maine seacoast cove, an Atlantic coral reef, and a tropical rain forest. It has a dolphin pool and a 200,000-gallon shark tank for lemon, bull, tiger, and sandbar sharks. Memorial Day-mid-Sept. Mon.-Tues., 10 A.M. to 6 P.M.; Wed.-Sun., 10 A.M. to 10 P.M.; other months, Sat.-Thurs., 10 A.M. to 6 P.M.; Fri., 10 A.M. to 9 P.M. Adults $4.50; students and persons 62 and over, $3.50; 3-12, $2.50; under 3, free. 301/727-3000 or 301/727-6900. **Peale Museum,** 225 N. Holliday St., was opened in 1814 by artist Rembrandt Peale (1778-1860), famous portrait painter as was his father, Charles Willson Peale (1741-1827). Year-round, Tues.-Sun., 10 A.M. to 4 P.M. Sat.-Sun., 1 to 5 P.M. Free. 301/396-3523. **U.S. Frigate *Constellation*,** Pratt St., Pier 1, Inner Harbor, is a full-masted sailing ship constructed in 1797 of Maryland oak. The first ship built for the U.S. Navy to go to sea, she served in actions from 1799 through the mid-1800s; and during the early days of World War II, Pres. Franklin D. Roosevelt designated her as the Flagship of the Atlantic Fleet. Mid-June-Labor Day, Mon.-Sat., 10 A.M. to 8 P.M.; mid-May-mid-June, after Labor Day-mid-Oct., 10 A.M. to 6 P.M.; other months, 10 A.M. to 4 P.M. Year-round, Sun., 10 A.M. to 5 P.M. Adults $1.50; persons 6-15 and 65 and over, 50¢; under 6, free. 301/539-1797. **Walters Art Gallery,** 600 N. Charles St., was built by Henry Walters (1849-1931) to house treasures which he and his father, William Thompson Walters, collected over a period of 80 years. Sept.-June, Mon., 1 to 5 P.M.; Tues.-Sat., 11 A.M. to 5 P.M.; Sun., 2 to 5 P.M.; other months, Mon.-Sat., 1 to 4 P.M.; Sun., 2 to 5 P.M. Free. 301/547-9000.

CENTERS: Baltimore City Hall, 100 N. Holliday St., has a 110-foot-high interior rotunda with a segmental dome. Built in 1867-75, many details have been restored. Year-round, Mon.-Fri. Call 301/752-8632 for tour information. **Charles Center,** bounded by Lombard, Charles, Saratoga, and Liberty Sts. and Hopkins Pl., is an architectural revitalization of downtown Baltimore and has won 18 national awards for excellence in design. It includes new buildings, renewal projects, fountains, sculpture, and a Central Plaza. **Civic Center,** 201 W. Baltimore St., is the site of circuses, ice shows, sporting events, and major entertainment. 301/837-0903. **World Trade Center,** Pratt St. between South and Gay Sts., rises some 423 feet above the waters in the Inner Harbor. ***Top of the World,*** an observation level on the 27th floor, has exhibits related to the city. Year-round, Mon.-Tues., 10 A.M. to 5 P.M.; Fri.-Sat., 10 A.M. to 10 P.M.; Sun., noon to 5 P.M. Adults $1, children 75¢. 301/659-4545.

PARKS AND GARDENS: Federal Hill, Warren Ave. near Key Hwy., was named for the celebration following the ratification of the U.S. Constitution and is a vantage point for a view of the harbor and skyline. **Sherwood Gardens,** Highfield Rd. and Greenway Dr., has seven acres of gardens, with flowers blooming sometime during the year in each. Peak season for the thousands of tulips, azaleas, and flowering shrubs is mid-May. Always open. **War Memorial Plaza,** Lexington St., across from City Hall, has daily entertainment during summer. Here "The Star-Spangled Banner" was first sung publicly.

SHOPPING: Harborplace, European-styled marketplace, is housed in two glass pavilions on the Inner Harbor and has restaurants, boutiques, and specialty shops. Year-round, Mon.-Sat., 10 A.M. to 10 P.M.; Sun., noon to 6 P.M. Restaurants are open

until 2 A.M. **Lexington Market,** between Eutaw and Paca Sts., one of the largest of Baltimore's markets, has been in existence since 1782 and features seafood, poultry, ethnic food, produce, meats, and specialty items. Shoppers can also lunch here. Year-round, Mon.-Sat., 8 A.M. to 6 P.M.

ZOO: Baltimore Zoo, Druid Hill Park, has over 1,000 specimens of animals, birds, and reptiles. Adjacent is the **Baltimore Children's Zoo,** which has farm animals, a petting zoo, swinging bridge, and zoo train. Year-round, daily, 10 A.M. to 4:30 P.M. Adults $1.50; children 2-11, 50¢; under 2, free. Mon., free. 301/396-7102.

See also **Brooklandville** and **Essex.**

BELTSVILLE, 9,000, north of College Park, C-5. **Beltsville Agricultural Research Center,** on Powder Mill Rd., east of Beltsville, is a U.S. Department of Agriculture facility where visitors can observe plant and animal science research, the milking parlor complex, beef cattle, swine, and sheep. Year-round, Mon.-Fri., 8 A.M. to 4:30 P.M. Free. 301/344-2483.

BETHESDA, 78,000, C-5. **The National Institutes of Health,** comprising 17 institutes and bureaus, is the federal agency responsible for health research. The Visitors Center, in Building 31A between Old Georgetown Rd. and Wisconsin Ave. at Cedar Lane, presents an orientation on the institutes, has a theater where slides and film on biomedical subjects are shown, a model laboratory, and publications room, with free literature on disease subjects. Year-round, Mon.-Fri., 10 A.M. to 4 P.M. Free. 301/496-

See also **Clara Barton House National Historic Site,** Glen Echo.

BOONSBORO, 1,908, B-4. Early settlers (1774) were George and William Boone, said to be relatives of Daniel Boone. **Scoper House Museum,** 113 N. Main St., has historic items related to Boonsboro. May-Sept., Sun., 1 to 5 P.M. Donations. 301/432-6969. **Crystal Grottos,** 1 mile southwest off St. 34, has limestone corridors of stalactites and stalagmites. Daily, Oct.-Feb., 11 A.M. to 5 P.M.; Mar.-Sept., 9 A.M. to 6 P.M. Adults $3, children $2. 301/432-6336. At **Washington Monument State Park,** 3 miles southeast off U.S. 40A, is the first completed monument to George Washington.

BOWIE, 33,695, C-5. **Bowie Race Course,** north of the city off Race Track Rd., has thoroughbred racing. Sept.-Oct., daily except Sun. 301/262-8111. **Belair Stables Museum,** Belair Dr. off St. 450, has racing memorabilia of the 1930s and 1940s. May, June, Sept., Sun., 2 to 4 P.M. Next door is **Belair Mansion,** built for Gov. Samuel Ogle (1694–1752), who owned the thoroughbreds Spark and Queen Mab, from whom many Maryland thoroughbreds have descended. Bowie is sometimes called the "home of racing." Open by request. Stables

and mansion, free. 301/262-0695.

BROOKLANDVILLE, 500, north of Baltimore on St. 130, B-6. **Cloisters Children's Museum and Creative Workshop,** 10440 Falls Rd., is in a French Gothic Tudor Revival castle built by Sumner Parker to house his collection of antiques. Children visiting the museum may play with the dollhouses and dress in the antique costumes. Year-round, Mon.-Fri., 10 A.M. to 4:30 P.M.; Sat.-Sun., noon to 5 P.M. Adults $1, children free. 301/823-2550.

BRUNSWICK, 4,572, southwest of Frederick on St. 464, B-4. Switchyards operate 24 hours a day in this early railroad town. **Brunswick Museum,** 40 W. Potomac St., has a replica of the railroad from Washington, D.C. to Brunswick, early maps, and pictures. Year-round, Sat., 10 A.M. to 4 P.M.; Sun., 1 to 4 P.M. Adults $1, children 50¢. 301/834-8400.

CAMBRIDGE, 11,703, D-7. Built in 1684, it was one of the towns provided for in a supplement to the 1683 Act for Advancement of Trade. In the graveyard of Christ Protestant Episcopal Church, High St., are graves of statesmen and heroes of the American Revolution and other wars. **Dorchester Heritage Museum,** off St. 343, has exhibits relating to Dorchester County history. Year-round, weekends, 1 to 4:30 P.M. Free. 301/228-5530.

CATOCTIN MOUNTAIN PARK, A-4. This 5,769-acre retreat, which is under the jurisdiction of the National Park Service, is part of the forested ridge that forms the eastern rampart of the Appalachian Mountains. The Visitors Center, 3 miles west of Thurmont on St. 77, is open daily from 8 A.M. to 5 P.M. 301/663-9330. Twelve miles of well-marked trails traverse the park, which has numerous streams and wooded areas. Hours and days for guided walks, talks, and campfire programs are posted in the Visitors Center. Also in the park is Camp David, presidential retreat established by Franklin D. Roosevelt; however, it is not open to the public.

CENTREVILLE, 2,018, C-7. On the green of **Queen Anne's County Courthouse** (1792) is a statue of Queen Anne, which was dedicated by Princess Anne of Great Britain during the Bicentennial. **Queen Anne County Historical Society** maintains **Tucker House** and **Wright's Chance,** both on S. Commerce St., as museums. Summer, Fri., 10 A.M. to 5 P.M.; other days by request. Admission $1 per house. 301/758-1637.

CHESAPEAKE AND OHIO CANAL NATIONAL HISTORICAL PARK, C-4 to A-2. The 184-mile-long canal follows a route along the Potomac River from Georgetown, in the District of Columbia, to Cumberland, Maryland. Promoters originally planned for the canal to extend from

Georgetown to Pittsburgh to share some of the trade with the rapidly growing West. On July 4, 1828, Pres. John Quincy Adams lifted the first shovelful of earth near Little Falls, officially starting the project. Navigation began as divisions were completed: Georgetown to Seneca in 1831; Seneca to Harper's Ferry in 1833; Harper's Ferry to Hancock, Maryland, in 1839; and Hancock to Cumberland in 1850. As a result of financial and legal difficulties, the project was abandoned at Cumberland. In the 1870s, as many as 540 boats carrying coal, flour, grains, and lumber were navigating the canal. A typical boat measured 92 feet long, 14½ feet wide, and carried 110 to 120 tons of cargo. Three and five mules pulled the boats; relief teams were carried on board, and the captain and his family and crew lived in the small aft cabin. As a result of modern transportation facilities available to carry supplies, the canals were abandoned in 1924. In 1938, the canal and adjoining right-of-ways were placed under the jurisdiction of the National Park Service. The park has numerous birds and wildflowers, making it ideal for nature study. At Great Falls are several locks, as well as Great Falls Tavern, built in 1830 as a rest stop for visitors using the canal. Today it houses exhibits. June-Labor Day, daily, noon to 6 P.M.; other months, weekends, same times. Park headquarters are 4 miles west of Sharpsburg, Md., on St. 34. Other centers and information offices are at 108 Main St., Hancock; North Branch, 8 miles south of Cumberland, off St. 51; and Great Falls Tavern. North Branch 301/777-8667; 24-hour emergency 301/339-4206.

CHESTERTOWN, 3,300, B-7. The courthouse was built in 1698 and streets were laid out in 1706 in this picturesque town of waterfront houses built during the American Revolution. **Washington College,** overlooking the river and town, was founded in 1782. In 1789, George Washington, in absentia, was given an honorary degree of doctor of laws; in 1933, Pres. Franklin D. Roosevelt delivered an address at the college and was given a similar degree. Several historic buildings, not open on a regular basis, may be seen on a walking tour. 301/758-2300. Among these are **Geddes-Piper House** (1730–54), Church Alley; **Customs House** (1730), Front and High Sts.; **Hynson-Ringgold House** (1735), Cannon and Front Sts.; **River House** (1784), 107 Water St.; and **Nicholson House** (1788), 111 Queen St.

CLARA BARTON HOUSE NATIONAL HISTORIC SITE, 5801 Oxford Rd., Glen Echo, southwest of Bethesda, C-5. This was the home of Clara Barton, founder of the American Red Cross. The 38-room house, was built in 1892 of lumber from the temporary warehouses and hotels built in Johnstown, Pennsylvania, to house victims of the 1889 flood. When the Johnstown buildings were torn down, Miss Bar-

ton had the lumber shipped to Washington, D.C. and stored. After acquiring the Glen Echo property in 1891, she had the Red Cross warehouse built from the lumber; and in 1897, she had the warehouse remodeled for use as Red Cross headquarters and her home. Year-round, Thurs.-Sat., 10 A.M. to 5 P.M.; Sun., 1 to 5 P.M. Reservations preferred. Free. 301/492-6245. **Glen Echo Park,** also under the jurisdiction of the National Park System, was once a Chautaqua meeting ground. In the park on Oxford Rd. is a half-century-old carousel and art gallery. Apr.-Sept., Mon.-Thurs., 10 A.M. to 5 P.M.; Sat.-Sun., noon to 6 P.M. Free. 301/492-6282.

COLLEGE PARK, C-5. *See* **Beltsville** and **Greenbelt.**

CUMBERLAND, 25,933, A-2. The first settlement here was an Ohio Company trading post in 1749. By 1754, it was enlarged to a fort after the governor of Virginia sent George Washington here with a small company of soldiers to protect Virginia's interests. It grew as an important point on the Cumberland Road (later called National Road, now U.S. 40), which was built as a link to the West. Cumberland is the western terminus of the Chesapeake and Ohio Canal. It is also one of the closest settlements to the Mason and Dixon Line, an imaginary line established in 1763-67 by two English astronomers, Charles Mason and Jeremiah Dixon, along the 39° 43′ latitude to settle a dispute between Pennsylvania and Maryland. Traditionally, this line is also referred to as the dividing line between the North and South. **Washington's Headquarters,** in Riverside Park, was where George Washington, then a colonel, served as post commander during the French and Indian War. **History House,** 218 Washington St., is a restored 18-room house. May-

Nov., Tues.-Sun., 1:30 to 5 P.M. Adults 50¢, students 25¢, children free. 301/777-8678.

EASTON, 7,536, C-7. **Third Haven Meeting House** (1682-83), S. Washington St., was the first structure in the Easton area, which began as a Quaker community. **Talbot County Historical Society,** 25 S. Washington St., has a museum open year-round, Tues.-Fri., 10 A.M. to 4 P.M.; Sat. and Sun., 1 to 4 P.M. Free. Group tours. 301/822-0773. **The Academy of Arts,** Harrison and South Sts., is the center for Talbot County and adjoining communities. Year-round, Mon.-Fri., 10 A.M. to 4 P.M.; Sept.-Nov., Mar.-early June, weekends, 2 to 4 P.M. Donations accepted. 301/822-0455.
See also **St. Michaels.**

EMMITSBURG, 1,552, A-4. Saint Elizabeth Seton, who was canonized in 1975 as the first American-born saint, is enshrined beneath the altar of *Saint Joseph's Provincial House,* in **Seton Shrine Center.** Also in the shrine center are *Stone House,* the first parochial school in the United States and the first residence of the Sisters of Charity, and *White House,* onetime residence of Mother Seton, who came to St. Joseph's Valley in 1809. Year-round, daily, 10 A.M. to 5 P.M.; closed first two weeks in Jan. Reservations preferred. Free. 301/447-6606.

ESSEX, 43,700, east of Baltimore, B-6. **Ballestone Mansion,** Rocky Point Park, was built prior to 1744 on property owned by George Washington's great-grandfather. It was enlarged in the middle 1800s and restored in keeping with the period as a Bicentennial project. Year-round, Mon.-Fri., 9 A.M. to noon, 1 to 4 P.M. Admission $1; persons 65 and over, 50¢. 301/574-3630.

FORT FREDERICK STATE PARK, west of Hagerstown, A-4. On St. 56 south of

---

Historic Churches: 1675-1798

Throughout Maryland are a number of historic churches, some noteworthy because they were the first of their denomination built in America, others because of unusual architectural features, and some because of both. The following, which are open daily or by request, are also noteworthy because they were built either in the 1600s or the 1700s: St. Paul's Church (1733-35), Baden; Bridgetown Church (1773), Bridgetown; St. John's Church (1723), Broad Creek; Emmanuel P.E. Church (1722), Chestertown; Old Trinity Church (c. 1675), near Church Creek; St. Luke's Episcopal Church (1732), Church Hill; St. Francis Xavier Church (1766), near Compton; St. Joseph's Church (c. 1763), near Cordova; St. Thomas (1732), Croom; Third Haven Meeting House (1682), Easton; All

Saints Episcopal Church (1742), Frederick; Green Hill Episcopal Church (1735), Green Hill; Zion Reform Church (1774), Hagerstown; Christ Church, Durham Parish (1732), Ironsides; Middleham Chapel (1748), Lusby; St. Ignatius Church (1798), near Port Tobacco; Christ P.E. Church (1772), Port Republic; St. Andrew's Episcopal Church (1770) and Manokin Presbyterian Church (1765), Princess Anne; Rehoboth Church (1706), Rehobeth; St. Paul's Church (1713), Rock Hill; St. Ignatius Church (1748), St. Inigoes; Spring Hill Episcopal Church (1773), Salisbury; Old Otterbein U.M. Church (1785-86), Sharp; All Hollows Episcopal Church (1756), Snow Hill; All Saints Church (1774), Sunderland; St. James Church (1763), Tracey's Landing; Old Bohemian (St. Francis Xavier) Church (1704), Warwick; Christ P.E. Church (c. 1750), Wayside; Wye Church (1721), Wye Mills.

Indian Springs, which is on Int. 70, 19 miles southwest of Hagerstown, the fort was built in 1756 during the French and Indian War. Garrisoned during the American Revolution and Civil War, it was never attacked. Its stone wall and two barracks have been restored to its early appearance. Year-round, daily, 9 A.M. to sunset.

FORT WASHINGTON PARK, C-5. Across the Potomac river from Mt. Vernon, the garrison, which was established to protect the nation's capital, has had a long and interrupted career since its completion in 1809. It was burned in 1814 when the British successfully attacked the capital and burned the White House, Capitol, and other buildings; but the fort was rebuilt and used as a military post until 1872. In 1939, it came under the jurisdiction of the U.S. Department of the Interior, where it has remained, except during World War II, when it was used by the War Department. Sept.-Apr., 7:30 A.M. to 5 P.M.; May-Aug., 7:30 A.M. to 8 P.M. Free. 301/292-2112.

FREDERICK, 27,557, B-4. In 1725, Benjamin Tasker surveyed a 30,000-acre tract of land and two years later was granted the land. In 1745, the townsite was laid out on property purchased from Tasker's heirs. **Barbara Fritchie Home,** 154 W. Patrick St., is a reproduction of the home of the heroine of John Greenleaf Whittier's poem. Described as sharp tongued, she was said to have defied Gen. Stonewall Jackson and his troops. Year-round, Mon.-Sat., 9 A.M. to 5 P.M.; Sun., 1 to 5 P.M. Adults $1, children 50¢. 301/662-3000. **The Historical Society of Frederick County,** 24 E. Church St., has exhibits of early American glass, pre-Columbian Indian artifacts, and antique dolls. June-Sept., Mon.-Thurs., 9 A.M. to 4 P.M.; Sun., 11 A.M. to 4 P.M. Donations. 301/663-1188. **Mount Olivet Cemetery,** S. Market St., near Int. 70, has near the entrance the monument marking the grave of Francis Scott Key, author of "The Star Spangled Banner." **Roger Brooke Taney House** and **Francis Scott Key Museum,** 123 S. Bentz St., was the residence of Roger Brooke Taney, chief justice of the U.S. Supreme Court (1835-64), who wrote the majority opinion in the Dred Scott case. By appointment. 301/293-2526. Adults $1; children 3 to 12, 50¢; under 3, free. **Rose Hill Manor Children's Museum,** 1611 N. Market St., is located on a 43-acre park. Rose Hill was the home of the first governor of Maryland. Today it houses a museum where children (and adults) can touch and see the historic items. In another park building are restored carriages and sleighs. Apr.-Oct., Mon.-Sat., 10 A.M. to 4 P.M.; Sun., 1 to 4 P.M.; Nov.-Dec., Sat., 10 A.M. to 4 P.M.; Sun., 1 to 4 P.M. Free. 301/694-1650. Historic houses open by request are **Schifferstadt** (c.1756), 1110 Rosemont Ave. and U.S. 15, 301/663-1515; and **Steiner House** (1807), 386 W. Patrick St., 301/663-8587.
See also **Brunswick.**

GAITHERSBURG, 26,424, B-5. **The National Bureau of Standards,** west off Int. 270, houses the nation's central measurement laboratory in a 26-building complex. Tours: Year-round, Tues., 1:30 P.M.; Fri., 9:30 A.M. Free. 301/921-2721.

GREENBELT, 16,000, east of College Park, C-5. **NASA Goddard Space Flight Center,** Greenbelt Rd., east of the Baltimore-Washington Pkwy., is the hub of NASA's tracking activities. Established in 1959, it was named for Robert Hutchings Goddard, rocket pioneer. The Visitors Center and Museum, on Soil Conservation Rd., adjacent to the flight center, relate the story of space and the relationship of space research to application on earth. Year-round, Wed.-Sun., 10 A.M. to 4 P.M. Free. 301/344-8101.

HAGERSTOWN, 34,132, A-4. In the center of Hagerstown valley, one of the first settlers was Jonathan Hager, a German, who came in 1737 and was granted a tract of land that he named Hager's Delight. **Jonathan Hager House and Museum,** a stone dwelling in City Park, was built by Hager over a spring so that when the family needed protection from maurauders, they could stay in the basement and still have water. May-Sept., Tues.-Sat., 10 A.M. to 4 P.M.; Sun., 2 to 5 P.M. Adults 50¢; children under 12, free. 301/739-8393. **Mansion House,** City Park, has a valley store and Civil War exhibits. June-Aug., Tues.-Sun., 10 A.M. to 5 P.M. Adults 50¢; persons 65 and over, 25¢; children, free. 301/797-8782. **Washington County Museum of Fine Arts,** City Park, has sculpture, works of 19th-century American artists, and American Indian artifacts. Concerts held periodically. Year-round, Tues.-Sat., 10 A.M. to 5 P.M.; Sun., 1 to 6 P.M. Free. 301/739-7889. **Washington County Courthouse,** Washington and Summit Sts., was designed by Benjamin H. Latrobe, who designed the nation's Capitol. Year-round, Mon.-Fri., 8 A.M. to 4 P.M. Free. 301/791-3090. **Miller House,** 135 W. Washington St., has an exhibit of clocks, dolls, and crafts, 1820-40 room settings, and a reference library. It is headquarters of the Washington County Historical Society. Apr.-Dec., Tues.-Fri., 1 to 4 P.M.; Sat.-Sun., 2 to 5 P.M. Adults 50¢; persons 65 and over, 25¢; children free. 301/797-8782.
See also **Fort Frederick State Park.**

JACKSONVILLE, 400, north of Towson, 14 miles north of Exit 27N off Int.695, B-6. **Ladew Topiary Gardens and Pleasant Valley Home,** 3535 Jarrettsville Pike, are the gardens and home of the late Harvey S. Ladew, who moved from Long Island to Maryland for the fox hunting. The gardens comprise 14 acres of topiary sculpture, featuring such figures as a huntsman riding to hounds, swans, and pheasants. **Pleasant Valley Home** is furnished with English antiques, rare books, and china;

among its special features are an Elizabethan room and an oval library, cited as one of the "100 most beautiful rooms in America." Seminars on gardening and concerts are also held on the grounds. House and gardens: Apr.-Oct., Wed., 10 A.M. to 4 P.M.; Sun., noon to 5 P.M. Adults $3.50, students $2.50, children free. Gardens only: Same months, Tues.-Sat., 10 A.M. to 4 P.M.; Sun., noon to 4 P.M. Adults $2, students $1.50, children 50¢. 301/557-9466.

KENT ISLAND, east of Annapolis, C-6. **Chesapeake Bay Hydraulic Model,** 2 miles south of U.S. 50 on St. 8, is an eight-acre concrete model of the Chesapeake Bay System housed in a 14-acre shelter. The model, under the jurisdiction of the Baltimore District of the Army Corps of Engineers, is used by engineers, scientists, and technicians to learn more about the largest estuary in the United States. It also serves as an educational aid to the public. Tours: Year-round, Mon.-Fri., 10 A.M., 1 and 3 P.M.; during summer, also weekends, tours at the same times. Free. 301/962-4616.

LAUREL, 12,103, C-5. The **Montpelier Mansion,** at the south edge of Laurel, is part of a land grant issued on February 26, 1686, to Richard Snowden, an officer in Cromwell's army. The classic Georgian mansion was built in the late 1700s for Thomas Snowden. Also on the estate are a carriage house, boxwood gardens, and a cemetery in which the Snowdens are buried. A recent addition is the *Montpelier Cultural Arts Center,* 12826 Laurel-Bowie Rd., which houses 30 resident artists (weavers, ceramists, painters, jewelers, etc.) in the restored estate barn. The center has three galleries, one exhibiting works of resident artists, another for community artists, and the third for major exhibits. Mansion: Early Apr.-late June, mid-Sept.-early Nov., Sat.-Sun., noon to 4 P.M. Admission $1; persons 6-13, 25¢; under 6, free. Cultural Arts Center: Year-round, daily, 10 A.M. to 5 P.M. Free. 301/953-1993. **Laurel Race Course,** northeast off St. 198, has thoroughbred racing late Oct.-Dec. 301/725-0400. **Freestate Raceway,** north on U.S. 1, has harness racing early June-mid-Sept. 301/725-2600.

LEONARDTOWN, 1,448, D-6. This town, where oxen once trundled tobacco along tree-lined lanes to the warehouses and boat landings, was laid out in 1708. **Old Jail Museum** has historic records, many available on microfilm. **St. Mary's County Historical Society** is also housed here. Mid-Jan.-Dec., Tues.-Sat., 10 A.M. to 4 P.M. Free. 301/475-2467. **Tudor Hall,** once the home of Abraham Barnes, a successful 18th-century tobacco planter, is now the **St. Mary's County Memorial Library.** Year-round, Mon.-Thurs., 9 A.M. to 8 P.M.; Fri.-Sat., 9 A.M. to 5 P.M. 301/475-2846.

LEXINGTON PARK, 11,000, D-6. **Naval Air Test & Evaluation Museum,** at the Patuxent Naval Air Test Center, St. 235

and Shangri-La Dr., relates information on the test and evaluation programs conducted at the center. Year-round, Tues.-Sat., 11 A.M. to 5 P.M.; Sun., noon to 5 P.M. Free. 301/863-7418.

OCEAN CITY, 4,946, D-8. This seashore resort was partially plotted in 1872 and the first hotel was built in 1875. Today it has 10 miles of beaches, a 3-mile-long boardwalk, and hundreds of accommodations. Activities include surf, bay, and deep-sea fishing; sunbathing; swimming; surfing; and in summer, the boardwalk miniature train. **Ocean City Life Saving Station Museum,** south end of the Boardwalk, is the original station commissioned by Congress in 1878. One room houses a saltwater aquarium with species native to Ocean City waters. May-Sept., daily, 9 A.M. to 5 P.M.; other months, weekends, noon to 4 P.M. Admission $1. 301/289-8559.

OXON HILL, 2,000, south of Washington, D.C. on St. 210, C-5. **Oxon Hill Children's Farm,** Oxon Hill Rd., off St. 210, has every kind of farm animal and demonstrations of farm chores and activities. Year-round, daily, 8:30 A.M. to 5 P.M. Free. 301/839-1177. **Rosecroft Raceway,** on Brinkley Rd., has harness racing early Mar.-June, daily except Sun. 301/567-4220.

PISCATAWAY PARK, C-5. This parkland preserves the tranquil view of the Maryland shore as seen from Mount Vernon. **National Colonial Farm,** in the park, is a living museum practicing the agricultural techniques of the 1700s. Year-round, Tues.-Sun., 10 A.M. to 5 P.M. Adults $1. 301/283-2113.

ROCKVILLE, 43,811, C-5. Seat of Montgomery County since 1777, it was first called Montgomery Court House and later Williamsburg before it was named Rockville in 1805. **Beall-Dawson House,** 103 W. Montgomery Ave., is headquarters for the Montgomery County Historical Society. The house and adjacent **Doctor's Museum,** which once housed a medical office, have been restored and refurnished. Year-round, Tues.-Sat., noon to 4 P.M.; first Sun. of each month, 2 to 5 P.M. Adults $1; children and persons 65 and over, 50¢. 301/762-1492.

ST. MARY'S CITY, 900, E-6. The first capital of Maryland, it was founded in 1634 by settlers from England. After the capital was moved to Annapolis (first state assembly held here February 28, 1694) and St. Mary's later lost its status as county seat to Leonard Town, it declined. Few traces of the town remained in 1934 when Maryland celebrated its tercentenary, but one of the ways the state observed its anniversary was by building a replica of the **Old State House.** The original structure, built in 1676, served as statehouse of Maryland Colony until 1694, when the seat of colonial government was moved to Annapolis. The replica built for Maryland's 300th anniversary is based on a meticulous study of the

original building and the times and conditions under which it served as a capitol. A replica of *Dove,* one of two ships that brought settlers to Maryland in 1634, is docked on the St. Mary's River below the State House in spring, summer, and fall. Old St. Mary's walking tours: Apr.-Oct., daily, 10 A.M. to 5 P.M.; other months, Tues.-Sun., 10:30 A.M. to 4:30 P.M. Free. 301/994-0779.

ST. MICHAELS, 1,301, west of Easton on St. 33, C-6. Located between the Miles and Broad rivers, St. Michaels produced many of the clipper ships in the early days. Today, it is a popular town for antiques, with many shops carrying these wares. **The Green** (St. Mary's Square) was laid out by Edward Braddock, commander of the British forces in America. **St. Mary's Square Museum** and adjoining building contain community artifacts. May-Oct., Sat.-Sun., 10 A.M. to 4 P.M.; other months, by request. Admission 50¢. 301/745-9561. **Chesapeake Bay Maritime Museum,** on Navy Point, comprises several exhibit buildings on 16 acres. Among the exhibits are racing log canoes, bugeyes, and skip jacks (oyster-dredging vessels); an aquarium; woodcarvings of waterfowl; marine items; a working boat shop; and the old Hooper Straight Lighthouse. May-Oct., daily, 10 A.M. to 5 P.M.; Jan.-Feb., Sat.-Sun., 10 A.M. to 4 P.M.; other months, Tues.-Sun., 10 A.M. to 4 P.M. Adults $2.50; persons 65 and over, $2; children $1; under 6, free. 301/745-2916.

SALISBURY, 16,429, D-7. In 1732, the Provincial Assembly of Maryland authorized the purchase of 15 acres to be surveyed and laid out into 20 lots and called Salisbury-Towne, but it took several decades before the town grew. In 1860 and again in 1866, the town was devastated by a fire that destroyed three-fourths of the buildings. Among those that escaped was **Poplar Hill Mansion,** 117 Elizabeth St. Year-round, Sun., 1 to 4 P.M.; other months, by appointment. 301/749-1776. **Newton Historic District,** which surrounds Poplar Hill, has several Victorian houses that were built after the two fires. **City Hall Museum,** on U.S. 50 near Division St., is the renovation of the old city hall. Year-round, Mon.-Fri., 10 A.M. to 4 P.M.; Sat., 10 A.M. to 2 P.M. Free. 301/546-9007. **North American Wildfowl Art Museum,** in Holloway Hall, Salisbury State College, has over 2,300 carvings relating the story of decoy and wildfowl carvings on the North American continent. Carvings are displayed in historic chronology from A.D. 1000 to the present and include the prize-winning carvings from the world championship carving contest held each spring in the Ocean City Convention Hall. Year-round, daily, 1 to 5 P.M. Adults $1, children under 13, free. 301/742-4988. **Salisbury Zoo,** City Park, has animals living in areas similar to their native habitat. Daily, Apr.-Nov., 8 A.M. to 5 P.M.; other months, 9 A.M. to 5 P.M. Free. 301/742-2123.

SOLOMONS, 500, D-6. **Calvert Marine Museum,** on St. 2/4, has extensive indoor and outdoor exhibits on maritime history and marine life in the Chesapeake Bay and Patuxent River. Some displays come from nearby Calvert Cliffs State Park, where sharks teeth and fossils are often found. In the museum are also a reconstructed seafood packers' shed and a shipbuilder's lean-to. **Drum Point Lighthouse** (1883), one of the remaining screwpile lights on Chesapeake Bay, is also part of the museum. During the summer months, visitors can take a cruise on the Patuxent River in the 1899 oyster buyboat *Wm. B. Tennison.* May-Sept., Mon.-Sat., 10:30 A.M. to 5 P.M.; Sun., 1 to 5 P.M.; Oct.-Dec., Mon.-Sat., 10:30 A.M. to 4:40 P.M.; Sun., 1 to 4:30 P.M. Free. 301/326-3719.

THURMONT, 2,934, A-4. **Catoctin Furnace Historic District,** east off St. 806 (which runs parallel to U.S. 15) and 4 miles south of Thurmont, opened in 1774 and supplied cannon balls for the siege of Yorktown. Homes of early iron workers are along the way. **Catoctin Mountain Zoological Park,** south off St. 806, has a large collection of lemurs, a reptile house, and petting zoo. Daily, Apr.-May, 10 A.M. to 5 P.M.; June-Aug., 9 A.M. to 8 P.M. Adults $3.50, children $2.25. 301/271-7488.

TOWSON, 84,500, B-6. Seat of Baltimore County since 1854, Towson was founded in 1750 by Ezekiel Towson. Among the historic buildings here are **Auburn House** (1799), on the Towson State University campus; **Sheppard-Pratt Hospital Buildings** (1862); and the original **Courthouse** (1855). **Roberts Gallery,** Fine Arts Building, Towson State University, has Asian, African, and pre-Columbian art. Sept.-May, Mon.-Fri., 10 A.M. to noon and 2 to 4 P.M.; other months, hours vary. Free. 301/321-2807. **Hampton National Historic Site,** 535 Hampton Lane, is a fine example of the lavish Georgian mansions built in America during the latter part of the 19th century. Formal gardens and other plantation buildings surround the mansion. Year-round, Tues.-Sat., 11 A.M. to 5 P.M.; Sun., 1 to 5 P.M. Free. 301/823-7054. *See* also **Jacksonville.**

WESTMINSTER, 8,808, B-5. Carroll County seat, Westminster was founded in 1764 and named for its founder, William Winchester. It was given its present name shortly after the American Revolution began. Among the historic buildings are **Kimmey House,** 210 E. Main St., and **Shellman House,** next door, which today houses the Carroll County Historical Society. Nov.-Apr., Tues.-Fri., 9:30 A.M. to 3:30 P.M.; weekends by request; other months, Sun., 2 to 4:30 P.M. Free. 301/848-6494. **Carroll County Farm Museum,** 500 S. Center St., features an 1850 farmhouse and barn with furnishings of the period. July-Aug., Tues.-Fri., 10 A.M. to 4 P.M.; Sat.-Sun., noon to 5 P.M.; late Apr.-June, Sept.-Oct., weekends and holidays, noon to 5 P.M. Adults $2; persons 6-18 and 65 and over, $1; under 6, free. 301/848-7775.

WHEATON, 73,800, north of Washington, D.C., C-5. **Brookside Gardens,** Wheaton Regional Park, east of St. 97 at 1500 Glenallen Ave., is a 90-acre botanic gardens with a conservatory and outdoor formal, rose, and Japanese gardens. Year-round, daily, 9 A.M. to 5 P.M. Free. 301/949-8230. **National Capital Trolley Museum,** Bonifant Rd., houses a collection of trolley cars from the United States and Europe. Visitors can also ride the trolley on a two-mile-long track. Year-round, Sat.-Sun., noon to 5 P.M.; July and Aug., also Wed., noon to 5 P.M. Adults 75¢; persons under 18, 50¢. 301/384-9797.

Information Sources

Office of Tourist Development
State of Maryland
1748 Forest Dr.
Annapolis, MD 21401
301/269-3517

Tourism Council
Annapolis and Anne
Arundel Co.
171 Conduit St.
Annapolis, MD 21401
301/268-8687

Baltimore Office
of Promotion & Tourism
110 W. Baltimore St.
Baltimore, MD 21201
301/752-8632 or
301/685-8689

Tourism Council
of the Upper Chesapeake
P.O. Box 66
Centerville, MD 21617
301/758-2300

Allegany County Tourism
Baltimore at Green Street
Cumberland, MD 21502
301/777-5905

Howard County
Public Information Office
3430 Court House Dr.
Ellicott City, MD 21043
301/992-2027

Tourism Council
of Frederick County, Inc.
19 E. Church St.
Frederick, MD 21701
301/663-8687 or
301/663-8703

Washington County
Tourism Office
Court House Annex
Hagerstown, MD 21740
301/791-3130

Deep Creek Lake—
Garrett County
Promotion Council
Garrett County Court House
Oakland, MD 21550
301/334-3888

Ocean City Convention
& Visitors Bureau, Inc.
P.O. Box 116
Ocean City, MD 21842
301/289-8181

Prince George's Travel
Promotion Council, Inc.
6600 Kenilworth Ave.
Riverdale, MD 20840
301/927-0700

Baltimore County
Chamber of Commerce
100 W. Pennsylvania Ave.
Towson, MD 21204
301/825-6200

Tri-County Council
for Southern Maryland
(Charles, St. Mary's,
and Calvert counties)
P.O. Box 301
Waldorf, MD 20601
301/645-2693

Carroll County Economic
Development Commission
225 N. Center St.
Westminster, MD 21157
301/848-4500

Somerset County
Tourism Commission
P.O. Box 100
Westover, MD 21871
301/651-2968

Maryland Campgrounds

FEES REFLECT MINIMUM RATE FOR 2 ADULTS AND ARE SUBJECT TO INCREASE OR SEASONAL CHANGES

•	at the campground	E	tents rented	U	unlimited	g	public golf course within 5 miles	p	motor bikes prohibited
○	within one mile of campground	F	entrance fee or premit required	V	trailers rented	h	horseback riding	r	boat rental
$	extra charge	N	no specific number, limited by size of area only	Z	reservations accepted	j	whitewater running craft only	s	stream, lake or creek water only
**	limited facilities during winter months	P	primitive	LD	Labor Day	k	snow skiing within 25 miles	t	tennis
A	adults only	R	reservation required	MD	Memorial Day	l	boat launch	u	snowmobile trails
B	10,000 acres or more	S	self-contained units only	UC	under construction	m	area north of map	w	open certain off-season weekends
C	contribution			d	boat dock	n	no drinking water	y	drinking water must be boiled

Map Reference	Park Name	Access	Acres	Tent Spaces	Trailer Spaces	Approximate Fee	Season	Other Swimming Swimming Pool	Fishing	Boating	Playground Other	Telephone Number	Mail Address
	STATE PARKS												
B1	Deep Creek Lake	Fr Thayerville, 1 mi N, on N side of lk	1826	112	112	5.00	5/15-10/1	• •		lr	•	301/387-5563	Rt 2 Swanton 21561
A3	Fort Frederick	Fr Indian Spgs, 3 mi S on Hwy 56	275	28	28	2.50	4/15-10/31		•	lr	•	301/842-2504	Box 1, Big Pool 21711
B6	Patapsco Val-Hilton Area	In Baltimore at 1100 Hilton Rd		24	S24	4.50	4/15-10/31				•	301/747-6602	1100 Hilton, Baltimore 21228
B4	Gambrill	Fr Frederick, 6 mi NW on Hwy 40, E to pk	1139	45	45	4.50	All year				•	310/473-8360	Rt 8, Frederick 21701
B4	Cunningham Falls	Fr Frederick, 15 mi N on US 15	4985	31	AS31	5.00	4/15-10/31	• •		lr		301/271-2495	Rt 3, Thurmont 21788
B4	Washington Monument	Fr Boonsboro, 2 mi E on Hwy 40A	104	13	13	2.50	4/1-10/31				•	301/432-8065	Rt 1, Middletown 21769
	Patapsco		7169									301/747-6602	1100 Hilton, Baltimore 21228
B5	Glen Artney Area	Fr US 1 in Elkridge, 2 mi NW on Levering Ave		98	98	2.50	4/15-10/31		•				
B5	Hollofield Area	Fr Baltimore, 7 mi W on US 40		60	60	4.50	4/15-10/31		•				
B1	Big Run	Fr Grantsville, 1 mi E on US 40, 12 mi S	300	37	37	2.50	5/15-10/1		•			301/895-5453	Rt 2, Grantsville 21536
C7	Martinak	Fr Denton, 2 mi S on Hwy 404 & Deep Shore Rd	99	60	60	4.50	All year			l		301/479-1619	Denton 21629
B7	Elk Neck	Fr North East, 10 mi S on Hwy 272	1575	330	330	5.00	All year	•		lr	•	301/287-5333	North East 21901
D8	Assateague	Fr Ocean City, 9 mi S on Hwy 611	756	311	311	6.00	All year	• •			•	301/641-2120	PO Bx 246, Berlin 21811
B1	Swallow Falls	Fr Oakland, 9 mi NW	257	125	125	4.50	5/15-10/1		•		•	301/334-9180	Rt 1, Oakland 21550
A1	New Germany	Fr Grantsville, 1 mi E	220	38	38	5.00	5/15-10/1		•	r	•	301/895-5453	Rt 2, Grantsville 21536
E6	Point Lookout	Fr Lexington Pk, 17 mi S on Hwy 5; 4 mi S of Scotland	513	146	146	7.00	All year	•		lr	•	301/872-5688	Scotland 20867
A6	Susquehanna	Fr Harve de Grace, 3 mi N on Hwy 155	2000	70	70	4.50	4/1-10/31		•	l		301/939-0643	801 Stafford, Harve de Grace
C5	Cedarville	Fr Townsend, 5 mi E on US 301	340	130	130	4.50	4/1-11/1		•		•	301/898-1622	Brandywine 20613
E7	Jane's Island	Fr Hwy 413 at Crisfield, 2 mi SW	2874	50	50	4.50	All year		•	r	•	301/968-1565	Crisfield 21817
E8	Shad Landing	Fr Snow Hill, 4 mi SW on Hwy 113	545	200	200	4.50	All year	•		lr	•	301/632-2566	Rt 1 Snow Hill 21863
E8	Milburn Landing	Fr Pokomoke City, 7 mi NE on Hwy 364	370	50	50	2.50	3/15-12/1		•		•	301/957-2580	Pokomoke City 21851
C7	Tuckahoe	Fr Queen Anne, 5 mi N off Hwy 404	3349	71	S71	4.50	4/1-12/5		•		•	301/634-2810	Rt 1, Box 31 Queen Anne 21657
B4	Greenbrier	Fr Hagerstown, 10 mi E on US 40	1148	200	S200	4.50	4/15-10/31			r•		301/739-7877	Rt 2 Box 234A, Boonsboro 21713
	STATE FORESTS												
A1	Savage River	Fr Grantsville, 5 mi S on New Germany Rd (Contact Forest Supt)	B	P36			All year		•				Grantsville 21536
A2	Green Ridge	Fr Cumberland, approx 20 mi E on US 40 (Contact Forest Supt)	B	P134			All year		•				Flintstone 21530
B1	Potomac	Fr Oakland, 3-1/2 mi SE on Hwy 560, approx 3 mi E on Bethlehem Rd, E & N to forest hdqtrs	B	P12			All year		•				Deer Park 21550
	NATIONAL PARKS												
C5	Greenbelt Pk	Fr College Park, 2 mi E on Hwy 193	1100	178	178	2.00	4/1-11/30						Greenbelt
A4	Catoctin Mountain Pk Owens Creek	Fr Thurmont, 6 mi W on Hwy 77, 2 mi N on Foxville- Deerfield Rd		51	51	2.00	4/15-10/31	•				301/271-7447	Thurmont MD 21788
	NATIONAL MONUMENTS												
	Chesapeake & Ohio Cl NHD		4472									301/739-4200	Box 4, Sharpsburg 21782
B4	Antietam Creek Camp Area	Fr Sharpsburg, 3 mi S on Harpers Ferry Rd, 1/4 mi on Canal Rd to parking (walk-in)	15	44			5/15-10/15	•			p	301/739-4200	Sharpsburg
B4	Mountain Lock CA	Fr Sharpsburg, S on Harpers Ferry Rd to Limekiln Rd, 1/2 mi to parking (walk-in)	2	11			5/15-10/15	•			p		Harpers Ferry, W Va
A3	Fifteen Mile Creek CA	Fr Hancock, 2-1/2 mi W on US 40, 10 mi S on Woodmont Rd	1	16	16	None	5/1-10/15	•		l			Hancock
B2	Spring Gap	Fr Cumberland, 11 mi E on Hwy 51		P20	PS20	None	5/15-10/15	•			np		Spring Gap
B3	McCoy's Ferry	Fr I-70, Clear Sprgs ext, 5 mi SE on Hwy 68, W on Hwy 56, 3 mi on 4 Lock Rd		P19	PS19	None	5/1-10/15	•			np		Clear Springs
	NATIONAL SEASHORES												
E8	Assateague Island	Berlin, 5 mi E on Hwy 376, 4 mi S on Hwy 611, 2 mi SE	B	61	65	3.00	4/15-10/30	• •					Berlin MD 21811

Mississippi

Major Events

See state map, page 33

Dixie National Livestock Show, early to mid-Feb., Jackson. This is one of the largest livestock shows east of the Mississippi River. Other activities include a junior round up and a rodeo. Admission is charged for the rodeo. 601/961-4000.

Mississippi Gem and Mineral Society Show, late Feb., Jackson. Working artisans display a wide variety of cut stones and jewelry. There are competitive and non-competitive exhibits, and movies are shown. Admission. 601/961-4000.

Mardi Gras, late Feb., Biloxi. Parades and a coronation and ball highlight the carnival season in Biloxi. Free. 601/374-2717.

Natchez Pilgrimage Tours, early Mar. to early Apr. and early to late Oct., Natchez. Many handsome antebellum homes in Natchez are opened to the public on several different tours. There are six daylight tours and one candlelight tour, all conducted numerous times during the pilgrimage. Maps and brochures are provided for the self-guided tours. The Confederate Pageant is held at the City Auditorium four nights a week. Admission. 601/446-6631.

Gulf Coast Pilgrimage, late Mar., various Gulf Coast towns. Selected homes, churches, and historic sites are featured in Gulf Coast communities from Waveland to Pascagoula. Each day features a particular town or towns. Admission. 601/436-4060.

Woodville Pilgrimage, late Mar., Woodville. Four homes may be toured, and a reenactment is presented of the "Burning of Bowling Green," which was a plantation house burned down by Union troops in 1864. Admission. 601/888-6809.

Vicksburg Pilgrimage, late Mar. to early Apr., Vicksburg. Morning and afternoon tours of four Southern homes are available. Admission. 601/636-9421.

Port Gibson Pilgrimage, late Mar., Port Gibson. Eight homes and several gardens, churches, and historic sites are open to the public for tours. Admission. 601/437-4351.

Columbus Pilgrimage, early Apr., Columbus. Five separate tours present three houses each in this antebellum town. Admission. 601/328-4491.

World Catfish Festival, early Apr., Belzoni. A canoe race opens this springtime celebration at the "Catfish Capital of the World." Other festivities include a 10,000-meter run, catfish-eating and fiddling contests, live entertainment, tours of the fish ponds, and catfish dinners. Free (except food). 601/247-2616.

Holly Springs Pilgrimage, late Apr., Holly Springs. Ten antebellum homes and four churches are included on this springtime walk. Admission. 601/252-3867.

Landing of d'Iberville, late Apr., Ocean Springs. Townspeople dress in period costumes for a weekend of festivities centering around the reenactment of the 1699 landing of d'Iberville at the town's present site. Following the landing, there is an arts and crafts show, a street fair, a parade, and a ball. Admission is charged for the ball. 601/875-8955.

Gum Tree Festival, early May, Tupelo. A competitive art show, arts and crafts exhibits, and live entertainment all take place on the lawn around the town courthouse. Admission is charged for several events. 601/842-4521.

Flea Market and Crafts Show, mid-May and early Oct., Canton. Courthouse Square is the site where arts and crafts are demonstrated and exhibited twice a year. Free. 601/859-1606.

Annual Commemorative Battle of Champion Hill, mid-May, Edwards. Cactus Plantation sponsors this re-creation of the decisive Civil War battle which preceded the siege of Vicksburg. Twenty-seven states are represented with mock troops who form encampments and stage a reenactment of the battle. A large barn dance is held, and worship services take place on the last day. 601/852-5110.

Blessing of the Fleet, mid-May, Pass Christian. The town's fishing fleet is blessed by a priest, and the decorated boats compete for prizes. There is live music, dancing, and free seafood. Free. 601/452-2252.

Jimmie Rodgers Festival, late May, Meridian. Country and western stars salute the "Father of Country Music" with live performances. Admission. 601/693-1306.

Biloxi Shrimp Festival and Blessing of the Fleet, early June, Biloxi. The coronation of the Shrimp Queen takes place at night along with a dance and a shrimp dinner. A parade of decorated boats and a blessing of the fleet take place the next day. Free. 601/374-2717.

Art Mart/Pecan Grove Festival, late June, Batesville. Demonstrations and displays of arts and crafts are featured along with a fiddle contest, a pancake breakfast, and live entertainment. Free (except food). 601/563-3126.

Mississippi Deep-Sea Fishing Rodeo, early July, Gulfport. Fishing competition is open to the public at this event, which is one of the largest fishing contests in the South. Prizes are awarded to fishermen, and a carnival and food are also available. Admission is charged for several events. 601/863-2713.

Choctaw Indian Fair, mid-July, Philadelphia. The Choctaw Indian Reservation presents native arts and crafts, social dancing, stickball, archery, blowguns, rabbit stick competition, and Choctaw foods. Admission. 601/656-5251.

National Tobacco Spit, late July, Raleigh. People gather at Billy John Crumpton's Farm for a tobacco-spitting contest, country music, children's contests, and food. Admission. 601/782-4339.

Neshoba County Fair, late July to early Aug., Philadelphia. This is the only remaining campground fair in the country, and it has been an annual event since 1889. Among the more unusual events that take place are political speaking, harness racing, and grandstand shows. There are displays of folk crafts and home-canned goods and several different types of live music. Admission. 601/656-1742.

Ole Brook Festival, early Aug., Brookhaven. Whitworth College sponsors an arts and crafts show, a flea market, an antique auto show, and a cross-country footrace. Free. 601/833-1411.

Delta Blues Festival, mid-Sept., Greenville. Seven miles north of town at Freedom Village, blues artists perform their distinctive musical art form in the land where the blues was born. Admission. 601/335-3523.

EXPO 1850, late Sept., Greenwood. Florewood River Plantation hosts this event where crafts, food, and entertainment are enjoyed on the grounds of the plantation. Admission. 601/455-3821.

Gumbo Festival of the Universe, early Oct., Necaise Crossing, north of Bay St. Louis. Seafood and chicken gumbo are cooked up at this festival which also features country and western entertainment, crafts booths, a tobacco-spitting contest, gumbo-cooking and -eating contests, a coronation of the queen, and baby contests, including the crowning of Little Miss Gumbo. Admission. 601/255-1635.

Mississippi State Fair, early to mid-Oct., Jackson. A typical Southern country fair is staged at the State Fairgrounds with a livestock show, domestic arts exhibits, horse shows, horse-pulling competition, nightly entertainment, and three midways. Admission. 601/961-4000.

Chimneyville Crafts Festival, early Dec., Jackson. The Craftsmen's Guild of Mississippi sponsors this festival of the performing arts at the Trade Mart. Music, drama, arts and crafts demonstrations, and educational workshops are presented. Admission. 601/969-2830.

Trees of Christmas, early to mid-Dec., Meridian. On display at Merrehope Plantation are traditional and contemporary Christmas trees decorated with hundreds of ornaments from around the world. Admission. 601/483-8439.

Mississippi Destinations

BILOXI, 49,311, H-4. One of the oldest colonial settlements in the Mississippi Valley, Biloxi dates back to the early 18th century. From 1721 to 1723, Biloxi served as the territorial capital of the Louisiana Territory. When the capital was moved to New Orleans, Biloxi became a quiet fishing town. Around 1840, people began to vacation in the seaside town, enjoying the warm climate and the Gulf of Mexico. It is still a tourist center with many hotels and resorts, as well as a long beach where swimming, fishing, and boating are popular. **Beauvoir,** 200 W. Beach Blvd., was the last home of the president of the Confederacy, Jefferson Davis. Built in the 1850s, it has the original furnishings, 74 acres of landscaped grounds, two museums, and a Confederate cemetery. Year-round, daily, 8:30 A.M. to 5 P.M. Adults $3; military and persons 65 and over, $2; persons 8-16, $1; under 8, free. 601/388-1313. **Biloxi Lighthouse,** U.S. 90, was built in 1848. There is a historical display inside. May-Sept., Sat.-Sun., 10 A.M. to 4 P.M.; other months by appointment. Admission 25¢. 601/374-4355. The **Vieux Marché** is a restored section of Biloxi with many 18th- and 19th-century buildings. A pedestrian mall runs through the center of the district, and there are restaurants, shops, and courtyards. Always open. **Magnolia Hotel and Museum,** Rue Magnolia, was built in 1847 and now houses an art gallery and historical exhibits. Year-round, Tues.-Sat., 10:30 A.M. to 5:30 P.M. Free. Museum: By appointment. 601/435-3521. **Tullis Manor** (1856), on U.S. 90, has a cabinet gallery and Federalist furnishings. Year-round, Mon.-Fri., noon to 5 P.M. Admission $1. 601/374-8600.

BRICES CROSS ROADS NATIONAL BATTLEFIELD SITE, B-4. On June 10, 1864, Union forces under the command of Gen. Samuel D. Sturgis were defeated in an attempt to check the advance of Confederate Gen. Nathan Bedford Forrest and his cavalry. There are no facilities or personnel at Brices, but park interpreters at the Tupelo Visitors Center of the Natchez Trace Parkway can answer questions concerning the battle. (*See* **Tupelo**).

CLEVELAND, 14,524, C-2. The **Fielding L. Wright Art Center** contains contemporary art exhibits which are changed monthly. A collection of original prints and other contemporary art make up the center's permanent exhibits. Year-round, Mon.-Thurs., 8 A.M. to 10 P.M.; Fri., 8 A.M. to 5 P.M.; Sun., 3 to 5 P.M. Free. 601/843-2151.

COLUMBUS, 27,383, C-5. A trading post and a tavern were built at the confluence of the Tombigbee and Luxapalila rivers in 1817, and over the next several years the site grew into the town of Columbus. Planters settled in the area, growing cotton in the rich prairie soil and building homes in town. During the Civil War, a large arsenal was maintained here. When Jackson fell to the Union in 1863, the state legislature was moved to Columbus. The town was never attacked during the war, and many fine antebellum homes still remain. **Columbus and Lowndes County Historical Museum,** 316 Seventh St. N, is housed in the *Blewett-Harrison-Lee Home* and contains memorabilia from 1832 to 1908. There are examples of crystal, costumes, silver, documents, and 100 years of wedding dresses. Year-round, Tues., Thurs., 1 to 4 P.M. Free. 601/328-5437. **Waverley Plantation,** 10 miles northwest off St. 50, was built in the 1850s and is representative of a plantation complex of its time. The style is winged pavilion and features a 64-foot-tall entrance hall embraced by four spiral staircases. Year-round, daily, dawn to dusk. Adults $2.50; under 6, free. 601/494-1399.

CORINTH, 13,839, A-5. This northern Mississippi town was the scene of much Civil War activity. The Battle of Corinth in October, 1862, ended in a Union victory. **Jacinto Courthouse,** 13 miles southeast off U.S. 45 near Jacinto, is a restored two-story brick courthouse built in 1854 in the Federal style. It was the courthouse for old Tishomingo County; it also served as a church and a school. Year-round, Mon.-Sat., 8 A.M. to 5 P.M.; Sun., 1 to 5 P.M. Free. 601/462-7204.

FLORA, 1,507, E-3. **Mississippi Petrified Forest,** Petrified Forest Rd., has self-guiding trails leading through an area with stone trees dating back 30 million years. A geological museum has fossils, crystals, and minerals from around the world. Daily, Memorial Day-Labor Day, 9 A.M. to 7 P.M.; other months, 9 A.M. to 5 P.M. Adults $2; persons 6-18 and 65 and over, $1.50; under 6, free. 601/879-8189.

GREENVILLE, 40,613, C-2. Over 40 towboat and barge fleets serve this chief river port of the Delta region, which is rich in cotton, soybeans, and other crops. **Winterville Mounds State Park and Museum,** 4 miles north on St. 1, contains 17 mounds which were constructed around A.D. 1300. It is one of the largest prehistoric Indian sites in the Mississippi Valley. The museum has displays on Indian life and many artifacts that were uncovered during the archaeological dig of the site. Park: Year-round, daily, 8 A.M. to sunset. Free. Museum: Year-round, Tues.-Sat., 9 A.M. to 6 P.M.; Sun., 1 to 5 P.M. Adults 50¢; children 35¢; under 6, free. 601/334-4684.

GREENWOOD, 20,115, C-3. **Florewood River Plantation,** 2 miles west on U.S. 82, is a reconstruction of a typical Delta cotton farm in the 1850s. Authentically attired plantation family members

Steamboats first traveled on the Mississippi River about 1812. They also traveled up the Tombigbee, Pearl, and Pascagoula rivers. Packet boats carrying mail and dispatches traveled daily between New Orleans and Vicksburg and Natchez and Vicksburg. Flatboats and arks, known as broadhorns, were used for downstream traffic. And brightening the rivers were pleasure boats, with their calliopes.

and workers perform daily tasks such as weaving, candle and soapmaking, cabinetmaking, and craft demonstrations. Plantation: Mar.-Nov., Tues.-Sat., 9 A.M. to 4:30 P.M.; Sun., 1 to 5 P.M. Cotton Museum: Year-round, same days and hours. Adults $2.50; persons 6-16, $1.50; students 50¢; under 6, free. 601/455-3821. **Cottonlandia Museum,** U.S. 82 Bypass West, displays artifacts and relics from early Indian culture and a collection of farm implements, changing art exhibits, and ceramics. There is also a diorama of the natural history of the Delta region. Year-round, Mon.-Fri., 9 A.M. to 5 P.M.; Sat.-Sun., 2 to 5 P.M. Adults $1.50; persons 7-18, 75¢; over 65, $1; under 7, free. 601/453-0925.

GULF ISLANDS NATIONAL SEASHORE, H-5. Three barrier islands and a Visitors Center on the mainland make up the Mississippi section of the Gulf Islands National Seashore (*see* Florida). The islands, accessible only by boat, contain beaches, historic ruins, and wildlife sanctuaries. **Fort Massachusetts** was built on Ship Island in the 1850s and was occupied briefly by the Confederates during the Civil War. Union forces took over the fort in 1861 and used it as a base to attack New Orleans. The shell of the fort still stands and may be toured from June through Labor Day. The Visitors Center on the mainland is on Davis Bayou, 1 mile south of U.S. 90, in Ocean Springs. There is an information center and a self-guiding nature trail. Year-round, daily, 8 A.M. to 4:30 P.M. Free. 601/875-1864. **Excursion boats:** The *Pan American* leaves from the Buena Vista Hotel, U.S. 90, Apr.-Sept., Mon.-Fri., 2:30 P.M.; Sat.-Sun., 9 A.M., 2:30 P.M. Round trip: Adults $8; children 3-10, $4; under 3, free. 601/432-2197. The *Pan American Clipper* leaves from the Gulfport Small Craft Harbor Mar.-Labor Day, daily, 9 A.M., 2:30 P.M.; other months, call for information. Round trip: Adults $8; children 3-10, $4; under 3, free. 601/436-6010.

GULFPORT, 39,676, H-4. Originally planned as a shipping and industrial center by the Gulf & Ship Island Company, Gulfport has also become a popular seaside resort community. The city has had its ups and downs with land booms, hurricanes, and fluctuating activity at its harbor, yet Gulfport's ability to adjust to changing times has been proven often. Gulfport's harbor is Mississippi's largest as well as one of the largest import points for bananas on the Gulf Coast. **Marine Life Aquadome,** south of U.S. 90 and east of 25th Ave., has six shows a day featuring trained porpoises and seals, skin divers, giant sea turtles, and sharks. Daily, Memorial Day-Labor Day, 9 A.M. to 6 P.M.; other months, 9 A.M. to 5 P.M. Adults $5.50; children 4-12, $4; under 4, free. 601/863-0651. Marine Life also operates the **Harbor Tour Train,** a 25-minute narrated tour of the small craft harbor, the deep seaport and its banana terminal, and the Commercial Harbor of Gulfport. Year-round, daily, departs at the end of each show at the Aquadome. Free with paid admission to Marine Life. Tour Train only: Adults and children $1.55. 601/863-0651.

HATTIESBURG, 40,829, F-4. This southern Mississippi town was established during the railroad and lumber booms from 1880 to 1920. **Civic Arts Council Gallery,** in the Saenger Center on W. Front St., houses a permanent collection of Mississippi art as well as periodically changing art exhibitions. Year-round, Mon.-Fri., 9:30 A.M. to 2:30 P.M. and by appointment. Free. 601/583-6005. The **Lena Y. de Grummond Collection of Children's Literature,** in the McCain Graduate Library on the campus of the University of Southern Mississippi, contains over 16,000 volumes of old and new children's books as well as an extensive collection of original manuscripts and artwork for children's books. Open during the academic terms, daily, 8 A.M. to 5 P.M. Free. 601/266-4172.

HOLLY SPRINGS, 7,285, A-4. **Montrose,** on Salem Ave., is a two-story Classic-Revival brick mansion and the home of the Holly Springs Garden Club. Year-round by appointment. Admission $2. 601/252-2943.

JACKSON, 202,895, E-3. Louis Le Fleur, an adventurous French-Canadian, established a trading post on the bluffs along the Pearl River in 1792, and 29 years later the site was chosen to be the new state capital. Le Fleur's Bluff was renamed Jackson, in honor of Maj. Gen. Andrew Jackson. During the next 20 years, much of the groundwork for the city's future prosperity was laid. Railroads were built, linking Jackson with numerous towns like Vicksburg, Natchez, and New Orleans. The Ordinance of Secession was drawn up in the Old Capitol in 1861, and Mississippi became the second state to secede from the Union. During the Civil War, Union forces invaded Jackson four times. General Sherman burned the city in 1863, and the remains prompted the nickname "Chimneyville" for what was left of Jackson. Railroads, colleges, and incentives to industry all helped to rebuild the city to its present stature. Still the state's capital, Jackson is also a major distribution and wholesale center for the southeastern and south central states.

GOVERNMENT BUILDINGS: Governor's Mansion, 300 E. Captiol St., was commissioned in 1833, making it the second oldest executive mansion in the nation. The residence of state governors since 1842, the building was restored in 1908 and again in 1975. There are changing exhibits of Mississippi art on display. Year-round, Tues.-Fri., 9:30 to 11:30 A.M. Free. 601/354-7650. The **New State Capitol,** on Mississippi St., is undergoing extensive renovation, with completion scheduled for 1982-83. All executive and legislative offices have been temporarily moved to **Central High School** at N. West and Griffin Sts., and they may be visited. Year-round, Mon.-Fri., 8 A.M. to 5 P.M. Free. 601/354-7294. **Manship House,** Fortification and Northwest Sts., was one of the few houses left standing after the Civil War. Built in 1857, the Gothic-Revival style house has been restored and is operated by the State Department of Archives and History. Year-round, Tues.-Sat., 9 A.M. to 4 P.M.; Sun., 1 to 4 P.M. Free. 601/961-4724.

MUSEUMS: Mississippi Museum of Art, 201 E. Pascagoula St., the state's newest and largest museum, is housed in the Mississippi Arts Center, which has facilities for concerts, opera, and ballet. The museum's four galleries contain a constantly changing spectrum of art, both contemporary and traditional. Its permanent collections include famous international artwork, and there is a changing exhibit of work for sale by selected Mississippi artists. One gallery is devoted to experimental and conceptual art. Year-round, Tues.-Thurs., 10 A.M. to 3 P.M.; Fri., 10 A.M. to 8 P.M.; Sat.-Sun., noon to 4 P.M. Nonmembers: Adults $1, children 25¢. 601/960-1515. **Davis Planetarium,** 201 E. Pascagoula St., presents star shows and programs of general interest. It also contains an atmospherium—a motion picture system that projects images over the entire dome, creating an effect of being totally

surrounded. June-Aug., Tues.-Fri., noon, 2, and 8 P.M.; other months, Tues.-Fri., 8 P.M.; year-round, Sat., 2, 4, and 8 P.M.; Sun., 2 and 4 P.M. Adults $2.50; persons 17 and under and over 65, $1.50. 601/960-1540 or 601/960-1550. **Mississippi Museum of Natural Science,** 111 N. Jefferson St., has ecological exhibits, including dioramas, aquariums, and natural science collections. Year-round, Mon.-Fri., 8 A.M. to 5 P.M. Free. 601/354-7303. **Mississippi State Historical Museum/Old Capitol Restoration,** 100 State St., features the restored 1833 Capitol, a Greek-Revival structure which housed the state government until 1903 and now houses the state historical museum. There are permanent and changing historical and art exhibits, dioramas, antebellum furnishings, folklife presentations, musical performances, and archives. Year-round, Mon.-Fri., 8 A.M. to 5 P.M.; Sat., 9:30 A.M. to 4:30 P.M.; Sun., 12:30 to 4:30 P.M. Free. 601/354-6222.

PARKS AND GARDENS: Jackson Zoological Park, 2918 W. Capitol St., has over 800 animals and 115 different species maintained in 40 acres of landscaped park terrain designed to re-create each animal's natural habitat. Daily, Mar.-Sept., 9 A.M. to 6 P.M.; other months, 9 A.M. to 5 P.M. Adults $1.50; persons 4-12, 75¢; under 4, 65 and over, and handicapped, free. 601/960-1575. **Mynelle Gardens,** 4736 Clinton Blvd., is a bird sanctuary with thousands of azaleas, camellias, flowering trees and shrubs, pathways, ponds, and streams. Mar.-Oct., Mon.-Fri., 8 A.M. to 5 P.M.; Sat.-Sun., 9 A.M. to 5 P.M.; other months, Mon.-Fri., 8 A.M. to 4:30 P.M.; Sat.-Sun., 9 A.M. to 5 P.M. Adults $1; under 12 with adult, free. 601/960-1894. *See* also **Ridgeland.**

LAUREL, 21,897, F-4. **The Lauren Rogers Library and Museum of Art,** Fifth Ave. at Seventh St., contains a collection of 19th-century American and European art, Georgian silver, and an Indian basket collection. Changing contemporary art exhibits and gallery concerts are also featured here. Year-round, Tues.-Sat., 10 A.M. to noon, 1 to 5 P.M.; Sun., 2 to 5 P.M. Free. 601/428-4875.

MERIDIAN, 46,577, E-4. From its beginnings as a railroad crossing, Meridian has grown into the major industrial center of eastern Mississippi. **Jimmie Rodgers Memorial and Museum,** in Highland Park, honors the "Father of Country Music," who was a native of Meridian. The museum contains his personal effects and memorabilia. Year-round, Mon.-Sat., 10 A.M. to 4 P.M.; Sun., noon to 6 P.M. Adults $1; under 10 with adult, free. 601/483-5202. **Meridian Museum of Art,** 25th Ave. and 7th St., houses six galleries and a permanent collection of over 100 pieces of art. Openings are held in conjunction with the changing exhibition schedule, which focuses on regional contemporary art. Aug.-June, Tues.-Sun., 1 to 5 P.M.; Tues., also 10 A.M. to noon; other

Kudzu has transformed fences, trees, bushes, utility poles, and many other stationary objects in the South into a topiary landscape. Along portions of U.S. 72, which runs through Holly Springs National Forest in northern Mississippi, it has so completely covered the trees and bushes, that only their outline is visible. This spreading plant has transformed other areas of the South in the same way. Kudzu was introduced from Japan in the 1930s as a forage crop and as a valuable soil conserving plant. Although it gives the impression that it is a thick growth, it produces relatively low forage yields. It is also difficult to cut and bale because of its viney growth. It will grow in a wide range of soil types, but does best in a deep loamy soil. According to the state agricultural department, kudzu is seldom planted intentionally. For the first-time visitor to the South, its appearance is awesome.

mornings, by appointment; Thurs., also 7 to 9 P.M. Free. 601/693-1501.

NANIH WAIYA STATE HISTORIC SITE, D-4. The legendary birthplace of the Choctaw Indians and site of their Sacred Mound, Nanih Waiya was occupied from the time of Christ until European contact. A swinging bridge leads to a cave under the mound. Graphic explanations of the conflicting legends surrounding the mound and cave are provided, and a burial mound is nearby. Year-round, daily, 5 A.M. to 10 P.M.; office hours, 8 A.M. to 5 P.M. Free. 601/773-7988 or 601/961-5014.

NATCHEZ, 22,015, F-1. Since its initial settlement in 1716, Natchez has been one of the most noteworthy cities on the Mississippi River. It has been ruled by the Natchez Indians, France, Spain, England, the Confederacy, and the United States. Cotton and shipping brought great wealth to Natchez from 1820 to 1860. Planters spent their money building distinctive homes and accumulating libraries and art collections. The Civil War brought an end to the city's lavish culture, as slaves were freed and economic and social structures were overturned completely. Reminders of Natchez' past are still present, especially in the numerous gracious homes built before the Civil War.

HISTORIC HOMES: Connelly's Tavern, Canal and Jefferson Sts., is an old frame house built in 1798 and restored by the Natchez Garden Club. Year-round, daily, 9 A.M. to 5 P.M. Adults $3; persons 10-18, $1.25; under 10, free. 601/442-2011. **The Burn,** 712 N. Union St., is a three-story Greek-Revival structure built in 1832, occupied by Union troops, and used as a hospital during the Civil War. Year-round, daily, 9 A.M. to 5 P.M. Adults $3.50; children 12 and under, $1.50. The home has six antique-furnished rooms for overnight guests. 601/445-8566 or 442-1344. **Longwood,** Lower Woodville Rd., was still under construction when the Civil War broke out and was never completed. It is the largest octagonal house in the country; the nine-room basement, the only floor completed, is furnished with period pieces. Year-round, daily, 9 A.M. to 5 P.M. Adults $3.50; persons 10-18, $1.25; under 10, free. 601/442-5193. **Melrose,** Melrose Ave., was built in 1845 and is known for its impeccable architecture and gardens. It is furnished with original early 19th-century furniture and has painted floor cloths in two rooms. Year-round, daily, 9 A.M. to 5 P.M. Adults $5; persons 12-18, $2; under 12 with adult, free. 601/446-9408. **Stanton Hall,** 401 N. High St., is the most palatial mansion in Natchez. Built in 1857, many of the materials used in the construction were imported on a chartered boat from Europe. Year-round, daily, 9 A.M. to 5 P.M. Adults $3.50; persons 10-18, $1.25; under 10, free. 601/446-6631.

MUSEUMS: Grand Village of the Natchez Indians, 400 Jefferson Davis Blvd., has a museum with archaeological artifacts taken from this site, which was the center of activities for the Natchez Indians from 1682 to 1729. A film is presented in an auditorium. Year-round, Mon.-Sat., 9 A.M. to 5 P.M.; Sun., 1:30 to 5 P.M. Free. 601/446-6502. **Mount Locust Inn,** 15 miles northeast on the Natchez Trace Parkway, was built in 1777 and used as an inn. It has been completely restored and furnished to 1829 authenticity. Craftsmen in period clothing demonstrate the various activities of the early 19th century, such as rail splitting, spinning, and soapmaking. Feb.-Nov., daily, 8:30 A.M. to 5:30 P.M. Grounds: Always open. Free. 601/445-4211 or 601/842-1572.

HISTORIC SITE: Emerald Mound, 12 miles northeast on St. 553, is one of the largest Indian temple mounds in the country. Archaeologists believe it was built between A.D. 1300 and 1600 by ancestors of the Natchez Indians. Always open. Free.

NATCHEZ TRACE PARKWAY, F-1 to A-5. *See* **Tupelo.**

OCEAN SPRINGS, 14,504, H-4. This resort town on Biloxi Bay is on the site of Old Biloxi, the first European settlement in the lower Mississippi River Valley. Pierre le Moyne, Sieur d'Iberville, founded the colony in 1699. **Shearwater Pottery,** 102 Shearwater Dr., contains artistic creations by members of the Shearwater family. These creations, along with other pottery and art, are on exhibit at the combination showroom and studio. Showroom: Year-round, Mon.-Fri., 9 A.M. to 5:30 P.M.; Sun., 1 to 5:30 P.M. Tours: By appointment. Workshop: Year-round, Mon.-Fri., 9 A.M. to noon, 1 to 4 P.M. Free. 601/875-7320.

OXFORD, 9,882, B-3. The University of Mississippi opened its doors here in 1848, and Oxford has been primarily a college town ever since. William Faulkner grew up and eventually made his permanent home in Oxford. **Rowan Oak,** Old Taylor Rd., is an antebellum home begun about 1840 and purchased by William Faulkner, who enlarged it and gave it its name. A clapboard house of modified Greek-Revival style, it contains many of Faulkner's personal effects. Year-round, Mon.-Fri., 10 A.M. to noon, 2 to 4 P.M.; Sat., 2 to 4 P.M. Free. 601/234-3284. **University Museums,** University Blvd. and Fifth St., contain Greek and Roman antiquities, scientific instruments, paintings, and changing exhibitions. This institution now incorporates the *Mary Buie Museum,* which contains, among other items, an extensive doll collection. Year-round, Tues.-Sat., 10 A.M. to 4 P.M.; Sun., 1 to 4 P.M. Free. 601/232-7073.

PASCAGOULA, 29,318, H-5. **Old Spanish Fort,** 4602 Fort St., was built around 1718 and is said to be the oldest building in the Mississippi River Valley. The fort museum displays 18th-century artifacts. Year-round, daily, 9 A.M. to 4:30 P.M. Adults $1; persons 6-16, 50¢; under 6, free. 601/769-1505.

PICKENS, D-3. *See* **Vaughan.**

PORT GIBSON, 2,371, E-2. Purely antebellum in tone, Port Gibson's quiet oak-lined streets and white frame homes support the story that General Grant, when he passed through on his march to Vicksburg in 1863, said, "Port Gibson is too beautiful to burn." **Ruins of Windsor,** 12 miles southwest on St. 552, are the remains of the home built by Smith Coffee Daniel II in 1861 and destroyed by fire in 1890. Massive Corinthian columns made of stone and joined by Italian wrought-iron railings are all that remain as testimony to one of the finest examples of antebellum Greek-Revival architecture in the state. Always open. Free.

RIDGELAND, 5,461, north of Jackson, E-3. The **Mississippi Crafts Center,** on the Natchez Trace Parkway, is housed in a reproduction of a dogtrot cabin. Mississippi handcrafted items are for sale in a changing exhibition; periodic crafts demonstrations are held. Year-round, daily, 9 A.M. to 5 P.M. Free. 601/856-7546.

STARKVILLE, 15,169, C-4. **Cobb Institute of Archaeology,** Mississippi State University Campus, teaches archaeology and museology with treasures from civilizations of the Mesopotamian era (3000 B.C.) to the early Christian era. The Mississippian period of Indian objects is also depicted by exhibits. Year-round, Mon.-Fri., 8 A.M. to 4 P.M.; by appointment on weekends. Free. 601/325-3826.

TUPELO, 23,905, B-4. At the outbreak of the Civil War, Tupelo was a small village at a railroad junction. Much of the military activity in northern Mississippi, including one battle within the town limits, revolved around the town. Today, Tupelo is the major industrial and marketing center for northern Mississippi. **Chickasaw Village Site,** 3 miles northwest on the Natchez Trace Parkway, has been archaeologically researched. Foundations of an Indian fort and summer and winter houses have been marked with concrete, and there are exhibits depicting the daily life of the Indians. Always open. Free. Questions may be answered at the Tupelo Visitors Center of the Natchez Trace Parkway. **Elvis Presley Birthplace,** in Elvis Presley Park, was the childhood home of the famed rock-'n-roll singer. The two-room white frame house is restored and furnished. June-Oct., Mon.-Sat., 9 A.M. to 5:30 P.M.; Sun., 1 to 5:30 P.M.; other months, Mon.-Sat., 10 A.M. to 5 P.M.; Sun., 2 to 5 P.M. Adults $1; under 12, 50¢. 601/842-9796. **Tupelo National Battlefield,** on St. 6, 1 mile west of U.S. 45, was the site of several Civil War clashes on July 13-14, 1864. Lt. General Forrest's Confed-

Natchez Trace Parkway

The Natchez Trace Parkway, now under the jurisdiction of the National Park Service, preserves a roadway used by Indians, boatmen, soldiers, postmen, missionaries, and pioneer settlers. Beginning about 1785, men from Ohio, Kentucky, and other parts of the western frontier floated products down the Mississippi River to the markets in Natchez and New Orleans. Once downriver, the only way home on the 450-mile trail from Natchez to Nashville was either on foot or on horseback. From 1800 to 1820 the trace was the most heavily traveled road in the Old Southwest; however, its usefulness disappeared with the coming of the steamboats. Today only a few sections of the historic trace remain and a paved parkway takes you through this land of historic adventure and beauty.

1. **Southern Terminus.**
2. **Emerald Mound.** Built about 1600 by Creek, Choctaw, Natchez ancestors.
3. **Mount Locust.** One of the first inns (called *stands*) in Mississippi. Now restored. Living history program.
4. **Port Gibson.** Ranger station.
5. **Mangum Mound.** Hilltop graves. Burnett's stand once near Bayou Pierre at Grandstone Ford.
6. **Lower Choctaw Boundary.** North-south line between earliest settled part of Mississippi and Choctaw's land.
7. **Battle of Raymond.** Part of Vicksburg campaign fought here (1863).
8. **Ridgeland.** Mississippi crafts.
9. **Ross Barnett Reservoir.**
10. **Boyd Mounds.** Built by Indians more than 500 years ago.
11. **West Florida Boundary.** Drawn in 1763 after French and Indian War.
12. **Cypress Swamp.** Nature Trail.
13. **Red Dog Road.** Opened 1834.
14. **Kosciusko.** Ranger station.
15. **Hurricane Creek.** Nature trail.
16. **Cole Creek.** Nature trail through changing Tupelo-bald cypress swamp.
17. **Bethal Mission.** Site of one of 13 missions built for Choctaw Indians.
18. **French Camp.** School since 1822, stand in 1812.
19. **Jeff Busby.** Overlook one of highest points (603 feet) in Mississippi.
20. **Old Trace.** Portion of old road.
21. **Dancy.** Ranger station.
22. **Bynum Mounds.** Built A.D. 700.
23. **Fossil Display.** Once an inland sea. Displays of marine animals.
24. **Chickasaw.** Pontatok, capital of Chickasaw nation 1820s, was nearby.
25. **Tupelo National Battlefield.** East on Mississippi 6. Site of attack on Union Forces in Civil War.
26. **Chickasaw Village.** Exhibits in nearby site of Chickasaw village.
27. **Tupelo Visitor Center.** Parkway headquarters. Exhibits, orientation programs. Sorghum made last week in September; all October weekends.
28. **Cherokee.** Ranger station. Nearby Buzzard Roost exhibits tell the story of Chickasaw chief Colbert, who owned an inn near here.
29. **Colbert Park.** Swimming, fishing, boat launching. Colbert Stand and ferry and section of Old Trace here. Colbert is said to have charged Andrew Jackson $75,000 to ferry his army across the river here.
30. **Rock Spring.** Nature trail.
31. **Old Trace.** Three sections of original trace can be seen here.
32. **Sweetwater Branch.** Nature trail.
33. **Old Trace Drive.** One-way road follows original (2.5 miles long).
34. **Napier Mine.** Open pit mine. Exhibits explain 19th century operation.
35. **Metal Ford.** Site of early iron industry. McLish's Stand. Travelers forded Buffalo River here.
36. **Meriwether Lewis.** Lewis of Lewis and Clark died on the trace and is buried here.
37. **Phosphate Mines.** Center of short-lived local industry based on mining.
38. **Northern Terminus.**

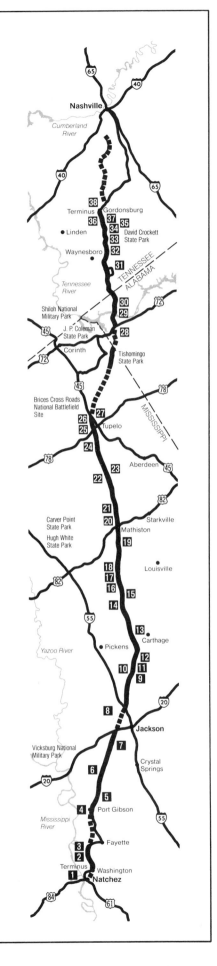

erate cavalry battled a Union force of 14,000 sent to keep them from cutting off the railroad supplying General Sherman's march on Atlanta. Although Union troops successfully thwarted the Confederate assaults, their lack of supplies forced them to retreat and leave their wounded behind. There are no facilities at the battlefield; but interpreters at the Tupelo Visitors Center of the Natchez Trace Parkway, a scenic road running from Natchez to Nashville, can answer questions about the battle. The **Tupelo Visitors Center,** 5 miles north on U.S. 45, is the National Park Service headquarters for the **Natchez Trace Parkway.** A small museum contains items relating to the history of the Natchez Trace; a film depicting the history is also shown. Interpreters are on hand to answer questions. Year-round, daily, 8 A.M. to 5 P.M. Free. 601/842-1572.

See also **Brices Cross Roads National Battlefield.**

VAUGHAN, 40, south of Pickens, D-3. **Casey Jones Museum,** Int. 55 at Exit 133, commemorates the life and death of the legendary John Luther "Casey" Jones. The museum, in a restored depot near the site of the famous wreck, houses railroad memorabilia. Year-round, Wed.-Sat., 9 A.M. to 5 P.M.; Sun., 1 to 5 P.M. Adults 50¢, children 35¢. 601/961-5014.

VICKSBURG, 25,434, E-2. During the Civil War, Vicksburg was called the "Gibraltar of the Confederacy" because of its strategic location on a large bend in the Mississippi River. Its bluffs provided a natural lookout and stronghold over all river traffic below. Prior to the war, Vicksburg was an important steamboat port. In 1863, General Grant made several unsuccessful attempts to attack the city; but on May 19,

he managed to surround Vicksburg, and a 47-day siege began. On July 4, Confederate Gen. J. C. Pemberton surrendered to Grant, and a major blow was dealt to the Confederate cause, as the Union gained control of the Mississippi River. River traffic eventually returned to the city, and industry has been established as well. **Old Courthouse Museum,** 1008 Cherry St., is housed in a columned edifice and contains a large collection of Southern memorabilia with emphasis on the Confederate way of life and the Battle of Vicksburg. Year-round, Mon.-Sat., 8:30 A.M. to 4:30 P.M.; Sun., 1:30 to 4:30 P.M. Adults $1; persons 13-18 and college students with I.D., 50¢; persons 6-12, 25¢; under 6, free. 601/636-0741. **Vicksburg National Military Park,** which nearly surrounds the city, has a Visitors Center near U.S. 80 that offers a 16-mile tour of the park and an 18-minute film on the siege of Vicksburg. Living history demonstrations are given June-August. The U.S.S. *Cairo,* a Union ironclad gunboat, is also being reconstructed in the park; a nearby museum contains artifacts from the boat. Daily, June-Aug., 7 A.M. to 7 P.M.; other months, 8 A.M. to 5 P.M. Free. 601/636-0583. **Biedenharn Candy Company Museum,** 1105 Washington St., is on the site where Joseph A. Biedenharn bottled the first Coca-Cola in 1894. The restored building has Coca-Cola memorabilia and two old-fashioned soda fountains. Year-round, Mon.-Sat., 9 A.M. to 5 P.M.; Sun., 1:30 to 4:30 P.M. Adults $1, children 50¢. 601/638-6514. **Waterways Experiment Station,** 2 miles south of Int. 20 on Halls Ferry Rd., is the principal consulting and laboratory complex of the U.S. Army Corps of Engineers. There are scale models of many rivers and dams and a scale model of Niagara Falls. Visitors Facilities: Year-round,

Mon.-Fri., 7:45 A.M. to 4:15 P.M. Free. Guided tours at 10 A.M. and 2 P.M. Free. 601/634-2502.

WASHINGTON, 400, F-1. **Jefferson College,** on U.S. 61, was chartered in 1802 as Mississippi's first institution of higher learning. Although the school closed its doors in 1964, several restored buildings include exhibitions of historical archives, uniforms, and other memorabilia. Year-round, Mon.-Sat., 9 A.M. to 5 P.M.; Sun., 1 to 5 P.M. Free. 601/442-2901. Washington was also the site of the state constitutional convention in 1817 and Aaron Burr's arraignment in 1807 for treason.

WOODVILLE, 1,512, G-1. **Rosemont Plantation,** 1 mile east on St. 24, was the boyhood home of Jefferson Davis. Completed in 1810, it is a Mississippi planter-style home. Much of the original furniture remains. Mar.-Dec., Mon.-Fri., 9 A.M. to 5 P.M. Adults $3; persons 6-18 and college students with I.D., $1; under 6, free. 601/888-6809.

Information Sources

Mississippi Gulf Coast Visitors Bureau
P.O. Box 4554
Biloxi, MS 39531

Mississippi Agricultural & Industrial Board Division of Tourism
P.O. Box 849
Jackson, MS 39205
601/961-4200

Columbus-Lowndes Chamber of Commerce
P.O. Box 1016
Columbus, MS 39701
601/328-4491

Jackson Chamber of Commerce
P.O. Box 22548
Jackson, MS 39205
601/948-7575

Natchez-Adams County Chamber of Commerce
P.O. Box 725
Natchez, MS 39120
601/445-4611

Warren County Tourist Promotion Commission
P.O. Box 110
Vicksburg, MS 39180
601/636-9421

Mississippi Campgrounds

FEES REFLECT MINIMUM RATE FOR 2 ADULTS AND ARE SUBJECT TO INCREASE OR SEASONAL CHANGES

- • – at the campground
- ○ – within one mile of campground
- $ – extra charge
- ** – limited facilities during winter months
- A – adults only
- B – 10,000 acres or more
- C – contribution
- E – tents rented
- F – entrance fee or premit required
- N – no specific number, limited by size of area only
- P – primitive
- R – reservation required
- S – self-contained units only
- U – unlimited
- V – trailers rented
- Z – reservations accepted
- LD – Labor Day
- MD – Memorial Day
- UC – under construction
- d – boat dock
- g – public golf course within 5 miles
- h – horseback riding
- j – whitewater running craft only
- k – snow skiing within 25 miles
- l – boat launch
- m – area north of map
- n – no drinking water
- p – motor bikes prohibited
- r – boat rental
- s – stream, lake or creek water only
- t – tennis
- u – snowmobile trails
- w – open certain off-season weekends
- y – drinking water must be boiled

Map Reference	Park Name	Access	Acres	Tent Spaces	Trailer Spaces	Approximate Fee	Season	Other Swimming Swimming Pool	Fishing	Boating	Playground	Other	Telephone Number	Mail Address
	STATE PARKS													
C3	Hugh White	Fr Grenada, 7 mi E on Hwy 8/7 & access rd	B	62	111	4.00	All year	• •	•	lr			601/226-4934	Grenada 38901
C5	Lake Lowndes	Fr Columbus, 6 mi SE on Hwy 69	751	N	50	4.00	All year	$ •	$	lr		t	601/328-2110	PO Box 2331, Columbus 39701
B3	John W. Kyle	Fr Sardis, 9 mi E on Hwy 315	784	55	200	4.00	All year	$ $	$	lr			601/487-1345	Sardis 38666
B5	Tombigbee	Fr Tupelo, 6 mi SE on US 78 & Hwy 6	822	N	22	4.00	All year		$ $	lr	•	t	601/842-7669	Rt 2, Box 336E, Tupelo 38801
A5	Tishomingo	Fr Dennis, 3 mi N on Hwy 25 to pk access rd	1500	N	25	4.00	All year	$	•	lr			601/438-6914	Tishomingo 33838
A4	Wall Doxey	Fr Holly Springs, 7 mi S on Hwy 7	855	10	15	4.00	All year	$ $		lr			601/252-4231	Holly Springs 38635
G4	Paul B. Johnson	Fr Hattiesburg, 15 mi S on US 49	805	100	100	4.00	All year	$ $	$	lr	•		601/582-7721	Hattiesburg 39401
E3	Roosevelt	Fr Morton, 2 mi S on Hwy 13	562	N	108	4.00	All year	$ $	$	lr	•	t	601/732-6316	Morton 39117
G2	Percy Quin	Fr McComb, 6 mi W on Hwy 48/24 to pk access rd	1500	N	109	4.00	All year	$ $	$	lr	•		601/684-3938	McComb 39648

Map Reference	Park Name	Access	Acres	Tent Spaces	Trailer Spaces	Approximate Fee	Season	Other Swimming	Swimming Pool	Fishing	Boating	Playground	Other	Telephone Number	Mail Address
D2	Leroy Percy	Fr Hollandale, 5 mi W on Hwy 12	2442	N	16	4.00	All year	$	$			•	lr	601/827-5436	Hollandale 38748
D3	Holmes County	Fr Durant, 5 mi S on US 51, W on access rd	463	N	28	4.00	All year	$	$			•	lr	601/653-3351	Durant 39063
E5	Clarkco	Fr Quitman, 6 mi N on US 45	800	N	26	4.00	All year	$	$			•	lr t	601/776-6651	Quitman 39355
A5	J. P. Coleman	Fr Iuka, 5 mi N on Hwy 25, 8 mi NE to pk	1468	N	47	4.00	All year	$	$	$		•	dlr	601/423-6515	Iuka 38852
A3	Arkabutla	Fr I-55 at Coldwater, W on access rd	5160	N	55	4.50	All year					•	dlr	601/562-4385	PO Box 24, Arkabutla 38602
D4	Golden Memorial	Fr Walnut Grove, 5 mi E on Hwy 35	120	N	6	4.50	All year	$	$				dlr	601/253-2237	Walnut Grove 39189
B3	George Payne Cossar	Fr Oakland, 5 mi NE on Hwy 32 To pk access rd	7000	N	159	4.00	All year	$	$			•	lr	601/623-7356	Rt 1, Oakland 38948
B3	George P Cossar-Lower	Fr Oakland, 5 mi NE on Hwy 32, adj to dam		N	159	4.00	All year	$	$			•	lr		Oakland
H4	Buccaneer	Fr Bay St Louis, 10 mi on US 90	365	N	104	4.50	All year		$	•	•		t	601/467-3822	PO Box 180, Waveland 39576
D4	Nanih Waiya Hist Site	Fr Noxapater, 12 mi E on Hwy 490	85	N		2.25	All year						p	601/773-7988	Rt 3, Louisville 39339
F1	Natchez(UC)	Fr Natchez, 10 mi NE on US 61	B	N	35	None	All year						h	601/442-2658	Rt 5 Bx 465, Natchez
C2	Great River Rd	In Rosedale	756	60	61	6.00	All year			•			dlr	601/759-6762	PO Box 292, Rosedale 38769
	STATE AREAS														
	Pat Harrison Wtrwy Dist													601/264-5951	PO Drawer 1509, Httsbrg 39401
G4	Flint Creek Water Pk	NE outskirts of Wiggins, on Hwy 29	1900	P50	131	5.00	All year					•	dlr	601/928-3051	Rt3 Box 309, Wiggins 39577
F4	Big Creek Water Pk	Fr Laurel, 15 mi W on Hwy 84, 1 mi S of Hwy 84	450		28	3.00	All year						lr		Rt 1, Soso 39480
F4	Maynor Creek	Fr Waynesboro, 2 mi W on Hwy 84	1400		69	5.00	All year			•	•	•	dlr	601/735-4365	Box 591, Waynesboro 39367
	Okatibbee Lake														
E4	Okatibbee Lake Water Pk	Fr Meridian, 12 mi N on Hwy 19, access rd to pk	1500	P30	106	5.00	All year			•	•		dlr	601/626-8431	Rt 12 Bx 277, Meridian 39301
E4	Twiltley Branch CG	Fr Meridian, 10 mi N on Hwy 19, 2 mi E on Co Hwy 17	345	40	40	None	All year			•	•	•	d r	601/626-8431	PO Bx 98, Collinsville 39325
E5	Archusa Creek Water Pk	In Quitman, off US 45ark	1000	68	58	5.00	All year			•	•	•	dlr g	601/776-6956	PO Box 95, Quitman 39355
G4	Little Black Creek	Fr Lumberton, N on Hwy 13	1100	50	100	5.00	All year			•	•	•	dlr	601/794-2957	Rt 2, Lumberton 39455
	NATIONAL PARKS														
	Natchez Trace Parkway	(See Tennessee for additional CGs)												601/842-1572	RR1 NT143, Tupelo 38801
C4	Jeff Busby	Fr Mathiston, 10 mi SW on Parkway	300	18	10	None	All year								
E2	Rocky Springs	Fr Port Gibson, 17 mi NE on Parkway	600	22	18	None									
	NATIONAL SEASHORES														
	Gulf Isl Nat'l Seashore		400												
H4	Davis Bayou	Fr Ocean Springs, 3 mi E on US 90, 1-1/4 mi S on Hanley Rd	400		51	4.00	All year			•		•	dl g	601/875-3962	4000 Hanley Rd, Ocean Sp 39564
	NATIONAL FORESTS														
	Bienville NF														
E4	Marathon Lake	Fr Forest, 11 mi SE on Hwy 501, 3.8 mi E on FR 506, .3 mi S on FR 520.	10	55	55	2.00	All year			•	•		dl		Forest
	Desota NF														
G4	Cypress Creek	Fr Brooklyn, 10.2 mi E on Co 301, .2 mi E on Hwy 29, 3.6 mi SE on FR 305, 1.4 mi S on 305B.	3	7	7	None	All year			•			dl h		Brooklyn
F5	Turkey Fork	Fr Richton, 12 mi E on Hwy 42, 2 mi S on Hwy 63, 3 mi E on Co Rd, 2 mi N on FR 232	21	16	16	2.00	4/1-10/31			•			dl		Richton
G4	Big Biloxi	Fr Gulfport, 14 mi N on US 49, .5 mi W on Co 416.	10	10	10	None	3/1-11/30			•	•		dl		Gulfport
	Homochito NF														
F2	Clear Springs	Fr Meadville, 4.6 mi W on US 84, 4.1 mi S on Co 104.	12	26	26	2.00	All year			•	•		d		Meadville
	Holly Springs NF														
A4	Chewalla Lake	Fr Holly Spring, 5 mi NE on Hwy 4, 1 mi S on Co, 1 mi E on FR 611.	46	65	42	2.00	4/1-1/15			•			dl		Holly Spring
B4	Puskus	Fr Oxford, 1.5 mi NE on Hwy 7, 9.3 mi E on Hwy 30, 2.8 mi N on FR 838.	8	21	18	None	All year			•			dl		Oxford
	Tombigee NF														
C4	Choctaw Lake	Fr Ackerman, 4 mi S on Hwy 15, 1 mi E on Hwy 967.	5	12	11	2.00	All year			•	•		dl		Ackerman
B4	Davis Lake	Fr Houston, 10 mi NE on Hwy 15, 3 mi E on FR 903.	15	29	29	2.00	All year			•	•		dl		Houston
	CORPS OF ENGINEERS														
	Arkabutla Lake		B											601/562-6261	Hernando
A3	Pleasant Hill	Fr Hernando, 5 mi W on Hwy 304, 5 mi S on Fogg Rd	115	11	11	None	All year			•	•	•	l		Hernando
A3	South Abutment	Fr Coldwater, 9.5 mi W on paved hwy, 4 mi N on paved rd	103	85	80	4.00	All year			•	•	•			Coldwater
A3	Outlet Channel	Fr Arkabutla, 4.5 mi N on paved rd, 1/2 mi W	21	47	47	None	All year					•			Coldwater
A3	North Abutment	Fr Coldwater, 9.5 mi W on paved hwy, 5.1 mi N on paved rd	149	66	66	4.00	All year			•	•		l		Coldwater
A3	Hernando Point	Fr Coldwater, 4 mi N on US 51, 5 mi W on paved Wheeler Rd	149	54	54	6.00	All year			o	•		l		Hernando
	Sardis Lake													601/563-4531	
B3	Pat's Bluff	Fr Batesville, 11 mi E on Hwy 6, 3/4 mi N on Hwy 315, 7 mi NE	163	10	10	None	All year			•	•		l		Batesville
B3	Dam Area	Fr Sardis, 8 mi SE on Hwy 315 to N end of dam		201	201	4.00	All year			•	•	•	l		Sardis
B3	Dam Area	Fr Sardis, 8 mi SE on Hwy 315 to N end of dam	65	90	90	2.00	5/1-9/1			•	•	•	l		Sardis
B3	Wyatt Crossing	Fr I-55, 21.5 mi E on Hwy 310, 3.3 mi SE on gravel rd		10	10	None	All year			•	•		l		Sardis
B3	Teckville	Fr Como, 16 mi E on Hwy 310, 3 mi SE on gravel rd	57	12	12	None	All year			•	•		lr		Sardis
B3	Hurricane Landing	Fr Oxford, 11 mi N on Hwy 7		12	12	None	All year			•			l		Abbeville
	Enid Lake		B											601/563-4571	
B3	Riverview	Fr I-55 Enid, ext 1/2 mi E, 1 mi S	90	90	90	5.00	All year			o	•	•			Enid
B3	Plum Point	Fr Pope, 7-1/2 mi E on paved rd, 1/2 mi S on access rd	150	15	15	None	All year			•	•		l		Pope
B3	S Abutment-Persimmon Hill	Fr US 55, 2 mi on access rd	243	72	72	5.00	All year			•	•		l		
B3	Point Pleasant	Fr I-55, 6-1/2 mi NE on Hwy 32, 3 mi NW on paved access rd	235	5	5	None	All year			•	•		l		Oakland
B3	George Payne Cossar St Pk	Fr US 55, NE 5.1 mi on Hwy 32, 3 mi on paved access rd	836	81	81	5.00	All year			•	•	•	l		Oakland
B3	Wallace Creek	Fr I-55, Enid ext, 2 mi E, 1/2 mi S	159	99	99	4.50	All year			•	•		l		Enid
B3	Bynum Creek	Fr Water Val, 8.3 mi NW on Hwy 315, 2.8 mi SW on paved rd, 2.4 mi on gravel access rd	64	5	5	None	All year			•	•		l		Water Valley
B3	Chicksaw Hill	Fr Pope, 9 mi E, 2 mi SW on gravel rd	86	17	17	4.50	All year			•	•		l		Pope
B3	Long Branch	Fr I-55, 3 mi NE on Hwy 32, 2 mi N	107	8	8	None	All year			•	•		lr		Oakland
B3	Water Valley Landing	Fr Water Val, S on Hwy 7, 5.3 mi W on Hwy 32, 3 mi NW	66	28	28	3.00	All year			•	•		l		Water Valley
	Grenada Lake		B											601/226-5911	
C3	Gum's Crossing	Fr Grenada, 12 mi E on Hwy 8, 11-1/2 mi N	109	5	10	None	All year			•	•		lr		Grenada
C3	Grenada Landing	Fr Grenada, 2.1 mi NE on Hwy 8, 1.5 mi NE on paved rd, fol signs	250	45	21	None	All year			•	•		lr		Grenada
C3	South Abutment	Fr Grenada, 2.1 mi NE on Hwy 8, 2 mi N on paved rd	41	61	110	6.00	All year			•			l		Grenada
C3	North Graysport	Fr Grenada, 8 mi E on Hwy 8, 5 mi N		95	95	4.50	3/1-12/1			•	•		l		Grenada
C3	Skuna-Turkey Creek	Fr Coffeeville, 4.5 mi SE on Hwy 330, 2.1 mi S on paved rd, 1.5 mi W, 2.8 mi S & 1.5 mi W on gravel rds	129	4	5	None	All year			•			lr		Coffeeville
C3	Hugh White St Pk	Fr Grenada, 4.7 mi W on Hwy 8, 3.4 mi N on paved rd	747	30		4.50	All year			•	•		l		Grenada

North Carolina

Major Events

See state map, pages 36-37

The Carolina 500, late Feb., Rockingham. New model stock cars compete in this 500-mile race at the N.C. Motor Speedway. Admission. 919/582-2861.

Greater Greensboro Open, late Mar. to early Apr., Greensboro. This PGA tournament at the Forest Oaks Country Club is one of the premier matches of the tour. It is a testing ground for top pros on their way to the Masters. Admission. 919/379-1570.

N.C. Azalea Festival, mid-Apr., Wilmington. Garden tours, a parade, art shows, arts and crafts, a beauty pageant, live music, big-name entertainment, an air show, and boat races are some of the activities at this festival. Admission is charged for several events. 919/343-2287.

Moravian Easter Sunrise Service, Easter, Winston-Salem. A traditional Moravian service and love feast are held in Old Salem. Free. 919/722-6171.

Carolina Dogwood Festival, late Apr., Statesville. The blooming of the town's dogwood trees is celebrated with athletic events, music, a parade, food, and a beauty pageant. Admission is charged for several events. 704/873-6501.

Earl of Granville Festival, late Apr., Oxford. This townwide festival features an antique car show, athletic events, arts and crafts, a parade, street dances, and a large fireworks show. Free. 919/693-6125.

Raleigh Artsplosure, late Apr. to early May, Raleigh. The visual, performing, and literary arts are presented in various indoor and outdoor locations throughout the city. Free. 919/755-6154.

Springfest, early May, Raleigh. A German festival of spring is held at the Civic Center with authentic German cultural events and food. Admission. 919/755-6011.

Spring Wildflower Pilgrimage, early May, Asheville. There are guided field trips along the Blue Ridge Pkwy. to see wildflowers and birdlife. Admission. 704/258-6623.

"May Fair," early May, Wilmington. The Governor Dudley Mansion celebrates the month of May with arts and crafts, children's games, a country store, and attic treasures. Admission. 919/762-2511.

Hang-Gliding Spectacular, late May, Nags Head, northeast of Manteo. Hang-gliding pilots from all over the country come to compete in the event at Jockey's Ridge State Park. Free. 919/441-6247.

The Lost Colony **Outdoor Drama,** mid-June to late Aug., Manteo. The story of the first English settlement in the New World is told daily except Sunday at the Fort Raleigh National Historic Site. Admission. 919/473-2127.

Unto These Hills **Outdoor Drama,** mid-June to late Aug., Cherokee. The history of the Cherokee Indians from 1540 through their removal from their homeland (and subsequent march on the Trail of Tears) is told daily except Sunday at the Mountainside Theatre. Admission. 704/497-2111.

N.C. Rhododendron Festival, mid-June, Bakersville. Beauty pageants, food, athletic events, and arts and crafts exhibits are all held at the Bowman Middle School. Admission. 704/688-2113.

Highland Heritage Arts and Crafts Show, mid-June, Asheville. Some 65 exhibitors in 35 different mediums demonstrate and sell their goods, which include wood carvings, woven goods, pottery, glasswork, and mountain furniture, at the Asheville shopping mall. Free. 704/253-6893.

National Hollerin' Contest, mid-June, Spivey's Corner, southeast of Dunn. This unique event pays homage to the lost art of hollerin' and features contests in ham hollerin', junior hollerin', conch shell and foxhorn blowin', whistlin', and ladies callin'. Also featured is a clogging demonstration and other forms of entertainment. Admission. 919/892-4133.

Pirate Invasion, late June, Beaufort. Pirates invade the town and carry off maidens in an unrehearsed free-for-all on Beaufort's waterfront. Free. 919/726-6831.

Blue Ridge Mountain Fair, early July, Sparta. A horse show, a crafts fair, a pet show, a parade, sports events, food, contests, and musical entertainment all take place on the lawn of the Methodist Church in Sparta. Free (except food). 919/372-8840.

Greater Raleigh Antique Show, early to mid-July, Raleigh. Thousands of antique items are on display and for sale for three days at Raleigh Civic Center. Admission. 919/755-6011.

Grandfather Mountain Highland Games and Gathering of Scottish Clans, mid-July, Linville, southwest of Blowing Rock. Representatives of over 100 Scottish clans gather at Grandfather Mountain for traditional sports, dances, ceremonies, and pageantry. Admission. 704/898-4720.

Guild Fair of the Southern Highlands, late July, Asheville. Craft sales, exhibits, folk music, and folk dancing are all featured at the Civic Center. Admission. 704/298-7928.

Smoky Mountain Folk Festival, late July, Waynesville. Mountain ways are celebrated with crafts, square dancing, music, and an old-time muzzle-loading shoot. Admission. 704/456-6834.

Bluegrass and Old-Time Fiddlers Convention, early Aug., Jefferson. Ash Park is the site for food, bluegrass music, and fiddling competition in several different categories. Admission. 919/246-9945.

North Carolina Apple Festival, late Aug. to early Sept., Hendersonville. There are beauty pageants, parades, athletic events, arts and crafts, street dances, apple-bobbing and -baking contests, and lots of food at this festival. Admission is charged for several events. 704/692-1413.

Coharie Indian Pow-Wow, mid-Sept., Clinton. The Coharie Indian Center holds this event which features Indian cultural activities, drumming, dancing and singing, arts and crafts, and games. Parking: Fee. Festival: Free. 919/564-6901.

Festival in the Park, mid-Sept., Charlotte. This large festival is held in Freedom Park and features arts and crafts, music, drama, various contests, and children's activities. Free. 704/372-8900.

Masters of Hang-Gliding Championship, mid-Sept., Linville, southwest of Blowing Rock. The top 28 pilots in the world are invited to compete in this major international hang-gliding tournament which is held at Grandfather Mountain. Admission. 704/898-4720.

Traditional Wooden Boat Show, late Sept., Beaufort. Handmade wooden boats of many different types and designs are on display both in and out of the water. Admission. 919/728-7317.

Cherokee Fall Festival, early Oct., Cherokee. The Cherokee Ceremonial Grounds come alive with Indian food, an archery and blowgun competition, a grandstand show, a band competition, and arts and crafts exhibits. Admission is charged for several events. 704/497-9195.

N.C. State Fair, mid- to late Oct., Raleigh. Livestock shows, live entertainment, a carnival midway, and agricultural and industrial displays are featured at the State Fairgrounds just west of the city. Free. 919/733-2145.

Southern Flue-Cured Tobacco Festival, mid-Nov., Greenville. This harvest festival features a beauty pageant, athletic events, a tractor-driving contest, a pipe-smoking contest, a quilting seminar, a clogging contest, and an agricultural art contest. Free. 919/756-9687.

Old Wilmington by Candlelight, mid-Dec., Wilmington. Thousands of candles light the way through town where tours of historic houses and churches are conducted and music and refreshments may be enjoyed. Admission. 919/762-0492.

Salem Christmas, mid-Dec., Winston-Salem. The sights, sounds, and smells of Christmas in Salem as it was in the 19th century are re-created at the Old Salem Village. Admission. 919/723-3688.

North Carolina Destinations

ALAMANCE, 320, southwest of Burlington on St. 62, B-6. This small town was the site of a skirmish which some historians say was the first blow for liberty in the American Revolution. A group of 2,000 homesteaders called the "Regulators" fought the militia of Royal Gov. William Tryon on May 16, 1771, five years before the Declaration of Independence was signed. **Alamance Battlefield** is now a state historic site. Year-round, Tues.-Sat., 9 A.M. to 5 P.M.; Sun., 1 to 5 P.M. Free. 919/227-4785.

ASHEBORO, 15,252, C-6. At the geographical center of North Carolina, Asheboro is also the seat of Randolph County and was named for Samuel Ashe, governor of North Carolina from 1795 to 1798. The **North Carolina Zoological Park,** on Cox Rd. (St. 2834) southeast of Asheboro, will cover 1,371 acres upon its completion. Presently open is the African section, where native species are in an area surrounded by a moat; other species are housed in buildings. The completed zoo will display animals and plants by continent. Apr.-Sept., Mon.-Fri., 9 A.M. to 5 P.M.; Sat.-Sun., 10 A.M. to 6 P.M.; other months, daily, 9 A.M. to 5 P.M. Adults $1; persons 2-15, 50¢; under 2 and over 62, free. 919/879-5606. **Petty Enterprises,** at Level Cross, north of Asheboro off U.S. 220, is the home of stock car racer Richard Petty. Here are displays of racing cars and other items relative to racing. Open by appointment. Free. 919/498-3745 or 919/498-2743. **Seagrove Potters Museum,** 10 miles south of Asheboro on U.S. 220, displays traditional pottery and wares from 1750 to the present. Feb.-mid-Dec., Mon.-Sat., 10 A.M. to 4 P.M. Free. 919/873-7406.

ASHEVILLE, 53,281, C-3. Located on the Blue Ridge Parkway and not far from Great Smoky Mountains National Park, this city is often referred to as "The Land of the Sky." The city was laid out in 1796, originally named Morristown, and later renamed in honor of North Carolina governor Samuel Ashe. **Biltmore House and Gardens,** south on U.S. 25, was the home of George Washington Vanderbilt, who began land purchases in 1888 after visiting Asheville the year before in search of "the most beautiful spot in the world" for his home. The estate now includes 12,000 acres. Biltmore House, a French Renaissance mansion of hand-tooled and -carved limestone, has 365 rooms. Among them are a banquet hall with a 75-foot ceiling and a library, with some 20,000 volumes of books and a spiral staircase leading to the upper shelves. The gardens feature such special areas as the azalea, Italian, walled (considered one of the finest English gardens in America), and rose gardens, as well as all-season greenhouses. Other areas of the estate are a wildlife refuge, deer park, Biltmore Dairy

Farms, and restaurant facilities. Year-round, daily, 9 A.M. to 5 P.M. Grounds are open until 6 P.M. Upstairs or downstairs tour: Adults $8; persons 12-18, $16; under 12, free. Both tours: Adults $12; persons 12-18, $9; under 12, free. 704/274-1776. **Thomas Wolfe Memorial,** 48 Spruce St., is the boyhood home of Thomas Clayton Wolfe (1900-38), author of *Look Homeward, Angel* and other novels. Year-round, Tues.-Sat., 9 A.M. to 5 P.M.; Sun., 1 to 5 P.M. Adults $1, students 50¢; children under 12, free. 704/253-8304. Wolfe and O. Henry (William Sidney Porter), who also wrote in Asheville, are buried in nearby Riverside Cemetery. **Asheville Botanical Gardens,** at the University of North Carolina at Asheville, near the center of the city, contains hundreds of species of wildflowers, plants, trees, ferns, and mosses native to the Southern Highlands. Always open. Free. 704/258-6600. **Coburn Mineral Museum,** Civic Center, on Haywood St., has a collection of gems and minerals of North Carolina plus others from around the world. Year-round, Tues.-Fri., 10 A.M. to 5 P.M.; Sat.-Sun., 1 to 5 P.M. Free. 704/254-7162. **Vance Homestead,** Weaverville, 10 miles north of Asheville off U.S. 19/23 and 5 miles east on Reems Creek Rd., is the birthplace of Zebulon Baird Vance, governor of North Carolina during the Civil War. Built in 1786, the house is now a state historic site. Year-round, Tues.-Sat., 9 A.M. to 5 P.M.; Sun., 1 to 5 P.M. Free. 704/645-6706.

BATH, 207, C-9. Located on the banks of the Pamlico River, Bath, which was incorporated March 8, 1705, is the state's oldest town. Several of the town's 18th-century structures have been preserved. Among these are **St. Thomas Church,** the earliest North Carolina church still in existence; **Palmer-Marsh House** (1744) and **Bonner House** (1825). Tours to these places start at the Visitors Center, Cartaret St. Tours: Year-round, Tues.-Sat., 9 A.M. to 5 P.M.; Sun., 1 to 5 P.M. Adults $1, children 50¢. 919/923-3971.

BLOWING ROCK, 1,337, B-4. First settled in 1870, it was incorporated in 1889 and named for a rock formation which causes air currents from the Johns River Gorge to return lightweight objects. For example, one can throw a piece of paper over Blowing Rock, 2 miles southeast of town on U.S. 321, and an updraft will blow it back. **Tweetsie Railroad,** 4 miles north on U.S. 321, is the focal point of a park which also has a western town, country store, magic shows, petting zoo, and chair lift. Tweetsie Railroad, an old narrow-gauge line which celebrate its 100th anniversary in 1981, takes visitors on a three-mile excursion. Late May-Oct., daily, 9 A.M. to 6 P.M. Adults $7; children 4-12, $6; under 4, free. 704/264-9061.

BLUE RIDGE PARKWAY, A-4/C-2. This 469-mile parkway through the southern Appalachians follows mountain crests to link Shenandoah National Park in northern Virginia and Great Smoky Mountains National Park in North Carolina and Tennessee. In North Carolina, the parkway threads the Blue Ridge from Virginia, going in and out of Pisgah National Forest from Grandfather Mountain (5,964 ft.) to the Great Smoky Mountains. The parkway also skirts 5,721-foot-high Mount Pisgah. Several points of interest can be seen along the way. **Cradle of Forestry in America,** Milepost 408.6 and U.S. 276 several miles southeast of Asheville, is a reconstruction of America's first forestry school. Close by are picnic areas, waterfalls, and trout-fishing streams. Early Apr.-Oct., daily, 10 A.M. to 6 P.M. Free. 704/253-2352. **The Folk Art Center,** home of the Southern Highlands Handicraft Guild, is situated at Milepost 382, one-half mile from its intersection with U.S. 70 and 5 miles east of Asheville. At the center are crafts native to the area and tools used by the early settlers. Exhibitions also include folk dancing, folk music, and film programs. Year-round, daily, 9 A.M. to 5 P.M. Free. 704/298-7928. **Craggy Gardens,** Milepost 363.4 to 369.6 about 10 miles north of Asheville, includes more than 1,500 species of wildflowers which bloom from late spring through fall. May-Oct., daily, 24 hours. Free. 704/258-2850. **Mt. Mitchell State Park,** Milepost 355.4, contains virgin balsam forests, hiking and nature trails, and picnicking and camping facilities. In the park is 6,684-foot-high Mt. Mitchell, highest point in North Carolina. Always open. Free. 704/675-4611. **Museum of North Carolina Minerals,** south of Milepost 330, displays some of North Carolina's abundance of gems and minerals. May-Oct., daily, 9 A.M. to 5 P.M.; Sat.-Sun., 1 to 5 P.M. Free. 704/765-2761.

BREVARD, 5,323, C-2. Situated in North Carolina's northwestern mountains, Brevard is known as the "Land of Waterfalls." The most famous of the falls are **Looking Glass** (85 feet high); **Connestee** (twin falls, each about 110 feet high); **High** (125 feet high); and **Whitewater,** whose upper falls drop some 411 feet and are believed to be the highest in eastern America. Many of the falls are along U.S. 64, which is known as the "Waterfalls Highway." **Bridal Veil Falls** (120 feet high), southwest of Brevard near Highlands in Macon County, cascades over old U.S. 64. **Brevard Music Center,** Probart St., is the site of the annual *Brevard Music Festival,* a six-week series of presentations by music center students and faculty and guest performers. Events include recitals, operas, operettas, and concerts (rehearsals are also open to the public). Early July-mid-Aug., Mon.-Sat., 8:15 P.M.; Sun., 3 P.M. Season ticket $87.50. Individual performances: Adults $3.75 to $7.50; persons 16 and under, $2 to $4. 704/884-2011.

CAPE HATTERAS NATIONAL SEASHORE, C-10.

Eighty miles of beachland, from Whalebone Junction south and southwest to Ocracoke Inlet, are preserved in this national seashore. It is divided into four sections: Bodie, Hatteras, and Ocracoke islands, and Pea Island National Wildlife Refuge. Eight villages and several lighthouses are also within the natural boundaries. Recreational activities include beachcombing, swimming, camping, boating, sailing, fishing, history and nature study, and bird-watching. Wildflowers grow profusely, and more than 300 species of birds have been recorded in the area. The national seashore has three Visitors Centers, all on St. 12, which extends from U.S. 158 and U.S. 64 on the north, south through the national seashore to Ocracoke. **Bodie Island Visitors Center,** south of Whalebone Junction: Apr.-Oct., daily, 9 A.M. to 5 P.M.; Nov.-Dec., Apr., Fri.-Sun., 9 A.M. to 5 P.M. Free. 919/441-5711. **Hatteras Visitors Center,** in Buxton: Year-round, daily, 9 A.M. to 5 P.M. Free. 919/995-5209. **Ocracoke Visitors Center**: June-Oct., daily, 9 A.M. to 5 P.M.; other months, Sun.-Tues., 9 A.M. to 5 P.M. Free. 919/928-4531. **Pea Island Wildlife Refuge,** along St. 12 between Oregon Inlet and Rodanthe, is the winter home of snow geese and other species of waterfowl. Observation platforms and Visitors Center are on St. 12, 17 miles south of U.S. 158 and U.S. 64. Year-round, daily, 9 A.M. to 5 P.M. Free. 919/987-2394. **Ocracoke Island,** settled in the 17th century, was supposedly used as the headquarters for Blackbeard. The lighthouse, built in 1823, is still in use; it is accessible only by ferry from Hatteras and the mainland. Toll ferryboats operate between Ocracoke and Cedar Island every 2¼ hours and between Ocracoke and Swanquarter every 2 hours, connecting the park (Cape Hatteras National Seashore) with the mainland. Reservations required. Ocracoke: 919/928-3841. Cedar Island: 919/225-3551.

CAPE LOOKOUT NATIONAL SEASHORE, D-10.

This series of islands of the lower Outer Banks embrace beaches, dunes, salt marshes, and Cape Lookout Lighthouse. To the mariner, Cape Lookout was known as a danger, a safe refuge, and a good place to fish. The danger was the treacherous shoals that project far out to sea; the safe refuge was the cape past the shoals which provides a safe, sheltered anchorage to shield a vessel from a northeaster. Now accessible only by private boat, the area includes natural and historical features; National Park Services facilities are being developed. 919/728-2121.

CASHIERS, 553, C-2. A resort area, the town is located in the mountains of south-

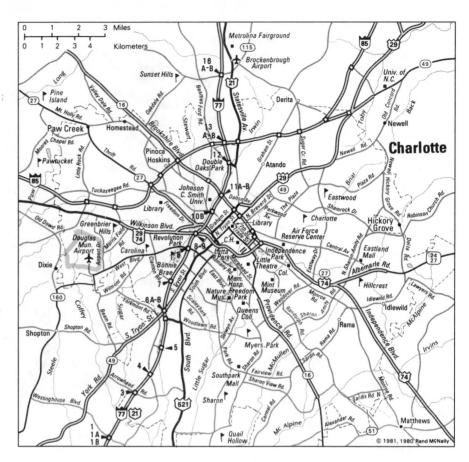

western North Carolina, where there are many small lakes. One of many rustic inns in North Carolina, **High Hampton Inn** was built on the estate of Confederate Gen. Wade Hampton about 1850, destroyed by fire in 1932, and rebuilt in 1933.

CHAPEL HILL, 32,421, B-6. Site of the University of North Carolina, Chapel Hill was named for the Church of New England New Hope Chapel, which once stood at the crossroads on this wooded hill.

UNIVERSITY OF NORTH CAROLINA: Authorized in 1776, chartered in 1789, and opened for classes in 1795 (the first student walked 125 miles to enroll and attend school), the University of North Carolina is one of the oldest state-supported universities in the country. The university is divided into two campuses—north campus, the older part of the university, is north of St. 54; and south campus, which includes the five schools of the Division of Health Affairs, is south of St. 54. Walking tours of the historic north campus are available, starting in the rotunda of the Morehead Building on Franklin St. Mar.-Oct., daily, 2 P.M. Free. 919/933-2211. Several places of historic and academic interest are located in north campus. The **Old Well,** on Cameron St., is at the center of north campus and has long been a meeting place for students and alumni. **Old East,** a dormitory near Old Well, is the oldest building on campus (its cornerstone was laid in 1793) and is now a National Historic Landmark. The **Ackland Art Center,** west of the Old Well, has per-

manent collections of artworks of all media as well as changing exhibits. Year-round, Tues.-Sat., 10 A.M. to 5 P.M.; Sun., 2 to 6 P.M. Free. 919/966-5736. **South Building,** across the street from Old Well, was where Pres. James K. Polk lived while a student at the university. Today, it houses the university administrative offices. The **Davie Poplar,** just north of the Old Well, is said to have been only a small sapling when the university opened its doors to students in 1795. Today, it is still standing, its trunk covered with ivy. **Coker Arboretum,** east of Old Well, has an abundance of flowering plants; more bloom in mid-May than any other time. **Morehead Planetarium,** in the Morehead Building, includes a 24-inch telescope available to the public for stargazing by advance reservation, and it is one of the training sites for the astronauts. In the planetarium also are scientific exhibits open to the public. Year-round, Mon.-Fri., 2 to 5 P.M., 7:30 to 10 P.M.; Sat., 10 A.M. to 5 P.M.; 7:30 to 10 P.M.; Sun., holidays, 1 to 5 P.M., 7:30 to 10 P.M. Adults $2.75; students, persons 65 and over, and military personnel $2; children under 12, $1.35. 919/933-1236. **North Carolina Botanical Gardens,** about 2 miles south of the campus at U.S. 15/501 bypass, contain hundreds of species of flowers and plants native to North Carolina. Nature trails: Year-round, daily, 8 A.M. to 5 P.M.. Totten Center and greenhouses: Mid-Mar.-mid-Nov., Mon.-Fri., 8 A.M. to 5 P.M.; Sat., 10 A.M. to 4 P.M.; Sun., 2 to 5 P.M.; other months, Mon.-Fri., 8 A.M. to 5 P.M. Free. 919/967-2246.

CHARLOTTE, 314,447, C-5. North Carolina's largest city, Charlotte was settled in 1750 and incorporated in 1768. The city played an important role in the state's history starting with the Revolutionary War period. One of the early events occurred on May 20, 1775; local citizens, dissatisfied with British rule, met and affixed their signature to the Mecklenburg Declaration of Independence and declared themselves "a free and independent people." The date is on the North Carolina flag and state seal. **McIntyre Historic Site,** on Beatties Ford Rd. at McIntyre Ave., is the site of the October 4, 1780, skirmish which earned the people of Charlotte the nickname "Hornets." State troops under the command of Brig. Gen. William R. Davie harassed the British outpost, under the command of Lord Cornwallis, with such fury that Cornwallis described it as like "fighting a hornet's nest." Always open. Free. 704/374-2475. **Hezekiah Alexander House,** 3500 Shamrock Dr., the oldest dwelling still standing in Mecklenburg County, was completed in 1774. Alexander, a blacksmith who called himself a "planter" after gaining some position in the community, was a founding trustee of Queens College (Colonial), the first college south of Virginia. House tours: June-Aug., Sat.-Sun., 2 to 5 P.M.; Tues.-Fri., by appointment two weeks in advance; other months, Sat.-Sun., 2 to 4 P.M. Adults $1; children 6-18, 50¢; under 6, free. 704/568-1774. **Mint Museum of Art,** 501 Hempstead Pl., had its beginning as a branch of the United States Mint serving the gold mines around Charlotte in the early 1800s. It contains more than 5,000 pieces in its permanent collection. Year-round, Tues.-Fri., 10 A.M. to 5 P.M.; Sat.-Sun., 2 to 5 P.M. Free. 704/334-9725. The **Mint Museum of History,** 3500 Shamrock Dr., has extensive collections and exhibits which reflect America's past and emphasizes the history of North Carolina. Year-round, Tues.-Fri., 10 A.M. to 5 P.M.; Sat.-Sun., 2 to 5 P.M. Free. 704/568-1774. **Spirit Square Arts Center,** 110 E. Seventh St., is a center for community and performing arts. It includes classes, plays, workshops, films, concerts, and lectures. Year-round, Mon.-Fri., 9 A.M. to 11 P.M.; Sat.-Sun., 10 A.M. to 11 P.M. 704/372-9664. **Charlotte Nature Museum,** 1650 Sterling Rd., is a natural history museum with live animals native to North Carolina; a nature hall; a learning theater for archaeological and geological subjects; nature trails; a salt-marsh exhibit; puppet theater; and the *Charlotte Kelly Planetarium.* Museum: Year-round, Mon.-Sat., 9 A.M. to 5 P.M.; Sun., 2 to 5 P.M. Free. Planetarium shows for children 7 and under: Sat., 1:30 and 2:30 P.M., Sun., 2:30 P.M. Admission 75¢. General planetarium shows: Sat.-Sun., 3 and 4 P.M. Adults $1; students over 7, 75¢. 704/333-0506. **Discovery Place,** 301 N. Tryon St., is another unit of the Charlotte Nature Museum. This "hands-on" museum has exhibits relating to physical science. It also has an aquarium

and a rain forest. Year-round, Mon.-Thurs., Sat., 9 A.M. to 6 P.M.; Fri., 9 A.M. to 9 P.M.; Sun., 1 to 6 P.M. Adults $2.50; students and persons 60 and over, $1.50; under 5, free. 704/362-6261. **Carowinds,** 6 miles south of Charlotte on Int. 77, is a 73-acre theme park with eight different themes, each covering a historic period of the Carolinas (the park is also in South Carolina). The park has 30 rides, including five roller coasters, and live shows. Apr.-mid-June, Sat.-Sun., 10 A.M. to 8 P.M.; mid-June-mid-Aug., Sat.-Thurs., 10 A.M. to 8 P.M.; mid-Aug.-mid-Oct., Sat.-Sun., 10 A.M. to 8 P.M. Admission $9.50 (includes all entertainment); children under 3, free. 704/588-2606. **James K. Polk Memorial State Historic Site,** 12 miles south of Charlotte on U.S. 521 in Pineville, has a log house (and outbuilding) reconstructed to resemble the place where the eleventh president of the United States was born in 1795. In the Visitors Center are exhibits relating to the life and times of James K. Polk. Year-round, Tues.-Sat., 9 A.M. to 5 P.M.; Sun., 1 to 5 P.M. Free. 704/889-7145. **Reed Gold Mine State Historic Site,** 20 miles northeast of Charlotte on St. 200, is the site of the first authenticated gold discovery in America. The Visitors Center features a museum and an old assay office. Guided tours include about 400 linear feet of underground mine. Year-round, Tues.-Sat., 9 A.M. to 5 P.M.; Sun., 1 to 5 P.M. Free. 704/786-8337. **Charlotte Motor Speedway,** 12 miles north of Charlotte on U.S. 29, is the site of the *NASCAR World 600* in May and the *National 500* in October. 704/455-2121.

CHEROKEE, 309, C-2. This small town is the capital of the eastern band of the

National Portrait Gallery, London

Sir Walter Raleigh left an indelible mark on North Carolina. The state capital, a bay, and a fort are named for him. And his plan to establish a colony in the New World pleased Queen Elizabeth I so much she knighted him *Sir Walter Raleigh.* Colonists sent by Raleigh left England in April, 1585, and arrived three months later, landing on Roanoke Island. The colony, which they named Fort Raleigh, was short-lived, earning for it today the title "Lost Colony." This failure was attributed partially to the inaccessibility of the island. Three contributions as a result of the colony were the development of three crops — tobacco, corn, and potatoes. Today, the site of the colony, which was the first English settlement in North America, is a national historic site. Each summer an outdoor drama, *The Lost Colony,* recounting this event, is presented at Waterside Theatre at the site of the settlement.

Cherokees who live in Qualla Reservation, which adjoins Great Smoky Mountains National Park. **Oconaluftee Indian Village,** one-half mile north on U.S. 441, is a replica of an 18th-century Cherokee community. Here Indian artisans make items used by their ancestors. Huts, cabins, and the seven-sided council house have furnishings and trappings used 200 years ago. Guided tours: Mid-May-late Oct., daily, 9 A.M. to 5 P.M. Adults $4; children 6-12, $2.50; under 6, free. 704/497-2111. **Museum of the Cherokee Indians,** U.S. 441 on the reservation, has arts, crafts, and prehistoric artifacts. Daily, mid-June-Aug., 9 A.M. to 8 P.M.; other months, 9 A.M. to 5:30 P.M. Adults $3, children $1.50. 704/497-3481.

DURHAM, 100,831, B-7. A tobacco manufacturing center, Durham was incorporated in 1867; however, tobacco was being manufactured in the area as early as 1858 by Robert F. Morris. And in 1865, Washington Duke mustered out of the army and began grinding tobacco and laying the foundation for the company. It would eventually embrace practically the entire tobacco industry, with James B. Duke, Washington's son, at the helm.

DUKE UNIVERSITY: An endowment by the Duke family, Duke University is divided into two campuses—east and west. **Duke Art Museum,** on east campus, features collections of a variety of artworks. Year-round, Mon.-Fri., 9 A.M. to 5 P.M.; Sat., 10 A.M. to 1 P.M.; Sun., 2 to 5 P.M. Free. 919/684-5135. West campus is noted for its Gothic architecture. **Duke Chapel,** on west campus, features 77 inspirational stained-glass windows and a 210-foot bell tower patterned after one at Canterbury Cathedral in England. Year-round, daily, 8 A.M. to 11 P.M. Free. 919/684-2572. **Duke Medical Center,** on west campus, is renowned as a research and teaching center. Tours and information: 919/684-3384. **Botany Department Greenhouses** have 13 rooms of diverse plants open to the public. Year-round, Mon.-Fri., 8 A.M. to 5 P.M. Guided tours: 919/684-5638. The **Sarah P. Duke Gardens,** a 55-acre garden on west campus, has a constant display of flowers in formal, informal, and Oriental gardens. Year-round, daily, 8 A.M. to sunset. Free. Guided tours: 919/684-3698. Duke University Information: Office of Community Relations, 919/684-3710.

MUSEUMS AND HISTORIC AREAS: North Carolina Museum of Life and Science, 433 Murray Ave., has extensive exhibits of prehistoric material and an aerospace collection. The 78-acre site also includes a zoo, wildlife sanctuary, and a mile-long narrow-gauge railroad. Year-round, Tues.-Sat., 10 A.M. to 5 P.M.; Sun., 2 to 5 P.M. Adults $2; persons 6-18, $1; over 65, 50¢; under 6, free. 919/477-0431. **Duke Homestead State Historic Site,** Duke Homestead Rd., near Int. 85, is the Duke family ancestral home, where Washington Duke established the first tobacco "factory" after the Civil War. A *Tobacco Museum* here traces the history of tobacco from its use by the early Indians to today. Year-round, Tues.-Sat., 9 A.M. to 5 P.M.; Sun., 1 to 5 P.M. Free. 919/477-5498. **Bennett Place State Historic Site,** 6 miles west and one-half mile south of Durham on U.S. 70, just off Int. 85, is the location where surrender negotiations took place between Confederate Gen. Joseph E. Johnston and Union Gen. William T. Sherman after the Appomattox capitulations of the Civil War in 1865. The site has displays of furnishings of the period in a restored log house and other buildings. Picnicking is permitted on the grounds. Buildings: Year-round, Tues.-Sat., 9 A.M. to 5 P.M.; Sun., 1 to 5 P.M. Free. 919/383-4345. **Stagville Preservation Center,** 7 miles northeast of Durham on Old Oxford Hwy. (Co. 1004), is a state-owned research center for the study of historic and archaeological preservation technology. It occupies several historic late 18th- and early 19th-century plantation buildings on 71 acres. Year-round, Mon.-Fri., 9 A.M. to 4 P.M. Free. 919/477-9835.

EDENTON, 5,264, B-9. In Chowan County along the shores of Albemarle Sound and the Chowan River, Edenton is the third oldest city in North Carolina. It was settled as early as 1685, planned in 1712, incorporated in 1722; and it was capital of the colony from 1722 to 1743. The pirate Blackbeard (Edward Teach) sailed into Edenton, and many noted American patriots have lived here. In 1774, in an event that became known as the Edenton Tea Party, 51 women of the area signed a resolution supporting the protest of the Provincial Congress against British injustice.

Historic Edenton, in Barker House, N. Broad St., conducts tours to several historic places. *Barker House* (1782), Historic Edenton Visitors Center, was the home of Thomas Barker, a colonial agent in England, and his wife, Penelope, who participated in the Edenton Tea Party. Other buildings on the tour are *Cupola House* (c. 1724), the home of Francis Corbin, agent for Lord Granville, who retained property in 1729 when other Lords Proprietors surrendered their charters; *Chowan County Courthouse* (c. 1767), a Georgian-style structure; *Iredell House* (c. 1776), home of James Iredell and his son James, Jr., who became governor of North Carolina; and *St. Paul's Episcopal Church,* built between 1736 and 1760, which has served an active congregation since it was organized. Historic Edenton tours (all buildings listed): Year-round, Mon.-Sat., 10 A.M. to 4:30 P.M.; Sun., 2 to 5 P.M. Adults $2.50; students $1; children under 6, free; tours, extra. 919/482-3663.

FAYETTEVILLE, 59,507, D-7. Incorporated in 1762 as Campbellton, for Farquhard Campbell, the name was changed in 1783 to Fayetteville. Next door is Fort Bragg, one of the world's largest military installations. **Fort Bragg,** 10 miles northwest on St. 87, is headquarters for special forces (Green Berets) and home of the Golden Knights, the army's official parachute demonstration team, which has held 96 of the 128 world parachuting records. *Iron Mike,* a giant statue which is a monument to all American soldiers, overlooks the military installation. Fort Bragg Visitors Center: Always open. Free. 919/396-0011. *82nd Airborne War Memorial Museum,* Ardennes Rd. and Gela St., has weapons from wars and conflicts since World War I. Year-round, Tues.-Sun., 11:30 A.M. to 4 P.M. Free. 919/396-2328. The *U.S. Army John F. Kennedy Center for Military Assistance Museum,* Ardennes St. in Smoke Bomb Hill Area, has a display of guerilla warfare weapons. Year-round, Tues.-Fri., 9 A.M. to 4 P.M.; Sat.-Sun., holidays, noon to 5 P.M. Free. 919/396-1524. **Arsenal House,** headquarters of the Art Council of Fayetteville/ Cumberland County, 822 Arsenal Ave. in Fayetteville, is at the site of the North Carolina Arsenal; it was built between 1838 and 1856 and destroyed when Gen. William Tecumseh Sherman ordered it burned. The historical park has self-guided tours. Arsenal House: Year-round, Mon.-Fri., 9 A.M. to 5 P.M.; Sat.-Sun., 1 to 5 P.M. Historic site: Year-round, daily, sunrise to sunset. Free. 919/323-1776.

FLAT ROCK, C-3. *See* **Hendersonville** for **Carl Sandburg Home National Historic Site,** and **Tryon.**

FONTANA DAM, 130, C-1. This 480-foot-high dam, highest in the TVA system, forms a 30-mile-long lake which offers boating, fishing, water-skiing, and camping areas. Guided tours of the dam and gener-

ating facilities: Year-round, daily, 9 A.M. to 5 P.M. Free. 704/498-2211.

FRANKLIN, 2,640, C-2. This area of the state has many mines rich in gems and minerals. Some are open year-round as weather permits. Others are open April through October. **Gibson Ruby Mine** is 9 miles northeast via St. 28. May-Oct., Mon.-Sat., 8 A.M. to 5 P.M. Adults $5; children 9-12, $2; under 9, free. 704/524-3546. **Shuler Ruby Mine,** 10 miles north via St. 28, permits digging for rubies and other gems. Apr.-Oct., Mon.-Sat., 8 A.M. to 5 P.M. Adults $5; children 6-12, $2; under 6, free. 704/524-3155. **Franklin Gem and Mineral Museum,** 2 W. Main St., displays gems, minerals, Indian artifacts, and fossils. May-Oct., Mon.-Sat., 10 A.M. to 4 P.M. Free. 704/524-3161. **Heritage Hollow,** between Phillips and Porter Sts., is a village of shops and restaurants built of weathered wood. Paved walkways and rail-tie steps follow the contour of the parklike area where visitors can browse for handcrafted and imported gifts. 704/369-9400. **Nantahala National Forest,** once home of the Cherokee Nation, has many drives; some trace the *Trail of Tears* over which Indians marched from North Carolina to a new reservation in Oklahoma.

GASTONIA, 47,333, C-4. Incorporated in 1877 and named for the county in which it is located, Gastonia is an industrial city. **Schiele Museum of Natural History and Planetarium,** 1500 E. Garrison Blvd., has more than 6,000 mounted birds, mammals, reptiles, and fish; Indian arts and crafts; a 20-acre nature park; living-history farms; and a planetarium. Year-round, Tues.-Fri., 9 A.M. to 5 P.M.; Sat.-Sun., 2 to 5 P.M. Free. Planetarium shows: Year-round, Sat.-Sun., 3 to 4 P.M. Free. 704/864-3962 or 704/865-6131.

GREAT SMOKY MOUNTAINS NATIONAL PARK, C-1. The Great Smoky Mountains, which form the boundary between North Carolina and Tennessee, are preserved in a national park, also located in both states. The park covers 517,368 acres, with 273,757 acres in North Carolina. In the park are over 600 miles of horse and foot trails, ranging from short nature walks to a 71-mile section of the Appalachian Trail, which follows the mountain crest. Seven developed campgrounds and three primitive camping areas are in the area. Evening programs and nature walks at or starting from the Visitors Centers are conducted by park rangers during the summer months. **Oconaluftee Visitors Center,** 3 miles north of Cherokee on U.S. 441, is the main entrance to the park in North Carolina. Daily, May-Oct., 8 A.M. to 6 P.M.; other months, 8 A.M. to 4 P.M. Free. Park: Always open. 704/497-7211.

See also **Great Smoky Mountains National Park** in Tennessee.

GREENSBORO, 155,642, B-6. Established in 1808 and incorporated in 1810,

Greensboro is named for Gen. Nathanael Greene, the American leader of the Battle of Guilford Court House. **Guilford Court House National Military Park,** north off U.S. 220, is the site of the March 15, 1781, battle which opened the campaign that led to Yorktown and the end of the American Revolution. The Visitors Center has exhibits and slides relating the battle. Daily, May-Labor Day, 8:30 A.M. to 6 P.M.; other months, 8:30 A.M. to 5 P.M. Free. 919/288-1776. **Old Mill,** 5 miles north of the airport on St. 68, was seized by British troops for grain before the March 15 battle. Built in 1745, it is one of the oldest continuously operating mills in the nation. Year-round, daily, 9 A.M. to 6 P.M. Free. 919/274-8675. **Greensboro Historical Museum,** 130 Summit Ave., features costumes, household furnishings, old currency, and relics from seven major wars. Also on exhibit are items relating to two of Greensboro's famous natives—Dolley Madison, wife of Pres. James Madison, and O. Henry (William Sydney Porter), short-story writer and novelist. Year-round, Tues.-Sat., 10 A.M. to 5 P.M.; Sun., 2 to 5 P.M. Free. 919/373-2043. **Guilford College,** 5800 W. Friendly Ave., is the summer home of the *Eastern Music Festival,* which provides a six-week series by internationally known musicians and about 200 young musicians from across the nation. 919/292-5511. **Weatherspoon Art Gallery,** University of North Carolina at Greensboro campus, has exhibits of more than 2,000 art items. Academic year, Tues.-Fri., 10 A.M. to 5 P.M.; Sat.-Sun., 2 to 6 P.M. Free. 919/379-5770.

HENDERSONVILLE, 6,862, C-3. In Henderson County, Hendersonville is considered the "apple capital" of North Carolina. **Carl Sandburg Home National Historic Site,** on Little River Rd., 5 miles south on U.S. 25 in Flat Rock, was the farm home of the poet and author for the last 22 years of his life. Several of his books were published while he lived here. *Connemara,* the farm home, was originally the summer home of C. G. Menninger, first secretary of the Confederate Treasury. Next to the home is an amphitheater where two productions by the Vagabond Players of the North Carolina State Theatre are presented during the summer. *The World of Carl Sandburg,* an abbreviated version of Norman Corwin's Broadway production: Late June-early Sept., Mon.-Tues., Thurs.-Fri., Sun., 2:30 P.M. Free. *The Rootabaga Stories,* a production of Mr. Sandburg's stories for "children of all ages,": Early July-mid-Aug., Mon., Thurs., 11 A.M. Free. National Historic Site: Year-round, daily, 9 A.M. to 5 P.M. Free. 704/693-4178. **Flat Rock Playhouse,** also in Flat Rock, is the North Carolina State Theatre, oldest professional summer theater in the state. Performances: Late June-early Sept., Tues., 8:30 P.M.; Wed., 2:30 and 8:30 P.M.; Thurs.-Fri., 8:30 P.M.; Sat., 2:30 and 8:30 P.M. Adults $7 to $8; children, half price at matinee. 704/693-0731.

HIDDENITE, 600, west of Statesville, B-5. The town is a mining center for gems and minerals, such as emeralds, hiddenite, quartz, rutile, tourmaline, moonstones, and garnets. The Carolina Emerald (13.14 carats), now owned by Tiffany & Company (New York City), was discovered at one of the mines in Hiddenite in the early 1970s. Gem shops at the mine sites feature gem and mineral specimens, lapidary supplies, and jewelry. Mar.-Oct., daily, 9 A.M. to 5 P.M. Mines are open for digging: Mar.-Oct., 8 A.M. to sunset. Admission $4 a day. Hiddenite Chamber of Commerce: 704/632-3132.

HIGH POINT, 64,107, B-6. A large industrial center, it is home of the Southern Furniture Market, 508 N. Hamilton St. **High Point Museum,** 1805 E. Lexington Ave., has exhibits reflecting the area's military, industrial, social, and civic history. It also includes *John Haley House* (1786), a blacksmith shop, and a weaving house. Museum: Year-round, Mon.-Fri., 9 A.M. to 4:30 P.M.; Sat.-Sun., 1 to 5 P.M. Other buildings: Sun., 1 to 5 P.M.; Mon.-Fri., by appointment. Free. 919/885-6859.

HILLSBOROUGH, 3,019, B-6. Hillsborough, formerly known as Hillsboro, was the site of several important historic events: War of the Regulation (1768-1771), during which a group called the Regulators took possession of the town, held mock trials, and plundered and burned homes of officials; Third Provincial Congress (1775); and the nearby site of Gen. Joseph E. Johnston's surrender to Gen. William Tecumseh Sherman that effectively ended the Civil War. **Orange County Historical Museum,** on the second floor of the Old Courthouse, offers tours by appointment. 919/732-8648.

KINGS MOUNTAIN, 9,080, C-4. Located here is the National Park Service headquarters for **Kings Mountain National Military Park,** which preserves the site of the October 7, 1780, Battle of Kings Mountain fought nearby in South Carolina. 803/936-7508.
See also **Kings Mountain National Military Park** in South Carolina.

LINVILLE, 244, B-3. Located in North Carolina's highlands just off the Blue Ridge Parkway, Linville has a very old neighbor—**Grandfather Mountain**—which reaches 5,964 feet skyward. Geologists say it is a billion years old, making it probably the oldest mountain in the world. A mile-high swinging bridge connects its two peaks. The mountain is also a popular hang-gliding area. Visitors Center, U.S. 221 and Blue Ridge Pkwy.: Late Mar.-mid-Nov., daily, 9 A.M. to 5 P.M.; winter weekends (weather permitting), same times. Adults $4; children 4-12, $3; under 4, free. 704/733-2800.

MANTEO, 902, B-10. Located on Roanoke Island, site of the first English settlement (1584) in America, the town was named for Indian chief Manteo. An outdoor

drama, *The Lost Colony* is presented each summer from mid-June through August in Waterside Theatre at the site of the settlement. Manteo is also National Park Service headquarters for two facilities: **Cape Hatteras National Seashore** and Fort Raleigh National Historic Site. **Fort Raleigh National Historic Site,** at the north end of Roanoke Island, preserves the site of the first English settlement (1584). Park and Visitors Center: Memorial Day-Labor Day, Mon.-Sat., 8:30 A.M. to 8:15 P.M.; Sun., 8:30 A.M. to 6 P.M.; other months, daily, 8:30 A.M. to 4:30 P.M. Free. 919/473-2111. **Elizabethan Gardens,** 5 miles southeast of Manteo on U.S. 26, near Waterside Theatre, commemorates 16th-century Queen Elizabeth and the Lost Colony. Gardens include an herb garden, wildflower area, trees, plants, and antique statuary. The House Reception Center displays period furniture, English portraits, and coats of arms. Daily, Sept.-May, 9 A.M. to 5 P.M.; other months, 9 A.M. to 8 P.M. Adults $1.50; persons 65 and over, $1.35; children under 12, free. 919/473-3234. **Marine Resources Center,** on Airport Rd., near Manteo, is a marine-oriented educational and research facility, which has public aquariums and exhibits, field trips, and guided tours. Year-round, Mon.-Sat., 9 A.M. to 5 P.M.; Sun., 1 to 5 P.M. Free. 919/473-3493.
See also **Cape Hatteras National Seashore.**

MURFREESBORO, 3,007, A-9. In Hertford County, Murfreesboro dates back to the 18th century. It is the birthplace of Richard Jordon Gatling, inventor of the Gatling gun. Dr. Walter Reed, who discovered a cure for yellow fever, spent several of his childhood years here; and novelist William Hill Brown died here in 1793. **William Rea Store,** built in 1790, is said to be the oldest brick structure in North Carolina. The restored building houses a museum, which features a Gatling gun. Tours: Apr.-Oct., hours flexible. 919/398-4886.

NEW BERN, 14,557, C-9. North Carolina's second oldest city, New Bern was settled in 1710 by German and Swiss colonists led by Baron Christoph von Graffenried. Named for the city of Berne, Switzerland, the town was designated by Royal Governor William Tryon as the first capital of the state, hosting the colonial assembly in 1737. **Tryon Palace and Gardens,** 610 Pollock St., completed in 1770, made New Bern the political center of North Carolina. The first publicly initiated assembly was called here on August 24, 1775. A reconstructed Tryon Palace, with furniture of the period, is open. Here also are 18th-century authentic English gardens. Costumed guides conduct tours: Year-round, Tues.-Sat., 9:30 A.M. to 4 P.M.; Sun., 1:30 to 4 P.M. Palace and gardens: Adults $4; students $1; under 6, free. 919/638-5109. **New Bern's Firemen's Museum,** 420 Broad St., was founded by the two oldest continuously operating fire companies in the United States. Its exhibits include historic flags, old maps, antique fire engines, equipment, and other memorabilia. Year-round, Tues.-Sat., 9:30 A.M. to 5:30 P.M.; Sun., 1 to 5:30 P.M. Adults 50¢; children 3-12, 25¢; under 3, free. 919/637-3407.

OUTER BANKS, A-10/D-9. The Outer Banks is a chain of narrow, sandy islands stretching from Back Bay, Virginia, south to Cape Lookout. Parts of the chain are 30 miles from the mainland. The islands may be reached by bridge from Point Harbor and Manteo or by ferry from Cedar Island to Ocracoke or Swanquarter to Ocracoke. Located here are several points of interest. **Cape Hatteras Lighthouse,** off St. 12, near Buxton, is the tallest (208 feet) lighthouse in America. The former keeper's residence is now a museum. Year-round, daily, 8 A.M. to 5 P.M. Free. 919/995-5209. **Cape Hatteras Post Office,** one of the smallest in the United States, is located in the postmaster's house. **Bodie Island Lighthouse,** with its Visitors Center, provides seashore information and natural history exhibits. A self-guided trail is nearby. 919/441-5711. At **Coquina Beach,** the remains of the *Laura Barnes,* shipwrecked in 1921, can be seen. **Oregon Inlet Fishing Center,** on St. 12, is the home of one of the largest fleets of charter sport-fishing boats on the mid-Atlantic Coast. 919/441-6301. **Chicamacomico Station,** an early lifesaving station at Rodanthe, stands as a historical monument to the men who manned the stations, which were situated every 7 miles along the Outer Banks. More than 300 shipwrecks have been recorded along the Outer Banks, giving it the epithet "Graveyard of the Atlantic."

See also **Cape Hatteras National Seashore** and **Wright Brothers National Memorial.**

PINEHURST, 1,056, C-6. Named for its location in a pine forest, this resort town was incorporated in 1949 for golf and golfers; and today its golf courses rank among the finest in the world. The **World Golf Hall of Fame,** Gerald R. Ford Blvd., was officially opened in 1974 by former Pres. Gerald R. Ford in ceremonies which also inducted 13 golfers into the Hall of Fame. Comprising several units, World Golf Hall of Fame gives the history of golf and Pinehurst. Year-round, daily, 9 A.M. to 5 P.M. Adults $2; children 8-12, 50¢; under 8, free. 919/295-6651.

RALEIGH, 149,771, B-7. The capital of North Carolina, the city was named for Sir Walter Raleigh, who in the 16th century was responsible for the establishment of the first English colony in the New World.

GOVERNMENT BUILDINGS: State Capitol, Capitol Square, completed in 1840, is in the center of a six-acre parklike square. Regarded as a fine example of Greek-Revival Doric architecture, it is a National Historic Landmark. The *Legislative Chambers* and

offices, *Supreme Court, Cabinet of Minerals Room,* and *State Library Room* are open for viewing. Also located in the building are the offices of the governor and secretary of state. Year-round, Mon.-Sat., 8:30 A.M. to 5:30 P.M.; Sun., 1 to 6 P.M. 919/733-4994. **State Legislative Building,** on Jones St., was constructed in 1963 to house the state general assembly. Year-round, Mon.-Fri., 8 A.M. to 5 P.M.; Sat., 9 A.M. to 5 P.M.; Sun., 1 to 5 P.M. **Governor's Executive Mansion,** begun in 1883 and completed in 1891, is considered an outstanding example of Queen Anne Cottage style of Victorian architecture. Open by appointment only. All government buildings: Capital Area Visitors Center, 919/733-3456.

MUSEUMS AND ART GALLERY: North Carolina Museum of History, in the east wing of the Archives and History Building, 109 E. Jones St., features a collection of more than 100,000 artifacts, including clothing and documents reflecting the state's heritage. Year-round, Tues.-Sat., 9 A.M. to 5 P.M.; Sun., 1 to 6 P.M. Free. 919/733-3894. **North Carolina Museum of Natural History,** in the Bicentennial Mall, 101 Halifax St., includes nature displays from astronomy to zoology. Year-round, Mon.-Sat., 9 A.M. to 5 P.M.; Sun., 2 to 6 P.M. Free. 919/733-7450. **North Carolina Museum of Art,** 107 E. Morgan St., has a collection of Western European art, including paintings, sculpture, prints, drawings, and decorative art. Its Samuel H. Kress Collection of Renaissance and Baroque art is one of the largest in the country. Year-round, Tues.-Sat., 10 A.M. to 5 P.M.; Sun., 2 to 6 P.M. Free. 919/733-3248.

OTHER PLACES OF INTEREST: Mordecai Historic Park, at the corner of Wake Forest Rd. and Mimosa St., is the location of the house in which Pres. Andrew Johnson was born. The 12-by-18-foot house, built around 1795, was moved to this site in 1975. Also in the park are Raleigh's first post office (c. 1847) and the *Iredell-Badger Law Office* (c. 1815). Tours: Oct.-May, Tues.-Thurs., 10 A.M. to 1 P.M.; Sun., 2 to 4 P.M.; other months, Wed., 10 A.M. to noon; Sun., 2 to 4 P.M. Free. 919/834-4844. **Henry Clay Oak,** 407 N. Blount St., is a huge oak tree at the place where Henry Clay chose to sit and think and write his "Texas Question" letter to the *National Intelligencer,* which became a factor in his defeat for presidency in 1844. The **Raleigh Memorial Auditorium,** 500 Fayetteville Mall, was built by the city in 1932 as a memorial to those killed in the American Revolution, War of 1812, Spanish-American War, and World War I. It has been the home of the North Carolina Symphony Orchestra since 1975. 919/733-2750.

TRYON, 1,796, on U.S. 176 southeast of Flat Rock, C-3. Named for **Tryon Mountain,** it was established in 1882. Located in Polk County, its fox hunts, horse shows, and steeplechases are known throughout the country. A major event is the **Block House**

Dolley Payne Madison, famous Washington, D.C. hostess while her husband was secretary of state and later president of the United States, was born June 20, 1768, in a two-room log house in Greensboro, North Carolina. Her birthplace was near present-day Guilford College in a Quaker settlement to which her parents had come from Virginia.

Steeplechase run each spring. (**Block House,** the building, includes portions of a fort used during the French and Indian War.) **Pearson Falls,** 5 miles north off U.S. 176, is a botanical sanctuary with a wide variety of flora and fauna. The falls are one of many in the area. Apr.-Oct., daily, 10 A.M. to 6 P.M.; other months, Tues.-Sun., same times. Adults $1; children 6-12, 50¢; under 6, free. Tryon Chamber of Commerce: 704/859-6236.

WILMINGTON, 44,000, E-8. Although recorded history of the area of North Carolina's largest port city dates back to 1524 when explorer Giovanni da Verrazzano landed nearby, no serious attempts were made to settle the area until the English landed at Town Creek in 1664 and Brunswick Town in 1726. Wilmington, the first permanent settlement in the area, was founded in 1732.

WILMINGTON HISTORIC SITES: Wilmington Historic Tour includes five buildings and begins at *Thalian Hall,* Third and Princess Sts., now the Wilmington City Hall, a restored 19th-century community theater and home of the city's arts council. The tour includes the following: *Burgwin-Wright House,* Third and Market Sts., built in 1771 and occupied in 1781 by Lord Cornwallis prior to his surrender at Yorktown; *Zebulon Latimer House,* Third and Orange Sts., a four-story residence which symbolizes the mid-19th-century opulence enjoyed in Wilmington; and *Governor Dudley Mansion,* Front and Nun Sts., built in 1832 as the home of the first elected governor of North Carolina. Tours: Year-round, Tues.-Sat., 10 A.M. to 5 P.M. Adults $5; students and children 6-8, $1; under 6, free. 919/763-9328. **New Hanover County Museum,** 814 Market St., was established in 1897 and is dedicated to cultural education in the arts, science, and history. Year-round, Tues.-Sat.,

9 A.M. to 5 P.M.; Sun., 2 to 5 P.M. Free. 919/763-0852. **U.S.S. *North Carolina* Battleship Memorial,** permanently berthed on the west bank of Cape Fear River, is a memorial to North Carolinians who died in World War II. Ship tours: Daily, June-Aug., 8 A.M. to 8 P.M.; Sept.-May, 8 A.M. to sunset. Adults $2.50; children 6-11, $1; under 6, free. Outdoor sound and light show: Daily, June-Aug., 9 P.M. Adults $2.50, children $1. 919/762-1829. **Chandler's Wharf,** No. 2 Ann St., on the city's waterfront, includes shops, restaurants, a nautical museum, and harbor rides. Year-round, daily, 9 A.M. to 5:30 P.M. Adults $2; children under 12, $1. 919/343-1406. **Cotton Exchange,** Nutt St., a center for exporting cotton particularly during the colonial period, has been converted into shops and restaurants. Year-round, Mon.-Sat., 10 A.M. to 6 P.M. Free. 919/799-1222.

NEARBY GARDENS AND HISTORIC AREAS: Arlie Gardens, 7 miles east and 2 miles southeast of Wilmington on U.S. 17, now a private residence, was once the estate of a wealthy 19th-century rice magnate. Gardens only: Spring flowering season, daylight hours. Admission $1. **Greenfield Gardens,** 2½ miles south on U.S. 421, is a 185-acre park with a 125-acre lake, scenic drives, and a zoo. Year-round, daily, 8 A.M. to 11 P.M.. Free. 919/763-9871. **Orton Plantation Gardens,** 18 miles south off St. 133, now a private residence, is an antebellum mansion on an 18th-century rice plantation. Overlooking Cape Fear River, the plantation gardens, open to the public, have avenues of live oaks, hundreds of camellias and azaleas, various types of gardens, and a memorial chapel built in 1915. Daily, Mar.-early Sept., 8 A.M. to 6 P.M.; other months, 8 A.M. to 5 P.M. Adults $3; children 6-12, $1; under 6, free. 919/762-2611. **Brunswick Town Historic Site,** just south of Orton Plantation, was planned in 1726 (first dwelling was constructed in 1728) and quickly became a major port of the first capital of the colony. Its townspeople were the first to resist British authority as the American Revolution approached. Two of the colony's royal governors—Arthur Dobbs and William Tryon—lived at Brunswick Town until Tryon Palace was completed in New Bern. The excavation of the house in which they lived remains. Visitors Center: Year-round, Tues.-Sat., 9 A.M. to 5 P.M.; Sun., 1 to 5 P.M. Free. 919/371-6613. **Poplar Grove Plantation,** 12 miles northeast of Wilmington on U.S. 17, is an example of a coastal North Carolina plantation house of the 1850s. Mar.-Jan., Mon.-Sat., 9 A.M. to 5 P.M.; Sun., noon to 6 P.M. Adults $2, children 75¢. 919/686-0172. **Moore's Creek National Military Park,** 17 miles north on U.S. 421, 3 miles west on St. 210, commemorates the February 27, 1776, battle between North Carolina Patriots and Loyalists. Exhibits in the Visitors Center describe the conflict. Walking tours of the battlefield start from this point. Nov.-Apr., daily, 8 A.M. to 5 P.M.;

other months, Mon.-Fri., 8 A.M. to 5 P.M.; Sat.-Sun., 8 A.M. to 6 P.M. Free. 919/283-5591.

WINSTON-SALEM, 131,885, B-5. A Moravian settlement, Salem was incorporated by the assembly of 1856-57 and Winston by the assembly of 1859. In 1913, they were consolidated to become Winston-Salem, an industrial center with historic places of interest. **Historic Bethbara** (House of Passage) **Park,** 2147 Bethbara Rd., is the site of the first Moravian settlement, established November 17, 1753. The founders included about 15 men who had walked to the site from Pennsylvania. Foundations of the 18th-century buildings have been located and labeled. A reconstructed fort is in the original 1756 trench. Picnic facilities are in the area. Easter-Nov., Mon.-Fri., 9:30 A.M. to 4:30 P.M.; Sat.-Sun., 1:30 to 4:30 P.M. Free. 919/924-8191 or 919/727-2063. **Old Salem,** south of the business district on Old Salem Rd., was founded in 1766 around a public square by Moravians as a religious, cultural, and trade center. Restoration of the old village portrays the pioneer life of the Moravians. Many structures have been restored and furnished with original period pieces. Crafts are demonstrated in *Single Brothers House* (some houses are privately occupied). *Museum of Early Southern Decorative Arts,* 924 S. Main St., has four galleries and period rooms with decorative art from several Southern states. Year-round, Mon.-Sat., 10:30 A.M. to 5 P.M.; Sun., 1:30 to 4:30 P.M. Adults $3; persons 6-14, $1.50; under 6, free. 919/722-6148. Old Salem: Tours start from the Reception Center on Old Salem Rd. Year-round, Mon.-Sat., 9:30 A.M. to 4:30 P.M.; Sun., 1:30 to 4:30 P.M. Buildings: Adults $5; persons 6-14, $2.50; under 6, free. **Reynolda House,** 2 miles northwest of Winston-Salem on St. 67, was the estate of the late Joshua Reynolds, founder of R. J. Reynolds Tobacco Co. Outstanding are the traditional Ámerican paintings. *Reynolda Gardens* is a 125-acre area of formal gardens, natural woodlands, and greenhouses. House: Year-round, Tues.-Sat., 9:30 A.M. to 4:30 P.M.; Sun., 1:30 to 4:30 P.M. Adults $3; students and persons 65 and over, $2; students $1. Gardens: Free. 919/725-5325. **Tanglewood Park,** 12 miles southwest off U.S. 158, was once the estate of William and Kate B. Reynolds. Now the 1,110-acre park, which was bequeathed by the Reynolds for recreational use, has public facilities for golfing, tennis, swimming, horseback riding, steeplechases, and fishing; plus gardens, a summer theater, restaurants, and lodging. Park: Year-round, daily, 8 A.M. to 11 P.M. Admission $1 per vehicle. 919/766-6421. **Nature Science Center,** Museum Dr., has exhibits on early man, man in space, and the natural history of North Carolina; a model railroad, ham radio station, and other scientific displays. Lectures: Sept.-June, Sun., 3 P.M. Free. Center: Year-round, Mon.-Sat., 9 A.M. to 5 P.M.; June-

Aug., Sun., 1 to 6 P.M.; other months, Sun., 1 to 5 P.M. Free. 919/767-6730. **R. J. Reynolds Tobacco Co. Whitaker Park,** 2½ miles north on Int. 40, offers tours: Year-round, Mon.-Fri., 8 A.M. to 10 P.M. Free. 919/748-3571. **Joseph Schlitz Brewing Co.,** off U.S. 52, 5½ miles south of Int. 40, is one of the largest plants in North Carolina under one roof. Tours: Year-round, Mon.-Fri., 9 A.M. to 5 P.M. Free. 919/788-6710.

WRIGHT BROTHERS NATIONAL MEMORIAL, B-10. On the Outer Banks midway between Kitty Hawk and Nags Head, Wilbur and Orville Wright began an adventure in 1900 that three years later was to culminate in man's first powered flight. In 1900, they came to the Outer Banks from Dayton, Ohio, and spent windy autumn days flying their glider as a kite; in 1901, with a larger glider, they returned to the Outer Banks and continued their testing. Finally in 1903, they were ready for the final test. On the morning of December 17, they moved to a spot on level ground, Orville took the pilot's position and started the engines and propellers. At 10:35 A.M., the machine moved slowly forward under its own power and lifted into the air. The flight covered 120 feet and lasted only 12 seconds. A granite shaft on top of Kill Devil Hill stands on the site of many glider experiments made by the Wright brothers. A larger granite boulder marks the spot where the first plane left the ground. The area, which is actually a large sand dune, is listed on the National Registry of Natural Landmarks. The Visitors Center has a replica of the first plane and a history of the Wright brothers and aviation. Daily, June-Aug., 8:30 A.M. to 6:30 P.M.; other months, 8:30 A.M. to 4:30 P.M. Free. 919/441-7430. **Jockey's Ridge State Park,** 1 mile south of the national memorial along U.S. 158 and St. 12, encompasses the largest natural sand dune on the East Coast and is a popular hang-gliding site. 919/261-2626.

North Carolina Campgrounds

FEES REFLECT MINIMUM RATE FOR 2 ADULTS AND ARE SUBJECT TO INCREASE OR SEASONAL CHANGES

•	at the campground	E	tents rented	U	unlimited	g	public golf course within 5 miles	p	motor bikes prohibited
○	within one mile of campground	F	entrance fee or premit required	V	trailers rented	h	horseback riding	r	boat rental
$	extra charge	N	no specific number, limited by size of area only	Z	reservations accepted	j	whitewater running craft only	s	stream, lake or creek water only
**	limited facilities during winter months	P	primitive	LD	Labor Day	k	snow skiing within 25 miles	t	tennis
B	10,000 acres or more	R	reservation required	MD	Memorial Day	l	boat launch	u	snowmobile trails
C	contribution	S	self-contained units only	UC	under construction	m	area north of map	w	open certain off-season weekends
				d	boat dock	n	no drinking water	y	drinking water must be boiled

Map Reference	Park Name	Access	Acres	Tent Spaces	Trailer Spaces	Approximate Fee	Season	Swimming Pool	Fishing/Swimming	Boating	Playground	Other	Telephone Number	Mail Address
	STATE PARKS													
B7	Wm B Umstead	Fr*Raleigh, 12 mi NW on US 70	5231	28	28	3.50	All year		○	r		h	919/787-8915	Rt 8, Bx 130, Raleigh 27612
C8	Cliffs of the Neuse	Fr Goldsboro, 1 mi E on US 70, 13 mi SE on Hwys 111 & 55	604	35	35	3.50	All year	○	○	r			919/778-6234	Rt 2, Bx 50, Seven Spgs 28578
B5	Hanging Rock	Fr Winston-Salem, 32 mi N on Hwy 66	4819	74	74	3.50	All year	○	○	r			919/593-8480	Box 128, Danbury 27016
B5	Pilot Mountain	Fr Winston Salem, 13 miles N on US 52	3802	49	49	3.50	All year					h	919/325-2355	Rt 1, Bx 13, Pinnacle 27043
D7	Jones Lake	Fr Elizabethtown, 4 mi N on Hwy 242	2208	18	18	3.50	All year	○	○	l			919/588-4550	Rt 1,Bx 945,Elizabethtwn 28337
C5	Morrow Mountain	Fr Albemarle, 2-1/2 mi NE on Hwys 24/27, E on access rd	4508	106	106	3.50	All year	○	○	l			704/982-4402	Rt 2, Bx 204, Albemarle
C3	Mount Mitchell	Fr Asheville, 33 mi NE on Blue Ridge Pkwy	1469	7		3.50	4/15-10/15						704/675-4611	R 5 Bx 700, Burnsville 28714
B9	Pettigrew	Fr US 64 in Creswell, 9 mi S	B	13	13	3.50	All year	•		lr			919/797-4475	Rt 1 Bx 336, Creswell 27928
E8	Carolina Beach	Fr Wilmington, 14 mi S on US 421	1770	83	83	3.50	All year	•		l			919/458-8206	Box 475, Carolina Bch 28428
C4	Duke Power	Fr Statesville, 10 mi S on US 21, Co 1303 & 1321	1432	33	33	3.50	All year	•		lr			704/528-6350	R2, Bx 199, Troutman 28166
	STATE RECREATION AREAS													
	Kerr Reservoir												919/438-7791	Rt3 Box 800, Henderson 27536
B7	Bullocksville	Fr Drewry, 2.5 mi W on Co 1366	455	68	68	3.50	4/1-11/1	•	•	l •				Manson
B7	County Line	Fr Drewry, 2-1/2 mi N on Co 1200, 1/2 mi W on Co 1202, 1 mi N on 1361	225	75	75	3.50	4/1-11/1	•	•	l •				Norlina
B7	Henderson Point	Fr Townsville, 2 mi N on Hwy 39, 2-1/2 mi NE on Co 1356, 1 mi E on Co 1359	329	79	79	3.50	4/1-11/1	•	•	l •				Townsville
B7	Hibernia	Fr Townsville, 1 mi NE on Hwy 39, 1-1/2 mi E on Co 1347	446	150	150	4.50	All year	•	•	l •				Townsville
B7	Kimball Point	Fr Drewry, 4 mi N on Co 1200, 1 mi NW on Co 1204	95	100	100	3.50	4/1-11/1	•	•	l •				Norlina
B7	Nutbush Bridge	Fr Henderson, 5 mi N on Hwy 39, 1 mi NE on Co 1308	363	109	109	4.50	All year	•	•	l •		g		Henderson
B7	Satterwhite Point	Fr Henderson, 1 mi N on I-85, 7 mi N on Co 1319	390	115	115	4.50	All year	•	•	dlr		g		Henderson
	NATIONAL PARKS													
	Blue Ridge Parkway	(See Virginia for additional campgrounds)											704/258-2880	700 NWstrn Bnk Bldg,Asheville
B3	Crabtree Meadows	Fr Asheville, 45 mi NE on Pkwy, mi Post 339.5	250	71	22	3.00	5/1-10/31							Little Switzerland
B4	Julian Price	Fr Blowing Rock, 5 mi W on Blue Ridge Pkwy to Mi 297.1	4300	129	68	3.00	All year		•					Blowing Rock
B3	Linville Falls	Fr Marion, 23 mi W on US 221, Mi 316.3	1000	55	20	3.00	All year							Linville Falls, NC 28647
C2	Mt. Pisgah	Fr Asheville, 26 mi SW on Pkwy, Mi 408.6	690	70	70	3.00	5/1-10/31							Canton
B4	Doughton Pk	Nr Laurel Springs, at mi 241.1 on Pkwy	6000	110	26	3.00	5/1-10/31							Laurel Springs
	Cape Hatteras Natl Seash												919/473-2111	Rt 1 Box 675, Manteo 27954
C10	Cape Point	Fr Buxton, S on Hwy 12, 2 mi E on Pk Rd		101	102	4.00	4/1-11/1	•	•					Rt 1, Bx 675 Manteo 27954
C10	Frisco	Fr Buxton, 4 mi W on Hwy 12		65	71	4.00	6/15-LD	•	•					Rt 1, Bx 675 Manteo 27954
C10	Ocracoke Beach	Fr Ocracoke, 3 mi NE, on Ocracoke Is		66	66	2.00	4/1-12/1	•	•					Rt 1, Bx 675 Manteo 27954
C10	Salvo	Fr Nag's Head, 30 mi S on Hwy 12		70	70	4.00	6/15-LD	•	•					Rt 1, Bx 675 Manteo 27954
B10	Oregon Inlet	Fr Nag's Head, 8 mi S on Hwy 12		60	60	4.00	4/1-12/1	•	•					RT 1, Bx 675 Manteo 27954
	Great Smoky Mountains NP	Tennessee)	B										615/436-5615	Supt,Gatlinburg,TN 37738
C2	Balsam Mountain	Fr Soco Gap, 10 mi NE on US 19		46	15	4.00	5/18-10/18							Gatlinburg 37738
C2	Deep Creek	Fr Bryson City, 2 mi N		119	122	4.00	3/16-10/31		•			h		Gatlinburg 37738
C2	Smokemont	Fr Cherokee, 5 mi N on US 441		152	103	4.00	All year		•			h		Gatlinburg 37738
	NATIONAL FORESTS													
	Pisgah NF													
B2	Rocky Bluff	Fr Hot Springs, 3 mi S on Hwy 209	5	31	25	None	4/2-12/15		•	dr		n		Hot Springs
B4	Boone Fork	Fr Lenoir, 7 mi NW on Hwy 90, 4.7 mi NW on Hwy 1368, 2 mi NE on FR 2055.	10	35	31	None	4/1-10/31							Lenoir
B4	Mortimer	Fr Edgemont, 2 mi NW on Hwy 90.	3	16	16	None	All year	•	•					Edgemont
C3	Curtis Creek	Fr Old Fort, 1.7 mi E on US 70, 3 mi N on Hwy 1227, 1.7 mi N on Fr 482.	1	6		None	4/1-10/31		1					Old Fort
B3	Black Mountain	Fr Micaville, 11.9 mi S on Hwy 80, 3 mi SW on FR 472.	10	45	45	2.00	5/2-12/15		•					Micaville
B3	Carolina Hemlock	Fr Micaville, 8.7 mi S on Hwy 80.	6	25	25	2.00	5/27-9/5	•	•			h		Micaville
	Nantahala NF													
D2	East Fork	Fr Highlands, 2.5 mi S on Hwy 28, 1 mi W on Hwy 1618	3	6		None								Highlands
C2	Davidson River	Fr Brevard, 3.4 mi N on US 64, 1.4 mi N on US 276.	86	137	137	4.00	All year	2	•					Brevard
C2	Sunburst	Fr Waynesville, 7 mi E on US 276, 6 mi S on Hwy 215.	2	12	12	None	4/1-12/10		•			n		Waynesville
C2	Lake Powhatan	Fr Asheville, 4 mi SW on Hwy 191, 3.4 mi W on FR 806	30	97	97	3.00	5/1-12/10	•	•					Asheville
C2	North Mills River	Fr Asheville, 13.3 mi S on Hwy 191, 5 mi NW on FR 478.	8	25	25	3.00	5/1-12/10	•	•					Asheville
C2	Standing Indian	Fr Franklin, 13.6 mi SW on US 64, 1.9 mi S on FR 67	22	60	60	3.00	All year	•	•					Franklin
C1	Bob Allison	Fr Hayesville, 8.8 mi NE on Hwy 1307, 4.5 mi N on FR 440	2	12		None	All year		•					Hayesville
C1	Hanging Dog	Fr Murphy, 5 mi NW on Hwy 1326.	21	69	69	2.00	2/1-12/31		•	dlr				Murphy
D1	Jackrabbit Mountain	Fr Hayesville, 6.2 mi E on US 64, 2.5 mi S on Hwy 175, 1.4 mi W on Co 1155.	28	103	103	3.00	5/23-10/31	•	•	dlr		h		Hayesville
C1	Tsali	Fr Bryson City, 9 mi S on US 19, 5.5 mi W on Hwy 28, 1.5 mi N on FR 361.	10	42	42	2.00	5/1-10/31		•	dlr				Bryson City
C1	Horse Cove	Fr Robbinsville, 8 mi NW on US 129, 2.5 mi SW on Hwy 1134, 3.7 mi SW on FR 416.	4	17	17	2.00	All year		•	d				Robbinsville
C1	Cheoah Point	Fr Robbinsville, 7 mi NW on US 129.	10	23	23	2.00	4/15-10/31	1	1	dlr				Robbinsville
D2	Vanhook Glade	Fr Highlands, 4.5 mi NW on US 64.	6	19		2.00	5/1-9/30	1	1			h		Highlands
D2	Cliffside Lake	Fr Highlands, 4.6 mi NW on US 64, 1.3 mi N on FR 57.	5	110	100	2.00	5/1-9/30	•	•			h		Highlands
D9	Cedar Point	Fr Swansboro, 3.3 mi SE on Hwy 24, .8 mi NE on Hwy 58, .5 mi NW on Co 1114, .7 mi SW on FR 153A.	20	43	43	None	All year	5	•	dlr				Swansboro
	Croatan NF													
D9	Neuse River	Fr New Bern, 11.1 mi SE on US 70, 1.5 mi NE on Hwy 1107.	4	22	22	3.00	3/1-10/31	•	•	d				New Bern
	CORPS OF ENGINEERS													
	John H Kerr Proj	See Virginia for additional CG's	B											Rt 1 Box 76, Boydton,Va 23917
A7	Grassy Creek	Fr Oxford, 10 mi NW on US 15 to Bullock, 5 mi NW	17	10	10	None	4/1-10/30			l				Boydton
	W Kerr Scott Res		2000										919/921-3750	PO Box 182, Wilkesboro 28697
B4	Bandits Roost	Fr Wilkesboro, 6 mi SW on Hwy 268, N on access		35	61	3.00	All year	•	•	dlr •		p	919/921-3750	Wilkesboro
B4	Warrior Creek	Fr Wilkesboro, 9 mi SW on Hwy 268, N on Co		39	49	3.00	All year	•	•	dlr •		p	919/921-3750	Wilkesboro
B4	Warrior Creek	Fr Wilkesboro, 11 mi SW on Hwy 268, N on access rd		10	11	3.00	All year	○	•	dl		p	919/921-3750	Wilkesboro 28697

Oxlahoma

See state map, page 39

Major Events

International Finals Rodeo, mid- to late Jan., Tulsa. This rodeo attracts the top 15 international money winners in the following categories: bull riding, saddle-bronc riding, steer wrestling, bareback-bronc riding, team roping, calf roping, and barrel racing. Admission. 405/238-6488.

Waurika Rattlesnake Hunt, early Apr., Waurika. Rattlesnake hunts are conducted, and contests are held for sizes and weights of snakes. A carnival is also part of the festivities. Free. 405/228-2802.

Azalea Festival, mid- to late Apr., Muskogee. Honor Heights Park is the site of thousands of azaleas in bloom. A parade and an art show supplement the tours of the park and the tours of private gardens. Free. 918/682-2401.

Wichita Mountains Easter Sunrise Service, Easter, Lawton. The life of Jesus is retold by hundreds of actors against a background of permanent outdoor granite sets at the Holy City in the Wichita Mountains Wildlife Refuge. Free. 405/429-3361.

'89er Day Celebration, mid- to late Apr., Guthrie. This event celebrates the settlement of the part of Oklahoma once known as the "unassigned lands" which were opened with a land run on April 22, 1889. There is a parade, a rodeo, a carnival, and craft demonstrations. Admission is charged for several events. 405/282-1947.

Cimarron Territory Celebration, late Apr., Beaver. Among the many forms of entertainment at this homesteader festival, the most unusual is the World Championship Cow-Chip Throwing Contest. Other activities include live entertainment, a square dance, a parade, a barbecue, and a rodeo. Admission is free to all events except the rodeo. 405/625-4726.

Oklahoma City Festival of the Arts, late Apr., Oklahoma City. There are outdoor displays of visual arts in all media, live entertainment, and various types of ethnic foods. Free (except food). 405/521-1426.

Kolache Festival, early May, Prague. Kolaches (sweet rolls filled with fruit and other delicacies) are the focus of this event. Thousands are served hot from the ovens. Other activities are a parade, folk dancing, and a display of native Czechoslovakian costumes. Free. 405/567-4077.

Strawberry Festival, early May, Stilwell. This celebration in the state's largest strawberry-producing region features a parade, a berry-judging contest, an auction, and free strawberries and ice cream for everyone. Free. 918/774-7143.

Tulsa International Mayfest '81, mid- to late May, Tulsa. Tulsa's annual four-day arts festival features artwork by many of the finest artists in the South.

There are food booths and workshops where visitors may try their hand at different types of crafts. Free. 918/583-5794.

Italian Festival, late May, McAlester. Italian coal miners settled here in the 1880s, and descendants celebrate their heritage with folk music, dances, native costumes, and Italian food. Free (except food). 918/423-2550.

Santa Fe Trail Daze, early June, Boise City. The Santa Fe Trail used to pass through this panhandle town, and the trail days are remembered with bus tours of the trail, a tug-of-war, a watermelon feed, live music, a square dance, and a rodeo. Free. 405/544-3344.

***Oklahoma!* Outdoor Drama,** early June to mid-Aug., Tulsa. Rogers' and Hammerstein's famous musical *Oklahoma!* is performed daily except Sunday. Admission. 918/587-4481.

***Will Rogers at Home* Outdoor Drama,** mid-June to mid-Aug., Claremore. This drama, a biographical sketch of Oklahoma's most famous native, is presented at the Will Rogers Amphitheatre. Performances are Wed.-Sat. Admission. 918/341-7510.

"Trail of Tears" Art Show, late June to early July, Tahlequah. Paintings, graphics, and sculpture done by artists of American Indian descent are on display at the Cherokee National Museum. Many art pieces depict interpretations of the Trail of Tears march which took place in the 19th century. Admission. 918/456-6007.

Tsa-La-Gi *Trail of Tears* Drama, late June to mid-Aug., Tahlequah. This drama explains the plight of the Cherokee people, who were forced from their native homeland and given land for settlement in northeastern Oklahoma. Performances are daily except Sunday. Admission. 918/456-6007.

Kiamichi Owa Chito Festival of the Forest, late June, Broken Bow. This festival recalls Choctaw Indian heritage and celebrates the culture and industry of this forested region. Native American foods and ceremonies, lumbermen's contests, and an art show are just some of the activities. Free (except food). 405/584-3393.

International Brick- and Rolling Pin-Throwing Competition, early to mid-July, Stroud. This competition is celebrated with a baseball tournament, fireworks display, Sac and Fox Indian Pow-Wow and Rodeo, Miss Stroud Pageant, parade, and sidewalk sales. Admission is charged for several events. 918/968-3321.

Tulsa Pow-Wow, early to mid-July, Tulsa. Local Indians perform various dances and ceremonies, and they display and sell native American arts and crafts. Free. 918/585-1201.

Lawton Rangers Rodeo, early Aug., Lawton. Lawton's birthday is commemorated with a parade and a rodeo featuring bareback- and saddle-bronc riding, bull riding, steer wrestling, calf roping, and barrel racing. Admission. 405/353-6047.

Grant's Bluegrass and Old-Time Music Festival, early Aug., Hugo. There are band and instrument contests for all ages. Top U.S. groups perform, and jam sessions are held throughout the day. Admission. 405/326-5598.

American Indian Exposition, mid-Aug., Anadarko. The National Championship War Dance Contest, pageants, horse racing, a parade, and arts and crafts are some of the activities at this event, which is one of the largest annual gatherings of American Indians in the nation. Admission is charged for several events. 405/247-6652.

Great Raft Race, early Sept., Sand Springs to Tulsa. Hundreds of homemade rafts in all shapes and sizes will challenge a nine-mile course along the Arkansas River. Trophies are awarded for the fastest times in several categories. Free. 918/583-7400.

State Fair of Oklahoma, late Sept. to early Oct., Oklahoma City. The attractions at the State Fairgrounds include rodeos; ice-skating performances; a giant midway; international, cultural, and industrial exhibits; a livestock show; and continuous outdoor stage performances. Admission. 405/942-5511.

Tulsa State Fair, early Oct., Tulsa. Statewide, national, and international exhibits are on display; other attractions are live performances and a giant midway. Admission. 918/744-1113.

Czech Festival, early Oct., Yukon, west of Oklahoma City. This festival features polka bands, native costumes, folk dances, and food booths. Free. 405/354-3567.

Bushyhead World's Richest Roping and Western Art Show, early Oct., Chelsea. Only former world champion ropers, National Finals Rodeo all-round cowboys, or National Finals Rodeo participants are eligible to compete in the World's Richest Roping event. The Western Art Show features an art auction, a barbecue, and other festivities. Admission is charged for several events. 918/789-2408.

Will Rogers Days, early Nov., Claremore. Various events recall the life and times of Oklahoma's most famous native son, who was born 12 miles north of town. Free. 918/341-2818.

National Finals Rodeo, early Dec., Oklahoma City. This is the "Olympics" of rodeo, and only the top 15 Professional Rodeo Cowboys Association money winners compete. Admission. 405/232-6381.

Oklahoma Destinations

ALABASTER CAVERNS STATE PARK, A-4. Daily guided tours take visitors past gleaming selenite crystals and white- and pink-alabaster walls of one of the world's largest gypsum caves. The park, south of U.S. 64 on St. 50, midway between St. 34 and St. 14, also has a 150-foot-high natural bridge. Daily, May-Sept., 9 A.M. to 5 P.M.; other months, 9 A.M. to 4 P.M. Adults $1.50; children 12-15, $1; 6-11, 75¢; persons under 6 and 62 or older, free. 405/621-3381.

ALTUS, 23,101, C-4. When Bitter Creek flooded in 1891 and washed away the little settlement of Frazier, people moved to higher ground and called it Altus. Great herds of longhorn cattle moved through the area in the 1870s and 1880s on the way to Dodge City, Kansas. **The Museum of the Western Prairie,** 1100 N. Hightower St., was designed in the form of the dugouts in which the first settlers lived. It features artifacts of Indians and early white settlers. Year-round, Tues.-Fri., 9 A.M. to 5 P.M.; Sat.-Sun., 2 to 5 P.M. Free. 405/482-1044.

ANADARKO, 6,378, C-5. For many years, Anadarko has been the center of Plains Indian culture in Oklahoma. The Wichita Agency, first Indian agency in western Oklahoma, was opened in 1859. It was occupied by Confederate Indians during the Civil War; and on October 23, 1862, it was attacked and destroyed by northern Indians from Kansas who massacred 100 Tonkowa Indians living nearby. When the Kiowa-Comanche Indian Reservation was opened to white settlement in 1901, Anadarko was named a county seat town. The Anadarko office of the Bureau of Indian Affairs still serves Indians in Oklahoma, Kansas, and Texas. Indian events are held regularly, including the week-long **American Indian Exposition,** second week in August, at Caddo County Fairgrounds. Indians from across the country assemble for ceremonial dances, pageants, and contests, drawing up to 40,000 spectators. Free. 405/247-6673. **Indian City, U.S.A.,** 2½ miles southeast on St. 8, re-creates the life of the Plains Indians through faithfully reproduced Indian villages. Daily, Labor Day-Memorial Day, 9 A.M. to 6 P.M.; other months, 9 A.M. to 5 P.M. Adults $4; persons 6-16, $2; under 6, free. 405/247-5661. **Southern Plains Indian Museum and Crafts Center,** 1 mile east on U.S. 62, exhibits artifacts of the history and culture of the Plains Indians. Early June-late Sept., Mon.-Sat., 9 A.M. to 5 P.M.; Sun., 1 to 5 P.M.; closed Monday other months. Free. 405/247-6221. The **National Hall of Fame for Famous Indians,** an outdoor display of bronze busts of famous Indians, adjoins it. **Anadarko Philomathic Museum,** 311 E. Main St. in the Rock Island depot, features typical rooms in frontier homes and stores. Year-round, daily, 1 to 5 P.M. Free. 405/247-3240.

ARMSTRONG, D-7. *See* **Fort Washita.**

BARTLESVILLE, 34,568, A-7. This oil-rich city had its beginning in a gristmill built on the Caney River in 1870. Five years later, Jacob Bartles bought it and opened a store to trade with the Indians, and the town built up around it. On April 15, 1897, the state's first commercially successful oil well was discovered here. The Nellie Johnstone #1 produced 100,000 barrels of oil before it was shut down in 1957. **Woolaroc Museum,** 14 miles southwest on St. 123, is a game preserve and museum located on the ranch of Frank Phillips, co-founder of Phillips Petroleum Company. Herds of buffalo, elk, and deer roam freely, and guests are warned to stay in their cars until they reach the museum. This is an impressive 300-foot-long sandstone building which houses 55,000 exhibits showing the full scope of Indian culture from prehistory to the present. Paintings by Charles M. Russell, Frederic Remington, and many other western artists are featured. Apr.-Oct., daily, 10 A.M. to 5 P.M.; other months, Tues.-Sun., 10 A.M. to 5 P.M. Free. 918/336-6747. **Frank Phillips Home,** 1107 S.E. Cherokee Ave., is a 26-room mansion built in 1909 in Greek-Revival style, and it has its original furnishings. Year-round, Tues.-Fri., 9 A.M. to 4:20 P.M.; Sat.-Sun., 2 to 5 P.M. Free. 918/336-2491. **Nellie Johnstone #1,** the rig that started it all, is on display in what is now Johnstone Park, 300 N. Cherokee Ave., on the banks of the Caney River, where the town's history began.

BLACK MESA STATE PARK, A-1. In this far western part of the Oklahoma Panhandle, the country is rocky and rugged with sweeping vistas like that of adjoining New Mexico. Looming above it all is the great **Black Mesa,** formed from lava flow from an ancient volcano, and rising to 4,972 feet, highest point in Oklahoma. Petrified wood and dinosaur bones have been found in the area, which was once a robbers' stronghold. The park, 30 miles northwest of Boise City via paved and unpaved roads, surrounds a small lake for boating and fishing. South of the park on private land lie the ruins of old Fort Nichols, established by Kit Carson in 1865 to protect the Sante Fe Trail, on which deep ruts can still be seen. The park has camping and picnic facilities. Year-round. Free. 405/426-2222.

CHEYENNE, 1,207, B-4. On the dark, bitter cold night of November 26, 1868, Gen. George A. Custer and his Seventh Cavalry surrounded the sleeping Cheyenne camp of Chief Black Kettle. At dawn they attacked, killing more than 100 Indians and destroying the village. The site of the battle, known variously as the Battle of Washita and the Black Kettle Massacre, lies near the Washita River, 2 miles west of Cheyenne on St. 47A. A stone monument describing the battle stands on an overlook of the battleground. Free. **Black Kettle Museum,** U.S. 283 and St. 47 in Cheyenne, exhibits artifacts of the Indians, Seventh Cavalry, early white pioneers, and a diorama of the battle. Late Apr.-late Oct., Mon.-

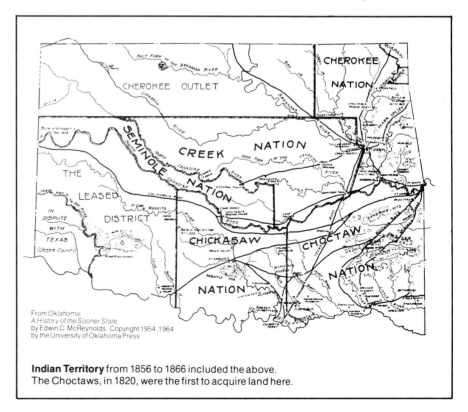

From *Oklahoma:*
A History of the Sooner State,
by Edwin C. McReynolds. Copyright 1954, 1964
by the University of Oklahoma Press

Indian Territory from 1856 to 1866 included the above.
The Choctaws, in 1820, were the first to acquire land here.

Sat., 9 A.M. to 7 P.M.; Sun., 1 to 7 P.M.; other months, closes 5 P.M. Free. 405/497-3929.

CHICKASAW NATIONAL RECREATIONAL AREA, D-6. This combines the former Platt National Park and the Arbuckle Recreational Area in a sylvan setting of trees, streams, wildflowers, fresh and mineral springs, and the Arbuckle Reservoir. **The Travertine Nature Center** has special programs explaining the ecology of the area. Daily, Memorial Day-Labor Day, 8 A.M. to 9 P.M.; other months, 8 A.M. to 5 P.M. Free. 405/622-3165.

CLAREMORE, 12,058, B-7. This early Cherokee settlement was claimed as hometown by humorist Will Rogers and dramatist Lynn Riggs, whose *Green Grow the Lilacs* was made into the musical *Oklahoma!* Actually, Rogers was born between Claremore and Oologah but claimed Claremore, he said, because "nobody but an Indian could pronounce Oologah." **Will Rogers Memorial,** 1 mile west on Will Rogers Blvd., contains many personal belongings of the humorist. His tomb is in the museum's garden. Year-round, daily, 8 A.M. to 5 P.M. Free. 918/341-0719. **Will Rogers Birthplace,** 10 miles northwest on St. 88, is a two-story white house on a hill overlooking Lake Oologah and the Will Rogers State Park. Year-round, daily, 8 A.M. to 5 P.M. Free. 918/275-4201. **Lynn Riggs Memorial,** in the Claremore College Library, exhibits Riggs' original manuscripts, personal belongings, and the surrey with the fringe on top. Open when school is in session, Mon.-Thurs., 8 A.M. to 10 P.M.; Fri., 8 A.M. to 4:30 P.M.; Sat., noon to 5 P.M.; Sun., 2 to 5 P.M. Free. 918/341-7510, ext. 264. **J. M. Davis Gun Museum,** 333 N. Lynn Riggs Blvd., displays collections of 30,000 guns, Indian weapons, and many trophy heads. Year-round, Mon.-Sat., 8:30 A.M. to 5 P.M.; Sun., 1 to 5 P.M. Free. 918/341-5707.

DEWEY, 3,545, A-7. **Tom Mix Museum,** 721 N. Delaware St., displays the early movie cowboy's fancy clothes, boots, saddles, guns, and a replica of his horse Tony wearing a $15,000 sterling silver and hand-tooled leather saddle. Tom Mix was once city marshal of Dewey before he became famous as a movie cowboy. Year-round, Tues.-Fri., 9 A.M. to 5 P.M.; Sat., 1 to 5 P.M.; Sun., 2 to 5 P.M. Free. 918/534-1555.

ENID, 50,363, A-5. Enid was one of the towns that sprang up when the Cherokee Outlet was opened for settlement on September 16, 1893, and 100,000 settlers scrambled for homesteads. **Museum of the Cherokee Strip,** 507 S. 4th St., exhibits belongings of those early settlers. Year-round, Tues.-Fri., 9 A.M. to 5 P.M.; Sat.-Sun., 2 to 5 P.M. Free. 405/237-1907. **Homesteader's Sod House Museum,** 30 miles west on U.S. 60 and 6 miles north on St. 8, is the only original sod house remaining from the thousands that once dotted the prairies. When no timber was available,

homesteaders built temporary homes out of strips of sod. Year-round, Tues.-Fri., 9 A.M. to 5 P.M.; Sat.-Sun., 2 to 5 P.M. Free. 405/463-2441.

FORT GIBSON, 2,483, B-8. Established in 1824, Fort Gibson was the center of military power in the Indian Territory and a base for explorations into the Southwest. Lt. Jefferson Davis was court-martialed here for sassing a superior in 1834 but was acquitted. Sam Houston lived near the fort before going on to Texas and fame. Many Civil War generals were stationed here. The first fort was built of logs near the Grand River, but later it was rebuilt of stones farther up the hill. **Fort Gibson Stockade,** reconstructed in the 1930s, houses a museum of related artifacts. Year-round, Mon.-Sat., 9 A.M. to 5 P.M.; Sun., 1 to 5 P.M. Free. 918/478-2669. **Fort Gibson National Cemetery,** 1 mile north off U.S. 62, contains graves of veterans of every American war and of early Oklahomans. Year-round, daily, 8 A.M. to 5 P.M. 918/478-2334. **Cherokee National Cemetery,** 1½ miles north on U.S. 62, contains the graves of Principal Chief William P. Ross and other Cherokee officials.

FORT WASHITA, between Madill and Armstrong on St. 199, D-6. Ghostly stone ruins beneath gnarled oak trees mark the site of Fort Washita, established in 1842 to protect the Chickasaw Indians from the Plains Indians to the west. Years ago, people believed the old fort actually was haunted, and many claimed to have seen the headless ghost of Aunt Jane, a pioneer woman beheaded by robbers and buried on the post. The old fort has been abandoned for more than a century. It was occupied by Confederate forces during the Civil War. After the war it was not reactivated, but became the home of Confederate Gen. Douglas H. Cooper until his death in 1879. The double log cabin where he lived is still standing. Two old cemeteries and the ruins of more than 40 buildings are on the grounds. Year-round, Tues.-Fri., 9 A.M. to 5 P.M.; Sat.-Sun., 2 to 5 P.M. Free. 405/924-6502.

GROVE, 3,378, A-8. **Har-Ber Village,** 3½ miles west on Lake Rd. 1, re-creates a whole frontier town on the shores of the Lake of the Cherokees. Some 70 buildings are on display; many were moved from other sites, with authentic furnishings. May-Oct., daily, 9 A.M. to 6 P.M. Free. 918/786-5882.

GUTHRIE, 10,312, B-6. Guthrie was once the biggest city in Oklahoma and its territorial and state capital. In 1910, it lost the capital to Oklahoma City and ever since it has been like a city frozen in time. Its population remained unchanged; so there was no need to tear down old buildings and replace them. The downtown resembles a Victorian town, with brick and sandstone

buildings topped by exotic cupolas and towers and turrets. The entire original townsite is listed in the National Register of Historic Places as the nation's only surviving territorial capital. Tom Mix, Lon Chaney, and Carry Nation lived here. It came to dominance in a single day during the land run of April 22, 1889, and now it is a relic of that past. **Oklahoma Territorial Museum,** 402 E. Oklahoma Ave., exhibits many household, farm, and personal items of the '89ers. Brochures for a walking tour and a driving tour of the town are available. Year-round, Tues.-Fri., 9 A.M. to 5 P.M.; Sat.-Sun., noon to 4:30 P.M. Free. 405/282-1889. **State Capital Publishing Museum,** Oklahoma Ave. and 2nd St., displays cases of hand-set type and printing equipment used in territorial days. A new museum, it is located in the office of the first daily newspaper in Oklahoma. Year-round, Tues.-Fri., 9 A.M. to 5 P.M.; Sat.-Sun., 2 to 5 P.M. Free. 405/282-4123.

HEAVENER, 2,776, C-8. **Heavener Runestone,** 1 mile east, is a huge sandstone slab bearing runic letters originally believed to have been carved by Viking explorers. It is high on wooded Poteau Mountain in *Heavener Runestone State Park*. Daily, late Apr.-late Oct., 8 A.M. to 8 P.M.; other months, 8 A.M. to 5 P.M. Free. 918/653-2241. **Peter Conser House,** 7 miles southwest off U.S. 59, was built in 1894 by the leader of the Choctaw Lighthorsemen, an early Indian law enforcement group. The two-story frame house has original furnishings showing how Indian officials lived just before statehood. Year-round, Tues.-Fri., 9 A.M. to 5 P.M.; Sat.-Sun., 2 to 5 P.M. Free. 918/653-2943.

KINGFISHER, 4,245, B-5. King Fisher ran a state station here on the Chisholm Trail in the early 1870s. It was one of the instant towns formed during the land run of April 22, 1889. Abraham J. Seay, second governor of the Oklahoma Territory, lived here in a mansion with a unique circular tower, which has been restored as a museum. **Chisholm Trail Museum,** close by at 605 Zellers Ave., has displays of frontier life and a restored frontier town. Mansion and museum: Late Apr.-late Oct., Mon.-Sat., 9 A.M. to 7 P.M.; Sun., 1 to 7 P.M.; other months, closes 5 P.M. Free. 405/375-5176.

LAWTON, 80,054, C-5. For centuries the country around the rugged Wichita Mountains northwest of Lawton has been the homeland of Plains Indians. **Fort Sill** was established in 1869 as a cavalry post during a campaign against hostile tribes, and the defeated tribesmen were taken there. Lawton, now the third largest city in Oklahoma, was founded on August 6, 1901, when the Kiowa-Comanche Indian Reservation was opened to white settlement. Since 1911, the fort has been the home of the U.S. Field Artillery Center and School. Most of the original stone buildings are still standing, and seven of them make up the *U.S. Army Field Artillery and Fort Sill Museum*. Among them are the guardhouse where Geronimo and other famous Indian chiefs were imprisoned, and McLain and Hamilton Halls, where weapons, uniforms, and equipment from early colonial days through the Vietnam War are displayed. On *Cannon Walk* around the buildings are weapons ranging from primitive cannons to 85-ton Atomic Annie, which fired the first atomic artillery round in 1957. Entrance to the old post is through the Key Gate, 4 miles north on U.S. 62. Year-round, daily, 9 A.M. to 4:30 P.M. Free. 405/351-5123. **Wichita Mountains Wildlife Refuge**, 13 miles west on U.S. 62 and 3 miles north on St. 115, has herds of buffalo, elk, deer, and longhorn cattle, along with lakes, scenic drives, and hiking trails. A road to the top of *Mt. Scott* gives a wide panoramic view. Visitors Center: Year-round, Sat.-Sun., noon to 5 P.M. Free. 405/429-3222. **Museum of the Great Plains**, 601 Ferris Blvd., has displays about buffalo hunters, fur traders, cowboys, law officers, and Plains Indians. Year-round, Mon.-Fri., 8 A.M. to 5 P.M.; Sat., 10 A.M. to 5:30 P.M.; Sun., 1:30 to 5:30 P.M. Free. 405/353-5675.

MADILL, D-6. *See* **Fort Washita.**

MUSKOGEE, 40,011, B-7. An early Creek Indian settlement, Muskogee was chosen in 1874 as site of the Union Agency supervising affairs of the Five Civilized Tribes. The **Five Civilized Tribes Museum,** Agency Hill above Honor Heights Park, focuses on the history and culture of the tribes. Year-round, Mon.-Sat., 10 A.M. to 5 P.M.; Sun., 1 to 5 P.M. Adults 50¢; persons 6-16, 25¢; under 6, free. 918/683-1701. The museum has lakes, lily pools, and flower gardens, and in mid-April it is a blaze of red, purple, pink, and white from 22,000 azalea plants. **Ataloa Lodge,** on the Bacone College campus, Shawnee Ave. and St. 16, has displays of Indian jewelry, pottery, clothes, and toys. School year, Mon.-Fri., 10 A.M. to noon, 1 to 4 P.M. Free. 918/683-4581. **Antiques, Inc., Car Museum,** 2215 W. Shawnee Ave., has a collection of 70 classic antique cars, including Rolls Royces. Year-round, daily, 10 A.M. to 5 P.M. Adults $3.50; persons 6-16, $2; under 6, free. 918/687-4447. **U.S.S.** *Batfish*, a World War II submarine, is permanently moored at **War Memorial Park,** 4 miles north on the Muskogee Turnpike. Mid-Mar.-late Sept.,

Mon.-Sat., 9 A.M. to 6 P.M.; Sun., noon to 6 P.M. Adults $1.50; persons 6-16, 75¢; under 6, free. 918/687-4447.

NORMAN, 68,020, C-6. Like Oklahoma City and Guthrie, Norman was founded on April 22, 1889, in the great Oklahoma land run. **Stovall Museum,** University of Oklahoma, 1335 Asp Ave., has displays of mounted animals and birds in their natural habitats and exhibits of fossils dug mostly in Oklahoma. Year-round, Mon.-Fri., 9 A.M. to 5 P.M.; Sat.-Sun., 1 to 5 P.M. Free. 405/325-4711. **Museum of Art,** University of Oklahoma, 410 W. Boyd St., has permanent collections of American, European, and Oriental art, and changing exhibits in many media. Year-round, Tues.-Fri., 10 A.M. to 4 P.M.; Sat., 10 A.M. to 1 P.M.; Sun., 1 to 4 P.M. Free. 405/325-3272.

OKLAHOMA CITY, 403,213, B-6. On the morning of April 22, 1889, Oklahoma City was only a Sante Fe station and several small houses. That afternoon, settlers in the great land run increased the population to 10,000 people, and the town was on its way toward being the largest city in Oklahoma. Guthrie, the territorial capital, was the largest city for awhile; but by 1900,

Oklahoma City had overtaken it and in the election of 1910 won the capital for itself. First, it became a railway and trade center, then an oil center. In 1928, oil was discovered under the city, and a forest of oil rigs suddenly appeared in backyards. Many of them are still working, spread out across the city and even onto the State Capitol grounds. The city's downtown is now under reconstruction as old areas are replaced with the new, such as the Myriad Gardens and the Retail Galleria.

GOVERNMENT BUILDINGS: State Capitol, Lincoln Dr. at N.E. 23rd St., was completed in 1917 of Indiana limestone with Greco-Roman columns and a base of pink-and-black granite. The floors are of Alabama marble and the stairs of Vermont marble. At the top of the grand stairway are murals and portraits of famous Oklahomans painted by Charles Banks Wilson. Tours: Year-round, daily, 8 A.M. to 3:30 P.M. at the Visitors Center on the first floor. Free. 405/521-3356. **Governor's Mansion,** 820 N.E. 23rd St. just east of the Capitol, is a 19-room, Indiana limestone house built in 1928. Open house, year-round, Wed., 1 to 3 P.M. Free. 405/521-3356. **Wiley Post Historical Building,** 2100 Lincoln Blvd. opposite the Capitol, houses the Oklahoma Historical Society and its huge collections pertaining to all periods of the state's history. Many of the state's museums, monuments, and historic homes are under its management. Year-round, Mon.-Sat., 9 A.M. to 5 P.M. Free. 405/521-2491.

MUSEUMS AND ART CENTERS: National Cowboy Hall of Fame and Western Heritage Center, 1700 N.E. 63rd St., presents a composite picture of the Old West through famous paintings and sculptures and historical exhibits. It was opened in 1967 with an initial $5 million raised in 17 western states. Daily, Memorial Day-Labor Day, 8:30 A.M. to 6 P.M.; other months, 9:30 A.M. to 5:30 P.M. Adults $3; children 6-12, $1; under 6, free. 405/478-2250. **Kirkpatrick Center,** 2100 N.E. 52nd St., has galleries of African, American Indian, and Japanese art. It also houses the Kirkpatrick Planetarium, the Omniplex Science Museum, and the Air-Space Museum. Center: Year-round, Mon.-Sat., 10 A.M. to 5 P.M.; Sun., noon to 5 P.M. Free. 405/427-5461. **Omniplex** and **Planetarium:** Year-round, Mon.-Sat., 10 A.M. to 5 P.M.; Sun., noon to 5 P.M. Adults $2.50; children under 13, $1.25. 405/424-5545. **Air-Space Museum:** Year-round, Tues.-Fri., 10 A.M. to 4:30 P.M.; Sat.-Sun., 1 to 5 P.M. Adults $1; students 50¢; under 5, free. 405/424-1443. **Oklahoma Museum of Art,** 7316 Nichols Rd., has permanent collections of early and contemporary European, American, and Oriental art displayed in the mansion of early-day oilman Frank Buttram. Year-round, Tues.-Sat., 10 A.M. to 5 P.M.; Sun., 1 to 5 P.M. Adults $1, children free. 405/840-2759. **Oklahoma Art Center,** 3113 Pershing Blvd. in State Fair Park, has changing exhibits of contemporary art and

a sales and rental gallery. Year-round, Tues.-Sat., 10 A.M. to 5 P.M.; Sun., 1 to 5 P.M. Adults $1.50; under 18, free. 405/946-4477. **Oklahoma Heritage Center,** 201 N.W. 14th St., has formal gardens, period furniture, and American and European paintings in the 1920 mansion of Judge R. A. Hefner. Year-round, Mon.-Sat., 9 A.M. to 5 P.M.; Sun., 1 to 5 P.M. Adults $2; children 6-12, $1.50; under 6, free. 405/235-4458. **Oklahoma Firefighters Museum,** 2716 N.E. 50th St., displays collections of antique fire-fighting equipment dating back to the mid-1700s. Year-round, daily, 10 A.M. to 5 P.M. Adults $1; children under 12, 50¢. 405/424-3440. **45th Infantry Division Museum,** 2145 N.E. 36th St., has exhibits showing the history of the state militia from territorial days to the present. Memorial Day-Labor Day, Mon.-Sat., 9 A.M. to 6 P.M.; other months, Tues.-Sat., 9 A.M. to 5 P.M.; Sun., 1 to 5 P.M. Free. 405/424-5313. **National Softball Hall of Fame and Museum,** 2801 N.E. 50th St., depicts the sport's history. Apr.-Oct., Mon.-Fri., 9 A.M. to 4:30 P.M.; Sat.-Sun., 10 A.M. to 4 P.M.; other months, closed Sat.-Sun. Adults $1, children 50¢. 405/424-5266.

PARKS: Martin Park Nature Center, 5000 W. Memorial Rd., has a nature trail, a lake, and a nature center. Daily, May-Oct., 8 A.M. to 8 P.M.; other months, 9 A.M. to 6 P.M. Free. 405/755-0676. **Will Rogers Tennis Center,** N.W. 35th St. and Portland Ave., has a tropical plant conservatory and an exhibition building for periodic garden shows. It has 24 tennis courts, a playground, and picnic areas. **Earlywine Park,** S.W. 119th St. and May Ave., is another tennis center. City golf courses are at **Lincoln Park,** 4001 N.E. Grand Blvd.; **Lake Hefner,** N.W. Highway and Meridan Ave.; **Trosper,** 2301 S.E. 29th St.; **Eastern,** N.E. 4th St. and Eastern Ave.; and **Earlywine.** Boating and fishing permits are available at city ranger stations on Lakes Hefner, Draper, and Overholser. Golf courses: 405/691-1727. Tennis courts: 405/691-5430.

SHOPPING: The Crossroads, Int. 35 and Int. 240, is an enclosed air-conditioned mall with over 100 stores and 1.5 million square feet of shopping space. **Metro Concourse,** a 12-block downtown tunnel system, is carpeted, brightly lighted and decorated, and lined with restaurants and small shops.

ZOO: Oklahoma City Zoo, 2101 N.E. 52nd St., covers 500 acres and has 436 species of animals, birds, and reptiles, many in cageless, native-habitat displays. There are train rides, paddle-wheel steamboat rides, and a children's zoo. May-Aug., Mon.-Fri., 9 A.M. to 6 P.M.; Sat.-Sun., 9 A.M. to 7 P.M.; other months, daily, 9 A.M. to 5 P.M. Adults $2; children 3-11, $1; under 3, free. 405/424-3343.

OKMULGEE, 16,263, B-7. This was the capital of the Creek Indian Nation before statehood. **Creek Nation Council House and Museum,** 6th St. and Grand Ave., was

The **American Cowboy** is real, historical, and fictional. Even though the open range on which he trailed cattle has almost disappeared, cowboys still ride in roundups and rodeos. And in Oklahoma City, the National Cowboy Hall of Fame and Western Heritage Center honors over 300 cowboys. Over 250 are honored as great westerners, 20 as great western performers, and 60 as rodeo performers.

the two-story sandstone building which replaced the first capitol, a log structure. It has displays of Indian tools, weapons, clothing, arts, and crafts. Two rooms are filled with household goods of a typical Creek home of 1885. Year-round, Tues.-Sat., 9 A.M. to 5 P.M. Free. 918/756-2324.

PAWHUSKA, 4,771, A-7. After the Civil War, the Osage Indians agreed to give up their land in Kansas and take land in Oklahoma (then known as Indian Territory). Pawhuska, seat of Osage County today, was once the tribal capital. Oil was struck in 1895; and between 1905 and 1945, more than $300 million in oil royalty was divided among the 2,229 original allottees on the tribal rolls. Tribunal business is still handled at the Osage Agency on Agency Hill, north of town. **Osage Tribal Museum,** on the agency campus, exhibits Osage treaties, costumes, arts, and crafts in a sandstone building erected in 1938. Year-round, Mon.-Fri., 8 A.M. to 4:30 P.M. Free. 918/287-2414.

Osage County Historical Society Museum, 700 N. Lynn Ave., exhibits belongings of the Indian and white pioneers. It is in the old Sante Fe Depot. Year-round, daily, 9 A.M. to 5 P.M. Free. 918/287-9924.

PAWNEE, 1,688, B-6. Once an Indian trading post, Pawnee was the home of Maj. Gordon W. Lillie, known as Pawnee Bill, whose Wild West Circus toured widely in the United States and Europe about the turn of the century. **Pawnee Bill's Museum**, 1 mile west on U.S. 64, is housed in the 14-room brick home he built in 1910. It contains the original furnishings and his personal effects and mementos from the show. On the ranch are herds of buffalo and longhorn cattle. Late Apr.-late Oct., Mon.-Sat., 9 A.M. to 7 P.M.; Sun., 1 to 7 P.M.; other months, Mon.-Sat., 9 A.M. to 5 P.M.; Sun., 1 to 5 P.M. Free. 918/762-2513.

PONCA CITY, 26,238, A-6. Water and oil were the founding genius of Ponca City. A running spring drew some 3,000 settlers during the opening of the Cherokee Outlet on September 16, 1893. Then oil discoveries in the 1920s made it a boom town. Oilman E. W. Marland, its most famous citizen, was elected governor of Oklahoma in 1934. His Marland Oil Co. later became Continental Oil Co., which operates a refinery here. Marland was responsible for the city's main tourist attractions. Two museums are in his former homes, and he commissioned the famous *Pioneer Woman* statue. **Pioneer Woman Museum**, 701 Monument Rd., preserves artifacts of the frontier days. Late Apr.-late Oct., Mon.-Sat., 9 A.M. to 7 P.M.; Sun., 1 to 7 P.M.; other months, Mon.-Sat., 9 A.M. to 5 P.M.; Sun., 1 to 5 P.M. Free. 405/765-6108. The 17-foot-tall bronze *Pioneer Woman* is set in a rose garden and may be seen at any time. **Marland Estate**, 901 Monument Rd., consists of the Florentine Renaissance mansion and 30-acre estate of Marland. Daily, June-late Aug., 10 A.M. to 4 P.M.; other months, noon to 4 P.M. Adults $3; children 6-18, $1.50; persons under 6, free. 405/765-2422. **Ponca City Cultural Center**, 1000 E. Grand Ave., displays period furnishings and Indian artifacts in an earlier home of Governor Marland. Year-round, Mon., Wed.-Sat., 10 A.M. to 5 P.M.; Sun., 1 to 5 P.M. Free; non-residents $1. 405/762-6123.

SALLISAW, 6,403, B-8. **Sequoyah's Log Cabin**, 11 miles northeast on St. 101, stands as a monument to that American Indian genius. The Cherokee Indians had no written language; and Sequoyah, while living in Georgia, set out to invent one, reducing the spoken language to 86 consonant and vowel sounds and giving a character for each. His alphabet was so simple that most of his tribe learned to read and write in a few months in 1821. The only tribe with a written language, the Cherokees quickly became the most advanced of the Five Civilized Tribes, starting their own schools, newspaper, and a democratic government. Sequoyah built the cabin in 1829. On the

grounds, the **Indian Contemporary Arts Building** displays Cherokee arts and crafts. Year-round, Tues.-Fri., 9 A.M. to 5 P.M.; Sat.-Sun., 2 to 5 P.M. Free. 918/775-2413. **Dwight Mission**, 8 miles northwest, was established in 1829 to teach the Cherokee Indians, and did so for more than a century. It is now a Presbyterian retreat with a small museum. Grounds: Always open. Buildings: By appointment. 918/775-2144.

TAHLEQUAH, 9,708, B-8. The flavor of the old Cherokee Indian Nation remains strong in Tahlequah, the Cherokee capital before statehood. A number of buildings still stand from the days when the Cherokees governed themselves. Among them are the **Capitol Building**, dating from 1869, on the public square at Muskogee Ave. and Keetohaw St., and the nearby **Supreme Court Building**, built in 1844. **Seminary Hall**, on the Northeastern State University campus, impressively Victorian, was once the Cherokee Female Seminary, completed in 1888. The **George Murrell Home**, built in 1844 in Park Hill, 4 miles southeast off U.S. 82, is open for display with many original furnishings. Late Apr.-late Oct., Mon.-Sat., 9 A.M. to 7 P.M.; Sun., 1 to 7 P.M.; other months, Mon.-Sat., 9 A.M. to 5 P.M.; Sun., 1 to 5 P.M. Free. 918/456-2751. **Tsa-La-Gi**, the Cherokee Heritage Center, 3½ miles south off St. 82, is made up of two reconstructed villages, a museum, and an outdoor drama staged by the Cherokees. *Ancient Village*, at Tsa-La-Gi, is a reconstructed village peopled by Cherokees who enact typical Cherokee life about 1700. Early May-late Aug., Tues.-Sat., 10 A.M. to 5 P.M.; Sun., 1 to 5 P.M.; late Aug.-Labor Day, Sat.-Sun., 1 to 5 P.M. Adults $2.50; children under 16, 50¢. 918/456-6007. *Cherokee National Museum and Rural Village* shows the full range of Cherokee history, including a rural village of 1875-90 when the Cherokees lived much as white settlers did. Mid-June-late Aug., Mon.-Sat., 10 A.M. to 8 P.M.; Sun., 1 to 6 P.M.; other months, Tues.-Sat., 10 A.M. to 5 P.M.; Sun., 1 to 5 P.M. Adults $1; children under 16, 50¢. The *Theatre at Tsa-La-Gi* stages the musical drama, *Trail of Tears*, depicting Cherokee life from the forced removal to Indian Territory until statehood in 1907. Late June-late Aug., Mon.-Sat., 8:30 P.M. Adults $7 and $6.50; persons under 16, half price. Tsa-La-Gi Cherokee Heritage Center: 918/456-6007.

TALIHINA, 1,387, C-8. **Talimena Skyline Drive** extends east, from Talihina to Mena, Ark., on St. 1 in Oklahoma and St. 88 in Arkansas, and crosses the heavily wooded Winding Stair Mountains through the Ouachita National Forest. Bordering the drive are some 30 miles of hiking and backpacking trails.

TULSA, 360,919, B-7. Tulsa, second largest city in Oklahoma and known as the "Oil Capital of the World," got its start as a typical western cow town in the Creek Indian Nation. In 1882, the Atlantic and Pacific

Railway built a terminus at Tulsa, a post office in a ranch house near the Arkansas River. Great herds of Texas cattle were driven here for shipment to St. Louis and Chicago. The first of several rich oil strikes was made in 1901, and Tulsa became home base for the oilmen. Today, the city has more than 800 oil-related industries and tall downtown buildings bearing oil names. In 1971, the $1.2 billion Arkansas River Navigation System was completed, joining Tulsa's Port of Catoosa to the Mississippi River and the Great Lakes and Gulf of Mexico. A downtown landmark is the **Williams Center**, an urban renewal project with an office tower, a hotel, and an enclosed mall with ice skating rink, cinema, restaurants, and shops. Between the Center and the Civic Center, where government buildings are clustered, is a pedestrian mall with fountains, benches, and greenery. Near Williams Center is the **Tulsa Performing Arts Center**, with three theatres and a 2,400-seat music hall. 918/585-1111.

MUSEUMS AND ART CENTERS: Thomas Gilcrease Institute of American History and Art, 2500 W. Newton St., contains more than 5,000 artworks, 300,000 Indian artifacts, and 70,000 books and documents on Western Americana. It has the world's largest collection of works by Frederic Remington, Charles M. Russell, and Thomas Moran. The institute was built around the private collections of oilman Thomas Gilcrease. Year-round, Mon.-Sat., 9 A.M. to 5 P.M.; Sun., 1 to 5 P.M. Free. 918/581-5311. **Philbrook Art Center**, 2727 Rockford Rd., is housed in the Italian Renaissance villa built by oilman Waite Phillips in 1926. It contains a Samuel H. Kress collection of Italian Renaissance paintings and sculp-

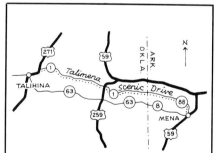

Talimena Scenic Drive got its name from its terminal points, Talihina, Oklahoma, and Mena, Arkansas, and its unusual scenery. This 55-mile route from Talihina on St. 1 in Oklahoma to Mena on St. 88 in Arkansas winds across the crests of Rich and Winding Stair mountains in the Ouachita (Wash-ee-taw) National Forest and Mountains. The fall colors along the drive are at their peak during mid-October and early November. The trees include oak, gum, maple, sycamore, dogwood, and persimmon. And at the pinnacle of Rich Mountain is Queen Wilhemina State Park, overlooking the mountains and valleys.

ture, the George H. Tabor collection of Chinese jades, and major collections of American Indian art. Year-round, Tues.-Sat., 10 A.M. to 5 P.M.; Sun., 1 to 5 P.M. Adults $2; college students and persons 65 and over, $1; children and high school students, free. 918/749-7941. **Tulsa Historical Society Museum,** 831 S. Gary Pl., displays furniture, tools, and household goods of early Oklahomans. Year-round, Wed., Fri., 11 A.M. to 4 P.M.; other days, by appointment. Free. 918/592-2595. **Rebecca and Gershon Fenster Gallery of Jewish Art,** 1719 Owasso Ave., contains Jewish art and ritual objects from 5000 B.C. to the present in B'Nai Emunah Synagogue. Mid-Oct.-late May, Sun., 2 to 4 P.M. Free. 918/583-7121.

PARKS AND ZOO: Mohawk Park, 5701 E. 36th St. N., is 2,800 acres of scenic drives, picnic grounds, a lake for fishing and boating, two 18-hole golf courses, and the *Tulsa Zoological Park*. This contains a main zoo of more than 600 animals, a children's zoo, and the *Robert J. LaFortune North American Living Museum*. Daily, mid-May-Sept., 10 A.M. to 6:30 P.M.; other months, 10 A.M.

to 5:30 P.M. Adults $2; persons 6-12 and over 65, $1; under 6, free. 918/835-8471. **River Park** along the Arkansas River in Tulsa has picnic and playgrounds; a 5-mile lighted, hard-surfaced jogging and bicycle trail; and a pedestrian bridge across the river. **Woodward Park,** at Peoria Ave. and 23rd St., has a garden center, a conservatory, extensive dogwood and azalea growth, and a rose garden that has won national awards. **Swan Park,** 17th Pl. and Utica Ave., is a residential park with a lake filled with swans, geese, and ducks. City parks: 918/581-5401.

SHOPPING: Woodland Hills Mall, 7021 S. Memorial Dr., has 100 stores in an enclosed air-conditioned mall. **Southroads Mall,** 4945 E. 41st St., has 69 stores in an enclosed mall.

WEWOKA, 5,408, C-7. The old pecan tree on the courthouse lawn, 204 S. Wewoka Ave., was the whipping tree where offenders were punished when Wewoka was capital of the Seminole Nation. In the 1920s it was an oil-boom town. **Seminole Nation Museum,** 524 S. Wewoka Ave., has displays

of Seminole life in Florida, their forced removal to the Indian Territory, and the life of area pioneers. Feb.-Dec., daily, 1 to 5 P.M. Free. 405/257-5580.

Information Sources

Oklahoma Tourism and Recreation Department Division of Marketing Services 500 Will Rogers Building Oklahoma City, OK 73105 405/521-2406

Oklahoma Department of Wildlife Conservation 1801 N. Lincoln Blvd. Oklahoma City, OK 73105 405/521-2221 or 405/521-3855

Claremore Area Chamber of Commerce 419 W. Will Rogers Blvd. Claremore, OK 74017 918/341-2821

Lawton Chamber of Commerce P.O. Box 1367 Lawton, OK 73501 405/355-3541

Oklahoma City Visitor Information Center State Capitol Building Oklahoma City, OK 73105 405/521-3356

Oklahoma City Convention & Tourism Center 4 Santa Fe Plaza Oklahoma City, OK 73102 405/232-2211

Stillwater Chamber of Commerce P.O. Box 112 502 S. Main St. Stillwater, OK 74074 405/372-5573

Metro Tulsa Chamber of Commerce 616 S. Boston Ave. Tulsa, OK 74119 918/585-1201

Oklahoma Campgrounds

FEES REFLECT MINIMUM RATE FOR 2 ADULTS AND ARE SUBJECT TO INCREASE OR SEASONAL CHANGES

- • – at the campground
- ○ – within one mile of campground
- $ – extra charge
- ** – limited facilities during winter months
- A – adults only
- B – 10,000 acres or more
- C – contribution

- E – tents rented
- F – entrance fee or premit required
- N – no specific number, limited by size of area only
- P – primitive
- R – reservation required
- S – self-contained units only

- U – unlimited
- V – trailers rented
- Z – reservations accepted
- LD – Labor Day
- MD – Memorial Day
- UC – under construction
- d – boat dock

- g – public golf course within 5 miles
- h – horseback riding
- j – whitewater running craft only
- k – snow skiing within 25 miles
- l – boat launch
- m – area north of map
- n – no drinking water

- p – motor bikes prohibited
- r – boat rental
- s – stream, lake or creek water only
- t – tennis
- u – snowmobile trails
- w – open certain off-season weekends
- y – drinking water must be boiled

Map Reference	Park Name	Access	Acres	Tent Spaces	Trailer Spaces	Approximate Fee	Season	Swimming Pool	Other Swimming	Fishing	Boating	Playground	Other	Telephone Number	Mail Address
	STATE PARKS														
D6	Lake Texoma	Fr Kingston, 5 mi E on US 70	1882	218	174	6.50	All year	•	•	•	lr		ght	405/564-2566	Kingston 73439
C4	Quartz Mtn (Lake Altus)	Fr Lone Wolf, 7 mi S on Hwy 44	4284	75	71	6.50	All year	•	•	•	dl		gt	405/563-2238	Rt 1,Box 21,Lone Wolf 73655
B5	Roman Nose	Fr Watonga, 7 mi NW on Hwy 8 & 8A	515	25	34	4.50	All year	•		•	l		ght	405/623-4215	P.O. Box 227, Watonga 73772
D6	Lake Murray	Fr Ardmore, 7 mi S on I-35, 2 mi E on Hwy 77S	B	100	235	6.50	All year	•	•	•	lr		ght	405/223-4044	Ardmore 12496
B8	Sequoyah	Fr Wagoner, 6 mi E on Hwy 51	2876	321	252	5.00	All year	•	•	•	dlr		ght	918/772-2046	Rt 3 Box 112, Hulbert 74441
D8	Beavers Bend-3 areas	Fr Broken Bow, 7 mi N on Hwy 259, E on 259A	3482	58	92	5.50	All year	•		•	•			405/494-6538	P.O. Box 10,Broken Bow 74728
A7	Osage Hills	Fr Bartlesville, 11 mi W on US 60, 2 mi S on Hwy 35	1199	25	34	3.50	All year	•		•	l			918/336-4141	Pawhuska 74057
C5	Red Rock Canyon	Fr Hinton, 1/2 mi S on US 281	310	25	44	4.50	All year	•						405/542-6344	Box 502,Hinton 73047
A4	Boiling Springs	Fr Woodward, 3 mi N on Hwy 34, 5 mi E on Hwy 34C	790	35	50	6.50	All year	•						405/256-7664	Box 965, Woodward 73801
B8	Greenleaf Lake	Fr Braggs, 3 mi S on Hwy 10	565	25	66	6.50	All year	•	•	•	dlr			918/487-5196	Rt 1, Bx 119, Braggs 74423
B8	Lake Tenkiller	Fr Gore, 9 mi N on Hwy 100	1188	25	125	6.50	All year		•	•	dlr			918/489-5643	Star Rt, Box 169 Vian 74962
C8	Lake Wister	Fr Poteau, 9 mi SW on US 270	3040	50	65	4.00	All year		•	•	lr			918/655-7212	Rt 2, Bx 6B,Wister 74966
C8	Robber's Cave	Fr Wilburton, 5 mi N on Hwy 2	8246	75	50	5.50	All year	•	•	•	l			918/465-2565	Bx 9, Wilburton 74578
A7	Wah-Sha-She	Fr Hulah, 4 mi W on US 10	266	30	26	3.50	All year			•	l			918/532-4627	Rt 1, Box 161, Copan 74022
A5	Great Salt Plains	Fr Jet, N on Hwy 38	840	50	61	5.50	All year		•	•	l			405/626-4731	Rt 1, Jet 73749
A4	Alabaster Caverns	Fr Freedom, 6 mi S on Hwy 50, 1 mi E on Hwy 50A	200	15	10	3.50	All year							405/621-3381	Freedom 73842
A1	Black Mesa	Fr Boise City, 22 mi NW on paved rd, 8 mi W on gravel rd	349	20	20	3.50	All year			•	l			405/426-2222	Kenton 73946
C7	Arrowhead	Fr McAlester, US 69, 15 mi N	2459	186	60	6.50	All year	•	•	•	dl		ght	918/339-2204	PO Bx 57, Canadian 74425
C7	Fountainhead	Fr Checotah, 9 mi S on US 69, W on Hwy 150	3401	275	89	6.50	All year	•	•	•	dlr		ght	918/689-5311	Bx 185,W Str Rt,Checotah 74426
B7	Keystone	Fr Tulsa, 16 mi W on Hwy 51, 1/2 mi N on Hwy 151	715	50	53	5.50	All year		•	•	dl			918/865-4477	Box 147, Mannford 74044
B7	Walnut Cr Pk	Between Tulsa and Cleveland on N.Loop Hwy off Hwy 99	1429	25	78	5.50	All year		•	•	l			918/242-3362	Bx 112, Prue 74060
C6	Little River	Fr Norman, 12 mi E on Hwy 9	1834	100	192	5.50	All year		•	•	dlr	h		405/364-7634	Rt 4, Box 227 Norman 73071
C4	Great Plains	Fr Snyder, 6 mi N on US 183	487	25	18	4.50	All year		•	•	dl				Rt 1, Box 50A, Mt Pk 73559
A3	Beaver	Fr Beaver, 1 mi N on US 270	370	10	7	4.50	All year							405/625-3373	PO Box 1190, Beaver 73932
C8	Talimena	Fr Talihina, 7-1/2 mi E on Hwy 1	20	20	6	3.00	All year							918/567-2052	Bx 318, Talihina 74571
C5	Fort Cobb	Fr Fort Cobb, 4 mi NW on Hwy 9	4070	50	211	5.50	All year		•	•	lr		g	405/643-2249	Bx 297, Ft Cobb 73038
B4	Foss Reservoir	Fr Clinton, 14 mi NW on Hwy 73	1749	35	57	5.50	All year		•	•	dlr			405/592-3171	Rt 1, Bx 59C, Foss 73647
D8	Hochatown State Pk	Fr Broken Bow, 12 mi N on Hwy 259, 3 mi E	1713	25	46	4.50	All year		•	•	dlr		g	405/494-6452	PO Box 218, Broken Bow 74728
	STATE RECREATION AREAS														
B8	Cherokee Landing	Fr Tahlequah, 10 mi SE on Hwy 82	20	51	31	3.50	All year		•	•	l			918/457-5716	PO Box 186, Park Hill 74451
B7	Feyodi Creek	Fr Cleveland, 2 mi SE on US 64	140	25	18	4.50	All year		•	•	l			918/358-2844	Box 258, Cleveland 74020
D7	Boggy Depot	Fr Atoka, 8 mi W on Hwy 7, 3-1/2 mi S	229	100	12	4.50	All year							405/937-4606	Bx 116, Atoka 74525
D8	Raymond Gary	Fr Hugo, 16 mi E on US 70, S on Hwy 209	46	100	5	4.50	All year			•	l			405/873-2307	Rt 2, Ft Towson 74735
B8	Sequoyah Bay	Fr Okay, 1 mi E on Hwy 16, 4 mi NE on blcktp rd	303	50	32	5.50	All year		•	•	dlr			918/683-0878	Rt 2, Wagoner 74467
A8	Spavinaw	S of Spavinaw	35	25	24	3.50	All year			•	l			918/435-8066	Box 220, Disney 74340
C8	Clayton Lake	Fr Clayton, 6 mi S on US 271	595	15	59	4.00	All year			•	lr			918/569-7981	Clayton 74536
A8	Twin Bridges	Fr Fairland, 7 mi E on US 60	63	25	20	3.50	All year		•	•	dlr			918/542-6969	Rt 1 Box 170, Fairland 74343
A8	Honey Creek	Fr Grove, 1 mi S on US 59, 1 mi W on blcktp rd	30	15	16	3.50	All year			•	l			918/542-6969	Rt 1 Box 170, Fairland 74343
A8	Cherokee	Fr Spavinaw, N on Hwy 82 to Langley, 1/2 mi E on Hwy 28	59	68	16	3.00	All year		•	•	l			918/435-8066	Box 220, Disney 74340

Map Reference	Park Name	Access	Acres	Tent Spaces	Trailer Spaces	Approximate Fee	Season	Swimming Pool	Fishing	Boating	Playground	Other	Telephone Number	Mail Address
B7	Heyburn Lake	Fr Sapulpa, 12 mi W on Hwy 33	438	25	41	5.50	All year		•	•		I •	918/247-6695	Rt 3 Box 264, Bristow 74010
A8	Bernice	Fr Bernice, N on Hwy 60	10	20		None	All year		•	•		I	918/542-6969	Rt 1, Box 170, Fairland 74343
A4	Little Sahara	Fr Waynoka, 4 mi S on US 281	345	25	12	3.50	All year		•	•			405/824-1471	Rt 2 Box 147, Waynoka 73860
B8	Adair	Fr Stilwell, N on Hwy 51	40	20	12	3.50	All year		•	•			918/774-3785	Rt 1, Stilwell 74960
B7	Okmulgee Lake	Fr Okmulgee, 5 mi W on Hwy 56, S on access rd	535	25	38	3.50	All year		•	•		I •	918/756-5971	Rt 3 Box 140, Okmulgee 74447
B8	Snowdale	Fr Pryor, 6 mi E on Hwy 20	15	25	12	3.50	All year		•	•		dI	918/772-2047	Rt.3, Halbert 74441
B8	Salina	Fr Salina, E on US 20	18	20		None	All year		•	•		I •	918/772-2047	Rt 3, Hulbert 74441
B8	Sallisaw	Fr Sallisaw, 3 mi W on US 64	90	50		None	All year		•	•		I •	918/775-3897	Rt 2, Box 207, Sallisaw 74955
	NATIONAL PARKS & RECREATION AREAS													
	Chickasaw NRA												405/622-6121	PO Box 201, Sulphur 73086
	Travertine District		912											
D6	Cold Springs	Fr jct Hwy 7, S on US 177 to pk rd, 4/5 mi E		64	64	3.00	3/15-9/30**		•	•		g		Sulphur 73086
D6	Rock Creek	Fr jct Hwy 7, S on US 177 to pk ent, 2 mi W		106	106	3.00	3/15-9/30**		•	•		g		Sulphur 73086
	Lake District		8851											
D6	Guy Sandy	Fr Davis, 3 mi E on Hwy 7, 3-1/2 mi S		40	40	3.00	3/15-9/30**		•	•		dI		Sulphur 73086
D6	Buckhorn	Fr Sulphur, 5 mi S on US 177, 2 mi W		176	176	3.00	3/15-9/30**		•	•		dI		Sulphur 73086
D6	The Point	Fr Sulphur, 1/2 mi W on Hwy 7, 6 mi S		52	52	3.00			•	•		dI		Sulphur 73086
	NATIONAL FORESTS													
	Ouachita NF													
C8	Billy Creek	Fr Muse, 2 mi E on Hwy 63, 3 mi N on FR 22	3	14	14	None	All year		•					Muse
C8	Cedar Lake North Shore	Fr Heavener, 10 mi S on US 270, 3 mi W on Co 5, 1 mi N on FR 269	8	34	34	3.00	All year		•	•		dI		Heavener
C8	Cedar Lake South Shore	Fr Heavener, 10 mi S on US 270, 3 mi W on Co 5, 1 mi N on FR 269	3	54	54	3.00	4/4-9/8		•	•		dI		Heavener
C8	Winding Stair	Fr Talihina, 7.2 mi NE on US 271, 18 mi SE on Hwy 1	9	26	26	2.00	5/1-11/30	5	5			n		Talihina
	CORPS OF ENGINEERS													
	Canton Lake		175										405/886-2989	
B5	Big Bend	Fr Canton, 2 mi W on Hwy 51, 4 mi N on Co rd	60	N	126	4.00	All year		•	•	dI	•		Canton 73724
B5	Longdale	Fr Canton, 2 mi W on Co	10	N	42	1.00	All year		•	•	dI			Canton 73724
B5	Canadian	Fr Canton, 1 mi W on Hwy 51, 1-1/2 mi N on Hwy 58A	80	N	130	4.00	All year		•	•	dI	• g		Canton 73724
B5	Sandy Cove	Fr Canton, 3.5 mi NE on Hwy 58, 1.5 mi W on Hwy 58A	15	N	35	2.00	All year		•	•		I • g		Canton 73724
B5	Blaine Pk	Fr Canton, 1 mi W on Hwy 51, 5 mi NE on Hwy 58A	35	N	20	None	All year		•	•	dI	g		Canton 73724
B5	Fairview	Fr Longdale, 2 mi W on Co Rd, 1 mi N, 1 mi W on dirt rd	10	N	12	None	All year		•	•		gp	405/886-2989	PO Box 67, Canton 73724
B5	Primitive	Fr Canton, 1 mi W on Hwy 51, 1-1/2 mi N on Hwy 58A	30	N	S15	None	All year		•	•		ghp	405/886-3454	PO Box 67, Canton 73724
	Eufaula Lake		1000										918/799-5843	
C8	Belle Starr Pk	Fr Eufaula, 5 mi N on US 69, 2 mi E on Hwy 150	54	78	78	4.00	All year		•	•		dI		Stigler
C8	Brooken Cove	Fr Eufaula, 16 mi SE on Hwy 9, 3 mi N on Hwy 71	50	51	51	4.00	3/1-11/1		•	•		dI		Stigler
C8	Dam Site (South)	Fr Eufaula, 16 mi E on Hwy 9, 5 mi N on Hwy 71	25	49	49	3.00	All year		•	•		dI		Stigler
C8	Highway 9 Landing	Fr Eufaula, 9 mi SE on Hwy 9	22	72	72	4.00	All year		•	•		dI		Stigler
C8	Porum Landing	Fr Porum, 7 mi W on paved rd	22	44	44	4.00	All year		•	•		dI		Stigler
C7	Crowder Point (West)	Fr Eufaula, 12 mi S on US 69	9	5	5	None	All year		•			I		Stigler
C7	Crowder Point (East)	Fr Eufaula, 12 mi S on US 69	35	25	25	2.00	All year		•	•		dI		Stigler
C7	Cardinal Point	Fr Eufaula, 19 mi S on US 69	4	12	12	None	3/1-11/1		•			I		Stigler
C7	Gaines Creek	Fr Eufaula, 6 mi S on US 69, 2 mi NE on Hwy 9a, 3 mi S	20	17	17	None	3/1-11/1		•	•		I		Stigler
C7	Oak Ridge	Fr Eufaula, 5 mi S on US 69, 1 mi NE on Hwy 90	10	13	13	None	All year		•			n		Stigler
C7	Mill Creek Bay	Fr Eufaula, 6 mi W on Hwy 9, 2 mi S	6	11	11	None	All year		•			I		Stigler
C7	Elm Point	Fr McAlester, 12 mi NE on Hwy 31	5	7	7	None	All year		•			I		Stigler
C7	Hickory Point	Fr McAlester, 10 mi E on paved rd	14	10	10	None	All year		•			I		Stigler
C7	Highway 31 Landing	Fr McAlester, 7 mi NE on Hwy 31	20	23	23	None	3/1-11/1		•			I		Stigler
C7	Juniper Point	Fr McAlester, 5 mi N on US 69, 1 mi E on Hwy 113, 2 mi N, 1 mi E	14	16	16	2.00	All year		•	•		I		Stigler
B7	Gentry Creek Cove	Fr Checotah, 9 mi NW on US 266	17	42	42	2.00	All year		•	•		I		Stigler
B7	Holiday Cove	Fr Checotah, 7 mi W on I-40, 2 mi S on Hwy 150	10	15	15	None	3/1-11/1		•			I		Stigler
	Robert S Kerr Reservoir												918/775-4475	SR 4 Bx 182, Sallisaw 74955
C8	Little Sans Bois Cr	Fr Keota, 6 mi N on Co, 1 mi W on Co	147	27	S27	None	All year		•			I p	918/775-4476	Keota
C8	Keota Landing	Fr Keota, 2 mi N on Co	149	32	S32	2.00	All year		•			I p	918/775-4476	Keota
C8	Cowlington Point	Fr Sallisaw, 10 mi N on US 59, 3 mi W on Co	700	27	S27	2.00	All year		•	•		I p	918/775-4476	Sallisaw
C8	Short Mountain Cove	Fr Sallisaw, 10 mi N on US 59, 2 mi W on Co	748	82	S82	2.00	All year		•	•		I p	918/775-4476	Sallisaw
C8	Applegate Cove	Fr Sallisaw, 8 mi N on US 59, 3 mi W on Co	468	17	S17	2.00	All year		•	•		dlr p	918/775-4476	Sallisaw
C8	Sallisaw Creek	Fr Sallisaw, 5 mi N on US 64, 5 mi S on Co	1774	44	S44	2.00	All year		•	•		I p	918/775-4476	Sallisaw
	Fort Gibson Lake		B										918/687-2167	Box 370, Ft Gibson 74434
B8	Hulbert Landing	Fr Hulbert, 2 mi W on Blacktop rd	20	P9	S9	None	All year		•	•		I		Hulbert
B8	Dam Site Area	W side of Fort Gibson Dam	50	N		4.00	All year		•	•		p		Ft Gibson
B8	Wahoo Bay	Fr Okay, 1/2 mi E on Hwy 251A, 2 mi N, 1 mi E	175	P20	S20	1.00	All year		•	•		I		Okay
B8	Wildwood	Fr Hulbert, 3-1/2 mi W on Hwy 80	120	P51	S51	2.00	All year		•	•		I		Hulbert
B8	Mallard Bay	Fr Dam, 1/2 mi W on Hwy 251A, 2 mi E	643	N		None	All year		•	•		I p		Ft Gibson
B8	Rocky Point	Fr Wagoner, 3 mi N on US 69, 3 mi E, 1 mi N on blacktop rd	150	50	50	4.00	All year		•	•		I		Wagoner
B8	Snug Harbor	Fr Wagoner, 3 mi N on Hwy 69, 3-1/2 mi E	160	N		None	All year					p		Wagoner
B8	Blue Bill Point	Fr Wagoner, 4 mi N on US 69, 1 mi E, 1 mi N, 1 mi E	411	37	37	4.00	All year		•	•		I		Wagoner
B8	Long Bay Landing	Fr Wagoner, 5 mi N on Hwy 51, 1 mi N & 1 mi W on Co	57		S15	None	All year		•	•		dlr gp		Wagoner
B8	Taylor Ferry	Fr Wagoner, 5 mi E on Hwy 51	125	83	83	4.00	All year		•	•		dlr g		Wagoner
B8	Flat Rock	Fr Wagoner, 6-1/2 mi N on US 69, 3 mi E, 1 mi S, 1 mi W on blacktop rd	329	46	46	3.00	All year		•	•		dlr		Chouteau
B8	Jackson Bay	Fr Okay, 1/2 mi E on Hwy 251A, 2 mi N, 1 mi E, 1 mi N on blacktop rd	163	45	45	1.00	All year		•	•		I		Okay
B8	Whitehorn Cove	Fr Wagoner, 3 mi N on US 69, 6 mi E on blacktop rd	320	14	14	None	All year		•	•		dlr		Wagoner
B8	Mission Bend	Fr Chouteau, 5 mi S on US 69 to Mazie, 5 mi E, 2 mi N	177	P15	S15	None	All year		•	•		I		Chouteau
B8	Mazie Landing	Fr Chouteau, 3 mi S on US 69, 3 mi E on blacktop rd	186	P5	S5	None	All year		•	•		I		Chouteau
B8	Spring Creek	Fr Locust Grove, 3 mi W on Hwy 33, 5 mi S, 2 mi W on blacktop/gravel rd	316	14	14	None	All year		•	•		dlr		Locust Grove
B8	Big Hollow	Fr Locust Grove, 3 mi W to blacktop, 8-1/2 S on winding rd & gravel rd	318	P27	S27	None	All year		•	•		I		Locust Grove
B8	Chouteau Bend	Fr Chouteau, 3 mi E on Hwy 33	126	38	38	None	All year		•	•		dlr		Chouteau
	Fort Supply Dam		80										405/766-2701	Canton 73724
A4	Cottonwood Point	Fr US 270 in Ft Supply, 1.5 mi S on Co, 1.5 mi on project rd	75	N	76	2.00	All year		•	•		I	405/766-2701	Box 248, Fort Supply
A4	Wolf Creek Pk	Fr US 270 in Fort Supply, 1.5 mi S on Co, .5 mi on Project Rd	80	N	21	None	All year		•	•		I	405/766-2701	PO Box 248, Fort Supply 73841
A4	Beaver Point	Fr Ft Supply, 4 mi SE on US 270, 2 mi SW on project rd	50	N	10	1.00	All year		•	•		I	405/766-2701	Box 248, Fort Supply
A4	Supply Pk	Fr US 270 in Ft Supply, 1.5 mi S on Co	150	N	40	3.00	All year		•	•		I •		Box 248, Fort Supply
	Great Salt Plains Lake												405/626-4741	Jet 73749
A5	Great Salt Plains SP	Fr Cherokee, 18 mi E on Hwys 8 & 11, 8 mi N jct Hwy 38A	10	N	11	None	All year		•	•		I	405/626-4741	Jet
	Heyburn Lake		145											Kellyville 74039
B7	Sunset Bay	Fr Kellyville, 6 mi W on Co rd	41	N	N	None	All year		•	•		I p		Kellyville 74039
B7	Lake Heyburn Rec Area	Fr Sapulpa, 12 mi W on Hwy 33		N	N	None	All year		•	•	dI	I p		Kellyville 74039
B7	Heyburn Pk	Fr Kellyville, 6 mi W on Co Rd	133	N	N	3.00	All year		•	•		I p		Kellyville 74039
	Hulah Lake		B										918/532-4341	Rt 1 Bx 620, Copan 74022
A7	Caney River	Fr Chautauqua, Ks, 8 mi S on Hwy 99, 1-1/2 mi E & S	6	10	10	None	All year		•			I n	918/532-4341	Copan 74022
A7	Boulanger Landing	Fr Chautauqua, Ks, 7 mi S on Hwy 99, 1 mi W on access rd	4	7	7	None	4/1-12/1		•			n		Copan 74022

Map Reference	Park Name	Access	Acres	Tent Spaces	Trailer Spaces	Approximate Fee	Season	Swimming Pool	Other Swimming	Fishing	Boating	Playground	Other	Telephone Number	Mail Address
A7	Skull Creek	Fr Copan, 12 mi W on Hwy 10, 5 mi N	20	20	20	None	All year			•	l			918/532-4341	Copan 74022
A7	Pond Creek	Fr Chautauqua, Ks, 9 mi S on Hwy 99, E on Co	1	7	7	None	All year			•			n	918/532-4341	Copan 74022
A7	Turkey Creek	Fr Chautauqua, Ks, 15 mi SE on Co & access rd	240	20	20	None	All year		•	•	l			918/532-4341	Copan 74022
A7	Caney Bend	Fr Copan, 15 mi W on Hwy 10	172	7	7	None	4/1-9/1		•	•	lr			918/532-4341	Copan 74022
A7	Dam Site	Fr Copan, 12 mi W on Hwy 10	46	7	7	None	All year			•	l		p	918/532-4341	Copan 74022
	Chouteau & Newt Graham													918/489-5541	Rt 4, Bx 182, Sallisaw 74955
B7	Commodore Landing	Fr Inola, 7 mi W on old Hwy 33, 3 mi S on Co	85	23	23	3.00	All year		•	•	dl			918/489-5541	Sallisaw 74955
B7	Rocky Point	Fr Inola, 5 mi W on Hwy 33, 3 mi S on Co, 1 mi W	67	21	21	2.00	All year		•	•	d			918/489-5541	Sallisaw 74955
B7	Pecan Pk	Fr Muskogee, 7 mi N on US 69, .5 mi E on Chouteau L & D access rd	373	8	8	2.00	All year		•	•	dl			918/489-5541	Sallisaw 74955
B7	Tullahasee Loop	Fr Muskogee, 7 mi N on US 69, 2.5 mi fr US 69	176	9	9	None	All year		•	•	l			918/489-5541	Sallisaw 74955
B7	Verdigris Landing	Fr Wagoner, 7-1/2 mi W on Hwy 51, 1/4 mi N on Co	45	14	14	2.00	All year		•	•	l				Sallisaw 74955
B7	Afton Landing	Fr Wagoner, 6 mi W on Hwy 51, S on paved access rd	80	18	18	2.00	All year		•	•	dl			918/489-5541	Sallisaw 74955
B7	Rogers Point	Fr Catoosa, 4 mi E on US 66	9	23	23	None	All year			•	dl			918/489-5541	Sallisaw 74955
B7	Bluff View	Fr Broken Arrow, 12 mi E on 71st St, 1 mi N on Co	49	26	26	None	All year			•	dl			918/489-5541	Sallisaw 74955
	Keystone Lake		B											918/865-2621	Rt 1, Box 100, Sand Springs
B7	Washington Irving Cove S	Fr Sand Springs, 12 mi W on US 64, 1 mi NE on Co rd	75	42	42	4.00	All year		•	•	l	•			Sand Springs 74603
B7	Appalachia Bay	Fr Sand Springs, 12 mi W on US 64, 1-1/2 mi SW on Co rd	230	20	20	None	All year		•	•	dl				Sand Springs 74063
B7	Salt Creek Cove N	Fr Mannford, 1 mi E on US 51	320	60	60	3.00	All year		•	•	dl	•			Sand Springs 74063
B7	Old Mannford Ramp	Fr Mannford, 4 mi W on US 51, 2 mi N on Hwy 48, 1 mi E on Co rd	100	29	29	1.00	All year		•	•	l				Sand Springs 74063
B7	New Mannford Ramp	Fr Mannford, 1 mi N on Co rd	98	46	46	2.00	All year		•	•	l				Sand Springs 74063
B7	Washington Irving Cove N	Fr Sand Springs, 13 mi W on US 64, 2 mi SE on Co rd	280	17	17	1.00	All year		•	•	l				Sand Springs 74063
B7	Sandy Basin	Fr Mannford, 3 mi N on Co, 3 mi E on gravel Co	10	N	N	None	All year		•	•					Sand Springs 74063
B7	Keystone Ramp	Fr Sand Springs, 11 mi W on US 51, 1.5 mi N on Co rd	7	13	13	None	All year		•	•	l				Sand Springs 74063
B7	Cimarron	Fr Sand Sprgs, 19 mi W on Hwy 64, 1 mi S on Co	10	N	N	None	All year		•	•					Sand Springs 74063
B7	Pawnee Cove North	Fr Mannford, 3 mi N on Co rd, 1 mi W	428	15	15	1.00	All year		•	•	l				Sand Springs 74063
B7	Pawnee Cove South	Fr Mannford, 3 mi N on Co, 1 mi W	50	29	29	3.00	All year		•	•	l				Sand Springs 74063
B7	Osage Point	Fr Cleveland, 2 mi NE on Hwy 99, 4 mi E on Co rd	150	18	18	None	All year		•	•	l				Sand Springs 74063
B7	Osage Ramp	Fr Cleveland, 2 mi NE on Hwy 99, 4 mi E on Co	2	12	12	None	All year		•	•	l				Sand Springs 74063
B7	Cowskin Bay South	Fr Cleveland, 8 mi SE on US 64, 1 mi N on Co rd	324	33	33	1.00	All year		•	•	dl				Sand Springs 74063
B7	Cowskin Bay North	Fr Cleveland, 3-1/2 mi SE on US 64, 1-1/2 mi E on Co rd	174	22	22	None	All year		•	•	l		g		Sand Springs 74063
	Lake Texoma/Denison Dam	(See Texas for additional Campgrounds)	B												Denison, TX 75020
D6	Hickory Creek	Fr Marietta, 7 mi E on Hwy 32	120	10	10	None	All year			•	lr				Denison, TX 75020
D6	Lebanon	Fr Madill, 13 mi SW on Hwy 99c	390	18	18	None	All year			•	lr				Denison, TX 75020
D6	Arrowhead Point	Fr Madill, 15 mi S	280	18	18	None	All year			•	lr				Denison, TX 75020
D6	Briar Creek	Fr Madill, 13 mi SW on Hwy 99, 1-1/2 mi W	240			None	All year			•	lr				Denison, TX 75020
D6	Buncombe Creek	Fr Madill, 13 mi SW on Hwy 99, 1-1/2 mi E	280	56	56	3.00	All year			•	l				Denison, TX 75020
D6	Alberta Creek	Fr Madill, 15 mi SE on US 70 & 70A	320	14	14	None	All year			•	lr				Denison, TX 75020
D6	Little Glasses	Fr Madill, 4 mi SE on US 70 to Hwy 106	270	32	32	3.00	All year			•	lr				Denison, TX 75020
D6	Caney Creek	Fr Madill, 11 mi S on US 70	390	28	28	3.00	All year			•	l				Denison, TX 75020
D6	Cumberland Cove	Fr Madill, 12 mi SE on Hwy 199, S on paved rd	75	11	11	None	All year			•	l				Denison, TX 75020
D6	Roads End	Fr Madill, 13 mi SE on US 70 & 70A	170	18	18	None	All year			•	lr				Denison, TX 75020
D6	Bridgeview	Fr Madill, 9 mi SE on Hwy 199 to Little City, 4 mi S on paved rd	280	21	21	2.00	All year			•	lr				Denison, TX 75020
D6	Soldier Creek	Fr Madill, 12 mi SE on US 70 & Hwy 70B	105	19	19	3.00	All year			•	lr				Denison, TX 75020
D6	Burns Run	Fr Colbert, 5 mi W on Hwy 75A	555	184	184	4.00	All year		•	•	l	•			Denison, Texas 75020
D6	Lakeside	Fr Durant, 8 mi W on US 70, 4 mi S	430	24	24	1.00	All year			•	l				Denison, TX 75020
D6	Platter Flats	Fr Platter, 1 mi N	185	17	17	None	All year			•	l				Denison, TX 75020
D6	Sunset	Fr Colbert, 4 mi W on Hwy 75A to Cartwright, 2 mi N	175	19	19	None	All year		•	•	l				Denison, TX 75020
D6	Willafa Woods	Fr Cartwright, 4 mi N	190	15	15	None	All year			•	lr				Denison, TX 75020
D6	Willow Springs	Fr Durant, 10 mi W on US 70, S on paved rd	200	46	46	3.00	All year		•	•	lr				Denison, TX 75020
D6	Johnson Creek	Fr Durant, 9 mi W on US 70	75	54	54	4.00	All year			•	l				Denison, TX 75020
D6	Newberry Creek	Fr Durant, 8 mi W on US 70, 2 mi N	280	27	27	None	All year			•	lr				Denison, TX 75020
D6	Butcher Pen	Fr Tishomingo, 11 mi SE on Hwys 78 & 22	110	11	11	None	All year			•	lr				Denison, TX 75020
D6	Kansas Creek	Fr Brown, 4 mi W on Hwy 199	655	3	3	None	All year			•	l				Denison, TX 75020
D6	Pennington Creek	W side of Tishomingo	60	9	9	None	All year			•	lr				Denison, TX 75020
	Webbers Falls Dam													918/489-5541	c/o Robt Kerr Res, Sallisaw
B8	Canyon Road	Fr Ft Gibson, 2 mi N & NE on Hwy 80 to pk rd	200	50	50	3.00	All year		•	•	dl		p		Sallisaw 74955
B8	Spaniard Creek	Fr Keefton, 1.5 mi SE on US 64, 3 mi E on Co	132	32	32	3.00	All year		•	•	dl		p		Sallisaw 74955
B8	Arrowhead Point	Fr Gore, 6 mi N to Hwy 10, fr Hwy 10, 1 mi W & 1 mi S on Co	1238	30	30	3.00	All year		•	•	dl		p		Sallisaw 74955
B8	Hopewell Pk	Fr Muskogee Tpke, 4-1/2 mi E on paved rd, 1/2 mi S on gravel rd	132	17	17	None	All year		•	•	dl		p		Sallisaw 74955
B8	Ft Gibson Pk	Fr Ft Gibson, across Co bridge to CG	26	9	9	None	All year			•	dl		p		Sallisaw 74955
B8	Brewers Bend	Fr Webbers Falls, 1.5 mi W, 1 mi N, 1 mi W, 3 mi NW on Co	205	50	50	3.00	All year		•	•	dl		p		Sallisaw 74955
	Oologah Lake													918/587-7927	Box 38, Oologah 74053
A7	Blue Creek Cove	Fr Foyil, 2 mi W, 1 mi N, 2 mi W	112		S61	3.00	All year		•	•	l	•	p		Oologah 74053
A7	Hawthorn Bluff	Fr Oologah, 2 mi SE on Hwy 88	207		80	3.00	All year		•	•	l	•	p		Oologah 74053
A7	Clermont Pks 1 & 2	Fr Foyil, 2 mi W, 3 mi N, 3 mi W,	320		S26	None	All year		•	•	l		p		Oologah 74053
A7	Redbud Bay	Fr Oologah, 3 mi SE on Hwy 88	102		S25	1.00	All year		•	•	dlr		p		Oologah 74053
A7	Winganon Ramp	Fr Chelsea, 8 mi NW on Hwy 28 to Winganon, 1 1/2 mi S	50		S15	None	All year		•	•	l		p		Oologah 74053
A7	Spencer Creek	Fr Foyil, 2 mi W on Co, 5 mi N on Co	348		93	3.00	All year		•	•	l		p		Oologah 74053
A7	Overlook No-2	Fr Oologah, 2-1/2 mi SE on Hwy 88	35		S5	None	All year			•					Oologah 74053
A7	Verdigris River Pk	Fr Oologah, 2 mi SE on Hwy 88	131		S9	None	All year		o	•			p		Oologah 74053
A7	Double Creek Cove	Fr Nowata, 2 mi S on Hwy 169, 2 mi E	350		S15	1.00	All year		•	•	l		p		Oologah 74053
A7	Big Creek Cove	Fr Nowata, 5 mi E on Hwy 60, 2-1/2 mi N	37		S8	None	All year		•	•	l		np		Oologah 74053
A7	Sunnyside Ramp	Fr Talala, 3-1/2 mi E on Co Rd	13		S8	None	All year			•	l		p		Oologah 74053
	Pine Creek Lake													405/933-4350	Box 170, Valliant 74764
D8	Lost Rapids Landing	Fr Rattan, 19-1/2 mi E on Hwys 3/7	10	7	7	F2.00	All year			•	l			405/933-4350	Box 170, Valliant 74764
D8	Little River Pk	Fr Rattan, 18-1/2 E on Hwys 3/7 & access rds	20	25	25	F2.00	All year		•	•	l			405/933-4350	Box 170, Valliant 74764
D8	Pine Creek Cove	Fr Valliant, 7 mi N to project office	10	8	8	None	All year		•	•	l			405/933-4350	Box 170, Valliant 74769
	Tenkiller Ferry		B											918/487-5252	Rt 1 Bx 259, Gore 74435
B8	Strayhorn Landing	Fr Gore, 6 mi NE on Hwy 100, 3 mi N on Hwy 10A	220	54	54	3.00	All year		•	•	l		p		Rt 1 Bx 259, Gore 74435
B8	Dam Site	Fr Gore, 7 mi NE on Hwy 100	396	10	10	None	All year		•	•	l				Rt 1 Bx 259, Gore 74435
B8	Snake Creek Cove	Fr Vian, 10 mi N on Hwy 82	451	105	105	3.00	All year		•	•	dlr				Rt 1 Bx 259, Gore 74435
B8	Chicken Creek Pt	Fr Gore, 11 mi NE on Hwy 82	135	89	89	3.00	All year		•	•	l				Rt 1 Bx 259, Gore 74435
B8	Sixshooter Camp	Fr Vian, 15 mi NE on Hwy 82	84	25	25	1.00	All year		•	•	dlr				For Gibson 74434
B8	Cookson Bend	Fr Vian, 17 mi NE on Hwy 82	275	113	113	3.00	All year		•	•	dlr				Rt 1 Bx 259, Gore 74435
B8	Carters Landing	Fr Tahlequah, 11 mi S on Hwy 82	225	31	31	None	All year		•	•	dlr				Rt 1 Bx 259, Gore 74435
B8	Petit Bay	Fr Tahlequah, 13 mi S on Hwy 82	280	75	75	3.00	All year		•	•	dlr				Rt 1 Bx 259, Gore 74435
B8	Sisemore Landing	Fr Tahlequah, 15 mi S on Hwy 82	87	32	32	None	All year		•	•	l				Rt 1 Bx 259, Gore 74435
B8	Standing Rock	Fr Tahlequah, 20 mi SE on Hwy 82	73	15	15	None	All year			•	l				Rt 1 Bx 259, Gore 74435
B8	Elk Creek	Fr Tahlequan, 17 mi SE on Hwy 82	218	35	35	2.00	All year		•	•	dlr				Rt 1 Bx 259, Gore 74435
B8	Horseshoe Bend	Fr Tahlequan, 8 mi S on Hwy 82, 5 mi E on paved rd	137	10	10	None	All year			•	l				Rt 1 Bx 259, Gore 74435
	W D Mayo Dam													918/962-3481	Sallisaw 74955
C8	LeFlore Landing	Fr Spiro, 3 mi E on Hwy 9, 4 mi N on Co	114	14	S14	3.00	All year			•	l		p	918/962-3481	Rt 4, Bx 182, Sallisaw 74955
C8	Arkoma Pk	Fr US 271, E to Hwy 9A, N to Arkoma (SW crnr)	1	14	14	None	All year			•			p	918/775-4478	Rt 4 Bx 182, Sallisaw 74955
C8	Lake Wister	Fr Poteau, 10 mi SW on US 270	B	20	30	3.00	All year	•	•	•	lr	•	p	918/655-7756	Rt 2 Bx 7B, Wister 74966

South Carolina

Major Events

See state map, pages 36-37

Aiken Triple Crown, three Saturdays in Mar., Aiken. The Triple Crown includes harness racing, thoroughbred racing, and a steeplechase hunt meet. Admission. 803/648-4631.

Festival of Houses, mid-Mar. to mid-Apr., Charleston. Seven different afternoon and candlelight tours of homes in Charleston's Historic District are offered. Each tour includes 10 different houses, and visitors walk at their own pace. Four evening galas are also presented with music and wine. Admission. 803/723-1623.

Heritage Golf Classic, late Mar., Hilton Head Island. Top professionals compete on the Harbour Town Golf Course. Admission. 803/785-3333.

Carolina Cup Races, late Mar., Camden. Thoroughbred steeplechase and flat racing take place each year at this historic event. Admission. 803/432-6513.

Canadian-American Days, late Mar., Myrtle Beach. The Grand Strand is the site for a parade, plantation tours, fishing tournaments, softball games, a volleyball tournament, and concerts. Admission is charged for several events. 803/448-5135.

Family Circle Magazine Cup, early to mid-Apr., Hilton Head Island. Top professional women tennis stars compete for a large purse of prize money. Admission. 803/785-3333.

Historic Beaufort Tours, early Apr., Beaufort. Several antebellum homes, gardens, plantations, and churches open their doors for both daytime and candlelight tours. Admission. 803/524-6334.

Georgetown Plantation Tours, early Apr., Georgetown. Sixteen different town houses and plantations are open to the public for tours of both the houses and their gardens. Admission. 803/546-8436.

Rebel 500 Race, mid-Apr., Darlington. NASCAR's second oldest race features 36 of the nation's top drivers at the Darlington Raceway. Admission. 803/393-4041.

Governor's Frog Jump and Egg-Striking Contest, mid-Apr., Springfield, west of Orangeburg. This festival features frog-jumping contests, a parade, family games, square dancing, live music, and an egg-striking contest. Free. 803/258-3225.

S.C. Festival of Roses, early May, Orangeburg. Flower shows, canoe races, road races, a rodeo, and a 2-mile fun run are only some of the events at this festival held in Edisto Gardens. Free. 803/534-6821.

Hell Hole Swamp Festival, early May, Jamestown. Activities at this event include moonshine-making demonstrations, the Miss Hell Hole Swamp Pageant, and a concert of spirituals. Free. 803/257-2310.

Lowland Fling, early to mid-May, Georgetown County. Boat races, harbor tours, sports events, antiques, parades, and concerts are scheduled in three areas across the county. Admission is charged for several events. 803/546-8436.

Spoleto Festival, U.S.A., late May to early June, Charleston. This is one of the largest and most comprehensive arts festivals in the South. Opera, ballet, modern dance, jazz, theater performances, and symphonic, choral, and chamber music are all presented in various parts of Charleston's historic old downtown section. Admission. 803/722-2764.

Iris Festival, late May, Sumter. The blooming of the irises is celebrated with a parade, a beauty pageant, and family fun. Free. 803/775-1231.

Sun Fun Festival, early June, Myrtle Beach. Events take place all along the Grand Strand. Beauty pageants, parades, concerts, and beach games are just some of the different types of activities. Free. 803/626-7444.

Lexington County Peach Festival, early July, Gilbert, southwest of Columbia. Parades, entertainment, and a peach-cooking contest are some of the day's activities. Free. 803/359-4265.

Mountain Rest Hillbilly Day, early July, northwest of Walhalla. This mountain-flavored celebration includes clogging, country music, and a barbecue. Free (except food). 803/638-5251.

Gold Rush Day, early July, McCormick. This festival features a parade, panning for gold, arts and crafts, and fireworks. Free. 803/465-2218.

S.C. Peach Festival, mid-July, Gaffney. Plenty of peaches are brought in from surrounding orchards for this festival which also features an arts and crafts show, a beauty pageant, peach-cooking contests, games, and live entertainment. Admission is charged for several events. 803/489-5721.

Beaufort Water Festival, mid- to late July, Beaufort. Beaufort's waterfront is the scene for water-related events and a blessing of the fleet. There are street dances and tennis and golf tournaments as well as a Low Country dinner which will be served to some 3,000 people. Admission is charged for several events. 803/524-3163.

S.C. Festival of Flowers, mid-July, Greenwood. This townwide event features a pageant, garden tours, an arts and crafts fair, a tennis tournament, musical entertainment, and Flower Day, which is held at the Park Seed Company. Admission is charged for several events. 803/223-8431.

S.C. Tobacco Festival, late July, Lake City. Various events celebrating the local tobacco crop include agricultural displays, an arts and crafts show, a parade of antique autos, and live entertainment. Free. 803/394-8611.

S.C. Grape Festival, mid-August (on the first weekend following the ripening of the grapes), York. Local vineyards offer tours of their fields and cellars, and there is grape stomping as well as art shows and a beauty pageant. Admission is charged for the beauty pageant. 803/684-2590.

Schuetzenfest, late Aug., Ehrhardt, south of Bamberg. This "Hunter's Festival" features folk dancing, German foods, turkey shoots, and clogging. Free. 803/267-5335.

Southern 500 Race and Festival, early Sept., Darlington. NASCAR drivers compete in one of the largest races in the South. A parade and a pageant precede the race. Admission. 803/393-4041.

Atalaya Arts and Crafts Festival, mid-Sept., Murrells Inlet. The Spanish-style Atalaya Castle at Huntington Beach State Park is the site for an arts and crafts and performing arts festival. Admission. 803/758-3622.

Pioneer Days, late Sept., Kings Mountain State Park, northeast of Gaffney. Life on an 1840s Up Country farm is re-created with a muzzle-loader's competition, colonial games, and crafts. Free. 803/758-3622.

House and Garden Tour, mid-Oct., Charleston. This is a tour of several of Charleston's oldest, most rarely seen homes. Admission. 803/722-4630.

Fall Festival of Arts, mid-Oct., Sumter. Swan Lake Gardens hosts this showcase for the visual and performing arts, including musical concerts and choral groups. Admission is charged for several events. 803/773-1581.

S.C. State Fair, mid- to late Oct., Columbia. Along with the numerous agricultural and industrial exhibits, there are contests, athletic events, a carnival midway, and grandstand entertainment. Admission. 803/799-3387.

Colonial Cup International Steeplechase, mid-Nov., Camden. Horses from around the world vie for a large cash purse on the two-mile steeplechase course at Springdale Race Course, north of town. Admission. 803/432-6513.

Chitlin' Strut, late Nov., Salley, south of Columbia. This one-day annual event features country music, dancing, a pig-calling contest, a parade, barbecued chicken and pork, and chitlins. Free (except food). 803/258-3309.

Elgin Catfish Stomp, early Dec., Elgin, northeast of Columbia. Catfish are stewed and served to hundreds of people. Also, there is a Christmas parade, a street dance, and live music. Free. 803/438-1729.

South Carolina Destinations

ABBEVILLE, 5,863, E-3. This seat of Abbeville County was the birthplace of John C. Calhoun and the site of the last meeting of Confederate Pres. Jefferson Davis and his cabinet on May 1, 1865. The focal point of the city is a large square, on which storefronts have been restored as a part of a restoration and preservation program. Several historic buildings are open to the public, some only one month a year, others almost daily. **Burt-Stark Mansion,** 1865 N. Main St., is where President Davis and his cabinet members held their last meeting in 1865. May (only), Wed., 2 P.M. Free. 803/459-4297. The **Opera House,** on the public square, was built in 1906. Now restored, theater productions are held throughout the year. In the early days, it was a popular place for road shows, which featured many well-known performers. Year-round, Mon.-Fri., 9 A.M. to 5 P.M. **Trinity Episcopal Church** (c. 1845), Church St., is a handsome Gothic structure. Always open. Free. Information regarding all historic buildings: 803/459-2181.

AIKEN, 14,987, F-4. Called "Thoroughbred Country," Aiken has been a center for wintering and training horses since the early 1900s. One of its best-known horses is Kelso, a five-time national champion. Aiken was also the site of the first outdoor game of polo, which was played at Whitney Field in 1882. **Thoroughbred Racing Hall of Fame** is located in Hopeland Gardens, Whiskey Rd. and Dupre Pl., a 14-acre area of flowers, trees, and shrubs. The hall of fame was founded to portray Aiken's role and success in the training of thoroughbreds. Mid-Sept.-July, Tues.-Sun., 2 to 5 P.M. Free. 803/649-7700. Among events in March are the *Aiken Horse Trials,* for horses not yet tested in national competition; the *Aiken Steeplechase* and *Hunt Meet,* with leading jockeys on mounts soon to be on tour; and the *Harness Races.*

ANDERSON, 27,313, D-2. The **Anderson County Arts Center,** 405 N. Main St., is downtown in this principal northwestern town of South Carolina. The focus of the center is visual arts, with changing monthly exhibits. Year-round, Mon.-Fri., 10 A.M. to 5 P.M.; Sat., 10 A.M. to noon; Sun., 2 to 5 P.M. Free. 803/224-8811.

AWENDAW, G-6. *See* **Cape Romain National Wildlife Refuge.**

BEAUFORT, 8,634, G-5. Pronounced *Bewfort,* this is the "capital" of South Carolina sea islands. For a small area, it has one of the largest concentrations of massive town houses in America. **Henry C. Chambers Park** spans eight acres on the shore of the Beaufort River. Beaufort's restored waterfront includes a marina, plaza, covered pavilion, playground, and sunken amphitheater. A walking tour along Bay, Federal, Pinckney, and adjacent streets will show many of the houses. **John Mark Verdier House** (c. 1790), 801 Bay St., of Federal style, is headquarters for the Historic Beaufort Foundation. The Marquis de Lafayette spoke from the balcony while on a visit to South Carolina in 1825. Mar.-mid-Dec., Thurs.-Sat., 11 A.M. to 3 P.M. Adults $1.50; persons 14 and under, 75¢. 803/524-6334. **George Parsons Elliott Museum** (c. 1840), Bay and Charles Sts., is a Beaufort-style house (eight rooms, with four on the first floor, four on the second floor, and each opening onto a piazza which runs the length of the house on both floors). Year-round, Mon.-Fri., 11 A.M. to 3 P.M. Adults $2; persons under 18, $1. 803/524-8450. **Beaufort Arsenal Museum,** 701 Craven St., was built in 1785 and rebuilt in 1852. It contains fossils, Indian pottery, Civil War relics, and plantation handicrafts. Year-round, Mon.-Fri., 10 A.M. to noon, 2 to 5 P.M.; Sat., 10 A.M. to noon. Donations. 803/879-4965. **St. Helena's Episcopal Church** (1724), Newcastle St., is of colonial architecture. Year-round, daily, 7 A.M. to 6 P.M. 803/524-7595. **Parris Island Museum,** Marine Corps Recruit Depot, on St. 281, 7 miles south of Beaufort, has exhibits highlighting the important events in the history of the marines. Also on the island are three famous monuments: the **Jean Ribault Monument** honoring the French Huguenot who established the fort in 1762, the **Iwo Jima Monument,** and the **Iron Mike** (World War I Marine) **Monument.** Museum: Year-round, daily, 7:30 A.M. to 4:30 P.M. Free. 803/525-2951.
See also **Fripp Island.**

CAMDEN, 7,462, E-5. **Historic Camden,** Broad and Wateree Sts., is a reconstructed colonial village and Revolutionary War fortifications. Tours of historic houses, children's farmyard, and other facilities: Year-round, Tues.-Fri., 10 A.M. to 4 P.M.; Sat., 10 A.M. to 5 P.M.; Sun., 1 to 5 P.M. Adults $1; children 50¢; under 6, free. 803/432-9841. **Bethesda Presbyterian Church,** Main St., was designed by Robert Mills, with a monument to Baron deKalb, foreign officer killed in the Battle of Camden. Year-round, Mon.-Fri., 9 A.M. to 4:30 P.M.; Sat., 9 A.M. to 1 P.M. Free. 803/432-4593. **The Carolina Cup** and **Colonial Cup International Steeplechases** are run at the Springdale Course in late March and late November, respectively.

CAPE ROMAIN NATIONAL WILDLIFE REFUGE, G-6. Northeast of Awendaw, this migratory refuge is an estaurine environment for nearly 400 species of birds and sea turtles, plus a breeding ground for marine species. It is accessible only by private boat. Tidal schedules are available at Moore's Landing. Year-round, daylight hours. Free. 803/928-3368.

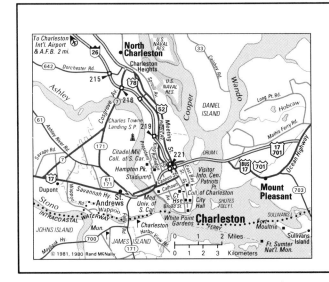

Walking Tour of Charleston

By planning wisely, it's possible to see enough of Charleston in a single day to understand why this is one of the South's most charming cities. Everything downtown is within easy walking or bicycling (rentals are available) distance. Begin at The Battery with a carriage tour. Trained drivers relate the city's history and lore while you sit back, relax, and look. The rest of the morning can be spent touring several of the houses and museums. The 1803 Joseph Manigault House, the Heyward-Washington House, Charleston Museum, and the Old Slave Market Museum and Gallery are a few possibilities. Lunchtime calls for a visit to one of the popular restaurants, such as the East Bay Trading Company, or to the City Market, which features shops and numerous restaurants. Afterwards, if you admired the historic houses, you may enjoy browsing among the antique shops along King Street. Or, if Civil War history beckons, tours of Fort Sumter, out in Charleston Harbor, depart from The Battery in early afternoon and last approximately two and a half hours. If time allows, drive out Scenic St. 61 to Drayton Hall, Magnolia Gardens, and Middleton Place.

CHARLESTON, 69,510, G-6. Founded and permanently settled by the English in 1670, Charleston was the original capital of South Carolina. Throughout the city are many places and events of historic and current interest. One of the major events is the **Spoleto Festival USA,** founded like its Italian counterpart by Gian Carlo Menotti, who is in residence during this festival of performing and visual arts by national and international entertainers. Late May to early June.

MUSEUMS: The **Charleston Museum** (1773), 360 Meeting St., is claimed to be the oldest museum in the United States. Year-round, 9 A.M. to 5 P.M. Adults $1.50; persons 4-18, 50¢; under 4, free. 803/722-2996. **Patriot's Point Museum,** Mt. Pleasant, is a naval and maritime museum with 15 rooms of exhibits related to ships, shipbuilding, and marine life. Year-round, 9 A.M. to 5 P.M. Admission $4; persons 65 and over, $3.50; 6-11, $2.50; under 6, free. 803/884-2727. The **Gibbes Memorial Art Gallery,** 135 Meeting St., has South Carolina art, portraits relative to Southern history, and a miniature collection. Year-round, Tues.-Sat., 10 A.M. to 5 P.M.; Sun., 1 to 5 P.M. Adults $2, children 50¢. 803/722-2706.

HISTORIC BUILDINGS: Joseph Manigault House (c. 1802), 350 Meeting St., is noted for its wood-carved mantels, molding, and wainscoting. Year-round, daily, 10 A.M. to 5 P.M. Adults $2.50; persons 6-18, $1; under 6, free. 803/723-2926. The **Heyward-Washington House,** 87 Church St., was built in 1770 by Daniel Heyward, founder of a rice dynasty and the father of Thomas Heyward, Jr., a signer of the Declaration of Independence. The house was leased by George Washington in 1791 during a state visit here. Year-round, daily, 10 A.M. to 5 P.M. Adults $2.50, persons 6-18, $1; under 6, free. 803/722-0354. **Edmonston-Alston House** (c. 1828), 21 E. Battery St., is a Greek-Revival mansion with a treasure of documents, silver, and china. Year-round, Mon.-Sat., 10 A.M. to 5 P.M.; Sun., 2 to 5 P.M. Admission $2.50. 803/722-7171. **Nathaniel Russell House** (1809), 51 Meeting St., is noted for its ornate detail, circular staircase, and furnishings. Year-round, Mon.-Sat., 10 A.M. to 5 P.M.; Sun., 2 to 5 P.M. Admission $2.50. 803/723-1624. **Dock Street Theatre,** 135 Church St., is said to be the first building in America designed solely for theatrical purposes. Spoleto USA and local performances are held here. Building: July-Aug., Mon.-Fri., 10 A.M. to 5 P.M.; Oct.-May, Mon.-Sat., 10 A.M. to 6 P.M. Free. Theater season: Oct.-May. 803/723-5648.

COLLEGES: The **College of Charleston** (1785), Calhoun St., is downtown. Tours: Year-round by appointment. 803/792-5507. **The Citadel,** at the foot of Moultrie St. in northwest Charleston, is a military college with a dress parade each Friday at 3:45 P.M. during the school year. Free. 803/792-5006.

HISTORIC PLACES: Fort Sumter National Monument, on a shoal at the entrance to Charleston Harbor, about 3½ miles from the Charleston Battery, commemorates the first shot fired (April 12, 1861) in the Civil War and the Confederate defense of 1863-65. The fort was one of a series of coastal fortifications built by the United States after the War of 1812. A boat to Fort Sumter leaves daily at 2:30 P.M. from the Municipal Marina, Lockwood Blvd., Charleston. Park and boat: Adults $5, children $2.75. 803/722-1691. The park also embraces **Fort Moultrie,** across River Bridge, via U.S. 17 and then St. 703. This fort was the scene of one of the early defeats (June 28, 1776) of the British in the Revolutionary War. Visitors Center: Daily, May-Sept., 9 A.M. to 6 P.M.; other months, 9 A.M. to 5 P.M. Free. Fort Sumter and Fort Moultrie: Year-round, daily, 9 A.M. to 5 P.M. Free. 803/883-3123.

SPECIAL AREAS: Cabbage Row (also known as Catfish Row), 89-91 Church St., is where vendors once peddled their wares. The area was the inspiration for *Porgy and Bess,* the opera with words by Dubose Heyward and music by George Gershwin. **City Market,** Market St. between Meeting and East Bay Sts., features small shops, restaurants, produce, Gullah basket weavers and their wares, and flower stalls. It was the original farmers' market. 803/722-8338. **The Battery,** East Bay St. and Murray Blvd., is the area at the tip of the peninsula around the harbor. Here, colonial homes look out over White Point Gardens onto the harbor and Fort Sumter.

NEARBY GARDENS, PARKS, AND PLANTATIONS: Magnolia Gardens, 10 miles northwest of Charleston on St. 61., was begun in 1680 as a plantation estate gardens for the American branch of the Drayton family. Thomas Drayton, first of the family to arrive in America, settled on the land and established the estate, which has been home to the Drayton family for ten generations. The gardens, acclaimed to be some of the most beautiful in America, are famous for their azaleas and camellias. They also include the plantation house, a waterfowl refuge, wildlife observation tower, herb garden, walking and bike trails, and other features. Year-round, daily, 8 A.M. to 6 P.M. Adults $5; persons 13-19, $4; 4-12, $3; under 4, free. 803/571-1266. **Drayton Hall,** on adjoining land on St. 61, was built by Thomas Drayton's youngest son, John, who named it for his family's ancestral seat in England. The hall, one of the oldest and finest examples of Georgian-Palladian architecture in the country, is still in excellent condition and retains many of its original features—in some areas even the original paint remains. The hall and land, originally owned by John Drayton, is now the property of the National Trust for Historic Preservation. Tours: Year-round, daily, 10 A.M. to 3 P.M. Adults $3; students $2; under 6, free. 803/766-0188. **Middleton Gardens,** 14 miles northwest on St. 61, were the first formal gardens in America. They were first

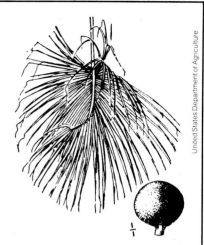

The cabbage palmetto is the state tree of South Carolina. It is a medium-sized palm tree of the south Atlantic and Gulf coasts from North Carolina to Florida. The trunk is stout and unbranched with a cluster of leaves at the top. The leaves are evergreen, coarse, fan-shaped, and 4 to 7 feet long. The fruits are in clusters, and each one is ⅜" to ½" in diameter, black, and one-seeded.

landscaped in 1740 with the assistance of an English landscape artist imported by Henry Middleton, later temporary president of the first Continental Congress. The gardens rise in terraces from the river; the landscape design includes intricate walks and extensive plantings of camellias, azaleas, magnolias, roses, and more. The plantation house tells the story of the Middleton family, which also included a signer of the Declaration of Independence. Year-round, Mon., 1:30 to 5 P.M.; Tues.-Sun., 10 A.M. to 5 P.M. Gardens and stable yards: Year-round, daily, 9 A.M. to 5 P.M. Adults $6; children 4-12, $3; under 4, free. House, $3 extra. 803/556-6020. **Cypress Gardens,** 26 miles north off U.S. 52, offers boat tours through the waterways. There are cypress trees, hundreds of azaleas, daffodils, and other flowers which bloom in the spring. Mid-Apr.-May, daily, 8 A.M. to 6 P.M. Adults $3; persons 13-16, $2; under 12, free. Boat ride 50¢. 803/577-6970. **Boone Hall Plantation,** 8 miles north on U.S. 17, originally was part of a 17,000-acre land grant made in 1681 by the Lords Proprietors of England to John Boone, an Englishman, in recognition of his services in the Royal Navy. The plantation, which was in the Boone family for 125 years and today includes 740 acres, is noted for its trees. The entrance is known as the "Avenue of the Oaks," for the three-quarter-mile-long drive is bordered by oak trees planted in 1743 by Thomas Boone, son of John Boone; Thomas is buried by the avenue. Also on the property are 140 pecan trees. Apr.-Sept., Mon.-Sat., 8:30 A.M. to 6:30 P.M.; Sun., 1 to 6:30 P.M.; other months, Mon.-Sat., 9 A.M. to 5 P.M.; Sun., 1 to 5:30 P.M. Adults $3.75; children 6-12, 50¢; under 6, free. 803/884-4371. **Charles Towne**

Landing Park, south off St. 171, is a historical state park on the site of the 1670 English settlement known as Charles Towne. In 1680, the settlement moved across the peninsula to the area which is now Charleston. The park includes historical and nature exhibits. Historical exhibits include displays in the pavilion; a 17th-century sailing vessel, which is still sailable; and Colonial Village, a living museum of replicas of the early dwellings, with costumed craftsmen demonstrating woodworking, printing, and blacksmithing. Nature areas include 100-acre English gardens, and a 22-acre natural habitat zoo. Daily, June-late Oct., 9 A.M. to 6 P.M.; other months, 9 A.M. to 5 P.M. Adults $3; persons 6-14, $1; under 6, free. Admission covers all park areas. 803/556-4450.

See also **Isle of Palms, Kiawah Island,** and **Seabrook Island.**

CLEMSON, 8,118, D-2. **Fort Hill,** on Clemson University campus, was the antebellum home of John C. Calhoun, 19th-century statesman who served as a U.S. senator, secretary of war, secretary of state, and vice president of the United States. Year-round, Tues.-Sat., 10 A.M. to noon, 1 to 5:30 P.M.; Sun., 2 to 6 P.M. Free. 803/656-2475. **Hanover House,** on the campus, is a Huguenot-style dwelling which was moved here from the lower part of the state when Moultrie and Marion lakes were impounded. Year-round, Tues.-Sat., 10 A.M. to noon, 1 to 5:30 P.M.; Sun., 2 to 6 P.M. Free. 803/656-2241. **Agricultural Sales Center,** in Newman Hall, is operated by the university's Department of Agriculture and is famous for Clemson's blue cheese and homemade ice cream. Year-round, Mon.-Fri., 9 A.M. to 5:30 P.M.; Sat., 9 A.M. to 1 P.M.; Sun., 2 to 5:30 P.M. 803/656-3242.

See also **Pendleton.**

COLUMBIA, 99,296, E-4. Known as "The City for All Seasons," Columbia is the capital of South Carolina. It sits on an eminence above the Broad, Saluda, and Congaree rivers; was rebuilt after the Civil War; and has received several All-America City awards. Columbia is the state's second capital city, the seat of government having been moved here from Charleston in the late 18th century.

STATE CAPITOL: The State House, Gervais St. between Assembly and Sumter Sts., occupies a city block, with palmetto trees on the grounds. Designed in the 1850s by John R. Niernsee, originally of Vienna, the Capitol houses the offices of the governor, lieutenant governor, and the general assembly. Tours: Year-round, daily, 9 A.M. to 5 P.M. Free. 803/758-0221.

LIBRARY AND ARCHIVES: University of South Carolina Library (1840), University Horseshoe, Sumter St., is devoted solely to the history, literature, and geography of South Carolina. Year-round, Mon.-Fri., 9 A.M. to 5 P.M.; Sat., 1 to 5 P.M. Free. 802/777-3131. **South Carolina Department of Archives and History,** 1430 Senate St., houses records dating back to the 17th century. It is an excellent resource for genealogical records. Year-round, Mon.-Sat., 9 A.M. to 9 P.M.; Sun., 1 to 9 P.M. Free. 803/758-5816.

MUSEUMS: The Columbia Museums of Art and Science, 1112 Bull St., includes collections from the Renaissance to the present time and the Gibbes Planetarium. Planetarium shows: Sat.-Sun., 2, 3, and 4 P.M. Adults 75¢; children under 6, 50¢. Museums: Year-round, Mon.-Fri., 10 A.M. to 5 P.M.; Sat.-Sun., 1 to 5 P.M. Free. 803/799-2810. **McKissick Museums,** University of South Carolina Horseshoe, Sumter St., includes five museums and an art gallery. Sept.-May, Mon.-Fri., 9 A.M. to 4 P.M.; Sun., 1 to 5 P.M.; other months, Mon.-Fri., 9 A.M. to 4 P.M. Free. 803/777-7251. **South Carolina Confederate Relic Room and Museum,** 900 Sumter St., is devoted to the Confederate era, with such items as civilian, military, and communication artifacts. Year-round, Mon.-Fri., 9 A.M. to 5 P.M. Free. 803/758-2144. **Fort Jackson Museum,** across from Fort Jackson post headquarters, contains artifacts from the life of Gen. Andrew Jackson, seventh president of the United States, and other exhibits of military history. Fort Jackson, which was named for President Jackson and is now an armed forces combat support training center, can be entered at the main gate in the 4400 block of Jackson Blvd., in eastern Columbia. Year-round, Tues.-Sun., 1 to 4 P.M. Free. 803/751-7511.

HISTORIC HOUSES: Robert Mills House and Park, 1616 Blanding St., is headquarters of the Historic Columbia Foundation and one of the few private homes designed by Robert Mills, who was the architect for several government buildings in Washington, D.C., as well as the Washington Monument. (Mills, one of the most highly regarded architects of his day, resided in Charleston, South Carolina; he died in 1855.) Year-round, Tues.-Sat., 10 A.M. to 4 P.M.; Sun., 2 to 5 P.M. Adults $2; students $1; under 6, free. 803/252-7742. **Governor's Mansion,** 800 Richland St., once served as the officers' quarters of a military academy. Tours: Year-round, Tues.-Thurs., 9:30 A.M. to 4 P.M. Free. 803/758-3452. **Hampton-Preston House,** 1615 Blanding St., was the antebellum home of South Carolina statesman Wade Hampton. Year-round, Tues.-Sat., 10 A.M. to 4 P.M.; Sun., 2 to 5 P.M. Adults $1.50; students 75¢; under 6, free. 803/252-0938. **Woodrow Wilson Boyhood Home,** 1705 Hampton St., is where President Wilson lived as a youth when his father was a professor at Columbia Theological Seminary. Year-round, Tues.-Sat., 10 A.M. to 4 P.M.; Sun., 2 to 5 P.M. Adults $1.50; students 75¢; under 6, free. 803/254-6333. **Manns-Simons Cottage,** 1403 Richland St., is the re-created home of a free black slave. Tours: Year-round, Tues., Fri., and weekends by appointment. Adults $1, stu-

Gullah basketry dates back to the times of the large plantations of the early 18th century. Low Country blacks wove baskets which were used for cleaning grain. Sweet grass and palmetto pine were the two basic weaving materials. Despite the declining use of Gullah baskets during the 19th century, mothers passed on the secrets of this unique form of basketry to their daughters. Artisans and collectors developed an interest in Gullah basketry in the early 1900s, and the baskets they exhibited caught the interest of the public. When U.S. 17 was paved between Charleston and Georgetown, Low Country basket weavers began to set up stands along the road and sell their handiwork. Today there are more than 60 stands along U.S. 17, north of Mt. Pleasant. The baskets are of the simple coil variety. The stitching radiates out from the center knot in straight rows. Sweet grass and palmetto pine are still the two basic weaving materials. Bulrushes and long needle pine straw are also used to strengthen and add color to the baskets.

dents and children 50¢. 803/252-1450.

ZOO: Riverbanks Park (also called the Columbia Zoo), Greystone exit off Int. 26, has more than 700 animals and birds. Year-round, daily, 9 A.M. to 5 P.M.; Sat.-Sun. (summer), 9 A.M. to 7 P.M. Adults $3; students, military, $2.25; children 6-12, $1.75; under 6, free. Parking 50¢. 803/779-8717.

MARKETS: State Farmers Market, Bluff and Stadium Rds., features fresh fruits and vegetables grown by local farmers. Year-round, Mon.-Sat., daylight to dusk.

COWPENS, 2,023, D-4. Cowpens National Battlefield, U.S. 221 and St. 11, was known as "Hannah's Cowpens" at the time of the Revolutionary War battle fought January 17, 1781. "The Battle that broke the back of the British" may now be relived at the Visitors Center through visuals, art, memorabilia, and a battlefield walking tour. Year-round, daylight hours. Free. 803/461-9930.

DARLINGTON, 7,989, E-6. Stock-car racing is the big attraction here, with such events as the *Southern 500 Stock Car Race and Festival,* the *Rebel 500 Stock Car Race,* the *Sandlapper 150 Stock Car Race,* and the *Swamp Fox 150 Stock Car Race.* They are held at Darlington Raceway, west on St. 151 and St. 34. 803/393-4041. Joe Weatherly Stock Car Museum, adjacent to Darlington Raceway, was named for the racing driver. The museum contains the *National Motorsports Hall of Fame;* a collection of stock-racing cars, said to be the world's largest collection; and a simulated drive-it-yourself racing car. June-Sept., daily, 9 A.M. to 5 P.M.; other months, Mon.-Fri., 9 A.M. to noon, 2 to 5 P.M. Free. 803/393-2103.

EDGEFIELD, 2,713, E-3. Some of South Carolina's famous citizens have lived in the Edgefield district. Among them are five state governors and five lieutenant governors. Oakley Park United Daughters of the Confederacy Shrine, 300 Columbia St., was the 19th-century home of former South Carolina governor John Gary Evans. Year-round, Mon.-Fri., 9 A.M. to noon, 1 to 4 P.M. Donations. 803/637-6576. Magnolia Dale, 320 Morris St., is another 19th-century dwelling. Open by appointment. Donations. 803/637-3335.

ELLOREE, 909, on St. 6 north of Santee, F-5. In the Elloree Trials, held in mid-March, participating mounts come from "Horse Country," between St. Matthews and Holly Hill. The animals are born, bred, and trained for national competition in the United States races here. The trials feature thoroughbred and quarter horse racing, and occasionally jousting. 803/496-7037.

FLORENCE, 30,062, E-6. Florence Museum, 558 Spruce St., features art and exhibits relating to the science and history of South Carolina. Year-round, Tues.-Sat., 10 A.M. to 5 P.M.; Sun., 2 to 5 P.M. Free. 803/662-3351. Florence Air and Missile Museum, east on U.S. 301 at the airport entrance, has exhibits of planes and missiles. Year-round, daily, 9 A.M. to sunset. Adults $2, children $1. 803/655-5118.

FRIPP ISLAND, 19 miles southeast of Beaufort and south of Hunting Island, H-5. This 3,000-acre-forested island has natural and resort attractions, with facilities for tennis, golf, sailing, cycling, jogging, fishing, or relaxing in the sun. Hotel rooms, condominiums, and oceanfront homes can be rented. 803/838-2411.

GEORGETOWN, 10,144, F-6. Established in 1735, many of its structures were built before the American Revolution. Among them is Prince George Winyah Episcopal Church, 300 Broad St., which was established in 1721; the building was erected in 1742–46. Year-round, daily, 8 A.M. to 5 P.M. Free. 803/546-4358. Georgetown Rice Museum, Front and Screven Sts., was once the Old Market Building, and the Clock Tower is the old timepiece of the historic building. Museum exhibits relate to the rice industry. Year-round, Mon.-Fri., 9:30 A.M. to 4:30 P.M.; Sun., 2 to 4:30 P.M.; Apr.-Sept., Sat., 10 A.M. to 4:30 P.M.; other months, Sat., 9:30 A.M. to 1 P.M. Adults $1; students and children under school age, free. 803/546-7423. Kaminski House, (c.1760), 1003 Front St., has a collection of antiques from the area. Year-round, Mon.-Fri., 10 A.M. to 5 P.M. Adults $2, children $1. 803/546-7706. Hopsewee Plantation House and Grounds, (c. 1740), south on U.S. 17, was the birthplace of Thomas Lynch, Jr., a signer of the Declaration of Independence. Mar.-Oct., Tues.-Fri., 10 A.M. to 5 P.M. Adults $2.50; persons 6-18, $1; under 6, free. Parking for grounds tour only, $1. 803/546-7891.

See also Murrells Inlet.

GREENVILLE, 58,242, D-3. Religious Art Museum, Bob Jones University, 1700 Wade Hampton Blvd., has a world-famous collection of sacred art and biblical antiquities. Year-round, Tues.-Sun., 2 to 5 P.M. Free. 803/242-5100. Greenville County Museum of Art, 420 College St., displays a large private collection of Andrew Wyeth paintings. Year-round, Mon.-Sat., 10 A.M. to 5 P.M.; Sun., 1 to 5 P.M. Free. 803/271-7570. Christ Episcopal Church, 10 N. Church St., was built in 1852; Pres. Millard Fillmore attended the cornerstone-laying ceremonies on May 2, 1852. Sundays and by appointment. 803/271-8773. Reedy River Falls Historic Park has footpaths along the river and can be reached by stairs from the 600 block on Main St. Year-round, daylight hours. Free. Cleveland Park and Zoo, 1200 E. Washington St., has animals, a playground, picnic facilities, and a garden. Year-round, daily, 9 A.M. to 5 P.M. Adults 50¢; persons 3-15, 25¢; 65 and older and under 3, free. Mon., Sat., 9 A.M. to noon, free. Zoo: 803/282-8079. Park: 803/242-1250.

GREENWOOD, 21,613, E-3. Greenwood Museum, Phoenix St., features 130 categories of displays, including a replica of Cinderella's coach; Indian war relics; mounted birds and animals; and the Frank Delano Gallery, with rare African artworks of the Katanga Tribe, now extinct. There is also a cotton culture and manufacturing exhibit. Year-round, Mon.-Fri., 9 A.M. to 5 P.M.; Sun., 2 to 5 P.M. Donations. 803/229-7083. George W. Park Seed Company, 7 miles north on St. 254, has trial gardens with 1,600 varieties of flowers and vegetables, including new species which are being introduced to the public for the first time. The company also has display areas and research greenhouses. Four tours daily from the garden shop, unless other activities conflict. Year-round, Mon.-Fri., 8 A.M. to 4:30 P.M. Free. 803/374-3341. The Railroad Historical Center, S. Main St., is for railroad buffs. Exhibits include a 1906 steam locomotive, a "President of the Railroad Car," and other equipment. By appointment. Donations. 803/229-5813 or 803/229-3828.

See also Ninety Six.

South Carolina Beaches

The Palmetto State has 281 miles of oceanfront beaches where a myriad of activities take place. You may swim in the ocean, stroll on the beach, fish, explore coastal islands, observe the abundant and unusual wildlife, and visit state parks. U.S. 17 is a good route to take while visiting the coast.

HARTSVILLE, 7,631, E-5. Cocker Pedigreed Seed Company and Coker Farms, on St. 151, is a Registered National Landmark. Begun in 1902 for scientific agricultural experiments and seed and plant breeding, its program has spread throughout the Southern states. Thousands of farmers visit here annually. Mid-March-Sept., daily, daylight hours. Free. 803/332-7531. The H. B. Robinson Plant, Carolina Power and Light Company's Nuclear Information Center, on St. 151 between McBee and Hartsville, has exhibits explaining how electricity is produced from fossil (coal) power and nuclear power. Year-round, Mon.-Fri., 9 A.M. to 5 P.M. Free. 803/332-2633.

HILTON HEAD ISLAND, H-5. One of the largest islands along the South Carolina coast, Hilton Head, on U.S. 278, was named for Capt. William Hilton, whose *Adventure* in 1663 was the first English ship to enter the waters of Port Royal Sound. Today Hilton Head is a resort island of championship golf courses and luxurious accommodations. In the heart of the island is 572-acre Sea Pines Forest Preserve, with miles of trails, grass marshes, and an abundance of wildflowers and birds, many of which winter here. A reminder of earlier inhabitants is a 150-foot-diameter oyster shell mound built more than 3,800 years ago. Originally the mound, thought to be a ceremonial place, contained some 150,000 bushels of shells. Also on the island is *Harbour Town,* a new port on the Intracoastal Waterway. At the mouth of the harbor is a lighthouse. In the town area are a yacht basin, golf course, and other recreational facilities.

HOLLY HILL, 1,785, F-5. **Francis Biedler Forest,** on St. 453 between U.S. 176 and Int. 26, south of Holly Hill, is an impressive 3,659-acre wilderness rich in virgin forests of cypress and tupelo. In the 1,783-acre virgin tract of this large stand of cypress-tupelo, bald cypresses reach as high as a 10-story building. The "jewel eco-system" is managed by the National Audubon Society. In the forest are an interpretive center, 40 miles of waterways, and a 6,500-foot-long boardwalk. Year-round, Tues.-Sun., 9 A.M. to 5 P.M. Adults $2, children 50¢. 803/462-2150.

ISLE OF PALMS, north of Charleston via U.S. 17, G-6. This densely forested, subtropical island has two miles of beach. The **Isle of Palms Beach and Racquet Club** has 14 tennis courts, an 18-hole golf course, supervised childrens' programs, and rental cottages and villas. 803/866-6000.

KIAWAH ISLAND, about 20 miles southwest of Charleston between Edisto Island and Folly Beach, G-5. This island is both a resort area and a natural area of woodlands, marshlands, and miles of empty beaches. The newly developed resort area has accommodations, restaurants, villas, shopping area, golf course, tennis courts, and natural beaches, all within walking distance. A Jeep Safari Tour takes visitors on a two-hour trek through the natural areas, which are still home to deer, bobcat, alligator, some 150 species of birds, and turtles. From late May through August, the turtle watch begins. From May through mid-July, the female Atlantic loggerhead turtles lay their eggs, which are protected by research scientists (and island residents and vacationers) who patrol the beaches each night to recover and relocate eggs which might be consumed by hungry hogs and raccoons. After the eggs are hatched, the baby turtles are sent back to sea. The island also has a haunted house—a shuttered 1800s Georgian-style house, said to be haunted by the ghost of Arnoldus Vanderhorst IV, whose family owned the island from 1772 through the mid-1900s. Jeep Safari Tour: Year-round, daily. Adults $8.50; children 4-11, $4.25; under 4, free. 803/768-2121, ext. 3500.

KINGS MOUNTAIN NATIONAL MILITARY PARK, C-4. North of St. 5, southeast of Int. 85, the military park was the site where the American frontiersmen defeated the pro-British forces on October 7, 1780, at a critical point during the American Revolution. Exhibits in the Visitors Center interpret the battle; a foot trail from the center leads to the chief features of the battlefield. Daily, Memorial Day-Labor Day, 9 A.M. to 6 P.M.; other months, 9 A.M. to 5 P.M. Free. 803/936-7508. The park is in both South Carolina and North Carolina; office of the park superintendent is in Kings Mountain, North Carolina.

LEXINGTON, 2,131, E-4. **Lexington County Museum,** U.S. 378 and Fox St., is a complex containing three 18th-century cabins, a 19th-century farm, and two antebellum houses (*John Fox House,* 1832; *Post House,* 1870). Museum: Year-round, Tues.-Sat., 10 A.M. to 3 P.M.; Sun., 1 to 3 P.M. Admission $1. 803/359-8369.

McBEE, 774, D-5. **Carolina Sandhills National Wildlife Refuge,** north on U.S. 1 and St. 145, is both a migratory bird refuge and a state forest. Living under the protection of the refuge is the red-cockaded woodpecker. An oddity is the location of Sugar Loaf Mountain in the sandhill terrain. Year-round, daily, daylight hours. Free. 803/335-8401.

McCLELLANVILLE, 436, F-6. **Francis Marion National Forest** was named for Francis Marion, Revolutionary War commander, who was known as "the Swamp Fox." He escaped into the swamps and forests when hard pressed in battle. In the forest are *Sewee Indian Mound,* a pre-Revolutionary War tar pit and kiln; and *Guillard Lake,* with campgrounds, primitive areas, and picnic sites. Always open. 803/887-3311.

MURRELLS INLET, 700, F-6. **Brookgreen Gardens,** on U.S. 17 between Myrtle Beach and Georgetown, includes a botanical garden, aviary, wildlife park, and outdoor museum. Founded by sculptor Anna Huntington and her husband, Archer, Brookgreen covers an area once occupied by five Low Country plantations. The garden's entrance is graced by Mrs. Huntington's "Fighting Stallions" and a long avenue of live oaks planted in the 1700s. Nearly 400 pieces of sculpture by leading 19th- and 20th-century Americans have been placed here. Year-round, daily, 9:30 A.M. to 4:45 P.M. Adults $2, children 50¢. 803/237-4218. **Atalaya Castle,** in Huntington Beach State Park across from Brookgreen, is a Moorish-appearing structure. In a lush growth of palmettoes, it was used at times by Mrs. Huntington for her sculpture work. Atalaya has many rooms, each with a fireplace; the Atlantic Ocean can be seen from the roof. Memorial Day-Labor Day, daylight hours. Admission 25¢. 803/237-2313.

MYRTLE BEACH, 18,785, F-7. Focal point of the **Grand Strand,** a 60-mile stretch of beaches from Little River south to Pawley's Island, Myrtle Beach offers golfing (some 29 courses), fishing, and facilities and accommodations for vacationers. Among the events here are the annual *Canadian-American Days* around late March and the *Sun Fun Festival* the first week of June. **Hall of Fame,** 21st and Oak Sts., in the Convention Center, is a shrine to famous South Carolinians recognized for their service to their state and nation. Among them are Astronaut Charles Duke, Jr., and several signers of the Declaration of Independence. Year-round, daily. Free. 803/448-4021.

NINETY SIX, 2,249, southeast of Greenwood on St. 34, E-3. **Ninety Six National Historic Site,** on St. 248, was the scene of the abortive siege of the British-held "Star Redoubt" by Gen. Nathanael Greene in 1781. The Visitors Center provides information on this onetime frontier settlement. An interpretive trail passes the trading post; a French and Indian fort; and construction and remnants of Revolutionary War fortifications, including tunnels excavated under the direction of Thaddeus Kosciusko, a Polish engineer who came to America to offer his services in the American Revolution. In 1781, he served as a colonel with General Greene. Year-round, daily, 8 A.M. to 5 P.M. Free. 803/543-4068.

ORANGEBURG, 14,933, F-5. **Edisto Memorial Gardens,** north off U.S. 301, are along the riverbank of the North Edisto River. Hundreds of species of roses, azaleas, flowering dogwood, crabapple trees, and more bloom throughout the spring and summer. Year-round, daily, 9 A.M. to 5 P.M. Free. 803/536-2337.

PENDLETON, 3,154, southeast of Clemson on St. 187, D-2. **Pendleton Historical and Recreational District Commission,** headquartered in the 19th-century Hunter Store, 125 E. Queen St., coordinates events and makes arrangements for tours in Oconee, Pickens, and Anderson counties. Among the historic homes which can be visited are *Woodburn House,* built in 1810 by Charles Cotesworthy Pinckney, Jr., member of a prominent South Carolina family (among them was one of the signers of the Federal Constitution), and *Astabula Plantation,* another 19th-century place of interest. Headquarters: Year-round, Sun.-Fri., 9 A.M. to 4:30 P.M. Admission $1. 803/646-3782.

PICKENS, 3,199, D-2. **Pickens Art and History Museum,** housed in the old Pickens County jail, has an outstanding collection of arrowheads. Year-round, Mon. and Fri., 2 to 5 P.M.; Wed., 9 A.M. to noon. Free. 803/878-4965.

RIDGELAND, 1,143, G-4. **Savannah National Wildlife Refuge,** south off U.S. 17, has 13,000 acres teeming with wildfowl, deer, and almost every other species east of the Mississippi River. Remains of rice levees, foundations of slave quarters, a small graveyard, a nature drive, and picnicking areas are also in the refuge. Year-round, daily, daylight hours. Free. 912/323-4321.

ROCK HILL, 35,344, D-4. **Carowinds,** 12 miles north on Int. 77, is a 73-acre park, with eight different themes, each covering a historic period of the Carolinas. (The park extends into North Carolina.) The park also has 30 rides, including five roller coasters, and live shows. Late Mar.-early June, Sat.-Sun., 10 A.M. to 8 P.M.; early June-late Aug., Sat.-Thurs., 10 A.M. to 8 P.M.; late Aug.-early Oct., Sat.-Sun., 10 A.M. to 8 P.M. Admission $9.50 (includes all entertainment); children under 3, free. 704/588-2606. **Glencairn Gardens,** Charlotte Ave. and Crest St., features terraced lawns and landscaped gardens that slope to a grassy plain, with fountains and pools that reflect the beautiful surroundings. Year-round, daily, daylight hours. Free. **Museum of York County,** Mt. Gallant Rd., has more than 500 animals from seven continents in natural settings, Hall of the Carolinas, and a planetarium. Year-round, Mon.-Fri., 9 A.M. to 5 P.M.; Sat.-Sun., 1 to 5 P.M. Admission 50¢. 803/366-4116.

SANTEE, 612, F-5. This small town hosts and advises anglers who pour into an area called Santee-Cooper Country to fish in Marion and Moultrie lakes. This is the home of the landlocked striped bass, in whose honor the **World's Championship Striped Bass Tournament** is held each year from April until July. Available to fishermen are 50 fishing camps, public landings, guides, rental boats, restaurants with menus devoted to fish, and many other accommodations. 803/854-2131.
See also **Elloree.**

SEABROOK ISLAND, 23 miles south of Charleston via U.S. 17, G-5. **Seabrook Island Resort** offers a variety of activities. Visitors can golf, play tennis, fish or crab, go horseback riding, or go sailing. Accommodations include rental villas and houses. 803/765-1000.

SPARTANBURG, 43,968, D-3. This city, which dates to around 1785, is an agricultural and industrial center. It is also a productive peach-growing area. **Morgan Square** is centered by a statue of Gen. Daniel Morgan, commander of the patriot forces at the Battle of Cowpens, fought north of here. **Walnut Grove Plantation,** south on Int. 26 to U.S. 221 and follow the signs, is the restored home of Kate Moore Barry, a scout for General Morgan. The home has a separate kitchen, grounds featuring an herb garden, schoolhouse, drover's house, doctor's office, barn, and cemetery. Apr.-Oct., Tues.-Sat., 11 A.M. to 5 P.M.; Sun., 2 to 5 P.M. Adults $2.50; persons under 19, $1.50. 803/576-6546. **Wofford College Planetarium,** N. Church and College Sts., features special sky shows produced by a simulation of the planetary system with celestial movements on the hemispherical ceiling of the planetarium. Sept.-May, by appointment. Free. 803/585-4821. **Spartanburg County Tours,** sponsored by the Jun-

These sketches of Beaufort in 1863 appeared in an 1895 Civil War atlas.

ior League, go from Spartanburg to Moore, Switzer, Woodruff, Reidville, Roebuck, North Spartanburg County, Croft State Park, and Glenn Springs. By appointment. 803/582-8564 or 803/585-8722.

STATEBURG, 75, west of Sumter on St. 261 off U.S. 76/378, E-5. The **Church of the Holy Cross** is one of the state's most photographed sanctuaries. Of Gothic Revival architecture, it was built of terreplein (earth), with lesser amounts of tabby, cypress, and stone. It is the burial place of Joel Roberts Poinsett (1779–1851), first U.S. Minister to Mexico. While serving there, Poinsett, a scientist, discovered the poinsettia and brought it back to the United States. It later was named for him. Open by appointment. 803/494-8101.

SUMMERTON, 1,173, F-5. **Santee National Wildlife Refuge,** southwest on St. 102, is a basic habitat for wildlife, including waterfowl. Migrant birds number from 6,000 to 40,000; many ducks winter here. In the refuge is a one-mile-long nature trail with interpretive signs and an observation tower. Year-round, daily, daylight hours. Free. 803/478-2217.

SUMTER, 24,890, E-5. **Williams-Brice House,** 122 N. Washington St., has collections of dolls, wedding gowns, toys, fossils, historic hand tools, period furniture, and art; also beautiful gardens. Year-round, Wed.-Sun., 2 to 5 P.M. Donations. 803/775-0908. **Sumter Gallery of Art,** 421 N. Main St., has exhibits by such nationally known artists as South Carolina's Jasper Johns. Mid-Sept.-late May, Tues.-Fri., 11 A.M. to 5 P.M.; Sat.-Sun., 3 to 5 P.M. Free. 803/775-0543. **Swan Lake, Iris Gardens,** W. Liberty St., is known for its thousands of Japanese iris; also azaleas and other plants. On the lake are Australian black and white

muted swan. Year-round, daily, 9 A.M. to sunset. Free. 803/775-1231.
See also **Stateburg.**

WALHALLA, 3,977, D-2. The **Blue Ridge Tunnel,** southeast on St. 28 at Stumphouse Mountain, was one of four begun in the mid-19th century to link South Carolina by railroad with areas beyond the Blue Ridge Mountains. About 1,600 feet of the tunnel are open to the public and partially lighted. A small campground, picnic shelter, and an old caboose are nearby. **Isaqueena Falls,** nearby, was named for an Indian maiden. Year-round, daily, daylight hours. Free. **Keowee-Toxaway Visitors Center (Duke Power Company),** east on St. 130 and 138, is on Lake Keowee in the Lower Nation of the Cherokee Indians. Displays tell the story of energy. Year-round, Mon.-Sat., 9 A.M. to 5 P.M.; Sun., noon to 5 P.M. Free. 803/882-5620. **Walhalla National Fish Hatchery,** north off St. 107, has exhibits, from fish eggs to brook and rainbow trout fingerlings. A picnic area and trail to Ellicott Rock Wilderness Area also are here. Year-round, daily, 9 A.M. to 5 P.M. Free. 803/638-2866. **Whitewater Falls,** a twin falls, is shared by South and North Carolina. On the state line, north of Walhalla, between St. 107 and U.S. 178, the South Carolina portion of the falls can be reached only on foot by backpacking or hiking. **Sumter National Forest,** northwest on St. 107, comprises three divisions: *Enoree,* in the South Carolina midlands, covers 157,140 acres and has its headquarters in Newberry; *Long Cane,* in the western portion, covers 111,909 acres and has its headquarters in Greenwood; and *Gen. Andrew Pickens,* in the northwestern part, covers 72,593 acres and has its headquarters in Walhalla. Sumter and Pickens were named for two South Carolina Revolutionary War

generals, Thomas Sumter and Andrew Pickens. Recreation areas, picnicking, camping, and primitive camping areas are in the forests. Year-round, daily, daylight hours. Free. 803/638-9568.

WINNSBORO, 2,919, E-4. In this quaint 18th-century town, three unusual buildings are located on Congress (Main) Street. The **Court House** (1820-23) was designed by Robert Mills, architect for several government buildings and the Washington Monument in Washington, D.C. Year-round, Mon.-Fri., 9 A.M. to 5 P.M. **Town Clock Building** (c. 1834) has a clock whose works were made in Alsace, France and has run continuously since 1837. Year-round, Mon.-Fri., 9 A.M. to 5 P.M. **Fairfield County Museum,** a Federal-style structure, has been restored to the 18th-century period when it was built. Year-round, Mon., Wed., Fri., 10:30 A.M. to 12:30 P.M.; 1:30 to 4:30 P.M.; second and fourth Sun. each month, 2 to 4 P.M. Free. 803/635-9811.

Information Sources

South Carolina
Department of Parks,
Recreation, and Tourism
Suite 113, Edgar
Brown Building
1205 Pendleton St.
Columbia, SC 29201
803/758-8735

South Carolina
Department of Wildlife
& Marine Resources
Dutch Plaza, Building D
P.O. Box 167
Columbia, SC 29202
803/758-6314

Beaufort Chamber
of Commerce
P.O. Box 910
Beaufort, SC
803/859-2693

Charleston
Visitors Center
85 Calhoun St.
Charleston, SC 29203
803/722-8338

Greater Convention
& Visitors Bureau,
1038 Laurel St.
Columbia, SC 29202
803/779-5350

Myrtle Beach Chamber
of Commerce
P.O. Box 2115
Myrtle Beach, SC 29577
803/448-5135

Spartanburg Chamber
of Commerce
P.O. Box 1636
Spartanburg, SC 29304
803/585-8722

South Carolina Campgrounds

FEES REFLECT MINIMUM RATE FOR 2 ADULTS AND ARE SUBJECT TO INCREASE OR SEASONAL CHANGES

•	at the campground	E	tents rented	U	unlimited	g	public golf course within 5 miles	p	motor bikes prohibited
○	within one mile of campground	F	entrance fee or premit required	V	trailers rented	h	horseback riding	r	boat rental
$	extra charge	N	no specific number, limited by size of area only	Z	reservations accepted	j	whitewater running craft only	s	stream, lake or creek water only
**	limited facilities during winter months			LD	Labor Day	k	snow skiing within 25 miles	t	tennis
A	adults only	P	primitive	MD	Memorial Day	l	boat launch	u	snowmobile trails
B	10,000 acres or more	R	reservation required	UC	under construction	m	area north of map	w	open certain off-season weekends
C	contribution	S	self-contained units only	d	boat dock	n	no drinking water	y	drinking water must be boiled

Map Reference	Park Name	Access	Acres	Tent Spaces	Trailer Spaces	Approximate Fee	Season	Swimming Pool	Other Swimming	Fishing	Boating	Playground	Other	Telephone Number	Mail Address
	STATE PARKS														
F4	Aiken	Fr Aiken, 16 mi E on US 78 & access rd	1067	25	25	5.00	All year		•	•	dr	•		803/649-2857	Windsor
F4	Barnwell	Fr Barnwell, 7 mi NE on Hwy 3	307	25	25	5.00	All year		•	•	dr	•		803/284-2212	Blackville
D6	Cheraw	Fr Cheraw, 4 mi SW on US 1	7361	25	25	5.00	All year		•	•	dlr	•	h	803/537-2215	Cheraw
D4	Chester	Fr Chester, 3 mi SW on Hwy 72	523	45	45	5.00	All year		•		r	•		803/385-2680	Chester
G5	Colleton	Fr Walterboro, 11 mi N on US 15	35	25	25	5.00	All year			•		•		803/538-8206	Canadys
G5	Givhans Ferry	Fr Summerville, 16 mi W on Hwy 61	1235	25	25	5.00	All year			•		•		803/873-0692	Ridgeville
E3	Greenwood	Fr Greenwood, 17 mi E on Hwy 702	914	100	100	5.00	All year		•	•	dlr	•		803/543-3535	Ninety-Six
H5	Hunting Island	Fr Beaufort, 16 mi SE on US 21	5000	200	200	7.50	All year		•	•	l	•		803/838-2011	Frogmore
C4	Kings Mountain	Fr York, 12 mi NW on Hwy 161	6141	125	125	5.00	All year		•	•	dr	•	h	803/222-3209	Kings Creek

Map Reference	Park Name	Access	Acres	Tent Spaces	Trailer Spaces	Approximate Fee	Season	Other Swimming / Swimming Pool	Fishing	Boating	Playground	Other	Telephone Number	Mail Address
E6	Little Pee Dee	Fr Dillon, 11 mi SE on Hwy 57	835	50	50	5.00	All year	• •	•		r •		803/774-8872	Dillon
F7	Myrtle Beach	Fr Myrtle Beach, 3 mi S on US 17	312	300	155	7.50	All year	$ •	$		r •		803/238-5325	Myrtle Beach
E5	Poinsett	Fr Sumter, 9 mi W on Hwy 763, 9 mi S on Hwy 261	1000	50	50	5.00	All year		•		r •		803/494-8177	Wedgefield
D2	Oconee	Fr Walhalla, 12 mi NW on Hwy 28	1165	140	140	5.00	All year	• •	•		r •		803/638-5353	Walhalla
G4	Rivers Bridge	Fr Ehrhardt, 7 mi SW on Hwy 64	390	25	25	5.00	All year	•			r		803/267-3675	Ehrhardt
F5	Santee	Fr US 301 in Santee, 3 mi NW	2364	150	150	6.00	All year	• •	•		dlr •	g	803/854-2408	Santee
E5	Sesquicentennial	Fr Columbia, 13 mi NE on US 1	1445	87	85	5.00	All year	• •			r •		803/788-2706	Columbia
D3	Table Rock	Fr Pickens, 16 mi N on Hwy 11	2860	100	100	5.00	All year	• •	•		r •		803/878-9813	Pickens
F6	Huntington Beach	Fr Murrells Inlet, 3 mi S on US 17	2500	128	128	7.50	All year	• •	•		r •		803/237-4440	Murrells Inlet
E5	Lee	Fr Bishopville, 7 mi E on US 15	2839	50	50	5.00	All year	• •			lr •		803/428-3833	Bishopville
D3	Croft	Fr Spartanburg, 3 mi SE on Hwy 56 & access rd	7088	50	50	5.00	All year	$ •	•		r •	h	803/585-1283	Pauline
D3	Paris Mountain	Fr Greenville, 9 mi N on US 25, E on paved rd	1275	50	50	5.00	All year	• •	•		r •		803/244-5565	Greenville
D3	Pleasant Ridge	Fr Greenville, 15 mi N on US 25 to Hwy 11, 3 mi W to pk	300	25	25	5.00	All year	• •	•		r •		803/836-6589	Cleveland
E2	Sadlers Creek	Fr Anderson, 13 mi SW on US 29, 2 mi N on Hwy 187	395	100	100	5.00	All year	•	•		l •		803/226-8950	Anderson
E3	Baker Creek	Fr McCormick, 4 mi SW on US 378	1305	100	100	5.00	All year	•	•		l •	h		McCormick
E3	Hickory Knob	Fr McCormick, 8 mi SW on US 378	1091	75	75	5.00	All year	• •	•		dlr •	h	803/443-2151	Rt 1,Bx 199B, McCormick 29835
G5	Edisto Beach	Fr US 17, 26 mi N on Hwy 174	1255	75	75	7.50	All year	• •	•		l •		803/869-2156	Edisto Island
D5	Andrew Jackson	Fr Lancaster, 8 mi N on US 521	360	25	25	5.00	All year	• •			r •		803/285-3344	Lancaster
E3	Hamilton Branch	Fr McCormick, 15 mi S on US 221, W to CG	731	200	83	5.00	All year	•	•		l •		803/333-2223	Plum Branch
	NATIONAL FORESTS													
	Francis Marion Sumter NF													
F6	Buck Hall	Fr McClellanville, .6 mi N on Hwy 9, 7 mi SW on US 17, .2 mi SE on FR 236	5	15	15	None	All year	•		dl ⌐				McClellanville
F4	Talatha	Fr New Ellenton, 4 mi S on Hwy 19, 1 mi SW on Fr SRP-1	10	8	8	None	10/1-12/31					n		New Ellenton
F4	Crackerneck Hunt	Fr Jackson, 7 mi SE on Hwy 125, 1 mi NW on Co 5, 4 mi SW on Co, 4 mi SE on FR 805.	2	5		None	10/1-12/31					n		Jackson
F6	Honey Hill	Fr McClellanville, .3 mi N on Hwy 9, .6 mi NW on Hwy 1189, 8.4 mi N on Hwy 45.	3	9	9	None	All year					n		McClellanville
F3	Lick Fork Lake	Fr Edgefield, 8.3 mi W on Hwy 23, .3 mi S on Hwy 230, 1.9 mi SE on Hwy 263, .4 mi W on Hwy 392.	5	12	12	2.00	5/3-11/30	• •		d				Edgefield
E3	Parsons Mtn Lake	Fr Abbeville, 2.2 mi SW on Hwy 72, 2.1 mi S on Hwy 28, 1.8 mi SE on Hwy 251, .8 mi S on FR 514.	7	26	26	2.00	4/1-10/31	• •		dl		h		Abbeville
E3	Midway Hunt	Fr Greenwood, 6.8 mi W on Hwy 72, .5 mi S on CO	4	25	25	None	10/1-12/31					n		Greenwood
E3	Morrows Bridge Hunt	Fr McCormick, 2.3 mi NW on Hwy 28, .5 mi NW on Co 37, .8 mi SW on Co 39.	4	25	25	None	10/1-12/31	1 1		d		n		McCormick
E3	Fell Hunt	Fr Abbeville, 8 mi SE on Hwy 33, 1.5 mi NE on Hwy 47.	40	40	40	None	10/1-12/31	3				n		Abbeville
D2	Cherry Hill	Fr Walhalla, 8.9 mi NW on Hwy 28, 7.2 mi N on Hwy 107.	13	29	21	2.00	5/1-10/15	•						Walhalla
D2	Cherokee Hunt Camp	Fr Salem, 5 mi W on Hwy 11, 4 mi NW on Hwy 375, 1 mi S on CO	5	5		None	10/15-12/15							Salem
D2	Cassidy Bridge Hunt Camp	Fr Walhalla, 5.5 mi NW on Hwy 28, .8 mi W on Hwy 193, 4.5 mi SW on Hwy 290, .5 mi SW on FR .	5	5		None		•						Walhalla
D2	Burrells Ford	Fr Walhalla, 8.9 mi NW on Hwy 28, 9.6 mi N on Hwy 107, 2.6 mi W on FR 708, .2 mi S on FR 7088	5	5		None	10/11-12/8	•						Walhalla
D4	Leeds	Fr Chester, 12.1 mi SW on Hwy 72, 2.1 mi N on Hwy 25, 3.6 mi N on Hwy 49, .3 mi NW on Hwy 574.	5	9		None	All year	•						Walhalla
D4	Woods Ferry	Fr Chester, 12.1 mi SW on Hwy 72, 2.1 mi N on Hwy 25, 3.6 mi N on Hwy 49, 3.6 mi NW on Hwy 574.	12	12	12	None	10/1-1/31					n		Chester
D4	Whiteoak Hunt	Fr Carlisle, .2 mi SE on Hwy 215, 3.6 mi SW on Hwy 72.	25	36	36	None	4/15-10/15	•		dl		n		Chester
D4	Poolus-Loop Hunt	Fr Lockhart, 5 mi SE on Hwy 9, .7 mi SW on Co 49, 3.1 mi W on FR 301, .5 mi N on FR .	5	12	12	None	10/1-1/31	2				n		Carlisle
F6	Guilliard Lake	Fr Jamestown, 3.8 mi SE on Hwy 45, 1.6 mi NE on FR 150, 1.2 mi N on FR 150G.	4	20	20	None	10/1-1/31	1				n		Lockhart
D4	Willow Oak Hunt	Fr Newberry, 10 mi N on Hwy 121, 3.8 mi SW on US 176, .3 mi TN on FR 387, 1.7 mi NE on FR 386.	2	6	6	None	All year	•		d				Jamestown
D4	Scenic Area Hunt	Fr Whitmire, 3.2 mi NE on Hwy 121, 7.2 mi SE on Hwy 45, 1.1 mi N on Hwy 54, 1.9 mi E on Co .	2	20	20	None	10/1-1/1					n		Newberry
D4	Rocky Branch Hunt	Fr Winnsboro, 14 mi W on Hwy 34, 1.3 mi N on Hwy 215, 2.4 mi SW on FR 412.	6	25	25	None	10/1-1/1	1 1				n		Whitmire
D4	Collins Creek Hunt	Fr Whitmire, 3.2 mi NE on Hwy 121, 4.2 mi SE on Hwy 45, .6 mi SW on FR FH393.	2	20	20	None	10/1-1/1					n		Winnsboro
D4	Beatty's Bridge Hunt Camp	Fr Union, 9 mi S on US 176, .2 mi E on Hwy 278	8	40	40	None	10/1-1/1					n		Whitmire
D4	Brick House	Fr Whitmire, 6.2 mi SW on Hwy 66, .3 mi S on FR 358.	2	10	10	None	10/1-1/2	1		d		hn		Union
D4	Tip Top Hunt	Fr Clinton, 7 mi E on Hwy 72.	12	20	20	None	4/1-12/31					hn		Whitmire
D4	Ridge Road Hunt Camp	Fr Whitmire, 5 mi W on Hwy 72, 1.5 mi N on Fr 355	10	40	40	None	10/1-1/1							Clinton
D4	Sedalia Tower Hunt Camp	Fr Union, 9 mi S on Hwy 16, 3 mi W on Hwy 63, 1 mi N on Hwy 79	2	10		None	10/1-1/2					n		Whitmore
D4	Long Lane Hunt	Fr Newberry, 9 mi N on Hwy 121, .9 mi W on Hwy 81.	2	20	20	None	10/1-1/2	2		d		n		Union
D4	Sedalia Hunt	Fr Union, 11 mi SW on Hwy 49, 1.9 mi SE on Co 18, .3 mi NE on Co .	8	20		None	10/1-1/1	2				n		Newberry
D4	Hickory Nut Hunt Camp	Fr Union, 10.6 mi S on Hwy 16, .5 mi E on Hwy 136	8	13	13	None	10/1-1/31	2				n		Union
D4	Fair Forest Hunt	Fr Union, .2 mi W on Hwy 49, 1 mi S on US 176, 6 mi SW on Co 16.	3	10	10	None	10/1-1/2	2		d		n		Union
D2	Pine Mountain Hunt Camp	Fr Westminster, 7 mi W on US 76, 5 mi SW on Hwy 90, 3 mi N on CO, 8 mi SW on FR 752	4	8	8	None	10/1-1/31	2				n		Union
			5	5		None	10/15-12/15	•				n		Westminster
	CORPS OF ENGINEERS													
	Clark Hill Reservoir	(See Georgia for additional campgrounds)											803/722-3770	Clarks Hill 29821
F3	Modoc	Fr Modoc, 5 mi on US 221, 1 mi W on paved rd	119	50	50	3.50	All year	• •		l				Modoc
E3	Leroy's Ferry	Fr jct Hwys 81 & 821, 3 mi NE, 3-1/2 mi W on Access Rd	92	15	15	None	All year	• •				p		Willington
E3	Mount Carmel	Fr Mt Carmel, 5 mi SW on paved rd	151	12	12	2.00	All year	• •		l				McCormick
E3	Haw Creek	Fr McCormick, 3.1 mi W on US 378, 1 mi S on paved rd, 2 mi S on dirt rd	86	28	28	2.00	All year	• •		l				McCormick
E3	Big Hart Creek Group Camp	Fr Thompson, GA, 12 mi N on US 78, 2-1/2 mi E on dirt rd	20	15	15	6.00	All year	• •		l			404/722-3770	Clark Hill 29821
E3	Parksville Wayside	Fr Parksville, 1/4 mi SE on US 221	59	8	8	2.00	All year	• •		l		p		Parksville
	Hartwell Reservoir	(See Georgia for additional campgrounds)											404/376-4788	Hartwell, Ga 30643
D2	Island Point	Fr Anderson, 15 mi S on US 29, 1 mi W on access rd	32	37	36	2.00	4/1-9/30	• •		l				Anderson
D2	Springfield	Fr Anderson, 10 mi SW on Hwy 80, S on Hwy 187, 1.5 mi W	60	69	69	3.00	4/1-9/30	• •		l				Anderson
D2	Crescent	Fr Starr, 7 mi W on Hwy 412, S on Hwy 29, 1 mi W on paved rd	41	42	42	3.00	4/1-9/30	• •						Starr
D2	Oconee Point	Fr Seneca, 6 mi SE on Co 21	29	50	50	3.00	4/1-9/30	• •		l				Seneca
D2	Twin Lakes	Fr Pendleton, 5 mi W on Hwy 104	107	25	25	3.00	4/1-9/30	• •		l				Pendleton
D2	Coneross	Fr Townville, 1-1/2 mi NW on Hwy 24, E on access rd	136	25	25	3.00	4/1-9/30	• •		l				Townville
D2	Asbury	Fr La France, 4.5 mi SE on Hwy 76, S on Co 102	27	46	46	2.00	4/1-9/30	• •						La France
D2	Glen Ferry	Fr Fair Play, 2 mi E on Hwy 243, S on access rd	164	5	5	None	4/1-9/30	• •		l				Fair Play
D2	Apple Island	Fr jct Hwys 24 & Co 86, 1-1/2 mi S	107	25	25	None	4/1-9/30	• •		l		p		Townville
D2	Weldon Island Pk	Fr Fair Play, E on Hwy 243, SE on Hwy 80, S on access rd	173	25	25	2.00	4/1-9/30	• •		l				Fair Play

Tennessee

Major Events

See state map, pages 28-29

Grand National Field Trials, mid-Feb., Grand Junction, east of Memphis. Bird dog owners from all over the country bring their pets to meet here for competition to determine the National Championship Hunting Dog. Free. 901/764-2167.

Valleydale 500, mid-Mar., Bristol. One of the premier NASCAR races in the South takes place at the Bristol International Raceway. Admission. 615/764-1161.

Dogwood Arts Festival, mid- to late Apr., Knoxville. This salute to spring centers around the blooming of the thousands of dogwood trees in the Knoxville area. There are arts and crafts shows, many different types of live music, parades, and sporting events. Admission is charged for several events. 615/637-4561.

Spring Wildflower Pilgrimage, mid-Apr., Gatlinburg. Hundreds of varieties of wildflowers are in bloom throughout the Great Smoky Mountains in late April, and there are guided tours through the mountains in the Gatlinburg area. Admission. 615/436-4178.

World's Largest Fish Fry, late Apr., Paris. Tennessee River catfish are prepared in large quantities at this festival which also features parades, beauty pageants, contests, live entertainment, and a rodeo. Admission is charged for several events. 901/642-3431.

Ramp Festival, late Apr., Cosby, northeast of Gatlinburg. The ramp is a wild plant which grows only in the higher elevations of the Appalachian Mountains. This festival features cooked ramps prepared in many different dishes, and there is plenty of live bluegrass, country and western, and gospel music. Admission. 615/487-5443.

Memphis in May, May, Memphis. This festival honors a different country each year with many different cultural programs: the Sunset Symphony on the banks of the Mississippi River, an international barbecue-cooking contest, several music festivals, the Cotton Carnival, pageants, contests, and numerous sporting events. Most of the activities take place during weekends in May, including the famous Beale Street Music Festival, which is usually held in mid-May. Admission is charged for several events. 901/525-4611.

Iroquois Steeplechase, early May, Nashville. This is one of the oldest and most important amateur steeplechase meets in the nation. Eight different races are held in Percy Warner Park. Free. 615/373-2130.

International Country Music Fan Fair, early to mid-June, Nashville. Top country recording artists mix and mingle with thousands of country music fans during a weeklong series of live shows, special concerts, autograph sessions, sporting events, and other special activities. The Grand Masters' Fiddling Contest is held on the last day, bringing together top musicians from all over the South. Admission. 615/889-7503.

Dulcimer Convention, mid-June, Cosby, northeast of Gatlinburg. The dulcimer, which is a traditional mountain musical instrument, is featured in workshops, demonstrations, and live performances at the Folk Life Center of the Smokies. Admission. 615/487-5543.

Rhododendron Festival, mid-June, Roan Mountain, southeast of Elizabethton. Six hundred acres of rhododendrons in bloom are the highlight of this festival which takes place in and around Roan Mountain State Park. Free. 615/772-3303.

Frontier Days, early July, Lynchburg, northeast of Fayetteville. Bluegrass music and square dancing are only two of the attractions at this July 4th celebration in the town best known as the home of Jack Daniels Sour Mash Whiskey. Free. 615/759-4221.

Old-Time Fiddler's Jamboree, early July, Smithville. There are two days of fiddling competition in 21 categories as well as an arts and crafts show, square dancing, and bluegrass music. Fiddlers also gather under the trees around the Smithville Courthouse where they perform for fun. Free. 615/597-4163.

Rugby Pilgrimage, early Aug., Rugby, southeast of Jamestown. This restored community, founded by Thomas Hughes, opens the doors of its historic homes and buildings in an event which also features lectures, slide shows, and musical performances. Admission. 615/628-2441.

International Grand Championship Walking Horse Show, mid-Aug., Murfreesboro. This show features the Tennessee Walking Horse, which is bred in central Tennessee and is known for its unusually comfortable riding gait. Admission. 615/890-9120.

International Banana Festival, mid-Aug., South Fulton. This town was once the distribution point for shipment of bananas to most of the country. Those days are recalled with parades, arts and crafts, street dances, and a 1-ton banana pudding made from 3,000 bananas. Free. 502/472-2975.

Tennessee Walking Horse National Celebration, late Aug. to early Sept., Shelbyville. "The Walking Horse Capital of the World" is the site for this 10-day show featuring beautiful horses, including the Grand Champion Tennessee Walking Horse. Old-fashioned pageantry is also part of the festivities. Admission. 615/684-5915.

Memphis Music Heritage Festival, early Sept., Memphis. Numerous musical acts provide continuous musical entertainment on four separate stages. Arts, crafts, and traditional foods are also featured. Free (except food). 901/526-6840.

TVA & I Fair, mid-Sept., Knoxville. This is an agricultural and industrial exhibition of the Tennessee Valley, and other events include rides, fireworks, and live entertainment. Admission is charged for several events. 615/637-5840.

Tennessee State Fair, mid- to late Sept., Nashville. The State Fairgrounds come alive with agricultural and livestock exhibits, a carnival, fireworks, and live entertainment. Admission. 615/255-6441.

Tennessee Grassroots Days, late Sept., Nashville. This celebration brings together the old-time survival ways of Tennessee working people. Music indigenous to Tennessee is also performed. Free. 615/331-0602.

National Storytelling Festival, early Oct., Jonesboro. Top storytellers from all over the country gather to swap tales in an event sponsored by the National Association for the Preservation and Perpetuation of Storytelling. One of the highlights is a ghost-story session around a bonfire in the old Jonesboro Cemetery. Admission. 615/753-2171.

Mid-South Crafts Fair, early Oct., Memphis. Some 100 craftsmen display and sell their goods at one of the largest crafts exhibitions in the South. Admission. 901/683-6707.

Craftsmen's Fall Exhibition, mid-Oct., Gatlinburg. This is an annual gathering of some of the nation's finest craftsmen displaying, demonstrating, and selling their wares. Continuous live entertainment is also provided. Admission. 615/436-9535.

Fall Color Cruise & Folk Festival, late Oct., Chattanooga. Two weekends of music, square dancing, live entertainment, and arts and crafts are held in the autumn beauty of eastern Tennessee and the Grand Canyon of the Tennessee River. The color cruise may be taken by boat, bus, or automobile. Free. 615/756-2121.

The 12 Days of Christmas, late Nov. to late Dec., Gatlinburg. There are special activities, sales, contests, and Christmas exhibits throughout the city. Free. 615/436-4178.

The Liberty Bowl Football Classic, late December, Memphis. This major bowl game pits two highly ranked NCAA teams against each other at the Liberty Bowl Memorial Stadium. A pregame brunch is served at the adjacent Mid-South Coliseum. Admission. 901/767-7700.

Tennessee Destinations

ANDREW JOHNSON NATIONAL HISTORIC SITE, E-10. In Greeneville, the site contains three separate sections. The tailor shop, Depot and College Sts., where Johnson worked as a young man also serves as a Visitors Center and museum. The **Andrew Johnson Homestead,** Main St., has been restored to the 1851-75 period when President Johnson lived in the house. The **Johnson Tomb and Monument,** Monument Ave., is also a national cemetery. Year-round, daily, 9 A.M. to 5 P.M. Free. The Johnson Homestead: Year-round, daily, 9 A.M. to 5 P.M. Adults 50¢; persons under 16 and over 62, free. 615/638-3551.

BRISTOL, 23,987, E-11. Located on the Tennessee-Virginia border, the city is bisected by the state line on its main street. **Bristol Caverns,** U.S. 421, is a large and spectacular dripstone cave. Year-round, June-Labor Day, Mon.-Sat., 9 A.M. to 8 P.M.; Sun., 12:30 to 8 P.M.; other months, Mon.-Sat., 9 A.M. to 6 P.M.; Sun., 12:30 to 6 P.M. Adults $3; children 7-12, $1.75; under 7, free. 615/878-2011. **Bristol International Raceway,** U.S. 11E, is a modern half-mile NASCAR track seating more than 30,000 people. Major races include the *Volunteer 500* in August and the *Valleydale 500* in March. 615/764-1161.

CHATTANOOGA, 169,565, G-7. Dominated by the imposing bulk of Lookout Mountain (elev. 2,126 ft.), Chattanooga is located in the Moccasin Bend of the Tennessee River. Beginning as a trading post on the river, the city grew into an important rail center in the mid-1800s and ranks today as a major center of manufacturing. **The Chattanooga Choo Choo,** 1400 Market St., was once the Southern Railroad Terminal in Chattanooga. Today it is the focal point of a complex of restaurants, lounges, a hotel with rooms in old rail cars, and Victorian-era shops. Year-round, daily. 615/266-5000. **Lookout Mountain,** south and southwest of downtown, is accessible by St. 57, St. 148, and an incline railway. On the mountain are several places of interest. *Incline Railway,* 3917 St. Elmo Ave., reaches a grade of 72.7° on the mile journey to the top of Lookout Mountain. Daily, June-Sept., 9 A.M. to 9:30 P.M.; other months, 9 A.M. to 6 P.M. Round trip: Adults $3; children 6-12, $2.25; under 6, free. One way: Adults $1.75; children 6-12, $1.25; under 6, free. 615/821-4224. Inside *Lookout Mountain Caverns,* on St. 148, is 145-foot *Ruby Falls.* Daily, May-Labor Day, 7:30 A.M. to 9:30 P.M.; other months, 8 A.M. to 8 P.M. Adults $3; children 6-12, $1.50; under 6, free. 615/821-2544. *Rock City,* St. 58, embraces 10 acres of unusual rock formations, with swinging bridge and observation tower. (*See* also **Chickamauga-Chattanooga National Military Park.**) **Tennessee Valley Railroad and Museum,** 2202

N. Chamberlain Ave., contains working steam and diesel locomotives, rail cars, and other railroad equipment. Excursion trips by rail are available on museum grounds. May-Oct., Sat., 10 A.M. to 5 P.M.; Sun., 1 to 5 P.M. Adults $2.50; children 5-12, $1.50; under 5, free. 615/894-8028. **Hunter Museum of Art,** 10 Bluff View, carved into a bluff overlooking the Tennessee River, contains sculpture and American art of the 18th, 19th, and 20th centuries. Year-round, Tues.-Sat., 10 A.M. to 4:30 P.M.; Sun., 1 to 4:30 P.M. Donations. 615/267-0968. **Houston Antique Museum,** 201 High St., features antique glassware, quilts, music boxes, and 15,000 pitchers. Year-round, Tues.-Sat., 10 A.M. to 4:30 P.M.; Sun., 2 to 4:30 P.M. Adults $1.50, children 75¢. 615/267-7176. **Confederama,** 3742 Tennessee Ave., is an automated, three-dimensional display with more than 5,000 miniature soldiers re-creating the four critical Civil War battles in Chattanooga. Memorial Day-Labor Day, Mon.-Sat., 9 A.M. to 9 P.M.; Sun., 1 to 9 P.M.; other months, Mon.-Sat., 9 A.M. to 5 P.M.; Sun., 11 A.M. to 5 P.M. Adults $2.50; children 6-12, $1; under 6, free. 615/821-2812. **Reflection Riding,** off U.S. 41, is a 300-acre scenic nature park containing the *Chattanooga Nature Center* and portions of the *Great Indian Warpath.* Year-round, Mon.-Sat., 9 A.M. to 5 P.M.; Sun., 1 to 5 P.M. Adults $1; children 3-16, 50¢; under 3, free. $2 extra per car. 615/821-1160.

CHICKAMAUGA-CHATTANOOGA NATIONAL MILITARY PARK, G-7. Established in 1890, **Chickamauga-Chattanooga National Military Park** is in both Tennessee and Georgia and includes eight separate sections. The *Chickamauga Battlefield,* U.S. 27S, is the nation's oldest and largest national military park, with 8,092 acres. Self-guided auto tours originate at the Visitors Center, which also contains the Fuller Gun Collection. Year-round, daily, 8 A.M. to 5:45 P.M. Free. 404/866-9241. *Point Park* on Lookout Mountain (*see* **Chattanooga**), was the site of the 1863 "Battle Above the Clouds." The park has hiking trails and a sweeping view of the city. Daily, May-Sept., 9 A.M. to 8 P.M.; other months, 9 A.M. to 6 P.M. Free. 615/821-7786. *Cravens House,* off St. 148, was used as a headquarters for both sides during the 1863 battle on Lookout Mountain. Year-round, daily, 9 A.M. to 5 P.M. Admission 50¢. Other sections of the park are *Orchard Knob* in downtown Chattanooga and *Missionary Ridge* and *Signal Point* on Signal Mountain. The *Chattanooga National Cemetery,* 1080 Bailey Ave., contains the graves of Civil War soldiers. Year-round, daily. Free.

COLUMBIA, 25,767, F-5. The **James K. Polk Home,** W. 7th and N. High Sts., was the early family dwelling of the 11th president of the United States. The adjoining

home and gardens of Polk's two sisters are included in the historic property. Year-round, Mon.-Sat., 9 A.M. to 5 P.M.; Sun., 1 to 5 P.M. Adults $2; persons 12-18, 75¢; under 12, free. 615/388-2354.

CRUMP, G-3. *See* **Shiloh National Military Park.**

DAYTON, 5,913, G-8. The **Rhea County Courthouse** is where, in 1925, Rhea County high school teacher John T. Scopes was tried for violating a Tennessee statute making it unlawful "to teach any theory that denies the story of the divine creation of man as taught in the Bible." Year-round, Mon.-Tues., Thurs.-Fri., 8 A.M. to 4:30 P.M.; Wed., Sat., 8 A.M. to noon. Free. 615/775-0187.

DOVER, E-4. *See* **Fort Donelson National Military Park.**

FORT DONELSON NATIONAL MILITARY PARK, E-4. Off U.S. 79 east of Dover, this park was the scene of one of the first decisive battles of the Civil War. The Confederate fort controlling the Cum-

D U X **spells ducks.** DUX is the new restaurant in the renovated Peabody Hotel in Memphis. Ducks are those famous fowl who live in the hotel penthouse and waddle to the lobby fountain each morning to the tune of a Sousa march. They pose with their keeper.

berland River fell to Union gunboats under the command of Gen. Ulysses S. Grant in February, 1862. Asked for surrender terms, Grant replied "unconditional and immediate surrender," a remark which earned him wide public attention. **Dover Hotel,** where the surrender was made, has been restored and is open to visitors. Year-round, daily, 8 A.M. to 4 P.M. Free. 615/232-5348.

FRANKLIN, 12,407, F-5. Civil War battles around Franklin were some of the war's heaviest, and the lives of six Confederate generals were lost in the Battle of Franklin, November 30, 1864. The **Carter House,** U.S. 31, was a focal point of this battle and houses a museum containing Civil War relics. Year-round, Mon.-Sat., 9 A.M. to 4 P.M.; Sun., 2 to 4 P.M. Adults $1.50; persons under 16, 50¢. 615/794-1733. **Battle-O-Rama,** 1143 Columbia Ave., features a 30-minute mural and slide presentation of area history. Year-round, Mon.-Sat., 11 A.M. to 4 P.M. Adults $1.50, children 75¢. 615/790-2422. **Carter's Court,** 1143 Columbia Ave., contains a variety of gift and specialty shops, antique shops, and restaurants. Year-round, Mon.-Sat., 10 A.M. to 5 P.M. 615/794-7445.

GALLATIN, 17,191, E-6. One of Tennessee's oldest towns, it contains many fine old homes. **Cragfont** (1802), off St. 25, was the home of Gen. James Winchester. Apr.-Oct., Tues.-Sat., 10 A.M. to 5 P.M.; Sun., 1 to 6 P.M.; other months by appointment. Adults $1.50; children 6-11, 50¢; under 6, free. 615/452-7070. **Wynnewood** (1828), St. 25 at Castalian Springs, is the largest log building ever erected in Tennessee. It once served as a stagecoach stop and a health spa. Year-round, Mon.-Sat., 10 A.M. to 4 P.M.; Sun., 1 to 5 P.M. Admission $2.

GATLINBURG, 3,210, F-10. Located at the main entrance to the Great Smoky Mountains National Park, Gatlinburg's permanent population swells to more than 25,000 during the summer. The resort city has also developed a reputation as a major craft center. The **Arrowmont School of Arts and Crafts,** in the downtown area, is affiliated with the University of Tennessee. The **Smoky Mountain Craft Trail,** off St. 73 between Gatlinburg and Cosby, features scores of working craftsmen, studios, and galleries, and visitors are welcome. Gatlinburg is filled with small gift and specialty shops offering native crafts and other items. **Gatlinburg Place,** Airport Rd., features the 70mm film *To Fly,* shown on a movie screen seven stories tall and 100 feet wide; the animated *Backwoods Bear Jamboree;* and live entertainment shows each night during the summer. Memorial Day-Oct., daily, 8 A.M. to 10 P.M.; other months, Sat.-Sun., 10 A.M. to 8 P.M. Adults $7, children $5. 615/436-6766. **Ober Gatlinburg,** 1001 Pkwy., features a 2.1-mile aerial tram to the Old Heidelburg Castle Ski Lodge. In addition to three winter ski runs, the lodge offers a 200,000-square-foot artificial surface

for year-round skiing; ice skating; and an Alpine Slide. Year-round, Mon.-Sat., 9 A.M. to midnight; Sun., 9 A.M. to 6 P.M. Adults $3; children 6-11, $1; under 6, free. 615/436-5423. **Christus Gardens,** River Rd., has life-size dioramas highlighting the life of Christ. Daily, Apr.-Oct., 8 A.M. to 10 P.M.; other months, 9 A.M. to 5 P.M. Adults $3; children 7-11, $1; under 7, free. 615/436-5155.

GREAT SMOKY MOUNTAINS NATIONAL PARK, I-9. Named for the smokelike haze which usually envelops these mountains, the Smokies are the highest series of peaks in the eastern United States. A vast wilderness covering more than 500,000 acres, the park contains more than 600 miles of horse and foot trails, ranging from short nature walks to a 71-mile section of the Appalachian Trail. More than 1,400 species of flowering plants grow in the park boundaries, and vegetation at the higher elevations is similar to the conifer forests of central Canada. There are seven developed campgrounds within the park and three primitive camping areas. Evening programs and nature walks at and from the Visitors Centers are conducted by park rangers during the summer months. **Sugarlands Visitors Center,** 2 miles south of Gatlinburg at the junction of U.S. 441 and St. 73, is the main entrance to the park in Tennessee. Visitors Center: Daily, late May-Oct., 8 A.M. to 7:30 P.M.; other months, 8 A.M. to 4:30 P.M. Free. 615/436-6515. **Cades Cove Visitors Center,** Cades Cove, is also within the park. Apr.-Oct., daily, 9 A.M. to 5 P.M. Free. 615/436-5615. *See* also **Great Smoky Mountains National Park** in North Carolina.

JACKSON, 49,131, F-3. **Casey Jones Village,** on Int. 40, includes a country store with antique fountain; the Carl Perkins Museum; and the museum and home of Casey Jones, legendary railroad engineer, who died in a 1900 train collision. Many artifacts and exhibits pertain to railroads. Casey Jones Home and Museum: Mid-Apr.-mid-Sept., Mon.-Sat., 8 A.M. to 9 P.M.; Sun., 1 to 9 P.M.; other months, Mon.-Sat., 8 A.M. to 5 P.M.; Sun., 1 to 5 P.M. Adults $1.75; children 6-12, 75¢; under 6, free. 901/668-1222.

JOHNSON CITY, 39,753, E-11. **Rocky Mount** (1770), U.S. 11E, was the first capital of the "Territory of the United States South of the River Ohio" which was brought into being in 1790 and lasted nearly six years. The two-story log home was the focal point of much of the region's early history. Year-round, Mon.-Sat., 10 A.M. to 5 P.M.; Sun., 2 to 6 P.M. Adults $2; persons 6-16, $1; under 6, free. 615/538-7396. **Tipton-Haynes Farm,** U.S. 19, represents four periods of American history, beginning in 1769. Apr.-Oct., Mon.-Sat., 10 A.M. to 5 P.M.; Sun., 2 to 6 P.M. Adults $1; children 6-12, 50¢; under 6, free. 615/926-3631. **Carroll Reece Museum,** East Tennessee State University,

features exhibits of Tennessee crafts, music, textiles, history, and folklore. Year-round, Mon.-Fri., 8 A.M. to 4:30 P.M.; Sat.-Sun., 1 to 5 P.M. Free. 615/929-4392.

JONESBORO, 2,829, E-11. Chartered by the North Carolina legislature in 1779, Jonesboro is the oldest town west of the Allegheny Mountains. Many historic buildings along the town's main street have been restored, including the **Chester Inn** (1797), **Sister's Row** (1820s), and the **Hoss House** (1830s). Walking tours originate from the Jonesboro Public Library in the Chester Inn or the Christopher Taylor Visitors Center, a 200-year-old log cabin representing Jonesboro's earliest period. 615/753-5961.

KINGSPORT, 32,027, E-11. **Bays Mountain Park,** Bays Mountain Rd., is a 3,000-acre nature center with ecology exhibits, walking trails, interpretive programs, and a planetarium. Memorial Day-Labor Day, Mon.-Sat., 8:30 A.M. to 8 P.M.; Sun., 1 to 8 P.M.; other months, Mon.-Tues., Thurs.-Fri., 8:30 A.M. to 5 P.M.; Wed., Sat., 8:30 A.M. to 8 P.M.; Sun., 1 to 8 P.M. Planetarium: Adults $1, children 50¢. 615/245-4192.

KNOXVILLE, 183,139, F-9. Begun in 1786 as a log fort and trading post on the Tennessee River, Knoxville served as the capital of the "Territory of the United States South of the River Ohio" (1792-96) and as the first capital of Tennessee (1796-1811 and 1817). Modern Knoxville is the headquarters for the Tennessee Valley Authority and the main campus of the University of Tennessee. Modern Knoxville is also host to the **1982 World's Fair,** May 1 through October 31 (*see* boxed feature). **James White Fort,** 205 Hill Ave., is a replica of the original fort built in 1786 and contains portions of the original log buildings. Year-round, Mon.-Sat., 9:30 A.M. to 5 P.M.; Sun., 1 to 5 P.M. Adults $1; children 6-12, 25¢; under 6, free. 615/525-6514. **Blount Mansion and Craighead-Jackson House,** 200 Hill Ave., was built in 1792 for William Blount, territorial governor, and is said to be the oldest frame home west of the Allegheny Mountains. The adjacent Craighead-Jackson House represents the Federal style of 1818 and serves as a Visitors Center. Mar.-Oct., Tues.-Sat., 9:30 A.M. to 5 P.M.; Sun., 2 to 5 P.M.; other months, Tues.-Sat., 9:30 A.M. to 4:30 P.M. Adults $2; children 6-12, 50¢; under 6, free. 615/525-2375. **Marble Springs,** Neubert Springs Rd. and John Sevier Hwy., is a two-story log home built by Tennessee's first governor, John Sevier. Mar.-Oct., Tues.-Sat., 10 A.M. to noon, 2 to 5 P.M.; Sun., 2 to 5 P.M. Adults $1; children 6-12, 10¢; under 6, free. 615/573-5508. **Confederate Memorial Hall,** 3148 Kingston Pike, is an antebellum mansion used by Confederate Gen. James Longstreet during the Civil War siege of Knoxville. Apr.-Sept., Tues.-Sun., 2 to 5 P.M.; Oct.-Mar., 1 to 4 P.M. Adults $1, children 50¢. 615/522-2371. **Frank H. Mc-Clung Museum,** Circle Drive on the University of Tennessee campus, has exhibits and artifacts of Tennessee history, natural history, and fine arts. Year-round, Mon.-Fri., 9 A.M. to 5 P.M. Free. 615/974-2144. **Dulin Gallery of Art,** 3100 Kingston Pike, has a permanent collection of nine miniature rooms. The gallery is housed in a neoclassical mansion designed by John Russell Pope, architect of the Jefferson Memorial. Year-round, Tues.-Fri., noon to 4 P.M.; Sat.-Sun., 1 to 5 P.M. Free. 615/525-6101. **Knoxville Zoological Park,** Magnolia Ave., successfully bred the first African elephants born in the Western Hemisphere. The zoo is also noted for its collection of large cats and reptiles. Daily, Apr.-Sept., 10 A.M. to 6 P.M.; other months, 10 A.M. to 3 P.M. Adults $3; persons 3-12, $1.50; under 3,

LAND BETWEEN THE LAKES, D-4. TVA's huge recreational area on the Tennessee-Kentucky border features one of the largest herds of buffalo in the eastern United States. **The Homeplace-1850,** on the Trace (unmarked north-south road through Land Between the Lakes) 12½ miles south of U.S. 68, is a living-history farm which re-creates the life-style of the area's early settlers. Feb.-mid-Dec., Wed.-Sun., 9 A.M. to 5 P.M. Free. 502/924-5602. *See* also **Land Between the Lakes** in Kentucky.

LYNCHBURG, 668, G-6. Downtown Lynchburg retains much of its turn-of-the-century atmosphere. The **Jack Daniel Distillery,** on St. 55 north of town, is the oldest registered distillery in the United States (1866). Tours include the limestone cave which supplies water, the modern distillery, and the old offices of Jack Daniel. Year-round, daily, 8 A.M. to 4 P.M. Free. 615/759-4221.

McMINNVILLE, 10,638, F-7. **Cumberland Caverns,** on St. 8, is the second largest cave system in the eastern United States; one of the rooms measures 200 feet by 100 feet by 60 feet. June-Aug., daily, 9 A.M. to 5 P.M.; May, Sept., Oct., Sat.-Sun., 9 A.M. to 5 P.M. Adults $4; children 6-12, $2; under 6, free. 615/668-4396.

MARYVILLE, 17,480, F-9. The **Sam Houston Schoolhouse,** on St. 33, is the oldest (1794) original schoolhouse in Tennessee. It is the state's only remaining building having a close association with Texas hero Sam Houston, who is believed to have taught at the school in 1812. The Visitors Center museum contains artifacts, including a set of lead knuckles (discovered during a 1954 restoration) with Houston's name carved in the metal. Year-round, daily, 9 A.M. to sunset. Free. 615/983-1550.

MEMPHIS, 646,356, G-1. Founded in 1819 by Andrew Jackson and John Overton, Memphis grew into one of the great commercial cities on the Mississippi River, with cotton as the basis of its economy. The Mem-

phis waterfront is lined with cobblestones brought from England as ballast aboard the ships carrying Memphis cotton to the European textile mills. Memphis is also famous as the home of the blues-style music first written by W. C. Handy.

HISTORIC AREAS AND HOMES: Beale Street, now under restoration, was once the center of the blues movement. **Blues Alley,** 60 S. Front St., is a restaurant and bistro in a converted 115-year-old cotton warehouse and houses a stage where Memphis musi-

The 1982 World's Fair

When: May 1 through October 31.
Where: Knoxville, Tennessee, on a 72-acre site bordered on the south by the Tennessee River, on the east by downtown Knoxville, and on the west by the University of Tennessee and Fort Sanders Neighborhood.
Theme: Energy Turns the World. Energy was chosen because of the attention directed to it. East Tennessee is the world energy center. Knoxville is the home of the University of Tennessee, which conducts extensive energy-related research, and the Tennessee Valley Authority, one of the world's largest utility complexes. Oak Ridge National Laboratory is within an hour's drive.
Participants: Companies, governments, and trade and professional associations from around the world.
Hours: Fair site: Daily, 10 A.M. to 10 P.M. Family Fun Land: Daily, 10 A.M. to midnight.
Admission: One-day pass, adults, $9.95; persons 55 and over, $9.25; 4 to 11, $8.25; under 4, free. Two-day pass, everyone, except children under 4, $15.95.

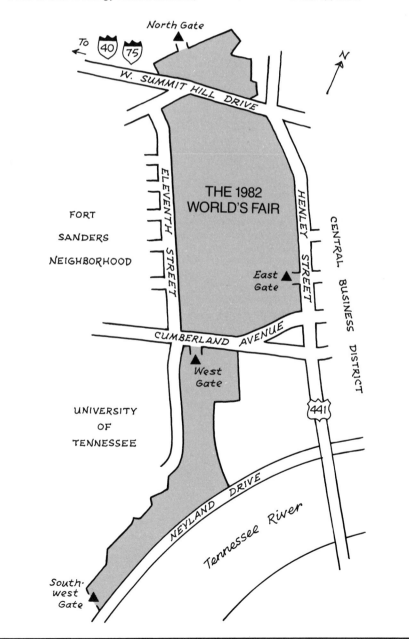

cians play the blues that made Memphis famous. **Handy Park,** Beale and Third Sts., honors blues musician W. C. Handy, whose compositions include "Memphis Blues," "Beale Street Blues," and "St. Louis Blues." A statue of Handy stands in the park, and impromptu blues concerts occur most summer afternoons. Donations. **Graceland,** 3764 Elvis Presley Blvd., is the Memphis home of Elvis Presley, who became an international star as "The King of Rock and Roll." Since his death, his home has become a shrine for his fans; he is buried in adjacent *Meditation Garden.* The mansion is not open to the public; but the garden is usually open, although it may be closed without notice. Year-round, Tues.-Sun., 9 A.M. to 4 P.M. Free. **Victorian Village Historical District,** 680 Adams Ave., contains several outstanding examples of late 19th-century architecture, including *The Fontaine House* (1870), 901/526-1469, and the *Mallory-Neely House* (1849), 901/523-1484. Both houses: Year-round, daily, 1 to 4 P.M. Adults $2; students and children $1; under 6, free. 901/526-1469.

MUSEUMS, GALLERIES, AND GARDENS: Chucalissa Indian Museum, Indian Village Dr., is a prehistoric Indian village restored by archaeologists from Memphis State University. The Visitors Center museum contains many artifacts and exhibits of Indian life of some three centuries ago. Year-round, Tues.-Sat., 9 A.M. to 5 P.M.; Sun., 1 to 5 P.M. Adults $1; children 6-11, 25¢; under 6, free. 901/785-3160. **Pink Palace Museum,** 3050 Central Ave., the home of Clarence Sanders, originator of the self-service supermarket, contains natural and cultural history exhibits. Year-round, Tues.-Fri., 9:30 A.M. to 4 P.M.; Sat., 9 A.M. to 4 P.M.; Sun., 1 to 4 P.M. Adults $1.50; persons 6-18 and 65 and over, 75¢; under 6, free. 901/454-5600. **Brooks Memorial Art Gallery,** Overton Park, houses a Kress collection of medieval religious art, as well as sculpture and porcelain exhibits. Year-round, Tues.-Sat., 10 A.M. to 5 P.M.; Sun., 1 to 5 P.M. Free. 901/726-5266. **Dixon Gallery and Gardens,** 4339 Park Ave., has a Georgian-style mansion housing French and American Impressionist art and 17th- and 18th-century British antiques. The gardens feature landscaped grounds, azaleas, and dogwoods. Year-round, Tues.-Sat., 11 A.M. to 5 P.M.; Sun., 1 to 5 P.M. Adults $1; persons 5-11 and 65 and over, 50¢; under 5, free. 901/761-5250. **Memphis Academy of Arts,** Overton Park, has student and professional art displays. Year-round, Mon.-Fri., 9 A.M. to 5 P.M. Free. 901/726-4085. **Memphis Botanic Gardens,** 750 Cherry St. at Audubon Park, contains a great variety of flowers, shrubs, and garden styles. Mar.-Sept., Mon.-Fri., 9 A.M. to 5 P.M.; other months, 9 A.M. to 4:30 P.M. Free. 901/685-1566.

ZOOS AND THEME PARK: Memphis Zoological Garden and Aquarium, Overton Park, contains more than 400 species of animals, birds, reptiles, and fish. Year-round, daily, 9 A.M. to 6 P.M. Adults $1.50; children 2-11, 50¢; under 2, free. 901/725-4768. **Libertyland,** Mid-South Fairgrounds, is a theme park with rides and live shows pertaining to American history. Late May-mid-Aug., daily, 11 A.M. to 8 P.M.; early Apr.-late May, mid-Aug.-mid-Sept., Sat., 11 A.M. to 8 P.M.; Sun., noon to 8 P.M. Admission $7. Adults $6.95; children 3-10, $4.95; under 3, free. Sun.-Fri., after 5 P.M., $5. 901/274-1776.

MARKETING AND SHOPPING AREAS: Memphis Cotton Exchange, Union and Front Sts., established in 1873, handles more than one-third of the nation's cotton crop each year. Year-round, Mon.-Fri., 8:30 A.M. to 4:30 P.M. Free. 901/525-3361. **Shelby Cotton Company,** 48 S. Front St., demonstrates cotton sorting and grading. **Cotton Row Gift Shop,** 48 S. Front St., includes thousands of items pertaining to cotton. Year-round, Mon.-Fri., 8:30 A.M. to 6 P.M.; Sat., 8:30 A.M. to 5 P.M. 901/526-3157. **Overton Square,** Madison Ave. and Cooper St., features many shops, restaurants, sidewalk cafes, art galleries, theaters, and an ice-skating rink. Year-round, daily. Free. 901/726-4656.

RIVERBOAT EXCURSION: *Memphis Queen,* Monroe St. and Riverside Dr., is a stern-wheel riverboat which offers daily excursions. Year-round, daily, 2:30 P.M.; June-Aug., Mon.-Sat., also 9:30 A.M., 6:30 P.M.; Apr.-Nov., Sat.-Sun., also 4:30 P.M. Adults $5; children 4-11, $2; under 4, free. 901/527-5694.

MORRISTOWN, 19,683, E-10. The **Crockett Tavern,** U.S. 11E, is a reproduction of the tavern operated in the 1790s by John Crockett, father of Davy Crockett. The tavern serves as a frontier museum honoring Davy Crockett and other early Tennessee pioneers. May-Oct., Mon.-Sat., 11 A.M. to 3 P.M.; Sun., 2 to 3 P.M. Adults $1.50; persons 6-17, 50¢; under 6, free.

MURFREESBORO, 32,845, F-6. The geographic center of Tennessee, Murfreesboro served as the state's capital from 1819 to 1825. **Cannonsburgh,** S. Front St., is a restored 19th-century village which features a blacksmith shop, general store, church, homes, and a river flatboat. Cannonsburgh was also the original name for Murfreesboro. May-Oct., Tues.-Sat., 10 A.M. to 5 P.M.; Sun., 1 to 5 P.M. Free. 615/893-6565. **Oaklands,** 900 N. Maney Ave., is a Romanesque-Revival mansion illustrating several 19th-century architectural styles. A Civil War landmark, the grounds also contain a medical museum. Year-round, Tues.-Sat., 10 A.M. to 4:30 P.M.; Sun., 1 to 4:30 P.M. Adults $1.50; persons 6-16, 75¢; under 6, free. 615/893-0022.

See also **Stones River National Military Park.**

NASHVILLE, 461,200, E-6. Internationally known as "Music City U.S.A.," Nashville recording studios are responsible for more than half of all the single records produced in the United States. The city's 17 colleges and universities, including Vanderbilt, Peabody, Scarritt, and Belmont, form one of the South's largest educational complexes. Many of Nashville's recording studios, music publishing firms, and talent agencies are located along a six-square-block area known as "Music Row." The focal point of the music industry is "The Grand Ole Opry," a live radio program broadcast each weekend since 1925 over WSM Radio.

COUNTRY MUSIC: Opryland U.S.A., 2802 Opryland Dr., is a 110-acre theme park dedicated to American music. Featured are 12 live musical shows. June-Aug., daily, 10 A.M. to 10 P.M.; Apr.-May, Sept.-Oct., Sat.-Sun., 10 A.M. to 10 P.M. One-day admission $10.75; two-day admission $15.25. 615/889-6611. *Grand Ole Opry,* Opryland U.S.A., is a live radio program featuring country music stars. Show times: Mid-June-mid-Aug., Fri.-Sat., 3, 6:30 and 9:30 P.M.; Sun., 3 P.M.; mid-Aug.-Oct., Fri.-Sat., 6:30 and 9:30 P.M.; Nov.-May, Fri., Sat., 6:30 and 9:30 P.M. Reserved seats $8, general admission $6. Sat. and Sun. matinees $5 and $4. 615/889-3060. **Ryman Auditorium,** 119 5th Ave., is where the "Grand Ole Opry" was broadcast from 1943 to 1974. Today, visitors can see the stage where performances were given and museum items related to the broadcast and stars. Year-round, daily, 8:30 A.M. to 4:30 P.M. Adults $1; children 6-12, 50¢; under 6, free. 615/749-1445. **Country Music Hall of Fame,** 4 Music Sq. E., at the head of "Music Row," has exhibits which trace the history and development of country music, as well as memorabilia of country stars and the Hall of Fame honoring the achievements of country music personalities. Daily, June-Aug., 8 A.M. to 8 P.M.; other months, 9 A.M. to 5 P.M. Adults $3.50; children 6-11, $1.25; under 6, free. 615/244-2527.

GOVERNMENT AND HISTORIC BUILDINGS AND SITES: Tennessee State Capitol, Capitol Hill, was designed by architect William Strickland, whose work also included the U.S. Capitol. Strickland died while construction was underway and is buried in the Capitol. Also on the grounds is the tomb of Pres. James K. Polk. Year-round, daily, 9 A.M. to 4 P.M. Free. 615/742-3211. **The Hermitage** (1819), U.S. 70E, was the home of Pres. Andrew Jackson and contains many of his personal possessions. The grounds include the tombs of Andrew and Rachel Jackson. **Tulip Grove** (1834), across the road, was the home of Rachel Jackson's nephew. Year-round, daily, 9 A.M. to 5 P.M. Adults $3; children 6-13, $1; under 6, free. 615/889-2941. **Belle Meade Mansion** (1853), Harding Rd. and Leake Ave., was known as the "Queen of Tennessee Plantations." Founded in 1807 by John Harding, the plantation was temporary headquarters for Confederate Gen. James R. Chalmers during the Civil War; later it was a famous thoroughbred horse nursery. Year-round, Mon.-Sat., 9 A.M. to 5 P.M.;

Sun., 1 to 5 P.M. Adults $2.50; persons 13-18, $2; 6-12, $1; under 6, free. 615/352-7350. **Travellers' Rest** (1799), Farrell Pkwy., was the home of John Overton, confidant and partner of Andrew Jackson. Year-round, Mon.-Sat., 9 A.M. to 4 P.M.; Sun., 1 to 4 P.M. Adults $2; children 6-12, 50¢; under 6, free. 615/832-2962. **Cheekwood and the Tennessee Botanical Gardens**, Cheek Rd., is a 60-room Georgian mansion built by the founders of the Maxwell House Hotel. Now a fine arts center, the grounds and gardens contain some of the finest boxwoods in America. Year-round, Tues.-Sat., 10 A.M. to 5 P.M.; Sun., 1 to 5 P.M. Adults $2; persons 7-17, $1; under 7, free. 615/352-5310. **Fort Nashboro**, 170 First Ave. N, is a reproduction of the stockade built in 1780 by Nashville's first settlers. Year-round, Tues.-Sat., 9 A.M. to 4 P.M. Free. 615/255-8192. **The Parthenon**, West End Ave. at Centennial Park, is an exact-size replica of the Greek Parthenon. Built for the Tennessee Centennial Exposition, it was dedicated in May, 1897. Year-round, Tues.-Sat., 9 A.M. to 4:30 P.M.; Sun., 1 to 4:30 P.M. Free. 615/259-6358.

MUSEUMS AND PERFORMING ARTS CENTER: Tennessee Performing Arts Center, Polk Cultural Complex, 505 Deaderick St., houses two theaters; a concert hall, home of the Nashville Symphony Orchestra; and a stage for a variety of theatrical groups. Schedule of events: 615/741-2787. **Tennessee State Museum**, Polk Cultural Complex, has exhibits of Tennessee history. An annex in the War Memorial Building con-

tains military exhibits. Year-round, Sun.-Mon., 1 to 5 P.M.; Tues.-Sat., 9 A.M. to 5 P.M. Free. 615/741-2692. **Tennessee Agricultural Museum**, Ellington Agricultural Center, Hogan Rd. off Franklin Pike in south Nashville, includes exhibits of farming tools, equipment, household instruments, and early farm artifacts. Year-round, Mon.-Fri., 8 A.M. to 4:30 P.M. Free. 615/741-1533. **Cumberland Museum and Science Center**, 800 Ridley Ave., includes exhibits of natural history, animals, arts, Indian life, and a planetarium. Year-round, Tues.-Sat., 10 A.M. to 5 P.M.; Sun., 1 to 5 P.M. Adults $2; persons 5-12, $1; under 5, free. 615/259-6099.

RIVERBOAT EXCURSION: *Belle Carol*, 170 First Ave. N, is a sternwheel riverboat with excursions on the Cumberland River. May, Fri.-Sat., 10:30 A.M., 2:30 P.M.; June-Sept., Mon.-Sat., 10:30 A.M., 2:30 P.M.; year-round, Sun., 2:30 P.M. Adults $5; children 2-11, $3; under 2, free. Dinner cruises: June-Aug., Thurs.-Sat., 8:30 P.M. $15 per person. 615/356-4120.

NATCHEZ TRACE PARKWAY, F-4. One of the nation's most important roads during the late 18th century, the Natchez Trace connected Nashville and Natchez, Mississippi. Year-round, daily. Free.
See also **Natchez Trace Parkway** in Mississippi.

NORRIS, 1,374, E-9. The **Museum of Appalachia**, Int. 75 at Norris exit, is an authentic replica of an early Appalachian Mountain village, with 30 original log

buildings and a museum housing more than 150,000 pioneer artifacts. Year-round, daily, 8 A.M. to sunset. Adults $2.50; children 6-12, $1.50; under 6, free. 615/494-7680.

OAK RIDGE, 27,662, F-9. This top-secret city, built during World War II as the base for the Manhattan Project to develop the atom bomb, contains many reminders of its military history. It is the location of the Oak Ridge National Laboratory. The **American Museum of Science and Energy**, Tulane and Illinois Aves., contains exhibits relating to energy. Year-round, Mon.-Sat., 9 A.M. to 5 P.M.; Sun., 12:30 to 5 P.M. Free. 615/576-3219. The **Graphite Reactor National Landmark**, Bethel Valley Rd. at the Oak Ridge National Laboratory, was the heart of the Manhattan Project and the world's first nuclear reactor. Year-round, Mon.-Sat., 9 A.M. to 4 P.M. Free. 615/574-4165.

PIGEON FORGE, 1,822, F-10. **Silver Dollar City**, a re-created mining village of the 1870s, serves as a theme for more than a dozen master craftsmen demonstrating skills ranging from blacksmithing to broom making and has rides and live shows. June-Aug., daily, 10 A.M. to 6 P.M.; May, Sept., Fri.-Wed., 10 A.M. to 6 P.M. Adults $7.95; children 6-11, $5.95. 615/453-4616. **Pigeon Forge Pottery**, 1 block off U.S. 441, uses natural clays in whimsical native animals and other varieties of pottery. Workshop demonstrations are given for visitors. Year-round, daily, 8 A.M. to 6 P.M. Free. 615/453-3883.

SHELBYVILLE, 13,530, G-6. Known as "The Tennessee Walking Horse Capital of the World," the city is surrounded by dozens of farms which raise and train the horses named for their unusually comfortable riding gait. Most farms welcome visitors at no charge. **Shadow Valley Farm**, U.S. 231N, is one of the most impressive. Year-round, Mon.-Fri., 9 A.M. to 4 P.M. Free. 615/684-0102.

SHILOH NATIONAL MILITARY PARK, G-3. On St. 22, south of Crump, the 3,753-acre park preserves the site of the first major battle of the western campaign of the Civil War. Union forces, under the command of Gen. Ulysses S. Grant, camped on the banks of the Tennessee River and were surprised by a Confederate attack on April 6, 1862. The Visitors Center contains artifacts and a film relating to the historic events. Daily, Memorial Day-Labor Day, 8 A.M. to 6 P.M.; other months, 8 A.M. to 5 P.M. Free. 901/689-5275.

SMYRNA, 8,839, F-6. The **Sam Davis Home**, St. 102, was the home of Confederate scout Sam Davis, who was executed as a spy during the Civil War and known as "The Boy Hero of the Confederacy." Davis is buried in the garden of the antebellum home. Year-round, Mon.-Sat., 9 A.M. to 5 P.M.; Sun., 1 to 5 P.M. Adults $2; children 6-16, $1; under 6, free. 615/459-2341.

STONES RIVER NATIONAL MILITARY PARK, F-6. Off U.S. 41/70 near Murfreesboro, the park includes a 331-acre portion of the Civil War battlefield. The battle, which took place from December 31, 1862, through January 2, 1863, marked the end of Confederate attempts to control Tennessee. Both sides suffered severe losses; of 38,000 Confederate troops, 10,000 were casualties; of 45,000 Union troops, about 13,000 were killed, wounded, or missing. In the park is a national cemetery with 6,831 burials and the **Hazen Brigade Monument** erected in 1863 and believed to be the oldest memorial of the Civil War. Self-guided auto tours originate at the Visitors Center, which also contains artifacts and orientation programs. Daily, Memorial Day-Labor Day, 8 A.M. to 8 P.M.; other months, 8 A.M. to 5 P.M. Free. 615/893-9501.

SWEETWATER, 4,728, F-8. The **Lost Sea,** St. 68, is the world's largest underground lake, according to the *Guinness Book of World Records*. Located in **Crag-** head **Caverns,** the cavern is also a Registered Natural Landmark because of its abundance of rare anthodium cave formations known as cave flowers. Year-round, daily, 9 A.M. to sunset. Adults $4; children 5-11, $2.25; under 5, free. 615/337-6616.

WAYNESBORO, 2,109, G-4. The **Natural Bridge,** off U.S. 64E, is a large double-span bridge. Country music shows are held here daily; square dancing, Saturday nights. Park: Mar.-Oct., daily, 9 A.M. to sunset. Adults $3, children $1. 615/722-3035.

Information Sources

Tennessee Department of Tourist Development
P.O. Box 23170
Nashville, TN 37202
615/741-2158

Tennessee Valley Authority
Information Office
400 Commerce St.
Knoxville, TN 37902
615/632-3257

U.S. Army Corps of Engineers
Nashville District
Public Affairs Office
P.O. Box 1070
Nashville, TN 37202
615/251-7161

Chattanooga Convention & Visitors Bureau
1001 Market St.
Chattanooga, TN 37402
615/756-2121

Gatlinburg Chamber of Commerce
520 Parkway
Gatlinburg, TN 37738
615/436-4178

Great Smoky Mountains National Park
Gatlinburg, TN 37738
615/436-5615

Knoxvisit
P.O. Box 15012
Knoxville, TN 37923
615/523-7263

Memphis Convention & Visitors Bureau
12 S. Main St., Suite 107
Memphis, TN 38103
901/526-1919

Nashville Area Chamber of Commerce
161 4th Ave. N.
Nashville, TN 37219
615/259-3900

Northwest Tennessee Tourist Association
P.O. Box 63
Martin, TN 38237
901/587-4215

South Central Tennessee Tourism Organization
245 E. Gaines St.
Lawrenceburg, TN 38464
615/762-6944

Southwest Tennessee Tourism Organization
Casey Jones Village
Jackson, TN 38301
901/668-1223

Tourist Association of the Upper Cumberlands
427 N. Willow Ave.
Cookeville, TN 38501
615/528-5077

Tennessee Campgrounds

FEES REFLECT MINIMUM RATE FOR 2 ADULTS AND ARE SUBJECT TO INCREASE OR SEASONAL CHANGES

- • – at the campground
- ○ – within one mile of campground
- $ – extra charge
- ** – limited facilities during winter months
- A – adults only
- B – 10,000 acres or more
- C – contribution
- E – tents rented
- F – entrance fee or premit required
- N – no specific number, limited by size of area only
- P – primitive
- R – reservation required
- S – self-contained units only
- U – unlimited
- V – trailers rented
- Z – reservations accepted
- LD – Labor Day
- MD – Memorial Day
- UC – under construction
- d – boat dock
- g – public golf course within 5 miles
- h – horseback riding
- j – whitewater running craft only
- k – snow skiing within 25 miles
- l – boat launch
- m – area north of map
- n – no drinking water
- p – motor bikes prohibited
- r – boat rental
- s – stream, lake or creek water only
- t – tennis
- u – snowmobile trails
- w – open certain off-season weekends
- y – drinking water must be boiled

Map Reference	Park Name	Access	Acres	Tent Spaces	Trailer Spaces	Approximate Fee	Season	Fishing Swimming	Other Swimming Swimming Pool	Boating	Playground	Other	Telephone Number	Mail Address
	STATE PARKS													
E9	Cove Lake	Fr Clinton, 10 mi N on US 25W	1500	100	100	6.00	All year	$ $		r	•		615/562-8355	Rt 2 Caryville 37714
E9	Big Ridge	Fr Norris, 11 mi NE on Hwy 61	3600	55	55	6.00	All year	$ $		lr	•	h	615/992-5523	Maynardville 37807
F6	Cedars of Lebanon	Fr Lebanon, 7 mi S on US 231 & Hwy 10	8900	120	50	6.00	4/1-10/31	$ $			•	h	615/444-9394	Rt 6 #, Lebanon 37087
G3	Chickasaw	Fr Henderson, 8 mi SW on Hwy 100	B	27	53	6.00		$ $			•		901/989-5141	Henderson 38340
F8	Cumberland Mtn	Fr Crossville, 6 mi S on Hwy 28	1425	146	146	6.00	All year	$ $		r	•		615/484-6138	Rt 8 Bx 330, Crossville 38555
G5	David Crockett	Fr Lawrenceburg, 1 mi W on US 64	950	108	108	6.00	All year	$ $		r	•		615/762-9408	Box 398 Lawrenceburg 38464
F7	Fall Creek Falls	Fr Pikeville, 11 mi NW on Hwy 30	B	57	143	6.00	All year	$ $		r	•	gh	615/881-3241	Rt 3 #, Pikeville 37367
G8	Harrison Bay	Fr Harrison, 11 mi NE on Hwy 58	1500	110	115	6.00	All year	$ $		dlr	•		615/344-6214	Harrison 37341
G8	Booker T Washington	Fr Chattanooga, 6 mi NE on Hwy 58	350	33	33	6.00	4/1-11/1	$ $		l	•		615/894-4955	5801 Champion, Chattanooga
F5	Montgomery Bell	Fr Dickson, 9 mi E on US 70	4600	51	52	6.00	All year	$ $ $		r	•		615/797-3101	Burns 37029
F4	Natchez Trace	Fr Hwy 20 at Lexington, 8 mi NE	B	140	140	6.00	All year	$ $			•		901/968-8176	Wildersville 38388
E9	Norris Dam	Fr Norris, 4 mi N on US 44	2400	8	91	6.00	All year	$ $		r	•		615/426-7461	Box 27, Norris 37828
E4	Paris Landing	Fr Paris, 15 mi E on US 79	1200	45	35	6.00	All year	$ $ $		dlr	•	g	901/642-4311	Rt 1#, Buchanan 38222
E8	Pickett	Fr Jamestown, 2 mi N on US 127, 11 mi NE on Hwy 154	B	27	5	6.00	All year	$ $		r	•		615/879-5821	Jamestown 38556
E2	Reelfoot Lake	Fr Tiptonville, 3 mi E on Hwy 21	50	95	95	6.00	All year	$ $		lr	•		901/253-7756	Tiptonville 38079
G1	Meeman-Shelby Forest	Fr Millington, 10 mi W on Shelby Rd	B	50	50	6.00	All year	$ $		lr	•	h	901/876-5201	Millington 38053
E7	Standing Stone	Fr Livingston, 10 mi NW on Hwy 52	B	34	16	6.00	All year	$ $		r	•		615/823-6347	Livingston 38570
E11	Warrior's Path	Fr Kingsport, 4 mi SE on US 23	1000	94	94	6.00	All year	$ $		dlr	•	gh	615/239-8531	Box 5026, Kingsport 37663
F6	Henry Horton	Fr Chapel Hill, 2-1/2 mi S on US 31A	1150	26	54	6.00	All year	$ $		•	•	gh	615/364-2222	Chapel Hill 37034
E6	Bledsoe Creek	Fr Gallatin, 7 mi E on Hwy 25	200	134	134	6.00	All year	$		l	•		615/452-3706	Rt 2 Box 60, Gallatin 37066
G1	T O Fuller	Fr Memphis, 5 mi SW on Hwy 61	1000	8	47	6.00	All year	$			•		901/785-3950	3269 Boxtown Rd, Memphis 38109
F4	Nathan Bedford Forrest	Fr Camden, 10 mi E on US 70	840	30	38	6.00	All year			l	•		901/584-6356	Eva 38333
G4	Pickwick Landing	Fr Savannah, 10 mi S on Hwy 128 at jct Hwy 57	500	48	48	6.00	All year	$ $		dlr	•	g	901/689-3135	Pickwick Dam 38365
F6	Old Stone Fort	Fr Manchester, 2 mi N on US 41	600	51	51	6.00	3/25-11/1	$			•		615/728-0751	Manchester 37355
F7	Edgar Evins	Fr Nashville, E on I-40	6100	60	60	6.00	All year	• •		l		p	615/858-2114	Rt 1#, Silver Point 38582
E11	Roan Mountain	Fr Roan Mtn, 5 mi S on Hwy 143	1450	50	50	6.00	All year	• •			•		615/772-3303	Rt 1# Box 50, Roan Mt 37687
F7	Rock Island	Fr Rock Island, 1 mi W on US 70 S	350	25	25	6.00	All year	$ $		l	•		615/686-2471	Rock Island 38581
E10	Panther Creek	Fr I-81, ext Morristown, N on US 25E, 4 mi S on US 11E, 2 mi W on Panther Cr Rd	1900	25	25	$4.00	4/1-12/31				•	p	615/581-2623	Rt 1 Bx 624, Morristown 37814
G6	Tim's Ford	Fr Winchester, 11 mi W on Hwy 50	720	50		None	All year	$ $ $		dlr	•	p	615/967-4457	Rt 4, Winchester 37398
	NATIONAL PARKS													
	Great Smoky Mtns NP	(See North Carolina for additional campgrounds)	B										615/436-5615	Supt, Gatlinburg 37738
F9	Cades Cove	Fr Townsend, 10 mi SW		180	160	4.00	All year					h		Gatlinburg
F10	Elkmont	Fr Gatlinburg, 8 mi W on Hwy 73		292	244	4.00	All year	○						Gatlinburg
F10	Look Rock CG	Fr Walland, 11 mi on Hwy 73 & Foothills Pkwy		92	92	4.00	5/31-9/4							Gatlinburg
F10	Cosby	Fr Cosby, 7 mi SE on Hwy 32 & access rd		174	164	4.00	4/6-10/26	○				h		Gatlinburg
	Natchez Trace Parkway	(See Mississippi for additional CGs)											601/842-1572	RR1 NT143, Tupelo 38801
F5	Meriwether Lewis	Fr Hohenwald, 7 mi E on Hwy 20	1000	32	32	None	All year					p		RR1 NT143, Tupelo 38801
	NATIONAL FORESTS													
	Cherokee NF													

Map Reference	Park Name	Access	Acres	Tent Spaces	Trailer Spaces	Approximate Fee	Season	Other Swimming / Swimming Pool	Fishing	Boating	Playground	Other	Telephone Number	Mail Address
E12	Jacobs Creek	Fr Shady Valley, 9 mi NW on US 421, 2 mi N on Co 32, .7 mi W on FR 337.	10	30	30	2.00	5/1-10/1	•	•			dlr		Shady Valley
E12	Little Oaks	Fr Bristol, 14 mi E on US 421, 7 mi SW on FR 87	35	72	72	3.00	4/1-10/1	•	•			dl		Bristol
E11	Dennis Cove	Fr Hampton, 1 mi E on US 321, 7 mi SE on FR 50.	2	18	18	None	4/14-11/27	•	•					Hampton
G8	Sylco	Fr Cleveland, 12.5 mi E on US 64, 3 mi SE on Co 75, 7.4 mi SE on FR 55.	4	12	12	None	All year	3				n		Cleveland
G8	Quinn Springs	Fr Etowah, 7 mi S on US 411, 3 mi E on Hwy 30.	4	12	12	2.00	All year	1				dlr		Etowah
G9	State Line	Fr Tellico Plains, 1.1 mi E on Co FH210, 21.7 mi SE on FR RH210.	3	7	7	2.00	All year	•	•			h		Tellico Plains
G9	Spivey Cove	Fr Tellico Plains, 1.1 mi E on Co FH210, 16.7 mi SE on FR FH210.	7	17	17	2.00	3/1-12/18	1	1			h		Tellico Plains
G9	Holly Flats	Fr Tellico Plains, 1.1 mi E on CO FH210, 18.7 mi SE on FR FH210, 5 mi W on FR126.	6	17	17	None	3/1-12/18	•	•			h		Tellico Plains
G9	North River	Fr Tellico Plains, 1.1 mi E on Co FH210, 13.7 mi SE on FR FH210, 2.5 mi NE on FR 217.	4	11	11	2.00	All year	•	•			h		Tellico Plains
G9	Big Oak Cove	Fr Tellico Plains, 1.1 mi E on CO FH210, 20.4 mi SE on FR FH210.	3	7	7	2.00	3/1-12/17	•	•			h		Tellico Plains
G8	Quinn Springs	Fr Etowah, 7 mi S on US 411, 3 mi E on Hwy 30.	3	5	5	2.00	All year	•	•		1	dlr		Etowah
G8	Lost Creek	Fr Etowah, 7 mi S on US 411, 6 mi SE on Hwy 30, 7 mi E on FR 103.	5	12	12	None	All year		•					Etowah
E11	Horse Creek	Fr Greeneville, 9 mi E on Hwy 107, 3 mi S on FR FH94.	4	10	9	2.00	5/1-10/31	•	•					Greeneville
E11	Old Forge	Fr Greeneville, 9 mi E on Hwy 107, 3 mi S on FR FH94, 3 mi SW on FR 331.	5	9		None	5/1-10/31		•			h		Greeneville
E11	Rock Creek	Fr Erwin, 1 mi N on US 23, 4 mi E on FR 30.	13	37	37	3.00	4/14-10/16	•	1					Erwin
E11	Limestone Cove	Fr Unicoi, 5 mi E on Hwy 107.	6	18	18	None	4/14-10/16	•						Unicoi
E12	Backbone Rock	Fr Damascus, 5 mi SW on Hwy 133.	5	13	13	None	All year	•	•					Damascus VA
G9	Jake Best	Fr Tellico Plains, 4 mi E on Co 165, .1 mi NE on Fr 35.	2	7	7	None	All year	•	•					Tellico Plains
G9	Double Camp	Fr Tellico Plains, 1.1 mi E on CO FH210, 18 mi NE on FR 35.	3	11	11	2.00	All year	•	•			dl		Tellico Plains
G9	Indian Boundary	Fr Tellico Plains, 1.1 mi E on Co FH210, 14 mi NE on FR 35.	20	100	100	3.00	3/1-10/15	•	•			dl		Tellico Plains
G9	Indian Boundary Overflow	Fr Tellico Plains, 14 mi E on Co 165, 1.1 mi NE on FR 35	5	25	25	2.00	All year	•	•			dl		Tellico Plains
G8	Tumbling Creek	Fr Copperhill, 1.8 mi NW on Hwy 68, 4.9 mi W on Co 5496, 2 mi N on FR 221.	3	8	8	None	All year	•						Copperhill
G8	Thunder Rock	Fr Cleveland, 28.5 mi E on US 64, .2 mi S on FR 45.	2	6	6	None	All year	•						Cleveland
G8	Parksville Lake	Fr Cleveland, 19.4 mi E on US 64, .4 mi NE on Hwy 30.	4	12	12	2.00	4/15-10/30	•	•			dlr		Cleveland
G8	Chilhowee	Fr Cleveland, 17.3 mi E on US 64, 7.4 mi NW on FR 77.	26	68	68	3.00	5/1-10/30	•	•			d		Cleveland
F10	Houston Valley	Fr Newport, 13 mi E on US 25, 5 mi NE on Hwy 107.	4	10	5	1.00	5/1-10/31	1						Newport
F10	Paint Creek	Fr Greeneville, 12 mi S on Hwy 70, 1.5 mi W on FR FH13, 1.5 mi SW on FR 31.	6	21	18	1.00	5/1-10/31	1	•					Greeneville
F10	Round Mountain	Fr Newport, 7 mi SE on US 25, 13 mi SE on Hwy 107.	6	16	14	1.00	5/1-10/31	1	•					Newport
E11	Cardens Bluff	Fr Hampton, 4 mi NE on US 321.	14	34	9	2.00	5/1-10/1	1	•			dlr		Hampton
	CORPS OF ENGINEERS													
	Cordell Hull Reservoir													Rt 1, Carthage, TN 37030
E7	Salt Lick Creek	Fr Carthage, 10 mi NE on Hwy 85 to Gladdice, 2 mi S	247	200	200	5.00	4/1-11/1	•	•		I			
	Cheatham Lake													
E5	Lock A Rec Area	Fr Ashland City, 11 mi NW on Hwy 12 & access	31	33	33	5.00	4/1-11/1		•		I	•		Ashland City
	Lake Barkley (See Ky for additional listings)													
E4	Bumpus Mills Rec Area	Fr Dover, 7 mi E on US 79, 5 mi N on Hwy 120, 6 mi W	10	33	33	None	4/1-11/1				I			Dover
E4	Hickman Creek Rec Area	Fr Dover, 4 mi NW, N of US 79	25	17	17	None	All year				I			Dover
E4	Blue Creek Rec Area	Fr Dover, 5 mi N on Hwy 20, W to access rd	10	20	20	None	All year				I	n		Dover
E4	Lick Creek Rec Area	Fr Dover, 2 mi E on Hwy 79	15	18	18	None	All year					n		Dover
E5	River Bend Rec Area	Fr Cumberland City, 3 mi N	15	15	15	None	All year					n		Dover
E5	Guises Creek Rec Area	Fr Cumberland City, 3 mi E on Hwy 149	10	20	20	None	All year				I	n		Cumberland City
	Old Hickory Lake													
E6	Shutes Branch	Fr Nashville, 8 mi NE on US 70, N on Saundersville Rd	100	84	84	4.00	4/1-11/1		•		I	•		Old Hickory
E6	Cages Bend	Fr Hendersonville, 3.5 mi E on US 31E, S on Cages Bend Rd	24	49	49	4.00	4/1-11/1		•		I	•		Hendersonville
E6	Cedar Creek	Fr Nashville, 12 mi NE on US 70, N on Saunders Ferry Rd	30	56	56	5.00	4/1-11/1		•		I	•		Old Hickory
	Center Hill Lake													
F7	Center Hill	Fr Gordonsville, 10 mi SE on Hwy 141	5	14	14	None	4/1-11/1		•		I			Silver Point
F7	Cove Hollow	Fr Smithville, 14 mi NE on US 70	6	25	25	None	4/1-11/1		•		I			Silver Point
F7	Hurricane Bridge	Fr Smithville, 12 mi N on Hwy 56	20	25	25	None	4/1-11/1		•		I			Silver Point
F7	Floating Mill Pk	Fr Smithville, 14 mi NE, off Hwy 56	30	120	120	4.00	4/1-11/1		•		I	•		Silver Point
F7	Holmes Creek	Fr Smithville, 5 mi NE on Hwy 70	30	150	150	4.00	4/1-11/1		•		I	•		Smithville
F7	Johnson Chapel	Fr Smithville, 3 mi NE on Hwy 70	8	22	22	None	4/1-11/1		•		I			Smithville
F7	Ragland Bottom	Fr Smithville, 8 mi NE, off Hwy 70	35	78	78	4.00	4/1-11/1		•		I	•		Smithville
	Cordell Hull Lake													
E7	Granville RA	Fr Granville, 2 mi S on Hwy 53	40	75	75	None	4/1-11/1		•		I	•		Granville
E7	Defeated Creek RA	Fr Carthage, 5 mi N on Hwy 85	150	150	150	5.00	4/1-11/1	•	•		I	•		Carthage 37030
E7	Roaring River RA	Fr Gainesboro, 3 mi NE on Hwy 135	50	75	75	None	4/1-11/1		•		I	•		Gainesboro
	Dale Hollow Lake (For additional CGs, see Kentucky & 'Backpack or Boat Access Areas')													
E7	Lillydale	Fr Livingston, 19 mi NE on Hwy 52 & Willow Grove Rd	20	92	92	4.00	4/11-11/1		•		I	•		Allons
E7	Willow Grove	Fr Allons, 1/2 mi N on Hwy 52, 15 mi NE on Willow Grove Rd	20	75	75	4.00	4/11-11/1		•		I	•		Allons
E7	Obey River	Fr Byrdstown, 6 mi SW on Hwy 42	40	157	157	3.50	4/11-11/1		•		I	•		Byrdstown
E7	Cove Creek	Fr Byrdstown, 2 mi SW on Hwy 42, 3 mi SE	3	12	12	None	All year		•		I			Byrdstown
E7	Pleasant Grove	Fr Celina, 4 mi E on Hwy 53, 1-1/2 mi SE	27	20	20	None	All year		•		I	n		Celina
E7	Dale Hollow Dam	Fr Celina, 3 mi W on Hwy 53	10	73	73	5.00	4/11-11/1		•		I	•		Celina
	J Percy Priest Reservoir													
E6	Cook	Fr Nashville, 10 mi E on I-40, 2 mi S on Old Hickory Blvd	145	57	57	4.00	4/1-11/1	•	•		I	•		Nashville
E6	Seven Points	Fr I-40, 1-1/2 mi S on Old Hickory Blvd, 1-1/2 mi SE	100	60	60	4.00	4/1-11/1	•	•		I	•		Nashville
F6	Fall Creek	Fr Walterhill, 1 mi N on US 231, 9 mi NW	90	37	37	None	All year		•		I	n		Nashville
F6	Poole Knob	Fr Smyrna, 2 mi NW on US 41, 5 mi NE	245	125	125	4.00	4/1-11/1	•	•		I	•		Nashville
F6	Anderson Road Rec Area	Fr Smyrna, 10 mi NW on US 41, 3 mi NE on Bell & Anderson Rds	70	37	37	4.00	4/1-11/1	•	•		I	•		Nashville
	NATIONAL WILDLIFE REFUGES													
F4	**Tennessee NWR**													
	Sugartree Marina	Fr Tn Riv, W on I-40, Birdsong ext #133, 4 mi S			15	3.50	All year	•	•		dlr	gp	901/584-7114	Sugartree 38380
	TENNESSEE VALLEY AUTHORITY													
E4	Land Between The Lakes	See Ky for Additional campgrounds											502/924-5602	Golden Pond KY 42231
	Rushing Creek CG	Fr Fenton Ky, 2 mi E, 9 mi SE on Hwy 453, 2 mi W	500	150	60	4.00	5/15-LD		•		I	•	502/924-5602	Golden Pond, KY 42231
E4	Lake Barkley Access Areas	Shore of Lake Barkley	*											Golden Pond, KY 42231
E4	Bards Dam	Fr Dover, 3 mi W on US79, 7 mi N on Hwy 49, 1.5 mi E		N	N	None	All year		•		I	p		
E4	Gatlin Point	Fr Dover, 3 mi W on US 79, 4 mi N on Hwy 49, 3.5 mi NE		S11	11	None	All year		•		I	p		
	Neville Bay	Fr Dover, 3 mi W on US 79, 9 mi N on Hwy 49, 2 mi E		S5	5	None	All year		•		I	p		
E4	Kentucky Lake Access Area	Shore of Kentucky Lake											502/924-5602	Golden Pond, KY 42231
	Blue Spring	Fr Dover, 3 mi W on US 79, 3 mi N on Hwy 49, 6 mi W		N	N	None	All year		•			p		
E4	Boswell Landing	Fr Dover, 9.5 mi W on US 79, 5 mi N		S10	10	None	All year		•		I	p		
E4	Piney CG	Fr Dover, 9.5 mi W on US 79, 2 mi N	200	200	200	4.00	All year		•		I	•		
E4	Ginger Rdge Back-Country	Southern Kentucky Lk Shoreline		P13	P13	1.00	All year		•			s	502/924-5602	Golden Pond 42231
E4	Grays Landing	Fr Dover, 10 mi W on US 79		6	S6	None	All year		•		I	ghp		

Texas

Major Events

The Cotton Bowl, Jan. 1, Dallas. This NCAA football classic features the Southwest Conference champion against a nationally ranked team. A large parade and several other events precede the game. Admission. 214/565-9931.

First Monday Trade Days, first Mon. (and preceding weekend) of each month, Canton. Each weekend of buying and selling features 60 acres of items for sale. Free. 214/567-4300.

Livestock Show and Rodeo, late Feb. to early Mar., Houston. The Houston Astrodome is the site for this large stock show with some 27,000 entries. Other events include a rodeo and live entertainment. Admission. 713/791-9000.

Shakespeare Festival, late Feb. to late Mar., Odessa. Staged in a faithful replica of Shakespeare's original Globe Theatre, a repertory company presents two Shakespearean plays along with one contemporary production. Admission. 915/332-1586.

Dogwood Trails Festival, late Mar. to early Apr., Palestine. A tour of homes, square dancing, a flea market, and an arts and crafts fair complement the 5-mile tour through a forest of flowering dogwood. Admission. 214/729-6066.

Fiesta San Antonio, mid-Apr., San Antonio. More than 140 events are at this year's fiesta, including a river parade, the Battle of Flowers Parade, Fiesta Flambeau Parade, the Parade of the Ugly King, Night in Old San Antonio, flower and fashion shows, fireworks, and concerts. Admission is charged for several events. 512/223-9133.

Brazos River Festival and Cotton Palace Pageant, late Apr., Waco. Waco's heritage is commemorated with a historic homes tour, an art show and auction, garden tours, children's events, international foods, and music. Admission is charged for several events. 817/772-1820.

Buccaneer Days Festival, late Apr. to early May, Corpus Christi. A music festival, an art jamboree, carnivals, parades, and fireworks highlight the festival. Admission is charged for several events. 512/882-3242.

Jefferson Historic Pilgrimage, early May, Jefferson. Tours of historic homes, horse-drawn surrey rides, and a play are some of the festivities at this pilgrimage. Admission is charged for several events. 214/665-2513.

Magnolia Homes Tour, mid-May, Columbus. Tours of homes and buildings are conducted, and shows are presented in the Stafford Opera House. Entertainment on Courthouse Square includes foods, rides, dances, antiques, an arts and crafts show, and buggy and surrey rides. Admission is charged for several events. 713/732-5881.

Texas State Arts & Crafts Fair, late May to early June, Kerrville. Some 200 Texas craftsmen and artists are invited to this fair on the campus of Schreiner College. There are demonstrations as well as exhibits, and historic crafts are shown along with contemporary works. Live music and food are also on hand. Admission. 512/896-5711.

The Lone Star **Outdoor Drama,** late May to late Aug., Galveston. The story of the war for Texas' independence and the heroes of the revolution is presented nightly except Monday in the Galveston Island State Park Amphitheater. Admission. 713/737-3442.

Fiesta del Concho, mid-June, San Angelo. This fiesta along the Concho River is highlighted by river parades, arts and crafts shows, and an antique automobile exhibit. Free. 915/653-1206.

TEXAS **Historical Musical Drama,** mid-June to mid-Aug., Canyon. This long-running play, written by playwright Paul Green, relives the joys and struggles of west Texas pioneers in the 1880s. Performances are nightly, except Sunday, at the Amphitheater located in nearby Palo Duro State Park. Admission. 806/655-2181.

Fort Griffin Fandangle, mid- to late June, Albany. First produced in 1938, this musical version of history as it lingers in the heads of old-timers is a blend of fantasy and realism set to music. The show is presented at an outdoor theater just outside of town. Admission. 915/762-2525.

Watermelon Thump, late June, Luling, south of Lockhart. The focus of this festival is on the local watermelon crop with watermelon-judging, -eating, and seed-spitting contests. Other events include a parade on Saturday, a street carnival, an auto rally, dances, a fiddler's contest, and golf and bowling tournaments. Free. 512/875-3214.

Texas Cowboy Reunion, late June to early July, Stamford. This event has attracted top amateur rodeo performers since 1930. Chuck wagon meals, music, and a Western art show are also featured. Admission. 915/773-3292.

Black-Eyed Pea Festival, mid-July, Athens. Contestants vie for valuable prizes in three categories of black-eyed pea cookery. Other events include country and western music, a pet parade, pea-shelling contests, and a carnival. Admission is charged for several events. 214/675-5181.

Aqua Festival, early to mid-Aug., Austin. Water-related activities take place on several lakes in the Austin area. Sporting events, a lighted night water parade, and fireworks are other activities. Admission is charged for several events. 512/472-5664.

Texas Folklife Festival, early Aug., San Antonio. The Institute of Texan Cultures is the site for this event which features the traditional folk performances, costumes, games, contests, demonstrations, crafts, art, food, music, and dancing of the 26 ethnic groups that settled Texas. Admission. 512/223-9133.

Republic of Texas Chilympiad, mid-Sept., San Marcos. CASI (Chili Appreciation Society, International) sanctions this cook-off which draws chili chefs from all over the state. An air show and other events also take place. Admission. 512/396-2495.

Texas Prison Rodeo, Sundays in Oct., Huntsville. Inmates compete in standard rodeo events, and there is live entertainment and an arts and crafts show featuring works by the inmates. Admission. 713/295-6371.

Heart O'Texas Fair and Rodeo, early Oct., Waco. There are traditional stock, farm, and home exhibits along with a large rodeo, horse shows, and live entertainment. Admission. 817/776-1660.

Autumn Trails Festival, weekends in Oct., Winnsboro, north of Quitman. Specially marked trails take visitors through the colorful autumn woodlands in the area. The five weekends of activity also include art shows and trail rides. Free. 214/342-6066.

State Fair of Texas, early to late Oct., Dallas. This is the largest state fair in the country. There are musicals, football games, shows, exhibits, and entertainment. Admission. 214/565-9931.

Wurstfest, late Oct. to early Nov., New Braunfels. The German heritage of New Braunfels is celebrated with a beer and sausage festival. Also featured are contests, live entertainment, and German singing, dancing, and music. Admission. 512/625-1886.

Chili Cook-off, early Nov., Terlingua, west of Big Bend National Park. Thousands of chili enthusiasts converge on a remote site near an abandoned mining town for a chili cook-off and many other events. Free. 214/522-4340.

Sun Bowl, late Nov. to late Dec., El Paso. The festivities begin with a parade on Thanksgiving Day, and many different events are held on both sides of the United States-Mexico border throughout December. The Sun Bowl Game is in late December, when two highly ranked NCAA football teams meet on the gridiron. Admission is charged for several events. 915/533-4416.

Bluebonnet Bowl, late Dec., Houston. Two top NCAA football teams play in the Astrodome on New Year's Eve. Admission. 713/799-9555.

Texas Destinations

ABILENE, 98,315, B-6. Named for Abilene, Kansas, this was a frontier settlement on the Chisholm Trail before the railroad came through here in 1881. **Fort Phantom Hill,** 10 miles north on Ranch Rd. 600, has the ruins of an old fort which was built to protect the gold miners traveling to California. Always open. Free. **Abilene Zoological Gardens,** in Nelson Park near the junction of Loop 332 and St. 36, has animals in their natural habitat. Year-round, Mon.-Fri., 10 A.M. to 5 P.M.; Memorial Day-Labor Day, Sat.-Sun., 10 A.M. to 7 P.M.; other months, 10 A.M. to 5 P.M. Adults $1; children 2-12, 50¢; under 2, free. 915/676-6222. **Old Abilene Town,** 4 miles northeast on Int. 120, is the replica of a frontier town, with shops, restaurant, saloon, and historical exhibits. Year-round, Mon.-Thurs., 10:30 A.M. to 9 P.M.; Fri.-Sun., 9 A.M. to 9 P.M. Adults $2; children $1.50; under 6, free. 915/677-2611. **Abilene Fine Arts Museum,** Oscar Rose Park, 7th and Barrow Sts., has permanent and changing exhibits. Year-round, Tues.-Fri., 9 A.M. to 5 P.M.; Sat.-Sun., 1 to 5 P.M. Free. 915/673-4587.

ALABAMA COUSHATTA INDIAN RESERVATION, on U.S. 90 east of Livingston, D-9. This major Indian reservation is on the fringe of the **Big Thicket National Preserve,** a 84,500-acre scenic, almost impenetrable cypress and streams area. In the **Living Indian Village** in the reservation, tribal members use traditional tools and techniques to make authentic jewelry, basketry, and leather items which are displayed and sold at the museum and arts and crafts shop. Tribal members also perform Indian dances. June-Aug., daily, 10 A.M. to 6 P.M.; Oct.-Nov., Fri.-Sun., 10 A.M. to 5 P.M.; Mar.-May, Tues.-Sun., 10 A.M. to 5 P.M. Adults $7, children $5. *Beyond the Sundown,* a historical musical drama, is presented during summer in the amphitheater. Performances: Mid-June-late Aug., Mon.-Sat., 8:30 P.M.. Adults $6, children $4. 713/563-4777.

AMARILLO, 149,230, G-2. This is the Texas Panhandle. Once known as *Llanos Estacados* ("staked plains"), it is open range, short-grass cattle country. The town, laid out in 1887 by land developer Henry B. Sandborn, was first settled by cattlemen and their families. **Amarillo Art Center,** 2200 Van Buren St. on Amarillo College campus, is a magnificent complex of three buildings designed by Edward Stone, architect for such famous structures as the John F. Kennedy Center for Performing Arts in Washington, D.C. Devoted to the fine arts, here are permanent collections of paintings and sculpture. Year-round, Tues., Thurs.-Fri., 10 A.M. to 5 P.M.; Wed., 10 A.M. to 5 P.M., 7:30 to 9:30 P.M.; Sat.-Sun., 1 to 5 P.M. Donations. 806/372-8356. **Amarillo Discovery Center,** at the Medical Center Complex on U.S. 66, is a planetarium with a small physical science museum. Year-round, Mon.-Fri., 9 A.M. to 4 P.M.; Sat., 2 to 4 P.M.; Sun., 2 to 5 P.M. Shows: Sat., 2, 3, and 8 P.M.; Sun., 2, 3, and 4 P.M. Adults $1.50; students under 18, $1. 803/355-9547. **Amarillo Livestock Auction,** 100 S. Manhattan St., is known as the "World's Largest Livestock Auction." It handles more than 5,000 cattle a day at weekly auctions which start on Monday and last two or three days. Auction times: 9 A.M. to about 9 P.M. Free. 806/373-7464.

See also **Fritch** for **Alibates Flint Quarries National Monument** and **Lake Meredith National Recreation Area.**

ARANSAS NATIONAL WILDLIFE REFUGE, south of Austwell on Farm Market Rd. 2040, F-8. **Aransas National Wildlife Refuge** is the winter home of the whooping cranes. Verging on extinction for many years, the cranes now number 80, migrating between Texas and Canada. The 47,261-acre refuge is also the habitat for more than 300 other species of migratory and native waterfowl. Information is available at the Visitor Center; a 16-mile loop goes by observation points and a tower where wildlife can be observed. Year-round, daily, sunrise to sunset. Free. Visitors Center: Year-round, daily, 8 A.M. to 5 P.M. 512/286-3559. A boat trip through the refuge offers another way to view its wildlife and birds, especially whoopers. The *Wharf Cat* leaves from Fisherman's Wharf in Port Aransas every Wednesday at 10 A.M. (Jan.-Mar.) for a five-hour cruise past tidal flats and salt marshes. Adults $12, children $6. 512/749-5760 or 512/888-8093. The *Whooping Crane* departs from Sea Gun Resort Marina off St. 35 north of Rockport for a three-hour cruise. Year-round, Wed., Fri.-Sun., 1:30 P.M. Adults $10; children under 10, $7. 512/729-2341.

ARLINGTON, 160,123, B-7. **Six Flags Over Texas,** midway between Dallas and Fort Worth at the junction of Int. 30 and St. 360, was the first regional theme park in the nation. This multifaceted entertainment complex has six theme areas containing more than 100 rides, shows, and attractions. Mid-May-Labor Day, daily, 10 A.M. to 10 P.M.; Sat.-Sun., Mar.-mid-May, Sept., 10 A.M. to 10 P.M.; Oct., 10 A.M. to 8 P.M.; Nov., 10 A.M. to 6 P.M. Admission (includes all rides and shows) $11.15; $19 for two consecutive days; children under 2, free. Parking $1.50. 817/461-1200.

AUSTIN, 345,496, D-7. When it was chosen the capital of the young Republic of Texas in 1839, this city changed its name from Waterloo to Austin in honor of Stephen F. Austin, the "Father of Texas." When Texas joined the Union as the 28th state in 1845, Austin continued as the capital. Today, it is a bustling governmental and com-

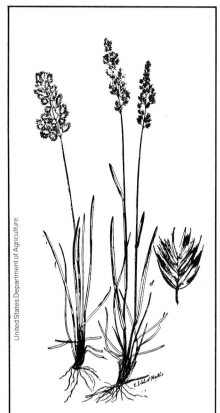

Texas bluegrass is a vigorous sodforming perennial that grows in the warmer parts of the Southern Great Plains. It grows to a height of 1 to 3 feet, with numerous leaves ¼ inch wide and from 6 to 12 inches long. Seed panicles are about 6 inches long, light green in color, and dense and somewhat spikelike in form. It grows in winter, producing an abundance of leafy forage when many range forages are less nutritious. This species is valuable for range and pasture in the area to which it is adapted. There are about 200 species of bluegrass *(poa).* Some of the others are Kentucky, Canada, roughstalk, bulbous, annual, big, Sandberg, and mutton.

mercial hub, yet it manages to retain much of the ease and charm of a small town. **GOVERNMENT BUILDINGS: State Capitol,** 11th St. and Congress Ave., is an impressive 311-foot-high domed statehouse constructed in 1888 of native pink granite and patterned after the nation's Capitol, although the Texas Capitol is seven feet taller. Statuary and memorials dominate the landscaped grounds. Year-round, daily, 8 A.M. to 5 P.M. Free. Free tours available from the Tourist Information Center in the rotunda during these hours. Walk-through rotunda: Always open. 512/475-3070. **Governor's Mansion,** 1010 Colorado St. across from the Capitol, with its white columns and broad verandas is a gracious example of antebellum Greek-Revival-style architecture, circa 1856, and the home of Texas governors; public rooms include historic items. Year-round, Mon., Wed., Fri., 10 A.M. to 11:40 A.M. Free. 512/475-2121. **Lyndon Baines Johnson Library,** 2313 Red River, has exhibit programs, a biography of LBJ, gifts from foreign heads of state, moon rocks, and a replica of the White House Oval Office. Year-round, daily, 9 A.M. to 5 P.M. Free. 512/397-5136.

MUSEUMS AND ART CENTERS: O. Henry Museum, 409 E. Fifth St., is a quaint Victorian cottage in which the writer lived in the 1900s. It contains many of his letters and photographs. Year-round, Tues.-Sat., 11 A.M. to 4:30 P.M.; Sun., 2 to 4:30 P.M. Free. 512/472-1903. **Texas Memorial Museum,** 2400 Trinity St. on the University of Texas campus, has four floors of exhibits including pre-Columbian pottery, native North American basketry, ethnographic collections, antique firearms, animals and plants, and minerals and gems of Texas. Year-round, Mon.-Fri., 9 A.M. to 5 P.M.; Sat.-Sun., 1 to 5 P.M. Adults $1, school-age children 50¢, preschool children 25¢. Sun., free. 512/471-1604. **French Legation,** 802 San Marcos St., is a cottage built in 1840 by Comte Alphonse de Saligny, chargé d'affaires to the Republic of Texas. Year-round, Tues.-Sun., 1 to 5 P.M. Adults $1; students 50¢; children 6-12, 25¢; children under 6, free. 512/472-8180. **Michener Galleries,** 21st and Guadalupe Sts. on the University of Texas campus, exhibits 20th-century American art as well as rare manuscripts donated from the personal collection of James and Mari Michener. Year-round, Mon.-Sat., 9 A.M. to 5 P.M.; Sun., 1 to 5 P.M. Free. 512/471-7324. **Daughters of the Republic of Texas Museum,** 112 E. 11th St. on the southeast corner of the Capitol grounds, houses memorabilia of the Confederacy and the Republic periods. Year-round, Mon.-Fri., 9 A.M. to noon, 1 to 5 P.M. Free. 512/477-1822.

HISTORIC AREA: East Sixth St., between Int. 35 and Congress Ave., is an interesting and varied part of a changing Austin; many of the old historic buildings are being restored and used as restaurants, galleries, offices, and shops.

PARKS: Zilker Park, Barton Springs Rd., features sports areas, extensive landscaping, picnic spots, a miniature train ride, and a spring-fed 1,000-foot-long swimming pool. Daily, summer, 7 A.M. to 10 P.M.; fall and spring, 10 A.M. to sunset. Adults $1.25; persons 12-17, 50¢; 4-12, 25¢; under 4, free. 512/476-9044. **Austin Area Garden Center,** 2200 Barton Springs Rd. in Zilker Park, is a lush complex featuring seasonal plants and flowers, rose garden, Japanese Gardens with Oriental bridge, Swedish pioneer log cabin with period furnishings, and a fragrance garden for the blind. Year-round, daily, 7:30 A.M. to dusk. Free, except $1 admission during spring flower show in late April. 512/477-8672.

AUSTWELL, F-8. *See* **Aransas National Wildlife Refuge.**

BEAUMONT, 118,102, D-10. An island port, the city sprawls along the winding Neches River. A lumber town and rice-farming area for many years, it became an oil-boom town in 1901. On January 10, 1901, with a deafening roar, a gusher drilled by Anthony B. Lucas released a geyser of oil 200 feet high. Oil gushed uncontrolled for five days; on the sixth, workers had it flowing through pipes (100,000 barrels a day). Land in Spindletop Oil Field, where the Lucas gusher was located, sold for $200,000 an acre; but oil was so plentiful, it sold for 3¢ a barrel. **Gladys City,** University Dr. and U.S. 69 S, built as a bicentennial project, recreates the oil-boom town, with clapboard buildings, wooden oil derricks, and artifacts associated with the oil industry in Texas. Year-round, Tues.-Fri., Sun., 1 to 5 P.M.; Sat., 9 A.M. to 5 P.M. Adults 50¢, children 25¢. 713/838-8122. **Lucas Gusher Monument,** a 58-foot granite shaft which once stood at the site of the Lucas gusher, has been moved next to Gladys City. **Spindletop Museum,** Florida and Callahan Sts., Lamar University campus, has historic items and artifacts of the early oil days in Beaumont. Year-round, Mon.-Fri., 1 to 5 P.M. Free. 713/838-8122. **Babe Didrikson Zaharias Memorial Museum,** Gulf St. exit off Int. 10E, honors Beaumont's famous woman golfer, the late Mildred "Babe" Didrikson Zaharias. Year-round, daily, 9 A.M. to 5 P.M. Free. 713/833-4622.

BIG BEND NATIONAL PARK, E-3. Established in 1944 to preserve this segment of the Chihuahuan Desert found along the Texan-Mexican border, the 1,100-square-mile park is in the giant bend of the Rio Grande River. Preserved in the park's 708,000 acres are colorful desert areas with unusual cacti, alpine meadows, contorted mountains, and three spectacular canyons—Santa Elena, Mariscal, and Bouquillas—carved by the Rio Grande River. The Chisos (Ghost) Mountains dominate the center of the park, and paved roads lead to most of its principal attractions. Big Bend has tourist facilities, but advance reservations at the **Chisos Mountains Lodge** in the park are recommended. Visitors may take a 14-mile trail ride to South Rim (year-round, daily, 8 A.M. to 3:30 P.M., $30), a two-and-one-half-hour jaunt to Window Rock (year-round, daily, 8 A.M., 1 and 4 P.M., $12), or float trips through the canyons. Park Administration Building is at Panther Junction. Daily, June-Aug., 8 A.M. to 7 P.M.; other months, 8 A.M. to 5 P.M. Free. 915/477-2251.

BIG THICKET NATIONAL PRESERVE, D-9. *See* **Alabama Coushatta Indian Reservation.**

BROWNSVILLE, 84,997, H-7. This southernmost city in Texas is just across the Rio Grande River international boundary from Mexico. **Gladys Porter Zoo,** 500 Ringgold St. at 6th St., is an elaborate zoological park without bars or cages for its

more than 1,500 rare and endangered animals, birds, and reptiles, which live in natural settings. Year-round, daily, 8:30 A.M. to 5:30 P.M. Adults $3, children $1. Guided train tours: Sun., 1:30 to 3:30 P.M. 50¢. 512/546-7187. **Matamoros, Mexico,** just across the border, is a popular place to shop for Mexican goods, where visitors can buy everything from paper flowers to a wool serape.

CANYON, 10,724, G-2. **Palo Duro Canyon State Park,** 12 miles east on St. 217 (between Int. 27 and St. 207) to Park Rd., is the largest state park in Texas. It is also one of the most spectacular. Here the Red River has carved spires and pinnacles, and walls in a variety of vivid colors drop a thousand feet to the floor of Palo Duro Canyon. A major attraction is the musical drama *Texas,* by Paul Green. Mid-June-late Aug., Mon.-Sat., first Sun., July, 8:45 P.M. Mon.-Thurs., adults $4 to $6, children $2 to $6; Fri.-Sun., adults $5 to $7, children $2.50 to $7. Park admission: $2 per car; theater patrons after 6 P.M., free. *Festival of Stars,* a singing, dancing, and sound and light show: Late Aug.-mid-Sept., Mon.-Tues., Thurs.-Sun., 8 P.M. Adults $5 to $6, children $2.50 to $3. Theater reservations: 806/655-2181. Park: 806/488-2227. **Panhandle-Plains Historical Museum,** 2501 4th Ave. on the West Texas State University campus, has historic brands, artifacts, fossils, and other mementoes of the Southwest. June-Aug., Mon.-Sat., 9 A.M. to 6 P.M.; Sun., 2 to 6 P.M.; other months, Mon.-Sat., 9 A.M. to 5 P.M.; Sun., 2 to 6 P.M. Free. 806/655-7191.

CLEAR LAKE, 22,000, 26 miles southeast of Houston, E-9. This is the site of NASA **Lyndon B. Johnson Space Center** (formerly named the Manned Spacecraft Center) on NASA Rd. 1 east of Clear Lake and 26 miles southeast of Houston. Exhibits, films, models, and other items relating to the space program can be viewed. Self-guided and guided tours of the complex's facilities are available. Year-round, daily, 9 A.M. to 4 P.M. Free. 713/483-4321.

CORPUS CHRISTI, 231,999, G-7. A major deep-water port and an industrial and agricultural center, Corpus Christi is a popular seacoast playground. Its roots go back to 1519 when the adjacent bay was discovered and named by Spanish explorer Alonzo Alvarez de Pineda on the Feast of Corpus Christi, hence the name. **Corpus Christi Museum,** 1919 N. Water St., is an award-winning general museum with exhibits on man, marine and earth sciences, and natural history, all with English and Spanish signs that say, "Yes, you may touch." Year-round, Tues.-Sat., 10 A.M. to 5 P.M.; Sun., 2 to 5 P.M. Free. 512/883-2862. **Art Museum of South Texas,** 1902 N. Shoreline Blvd., is a brilliant white building designed by architects Phillip Johnson of New York and Eugene Aubry of Houston. The museum has permanent exhibits which feature south Texas painters, with frequent touring exhibits by world-famous artists. Year-round, Tues.-Sat., 10 A.M. to 5 P.M.; Sun., 1 to 5 P.M. Free. 512/884-3844. **The Big Oak,** near Goose Island State Park (St. 35N through Rockport to Lamar, then east on Park Rd. 13), is the largest live oak in Texas. A 1,000-year-old giant, it measures 35 feet in circumference and is 44 feet tall. Free. 512/729-2858. **King Ranch Loop,** in nearby Kingsville, is the famed ranch and home of Santa Gertrudis cattle and Old Sorrel quarter horses. Stop at the entrance just west of Kingsville city limits on St. 141 for information and instructions. Loop road open year-round, daily, 8 A.M. to 4 P.M. Auto traffic only. Free. 512/592-6411. **Japanese Art Museum,** 426 S. Staples St., has hand-made Hakata dolls, rare masks from the Tang Dynasty, scale models of famous pagodas, and other Oriental art objects. Year-round, Mon.-Fri., 10 A.M. to 4 P.M.; Sun., 2 to 5 P.M. Adults $1, students 35¢, children 25¢. 512/883-1303.

See also **Padre Island National Seashore.**

DALLAS, 904,078, B-8. Founded as a trading post in 1841 by pioneer John Neely Bryan, Dallas today thrives on trade, manufacturing, transportation, aerospace, oil, finance, decorative and apparel wholesaling, and insurance, as well as culture.

HISTORICAL AREAS AND MEMORIALS: Dallas County Historical Plaza, Main and Market Sts., highlights John Neely Bryan's original 1841 log cabin. *Old Red Court House,* also in the Plaza, was built in 1860 of red Pecos limestone. **John F. Kennedy Memorial,** across the street from the Bryan cabin, is a four-walled, open-roofed, 30-foot cenotaph designed by architect Philip Johnson and situated 200 yards from the spot where the late president was assassinated. Plaza: Always open.

MUSEUMS AND ART CENTERS: Dallas Museum of Fine Arts, Fair Park, 2nd Ave. between Grand and Forest Sts., features exhibits from pre-Columbian artifacts to visiting contemporary collections. Year-round, Mon.-Sat., 10 A.M. to 5 P.M.; Sun., 1 to 5 P.M. Free. 214/421-4188. **Museum of Natural History,** Fair Park, 1st and Parry Sts., displays mounted Texas wildlife dioramas in natural habitat settings. Year-round, Mon.-Sat., 9 A.M. to 5 P.M.; Sun., noon to 5 P.M. Free. 214/421-2169. **Dallas Health and Science Museum,** Fair Park, 1st and Parry Sts., houses mineralogical, geological, and industrial exhibits. Planetarium shows reveal wonders of the heavens. Adults $1.50, children $1. Year-round, Tues.-Sat., 9 A.M. to 5 P.M.; Sun., 1 to 5 P.M. Free. 214/428-8351. **Texas Hall of State,** Fair Park, Nimitz and Grand Sts., records 400 years of the state's growth with murals of Texas' four distinct ecological regions, nostalgic exhibits of yesteryear, and a semi-circular *Hall of Heroes.* Year-round, Mon.-Sat., 9 A.M. to 5 P.M.; Sun., 1 to 5 P.M. Free. 214/421-5136. **Dallas Aquarium,** Fair Park, 1st St. and Forest Ave., has more than 300 species of exotic and tropical fish, rep-

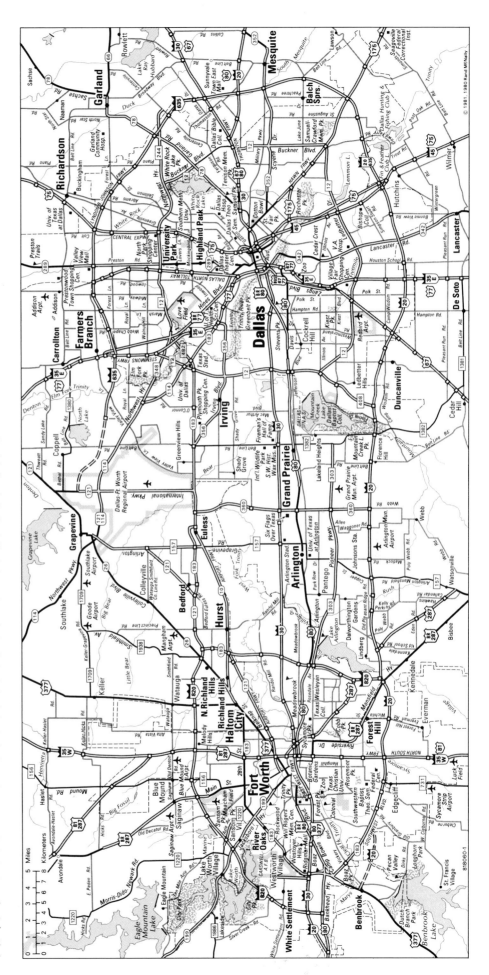

tiles, and amphibians. Year-round, Mon.-Sat., 9 A.M. to 5 P.M.; Sun., 1 to 5 P.M. Free. 214/428-3587. **Dallas Civic Garden Center,** Fair Park, 1st St. and Forest Ave., a two-story tropical conservatory with a waterfall, has plants gathered from around the world and a scent garden with braille markings for the blind. Year-round, Mon.-Fri., 10 A.M. to 5 P.M.; Sat.-Sun., 2 to 5 P.M. Free. 214/428-7476. **Age of Steam Museum,** Fair Park, 1st and Parry Sts., has trains from 1900 to 1950, the oldest depot in Dallas, and other railroad memorabilia. Year-round, Sun., 11 A.M. to 5 P.M. Adults $1, children 50¢. 214/826-1615. **Meadows Museum,** Southern Methodist University in Owens Fine Arts Center, Bishop and Binkley Sts., has a permanent collection of over 100 paintings, drawings, and etchings from the Renaissance to the 20th century. Year-round, Mon.-Sat., 10 A.M. to 5 P.M.; Sun., 1 to 5 P.M. Free. 214/692-2516.

PARKS: Fair Park, 1st and Parry Sts., has been a cultural and educational center since 1886 when its 250 acres first hosted the State Fair of Texas. The park includes seven museums; the *Cotton Bowl Stadium; State Fair Music Hall* where the *Dallas Symphony Orchestra* performs; and a midway with rides, restaurants, and concessions. Grounds: Always open. Free. 214/565-9931. **Biblical Arts Center,** 7500 Park Lane, houses a giant mural depicting "The Miracle at Pentecost." Year-round, Tues.-Sat., 10 A.M. to 5 P.M.; Sun., 1 to 5 P.M. Adults $2.50; children 6-12, $1; under 6, free. 214/691-4661. **Old City Park,** Gano and St. Paul Sts., depicts Dallas life in the 19th century with authentic restorations of a Southern mansion, clapboard hotel, log schoolhouse, general store, doctor's office, apothecary shop, church, and train depot. Year-round, Tues.-Fri., 10 A.M. to 4 P.M.; Sat.-Sun., 1:30 to 4:30 P.M. Adults $2, children 50¢. 214/421-5141. **Thanksgiving Square,** downtown at the intersections of Bryan, Pacific, and Ervay Sts., highlights an interfaith chapel. Outdoor concerts: Year-round, Sun., 3 P.M. Free. Chapel: Year-round, Mon.-Fri., 10 A.M. to 5 P.M.; Sat.-Sun., 1 to 5 P.M. Free. 214/651-1777.

THEATER CENTER: Dallas Theater Center, 3636 Turtle Creek Blvd., is a turretlike fortress of sweeping curves, chandeliers, and massive cantilevers designed by Frank Lloyd Wright. Presentations range from Shakespeare to the avant-garde. Tours: Year-round, Mon.-Sat., 1 P.M. with advance reservations. Donations. 214/526-8857.

ZOO: Dallas Zoo, Marsalis Park, 621 E. Clarendon Dr., has more than 2,000 birds, reptiles, amphibians, and mammals representing 800 species, all in a 50-acre setting with a petting zoo. Year-round, daily, 9 A.M. to 5 P.M. Adults, $1.50; children 5-11, $1; under 5, free. 214/946-5154.

SHOPPING: Farmers' Market, St. Louis St. between Pearl St. and Central Expwy., is a huge market where fresh fruits and vegetables from the Rio Grande Valley,

The Lighthouse, one of the most unusual geological formations in west Texas, helps to draw nearly half a million visitors a year to Palo Duro State Park, near the town of Canyon. The sandstone tower, along with an 800-foot-deep canyon, was carved by erosion, a process that has been changing the face of the area ever since it was formed 280 million years ago during the Permian Age. The Prairie Dog Town Fork of the Red River flows at the bottom of the canyon, nourishing birches and cottonwoods that grow along the banks, as well as a substantial animal population that includes deer, bobcats, cougars, coyotes, rabbits and an impressive variety of birds that range from meadowlarks and mockingbirds to red-tailed hawks and roadrunners. A 16-mile scenic drive (St. 217) provides a good way to orient yourself to the park. A five-mile hiking trail leads to the Lighthouse and back. For visitors wishing to stay overnight, there are 116 campsites, including 43 tent sites, 53 sites with electricity and water, and 20 with full hookups.

Mexico, and Florida are sold wholesale and retail in outdoor sheds. Early spring-late Nov., daily, sunrise to sunset; other months, Sat.-Sun., same times. Free. **Olla Podrida,** 12215 Coit Rd., resembles a rustic country store but is a mall where artists, craftsmen, and collectors offer some 70 shops and services. Year-round, Mon.-Wed., Fri.-Sat., 10 A.M. to 5:30 P.M.; Thurs., 10 A.M. to 9 P.M. 214/239-8541.

DENISON, 23,884, A-8. A transportation center, in 1858 it was on the Butterfield Stage Line; and in 1872 it became a stopping point for cattle when the Katy Railroad entered Texas. The **Eisenhower Birthplace State Historic Site,** 208 E. Day St., has been restored and furnished with some of the personal effects of the five-star general and 34th president of the United States, Dwight D. Eisenhower, who was born here. Daily, June-Labor Day, 8 A.M. to 5 P.M.; other months, 10 A.M. to 5 P.M. Adults 50¢; children 6-12, 25¢. 214/465-8908.

EL PASO, 425,259, C-1. In June, 1581, three Franciscans, Fray Agustin Rodriguez, Fray Francisco Lopez, and Fray Juan de Santa Maria, left Santa Barbara, Mexico, to explore the missionary possibilities in New Mexico. Accompanied by an armed escort under the command of Francisco Sanchez Chamuscado, they arrived at the Pass of the North in August, 1581. The Rodriguez-Chamuscado Expedition was the first party of Spaniards to reach the pass. In and near El Paso are several places of interest. **Ciudad Juárez,** connected to El Paso by three bridges over the Rio Grande River, is of particular interest to visitors because of the wide variety of items available at the Mexican shops and markets. **Aerial Tramway,** on McKinley St. off Alabama St., takes visitors in an enclosed cab to the top of 5,632-foot-high Ranger Peak. June-Labor Day, daily, noon to 9 P.M.; other months, Mon., Thurs.-Fri., noon to 6 P.M.; Sat.-Sun., noon to 9 P.M. Adults $2, children $1. 915/566-6622. **El Paso Centennial Museum,** University of Texas, El Paso campus, University Ave. and Wiggins Rd., has exhibits of archaeology, anthropology, and geology. Year-round, Tues.-Fri., 10 A.M. to 4:30 P.M.; Sun., 1:30 to 5:30 P.M. Free. 915/747-5565. **El Paso Museum of Art,** 1211 Montana St., has paintings and sculpture spanning six centuries. Year-round, Wed.-Sat., 10 A.M. to 5 P.M.; Sun., 1 to 5 P.M. Free. 915/541-4040. **McKelligon Canyon Theater,** Alabama and McKelligon Canyon Sts., is the site of the outdoor drama *Viva El Paso,* by the Southwest Repertory Organization. Performances: July-Aug., Wed.-Sat., 8 P.M. Admission: Wed., $2; Thurs., $3; Fri.-Sat., $3.50; $1 less for students, military, and persons under 12 and 65 and over. 915/533-1671. **Magoffin Home State Historic Site,** 1120 Magoffin Ave., is a one-story 1875 adobe surrounding an open patio. Its outside walls are four feet thick; its dividing walls are two feet thick. Year-round, Wed.-Sun., 9 A.M. to 4 P.M. Adults 50¢; children 6-12, 25¢; under 6, free. 915/533-5147. **Ysleta,** now part of the city of El Paso, was established in 1681 by refugees from the revolt of the pueblos in New Mexico. *Nuestra Señora de Carmen* (the Old Mission), Zaragosa Rd. and Alameda Ave., was established by Spanish missionaries and Tigua Indians in 1681 as Corpus Christi de la Isleta. The oldest of the Texas missions, it has been in continuous use as a house of worship Year-round, Mon.-Fri., 9 A.M. to noon, 3 to 5 P.M. Free. 915/859-9848. **Chamizal National Memorial,** Delta Dr. near Cordova Bridge, commemorates the peaceful settlement of the 99-year boundary dispute between the United States and Mexico in a treaty signed in 1963. Guided tours start from the Visitors Center. Year-round, daily, 8 A.M. to 5 P.M. Free. 915/543-7880. **Fort Bliss,** east of U.S. 54 between Fred Wilson Rd. and Montana Ave., is north of El Paso and located largely in New Mexico. Once the largest cavalry post in the nation, it is now home of the U.S. Army Air Defense Center. *Fort Bliss Replica Museum,* Pleasanton Rd. and Sheridan Dr., is a replica of an adobe fort. Exhibits relate the history of the Southwest and Fort Bliss. Year-round, daily, 9 A.M. to 4:30 P.M. Free. 915/568-4518 or 915/568-2804. *Army Air Defense and Artillery Museum,* Building 5000, Pleasanton Rd. near Robert E. Lee Rd., has displays of air defense missiles. Year-round, daily, 9 A.M. to 4:30 P.M. Free. 915/568-5412. **Hueco Tanks**

State Historical Park, 26 miles east of El Paso via U.S. 62/180, preserves an area where the infrequent rain is stored in natural basins (*huecos*). On the rocks in the park are petroglyphs by early Indians and the names of travelers to the California gold rush in 1849. Year-round, daily, 8 A.M. to 10 P.M. 915/859-4100.

FORT DAVIS, 850, D-3. **Fort Davis National Historic Site,** on St. 17/118, was a key post in the west Texas defense system. From 1854 to 1891, it guarded emigrants on the San Antonio-El Paso road. The Visitors Center offers a 17-minute audio dramatization of the 1875 full-dress retreat parade. More than 30 stone and adobe buildings have been restored, and costumed guides show visitors the refurbished officers' quarters, the commissary, and the kitchen. A bugler blows various calls, and mounted interpreters in cavalry uniforms patrol the post. Post: Daily, May-Aug., 8 A.M. to 6 P.M.; other months, 8 A.M. to 5 P.M. Free. 915/426-3225.

FORT WORTH, 385,141, B-7. Never a fort, this was originally an army camp established in 1849. It became a thriving cow town in post-Civil War days, serving as a major stop on the Chisholm Trail. Arrival of the Texas and Pacific Railroad in July, 1876, turned Fort Worth into a railhead. **SPECIAL AND HISTORIC AREAS: Stockyards,** on N. Main St. and Exchange Ave., are undergoing restorative work to depict the city as it was in the late 1800s. Home of the first indoor rodeo (1917) and restored Swift & Co. offices, the complex contains a corner drugstore, shops, and restaurants. **Auction Barn,** on Exchange Ave., has livestock and cattle auctions. Year-round, Mon.-Thurs., starting at 9 A.M. Free. 817/624-3101. **Thistle Hill,** 1509 Pennsylvania St., was built in 1802 and is the last remaining mansion of the cattle-baron era; it is currently being restored. Year-round, Mon.-Fri., 10 A.M. to 4 P.M.; Sun., 1 to 5 P.M. Adults $1.50, children 50¢. 817/336-1212. **Log Cabin Village,** University Dr. and Colonial Pkwy., provides authentic surroundings for a working gristmill and demonstrations of pioneer crafts. Year-round, Mon.-Fri., 8 A.M. to 4:30 P.M.; Sat., noon to 4:30 P.M.; Sun., 1 to 4:30 P.M. Adults 60¢, children 35¢. 817/926-5881. **Will Rogers Square,** W. Lancaster St. from University Dr. to Montgomery St., is the cultural heart of the city with theaters; art museums; the *Will Rogers Coliseum* where the *Southwestern Exposition, Fat Stock Show and Rodeo* are held every January; blocks of cattle barns and exhibition buildings; a planetarium; and ice-skating rink. **MUSEUMS AND ART CENTERS: Amon Carter Museum of Western Art,** 3501 Camp Bowie Rd., has an extensive collection of works by American artists. Tours: Year-round, Tues.-Sat., 10 A.M. to 5 P.M.; Sun., 1 to 5:30 P.M. Free. 817/738-1933. **Fort Worth Art Museum,** 1309 Montgom-

ery St., has 20th-century paintings, sculptures, and photographs. Year-round, Tues., 10 A.M. to 9 P.M.; Wed.-Sat., 10 A.M. to 5 P.M.; Sun., 1 to 5 P.M. Free. 817/738-9215. **Kimbell Art Museum,** 1101 Will Rogers Rd. W., houses an internationally acclaimed collection of classical European, Far Eastern, African, and pre-Columbian artworks. Year-round, Tues.-Sat., 10 A.M. to 5 P.M.; Sun., 1 to 5 P.M. Free. 817/332-8451. **Museum of Science and History,** 1501 Montgomery St., has halls exhibiting medicine, physiology, geology, Texas history, and laser technology. *Noble Planetarium,* in the museum, offers varied monthly shows explaining stars and constellations. Planetarium:

The armadillo, that odd-looking armored mammal so common in Texas, has recently been demonstrating an affinity for other parts of the South as well. The noisy, nearsighted, nearly deaf creatures have been turning up regularly in the peanut and watermelon patches of Mississippi, Alabama, Georgia, Florida, and parts of South Carolina. (They established themselves in Louisiana much earlier.) The reason for this expansionist activity is simply overcrowding — too many armadillos with too few places to go — even in Texas. And so the armadillos are going east. How do they manage to cross the Mississippi River? The best explanation seems to be that they simply fill themselves with air and float across. But some, in jest, have suggested that they merely take a deep breath and walk across the bottom.

An oil rig in a wheat field is a common sight to a native Texan, but visitors to the Lone Star State often find themselves doing a double take. Texas produced 931,078,275 barrels of oil in 1980, 31 percent of the U.S. total and by far the most oil of any state. As for the wheat that often surrounds the wells, it came to 183 million bushels in 1981, pushing Texas from fifth to third place.

Sat., 11 A.M., 1, 2:30, and 3:30 P.M.; Sun., 2:30 and 3:30 P.M. Adults $2.25; children $1.25; under 4, not admitted. Museum: Year-round, Mon.-Sat., 9 A.M. to 5 P.M.; Sun., 2 to 5 P.M. Non-residents 50¢, residents free. 817/732-1631.

PARKS: Fort Worth Botanic Gardens, University Dr. and W. Frwy., has over 2,500 species of plants in a 114-acre garden; picnic areas; and Japanese Garden. Japanese Garden: May-Labor Day, Tues.-Sat., 10 A.M. to 7 P.M.; Sun., 1 to 6 P.M.; other months, Tues.-Fri., 10 A.M. to 4 P.M.; Sat., 10 A.M. to 5 P.M.; Sun., 1 to 5 P.M. Botanic grounds: Year-round, daily, 8 A.M. to sunset. Free. 817/870-7686. **Nature Center and Refuge,** 2 miles west of Lake Worth on St. 199, is a 3,400-acre wildlife habitat with native animals, hiking trails, fishing, picnicking, and a Visitors Center. Year-round, Mon.-Fri., 8 A.M. to 5 P.M.; Sat.-Sun., 9 A.M. to 5 P.M. Free. 817/237-1111. **Fort Worth Water Gardens,** 1502 Commerce St., has mazelike walkways with pools, gardens, and a large tiered, concrete area over which thousands of gallons of water cascade every minute. Year-round, daily, 10 A.M. to 11 P.M. Free. 817/870-7699.

ZOO: Fort Worth Zoological Park, University Dr. and Colonial Pkwy. in Forest Park, features a rain forest, exotic birds, ape house, petting zoo, and a reptile collection. Year-round, daily, 9 A.M. to 5 P.M. Adults $1, children free. 817/870-7050.

FREDERICKSBURG, 6,412, D-6. Settled by Germans who came here in 1846 from New Braunfels, it is a diversified farming and ranching center with an Old-World atmosphere. Older buildings retain their traditional styles. Among the reminders of the past are the Sunday Houses, tiny dwellings built for weekend use by farmers and ranchers who lived several miles away and came to Fredericksburg to buy supplies on Saturday and attend church on Sunday. Several still stand but are not open to the public. **Admiral Nimitz Center,** 340 E. Main St., re-creates the career of Adm. Chester W. Nimitz. The one-half block area surrounds the restored Nimitz Hotel, constructed in 1847 by Admiral Nimitz's grandfather. Along with exhibits to the Pacific Theater of World War II, Japanese Peace Gardens were built by the Japanese. Year-round, daily, 8 A.M. to 5 P.M. Admission $1; under 6, free. 512/997-4379.

FRITCH, 2,299, G-2. **Alibates Flint Quarries National Monument,** off St. 136 about 10 miles south of Fritch and 30 miles north of Amarillo, preserves an area where for more than 10,000 years, pre-Columbian Indians dug agatized dolomite from quarries to make projectile points, knives, scrapers, and other tools. Access to the monument is via National Park Service tours which leave from Bates Canyon Infor-

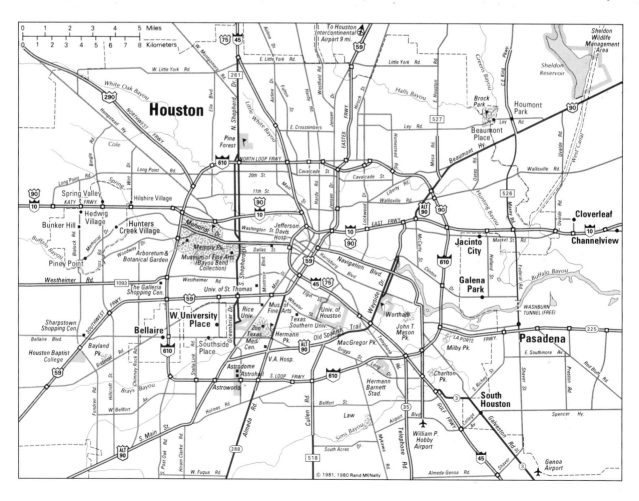

© 1981, 1980 Rand McNally

The whooping crane, distinguished and longtime member of the endangered species list, presently numbers about 100 in the wild. That's up from a low of 20 or so in 1941. About 75 of these majestic birds spend their winters at the Aransas National Wildlife Refuge on the Gulf Coast of Texas near Corpus Christi. They come here to escape the frigid winters of their other home in Wood Buffalo National Park in northern Alberta, a trip of roughly 2,500 miles as the crane flies. In 1981, U.S. and Canadian wildlife officials tracked the birds during their fall migration and made some interesting discoveries. For example, whooping cranes fly at an average altitude of 800 to 900 feet, can climb when necessary to 3,000 feet, and with a brisk tail wind can travel as much as 470 miles a day at a speed of 40 to 50 miles an hour. That same year, the cranes, who normally eschew civilization, chose to fly over Fort Sill, Oklahoma, necessitating an emergency halt to gunnery exercises on the artillery range. Oblivious to the scare they had caused their friends in the wildlife services, they subsequently flapped their unflappable way over downtown Fort Worth.

mation Station, 7½ miles south of Fritch on St. 136 to Cass Junction Rd. then west 5 miles. Tours: Memorial Day-Labor Day, daily, 10 A.M., 2 P.M. Free. **Lake Meredith National Recreation Area,** created by Sanford Dam on the Canadian River, is a 45,064-acre water-activity center. Always open. National Park Service headquarters, 419 E. Broadway, Fritch. 806/857-3151.

GALVESTON, 61,902, E-9. In the early 1800s, pirate Jean Lafitte made the subtropical island resort of Galveston his lair. Then cotton became king and money flowed into the city, filling the business district with ornate brick structures and the residential areas with elaborate Victorian and Greek-Revival-style mansions. Romantic memories of the boom times still linger in the seaside playground's 32 miles of sandy beaches on the Gulf of Mexico, connected to the mainland by the Int. 45 two-mile causeway. **The Strand,** a five-block-long, three-block-wide historic area between 20th and 25th Sts., once known as "The Wall Street of the Southwest," is now being restored with boutiques and restaurants in many of the gaslit buildings. One-hour walking tours conducted by the Galveston Historical Foundation leave from the Old Strand Emporium, 21st and Strand Sts., Sat., noon; Sun., 2 P.M. Free. 713/765-7834. **Ashton Villa,** 2328 Broadway at 24th St., is an 1859 three-story brick Italianate villa-style building restored to reflect the elegant Galveston life at the turn-of-the-century. *Carriagehouse* has a detailed 1890s dollhouse

presenting Galveston artifacts at a child's eye level, plus a multimedia presentation on the devastating hurricane of 1900. Year-round, Mon.-Fri., 10 A.M. to 4 P.M.; Sat.-Sun., noon to 5 P.M.; closed Tues. from Sept.-May. Adults $3; students and persons 65 and over, $2.25; children 6 to 12, $1.50; under 6, free. 713/762-3933. **Bishop's Palace,** 1492 Broadway, is an ornate four-story mansion built in 1886 with materials and furnishings gathered from all over the world. Guided tours: Memorial Day-Labor Day, Mon.-Sat., 10 A.M. to 4:45 P.M.; Sun., 1 to 5 P.M.; other months, Wed.-Mon., 1 to 4:45 P.M. Adults $2, teenagers $1.50, children 50¢. 713/762-2475. **Mary Moody Northern Amphitheater,** adjacent to Galveston Island State Park, Stewart Rd. at 13-Mile Rd., presents *Lone Star,* a musical drama by Paul Green about the struggle by Texas for independence. Performances: June-Aug., Tues.-Sun., 8:30 P.M. General admission: Adults $5 to $7, children $3 to $4. 713/737-3442.

GRAND PRAIRIE, 71,462, B-8. Located between Dallas and Forth Worth, Grand Prairie was established on the Texas & Pacific Railroad just after the Civil War. **Texas Sports Hall of Fame,** 401 E. Safari Pkwy., has exhibits relating to sports in the area. Memorial Day-Labor Day, daily, 10 A.M. to 7 P.M.; other months, Tues.-Fri., 10 A.M. to 5 P.M.; Sat.-Sun., 10 A.M. to 6 P.M. Adults $3; children 4-12, $1.50; under 4, free. 214/263-4255. **Fire Museum of Texas,** 702 E. Safari Pkwy., has new and

antique fire equipment. June-mid-Sept., daily, 9 A.M. to 5 P.M.; other months, Wed.-Sun., 9 A.M. to 5 P.M. Adults $3; students, military, and persons 65 and over, $2; children 4-12, $1.50; under 4, free. 214/263-1042. **Southwestern Historical Wax Museum,** 601 E. Safari Pkwy., has wax figures of famous Texans. Memorial Day-Labor Day, daily, 9 A.M. to 9 P.M.; other months, Mon.-Fri., 10 A.M. to 5 P.M.; Sat.-Sun., 10 A.M. to 6 P.M. Adults $3.95; children 4-12, $2.95; under 4, free. 214/263-2391. **International Wildlife Park,** 601 Wildlife Pkwy., has driving tours of the wildlife preserve. May-Sept., daily, 9:30 P.M. to 6 P.M.; other months (except Dec.), Sat.-Sun., 10 A.M. to 4:30 P.M. Admission $6.95; children under 2, free. 214/263-2203. **Traders Village,** 2602 Mayfield Rd., is one of the largest flea markets in the country; it covers 120 acres. Year-round, Sat.-Sun., 8 A.M. to sunset. Parking $1. 214/647-2331.

HARLINGEN, 43,543, H-7. This is a major distribution point for the Lower Rio Grande Valley vegetable, citrus fruit, cotton, and cane harvest. **Confederate Air Force Flying Museum,** Rebel Field at the Harlingen International Airport, has a flying collection of U. S. and foreign World War II combat aircraft, including many of the only aircraft of their type. Year-round, Mon.-Sat., 9 A.M. to 5 P.M.; Sun., noon to 5 P.M. Adults $3, children $1.50. 512/425-1057. Two air shows featuring all the planes in flying maneuvers are held in March and October.

HOUSTON, 1,594,086, E-9. Named after Sam Houston, general of the Texas army that won independence from Mexico in 1836, the state's largest city has experienced phenomenal growth since it was founded in August, 1836. In 1901 when the Spindletop oil field's Lucas Gusher blew in at neighboring Beaumont, producing several thousand times more oil than any previous well, the miracle happened. Crude oil began to be pumped into Houston, especially after the completion of the 50-mile-long Ship Channel as a deep-water port. Today, more than 122 million tons of cargo a year are moved through the Port of Houston, making it the nation's third largest port in total tonnage and the largest in foreign tonnage. **PORT: Port of Houston,** southeast of the city, was dredged to 40 feet deep and 400 feet wide to make the port, which was officially opened by President Wilson on November 10, 1914. Today, some 5,000 ships a year load and unload cargo; many fly the flag of a foreign nation. **Wharf 9 Observation Platform** offers a view of the port-turning basin and of the city skyline. *Sam Houston,* an excursion boat, takes visitors on a two-hour trip through the harbor and ship channel. Departure: Gate 8, Oct.-May, Tues.-Sat., 10 A.M. and 2:30 P.M.; Sun., 2:30 P.M. Free. In summer, advance reservations are recommended. 713/225-0671, Ext. 102.

MUSEUMS AND PLANETARIUM: Bayou Bend, 1 Westcott St., just off Memorial Dr., contains a collection of early American art and furniture in the home of the late Miss Ima Hogg, daughter of the first native-born governor of Texas, James S. Hogg. Approach to the estate is on a suspension bridge over Buffalo Bayou. Two-hour tours: Jan.-Feb., Apr.-July, Sept.-Dec., Tues.-Fri., 10 to 11:45 A.M., 12:45 to 2:30 P.M.; Sat., 10 A.M. to 12:45 P.M. Reservations required. Free. 713/529-8773. **Contemporary Arts Museum,** 5216 Montrose Blvd., is in a building of ultramodern design which allows the artist complete working freedom and space. Offered are exhibits, lectures, and art classes. Year-round, Tues.-Sat., 10 A.M. to 5 P.M.; Sun., noon to 6 P.M. Free. 713/526-3129. **Museum of Fine Arts,** 1001 Bissonnet St., has a collection of works ranging in time from ancient Greece to the present. The museum covers three acres, has several wings (the most recent was designed by the late Mies van der Rohe), a sculpture garden, and an art school. Year-round, Tues.-Sat., 10 A.M. to 5 P.M.; Sun., noon to 6 P.M. Free. 713/526-1361. **Rothko Chapel,** 1409 Sul Ross St., shelters several paintings by Mark Rothko, who worked closely with the chapel architects. Year-round, daily, 10 A.M. to 6 P.M. Free. 713/524-9839. **Museum of Natural Science,** Hermann Circle Dr., in northwest Hermann Park, has 13 large halls. Among its educational displays are the Hall of Space Science, Hall of Petroleum Science, and a dinosaur exhibit. Year-round, Tues.-Sat., 9 A.M. to 5 P.M.; Fri., also 7:30 to 9 P.M.; Sun.-Mon., noon to 5 P.M. Free. 713/526-4273. *Museum of Medical Science,* second floor of the Museum of Natural Science, has exhibits related to the human anatomy, life cycle, and medicine. Year-round, Tues.-Sat., 9 A.M. to 5 P.M.; Sun.-Mon., noon to 5 P.M. Free. 713/529-3766. *Burke Baker Planetarium,* in Hermann Park, has educational exhibits and planetarium shows related to astronomy, its history, and its development. Shows: Year-round, Wed., 4 P.M.; Fri., 4 and 8 P.M.; Sat.-Sun., 2, 3, and 4 P.M. Adults $1.25, children 50¢. 713/526-4273.

ARBORETUM AND GARDEN: Houston Arboretum, 4501 Woodway Dr. in Memorial Park, has 155 acres of woodland with five miles of trails, greenhouses, an herb and cactus garden, and a variety of other trees and shrubs. Year-round, Mon.-Sat., 9 A.M. to 5:30 P.M.; Sun., 1 to 5:30 P.M. Free. 713/681-8433. **Houston Garden Center,** 1500 Hermann Dr. in Hermann Park, features several thousand rose bushes, a garden of perennials grown in the Houston area, and a garden of bulbs and herbs. Building: Year-round, Mon.-Fri., 8 A.M. to 4 P.M.; other hours, by appointment. Grounds: May-Sept., Mon.-Fri., 8 A.M. to 8 P.M.; Sat.-Sun., 10 A.M. to 8 P.M.; other months, Mon.-Fri., 8 A.M. to 6 P.M.; Sat.-Sun., 10 A.M. to 6 P.M. Free. 713/529-5371.

PARKS: Hermann Park, Fannin St. and Hermann Dr., is a 410-acre wooded park

with several museums; a garden center; zoological gardens; theater; and many other facilities, including a golf course, two-mile jogging trail, and playground. **Sam Houston Historical Park,** 1100 Bagby St., literally in the front yard of downtown, is the site of several restored buildings. Year-round, Tues.-Fri., 10 A.M. to 3 P.M.; Sat., 11 A.M. to 3 P.M.; Sun., 2 to 5 P.M. Free. Tours every hour on the hour. Adults $2, children 35¢. Harris County Heritage Society headquarters: 713/223-8367.

SPORTS AND RECREATION CENTERS: Astrodome, southwest of downtown at Int. 610 and Kirby Dr., is a colossal amphitheater for sports events, concerts, and other special productions. Guided tours: Daily, June-Aug., 9 and 11 A.M., 1, 3, and 5 P.M.; other months, 11 A.M., 1 and 3 P.M. No tours when events are scheduled. Adults $2.50; children under 7, free. Parking $2. Ticket information: 713/799-9555. General information: 713/799-9500. **AstroWorld,** across the street from the Astrodome, is a 65-acre amusement park featuring 12 internationally themed areas with more than 100 rides, shows, and attractions. June-Aug., Tues.-Fri., noon to midnight; Sat.-Sun., 10 A.M. to midnight; other months, Sat.-Sun., 10 A.M. to 8 P.M. One-day ticket $11.50; two-day ticket $16.50; children under 3, free. Admission includes all rides and shows. 713/748-1234.

ZOO: Houston Zoological Gardens, Zoo Circle Dr. in Hermann Park, is a 42-acre zoo with a tropical birdhouse resembling an Asian jungle where more than 200 exotic birds fly freely through an aviary rain forest. Some 2,000 animals roam in surroundings similar to their natural habitats. Daily, May-Sept., 9:30 A.M. to 8 P.M.; other months, 9:30 A.M. to 6 P.M. Free. 713/523-0149.

SHOPPING: The **Galleria,** Westheimer Rd. at S. Post Oak Rd., is patterned after a shopping plaza built by Victor Emmanuel over a century ago in Milan, Italy. More than a hundred quality shops line the mall's three air-conditioned levels housing several cinemas, two hotels, numerous art galleries and restaurants, and an ice-skating rink. *See* also **San Jacinto Battleground State Historic Park.**

JOHNSON CITY, D-7. *See* **Lyndon B. Johnson National Historical Park.**

LANGTRY, 145, E-4. The original **Jersey Lilly Saloon,** billiard hall, and courtroom where Judge Roy Bean dispensed hard liquor and hard justice are on the Rio Grande River, 60 miles west of Del Rio on U.S. 90. The Visitors Center features six talking dioramas depicting his "Law West of the Pecos." Year-round, daily, 8 A.M. to 5 P.M. Free. 915/291-3340.

LBJ NATIONAL HISTORICAL PARK and **LBJ STATE HISTORICAL PARK,** D-6. These parks, one under the jurisdiction of the National Park Service and the other under the jurisdiction of

the state, preserve places related to the life of the 36th president of the United States. Both cover several areas and are often confused. **Lyndon B. Johnson National Historical Park** (previously known as a national historic site) includes two units—the *LBJ Ranch Unit,* near Stonewall, can be seen only by bus tours. Leaving from the state park Visitors Center, U.S. 290 east of Stonewall, free bus tours for LBJ Ranch unit go to the one-room Junction School first attended by Johnson in 1912; the reconstructed farmhouse birthplace; the Johnson family cemetery where President Johnson is buried; through LBJ Ranch past the white, two-story house formerly known as the "Texas White House"; and the working ranch area for a look at the Hereford cattle. Bus tours: Daily, June-Aug., 10 A.M. to 5:30 P.M.; other months, 10 A.M. to 4 P.M. Bus departure time (every 15 minutes during summer) depends on visitation. The *Johnson City Unit* includes President Johnson's boyhood home, his grandparents' ranch, and a small Visitors Center. Guided tours: Year-round, daily, 9 A.M. to 5 P.M. Free. *Johnson Settlement,* one-half mile away, is a restoration of the ranch owned in the mid-1800s by Samuel Ealy Johnson, President Johnson's grandfather. Johnson Settlement can be reached only by footpath or horse-drawn wagons. Year-round, daily, 9 A.M. to 5 P.M. Free. National historical park units: 512/868-7128. **LBJ State Historical Park,** east of Stonewall, comprises 710 acres and includes a Visitors Center; nature trails; an assortment of cattle and wildlife (Texas longhorns, white-tailed deer, and buffalo); and two historic buildings—*Behrens Cabin* (c. 1840), a dogtrot building with furnishings similar to those of the area and period; and the *Sauer-Beckmann Farmstead* (early 1900) that exhibits customs and farm life of early German settlers. Year-round, daily, 9 A.M. to 4:30 P.M. State Park Visitors Center: Daily, June-Aug., 9 A.M. to 6 P.M.; other months, 8 A.M. to 5 P.M. Free. 512/644-2252.

LIVINGSTON, D-9. *See* **Alabama Coushatta Indian Reservation.**

LUBBOCK, 173,979, A-4. Named after Col. Thomas S. Lubbock, Confederate officer and brother of a Texas Civil War governor, Lubbock originally was the headquarters for buffalo hunters, trail drivers, and early ranchers. Several places of interest are associated with Texas Tech University. **The Museum of Texas Tech University,** 4th and Indiana Sts., has exhibits on art, natural sciences, and history of the area. Also here is *Moody Planetarium.* Museum: Year-round, Mon.-Wed., Fri.-Sat., 9 A.M. to 4:30 P.M.; Thurs., 9 A.M. to 8:30 P.M.; Sun., 1 to 4:30 P.M. Free. Planetarium shows: Year-round, daily, 2:30 and 3:30 P.M. Adults $1.50, children 50¢. 806/742-2136. **Ranching Heritage Center,** adjacent to the university, has examples of almost every type of building in the West, (many moved here from other areas) which tell the story of Texas ranching from its beginning to the present time. Year-round, Mon.-Fri., 8:30 A.M. to 4:30 P.M.; Sat.-Sun., 1 to 4:30 P.M. Adults $1.50; persons 6 to college age, 50¢; under 6 and over 60, free. 806/742-2490. **Lubbock Lake Site,** 2 miles north of the campus, is a major archaeological excavation under the university's direction. Guides available, June-Aug.; reservations required. Free. 806/742-2442.

MIDLAND, 70,525, C-4. Administrative center for the Permian Oil Basin, hundreds of oil companies have their offices here. The city is also surrounded by cattle ranches. **Permian Basin Petroleum Museum, Library and Hall of Fame,** 1500 Int. 120W, traces the history and development of the oil industry in the Permian Basin. Year-round, Mon.-Sat., 9 A.M. to 5 P.M.; Sun., 2 to 5 P.M. Adults $1.50, children 75¢. 915/683-4403. **Museum of the Southwest,** 1705 W. Missouri Ave., has exhibits in art and anthropology. *Marian Blakemore Planetarium* is adjacent to the museum. Museum: Year-round, Mon.-Sat., 10 A.M. to 5 P.M.; Sun., 2 to 4 P.M. Free. Planetarium: Year-round, Sun., 2 and 3:30 P.M.; Tues., 7:30 and 9 P.M. Free. 915/683-2882.

ODESSA, 90,027, C-4. Established in 1881 as a stop on the Texas Pacific Railroad, Odessa is in the heart of the Permian Basin. An area geologically named for its anhydrite, potassium salt, natural gas, and oil, this is a petroleum supply center. **Globe of the Great Southwest,** Odessa College campus, Andrews Hwy. at 23rd St., is an authentic replica of the Shakespearean Globe Theatre in England. Performances include an annual *Shakespeare Festival* in February and March, other theatrical productions, and *Odessa Brand New Opree,* a country-western family show, every other weekend throughout the year. Evening performances, 8 P.M.; Sunday matinee, 2:30 P.M. 915/332-1586.

PADRE ISLAND NATIONAL SEASHORE, G-7. Padre Island stretches 110 miles from Corpus Christi almost to the Mexican border. **Padre Island National Seashore,** with well-preserved primitive beaches, covers 81 miles of the island. Visitors can drive about 15 miles down the northern tip of the island on a paved road via the JFK Causeway from Corpus Christi to Park Rd. 22, northern boundary of the seashore, and to Malaquite Beach (near the northern entrance of the park), which features a 450-foot concrete boardwalk, beach pavilion, observation tower, and other facilities. The Ranger Station, just north of the pavilion, has information on natural and historic points along the Grassland Trail. Five miles beyond Malaquite, only four-wheel vehicles can maneuver the narrow, trackless island. (Do not attempt to drive the length of the island in a conventional vehicle.) The entire length may also be hiked. Access to the southern tip is by the

Queen Isabella Causeway, which connects Port Isabel on the mainland with Park Rd. 100. This area is more developed, with hotels, restaurants, campsites, marinas, and fishing piers. Current weather, beach tide, and fishing information: 512/822-6161 (North Padre Island); 512/943-6433 (South Padre Island).

PALO DURO CANYON, G-2. *See* **Canyon.**

SAN ANTONIO, 785,410, E-7. On the San Antonio River, this city is rich in history, scenery, and atmosphere. It all began on June 13, 1691, when Don Domingo Terán de los Rios, accompanied by Father Damian Massanet and 50 soldiers, discovered a settlement of Indians at the headwaters of the river. The Indians called it *Yanaguana,* but Father Massanet rechristened it San Antonio in honor of St. Anthony of Padua. Permanent settlement began in 1718.

MISSIONS: Mission San Antonio de Valero (better known as the Alamo), between Commerce and Houston Sts. on the east side of Alamo Plaza, was founded on May 1, 1718, by Father Antonio de San Buenaventure Olivares on San Pedro Creek. Subsequently the mission was moved to the east bank of the San Antonio River, destroyed by a hurricane in 1724, and reestablished at its present location. From February 23 to March 6, 1836, it was the site of the tragic

Walking Tour of San Antonio

To walk in San Antonio is to head for the river which meanders through the heart of the city. Stop first, though, for a tour of the Alamo, the most revered of all Texas landmarks. Then head across Alamo Plaza, down some stairs, and onto the Paseo del Alamo, a pedestrian walkway linking Alamo Plaza with Paseo del Rio, the River Walk. Along the way, you'll stroll through the lobby of the Hyatt Hotel, past shops and lush plantings, and onto the River Walk. Paseo del Rio provides a mile and a half of walkways leading to the doors of fine restaurants such as the Little Rein Steakhouse, and places like The Landing, where Dixieland Jazz reigns supreme. Hotels, among them La Mansion and the Hilton, overlook the river, as do shops selling everything from designer clothes to Mexican crafts. At the bend in the river, Arneson River Theater is often the site of performances. Overlooking the theater is La Villita, its buildings recently rennovated and filled with new shopping opportunities. Next, walk across Alamo Street to Hemisfair Plaza, location of the Institute of Texan Cultures, Tower of the Americas, San Antonio Museum of Transportation, and the Convention Center. A walk down Alamo Street brings you back to Alamo Plaza.

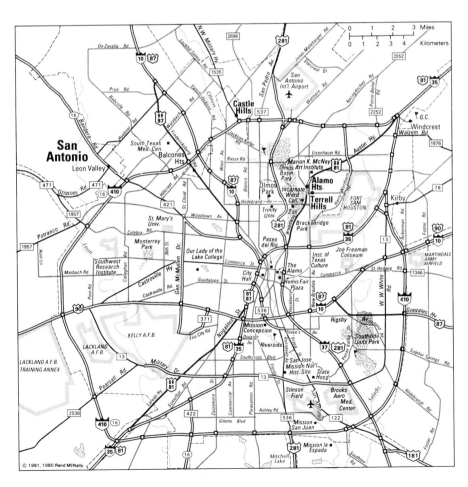

© 1981, 1980 Rand McNally

Battle of the Alamo. William Barret Travis, a South Carolina lawyer, led the defenders, who included such historic figures as James Bowie and Davy Crockett. All lost their lives in an effort to block the march of Mexican president and general, Santa Anna. The mission is now a museum containing relics and mementoes from the Republic of Texas days, a "Remember the Alamo" narration, and a Texas history library. Year-round, Mon.-Sat., 9 A.M. to 5:30 P.M.; Sun., 10 A.M. to 5:30 P.M. Free. 512/222-1693. **Remember the Alamo Theatre and Museum,** 315 Alamo Plaza, across the street from the Alamo, offers a visual presentation that literally surrounds the audience with the full story of the siege and its heroes. Shows every half hour. Year-round, daily, 9 A.M. to 5:30 P.M. Adults $2.50, children $1.25. 512/224-1836. **Mission Trail** is a specially marked roadway to four historic missions, starting at the intersection of Lone Star Blvd. and Roosevelt Ave. *Mission Concepción,* 807 Mission Rd., is the oldest church in Texas that has remained intact and in use for religious services. Completed in 1755, it was built of adobe and porous gray rock called tufa. Year-round, daily, 9:30 A.M. to 5:30 P.M. 512/532-3158. *Mission San José,* 6539 San Jose Dr., is called the "Queen of the Missions." Established February 23, 1720, it was the most beautiful, the most prosperous, and the best fortified of the Texas missions. Year-round, daily, 9:30 A.M. to 6 P.M. 512/922-2731. *Mission San Francisco de la Espada,* Espada Rd., is famed for its chapel with a sculptured stone door and the adjoining convent, its only surviving buildings; the nearby aqueduct built in 1720 is 37 miles long and still used for irrigation. Year-round, daily, 9:30 A.M. to 5:30 P.M. 512/627-2064. *Mission San Juan Capistrano,* 9101 Graf Rd., was established in 1731. It has a three-bell open tower with a bell hanging in the middle arch. Year-round, daily, 9:30 A.M. to 5:30 P.M. 512/532-3154. One mission: Adults $1, children 50¢. All four missions: Adults $2, children 50¢.

HISTORIC AREAS: Paseo del Rio (River Walk) lines the banks of the winding San Antonio River, some 20 feet below the city's downtown streets, for one and one-half miles. Winding stone stairways lead down to the river level where there are river-edge cobblestone walks, small shops, clubs, hotels, outdoor restaurants, and occasional scheduled entertainment. Tour boats leave every 10 minutes from well-marked stops for a 30-minute round trip of the river. Year-round, daily, 10 A.M. to 10 P.M. Adults $1.25, children 50¢. Paseo: Always open. Free. 512/227-4262. **King William Area,** King William and Alamo Sts., is a restored residential area and the state's first historic district. Victorian mansions are mixed in with Texas frame cottages built by early German settlers and highlighted by the Steves homestead with its mansard roof and one-foot-thick walls. Year-round, Mon.-Tues., 1 to 5 P.M.; Wed.-Sun., 10 A.M. to 5

P.M. Adults $1, children 50¢. A free walking tour is available from the San Antonio Conservation Society, 107 King William St. 512/227-8786. **La Villita** ("The Little Village"), S. Presa and Villita Sts., is an authentic restoration of the tiny settlement established two centuries ago by Canary Islanders and dedicated Franciscan padres. Among its attractions are the **Cos House,** an ancient adobe with a patio, and the **Little Church of La Villita,** built in 1876. Now the restored 19th-century enclave houses a variety of arts and craft shops. Year-round, daily, 10 A.M. to 5 P.M. Free. 512/299-8610. **Spanish Governor's Palace,** 105 Military Plaza, was the seat of Spanish government in Texas from 1772; the aristocratic Spanish home with its flagstone floors, three-foot-thick adobe walls, hand-hewn beamed ceilings, carved doors, and grape arbor in a mosaic patio, contains 18th-century Spanish furnishings and artifacts. Year-round, Mon.-Sat., 9 A.M. to 5 P.M.; Sun., 10 A.M. to 5 P.M. Adults 50¢, children 25¢. 512/224-0601. **San Fernando Cathedral,** 114 Military Plaza, is a French-Gothic, twin-towered cathedral which was the original parish church of the Canary Island settlers and the geographical and social center of San Antonio until the early 1900s. Interred here are remains thought to be those of the Alamo heroes. Year-round, daily. Free. 512/227-1297.

MUSEUMS AND ART CENTERS: McKay Art Institute, 6000 N. New Braunfels St., is a Spanish-style mission with patio and gardens containing a fine collection of post-Impressionist French and contemporary paintings. Year-round, Tues.-Sat., 9 A.M. to 5 P.M.; Sun., 2 to 5 P.M. Free. 512/824-5368. **Institute of Texan Cultures,** southeast corner, HemisFair Plaza, Durango St. and Int. 37, emphasizes the contributions of the racial and cultural groups that influenced Texas, with special exhibits featuring ethnic music and crafts. Year-round, Tues.-Sun., 9 A.M. to 5 P.M. Free. 512/226-7651. **Museum of Transportation,** HemisFair Plaza, S. Alamo and Durango Sts., highlights all modes of travel, especially by vintage vehicles on display. Year-round, daily, 10 A.M. to 5 P.M. Donations. 512/226-5544. **Hertzburg Circus Collection,** S. Presa and W. Market Sts., contains more than 20,000 items of big-top memorabilia. May-Oct., Mon.-Sat., 9 A.M. to 5:30 P.M.; Sun., 1 to 5 P.M.; other months, Mon.-Sat., 9 A.M. to 5:30 P.M. Free. 512/299-7810. **Witte Memorial Museum,** 3801 Broadway, has natural history, science, local history, and culture displays. Daily, June-Aug., 10 A.M. to 6 P.M.; other months, 10 A.M. to 5 P.M. Donations. 512/826-0647. **San Antonio Museum of Art,** 200 W. Jones Ave., opened recently in the Lone Star Brewery. Year-round, daily, 10 A.M. to 5 P.M. Adults $2; children under 12, $1. Free, Sat.-Sun., 10 A.M. to noon. 512/226-5544.

PARKS: Brackenridge Park, 2800 Block of N. Broadway, about 2 miles north of

downtown, is a 343-acre park with a wilderness area in a virgin oak forest. *Oriental Sunken Gardens* is another special area. Also in the park are a miniature train ride, aerial sky ride, golf course, polo field, bike trail, picnic area, paddleboats, and horseback-riding trails. Always open. Free, except for special rides. 512/299-8480.

ZOO: San Antonio Zoo, 3903 N. St. Mary's St., is in a setting of bluffs and lush vegetation. Among the inhabitants, many of which roam in natural areas separated from spectators only by moats, are 3,500 birds, animals, and reptiles. The zoo also has the only two whooping cranes in captivity. Daily, Apr.-Oct., 9:30 A.M. to 6:30 P.M.; other months, 9:30 A.M. to 5:30 P.M. Adults $2; persons 65 and over, $1.50; children 75¢. 512/734-7183.

PLAZA: HemisFair Plaza, 200 S. Alamo St., is the site of the 1968 World's Fair. In this 92-acre area are several outstanding buildings, including the *Institute of Texan Cultures, Museum of Transportation,* and the *Convention Complex.* The *Tower of the Americas,* also in the plaza, was the theme structure of the 1968 World's Fair. Glass-enclosed elevators take visitors to a popular restaurant and to the observation floor of this 760-foot-high tower for a view of the city. Observation deck: Year-round, daily, 10 A.M. to 11 P.M. Adults $1, children 50¢. 512/299-8570.

SHOPPING: Market Square, bounded by W. Commerce, Buena Vista, San Saba, and Santa Rosa Sts., is where area farmers sell their produce each day. Also here is *El Mercado,* with over 33 specialty shops featuring Mexican wares. Many fiestas, including *Fiesta de San Antonio,* are held here. 512/299-8600. Other shopping areas, described previously under Historic Areas, are La Villita and Paseo Del Rio.

SAN JACINTO BATTLEGROUND STATE HISTORIC PARK, E-9. Located 21 miles east of Houston via Int. 10, then St. 134, this is the site where on April 21, 1836, 910 Texans commanded by Sam Houston surprised and defeated 1,200 Mexican troops led by General Santa Anna. A 570-foot limestone monument topped by a 35-foot lone star commemorates the victory which gave Texas its independence. A museum at the base of the shaft displays items relative to Texas from the time it was a colony of New Spain through early statehood. Monument and museum: Year-round, Mon.-Sat., 9:30 A.M. to 5:30 P.M.; Sun., 9:30 A.M. to 5:30 P.M. Free. Elevator to top of monument: Adults $1.50, children 50¢. The **U.S.S.** *Texas,* flagship in the D-Day invasion, is moored nearby in permanent retirement. Built in 1914, it is a veteran of two wars and now is a museum. Year-round, daily, 10 A.M. to 6 P.M. Adults $1.50; children 50¢; under 6, free. Monument and battleship: 713/479-2421.

WACO, 101,261, C-7. **Fort Fisher Park,** Int. 35 and University Dr. at the Brazos

River in Waco, with its sloped-roof buildings of weathered fieldstone, is a restored fort near the site of the Texas Rangers 1837 outpost. It is now headquarters of Company F of the Rangers, a well-established part of the Texas State Police. The **Homer Garrison Memorial Museum** includes the Waco Tourist Information Center and a fine collection of western paintings and bronzes by Charles Russell and Frederic Remington, Jim Bowie knives, a saddle belonging to silent movie star William Hart, Texas Ranger memorabilia, and firearms. The **Texas Ranger Hall of Fame**, dedicated to the Texas Rangers, has exhibits depicting more than 150 years of Ranger history. Hall of Fame and Museum: Daily, June-Labor Day, 9 A.M. to 6 P.M.; other months, 9 A.M. to 5 P.M. Adults $2.50, children $1.50. 817/754-1433. **Brazos River Queen,** a paddlewheeler, Brazos River at Int. 35 Fort Fisher exit, has excursion cruises on the river. Year-round, daily, 2:30 P.M. (depending upon water level of the river). Adults $3.50; persons 12 and under and 65 and over, $2.50. 817/752-5800 or 817/752-9211.

Information Sources

Texas Tourist
Development Agency
P.O. Box 12008
Austin, TX 78711
512/475-4326

Texas Parks
and Wildlife Department
4200 Smith School Rd.
Austin, TX 78744
512/475-4845

Amarillo Board
of Convention &
Visitors Activities
1000 S. Polk St.
Amarillo, TX 79101
806/374-9812

Austin Chamber of
Commerce
P.O. Box 1967
Austin, TX 78767
512/478-9383

Corpus Christi Area
Convention
& Tourist Bureau
Box 2664
Corpus Christi, TX 78403
512/822-5603

Dallas Convention
& Visitors Bureau
1507 Pacific Ave.
Dallas, TX 75201
214/651-1020

El Paso Convention
& Visitors Bureau
5 Civic Center Plaza
El Paso, TX 79901
915/544-3650

Fort Worth Area Convention
& Visitors Bureau
700 Throckmorton Dr.
Fort Worth, TX 76102
817/336-2491

Galveston Convention
& Visitors Bureau
2106 Seawall Blvd.
Galveston, TX 77550
713/763-4311

Greater Houston
Convention
& Visitors Council
1522 Main St.
Houston, TX 77002
713/658-4200

San Antonio Convention
& Visitors Bureau
Box 2277
San Antonio, TX 78298
512/223-9133

Texas Campgrounds

FEES REFLECT MINIMUM RATE FOR 2 ADULTS AND ARE SUBJECT TO INCREASE OR SEASONAL CHANGES

- • – at the campground
- ○ – within one mile of campground
- $ – extra charge
- •• – limited facilities during winter months
- A – adults only
- B – 10,000 acres or more
- C – contribution

- E – tents rented
- F – entrance fee or premit required
- N – no specific number, limited by size of area only
- P – primitive
- R – reservation required
- S – self-contained units only

- U – unlimited
- V – trailers rented
- Z – reservations accepted
- LD – Labor Day
- MD – Memorial Day
- UC – under construction
- d – boat dock

- g – public golf course within 5 miles
- h – horseback riding
- j – whitewater running craft only
- k – snow skiing within 25 miles
- l – boat launch
- m – area north of map
- n – no drinking water

- p – motor bikes prohibited
- r – boat rental
- s – stream, lake or creek water only
- t – tennis
- u – snowmobile trails
- w – open certain off-season weekends
- y – drinking water must be boiled

Map Reference	Park Name	Access	Acres	Tent Spaces	Trailer Spaces	Approximate Fee	Season	Other Swimming / Swimming Pool	Fishing	Boating	Playground	Other	Telephone Number	Mail Address
	STATE PARKS													
C6	Abilene	Fr Abilene, 19 mi S on FM 89 to Buffalo Gap, 4.5 mi SW to Pk Rd 32	490	100		F3.00	All year	$ •		•			915/572-3204	Rt 1, Tuscola 79562
A10	Atlanta	Fr Atlanta, 12 mi NW on FM 77 & 96 to Pk Rd 42	1475	51	8	F3.00	All year	• •	l	•			214/796-6476	Rt 1, Box 116, Atlanta 75551
D3	Balmorhea	Fr Balmorhea, 5 mi SW on Hwy 17 to Toyahvale, S to Pk Rd 30												
H7	Bentsen - Rio Grande	Fr Mission, 6 mi SW on 83 & FM 2062 to Pk Rd 43	46	34		F3.00	All year	$ •		•			915/375-2370	Box 15, Toyahvale 79786
D10	Martin Dies	Fr Jasper, 13 mi W on US 190	587	65	77	F3.00	All year	• •	•	•			512/585-1107	Box 988, Mission 78572
E7	Blanco	Fr Blanco, 1 mi S on US 281 to Pk Rd 23	705	148	34	F3.00	All year	• •	lr	•			713/384-5231	Box 1108, Woodville 75979
A8	Bonham	Fr Bonham, 2 mi SE on Hwy 78 to FM 271, 2 mi SE to Pk Rd 24	110	23	10	F3.00	All year	• •		•			512/833-4333	Box 493, Blanco 78606
			257	9		F3.00	All year	• • ○	dl				214/583-5022	Rt 1 Box 337, Bonham 75418
E7	Buescher	Fr Smithville, 2.5 mi NW on Hwy 71/95 to FM 153, 1.5 mi N to Pk Rd 1	1013	30	40	F3.00	All year	• •		•			512/237-2241	Box 75, Smithville 78957
E7	Bastrop	Fr Bastrop, 1 mi SE on FM 21 to Pk Rd 1	3503	55	25	F3.00	All year	$ • •	l •	•	g		512/321-2101	Box 518, Bastrop 78602
B10	Caddo Lake	Fr Jefferson, 12 mi SE on FM 134	480	40	8	F3.00	All year	○ •	l •	•			214/679-3351	Rt 2, Box 15, Karnack 75661
C7	Cleburne	Fr Cleburne, 6 mi W on US 67 to Pk Rd 21, SW 8 mi	1068	61	27	F3.00	All year	• •	l •	•			817/645-4215	Rt 2, Box 90, Cleburne 76031
B9	Daingerfield	Fr Daingerfield, 2 mi E on Hwy 49 to Pk Rd 17	551	31	9	F3.00	All year	• •	dl •	•	g		214/645-2921	Box B, Daingerfield 75638
D3	Davis Mtns	Fr Fort Davis, 4 mi W on Hwy 118 to Pk Rd 3	1869	63	27	F3.00	All year	•		•			915/426-3337	Box 786, Ft Davis 79734
B6	Fort Griffin	Fr Albany, 15 mi N on US 283	503	20		F3.00	All year	•		•			915/762-3592	Rt 1, Albany 76430
C9	Mission Tejas	Fr Crockett, 22 mi NE on Hwy 21 to Pk Rd 44	118	10	5	F3.00	All year	•		•			713/687-2394	Rt 2 Box 108, Grapeland 75844
C8	Fort Parker	Fr Mexia, 7 mi S on Hwy 14 to Pk Rd 28	1485	27		F3.00	All year	○ •	l •	•			817/562-5751	Rt 3, Box 95, Mexia 76667
E6	Garner	Fr Concan, 7 mi N on US 83 to Pk Rd 29	912	143		F3.00	All year	○ •	•	•	h		512/232-6633	Concan 78838
C3	Monahans Sandhills	Fr Monahans, 6 mi NE on US 80 to Hwy 41	3840	28		F3.00	All year			•			915/943-2092	Box 1738, Monahans 79756
F8	Goose Island	Fr Rockport, 12 mi NE on Hwy 35 to Pk Rd 13	307	98		F3.00	All year	• •	l •	•			512/729-2858	Rt 1, Box 105, Rockport 78382
D9	Huntsville	Fr Huntsville, 6 mi S on I-45 to Pk Rd 40	2122	191		F3.00	All year	• •	dlr •	h			713/295-5644	Box 508, Huntsville 77340
B5	Lake Colorado City	Fr Colorado City, 6 mi W on I-20, 4 mi S on FM 2836	500	88		F3.00	All year		•	•			915/728-3931	Rt 2, Bx 232, Colo Cty 79512
E6	Kerrville	Fr Kerrville, 1/2 mi S on Hwy 16 to TX 173, SE 2.5 mi to Pk Rd 19	519	90	30	F3.00	All year	• •	l •	h			512/257-5392	2385 Bandera Hwy, Kerrvll 78028
C6	Lake Brownwood	Fr Brownwood, 15 mi NW on Hwy 279 to Pk Rd 15, 6 mi E on Pk Rd 15	538	70	20	F3.00	All year		dlr •				915/784-5223	Rt 5, Bx 160, Brownwood 76801
F7	Lake Corpus Christi	Fr Mathis, 4 mi SW on Hwy 359, 2 mi NW on Pk rd 25	365	83	25	F3.00	All year	• •	l •				512/547-2635	Box 1167, Mathis 78368
C7	Lake Whitney	Fr Whitney, 4 mi SW on FM 1244	955	95	42	F3.00	All year	• •	l •	g			817/694-3793	Box 1175, Whitney 76692
D7	Inks Lake	Fr Burnet, 9 mi W on Hwy 29 to Pk Rd 4	1200	197		F3.00	All year	• •	dlr •	g			512/793-2223	Box 117, Buchanan Dam 78609
C7	Meridian	Fr Meridan, 3 mi SW on Hwy 22 to Pk Rd 7	461	15	7	F3.00	All year	• •	l •				817/435-2536	Box 188, Meridian 76665
C7	Mother Neff	Fr Moody, 6.5 mi W on FM 107 to Hwy 236, S 1.8 mi to Pk Rd 14	259	15	6	F3.00	All year	•	•				817/853-2389	Rt 1, Bx 58, Moody 76557
E7	Palmetto	Fr Gonzales, NW 13 mi on US 183 to FM 1586, W 2 mi to Ottine	263	37	10	F3.00	All year	•	•				512/672-3266	Box 4, Ottine 78658
H2	Palo Duro Canyon	Fr Canyon, 12 mi E on Hwy 217 to Pk rd 5	B	94	20	F3.00	All year	•		h			806/488-2227	Rt 2 Box 285, Canyon 79015
B6	Possum Kingdom	Fr Caddo, 17 mi N on Pk rd 33	1528	116		F3.00	All year	• •	dlr	•			817/549-1803	Box 36, Caddo 76029
H6	Falcon	Fr Zapata, 25 mi SE on US 83 to FM 2098, SW 3 mi to Pk Rd 46	573	55	31	F3.00	All year	• •	lr				512/848-5327	Box 2, Falcon Heights 78545
E8	Stephen F Austin	Fr Sealy, 3 mi E on I-10, 2.5 mi N on FM 1458 to pk rd 38	664	40	40	F3.00	All year	$ • •	•	g			713/885-3613	Box 125, San Felipe 77473
B9	Tyler	Fr Tyler, 8 mi N on FM 14, 2 mi W on pk rd 16	994	80	39	F3.00	All year	• •	dlr				214/597-533P	Rt 9, Tyler 75706
F8	Goliad	Fr Goliad, 1 mi S on US 183 to Pk Rd 6	184	34	20	F3.00	All year	•	•				512/645-3405	Box 727, Goliad 77963
A8	Eisenhower	Fr Denison, 5 mi NW on Hwy 75A to FM 131D, 1.8 mi W on FM 1310 to Pk Rd 20	457	93	50	F3.00	All year	• •	dl				214/465-1956	Rt 2 Box 50K, Denison 75020
E7	Lockhart St Rec Pk	Fr Lockhart, 1 mi S on US 183, 2 mi SW on FM 20, 1 mi S on pk rd 10	263	14	10	F3.00	All year	$ •	•	g			512/398-3479	Rt 1 Box 69, Lockhart 78644

Map Reference	Park Name	Access	Acres	Tent Spaces	Trailer Spaces	Approximate Fee	Season	Other Swimming Pool	Swimming Pool	Fishing	Boating	Playground	Other	Telephone Number	Mail Address
B7	Ft Richardson Historic	In Jack County on US 281	383	23		F3.00	All year			•			p	817/567-3506	PO Box 4, Jacksboro 76056
	Lake Somerville														
D8	Birch Creek Unit	Fr Brenham, 15 mi NW on Hwy 36, 6 mi W on FM 60 to Pk Rd 57	640	133		F3.00	All year		•	•			l	713/535-7763	Rt 1 Box 192-A, Sommerville
D8	Nails Creek Unit	Fr Giddings, 8 mi E on US 290, 12 mi N on FM 180	300	40		F3.00	All year		•	•			l	713/289-2392	Rt 1 Bx 61C, Ledbetter 78946
A7	Lake Arrowhead	Fr Wichita Falls, 8 mi S on US 281, 6 mi E on FM 1954	524	67		F3.00	All year		•	•			dl	817/528-2211	Rt 2 Bx 260, Wichita Fls 76301
H8	Brazos Island	Fr Brownsville, 1 mi NE on Hwy 48, 22 mi E on Hwy 4	217	PN		None	All year		•	•					Boca Chica
A6	Copper Breaks	Fr Quanah, 12 mi S on Tx 6, in Hardeman Co	1944	40		F3.00	All year		•	•	•	l	• hp	817/839-4331	Rt 3, Quanah 79252
E9	Galveston Island	Fr Galveston, 6 mi SW on FM 3005	1950	170		F3.00	All year			•				713/737-1222	Rt 1 Bx 156A, Galveston 77550
C1	Hueco Tanks	Fr El Paso, 32 mi NE on US 62 to Ranch Rd 2775	860	12		F3.00	All year		•		•		p	915/533-8673	Bx 26502, El Paso 79926
G7	Lipantitlan Historical Pk	Fr Orange Grove, 9 mi E off Hwy 359/FM 624/FM 70	5	P6		F	All year								Orange Grove
A4	Mackenzie	In Lubbock, on Park Rd 18	542	10	10	F	All year		•	•			pt	806/762-6411	City Hall, Lubbock 79408
D7	Pedernales Falls	Fr Johnson City, 14 mi E on Ranch Rd 2766	4860	70		F3.00	All year			•		l	p	512/868-7304	Rt 1,Bx31A,Johnson City 78636
C7	Dinosaur Valley	Fr Glen Rose, 1 mi W on US 67, 4-1/2 mi on FM 205	1272	46		F3.00	All year			•			p	817/897-4588	Box 396, Glen Rose 76034
D7	McKinney Falls	Fr Austin, S on US-183 to Scenic Loop Dr, SW to Pk	726	84		F3.00	All year			•			gp	512/243-1643	Rt 2 Box 701B, Austin 78704
C8	Fairfield Lake	Fr Fairfield, 6 mi NE on FM 1124 to Pk Rd 64	1460	135		F3.00	All year		•	•		dl	• p	214/389-4514	Rt 2, Bx P30, Fairfield 75840
C9	Jim Hogg Historical Pk	Fr Rusk, 2 mi NE on US 84 & Pk Rd 50	177			F	All year							214/683-4850	Rt 2 Bx 29, Rusk 75785
E10	Sea Rim	Fr Sabine Pass, 10 mi W on Hwy 87	B	20		F3.00	All year			•		l		713/971-2559	P O Bx 1066,Sabine Pass 77655
E6	Lost Maples St NA	Fr Vanderpool 4 mi N on Ranch Rd 187	1280	20		4.00	All year			•			p	512/966-3413	Station C Rt,Vanderpool 78885
E5	Seminole Canyon St His Pk	Fr Comstock, 9 mi W on US 90	2182	31		3.00	All year							512/292-4464	PO Box 806 Comstock 78837
D9	Lake Livingston St RA	Fr Livingston 1 mi S on US 59, 4 mi W on FM 1988, 1/2 mi N on FM 3126 to Park Rd 65	635	147		4.00	All year	$	•	•	•	dlr	• p	713/365-2201	Rt 9 Box 1300,Livingston77351
G8	Mustang Island	Fr Port Aransas 14 mi S on Park Rd 53	3474	48		3.00	All year			•			p	512/749-5247	PO Box 326 Pt Aransas 78373
	NATIONAL PARKS														
	Lake Meredith RA		B											806/857-3151	Box 1438, Fritch 79036
G2	Blue West PUA	Fr Amarillo, N on Hwy 287 to 4 Way, 15 mi E on FM 1913		N	N	None	All year			•	dl		n		Masterson
G2	Sanford-Yake	Fr Fritch, 1 mi E on Hwy 136, 4 mi N on Hwy 687, W to CG		N	N	None	All year			•	dl				Fritch 79036
G2	Fritch Fortress PUA	Fr Fritch, E on Eagle Blvd, N on Co		N	N	None	All year			•	dl				Fritch
G2	McBride PUA	Fr Amarillo, 11 mi NE on Hwy 136 to Alibates rd, N to McBride cut-off, W		N	N	None	All year						n		Fritch
G2	Plum Creek PUA	Fr Four Way, 12 mi E on Fm 1913, S to Plum		N	N	None	All year			•	dl				Masterson
G2	Rosita Flats	Fr US 87-287 to Canadian Riv Brdg, E on dirt rd designated for off-road vehicles & motorcycle use		PN	PN	None	All year								Masterson
	Big Bend NP		B											915/477-2251	Big Bend NP 79834
E3	Chisos Mt Basin	Fr Marathon, 79 mi S on Hwy 385	35	72	72	2.00	All year						h	915/477-2251	Big Bend NP 79834
E3	Rio Grande Village Trl Pk	Fr Marathon, 69 mi S on Hwy 385, 20 mi E on Pk Rd #2	2		24	4.50	All year	o			dl			915/477-2293	Big Bend NP 79834
E3	Rio Grande Village	Fr Marathon, 69 mi S on Hwy 385, 20 mi E on Pk Rd 12	40	100	100	2.00	All year	o			dl			915/477-2251	Big Bend NP 79834
E3	Panther Jct Service Stati	Fr Marathon, 69 mi S on US 385	1		7	4.50	All year							915/477-8202	Big Bend NP 79834
E3	Cottonwood	Fr Marathon, 69 mi S on US 385, 40 mi SW on pk rds 5	3	8	8	1.00	All year								Big Bend NP 79834
	Guadalupe Mountains NP		B											915/828-3385	3225 Natl Pks Hwy,Carlsbad NM
C2	Pine Springs CG	Fr Carlsbad, NM, 55 mi SW on US 62/180		P10	P20	None	All year						p		Carlsbad, NM 88220
	Amistad Natl RA													512/775-7491	Box 1463, Del Rio 78840
E5	North, Highway 277	Fr Del Rio, 9 mi N on US 277	B		8	None	All year			•		l	n		Del Rio 78840
E5	Spur 406	Fr Del Rio, 20 mi W on Hwy 9, 4 mi S on Spur 406	B		12	None	All year			•		l	n		Del Rio 78840
E5	San Pedro Flats	Fr Del Rio, 6 mi W on US 90 to Spur 454, N on dirt rd	B	18	12	None	All year			•	•		n		Del Rio 78840
E5	Governor's Landing	Fr Del Rio, 9 mi E on US 90 to Amistead Dam, N on dirt rd	B	6	17	None	All year			•	•	d	n		Del Rio 78840
E5	South, Hwy 277	Fr Del Rio, 7 mi N on US 277	B		4	None	All year	o		•		dl	n		
	NATIONAL SEASHORES														
	Padre Isl Natl Seashore		B												S.Padre Is,Corp.Christi 78418
G7	Malaquite Beach CG	Fr Corpus Christi, SE on Hwy 358 to Hdqtrs, 20 mi SE on pk rd 22		100	70	2.00	All year			•					Corpus Christi
G7	North Beach	Fr Corpus Christi, SE on Hwy 358 to Hdqtrs, SE on pk rd 22 to Beach Access Road		P45	P45	None	All year			•			n		Corpus Christi
G7	South Beach	Fr Corpus Christi, SE on Hwy 358 to Hdqtrs, SE on pk rd 22 to end		P45	P45	None	All year			•					Corpus Christi
	NATIONAL FORESTS														
	Houston NF														
D9	Double Lake	Fr Coldspring, 1.5 mi W on Hwy 150, 1 mi S on Hwy 2025, 2 mi E on FR 210	20	53	53	2.00	All year		•	•		dr			Coldspring
D9	Stubblefield Lake	Fr New Waverly, 11 mi W on Hwy 1375, 2.9 mi NE on FR 215	10	28	28	2.00	All year			•					New Waverly
D9	Kelley Pond	Fr New Waverly, 11 mi W on Hwy 1375, .4 mi S on FR 204, .6 mi W on FR 271	6	8	8	None	All year			•					New Waverly
	Crockett NF														
C9	Ratcliff Lake	Fr Crockett, 20 mi NE on Hwy 7, .4 mi NE on FR 520	101	68	68	2.00	All year		•	•		dlr			Crockett
	Angelina NF														
D10	Letney	Fr Zavalla, 20 mi SE on Hwy 63, 3 mi E on Hwy 255, 2 mi N on FR 335	10	33	33	2.00	3/1-10/1			•	•	dl			Zavalla
D10	Boykin Springs	Fr Zavalla, 11 mi SE on Hwy 63, 2.5 mi SW on FR 313	14	36	36	2.00	All year			•	•	d			Zavalla
D10	Sandy Creek	Fr Zavalla, 17.5 mi SE on Hwy 63, 3 mi N on FR 333	10	27	19	2.00	3/1-10/1			•	•	dlr			Zavalla
D10	Caney Creek	Fr Zavalla, 5 mi E on Hwy 63, 4.5 mi SE on Hwy 2743, 1 mi N on FR 336	45	125	125	2.00	All year			•	•	dlr			Zavalla
D10	Bouton Lake	Fr Zavalla, 8 mi SE on Hwy 63, 7 mi S on FR 303	3	7		None	All year			•					Zavalla
C10	Townsend	Fr Broaddus, .7 mi NE on Hwy 147, 3 mi NW on Hwy 1277, 1 mi W on FR 2923	19	67	67	2.00	3/1-10/1			•	•	dl			Broaddus
C10	Harvey Creek	Fr Broaddus, 3.5 mi SE on Hwy 83, 5 mi SW on Hwy 2390	12	42	40	2.00	All year			•	•	dl			Broaddus
	Sabine NF														
C10	Red Hills Lake	Fr Hemphill, 10.5 mi N on Hwy 87, .2 mi E on FR 116	9	32	17	2.00	3/1-10/1			•		d			Hemphill
C10	Ragtown	Fr Center, 11 mi SE on Hwy 87, 6.5 mi W on Hwy 139, 3.7 mi E on Hwy 3184, 1.6 mi SE on FR 132	2	14	14	2.00	3/1-9/30			•	1	d			Center
C10	Indian Mounds	Fr Hemphill, 6 mi E on Hwy 83, 2 mi S on FR 115, 5 mi SE on FR 128, 1 mi E on FR 130	62	75	72	2.00	All year			•	•	dl			Hemphill
C10	Lakeview	Fr Hemphill, 9.2 mi SE on Hwy 87, 4.8 mi NE on Hwy 2928, 4.2 mi SE on FR 120	4	10	10	2.00	3/1-10/1			•		d			Hemphill
C10	Willow Oak	Fr Hemphill, 15 mi SE on Hwy 87, .2 mi E on FR 105	49	320	120	2.00	All year			•	•	dlr			Hemphill
G2	Lake McClellan	Fr Groom, 21 mi E on I-40, 2 mi N on Co 13438	12		10	None	4/15-9/15			•		dlr	n		Groom
	CORPS OF ENGINEERS														
	Belton Lake													817/939-1829	PO Box 209,Belton 76513
C7	Temple Lake	Fr Temple, 9 mi W on Hwy 2305	100	0	S23	4.00	MD-LD			•	•	l	p		Belton 76513
C7	Live Oak Ridge Pk	Fr Belton, 5 mi NW on Hwy 317	39	0	S48	4.00	MD-LD			•	•	l	p		Belton 76513
C7	Cedar Ridge	Fr Temple, 9 mi NW on Hwy 36	120		S55	3.00	MD-LD			•	•	dlr	p		Belton 76513
	Benbrook Lake													817/292-2400	PO Bx 26059, Ft Worth 76116
	Mustang Pk	Fr Benbrook, 1.5 mi S on US 377, 2.5 mi E on FM 1187, 1 mi on Co Rd 1041	440	0	S40	4.00	4/1-9/30			•	•	l	p		Benbrook 76126
B7	Holiday Pk	Fr Benbrook, 4 mi S on US 377, 1 mi E on FM 2376	486	0	S24	4.00	All year			•	•	l	p		Benbrook 76126
B7	Town Bluff Dam													713/429-3491	Str Rt 1 Bx 249,Wdville 75979
	Sandy Creek	Fr Jasper, 11 mi SW on US 190 & FM 777	70	0	S45	3.00	All year			•	•	l	p		Woodville 75979
D9	Magnolia Ridge	Fr Jasper, 15 mi SW on US 190, 1 mi N on Co rd	80	0	S35	3.00	All year			•	•	l	p		Woodville 75979
D9	Lewisville													214/434-1666	1801 N Mill,Lewisville 75067

Map Reference	Park Name	Access	Acres	Tent Spaces	Trailer Spaces	Approximate Fee	Season	Other Swimming	Swimming Pool	Fishing	Playground	Boating	Other	Telephone Number	Mail Address
B8	Oakland Pk	Fr Lake Dallas, 3 mi SE on old Hwy 24	62	0	S83	4.00	All year		•	•		l	p		Lake Dallas 75065
	Lavon Lake													214/442-5711	PO Box 429, Wylie 75098
B8	Lavonia Pk	Fr Wylie, 6 mi NE on Hwy 78, 1 mi W on Co Rd 6	76		S38	4.00	All year		•	•		l	p		Wylie
B8	Little Ridge	Fr Wylie, 8 mi NE on Hwy 78, 1 mi W on Co Rd	40	31		4	4/1-9/30		•	•		l	p		Wylie
B8	Collin	Fr Wylie, 2 mi N on FM 2514, 1 mi E on Co Rd	66		32	4.00	4/1-9/30		•	•		l	p		Wylie
B8	East Fork	Fr Wylie, 1/2 mi N on FM 2514, 2 mi E on Co Rd	46		50	4.00	All year		•	•		dl	p		Wylie
	Grapevine Lake													817/481-4541	Rt 1 Bx 10, Grapevine 76051
B7	Twin Coves	Fr Grapevine, 2 mi E on Hwy 121, 3 mi N on FM 2499, 2 mi W on FM 3040	243		S40	4.00	MD-LD	•	•	•		l			Grapevine 76051
	Hords Creek Lake													915/625-2322	Glen Cove Rt, Coleman 76834
C6	Lakeside Pk	Fr Coleman, 9 mi W on Hwy 53	157		S43	4.00	All year		•	•		l	p		Coleman 76834
C6	Flat Rock Pk	Fr Coleman, 8 mi SW on Hwy 53, 2 mi S on Dam Rd	192		S72	3.00	4/1-9/30		•	•		l	p		Coleman 76834
	Somerville Lake	Fr Brenham, 15 mi NW on Hwy 36 to Somerville, 1 mi W												713/596-1622	PO Bx 548, Somerville 77879
D8	Yegua	Fr Somerville, 2 mi S on Hwy 36, 2 mi W on FM 1948	93		S94	4.00	All year		•	•		l	np		Somerville 77879
D8	Rocky Creek	Fr Somerville, 2 mi S on Hwy 36, 3 mi W on FM 1948	195		S155	4.00	All year		•	•		l	p		Somerville 77879
D8	Big Creek	Fr Somerville, 2 mi N on Hwy 36, 3 mi W on FM 60, 2 mi S on R4	93		S66	3.00	All year		•	•		dlr	p		Somerville 77879
	O C Fisher Lake														PO Bx 3085, San Angelo 76902
C5	Red Arroyo Pk	Fr San Angelo, 2 mi W on FM 853	270		S48	None	All year		•	•		l	p		San Angelo 76902
C5	Dry Creek	Fr San Angelo, 5 mi NW on US 87, 1 mi S	180		S27	None	All year		•	•		l	p		San Angelo 76902
	Waco Lake													817/756-5359	Rt 10 Bx 173-G, Waco 76708
C7	Speegleville	Fr Waco, 2 mi W on Hwy 6	2473		S154	3.00	All year		•	•		dl			Waco 76708
C7	Airport Pk	Fr Waco, 2 mi NW on FM 1637, 1.5 mi SW on Flat Rock Rd	780		S92	3.00	All year		•	•		dl			Waco 76708
	Whitney Lake													817/694-3189	Bx 38, Laguna Pk Rr Sta, Clftn
C7	Loafers Bend	Fr Whitney, 6 mi SW on Hwy 22	550		S92	4.00	All year		•	•		dl			Whitney 76692
C7	Cedron Creek	Fr Whitney, 2 mi N on FM 933, 6 mi S on FM 1713	180		S56	4.00	All year		•	•		l			Whitney 76692
	Stillhouse Hollow Lake													817/939-1829	PO Bx 209, Belton 76513
D7	Dana Peak Pk	Fr Belton, 5 mi W on US 190, 5 mi W on FM 2410, 2.5 mi S on Commanche Gap Rd	110		S67	4.00	MD-LD		•	•		l	p		Belton 76513
D7	Union Grove Pk	Fr Belton, 5 mi W on US 190, 4 mi S on FM 1670, 3 mi W on FM 2786	51		S24	3.00	MD-LD		•	•		l	p		Belton 76513
	Lake Texoma (Denison Dam)	(See Oklahoma for additional campgrounds)													
A8	Big Mineral Camp	Fr Whitesboro, 14 mi N on US 377	990	20	20	2.00	All year			•		lr			Whitesboro
A8	Cedar Bayou	Fr Whitesboro, 13 mi N on US 377	435	12	12	None	All year			•		dlr			Whitesboro
A8	Cedar Mills	Fr Whitesboro, 14 mi N on US 377, 2 mi E	455	22	22	None	All year			•		lr			Whitesboro
A8	Flowing Wells	Fr Denison, 7 mi W on Hwy 120 to Pottsboro, 6 mi W on access rd	410	30	30	None	All year			•		lr			Denison
A8	Highport	Fr Denison, 6 mi W on Hwy 120, 5 mi N, 1 mi W	385	24	24	None	All year			•		dlr			Denison
A8	Mill Creek	Fr Denison, 16 mi W on Hwy 120, 3 mi N of Paradise Cove CG	75	13	13	None	All year			•		lr			Denison
A8	Paradise Cove	Fr Denison, 13 mi W on Hwy 120, 1 mi N of Flowing Wells CG	125	7	7	None	All year			•		lr			Denison
A8	Grandpappy Point	Fr Denison, 9 mi NW on Hwy 84	285	13	13	3.00	All year			•		lr			Denison
A8	Preston Fishing Camp	Fr Denison, 13 mi NW on Hwy 120	105	33	33	None	All year			•		lr			Denison
A8	Island View	Fr Denison, 13 mi NW on Hwy 120	65	N	N	None	All year			•		l			Denison
A8	Juniper Point	Fr Whitesboro, 14-1/2 mi N on US 377, S end Willis Bridge	390	77	77	4.00	All year			•		l			Whitesboro
A8	Paw Paw Point	Fr Whitesboro, 16 mi N on US 377 & access rds; 1 mi S of Rock Creek	210	N	N	None	All year			•		l			Whitesboro
A8	Preston Bend	Fr Denison, 14 mi NW on Hwy 120	115	44	44	4.00	3/1-6/30		•	•		lr			Denison
A8	Walnut Creek	Fr Whitesboro, 11 mi NE on US 377	455	31	31	None	All year			•		lr			Whitesboro
A8	Rock Creek	Fr Whitesboro, 17 mi NW on US 377 & access rds	280	20	20	None	All year			•		l			Whitesboro
A8	Damsite Area	Fr Denison, 5 mi NE on Hwy 75A	260	16	16	2.00	All year			•		l			Denison
	Pat Mayse Lake		6000											214/785-1510	Box 128, Powderly 75473
A9	Forest Point	Fr Arthur City, approx 7 mi W on Co 197, 1-1/2 mi S	20	24	24	2.00	All year		•	•		l	p		Chicota
A9	Pat Mayse Pk East	Fr Arthur City, approx 7 mi W on Co 197, 1-3/4 mi S	30	30	30	2.00	All year		•	•		l	p		Chicota
A9	Pat Mayse Pk West	Fr Arthur City, approx 7 mi W on Co 197, 1/2 mi S, 1/2 mi E, 1 mi S	60	86	86	2.00	All year		•	•		l	p		Chicota
A9	Sanders Cove	Fr Arthur City, 2 mi S on US 271, 3/4 mi W, 1 mi SW	85	79	79	2.00	All year		•	•		l	p		Powderly
A8	Lamar Point	Fr Paris, 5 mi N on Hwy 271, 5 mi W on Hwy 1499, 5 mi N on Hwy 1500	22	31	31	None	All year		•	•			p		Paris
	Lake O'The Pines		1194												Bx 17300, Fort Worth 76102
B9	Buckhorn Creek Pk	Fr Jefferson, 3 mi NW on Hwy 49, 3 mi W on FM 729, 3 mi SW on FM 726	45		75	4.00	MD-LD		•	•		l	p	214/665-2336	Bx 17300, Fortworth 76102
B9	Johnson Creek Pk	Fr Jefferson, 3 mi NW on Hwy 49, 5-1/2 mi W on FM 729	51		85	4.00	MD-LD		•	•		l	p	214/665-2336	Bx 17300, Fortworth 76102
B9	Alley Creek	Fr Jefferson, 3 mi NW on Hwy 49, 7 mi W on FM 729	50		S51	3.00	MD-LD		•	•		l	p	214/665-2336	Bx 17300, Fortworth 76102
B9	Brushy Creek	Fr Jefferson, 3 mi NW on Hwy 49, 3 mi W on FM 729, 5 mi SW on FM 726	60		100	4.00	All year		•	•		l	p	214/665-2336	Bx 17300, Fortworth 76102
	Wright Patman Lake		8712											214/838-8781	Bx 17300, Fort Worth 76102
A10	Rocky Point Pk	Fr Texarkana, 10 mi S on Hwy 59	40		120	4.00	All year		•	•		l	p	214/838-8781	Bx 17300, Fort Worth 76102
	Navarro Mills Lake													817/578-1431	Rt 1, Bx 33D, Purdon 76679
C8	Oak Pk	Fr Dawson, 4 mi E on Hwy 31, 1 mi N on FM 667	100		S42	4.00	All year		•	•		l	p		Dawson 76639
C8	Liberty Hill	Fr Dawson, 3 mi NE on FM 709	240		S98	4.00	All year		•	•		l	p		Dawson 76639
C8	Wolf Creek Pk	Fr Dawson, 4 mi On Hwy 31, 3 mi N on Hwy 677, 2 mi SW on FM 3164	278		S41	3.00	4/1-9/30		•	•		l	p		Dawson 76639
	Proctor Lake													817/879-2424	Rt 1 Bx 71A, Comanche 76442
C6	Copperas Creek	Fr Dublin, 14 mi SW on US 67/377, 1 mi N on FM 2861	176		S66	3.00	All year		•	•		l	p		Comanche 76442
C6	Promontory	Fr De Leon, 6 mi SW on Hwy 16, 4 mi SE on FM 2318	153		S40	3.00	MD-LD		•	•		l	p		De Leon 76444
C6	Sowell Creek	Fr Proctor, 1.5 mi W on FM 1476	76		S20	3.00	MD-LD		•	•		l	p		Proctor 76468
	Bardwell Lake													214/875-5711	Rt 4 Bx 33A, Ennis 75119
C8	Waxahachie Creek	Fr Bardwell, 2 mi NE on Hwy 984	63		S42	4.00	4/1-9/30		•	•		l	p		Bardwell 75101
C8	Mott Pk	Fr Bardwell, 3 mi NE on Hwy 34, 1/2 mi SE on Co Rd	54		S26	2.00	4/1-9/30		•	•		l	p		Bardwell 75101
C8	High View	Fr Bardwell, 1-1/2 mi NE on Hwy 34	79		S39	3.00	All year		•	•		l	p		Bardwell 75101
	Canyon Lake													512/964-3341	Canyon 78130
E7	Canyon	Fr New Braunfels, 19 mi NW on Hwy 306	433		S287	3.00	MD-LD		•	•		dlr	p		Canyon 78130
E7	Cranes Mill Pk	Fr New Braunfels, 14 mi NW on Hwy 306, 9 mi W on FM 2673	196		S80	3.00	MD-LD		•	•		dl	p		Canyon 78130
E7	Potters Creek	Fr New Braunfels, 21 mi NW on Hwy 306, 2 mi S on Co Rd	300		S89	3.00	MD-LD		•	•		l	p		Canyon 78130
	Sam Rayburn Lake													713/384-5716	Rt 3 Bx 320, Jasper 75951
C10	Hanks Creek	Fr Huntington, 8 mi E on Hwy 2109, 1 mi E on FM 2801	71		S30	3.00	MD-LD		•	•		dlr	p		Huntington 75949
C10	Jackson Hill Pk	Fr Zavalla, 11 mi NE on Hwy 147, 1 mi W on FM 3158	163		S60	3.00	MD-LD		•	•		dlr	p		Zavalla 75951
C10	Mill Creek Pk	Fr Jasper, 13 mi N on US 96 to Brookeland, 1 mi W on Spur 165	59		S95	4.00	All year		•	•		l	p		Jasper 75951
C10	Rayburn Pk	Fr Massie, 12 mi S on FM 705, 1 mi W on FM 3127	77		S77	3.00	MD-LD		•	•		l	p		Jasper 75951
C10	Powell Pk	Fr Massie, 12 mi S on FM 705	160		S98	3.00	MD-LD		•	•		dlr	p		Jasper 75951
C10	Twin Dikes Pk	Fr Jasper, 6 mi N on US 96, 5 mi W on Co 255	200		S47	3.00	MD-LD		•	•		l	p		Jasper 75951
C10	San Augustine	Fr Pineland, 5-1/2 mi W on Co 83, 4 mi S on FM 1751	77		S70	3.00	MD-LD		•	•		l	p		Pineland 75968
	INDIAN RESERVATIONS														
	Alabama-Coushatta													713/563-4391	Rt 3 Bx 640, Livingston 77351
D9	Big Sandy Creek CG	Fr Livingston, 17 mi E on US 190	4	11	31	3.00	All year			•			p		Livingston
D9	Tombigbee Lake Camp	Fr Livingston, 17 mi E on US 190, 1 mi S at Reservation ent	200	137	137	3.50	All year		•	•			p		Livingston

Virginia

Major Events

See state map, pages 46-47

Highland Maple Festival, mid- to late Mar., Monterey, northwest of Staunton. Festivities include tours of the local maple sugar farms, arts and crafts shows, country music, square dances, and lots of special foods, including pancakes with maple syrup. Admission is charged for several events. 703/468-2550.

Virginia State Horse Show, mid- to late Apr., Richmond. This horse show features hunters, jumpers, saddle horses, walking horses, roadster ponies, quarter horses, Appaloosas, Arabians, and Morgans. The Virginia Jumper Classic is the main event. Admission is charged for several events. 804/329-4437.

Historic Garden Week in Virginia, mid- to late Apr., statewide. For nine days visitors are invited to come to Virginia and visit privately owned homes, gardens, and historic landmarks in 33 areas of the state. Admission. 804/644-7776.

International Azalea Festival, mid- to late Apr., Norfolk. A grand parade, concerts, bicycle races, art shows, and the coronation and ball of Queen Azalea are all part of the festivities celebrating the blooming of thousands of azaleas at Norfolk's Gardens by the Sea. Free (except Grand Ball). 804/622-2312.

Shenandoah Apple Blossom Festival, late Apr. to early May, Winchester. Springtime is heralded with pageantry, arts and crafts, musical entertainment, band contests, a fire fighter's parade, and the Grand Feature Parade, which has over 50 floats and more than 80 marching bands participating. Admission is charged for several events. 703/662-3863.

Reenactment of the Battle of New Market, early May, New Market, west of Luray. Seven hundred mock soldiers, dressed in the uniforms of the North and South, reenact the charge of the Battle of New Market which took place in 1864. Free. 703/740-3101.

Jamestown Day, mid-May, Jamestown. This celebration commemorates the establishment of the first permanent English-speaking settlement in the New World. Free. 804/229-1733.

Festival in the Park, late May to early June, Roanoke. Elmwood Park is the site for this long weekend of outdoor art and music activities that include classical, jazz, bluegrass, and big band concerts; a sidewalk art show; and footraces. Free. 703/342-2640.

June Jubilee, early June, Richmond. This celebration of the arts, held in downtown Richmond, features entertainment provided by area musicians and theater groups, art exhibits, and many different types of food. Free (except food). 804/643-3982.

Harborfest, mid-June, Norfolk. Tall sailing ships, military ships, sailboats, and motorboats help to celebrate Norfolk's ties with the sea. Also, there are air shows, waterskiing shows, art shows, live entertainment, and a fireworks display. Free. 804/441-5266.

Antique Fly-In Air Show, late June, Fredericksburg. Nationally known stunt planes, antique aircraft, precision flying, and championship parachuting are all featured in this show held at Shannon Airport. Admission is charged for several events. 703/373-1776.

19th-Century Craft Days, early July, New Market, northeast of Harrisonburg. Demonstrations of different types of early crafts such as blacksmithing and bread baking in an outdoor oven are featured at the New Market Battlefield Park. Free. 703/740-3101.

Old-Fashioned Fourth of July in Yorktown, July 4, Yorktown, east of Williamsburg. Parades in the morning are followed by military demonstrations, arts and crafts shows, a fair, and fireworks over the York River. Free. 804/887-1776.

Pork, Peanut, and Pine Festival, mid-July, Surry, southwest of Williamsburg. Chippokes Plantation State Park is the site for this old-fashioned agricultural fair which features food, arts and crafts, displays, and live entertainment. Free (except food). 804/294-3116.

Belle Grove Annual Shenandoah Valley Farm Craft Days, mid-July, Middletown, south of Winchester. Some 75 craftsmen demonstrate many aspects of old folk art, including log splitting, basket weaving, loom weaving, pottery making, and candle dipping. The event is held on the Belle Grove Plantation. Admission. 703/869-2028.

Pony Penning, late July, Chincoteague. Wild ponies are rounded up from Assateague Island, herded to the town of Chincoteague, penned, and auctioned off the following day. Those not sold are returned to their refuge. Free. 804/336-6161.

Virginia Highlands Festival, early to mid-Aug., Abingdon. This arts and crafts festival features art, creative writing, and photography contests; craft demonstrations; a flea market; and an antique car show. Admission is charged for several events. 703/628-8141.

Annual Jousting Tournament, mid-Aug., Mount Solon, north of Staunton. One of America's oldest sporting events pits local riders against each other in order to test their skills at various jousting activities. Bluegrass music and a barbecue chicken dinner are also featured. Admission. 703/350-2510.

Annual Tour of Homes, late Sept., Alexandria. Several historic homes, most of them furnished with period pieces, in the Alexandria area are open to the public. Admission. 703/549-0205.

State Fair of Virginia, late Sept. to early Oct., Richmond. The State Fairgrounds showcases livestock and horse shows, commercial exhibits, arts and crafts, energy exhibits, a carnival midway, and nightly entertainment and fireworks. Admission. 804/329-4437.

Oktoberfest, late Sept. to early Oct., Wintergreen, southwest of Charlottesville. Adults celebrate at this festival with German music, dancing, costumes, food, and beer, while children are entertained with storytelling, games, songs, and puppet shows. Tours of the nearby mountain foliage are conducted, and crafts are demonstrated and sold. Admission is charged for several events. 804/325-2200.

Fredericksburg Dog Mart, early Oct., Fredericksburg. This event, first held in 1698 as a trade between Indians and settlers, is one of the oldest dog shows in the nation. In addition, there are Indian dances and crafts, music, and contests in hog calling, turkey calling, and fox horn blowing. Admission. 703/373-1776.

National Tobacco Festival, mid-Oct., Richmond. This tribute to the famous crop of Virginia includes the Grand Illuminated Parade, the Tobacco Bowl, and the Queen's Coronation Ball. Admission is charged for several events. 804/648-1234.

Medley of the Arts, late Oct., Hampton. This festival features a showcase of visual and performing arts, including a juried art show. Admission. 804/826-6066.

Virginia Thanksgiving Festival, early Nov., Charles City, northwest of Williamsburg. America's first Thanksgiving is reenacted with a landing, ceremonial Indian dances, music, and food. Admission. 804/353-3114.

Annual Scottish Christmas Walk, early Dec., Alexandria. Scottish clan chieftains, visitors, and residents parade through the streets in honor of Alexandria's Scottish founders. Special activities include highland dancing, bagpipe music, children's programs, and antiques and greens sales. Admission is charged for several events. 703/549-0111.

Grand Illumination, mid-Dec., Williamsburg. This official celebration marks the opening of Christmas fortnight. In the early evening is a fireworks show. Free. 804/229-1000.

Virginia Destinations

ABINGDON, 4,318, G-3. **Barter Theater,** at intersection of U.S. 11, U.S. 19, and U.S. 58, off Int. 81, Exit 8, was founded during the 1930s depression by Robert Porterfield, who believed that theatrical entertainment could be bartered. Patrons swapped hams, chickens, milk, and bread for tickets. Even playwrights accepted hams as royalty payment. Apr.-Oct., Tues.-Thurs., 8 P.M.; Sun., 7 P.M.; Wed., Sat., 2 P.M. Admission $5.75. Fri.-Sat., 8:30 P.M. Admission $7.50. 703/628-3991.

ALEXANDRIA, 103,217, D-9. One of Virginia's oldest and most historic cities, Alexandria was established in 1749 and named for John Alexander, who had purchased the land 80 years earlier. George Washington, a frequent visitor, helped lay out the streets and plan the building lots.
HISTORIC CHURCHES: Christ Church, Cameron and N. Washington Sts., had among its worshippers George Washington and Robert E. Lee. Mar.-Oct., Mon.-Sat., 9 A.M. to 5 P.M.; other months, Sun., 2 to 5 P.M. Donations. 703/549-1450. **Presbyterian Meetinghouse,** 321 S. Fairfax St., has in its churchyard the tomb of the Unknown Soldier of the American Revolution. Built in 1774 by Scottish sea captains, the meetinghouse was used for memorial sermons for George Washington on December 29, 1799, when bad weather made the road to his Christ Church impassable. Year-round, Mon.-Fri., Sun., 9 A.M. to 4 P.M. Donations. 703/549-6670. **Pohick Episcopal Church,** 12 miles south on U.S. 1, is the only remaining early church of colonial Truro Parish. It was built between 1769 and 1773 under the supervision of a committee which included George Washington, George Mason, and George William Fairfax. Mason served on the parish vestry for 35 years, and Washington, for 27 years. Year-round, daily, 8 A.M. to 4 P.M. Free. 703/399-6572.
HISTORIC HOMES: Carlyle House, 121 N. Fairfax St., is a restored Georgian mansion constructed in 1752 by John Carlyle. The house was the Alexandria headquarters of Gen. Edward Braddock, commander of the British Forces in America (1754-55). Year-round, Tues.-Sat., 10 A.M. to 5 P.M.; Sun., noon to 5 P.M. Adults $1.50; persons 65 and over, $1; 6-17, 75¢; under 6, free. 703/549-2997. **Gunston Hall,** 14 miles south on U.S. 1, was built in 1755-58 by George Mason, one of the framers of the U.S. Constitution and author of the Fairfax Resolves, which led to the Virginia Declaration of Rights of 1776. Year-round, daily, 9:30 A.M. to 5 P.M. Adults $2; persons 6-15, 50¢; under 6, free. 703/550-9220. **Woodlawn Plantation,** 7 miles south on U.S. 1, was a 2,000-acre gift from George Washington to his adopted granddaughter, Nellie Custis, and his nephew, Lawrence Lewis, at their marriage in 1799. Year-round, daily, 9:30 A.M. to

4:30 P.M. The **Pope-Leighey House,** a small residence designed by Frank Lloyd Wright as a model for low-cost housing in 1940, now stands on Woodlawn's grounds after being moved from its original site. Mar.-Oct., Sat.-Sun., 9:30 A.M. to 4:30 P.M. Woodlawn Plantation and Pope-Leighey House: Each, adults $2.50; persons 65 and over, $2; children and students through 12th grade, $1.25; under 2, free. Combination ticket with Woodlawn, adults $4, students $2. 703/557-7880. **Robert E. Lee Boyhood Home,** 607 Oronoco St., was built in 1795 and is noted for its central hall and stairs and its Adamesque woodwork. Feb.-mid-Dec., Mon.-Sat., 10 A.M. to 4 P.M.; Sun., noon to 4 P.M. Adults $1.50; persons 65 and over, $1; 6-12, 75¢; under 6, free. 703/548-8454.
MUSEUM: Fort Ward Museum and Park, 4301 W. Braddock Rd., contains a partial restoration of one of the largest Civil War forts constructed for the defense of Washington. The 40-acre park: Year-round, daily, 9 A.M. to sunset. Museum: Tues.-Sat., 9 A.M. to 5 P.M.; Sun., noon to 5 P.M. Free. 703/838-4848. **Gadsby's Tavern Museum,** 134 N. Royal St., once was the center of the city's social and political life. The museum consists of the original Georgian tavern built in 1752; the City Hotel, which was added in 1792 because of the tavern's popularity; and a popular restaurant. Year-round, Tues.-Sat., 10 A.M. to 5 P.M.; Sun., 1 to 5 P.M. Adults, $1.50; persons 65 and over, $1.25; 6-17, 75¢; under 6, free. 703/838-4242.
HISTORIC BUILDINGS: Friendship Engine House, 107 S. Alfred St., was the site of the city's first fire company, which was organized in 1775 and claimed George Washington as one of its members. A replica of the fire engine Washington gave the city in 1775 is on display. June-Aug., daily, 10 A.M. to 4 P.M. Adults $1; children under 12 and Scouts, free. **George Washington National Masonic Memorial,** located at the west end of King St., is a 333-foot-tall structure modeled after the ancient lighthouse in Alexandria, Egypt. Year-round, daily, 9 A.M. to 5 P.M. Free. 703/683-2007. **Stabler-Leadbetter Apothecary Shop,** 107 S. Fairfax St., founded in 1792, houses a collection of early medical ware and hand-blown glass containers. When the drugstore closed in 1933, it was the oldest in Virginia and the second oldest in America. Year-round, Mon.-Sat., 10 A.M. to 4:30 P.M. Donations. 703/836-3713. **Ramsay House Visitors Center,** 221 King St., is located in Alexandria's oldest house, built in 1724 by the city's first Lord Mayor, William Ramsay. Year-round, daily, 10 A.M. to 5 P.M. Free. 703/549-0205.
HISTORIC AREAS: George Washington's Grist Mill Historical State Park, 5514 Mt. Vernon Hwy., features a restored mill standing on the original foundation. The

history of the mill is shown through a slide presentation. Memorial Day-Labor Day, daily, 10 A.M. to 6 P.M. Adults 50¢; children 6-12, 25¢; under 6, free. 703/780-3383.

APPOMATTOX COURT HOUSE NATIONAL HISTORICAL PARK, F-7. Three miles northeast of Appomattox on St. 24, the park was established in 1940 to preserve the former village and county seat of Appomattox Court House. It was here that the Civil War formally ended on April 9, 1865, when Gen. Ulysses S. Grant's forces cut off Gen. Robert E. Lee's Confederate Army of Northern Virginia at the Appomattox Court House, signaling defeat for the South. Today, the village has been restored to its 1865 appearance and many buildings are open to the public. The courthouse contains a museum and auditorium where an audiovisual history of the area is presented. Year-round, daily, 8:30 A.M. to 6 P.M. Admission $1 per car. 804/352-8987.

ARLINGTON, 32,400, C-9. The **Pentagon,** on the south side of the Potomac River across from the District of Columbia, houses the Department of Defense. One of the world's largest office buildings, this five-sided structure covers 34 acres. Guided tours: Year-round, Mon.-Fri., 9 A.M. to 3:30 P.M. Free. 202/695-1776. **Arlington National Cemetery,** across the Potomac River from the District of Columbia, was established in 1864 as a place where those who had given their lives for their country could be buried. Daily, Apr.-Sept., 8 A.M. to 7 P.M.; other months, 8 A.M. to 5 P.M. Tourmobiles providing narration: Adults $2; children 3-11, $1; under 3, free. 202/692-0931. The *Tomb of the Unknown Soldier* commemorates those who died in World War I; remains of unknown soldiers from World War II and the Korean conflict also have been interred in this area. It is guarded 24 hours a day. Guard changes: Apr.-Sept., on the half hour; other months, every hour on the hour; year-round, nightly, every two hours on the hour. *Tomb of the Unknown Dead of the Civil War* marks the mass grave of more than 2,000 unidentified soldiers who were killed in the Civil War. The *Netherlands Carillon Tower,* near the cemetery, just off U.S. 50, is a gift from the Netherlands in appreciation for aid rendered by the United States. Concerts: Apr.-Sept., Sat. and holidays, 2 P.M. The *Memorial Amphitheater,* which can seat more than 4,000, is the site of Memorial Day services. Tributes from many foreign nations to the American Unknown Dead are contained in a special room in the marble structure. An *Eternal Flame* marks the grave of Pres. John F. Kennedy. Nearby is the gravesite of his brother Sen. Robert F. Kennedy. Both men were killed by assassins' bullets—the president on November 22, 1963, and Senator Kennedy on June 5, 1968. The *Marine Corps War Memorial,* at the north end of the cemetery, is a 78-foot, 100-ton monument of Joseph Rosenthal's picture of the flag-raising on Iwo Jima. **Arlington House,** overlooking the cemetery and the city of Washington, was made a permanent memorial to Gen. Robert E. Lee in 1955 by Act of Congress. General Lee and Mary Ann Randolph Custis were married and lived here from 1831 to 1861 (the property was owned by Mrs. Lee's family). The mansion has been restored and contains some of the original family furnishings. The *Tomb of Pierre L'Enfant,* the planner of the city of Washington, is in front of the mansion. Daily, Apr.-Sept., 8 A.M. to 7 P.M.; other months, 8 A.M. to 5 P.M. Free. 202/557-0613 or 202/557-3154.

ASHLAND, 4,640, E-9. **Scotchtown,** about 9 miles northwest of Ashland just off St. 54, was the home of Patrick Henry from 1771 to 1777 and the childhood home of Dolley Payne Madison. Apr.-Oct., Mon.-Sat., 10 A.M. to 4:30 P.M.; Sun., 1:30 to 4:30 P.M. Adults $2.50; persons 6-19, 75¢; under 6, free. 804/227-3500. **Kings Dominion,** north of Ashland on St. 30, one-half mile east of Int. 95, Doswell Exit, is a 1,300-acre theme park. Areas include the Land of Hanna-Barbera, International Street, Candy Apple Grove, Old Virginia, and Lion Country Safari. The park also features unusual rides, including a double roller coaster. Mid-June-Aug., daily, 9:30 A.M. to 10 P.M.; Apr.-May, Sept.-Oct., Sat.-Sun., 9:30 A.M. to 8 P.M. (closing time varies with season). Admission $10.95 per day includes monorail, parking $1. 804/876-5000.

Engraving made by John de Mare from a miniature painted by Charles Willson Peale. Chicago Historical Society

George Washington in 1755, at age 23, was in charge of all Virginia troops, a task so difficult and frustrating that it broke his health and forced him into temporary retirement in 1757. In the spring of 1758, he returned to duty. The following year, he married Martha Dandridge Custis, a widow with two children. The above engraving of Washington at age 25 was signed in the style of the times as "your most obedient humble servant" and dated "10th Sept. 1757."

BIG STONE GAP, 4,748, G-2. **June Tolliver House,** constructed in 1890 at Jerome and Clinton Sts., was the home of the heroine in the book *Trail of the Lonesome Pine* by John Fox, Jr. The house features mountain crafts and period pieces. Tours: Apr.-Christmas, Tues.-Sat., 10 A.M. to 5 P.M.; Sun., 2 to 6 P.M. Free. 703/523-1235. *Trail of the Lonesome Pine,* an outdoor musical drama, is presented at the June Tolliver Playhouse at Jerome and Clinton Sts. July-Aug., Thurs.-Sat., 8:30 P.M. Adults $3.50; children 6-12, $1.50; under 6, free. 703/523-1235. **John Fox, Jr. Museum,** Main St., was the home of the author of *Trail of the Lonesome Pine.* July-Aug., by appointment. Admission $1.50. 703/523-2747. **Southwest Virginia State Museum,** three blocks west of the center of town on W. First St. and Wood Ave., has dioramas, pioneer artifacts, miniature log houses, and folk art which trace the region's history from frontier days to the present. Year-round, Tues.-Sat., 9:30 A.M. to 5 P.M.; Sun., 2 to 5 P.M. Free. 703/523-1322.

BOOKER T. WASHINGTON NATIONAL MONUMENT, F-7. On St. 122 north, 20 miles southeast of Roanoke, the monument is a memorial to a former slave who became an educator and a leader of his people. Exhibits and a movie about Washington can be seen in the Visitors Center. Year-round, daily, 8:30 A.M. to 5 P.M. Free. 703/721-2094.

BROOKNEAL, 1,454, G-7. **Red Hill,** 5 miles southeast on Co. 600, was the last home and burial site of Patrick Henry and his wife, Dorothea Spotswood Dandridge. Henry's law office and the cook's cabin are the original buildings. Daily, Apr.-Oct., 9 A.M. to 5 P.M.; other months, 9 A.M. to 4 P.M. Adults $1.50; persons 65 and over, $1; 5-12, 75¢; under 5, free. 804/376-2044.

CHARLOTTESVILLE, 45,101, E-8. This was the home of Thomas Jefferson, who left an architectural legacy to the country; James Monroe; and Meriwether Lewis and William Clark, who led the expedition to find a route to the Pacific Ocean. **HISTORIC HOMES: Monticello,** on St. 53, 3 miles southeast of the city, was Jefferson's masterpiece. He began building the 35-room mansion, a classic example of American architecture, in 1769, but it was not completed until 1809. The dominating features are the dome; the parquet floors, some of the first in the nation; and the seven-day clock over the front door. Jefferson died at Monticello on July 4, 1826, on the fiftieth anniversary of Independence Day, and is buried here. Tours of the house, gardens, wine cellars, and Jefferson's tomb: Daily, Mar.-Oct., 8 A.M. to 5 P.M.; other months, 9 A.M. to 4:30 P.M. Adults $3; children 6-11, $1; under 6, free. 804/295-2657. **Ash Lawn,** off St. 53 on Co. 795, was the home of James Monroe, fifth president of the United States. Designed by Thomas Jefferson and

built in 1799-1826, the house contains many of Monroe's personal effects. The grounds are noted for their extensive boxwood gardens. Daily, Mar.-Oct., 9 A.M. to 6 P.M.; other months, 10 A.M. to 5 P.M. Adults $2.50; children 6-11, 75¢; under 6, free. 804/293-9539.

MUSEUM: Michie Tavern Museum, on St. 20, one-half mile south from Int. 64, was once a hostelry and tavern whose register included the names of Jefferson, Madison, Monroe, and Jackson. A part of the building ·is said to have been built in 1735 by Patrick Henry's father, Maj. John Henry. Year-round, daily, 9 A.M. to 5 P.M. Adults $2; college students $1.50; children 6-12, 75¢; under 6, free. 804/977-1234. *The Ordinary,* a 200-year-old converted slave house on the property, serves colonial food. Year-round, daily, 11:30 A.M. to 3 P.M. 804/977-1234.

UNIVERSITY: University of Virginia, U.S. 29 and U.S. 250 business routes, was founded and designed by Jefferson, who considered his role in founding the university of greater importance than his services as president of the United States. Edgar Allen Poe, whose room may be seen by appointment, and Woodrow Wilson were students there. Year-round. Free. 804/924-0311.

MEMORIALS: Lewis and Clark Memorial, Midway Park at Ridge and Main Sts., honors Meriwether Lewis and William Clark, who explored the Northwest. **George Rogers Clark Memorial,** W. Main St., is a tribute to George Clark, brother of William, the explorer.

COLONIAL NATIONAL HISTORICAL PARK, F-10. This park encompasses most of Jamestown Island, site of the first permanent English settlement; Yorktown, scene of the culminating battle of the American Revolution in 1781; a 23-mile parkway connecting these and other colonial sites with Williamsburg; and Cape Henry Memorial, which marks the approximate site of the first landing of Jamestown's colonists in 1607. **Jamestown National Historic Site,** on Jamestown Island, preserves the area of the first settlement, established in 1607. A walking tour from the Visitors Center, which also has an extensive series of exhibits related to the settlement, goes by several places of interest. Among them are *Old Tower,* which is believed to have been constructed as a part of the first brick church in 1639 (it is the only standing ruin in the settlement), and *Memorial Church,* erected in 1907 over the foundation of the early brick church. Colonial National Historical Park entrance at Jamestown Island (to Jamestown National Historic Site): Daily, Nov.-Mar., 8:30 A.M. to 4:30 P.M.; Apr.-mid-June, 8:30 A.M. to 5 P.M.; late June-Labor Day, 8:30 A.M. to 5:30 P.M.; early Sept.-Oct., 8:30 A.M. to 5 P.M. Admission $2 per vehicle. 804/898-3400. **Jamestown Festival Park,** adjacent to Jamestown National Historic Site, was constructed in 1957 for the 350th anniversary of the

Jamestown Landing and is under the jurisdiction of the Commonwealth of Virginia. In the park are *James Fort*, a full-scale reconstruction of the triangular palisade built by Capt. John Smith; the *New World Pavilion*, which has recorded the achievements of the settlers in the New World; the *Old World Pavilion*, which has exhibits showing the way of life the settlers brought with them from England; *Powhatan's Lodge*; crafts of the period; and full-scale reproductions of the ships *Susan Constant*, *Godspeed*, and *Discovery*, which carried the settlers to Virginia. Year-round, daily, 9 A.M. to 5 P.M. Adults $2.50; persons over 62, $2; 7-12, $1.25; under 7, free. 804/253-4838. *See* also **Yorktown**.

CUMBERLAND GAP NATIONAL HISTORICAL PARK, G-1. The park, southeast of Middlesboro, lies within the Kentucky, Tennessee, and Virginia borders. Travel from Virginia into Kentucky was difficult until this passage in southwestern Virginia was opened. It was explored by Dr. Thomas Walker and Daniel Boone in the mid-1700s; by 1795, a wagon trail called the Wilderness Road had been established. A Civil War and pioneer museum is housed in the Visitors Center. Daily, mid-June-Labor Day, 8 A.M. to 9 P.M.; other months, 8 A.M. to 5 P.M. Free. 606/248-2817.

DANVILLE, 45,642, G-7. Confederate Pres. Jefferson Davis and other government officials moved here after the evacuation of Richmond, making Danville the last capital of the Confederacy. Danville is believed to be the second largest tobacco auction center in the United States. Sales are held from September to November, and visitors are invited to attend. The **National Tobacco-Textile Museum**, 614 Lynn St., has displays of tobacco products and industry-related memorabilia and the history of textile manufacturing. Year-round, Tues.-Fri., 10 A.M. to 4 P.M.; Sat.-Sun., 2 to 4 P.M.; holidays, by appointment. Adults $1.50; children 3-12, 75¢; under 3, free. 804/797-9437.

DISMAL SWAMP, G-10. In southeastern Virginia and northeastern North Carolina, the swamp is a marshy region of some 750 square miles. Seven-mile-long *Lake Drummond* and *Dismal Swamp National Wildlife Refuge* are in it. Hunting and fishing are permitted here.

FAIRFAX, 19,390, D-9. **Sully Plantation**, on St. 28 north of U.S. 50, was built in 1794 by Richard Lee, uncle of Robert E. Lee. The house, which has the original flooring and paneling, has furnishings of the Federal period. Mid-Mar.-Dec., Mon., Wed.-Sat., 10 A.M. to 5 P.M.; Sun., noon to 5 P.M. Adults $1.50; persons 3-15 and over 59, 75¢; under 3, free. 703/437-1794.

FALLS CHURCH, 9,515, C-9. The city, a part of the Truro Parish where George Washington served as vestryman from 1762 to 1784, was named for the **Falls Church**,

Jamestown for the first few years of its existence in 1607 was James Fort, a cluster of crude buildings surrounded by a protective wall. The above reconstruction of the fort is now a part of Jamestown Festival Park. Like the original, the reconstruction includes 15 timber dwellings, a church, a storehouse, and a combination armory and barracks — all built with thatched roofs and wattle and daub walls. The 11-foot outer wall was surrounded by a 4-foot-deep moat.

on E. Fairfax St. The church has been restored to its 18th-century appearance. Year-round, daily, 9 A.M. to 4 P.M. Free. 703/532-7600. **National Memorial Park**, 2 miles west on U.S. 29, features *The Fountain of Faith*, which was designed by Carl Milles, a Swedish sculptor. Another sculpture is dedicated to the chaplains who lost their lives on the troopship *Dorchester* after they gave their life jackets away. Year-round, daily, 8 A.M. to sunset. Free. 703/560-4400 or 703/280-5076. **Wolf Trap Farm for the Performing Arts**, north of Falls Church in Vienna on Trap Rd., is the first National Park Service area established for the performing arts. In a setting of rolling hills and woods, *Filene Center*, where musical events are held, can accommodate an audience of 6,500, including 3,000 on the sloping lawn. Presented here from June through August are operas, symphony concerts, country-western music, jazz, and miscellaneous musicals. Park: Year-round, daily, sunrise to sunset. Free. Musical programs: June-Aug., daily, 8 P.M.; Sat.-Sun., also 2 P.M. Concert tickets: $5 to $25 per person. 703/938-3810.

FALMOUTH, 970, D-9. **Belmont—The Gari Melchers Memorial Gallery**, 224 Washington St., is an 18th-century manor house once owned by American artist Gari Melchers (1860-1932). Year-round, Mon., Wed., Fri.-Sun., 1 to 4 P.M.; other days, by appointment. Adults $1.50, children 50¢. 703/373-3634.

FREDERICKSBURG, 15,332, D-9. The area that was to become Fredericksburg was explored by Capt. John Smith in 1608. Founded in 1727, the town was well known

to Washington, Monroe, Lee, and others. Fredericksburg was a major seagoing port of Colonial Virginia and 17th-century America and was on the main road (the King's Highway) from North to South. During the Civil War, both sides fought for control of the principal land route between Richmond and Washington; and the battles of Fredericksburg, Chancellorsville, The Wilderness, and Spotsylvania Court House fought in and around Fredericksburg left the town nearly destroyed.

HISTORIC BUILDINGS: The Courthouse, 815 Princess Anne St., was completed in 1852 on the site of a structure dating from 1739. Paul Revere's foundry made the courthouse bell. Mary Washington's will is kept here. Year-round, Mon.-Fri., 8:30 A.M. to 4:30 P.M. Free. 703/373-4541. **Hugh Mercer Apothecary Shop**, 1020 Caroline St., belonged to Dr. Hugh Mercer, a Scotsman who arrived in this country in 1746 and practiced medicine here from 1771 to 1776. Daily, Apr.-Oct., 9 A.M. to 5 P.M.; other months, 9 A.M. to 4 P.M. Adults $1.50; persons 6-18, 50¢; under 6, free. 703/373-3362. **Masonic Lodge**, 803 Princess Anne St., was the site of George Washington's 1752 initiation as a Mason when he was 20 years old. Year-round, Mon.-Sat., 9 A.M. to noon, 1 to 4 P.M.; Sun., 1 to 4 P.M. Adults $1.50, children 50¢. 703/373-5885.

HISTORIC HOMES: Kenmore, 1201 Washington Ave., was owned by Col. Fielding Lewis and his wife, Betty Washington Lewis, the only sister of George. The Georgian manor house was built between 1752 and 1756 and once overlooked an 863-acre flax and tobacco plantation. Tours of the house end with tea and gingerbread baked from Mary Washington's recipe. Daily, Apr.-Oct., 9 A.M. to 5 P.M.; Nov.-Mar., 9 A.M. to 4 P.M. Adults $2.50, children $1. 703/373-3381. The **Mary Washington House**, 1200 Charles St., was purchased in 1772 by George Washington for his mother, who lived here until her death in 1789. Daily, Apr.-Oct., 9 A.M. to 5 P.M.; other months, 9 A.M. to 4 P.M. Adults $1.50, children 50¢. 703/373-1569. **George Washington's Birthplace**, 38 miles east of Fredericksburg off St. 3, is now a national monument. John, the first Washington to settle in the area, arrived about 1656. In 1731, his grandson Augustine married Mary Ball and the couple built the house in which George Washington was born in 1732. On Christmas Day, 1779, the house was destroyed by fire and was never rebuilt. A memorial house (and gardens) representing an 18th-century plantation was built here and furnished with items reflecting Washington's boyhood years. On the grounds are a working farm and a cemetery where 32 family members, including George Washington's father, grandfather, and great-grandfather, are buried. Year-round, daily, 9 A.M. to 5 P.M. Free. 804/224-0196.

MUSEUMS: Fredericksburg Museum, 623 Caroline St., is housed in The Chimneys, an 18th-century residence. Among its exhibits are items from Indian settlements and early Fredericksburg, 18th-century furnishings and costumes, a Civil War room, and a display on the history of transportation. Daily, Apr.-Oct., 9 A.M. to 5 P.M.; Nov.-Dec., Mar., 9 A.M. to 4 P.M. Adults $1.50, children 50¢. 703/371-4504. **James Monroe Museum and Memorial Library**, 908 Charles St., was built in 1758. Pres. James

Monroe began his public career here in 1786. Today it contains the personal effects of President and Mrs. Monroe and furniture originally used in the White House from 1817 to 1825. Year-round, daily, 9 A.M. to 5 P.M. Adults $1.50; persons 6-18, 50¢; under 6, free. 703/373-8426. **Shannon Air Museum**, 2½ miles southeast on U.S. 17, is a tribute to Sidney Shannon, Sr., former vice-president of Eastern Airlines. Year-round, daily, 9 A.M. to 5 P.M. Adults $2, children $1. 703/371-6611.

HISTORIC AREA: Fredericksburg and Spotsylvania County Battlefields Memorial National Military Park, southwest of Fredericksburg, comprises portions of four major Civil War battlefields—*Fredericksburg, Chancellorsville,* the *Wilderness,* and *Spotsylvania Court House.* On May 2, 1863, during the Battle of Chancellorsville, Gen. Stonewall Jackson was sent by General Lee to sever Union communications. While reconnoitering about 9 P.M., Jackson was accidentally wounded by fire from the guns of his own men, who mistook his party for a Federal patrol; he died a week later. *Stonewall Jackson Memorial Shrine,* 12 miles south on Int. 95 to Thornburg exit, then 5 miles east on St. 606 in Guinea, commemorates the spot where Jackson died. The park Visitors Center, west on St. 3 off Int. 95, has a documentary film and military exhibits related to the battles. Year-round, daily, 9 A.M. to 5 P.M. Free. 703/786-2880.

FRONT ROYAL, 11,126, C-8. Here is the northern gateway to the Skyline Drive, which winds through hardwood forests along the crest of the Blue Ridge Mountains in Shenandoah National Park. **Skyline**

Caverns, 1 mile south of the entrance to the Skyline Drive on U.S. 340, contains snow-white calcite formations known as "orchids of the mineral kingdom." Daily, Memorial Day-Labor Day, 8:30 A.M. to 6:30 P.M.; Sat. before Easter-Memorial Day, Labor Day-late Oct., 9 A.M. to 5:30 P.M.; other months, 9 A.M. to 5 P.M. Adults $4.75; persons 7-13, $2.25; under 7, free. 703/635-4545.

MUSEUMS: Confederate Museum, 95 Chester St., contains Civil War relics and records. Mid-Apr.-Oct., Mon.-Sat., 9 A.M. to 5 P.M.; Sun., noon to 5 P.M.; other months, by appointment. Adults $1, children free. 703/636-9068 or 703/635-2692. **Thunderbird Museum and Archaeological Park,** 7 miles south on U.S. 340, offers the opportunity to watch archaeologists at work. Major digs are reached by an amphibious vehicle across the Shenandoah River. Mid-Mar.-mid-Nov., daily, 10 A.M. to 5 P.M.; other months, by appointment. Adults $2; children and persons 65 and over, $1.50. 703/635-7337 or 703/635-3860.

HAMPTON, 122,617, G-10. One of the original boroughs in the Virginia Legislature, Hampton is the oldest English settlement still in existence in the United States. Hampton Roads was the scene of the famous battle between the *Merrimac* and the *Monitor,* two ironclad vessels. **St. John's Church**, 100 W. Queen's Way, housed British troops in the War of 1812 and was partially burned during the Civil War. It was built in 1728 in the nation's oldest continuous parish, which was founded in 1610. Year-round, daily, 9 A.M. to 4 P.M. Free. 804/722-2567. **NASA/Langley Research Center,** on St. 134 adjacent to Langley Air Force Base, is where astronauts practiced their moon landings and lunar lift-offs and scientists planned landings on Mars and the utilization of the space shuttle. Visitors Center: Year-round, Mon.-Sat., 8:30 A.M. to 4:30 P.M.; Sun., noon to 4:30 P.M. Free. 804/827-2855. **Fort Monroe**, designed by one of Napoleon's generals, was an important base for the Union forces during the Civil War. The Confederates' *Merrimac* and the Union's *Monitor* met in an epic sea battle here, but neither vessel was able to claim a decisive victory. Confederate Pres. Jefferson Davis was held at Fort Monroe two years after the war; his cell can be viewed today. Year-round, daily, 10:30 A.M. to 5 P.M. Free. 804/727-3973.

HARRISONBURG, 19,671, D-7. **Natural Chimneys Regional Park,** southwest off St. 42, has seven 120-foot natural limestone chimneys carved from solid rock by the waters of the Shenandoah River. Park facilities include campsites, playgrounds, bathhouse, laundry facilities, nature and bike trails, and swimming pool. Daily, Memorial Day-Labor Day, 8 A.M. to sunset; mid-Mar.-Memorial Day, Labor Day-late Nov., 9 A.M. to sunset. Adults $1; children 6-12, 50¢; under 6, free. 703/350-2510.

18th-Century Plantations Along the James River Were Accessible for Importing and Exporting Products Via English Ships

The James River, in southeastern Virginia, is the site of several 18th-century plantations, established here because of their accessibility for importing and exporting. In those days, English ships would tie up to the plantation wharfs, unload furniture, clothing, and wines, and take on tobacco, which was raised on the plantations. Some of the South's most stately homes are here. Today, several of these are open to the public year-round. Carter's Grove, 6 miles southwest of Williamsburg on U.S. 60, was built between 1750 and 1753 by Carter Burwell, grandson of Robert Carter, one of Virginia's wealthiest and most influential men and the original owner of the estate. Mar.-Nov., daily, 9 A.M. to 5 P.M. Adults $3; children 6-12, $1.50; under 6, free. Shirley Plantation, 20 miles southeast of Richmond on St. 5, has been the home of ten generations of Carters. Built in 1723, the mansion was the birthplace of Robert E. Lee's mother, Ann Hill

Carter. Year-round daily, 9 A.M. to 5 P.M. Adults $3.50; students $2.50; children 6-12, $1.75; under 6, free. Berkeley (1726) on St. 5 about 4 miles from Shirley, was the home of Benjamin Harrison, who signed the Declaration of Independence and whose son and grandson were the 9th and 23rd presidents, respectively, of the United States. Year-round, daily, 8 A.M. to 5 P.M. Adults $4.50; persons over 60, $3.50; 6-12, $1.75; under 6, free. Several other plantations are along the river. At some, only the gardens are open to the public; at others, homes are open only by appointment. Among these are Sherwood Forest, Riverview Farm, Westover, Belle Air, Weston Manor, Flowerdew Hundred, and Chippokes. All, plus other historic homes throughout Virginia, are open for Historic Garden Week, the last week of April. Historic Garden Week in Virginia, 12 E. Franklin St., Richmond, VA 23219. 804/644-7776 or 804/643-7141.

JAMESTOWN, F-10. *See* **Colonial National Historical Park**.

LEESBURG, 8,357, C-9. This town was named for Francis Lightfoot Lee, a local landowner and one of the signers of the Declaration of Independence. President Madison and his cabinet fled with 22 wagonloads of documents to this town when Washington, D.C. was burned during the War of 1812. **Morven Park**, north from St. 7 on Morven Park Rd., then northwest on Old Waterford Rd., is the estate of Westmoreland Davis, a former Virginia governor. Memorial Day-Labor Day, Tues.-Sat., 10 A.M. to 5 P.M.; Sun., 1 to 5 P.M. Adults $2.25; persons 65 and over, $2; 6-12, $1.25; under 6, free. 703/777-2414. **Oatlands**, about 6 miles south on U.S. 15, is a Classical-Revival mansion built by George Carter in the 1800s in the heart of the northern Virginia hunt country. The house has been restored and furnished to its original appearance. Apr.-Oct., Mon.-Sat., 10 A.M. to 5 P.M.; Sun., 1 to 5 P.M. Adults $3; persons over 60 and students over 6, $2.50; under 6, free. 703/777-3174.

LEXINGTON, 7,292, E-6. In the backdrop of mountains, Lexington offers two historic universities and the home of one of the Confederacy's great generals. The **Stonewall Jackson House**, 8 E. Washington St., has been restored to the way it looked when Thomas Jonathan Jackson, better known as Stonewall Jackson, lived here from 1859 to 1861. Year-round, Mon.-Sat., 9 A.M. to 4:30 P.M.; Sun., 1 to 4:30 P.M. Adults $1.50, children 75¢. 703/463-2552. **Virginia Military Institute**, founded in 1839, is the oldest state-supported military college in the United States. Weather permitting, there are dress parades spring and fall, Fri., 4:20 P.M. Free. 703/463-6207. *George C. Marshall Library and Museum*, at the west end of the parade ground, contains personal papers of the World War II chief of staff. Mid-Apr.-mid-Oct., Mon.-Sat., 9 A.M. to 5 P.M.; Sun., 2 to 5 P.M.; other months, Mon.-Sat., 9 A.M. to 4 P.M.; Sun., 2 to 4 P.M. Free. 703/463-7103. *Virginia Military Institute Museum*, Jackson Memorial Hall, contains many personal items of Stonewall Jackson, who taught here for 10 years before the Civil War. Year-round, Mon.-Fri., 9 A.M. to 4:30 P.M.; Sat., 9 A.M. to noon, 2 to 5 P.M.; Sun., 2 to 5 P.M. Free. 703/463-6232. **Washington and Lee University** was founded as Augusta Academy in 1749. Its present name honors George Washington, who endowed it, and Robert E. Lee, who served as its president. *Lee Chapel*, built in 1867 under General Lee's supervision, contains his office, preserved as he left it; the family crypt; Peale portraits of Washington and Lafayette; and a museum. Mid-Apr.-mid-Oct., Mon.-Sat., 9 A.M. to 5 P.M.; Sun., 2 to 5 P.M.; other months, Mon.-Sat., 9 A.M. to 4 P.M.; Sun., 2 to 5 P.M. Free. 703/463-9111, ext. 289. **Natural Bridge**, 15 miles south of Lexington

on U.S. 11 or 4 miles south of Exit 50 on Int. 81, is a 36,000-ton limestone structure 90 feet long and 215 feet high. George Washington carved his initials here as he surveyed it, and Thomas Jefferson bought the formation from King George III in 1774 for "20 shillings of good and lawful money." Daily, Apr.-Sept., 7 A.M. to 10 P.M.; other months, 7 A.M. to 7 P.M. Adults $3; children 6-12, $1.50; under 6, free. *The Drama of Creation* is presented under the arch. Nightly, May-Aug., 9 and 10 P.M.; Sept.-Oct., 8 and 9 P.M.; Nov., Mar.-Apr., 7 and 8 P.M.; Dec.-Feb., 6 and 7 P.M. Adults $3; children 6-12, $1.50; under 6, free. Bridge and drama: Adults $4; children 6-12, $2; under 6, free. 703/291-2121.

LURAY, 3,584, D-8. **Luray Caverns**, 1 mile west on U.S. 211 bypass, contain strange and colorful formations, including the *Great Stalacpipe Organ*, which produces music from the rocks, and the *Wishing Well*, which, through donations, provides thousands of dollars to national health research foundations. Guided tours: Daily, mid-Mar.-mid-June, 9 A.M. to 6 P.M.; mid-June-Labor Day, 9 A.M. to 7 P.M.; early Sept.-mid-Nov., 9 A.M. to 6 P.M.; mid-Nov.-mid-Mar., 9 A.M. to 4 P.M. Adults $6.75; children 7-13, $3; under 7, free. *Car and Carriage Caravan*, at Luray Caverns, presents the history of transportation. *Luray Singing Tower*, a carillon of 47 bells at the entrance to Luray Caverns, is a 117-foot tower; the largest bell weighs 7,640 pounds, the smallest, 12½ pounds. Concerts: Mar.-May, mid-Sept.-Oct., Tues., Thurs., Sat.-Sun., 2 P.M.; early June-mid-Sept., 8 P.M. Free. Luray Caverns: 703/743-6551.

MANASSAS NATIONAL BATTLE-FIELD PARK, C-9. The First and Second Battles of Manassas (the Battles of Bull Run) were fought here July 21, 1861, and August 28-30, 1862. It was in the First Battle of Manassas, in 1861, that Gen. Thomas J. Jackson earned his famous nickname, "Stonewall," because he so strongly resisted the Union advances. Visitors Center, St. 234 between Int. 66 and U.S. 29: Daily, June-Sept., 9 A.M. to 9 P.M.; other months, 9 A.M. to sunset. Park: Year-round, daily, 9 A.M. to sunset. Free. 703/754-7107.

MONTROSS, 456, E-10. **Stratford Hall**, north off St. 3 on Co. 214, is the birthplace of Gen. Robert E. Lee. In 1716, Thomas Lee, the first native-born Virginian to act as colonial governor, purchased Clifts Plantation, where he built Stratford Hall, in 1725-30. Six of Thomas Lee's eleven children were born on this estate. The most famous of them were Richard Henry and Francis Lightfoot, the only brothers to sign the Declaration of Independence. Thomas Lee's great-nephew, Henry "Light-Horse Harry" Lee, married the heiress to Stratford; one son was born before her death. Light-Horse Harry Lee continued on at Stratford and later married Ann Hill Carter of Shirley Plantation. Today Stratford Hall, a working

Stonewall Jackson, famed general of the Confederacy, was born in 1824 at Clarksville, Virginia (now West Virginia). Though best known for the effectiveness of his surprise attacks and rapid troop movements, Jackson earned his famous nickname in a defensive action. It occurred in July of 1861 at the First Battle of Bull Run (also known as First Manassas) where Jackson and his men held off Union forces "like a stone wall" until reinforcements arrived. As a result, the Confederates carried the day. On May 2, 1863, having just completed a brilliant flanking maneuver at the Battle of Chancellorsville, Jackson was accidentally shot by his own men. His death on May 10 deprived Robert E. Lee of his ablest general.

plantation, is run much as it was in colonial days. Year-round, daily, 9 A.M. to 4:30 P.M. Adults $2.50; persons 6-16, 75¢; under 6, free. 804/493-8038.

MOUNT VERNON, D-9. George Washington's home and burial site are 8 miles south of Alexandria at the southern terminus of the Mount Vernon Memorial Hwy. Washington inherited the Potomac River estate in 1752, and he and Martha Custis began their married life here in 1759. Washington stayed at Mount Vernon, living the peaceful life of a Southern planter until he was appointed commander-in-chief of the Continental Army in 1775. He returned in 1783 and except for his years as president lived here until his death in 1799. The walls of the rooms were recently restored to their original color. The grounds, stables, gardens, kitchen, greenhouse, and slave quarters are kept as they were in Washington's lifetime. Daily, Mar.-Oct., 9 A.M. to 5 P.M.; Nov.-Feb., 9 A.M. to 4 P.M. Adults $3; persons over 60 with I.D., $2.50; 6-11, $1.50; under 6, free. 703/780-2000.

NEW MARKET, 1,118, D-7. **New Market Battlefield Park**, 1 mile north of Int. 81, Exit 67, on St. 305, was the site of the battle where ten Virginia Military Institute cadets were killed and 47 wounded in 1864. This is said to have been the only battle in U.S. history in which schoolboy cadets fought as a unit under fire. The *Hall of Valor*, which commemorates the courage of the cadets, features models and dioramas presenting a history of the Civil War. Year-round, daily, 9 A.M. to 5 P.M. Adults $2; persons 7-13, 75¢; under 7, free. 703/740-3101. **Shenandoah Caverns,** 4 miles north and 1½ miles west of U.S. 11 or Exit 68 from Int. 81, contain formations called *Diamond Cascade, Hunter's Lodge,* the *Grove of the Druids,* and *Cathedral Hall.* Daily, mid-June-Sept., 9 A.M. to 6:15 P.M.; mid-Apr.-mid-June and Sept.-mid-Oct., 9 A.M. to 5:15 P.M.; other months, 9 A.M. to 4:15 P.M. Adults $4.50; persons 7-14, $2.50; under 7, free. 703/477-3115.

NEWPORT NEWS, 144,903, G-10. The Port of Hampton Roads, the nation's largest natural seaport, is made up of the cities of Newport News, Hampton, Portsmouth, and Norfolk. Shipbuilding, shipping, seafood processing, and naval yards are major economic activities. **Mariners Museum and Library,** south on U.S. 60 and Exit 9A from Int. 64 at J. Clyde Morris Blvd., is an internationally known museum with large collections of maritime artwork, figureheads, uniforms, weapons, photographs, ship models, and miniatures. The research library has thousands of books, photographs, ships' papers, maps, and charts. Museum and library: Year-round, Mon.-Sat., 9 A.M. to 5 P.M.; museum, also Sun., noon to 5 P.M. Museum: Adults $1.50; persons 6-16, 75¢; under 6, free. Library: Free. 804/595-0368. **Peninsula Nature and Science Center/Planetarium,** in Deer Park off J. Clyde Morris Blvd. between St. 143 and U.S. 60, contains exhibits on the natural history of the area and offers educational field trips. Year-round, Mon.-Sat., 9 A.M. to 5 P.M.; Thurs., 7 to 9 P.M.; Sun., 1 to 5 P.M. Admission 75¢; children under 6, free. Planetarium shows: Year-round, Thurs., 7:30 P.M.; Sat., 11 A.M., 2:15 and 3:45 P.M.; Sun., 1:30, 2:30, and 3:30 P.M. Admission $1; persons under 6, free. Museum and planetarium: Admission $1.75; children under 6, free. 804/595-1900.

NORFOLK, 266,979, G-11. Linked indelibly with naval facilities, Norfolk has one of the finest harbors in the world. The **Norfolk Naval Station,** the world's largest, is home port for more than 200 ships of the Atlantic and Mediterranean fleets. **HISTORIC HOMES: Myers House,** Freemason and Banks Sts., was built in 1792 by Moses Myers, one of the first American millionaires. Many of the original furnishings have been retained. Apr.-Nov., Tues.-Sat., 10 A.M. to 5 P.M.; Sun., noon to 5 P.M.; other months, Sun., noon to 5 P.M. Adults $2, students through high school $1. 804/622-1211, Ext. 55. **Willoughby-Baylor House,** Freemason and Cumberland Sts., was built by Captain Willoughby in 1794 near the home

of his friend Moses Myers. Apr.-Nov., Tues.-Sat., 10 A.M. to 5 P.M.; Sun., noon to 5 P.M.; other months, Sun., noon to 5 P.M. Adults $2; students through high school $1; under 6, free. 804/622-1211, Ext. 57. **MUSEUMS: Chrysler Museum,** Olney Rd. and Virginia Beach Blvd., contains art treasures from nearly every period of art history. Year-round, Tues.-Sat., 10 A.M. to 4 P.M.; Sun., 1 to 5 P.M. Free. 804/622-1211. **Hermitage Foundation Museum,** 7637 North Shore Rd., occupies a riverside estate built in 1906. Year-round, Mon.-Sat., 10 A.M. to 5 P.M.; Sun., 1 to 5 P.M. Adults $2; persons 6-18, 50¢; under 6 and military, free. 804/423-2052. **Douglas MacArthur Memorial,** City Hall Ave., is the final resting place of General MacArthur. It also contains a collection of exhibits and memorabilia tracing his life and military career. Year-round, Mon.-Sat., 10 A.M. to 5 P.M.; Sun., 11 A.M. to 5 P.M. Free. 804/441-2382. **Norfolk Gardens-By-The-Sea,** near the municipal airport, encompasses some 175 acres of flowers and plants. Trackless trains and canal boats carry passengers along the paths and waterways of the gardens. On *Treasure Island,* passengers can hunt for the hidden treasure and board the pirate ship *Hispanola,* anchored in a cove. Gardens: Year-round, daily, 8:30 A.M. to sunset. Admission $1. Boat and train tours: Mid-Mar.-Oct., daily, 9 A.M. to 5 P.M., leaving on the half hour. Boat and train fare $1.50. 804/853-6972.

PETERSBURG, 41,055, F-9. Founded in 1645 as a frontier trading post and incorporated as a city in 1850, Petersburg soon became an industrial and commercial center with tobacco warehouses, cotton and flour mills, and iron foundries. In 1864, Petersburg's strategic location and industrial importance made it a target for Union forces, and it became the site of the last major battle of the Civil War. Today, tobacco remains "King of Virginia Crops." The first tobacco warehouse inspection in Petersburg was authorized in 1730. **Brown & Williamson's Tobacco Factory,** 325 Brown St., shows visitors how cigarettes are made. Guided tours: Year-round, Mon.-Fri., 8:30 A.M. to 4 P.M. Free. 804/732-5221. **Farmers Bank,** 19 Bollingbrook St., which was built in 1817 and now restored, has Confederate bank notes printed on the original 100-year-old press. Year-round, Mon.-Sat., 9 A.M. to 5 P.M.; Sun., 1 to 5 P.M. Free. 804/861-1590. **Old Blandford Church,** Crater Rd., has 15 stained-glass windows designed and installed by Louis Comfort Tiffany. Built about 1735, the church served as a field hospital during the Civil War and was restored as a Confederate shrine in 1901, honoring the 30,000 soldiers buried here. Year-round, Mon.-Sat., 9 A.M. to 5 P.M.; Sun., noon to 5 P.M. Free. 804/732-2230. **Appomattox Iron Works,** 22-28 Old St., now houses a museum and crafts shops. Year-round, daily, 9:30 A.M. to 4 or 5 P.M. Free. 804/732-1553. **U.S. Army Quarter-**

master Museum, at Fort Lee, contains military relics dating back to the Revolutionary War, uniforms, and weapons. Year-round, Mon.-Fri., 9 A.M. to 5 P.M.; Sat.-Sun., 11 A.M. to 5 P.M. Free. 804/734-1854. **Siege Museum,** 15 W. Bank St., documents the human side of Petersburg during Gen. Ulysses S. Grant's ten-month siege, the longest in American history. Year-round, Mon.-Sat., 9 A.M. to 5 P.M.; Sun., 1 to 5 P.M. Free. 804/861-2904.

PETERSBURG NATIONAL BATTLEFIELD, F-9. The park was established to interpret Grant's siege of the city which began in June, 1864, and to trace the military encounters which led to the eventual fall of Richmond and Lee's surrender in 1865. The Visitors Center, park entrance off St. 35, has an audiovisual presentation of the Siege of Petersburg. Daily, June-Labor Day, 8 A.M. to 7 P.M.; other months, 8 A.M. to 5 P.M. Free. 804/732-3531.

RICHMOND, 219,214, F-9. The capital of Virginia is steeped in history, and familiar names are closely associated with the city. The land where Richmond now stands was explored by Capt. John Smith in 1607. In 1737, Col. William Byrd laid out the town, which was to become the capital in 1779. It was here, in 1775, at the Virginia Convention held in St. John's Church, that Patrick Henry made his famous "Give me liberty or give me death" speech. **HISTORIC BUILDINGS:** The **Capitol,** Capitol Square, was designed by Thomas Jefferson in 1785 and completed about 1788. Here Aaron Burr was tried and acquitted for treason in 1807, Robert E. Lee accepted the command of the Virginia armies, and the Confederate Congress met from July 20, 1861, until its final adjournment. Apr.-Nov., daily, 9 A.M. to 5 P.M.; Dec.-Mar., Mon.-Sat., 9 A.M. to 5 P.M.; Sun., 1 to 5 P.M. Free. 804/786-4344. **HISTORIC CHURCHES: St. John's Church,** 2400 E. Broad St., built in 1741 is the church in which Patrick Henry gave his "liberty or death" speech. Mid-Mar.-Nov., Mon.-Sat., 10 A.M. to 4 P.M. Free. 804/649-7938. **St. Paul's Church,** 815 E. Grace St., served many eminent men, including Confederate Pres. Jefferson Davis and Gen. Robert E. Lee. President Davis was in St. Paul's when he received the message in 1865 that Richmond had to be evacuated. Year-round, Mon.-Sat., 10 A.M. to 4 P.M.; Sun., 8 A.M. to 1 P.M. Free. 804/643-3589. **MUSEUMS AND GALLERIES: Valentine Museum,** 1015 E. Clay St., was built in 1812 and features an unusual free-standing stairway. Exhibits relate the history of Richmond. Year-round, Tues.-Sat., 10 A.M. to 5 P.M.; Sun., 1:30 to 5 P.M. Adults $2, students $1, family $5. 804/649-0711. **Virginia Museum of Fine Arts,** Grove and Boulevard Aves., houses collections of Oriental, European, American, and Art Nouveau in 15 galleries and has a sculpture garden. In the museum are also the *Virginia Museum*

Theatre and *Council Sale Shop*. Theater performances: Late Sept.-late Apr., late Oct.-late Mar., Tues.-Sun., 8:15 P.M. Admission $6 to $12. Wed., Sat.-Sun., 2 P.M. Admission $4 to $8. Museum and gift shop: Year-round, Tues.-Sat., 11 A.M. to 5 P.M.; Sun., 1 to 5 P.M. Museum: Minimum donation 50¢. 804/257-0844. **Virginia Historical Society**, 428 N. Boulevard Ave., has a collection of Civil War murals by Charles Hoffbauer, and Confederate flags. Year-round, Mon.-Fri., 9 A.M. to 5 P.M.; Sat.-Sun., 2 to 5 P.M. Adults $1, children free. 804/358-4901. **The Museum of the Confederacy**, 1201 E. Clay St., stands on the grounds of the Confederate White House. Exhibits relate to the history of the Confederacy. Year-round, Mon.-Sat., 10 A.M. to 5 P.M.; Sun., 2 to 5 P.M. Adults $1; children 7-12, 50¢; under 7, free. 804/649-1861. **Edgar Allan Poe Museum**, 1914 E. Main St., is believed to be the oldest surviving house (1685-88) in Richmond. Year-round, Tues.-Sat., 10 A.M. to 4 P.M.; Sun.-Mon., 1:30 to 4 P.M. Adults $2; students $1; children under 6, free. 804/648-5523.

HISTORIC HOMES: Agecroft Hall, 4305 Sulgrave Rd., is a 15th-century home, built in England, disassembed in the late 1920s and shipped to its present location on the James River. Formal gardens surround the house. Year-round, Tues.-Fri., 10 A.M. to 4 P.M.; Sat.-Sun., 2 to 5 P.M. Adults $1; persons 65 and over, 75¢; students 50¢; under 6, free. 804/353-4241. **John Marshall House**, 818 E. Marshall St., was built and occupied by Chief Justice John Marshall in 1789. Year-round, Wed.-Sat., 11 A.M. to 4 P.M.; Sun., 1 to 4 P.M. Adults $2; students $1; children under 6, free. 804/648-7998. **Virginia House**, 4301 Sulgrave Rd., was constructed in 1925-28 of materials brought from The Priory of the Holy Sepulchre, built in 1125 by the first earl of Warwick, England. Year-round, Tues.-Fri., 10 A.M. to 4 P.M.; Sat.-Sun., 2 to 5 P.M. Adults $1.50, children 75¢. 804/353-4251. **Wilton**, S. Wilton Rd., three blocks off Carey St., is a Georgian mansion built in 1753 by William Randolph, III. Today it is headquarters for the National Society of Colonial Dames in Virginia. Year-round, Tues.-Sat., 10 A.M. to 4 P.M.; Sun., 2:30 to 4:30 P.M. Adults $2; persons 12-17, $1; under 12, free. 804/282-5936.

HISTORIC AREAS: Fan District, west of downtown, is a residential area of restored 1890-1920 town houses. Also in the area are shops and restaurants. Fan District borders on mansion-lined Monument Ave., which has monuments of Civil War heroes along its central parkway. **Historic Schockoe Slip**, Cary and 13th Sts., is a two-block area of 18th- and 19th-century restored commercial and warehouse buildings which now house boutiques, restaurants, and shops.

SHENANDOAH NATIONAL PARK,

D-8. Along the crest of the Blue Ridge Mountains, **Shenandoah National Park** extends from Front Royal to Waynesboro.

The 105-mile *Skyline Drive* runs through the center of the park, and more than 70 overlooks provide spectacular panoramas of the Piedmont and the Shenandoah River Valley. Visitors Centers along the drive offer audiovisual and interpretive presentations, trail maps, brochures, and camping guides. Year-round (inclement weather may force closing for short periods). Admission $2 per private noncommercial vehicle, 50¢ per person by other means of transportation. 703/999-2266.

VIRGINIA BEACH, 262,199, G-11. A popular resort area, it has a 29-mile coastline, boardwalks, and beaches. Swimming, surfing, water-skiing, boating, and fishing are available. **Chesapeake Bay Bridge-Tunnel** is a 17.6-mile link between Virginia Beach, Norfolk, and Virginia's eastern shore. The bridge, which opened in 1964, took three and one-half years to build and cost $200 million. It goes over and under the bay, takes 23 minutes to cross, and has a rest area with fishing pier. Car toll $8. 804/464-3511.

WILLIAMSBURG, 9,870, F-10. The colonial captial of Virginia, 50 miles from Richmond on Int. 64, was named in honor of William III. The old town, **Colonial Williamsburg**, has been extensively restored to its 18th-century appearance by the Colonial Williamsburg Foundation. Nearly 100 original buildings, plus many others carefully reconstructed on their original sites after in-depth research, stretch a mile from the Capitol to the College of William and Mary, reflecting the Williamsburg of the 1700s. Many of the buildings are open to the public, and costumed craftsmen demonstrate 200-year-old methods used by the colonial silversmith, cooper, printer, baker, milliner, and many other tradesmen of the day. Visitors Center, Colonial Parkway, provides visitor information, including an orientation film, literature, maps for a self-guided tour, and tickets. Because many streets in the historic area are closed to vehicles, cars may be parked at the Visitors Center; a shuttle bus will transport visitors to Colonial Williamsburg. *The Capitol*, Duke of Gloucester St., is a reconstruction of the original building which was completed in 1705. The Virginia Legislature met here from 1704 to 1780, and here Patrick Henry denounced the British Stamp Act of 1765. *Bruton Parish Church*, Duke of Gloucester St. and Palace Green, is one of the oldest Episcopal churches in America. Completed in 1715, the church still serves the community, and its 1761 bell still calls people to worship. *Governor's Palace*, Palace Green, served as home to royal governors from 1720 to 1775. The mansion has been richly restored with mantels of imported French and Belgian marble, Chinese wallpaper, and crystal chandeliers from Canton. The kitchens, laundries, smoke-

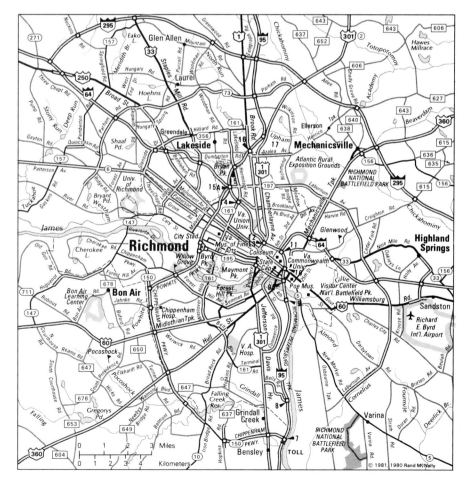

houses, and ten acres of gardens are just as they appeared nearly 300 years ago. *Magazine and Guardhouse*, Market Square, was built by the Crown-appointed Governor in 1715 for storing arms, gunpowder, and ammunition. *Public Gaol*, Nicholson St., features pillories and stocks for lawbreakers. *Raleigh Tavern*, Duke of Gloucester St., was built about 1742 and was only one of about 35 taverns and "ordinaries" that existed in Colonial Williamsburg. *Wythe House*, Palace Green, was the home of George Wythe, Thomas Jefferson's teacher. Wythe, one of the signers of the Declaration of Independence, was the first professor of law in an American college. *Abby Aldrich Rockefeller Folk Art Center*, 307 S. England St., has American folk painting, sculpture, and decorative wares. Williamsburg Information: 804/229-1000. **Busch Gardens**, 5 miles east on U.S. 60, is a 300-acre theme park. A miniature Europe, it is divided into English, German, Scottish, and French villages, with entertainment, food, and special events reflecting the old-world atmosphere. Memorial Day-Labor Day, daily, 10 A.M. to 7 P.M.; Apr.-May, Sept.-Oct., Sat.-Sun., 10 A.M. to 7 P.M. Admission $11.95; children under 3, free (includes all attractions and shows). 804/253-3350.

WYTHEVILLE, 7,135, G-4. **Big Walker Lookout Mountain**, 9 miles south of Bland and 12 miles north of Wytheville on U.S. 52, has a ski lift which takes passengers to the mountaintop picnic area for a panoramic view. Five states can be seen from the observation tower. Lift schedule: Mar.-late May, Sun., 9:30 A.M. to 5 P.M.; Memorial Day-Labor Day, daily, 8 A.M. to 8 P.M.; Sept.-Nov., Sat.-Sun., 9 A.M. to 5 P.M. Adults $2.75, children $1.75. 703/228-4401. **Shot Tower Historical Park**, 6 miles east on Int. 81, then 7 miles south on U.S. 52, is one of three shot towers still standing in the United States.

YORKTOWN, 311, F-10. This seaport town was established in 1691; however, it had long been known to Englishmen and was frequently visited by Capt. John Smith and his fellow settlers. The excellent harbor stimulated the growth of Yorktown, and at the peak of its prosperity in 1750, its population was 2,500. Yorktown also played an important role in both the American Revolution and the Civil War. The events of September and October, in 1781, in which General Cornwallis surrendered to General Washington, ended the siege, and for all purposes, the entire American Revolution. **Yorktown Battlefield**, a part of the Colonial National Historical Park, marks the site and encampments of these encounters. Historical markers line the battlefield tour, which begins at the Visitors Center. It passes restored *Moore House*, where surrender terms were drawn up by British, French, and American forces on October 18, 1781; the encampment area of French and American troops; and General Washington's headquarters site. The tour also goes through Yorktown past the headquarters of General Cornwallis and the cave where he sought protection as the siege ended. Battlefield: Year-round, daily, 8 A.M. to sunset. Free. Visitors Center: Daily, June-Labor Day, 8:30 A.M. to 6 P.M.; other months, 8:30 A.M. to 5:30 P.M. Free. 804/898-3400. **Yorktown Victory Center**, one-half mile west of Yorktown on St. 238, is the principal Bicentennial Center in the state. Exhibits and films depict the history of the Revolution from Bunker Hill to Yorktown. Year-round, daily, 9 A.M. to 5 P.M. Adults $2; persons 62 and over, $1; children 7-12, 75¢; under 7, free. 804/887-1776.

See also **Colonial National Historical Park.**

Information Sources

Department of Conservation & Economic Development
Virginia State Travel Service
6 N. 6th St.
Richmond, VA 23219
804/786-2051

National Capital
Regional Office
National Park Service
1100 Ohio Dr. SW
Washington, D.C. 20242
202/426-6700

Alexandria Tourist Council
221 King St.
Alexandria, VA 22314
703/549-0205

Colonial Williamsburg
Foundation
Box C
Williamsburg, VA 23187
804/229-1000

Fredericksburg
Visitors Center
706 Caroline St.
Fredericksburg, VA 22401
703/373-1776

Historic Garden Week
12 E. Franklin St.
Richmond, VA 23219
804/644-7776
or 804/643-7141

Lexington Visitors Center
107 E. Washington St.
Lexington, VA 24450
703/463-3777

Norfolk Convention & Visitors Bureau
Monticello Arcade
Norfolk, VA 23510
804/441-5266

Richmond Convention & Visitors Bureau
201 E. Franklin St.
Richmond, VA 23219
804/648-1234

Shenandoah Valley
Travel Association
P.O. Box 488
New Market, VA 22844
703/740-3132

Thomas Jefferson
Visitors Center
P.O. Box 161
Charlottesville, VA 22902
804/977-1783

Virginia Beach
Visitors Bureau
1000 19th St.
Virginia Beach, VA 23451
804/425-7511

Virginia Campgrounds

FEES REFLECT MINIMUM RATE FOR 2 ADULTS AND ARE SUBJECT TO INCREASE OR SEASONAL CHANGES

- • — at the campground
- ⊙ — within one mile of campground
- $ — extra charge
- ** — limited facilities during winter months
- A — adults only
- B — 10,000 acres or more
- C — contribution

- E — tents rented
- F — entrance fee or permit required
- N — no specific number, limited by size of area only
- P — primitive
- R — reservation required
- S — self-contained units only

- U — unlimited
- V — trailers rented
- Z — reservations accepted
- LD — Labor Day
- MD — Memorial Day
- UC — under construction
- d — boat dock

- g — public golf course within 5 miles
- h — horseback riding
- j — whitewater running craft only
- k — snow skiing within 25 miles
- l — boat launch
- m — area north of map
- n — no drinking water

- p — motor bikes prohibited
- r — boat rental
- s — stream, lake or creek water only
- t — tennis
- u — snowmobile trails
- w — open certain off-season weekends
- y — drinking water must be boiled

Map Reference	Park Name	Access	Acres	Tent Spaces	Trailer Spaces	Approximate Fee	Season	Other Swimming Swimming Pool	Fishing Boating	Playground Other	Telephone Number	Mail Address
	STATE PARKS											
G5	Claytor Lake	Fr Dublin or Radford, I-81 to ext 33, 2 mi S on Hwy 660	472	136	136	3.64	4/3-11/30	$ •	dlr	hp	703/674-5492	Dublin 24080
E6	Douthat	Fr E of Clifton Forge, 5-1/2 mi N on Hwy 629	4493	112	112	3.64	4/3-11/30	$ $	dlr	p	703/862-0612	Box 212, Milboro 24460
G6	Fairy Stone	Fr Bassett Forks, 13 mi W on Hwy 57 & 57A, 1 mi N on Hwy 346	4570	48	48	3.64	4/3-11/30	$ •	dlr	hp	703/930-2424	Rt 2 Box 134, Stuart 24171
G4	Hungry Mother	Fr I-81, ext 16, 6 mi N on Hwy 16 thru Marion	2180	89	99	3.64	4/3-11/30	$ •	dlr	hp	703/783-3422	Rt 5 Box 109, Marion 24354
F8	Goodwin Lk-Prince Edward	Fr Burkeville, 4 mi SW on US 360 bypass, 1-1/2 mi NW on Hwy 621	130	55	55	3.64	4/3-11/30	$ •	dlr	p		Rt 2 Box 70, Burkville 23922
G7	Staunton River	Fr S Boston, 8 mi NE on Hwy 304, 10 mi SE on Hwy 344	1287	45	45	3.64	4/3-11/30	$ •	dlr •	p	804/572-4623	Rt 2 Bx 295, Scottsburg 24589
E10	Westmoreland	Fr Montross, 5 mi NW on Hwy 3	1302	119	119	3.64	4/3-11/30	$ •	dlr •	p	804/493-6167	Rt 1 Box 53H, Montross 22520
F9	Pocahontas	Fr Chesterfield Courthouse, 4 mi SW on Hwy 655	2005	72	72	3.64	4/3-11/30	$ •	lr	hp	804/748-5929	10300 Bch Rd,Chestrfld 23832
G2	Natural Tunnel	Fr Duffield, 4 mi E on US 23, 1 mi N on Hwy 880	567	30	30	3.64	4/3-11/30			p	703/940-2674	Rt 2 Bx 250, Clinchport 24227
F8	Bear Creek Lake	Fr Cumberland, 1/4 mi E on US 60, 3-1/2 mi NW on Hwy 622, 1 mi S on Hwy 629	150	54	54	3.64	4/3-11/30	$ •		p	804/492-4410	Cumberland 23040
G11	Seashore	At Cape Henry, on US 60	2770	220	220	3.64	4/3-11/30	• •		l p	804/481-2131	2500 Shore Dr, Virginia Beach
F7	Holliday Lake	Fr Appomattox, NE on Hwy 24, 7 mi E on Hwy 626	250	60	60	3.64	4/3-11/30	$ •	dlr	p	804/248-6308	Rt 2 Bx 230, Appomattox 24522
G8	Occoneechee	Fr Clarksville, 1 1/2 mi E on US 58	2690	142	142	3.64	4/3-11/30		dlr	p	804/374-2210	Box 818, Clarksville 23927
G4	Grayson Highlands	Fr I-81 in Marion, 5 mi on Hwy 16 to Volney, W on US 58	4935	73	73	3.64	4/1-11/30			p	703/579-7092	Rt 2 Bx 141, Mouth of Wilson

Map Reference	Park Name	Access	Acres	Tent Spaces	Trailer Spaces	Approximate Fee	Season	Other Swimming / Swimming Pool	Fishing	Boating	Playground	Other	Telephone Number	Mail Address
G11	False Cape	Fr VA Bch, E on VA Bch Expy, SE on Pacific Ave, 5.5 mi S on Gen Booth Rd, 1.5 mi E on Princess Anne Rd, 5 mi N on Sandbridge Rd, 4 mi E on Sandpiper	4321	15		3.64	4/1-12/1	• •			l	p	804/426-9925	Bx 6273, Virginia Bch 23456
	STATE WILDLIFE MANAGEMENT													
G3	Clinch Mtn	Fr Saltville, 5 mi W on Hwy 613, 6 mi NE on Hwy 747		20	20	3.64	4/1-9/7	$			p		703/783-3422	Marion 24354
	NATIONAL PARKS Blue Ridge Parkway	(See North Carolina for additional campgrounds)											704/258-2850	700 Nrthwstrn Bnk,Ashville,NC
G5	Rocky Knob	Fr Roanoke, 51 mi SW on Pkwy, Mi 167	4000	81	28	3.00	All year	•					703/982-6490	Floyd
F6	Peaks of Otter	Fr Roanoke, 29 mi NE on Pkwy, Mi 86	4000	86	62	3.00	All year	•						Bedford
F7	Otter Creek	Fr Roanoke, 54 mi NE on Pkwy, Mi 60	500	42	25	3.00	All year	•						Big Island
F6	Roanoke Mtn	Fr Jct Pkwy & US 220, 2 mi N, at Roanoke City Limits	1142	74	31	3.00	All year	•						Roanoke
	Shenandoah NP		B										703/999-2266	Luray 22835
D8	Big Meadows	Fr Elkton, 22 mi NE on Skyline Dr, at Mile 51.2 (W)		255	193	F3.00	3/1-12/31					h		Luray 22835
D8	Lewis Mountain	Fr Elkton, 16 mi NE on Skyline Dr, at Mile 57.6		32	32	F3.00	5/22-10/31							Luray 22835
E7	Loft Mountain	Fr Elkton, 22 mi SW on Skyline Dr, at Mile 79.5		231	167	F3.00	5/1-10/31							Luray 22835
D8	Matthews Arm	Fr Luray, 18 mi NE on Skyline Dr, at Mile 22.2		186	167	F3.00	5/1-10/31		o					Luray 22835
	Cumberland Gap NHP	(For additional CGs, see 'Backpack or Boat Access Areas')	B											Box 840B, Middlesboro KY, 40965
G1	Wilderness Rd	Fr Middlesboro, 4 mi S on US 25E, 2 mi E on US 58 & pk rd		163	150	2.00	4/1-11/30				p		606/248-2817	Box 840B,Middlesboro KY, 40965
	Prince Wm Forest Pk	(for additional CGs, see 'Backpack and Boat Access Areas')	B										703/221-7181	Triangle 22172
G1	White Rocks Backcntry CA	Fr Middlesboro, 4 mi S on US 25E, 17 mi E on US 58		4		None	All year				p		606/248-2817	Bx 840, Middlesboro, KY 40965
G1	Gibson Gap Backcountry CA	Fr Middlesboro, 4 mi E on US 25E, 2 mi N on US 58 & Park Rd		3		None	All year				p		606/248-2817	Bx 840, Middlesboro, KY 40965
	Assateague Isl Natl Seas													
	NATIONAL FORESTS George Washington NF													
E6	Blowing Springs	Fr Warm Springs, 9 mi W on Hwy 39	3	12	3	None	4/1-12/1	• •						Warm Springs
E6	Hidden Valley	Fr Warm Springs, 2 mi W on Hwy 39, 1 mi N on Hwy 621, 1.8 N on FRR 24110	16	30	30	None	All year	• •						Warm Springs
D8	High Cliff Canoe Camp	Fr Rileyville, 8 mi S on Hwy 340, 3.3 mi NW on Hwy 675, 7.5 mi NE on Hwy 684, 2 mi E on Shenandoah	2	10		None	All year	•	dlr		h			Rileyville
D8	Elizabeth Furnace	Fr Strasburg, 5.1 mi E on Hwy 55, 4.8 mi SW on Hwy 678	22	29	9	3.00	All year	•			h			Strasburg
D8	Camp Roosevelt	Fr Luray, 8.5 mi NW on Hwy 675	5	10	10	2.00	4/15-10/15	2			hn			Luray
D8	Little Fort	Fr Sevenfountains, 1.2 mi SW on Hwy 678, 2.5 mi NW on Hwy 758	2	9		2.00	All year	•			h			Sevenfountains
C8	Hazard Mill	Fr Front Royal, 8.7 mi SW on US 340, .9 mi NW on Hwy 613, 3.2 mi W on FR 236	6	15	15	2.00	All year	1	dl		h			Front Royal
C8	Hazard Mill Canoe Camp	Fr Bentonville, 14 mi S on Hwy 340, 3.3 mi NW on Hwy 675, 7.5 mi NE on Hwy 684, 13 mi NE on Shenandoah	2	10		None	All year	•	dl					Bentonville
D7	North River	Fr Staunton, 20 mi W on US 250, 9 mi N on Hwy 715, 1 mi NE on FR 95, 1 mi SW on FR 95B	3	10	10	None	4/1-12/1	3	dl					Staunton
D7	Todd Lake	Fr Mt Solon, 1 mi NW on Hwy 731, 2.5 mi W on Hwy 730, 1 mi NW on Hwy 718, 5 mi W on FR 95	15	20	20	2.00	5/15-12/1	• •	dl					Mt Solon
D7	Hone Quarry	Fr Dayton, 11 mi NW on Hwy 257	4	10	10	None	4/1-12/1	• •	dl					Dayton
E7	Sherando Lake	Fr Waynesboro, 4 mi S on Hwy 624, 10 mi SW on Hwy 664, 2 mi W on FR 91	30	65	31	4.00	4/1-10/1	• •	dlr					Waynesboro
	Jefferson NF													
G3	Beartree	Fr Damascus, 5 mi SW on US 58	50	22	22	2.00	5/1-9/15	•						Damascus
F6	The Pines	Fr New Castle, 5 mi NE on Hwy 615, 4.9 mi W on Hwy 611, 5.5 mi NE on Hwy 617	4	17	3	None	All year	•						New Castle
G2	Bark Camp	Fr Norton, 6.3 mi E on US 58A, 4.1 mi S on Hwy 706, .3 mi E on Hwy 699, 1.7 mi SE on Hwy 822	15	11	11	2.00	5/1-10/15	•	dl					Norton
G2	High Knob	Fr Norton, 3.7 mi S on Hwy 619, 1.6 mi E on FR 238, 1.7 mi S on FR 233	15	13	3	2.00	5/1-10/15	• •						Norton
F6	North Creek	Fr Buchanan, 2.1 mi NE on I-81, 2.9 mi SE on Hwy 614, 2.4 mi E on FR 59	5	16	16	2.00	All year	5	•					Buchanan
F6	Cave Mountain Lake	Fr Natural Bridge Station, .3 mi E on Hwy 130, 3.1 mi SW on Hwy 759, 1.6 mi W on Hwy 781, 1 mi SW on FR 780	15	42	42	4.00	5/1-10/15	• 4	d		h			Natural Bridge Station
G4	Grindstone	Fr Trout Dale, 6.5 mi W on Hwy 603	55	90	90	2.00	5/1-12/1	• 1			h			Trout Dale
G4	Raccoon Branch	Fr Sugar Grove, 2.1 mi SW on Hwy 16	20	20	20	2.00	All year	•						Sugar Grove
G4	Hurricane	Fr Trout Dale, 2.5 mi NW on Hwy 16, 1.5 mi NW on Hwy 650, .4 mi N on FR 84	40	25	25	2.00	4/1-9/15	•						Trout Dale
G4	Comers Rock	Fr Speedwell, 5.4 mi SW on US 21, 4 mi W on FR 57	3	9		None	All year	•			n			Speedwell
G4	Fox Creek Trail Head	Fr Troutdale, 10 mi N on Hwy 16, 3.5 mi W on Hwy 603	5	15		None	All year				h			Troutdale
G2	Cave Springs	Fr Dryden, 2.4 mi SW on US 58, .8 mi N on Hwy 767, 3.7 mi NE on Hwy 621, .4 mi N on FR 1072	25	31	31	2.00	5/1-10/15	•						Dryden
F5	White Rocks	Fr Pearisburg, 3.8 mi E on US 460, 17 mi NE on Hwy 635, .8 mi S on Hwy 613, 1 mi E on FR 645	26	49	49	2.00	4/1-12/1	1						Pearisburg
F4	Stony Fork	Fr Wytheville, 1.5 mi E on US 11, 6.9 mi N on I-77, 4 mi W on Hwy 717	13	53	53	3.00	4/1-12/1	•						Wytheville
F6	Steel Bridge	Fr Paint Bank, .1 mi N on Hwy 311, 3.5 mi NE on Hwy 18	2	10		None	All year	• •						Paint Bank
	CORPS OF ENGINEERS Philpott Lake		9326										703/629-2703	Rt 6 Box 140, Bassett 24055
G6	Salthouse Branch	Fr Henry, 1-1/2 mi W on Co 605, 1-1/2 mi SW on Co 798 & 773	79	94	94	3.00	All year	• •	l					Bassett
G6	Goose Point	Fr Bassett, W on Hwy 57, N on Co 822	61	25	25	3.00	All year	• •	l					Bassett
G6	Bowens Creek	Fr Bassett, 4 mi W on Hwy 57, 1 mi N on Co 601	118	18	18	2.00	5/20-9/10	• •	l					Bassett
G6	Horseshoe Point	Fr Henry, 2-1/2 mi W on Co 605, SW on Co 903 & 934	108	46	46	3.00	4/1-10/30**	• •	l					Bassett
G6	Ryans Branch	Fr Ferrum, 7 mi SW on Co 623	120	13	13	None	5/10-9/30	• •	l					Bassett
G6	Jameson Mill	Fr Ferrum, 8 mi SW on Rt 623/605	50	12	12	2.00	All year	• •	l					Bassett
	North Fork of Pound Lake	(For additional CGs, see 'Backpack or Boat Access Areas')											703/796-5775	Rt 1, Box 369, Pound 24279
F2	Bee Bottom CG	Fr Pound, 9 mi W on Hwy 671	7	10	S12	None	All year	o o			np			Pound
F2	Canepatch	Fr Pound, 8-1/2 mi W on Hwy 671	12		35	3.00	5/1-10/15	o •	d					Pound
F2	Laurel Fork CG	Fr Pound, 9-1/2 mi W on Hwy 671	5	P8		None	All year	o •			p			Rt 1, Box 369, Pound 24279
	John H Kerr Res	See North Carolina for additional CG's	B										804/738-6662	Rt 1 Box 76,Boydton 23917
G8	Buffalo	Fr Clarksville, 7 mi W on US 58, 2 mi N on Co 767, 2 mi E on Co 722	24	15	15	2.00	4/1-10/30	• •	l					Boydton
G8	Rudd's Creek	Fr Boydton, 2 mi W on US 58	101	103	103	3.00	All year	• •	l					Boydton
G8	North Bend Pk	Fr Boydton, 4 mi N on US 58, S on Hwy 4 to dam	409	246	246	3.00	All year	• •	lr	•				Boydton
G8	Longwood	Fr Clarksville, 7 mi S on US 15	150	55	55	3.00	All year	• • •	l					Boydton
G8	Ivy Hill	Fr Townsville, NC, 7 mi NW on Hwy 39 & Co 825	1113	25	25	None	4/1-10/30	• •	l					Boydton
G8	Eastland Creek	Fr Boydton, 5 mi S on Co 707, 1 mi S on Co 824	119	28	28	2.00	4/1-10/30	• •	l					Boydton
	John W Flannagan Res												703/835-9544	Haysi
F3	Cranes Nest CA	Fr Clintwood, 3 mi NW on Hwy 83, 2-1/2 mi N on access rd	5	11	25	3.00	All year	o •	l		p			Haysi
F3	Pound River CG	Fr Clintwood, 2 mi N on Hwy 631, 2 mi E on SR 754	3		S16	3.00	All year	• •	l		p			Haysi
F3	Upper Twin CA	Fr Haysi 6 mi W on SR 63, 3 mi N on SR 614 & 739, 4 mi W on SR 611 to access rd	2		18	3.00	5/1-10/15	• •	l		p			Haysi
F3	Lower Twin CA	Fr Haysi, 6 mi W on SR 63, 3 mi N on 614 & 739, 3 mi W on SR 611 to access rd	5	8	29	3.00	5/1-10/15	• •	l		p			Rt 1 Bx 268, Haysi 24256

Washington, D.C.

Major Events

See maps, page 21 and 48

Washington International Art Fair, mid-Mar., Washington Convention Center. Fine art dealers gather in Washington where buyers and spectators may view a large display of many different types of art. Admission. 202/547-1080.

Kite Carnival, late Mar., Washington Monument Grounds. Contestants make and fly their own kites at this event. Free. 202/357-3030.

Cherry Blossom Festival, late Mar. to early Apr., Tidal Basin area. Each spring the cherry trees blossom, and daily festivities take place, including the Cherry Blossom Queen Pageant and the Cherry Blossom Parade. Free. 202/789-7000.

Annual Easter Egg Roll, the Monday following Easter, the White House. Children are invited onto the White House lawn for an Easter egg hunt and an Easter egg-rolling contest. Free. 202/456-7041.

Georgetown Garden Tour, late Apr., Georgetown. This is a self-guided walking tour of gardens in Georgetown. Hostesses are on duty at each garden in order to answer questions. Box lunches are available. Admission. 202/333-4953.

School Safety Patrol Parade, early May, Constitution Ave. Children from school safety patrols throughout the Mid-Atlantic and from various other parts of the United States come to participate in a large parade. Free. 703/222-6240.

Goodwill Industries Guild Embassy Tour, early May, various locations. Each year various embassies are open to the public. Admission. 202/842-5050.

The Evening Parade at Marine Barracks, Fri. evenings from early May to early Sept., Marine Barracks at 8th and I Sts. SE. Marines parade in a pageant of precision marching and drilling. Reservations necessary. 202/433-4074.

War Memorial Sunset Parade, Tues. evenings from early June to late Aug., Iwo Jima War Memorial. Parades and musical tributes are held at the base of the Iwo Jima Statue near Arlington National Cemetery. 202/433-4074.

Smithsonian Festival of American Folklife, late June to early July, the Mall. Craftsmen from around the country display crafts and perform various types of music and dance. Free. 202/381-6525.

Independence Day Celebration, July 4, citywide. There are concerts, lots of street activities, and a large fireworks display on the Mall. Free. 202/426-6700.

Frisbee Festival, early Sept., the Mall by the National Gallery of Art. Sponsored by the Smithsonian Institution, this event gives the pros a chance to demonstrate their skills, and amateurs get a chance to learn a few tricks. Free. 202/257-2700.

National Christmas Pageant of Peace, mid-Dec., on the Ellipse south of the White House. The National Christmas Tree is lighted by the President of the United States, and for the following two weeks there are musical performances, a Nativity drama, and a burning Yule log. Free. 202/426-6700.

Information Source

Washington Area Convention
and Visitors Association
1575 I St. NW, Suite 50
Washington, D.C. 20005
202/789-7000

Washington, D.C. Destinations

WASHINGTON, D.C., 637,651, C-5. Capital of the United States, the site was chosen by George Washington, for whom it was named. The site was authorized by Congressional Act in 1790, land was granted by Maryland and Virginia in 1790-91 and occupied by the United States Government in 1800. In the early 1700s, the area was still a swampland, but plantations were developed across the river. One of them was Mount Vernon, the home of George Washington. Soon after selecting the capital site, Washington hired Maj. Pierre Charles L'Enfant, a French-born engineer who had served under him during the American Revolution, to draw plans for the city. This L'Enfant did in 1791, developing a plan in which streets formed squares, with major diagonal avenues crisscrossing the design and leading to the center of government—the Capitol—like a wheel. Although Washington selected the site, was influential in its plans, and laid the cornerstone on September 18, 1793, he was inaugurated as first president of the United States on the balcony of the Federal Building in New York City and served his two terms of office in New York and later Philadelphia. Thomas Jefferson, third president of the United States, was the first president

inaugurated in Washington. The British burned many of the buildings in 1814, but reconstruction of much of the devastation was completed in 1819. The first great expansion occurred during the Civil War; the second during World War I; and during World War II, the government expanded its buildings into Maryland and Virginia.

U.S. GOVERNMENT BUILDINGS: U.S. Capitol, Capitol Hill. The nation's Capitol building stands on an 83-foot-high hill in a 131-acre park at a point where four sections of the city meet. The site for the Capitol was chosen by Maj. Pierre Charles L'Enfant, French-born military engineer, who also drew the plans for the city. The north section of the Capitol was completed in 1800 and in November of the same year, Congress held its first session here. In 1814, the Capitol was one of the buildings burned by the British in the War of 1812; however, construction began soon after under the supervision of Benjamin Henry Latrobe, who resigned in 1817 and was succeeded by Boston architect Charles Bulfinch. In the wings of the building are the *Senate Chambers* and *House of Representatives,* where galleries are open to visitors with passes, which may be obtained from the office of the visitor's U.S. Senator or Congressman.

Other features are the 4,500-ton cast-iron dome, Statuary Hall, the original Supreme Court and Senate Chambers, and the office of the Vice President of the United States. Year-round, daily, 9 A.M. to 4:30 P.M. Guided tours leave from the rotunda, 9 A.M. to 3:45 P.M. Free. 202/225-6827. **White House,** 1600 Pennsylvania Ave. NW. This had been the official residence of every American president except George Washington, who selected the site for the mansion. Burned by the British in 1814, the house was restored and painted white, thus accounting for its name, according to some authorities. James Hoban, who designed the building, oversaw its restoration after it was burned. Public rooms in the 132-room mansion are open to visitors. Year-round, Tues.-Sat., 10 A.M. to noon. Visitors entrance at East Gate, East Executive Ave. Free. 202/456-7041. **U.S. Senate and House Office Buildings.** The Senate offices, on 1st St. and Constitution Ave. NE., are connected to the Capitol by an underground "railroad" or subway which visitors may ride. The House offices are on Independence Ave. between 1st St. SW and 1st St. SE. Most congressmen will greet constituents if notified in advance of their visit to the Capitol. Senate offices: Year-round, Mon.-Fri., 8 A.M. to 5 P.M.; Sat., 8

A.M. to noon. House offices: Year-round, Mon.-Fri., 8 A.M. to 6 P.M.; Sat., 8 A.M. to 1 P.M. Free. 202/224-3121. **U.S. Supreme Court,** 1st St. and Maryland Ave. NE. The highest court in the land holds its sessions here. Established by the Judiciary Act of 1789, the Supreme Court originally was composed of the Chief Justice and five Associate Justices. Today the court has nine members. Year-round, Mon.-Fri., 9 A.M. to 4:30 P.M. Courtroom: Opens at 9:30 A.M. when court is in session, Oct.-June, Mon.-Wed., 10 A.M. to noon, 1 to 3 P.M. Free. 202/252-3200. **U.S. Treasury,** 15th St. and Pennsylvania Ave. NW, enter on Executive Ave. The oldest department building in Washington, its construction (1842) ruined L'Enfant's plan to have a broad, unobstructed avenue linking the Capitol with the President's residence. A U.S. Treasury draft for $7,200,000 which bought Alaska from Russia, along with other historic financial documents, can be seen here. Exhibit room: Year-round, Tues.-Sat., 9:30 A.M. to 3:30 P.M. Free. 202/566-2000. **U.S. Department of Agriculture,** 12th to 14th Sts. SW between Independence Ave. and Jefferson Dr. Temporary exhibits are displayed in the Administration Building, and department publications are available nearby. Year-round, Mon.-Fri., 8 A.M. to 4:30 P.M. Free. 202/447-2791. **U.S. Department of Commerce,** between Constitution Ave. and E St., 14th to 15th Sts. NW. One of the world's largest office buildings, it covers eight acres. An aquarium in the basement has many species of fish and other forms of aquatic life. Changing exhibits are featured in the lobby. Year-round, Mon.-Fri., 8:30 A.M. to 5 P.M. Free. 202/377-2000. **J. Edgar Hoover F.B.I. Building,** E St. between 9th and 10th Sts. NW (Visitors Entrance). One-hour tours include a history of the Bureau, explanation of work performed in F.B.I. laboratories, and a firearms demonstration. Year-round, Mon.-Fri., 9 A.M. to 4:15 P.M. Free. 202/324-3447. **Bureau of Engraving and Printing,** 14th and C Sts. SW. The bureau designs, engraves, and prints paper money, bonds, revenue, and postage stamps. A catwalk above the presses allows visitors to see the money and stamps being produced. Self-guided tours: Year-round, Mon.-Fri., 8 A.M. to 2 P.M. Free. 202/447-9709. **Bureau of Indian Affairs,** C St. between 18th and 19th Sts. NW. This agency, which has been a part of the Department of the Interior since 1849, was established to look after the interests of Indians who own lands under federal jurisdiction. On display in the museum are native arts and crafts, historic documents, and dioramas. Year-round, Mon.-Fri., 8 A.M. to 4 P.M. Free. 202/343-5116. **Library of Congress,** 10 1st St. SE. One of the world's largest libraries, it was established in 1800. During the War of 1812, it was burned by the British. In 1815, it was started again with about 6,500 volumes from Thomas Jefferson's personal collection. Today, the library contains more

than 85,000,000 reference materials, which require more than 36 acres of floor space and 340 miles of shelves. Musical and library programs are part of the library's services. Exhibit halls: Year-round, Mon.-Fri., 8:30 A.M. to 9:30 P.M.; Sat.-Sun., holidays, 8:30 A.M. to 6 P.M. Guided tours: Mon.-Fri., 9 A.M. to 4 P.M. Free. 202/287-5458. **National Archives,** Constitution Ave. at 8th St. NW. Government records of lasting value—treaties, census and land records, and fiscal accounts—are preserved here. Daily, Apr.-Labor Day, 10 A.M. to 9 P.M.; Sept.-Mar., 10 A.M. to 5:30 P.M. Free. 202/523-3099. **U.S. Naval Observatory,** 34th St. and Massachusetts Ave. NW. Fundamental positions of the principal celestial bodies are continuously studied in this observatory, called the nation's official timekeeper because it determines the correct time for the United States. Extensive astronomical and mathematical libraries also are maintained here. Tours: Year-round, Mon.-Fri., 12:30 P.M. and 2 P.M. Free. Evening tours by reservation only. Recorded message regarding evening tours 202/254-4569. Evening tour reservations 202/254-4567. General information 202/254-4533. **U.S. Postal Service,** 475 L'Enfant Plaza West SW. This building houses the official philatelic agency of the government. Year-round, Mon.-Sat., 9 A.M. to 5 P.M. Free. 202/245-4000. **Fort Lesley J. McNair,** 4th and P Sts. SW. This U.S. Army post encompasses the National War College, the Inter-American Defense College, and the Industrial College of the Armed Forces. Year-round, daily, daylight hours. Free. 202/693-8214. **MEMORIALS AND MONUMENTS: Franklin Delano Roosevelt Memorial,** 9th St. and Pennsylvania Ave. NW, near the National Archives. The small, 7½-ton white marble block dedicated to President Roosevelt was designed by Eric Gugler according to Roosevelt's wishes. **Jefferson Memorial,** southeast bank of the Tidal Basin. The circular pantheon building, designed by John Russell Pope, is of Vermont marble, with Ionic columns 41 feet tall. A 19-foot bronze statue of Jefferson by Rudolph Evans stands in the central room of the domed structure. Staffed year-round, daily, 8 A.M. to midnight. Free. 202/426-6841. **John F. Kennedy Center for the Performing Arts,** Rock Creek Pkwy. and New Hampshire Ave. NW. A living memorial to President Kennedy, who supported the establishment of a national cultural center in the Capital, the center offers music, drama, dance, and film in its theaters and concert halls. *Eisenhower Theater* has theatrical performances. The *Opera House* presents ballets, operas, and musical plays. *Concert Hall* is home of the National Symphony Orchestra and host to guest symphony orchestras. *Terrace Theater* presents chamber music, poetry readings, and children's programs. The *American Film Institute* also provides children's programs. The *Grand Foyer* of the center extends 192 feet

Thomas Jefferson was the first president of the United States to be inaugurated in Washington, D.C. History records show, however, that he was somewhat taken aback by his new home, then called the President's House, which he described as "a great stone house, big enough for two emperors, one pope, and a grand lama." Jefferson's dislike of pomp and formality was evident from the start. On the day of his inauguration, he walked to the Capitol from Mrs. Conrad's boarding house, accompanied by only a group of soldiers and civilians. That same year, at a reception in the President's House, he replaced bowing with handshaking. Even the presidency did not alter Jefferson's perspective. His epitaph, which he wrote, does not even mention that he held the office.

along the Potomac River side of the building. An outside balcony provides an expansive view of the river and beyond. Tours: Year-round, daily, 10 A.M. to 1 P.M. Free. Box office: Year-round, Mon.-Sat., 10 A.M. to 9 P.M.; Sun., holidays, noon to 9 P.M. Admission for performances varies with each event. 202/254-3600. **Lincoln Memorial,** West Potomac Park at the foot of 23rd St. NW. Designed by Henry Bacon, the Colorado marble memorial is dominated by a seated figure of Abraham Lincoln (19 feet by 19 feet) sculptured by Daniel Chester French. Supporting the structure in which the figure is located are 36 Doric columns, one for each state in existence in Lincoln's time. Staffed year-round, daily, 8 A.M. to midnight. Free. 202/426-6841. **Washington Monument,** Constitution Ave. at 15th St. NW. The cornerstone for this monument to the first President of the United States was laid on July 4, 1848; construction was completed in 1884. Rising 555 feet from the ground, it is the tallest structure in the city. The pinnacle of the marble obelisk, designed by Robert Mills, may be reached by a three-minute elevator ride, and visitors may walk down the 898 steps where 190 memorial stones can be viewed along the way. Daily, Memorial Day-Labor Day, 8 A.M.

The United States Capitol has undergone many metamorphoses since George Washington laid the cornerstone in 1793. This is the way it looked between 1825 and 1856 when construction was under the direction of Charles Bulfinch, the first native American architect to supervise construction on the Capitol. Bulfinch held the job from 1817 until 1829 and is credited with completing the Capitol as it was envisioned by his predecessors, chiefly William Thornton, the original designer of the building. Thornton was primarily a physician but also dabbled in painting, inventing, and architecture. In 1792, the District Commissioners decided to sponsor a competition for the best design of a Capitol. Thornton entered and captured first place. His design impressed not only the commissioners, but some other prominent gentlemen around the District of Columbia. Thomas Jefferson said Thornton's design "captivated the eyes and judgment of all." George Washington, in a letter recommending the design to the commissioners, wrote "Grandeur, Simplicity, and Convenience appear to be so well combined in this plan that I have no doubt of its meeting with . . . approbation from you." By September 18, 1793, Thornton's design was selected and modified. In addition to these honors, he received $500 and a city lot.

to midnight; other months, 9 A.M. to 5 P.M. Free. 202/426-6839.

SMITHSONIAN INSTITUTION: This is an "institution" of museums, many along the Mall, which extends from the U.S. Capitol to the Washington Monument. Sometimes called the "nation's attic" because of unusual collections bequeathed to it, the Smithsonian, itself, was an unusual bequest to the United States. James Smithson, an Englishman who could not inherit his father's title or position, willed his assets first to his nephew, and in case of his death, to the United States (which he had never visited), where he felt he might be recognized. His nephew preceded him in death. Smithson died in 1829, and it took the United States until 1846 to accept his bequest and until 1857 to formalize legislation designating Congress to appropriate money for its upkeep. Today, it is the largest complex of museums in the United States, ranging in architectural style from the turreted red sandstone Smithsonian Castle (1855) to the modern National Air and Space Museum. **Anacostia Neighborhood Museum,** 2405 Martin Luther King Ave. SE. This is a center for black heritage. Traveling exhibitions on Afro-American history and culture are supplemented with education programs of interest to the community. Year-round, Mon.-Fri., 10 A.M. to 6 P.M.; Sat.-Sun., 1 to 6 P.M. Free. 202/357-1300 or 202/357-2700. **Arts and Industries Building,** 900 Jefferson Dr. SW. Built to house exhibits from the 1876 Philadelphia Centennial Exhibition, the exhibit halls have been restored as nearly as possible to their original appearance. More than 25,000 objects are displayed in the collection of Victorian Americana. Costumed guides describe the exhibits. Year-round, daily, 10 A.M. to 5:30 P.M. Free. 202/357-1300 or 202/357-2700. **Freer Gallery of Art,** 12th St. and Jefferson Dr. SW. Housed here is one of the world's finest collections of Oriental art. The gallery also has a group of 19th- and early 20th-century American works. Year-round, daily, 10 A.M. to 5:30 P.M. Free. 202/357-1300 or 202/357-2700. **Hirshhorn Museum and Sculpture Garden,** 8th St. and Independence Ave. SW. The result of a gift in 1966 of paintings and sculptures assembled over 40 years by Joseph H. Hirshhorn, the museum and garden contain a comprehensive collection of 20th-century art. Regularly scheduled educational programs include films, lectures, and music recitals. Year-round, daily, 10 A.M. to 5:30 P.M. Free. 202/357-1300 or 202/357-2700. **National Air and Space Museum,** 7th St. and Independence Ave. SW. Here visitors can study the evolution of aviation from the 1903 *Wright Flyer* and the *Spirit of St. Louis* to *Friendship 7* and the *Apollo 11* command module. Special flight films, including the popular *To Fly,* can be seen in the museum's theater, and planetarium presentations can be viewed in the Albert Einstein Spacearium. Year-round, daily, 10 A.M. to 5:30 P.M. Museum: Free. Theater and Spacearium (each): Adults $1; students, children, and persons 65 and over, 50¢. 202/357-1300 or 202/357-2700. **National Museum of African Art,** 318 A St. NE. Exhibits reflecting the rich creative heritage of 20 African countries include art, musical instruments, and textiles. Year-round, Mon.-Fri., 11 A.M. to 5 P.M.; Sat.-Sun., noon to 5 P.M. Donations. 202/287-3490. **National Museum of American Art,** 9th and G Sts. NW. A center for the study and presentation of American arts, the collection of some 22,000 works comprises primarily American paintings, sculptures, and graphic arts from the 18th century to the present. Housed in the Old Patent Office Building, which is considered to be the finest Greek-Revival structure in the United States, the museum's Lincoln Gallery was the site of Abraham Lincoln's second inaugural reception. Year-round, daily, 10 A.M. to 5:30 P.M. Free. 202/357-1300 or 202/357-2700. **National Museum of American History,** 12th St. and Constitution Ave. NW. The nation's major cultural and technological achievements can be explored through a variety of exhibits in this museum. Among the items on display are the First Ladies' gowns, George Washington's uniform and tent, the flag which inspired Frances Scott Key to write "The Star-Spangled Banner," Bell's telephone, Ford's Model T, Whitney's model of the original cotton gin, Conestoga wagon, and antique cars. Year-round, daily, 10 A.M. to 5:30 P.M. Free. 202/357-1300 or 202/357-2700. **National Museum of Natural History,** 10th St. and Constitution Ave. NW. The museum has more than 65 million objects on anthropology and plants and animals in their natural surroundings. Year-round, daily, 10 A.M. to 5:30 P.M. Free. 202/357-1300 or 202/357-2700. **National Portrait Gallery,** 8th and F Sts. NW. The history of the United States can be traced through the portraits of the men and women who made significant contributions to the country's political, scientific, literary, artistic, and military development. Year-round, daily, 10 A.M. to 5:30 P.M. Free. 202/357-1300 or 202/357-2700. **National Zoological Park,** 3000 Connecticut Ave. NW. Some 2,500 animals representing about 800 species live at the zoo. Feeding times for the pandas are at 9 A.M. and 3 P.M. Trackless trains carry visitors past many of the exhibits. Buildings:

Daily, May-Sept., 9 A.M. to 6:30 P.M.; Oct.-Apr., 9 A.M. to 4:30 P.M. Grounds: Daily, May-Sept., 6 A.M. to 8 P.M.; Oct.-Apr., 6 A.M. to 5:30 P.M. Free. Parking $2. 202/357-1300 or 202/357-2700. **Renwick Gallery,** 17th St. and Pennsylvania Ave. NW. Contemporary and historic American crafts, decorative arts and design, and arts of other cultures are exhibited in the gallery. Completed in 1874, the building once housed the Corcoran Gallery. Year-round, daily, 10 A.M. to 5:30 P.M. Free. 202/357-1300 or 202/357-2700.

MUSEUMS, GALLERIES, LIBRARIES: Corcoran Gallery of Art, 17th St. and New York Ave. NW. The gallery has an extensive collection of early American paintings, drawings, prints, and sculpture, including the work of Gilbert Stuart and Samuel Morse. It also features temporary exhibits of modern art; a collection of European paintings, sculpture, rugs, tapestries, and pottery; and periodic exhibits of paintings, photography, and graphics by local artists and photographers. Year-round, Tues.-Wed., Fri.-Sun., 10 A.M. to 4:30 P.M.; Thurs., 10 A.M. to 9 P.M. Free. 202/638-3211. **Doll's House and Toy Museum,** 5236 44th St. NW. Antique dolls, dollhouses, toys, and games, many from the Victorian era, are beautifully displayed in this museum. Year-round, Tues.-Sat., 11 A.M. to 5 P.M.; Sun., noon to 5 P.M. Adults $2; persons under 14, $1. 202/244-0024. **Explorers Hall, National Geographic Society,** 17th and M Sts. NW. The hall contains exhibits of explorations, discoveries, and research sponsored by the society. Displays trace expeditions to every corner of the world and outer space. Taped recordings provide detailed explanations of the exhibits. Year-round, Mon.-Fri., 9 A.M. to 6 P.M.; Sat., 9 A.M. to 5 P.M.; Sun., 10 A.M. to 5 P.M. Free. 202/857-7589. **Folger Shakespeare Library,** 201 E. Capitol St. SE. The library contains one of the world's finest collections of Shakespearean and Renaissance books and manuscripts. It also has a full-scale reproduction of a 17th-century English playhouse where poetry readings, lectures, art exhibits, and concerts are held. Year-round, Mon.-Sat., 10 A.M. to 4 P.M.; May-Labor Day, Sun., 10 A.M. to 4 P.M. Free. 202/544-4600. **Library of Congress,** see **U.S. Government Buildings. Museum of Modern Art of Latin America,** 201 18th St. NW. The museum, located near the Organization of American States, contains a permanent collection of contemporary art from Latin America and the Caribbean. Year-round, Tues.-Sat., 10 A.M. to 5 P.M. Tours by appointment. Free. 202/789-6016. **National Gallery of Art,** 6th St. and Constitution Ave. NW. Two marble structures, the West Building and the new East Building, contain fine collections of European and American paintings, sculptures, and graphic arts from the 13th century to the present. Year-round, Mon.-Sat., 10 A.M. to 5 P.M.; Sun., noon to 9 P.M. Free. 202/737-4215. **Organi-**

zation of American States, 17th St. and Constitution Ave. NW. Formerly the Pan American Union, O.A.S. features the Gallery of Heroes, the Council Chamber, the Hall of the Americas, and an Aztec Garden. Concerts and art shows representing the member countries are organized here. Year-round, Mon.-Fri., 9:30 A.M. to 5 P.M. Free. 202/789-3751. **Phillips Collection,** 1600-1612 21st St. NW. This collection of 19th- and 20th-century art, many examples from the French Impressionists and Postimpressionists, is housed in the former home of the late art collector, Duncan Phillips. Year-round, Tues.-Sat., 10 A.M. to 5 P.M.; Sun., 2 to 7 P.M. Free. 202/387-2151. **Smithsonian Institution,** see separate entries. **Truxton-Decatur Naval Museum,** 1610 H St. NW. The history of the navy is depicted from its inception in 1775 to the present in this museum named for Thomas Truxton and Stephen Decatur, naval heroes. Year-round, daily, 10 A.M. to 4 P.M. Free. 202/842-0050. **U.S. Navy Memorial Museum,** 9th and M Sts. SE (Washington Navy Yard). More than 4,000 articles representing the history, battles, weapons, heroes, vessels, and achievements of the U.S. Navy from the Revolutionary War to the space age are in this museum. Year-round, Mon.-Fri., 9 A.M. to 4 P.M.; Sat.-Sun., 10 A.M. to 5 P.M. Free. 202/433-4882 or 202/433-2651.

HISTORIC BUILDINGS AND HOUSES: American Red Cross Building, 17th and D Sts. NW. Headquarters for the American Red Cross, the building is dedicated to the women of the Civil War. Exhibits tracing the history of the Red Cross from the Civil War to the present can be viewed. Year-round, Mon.-Fri., 9 A.M. to 4 P.M. Free. 202/737-8300. **Constitution Hall,** 18th St. between C and D Sts. NW. Concerts, lectures, meetings, and other events are held in this hall, which will seat nearly 4,000 persons. A recorded message provides visitors with information on upcoming programs. Adjacent to Constitution Hall is *Memorial Continental Hall,* headquarters of the Daughters of the American Revolution, who own the auditorium. A *Revolutionary War Museum* is in the adjoining Administration Building. Year-round, Mon.-Fri., 9 A.M. to 4 P.M. Free. 202/627-4780 or 202/638-2661. **Decatur House,** 748 Jackson Pl. NW. The Georgian town house, a block from the White House, was designed in 1818 by Benjamin Henry Latrobe, architect for the United States Capitol and many other famous buildings. Year-round, Tues.-Fri., 10 A.M. to 2 P.M.; Sat.-Sun., noon to 4 P.M. Adults $2; persons 6-18 and 65 and over, $1; under 6 and members of the National Trust, free. 202/673-4030. **Dumbarton House,** 2715 Q St. NW. Headquarters for the National Society of Colonial Dames of America, the Georgian house was built about 1800 and contains a collection of colonial furniture and accessories. Sept.-June, Mon.-Sat., 9 A.M. to noon. Donations. 202/337-2288. **Dumbarton Oaks,** 1703 32nd St. NW. Housed here are

the center for Byzantine Studies, art collections of the early Christian and Byzantine periods, and extensive libraries. Of Georgian design and set in a grove of oak trees, the mansion was given to Harvard University in 1940 by Robert Woods Bliss, U.S. Ambassador to Argentina. In 1944, the estate was used as headquarters for the Dumbarton Oaks Conference, which led to the organization of the United Nations. Year-round, Tues.-Sun., 2 to 5 P.M. Free. 202/342-3200. Recorded message 202/338-8278. **Ford's Theatre National Historic Site,** 511 10th St. NW. The theater where Pres. Abraham Lincoln was fatally wounded by John Wilkes Booth on April 14, 1865, has been restored to its appearance then. Historical lectures recalling the event are given in the auditorium by the National Park Service every hour on the half hour. Year-round, daily, 9:30 A.M. to 4:30 P.M. Theater performances are Oct.-June, Tues.-

Fri., 7:30 P.M.; Sat., 6 and 9:30 P.M.; Thurs., 1 P.M.; Sun., 3 P.M. During this season, the theater closes for rehearsals and one hour before matinees. Box office: 202/347-4833. *Lincoln Museum,* in the theater's basement, contains Lincoln memorabilia. Theater and museum: Year-round, daily, 9 A.M. to 5 P.M. Free. 202/426-6925. *The Petersen House,* 516 10th St. NW, where Lincoln died, is a four-story brick house just across the street from the theater. The President was taken here after he was wounded; he died the following morning. Year-round, daily, 9 A.M. to 5 P.M. Free. 202/426-6830. **Frederick Douglass Memorial Home,** 1411 W St. SE. Completed in 1854, this Victorian house was the last home of the noted black orator, educator, diplomat, and human rights activist. Daily, Sept.-Mar., 9 A.M. to 4 P.M.; Apr.-Aug., 9 A.M. to 5 P.M. Free. 202/889-1736. **Hillwood,** 4155 Linnean Ave. NW. Once the home of Marjorie Merriweather Post, the mansion features china services used by Catherine the Great and 18th- and 19th-century French and Russian art and furniture. Formal gardens surround the estate. Tours: Year-round, Mon., Wed.-Sat., 9 A.M., 10:30 A.M., noon, 1:30 P.M. Reservations required; children under 12 not permitted. House and garden tour: $7. 202/686-5807. **Octagon House,** 1799 New York Ave. NW. Designed in 1800 by William Thornton, the architect of the Capitol, the six-sided (not eight) Georgian mansion was the residence of President Madison in 1814 after the White House was burned by the British. Year-round, Tues.-Fri., 10 A.M. to 4 P.M.; Sat.-Sun., 1 to 4 P.M. Donations. 202/638-3105. **Old Stone House,** 3051 M St. NW. Built in 1765, the house is the oldest surviving structure in Georgetown and is a fine example of pre-Revolutionary architecture. Crafts are demonstrated on the premises. Year-round, Wed.-Sun., 9:30 A.M. to 5 P.M. Free. 202/426-6851. **Woodrow Wilson House,** 2340 S St. NW. This Georgian-Revival town house, built in 1915, was the retirement home of President Wilson from 1921 to 1924. Year-round, Tues.-Fri., 10 A.M. to 2 P.M.; Sat.-Sun., noon to 4 P.M. Adults $2; students, children, and persons 65 and over, $1; members of the National Trust, free. 202/387-4062.

CHURCHES AND RELIGIOUS CENTERS: Franciscan Monastery, 14th and Quincy Sts. NE. Called Mount St. Sepulchre, the monastery contains reproductions of early Christian art and full-scale replicas of Christian shrines in the Holy Land. A special feature is the rose garden. Year-round, daily, 8 A.M. to 5 P.M. Tours: 8:30 A.M. to 4 P.M. Free. 202/526-6800. **House of the Temple,** 1733 16th St. NW. Collections of general and Masonic interest can be seen at the headquarters for the Supreme Council of the 33rd and last degree of the Ancient and Accepted Scottish Rite of Freemasonry, Southern Jurisdiction, U.S.A. Year-round, Mon.-Fri., 9 A.M. to 4 P.M.; Sat., 9 A.M. to

noon. Guided tours. Free. 202/232-3579. **Islamic Center (Moslem Mosque),** 2551 Massachusetts Ave. NW. An institution of Moslem worship, education, and culture, it has Turkish tiles, Oriental rugs, and an Egyptian pulpit constructed of more than 10,000 separate pieces of wood. Visitors are asked to remove their shoes before entering. Year-round, daily, 9 A.M. to 4 P.M. Free. 202/332-3451. **National Shrine of the Immaculate Conception,** Michigan Ave. at 4th St. NE. Adjacent to the campus of Catholic University, it is the largest Catholic church in the United States and one of the largest in the world. The Romanesque and Byzantine structure is built entirely of stone and masonry and is shaped in the form of a Latin cross. Special features are the 329-foot bell tower, the Lourdes Chapel, and the Mary Altar made of semitransparent golden onyx. Year-round, daily, 7 A.M. to 6 P.M.; services daily. Guided tours: Mon.-Fri., 9 A.M. to 5 P.M.; Sat., 9 A.M. to 4 P.M.; Sun., 1:30 to 4 P.M. Free. 202/526-8300. **St. John's Episcopal Church,** 16th and H Sts. NW., opposite Lafayette Sq. Known as the "Church of the Presidents," it was designed by Benjamin Latrobe and has been in continuous use since 1816. Latrobe, architect of many famous buildings, also served as the first organist. James Madison, the first President to worship here, selected Pew 54 for his use. Traditionally, the pew has been set aside for the Chief Executive. Year-round, daily, 7 A.M. to 5 P.M. Free. 202/347-8766. **St. Matthew's Cathedral,** 1725 Rhode Island Ave. NW. The structure has a Romanesque exterior, a vast interior, and ornate ceilings. Pres. John Kennedy attended this church, which was also the site of his funeral mass. Year-round, daily, 6:30 A.M. to 6:30 P.M. Free. 202/347-3215. **Washington National Cathedral,** Massachusetts and Wisconsin Aves. NW., on Mount St. Alban. The structure is a fine example of 14th-century French- and English-Gothic styles. Of special interest is the Gloria in Excelsis central tower containing a unique combination of a 53-bell carillon and a 10-bell English ring; a high altar built of stones from Solomon's quarry near Jerusalem; stained-glass rose windows; hand-wrought silver altar cross and candlesticks, the gift of King George VI; and a museum with exhibits of stained-glass and stonecutting methods. On the grounds is the Bishop's Garden developed with boxwood, holly, and yew. Hundreds of herbs, which can be purchased in the Herb Cottage near the Bishop's Garden, are grown here. Also located here is a brass-rubbing center where, for a fee, visitors can receive materials and instructions in brass rubbing, using brass figures housed here. Year-round, daily, 10 A.M. to 4:30 P.M. Guided tours: Mon.-Sat., 10 A.M. to noon, 1 to 3:15 P.M.; Sun., 12:15 and 2:30 P.M. Donation $1. Services: Mon.-Sat., 7:30 A.M., noon, 4 P.M.; Sun., 8, 9, 10, and 11 A.M. and 4 P.M. 202/537-6200.

NATURAL AREAS: Anacostia Park, north and southeast sections of the city on both sides of the Anacostia River. Once an Indian village, the park now covers 750 acres and contains tennis courts, skating rink, golf, basketball courts, swimming pool, and a recreation center. Park: Year-round, daily. Activities vary according to the season. Free. 202/472-9227 or 202/472-9228. **National Zoological Park,** *see* under **Smithsonian Institution. Potomac Park,** along the north bank of the Potomac River, south of Constitution Ave. The park is divided into West and East Potomac Parks. Displayed to best advantage are the Washington Monument, the Jefferson Memorial, and the Lincoln Memorial. The irregularly shaped Tidal Basin, between the parks, is bordered by 3,000 Japanese cherry trees, which bloom in April. Golf, picnicking, swimming, tennis, baseball, and boating are available in this section of the city. **Rock Creek Park,** northwest along Rock Creek in the heart of the city. The 1,754-acre park, largest in the district, can be reached via the Rock Creek Parkway on the south or from 16th St. or Connecticut Ave. on the north. Recreation in the park includes horseback riding, tennis, bike and hiking trails, golf, and picnicking. Also in the park is *Pierce Mill,* Tilden St. and Beach Dr. NW, a working restoration of a waterwheel gristmill believed to have been built about 1820. Year-round, Wed.-Sun., 9 A.M. to 5 P.M. Free. 202/426-6908. *Rock Creek Nature Center,* 5200 Glover Rd. NW., has a planetarium and displays of wild animals, plant life, geology, weather, and conservation. A well-marked nature trail is open to those who want to explore on their own. Free. 202/426-6829. **Theodore Roosevelt Island,** Potomac River between Key and Memorial bridges. The 88-acre island is an unspoiled wilderness with several miles of hiking trails. It can be reached by a foot bridge over the west arm of the Potomac River. Year-round, daily, sunrise to sunset. Tours with ranger, Sat.-Sun., 11 A.M. and 2 P.M. Weekday tours can be arranged by calling 202/557-8991. Free. **U.S. Botanic Garden,** Maryland Ave, between 1st and 2nd Sts. SW. The garden has an international representation of more than 8,000 species of tropical and subtropical plants. Also of interest are a waterfall, reproduction of a tropical jungle, and special seasonal shows. Plants for the Capitol grounds are grown here. Daily, June-Aug., 9 A.M. to 9 P.M.; Sept.-May, 9 A.M. to 5 P.M. Free. 202/225-8333. Recorded message 202/225-7099. **U.S. National Arboretum,** 24th and R Sts. NE., off Bladensburg Rd. A wide variety of trees, shrubs, and plants are grown in this arboretum of more than 400 acres on the banks of the Anacostia River. Year-round, Mon.-Fri., 8 A.M. to 5 P.M.; Sat.-Sun., 10 A.M. to 5 P.M. Bonsai Collection: Daily, 10 A.M. to 2:30 P.M. Free. 202/472-9100.

OTHER PLACES OF INTEREST: Lafayette Square, Pennsylvania Ave. across from the

White House. Named for the Marquis de Lafayette, this well-known square is a good place to watch important people arriving at the White House. **L'Enfant Plaza,** 10th St. Mall between Independence and Maine Aves. The plaza, a model of urban renewal, is a three-level complex consisting of a shopping mall, movie theater, and parking facilities. **Voice of America,** 330 Independence Ave. SW. American ideas and ideals are broadcast in 38 languages through this worldwide radio service. The tour explains how short-wave radio, TV, and literature are used to relate information regarding U.S. policies. Tours: Year-round, Mon.-Fri., 8:45, 9:45, and 10:45 A.M., 1:45, 2:45, and 3:45 P.M. Free. 202/755-4744. **Arlington,** *see* **Virginia. Georgetown,** west of Rock Creek Park. In this colonial section of Washington are approximately 100 square blocks of historic buildings. Originally a Maryland tobacco shipping town, it was incorporated into Washington by Congress in 1871. The area, one of the most important single groups of historic buildings in the nation, is protected by an Act of Congress passed in 1950. Georgetown is the site of the spring Home and Garden Tours, a portion of the Chesapeake and Ohio Canal, and Georgetown University. Shopping boutiques, restaurants, and nightclubs draw both residents and visitors.

Museums and Government Buildings Line the Mall

The National Mall is a landscaped park extending from the United States Capitol to the Washington Monument. It is bounded on the east by 3rd St., on the west by 14th St., on the north by Constitution Ave., and on the south by Independence Ave., with Madison and Jefferson drives running east and west inside the mall. Envisioned as a formal park by L'Enfant in his 1791 plan for the city of Washington, today it is 145 acres of lawns, reflecting pools, museums, and hiking trails. Places of interest on the north side of the mall along Madison Dr. (east to west) are the National Gallery of Art Annex, National Gallery of Art, National Sculpture Garden (a circle area with concessions), National Museum of Natural History, National Museum of American History (formerly called Museum of History and Technology), and the Washington Monument. Places of interest on the south side of the mall along Jefferson Dr. (west to east) are the Sylvan Amphitheater, at the southeast corner of the Washington Monument, U.S. Department of Agriculture (north building), Freer Gallery of Art, Smithsonian Castle, Arts and Industries Building, Hirschhorn Museum, National Air and Space Museum, U.S. Botanic Gardens, and the U.S. Capitol.

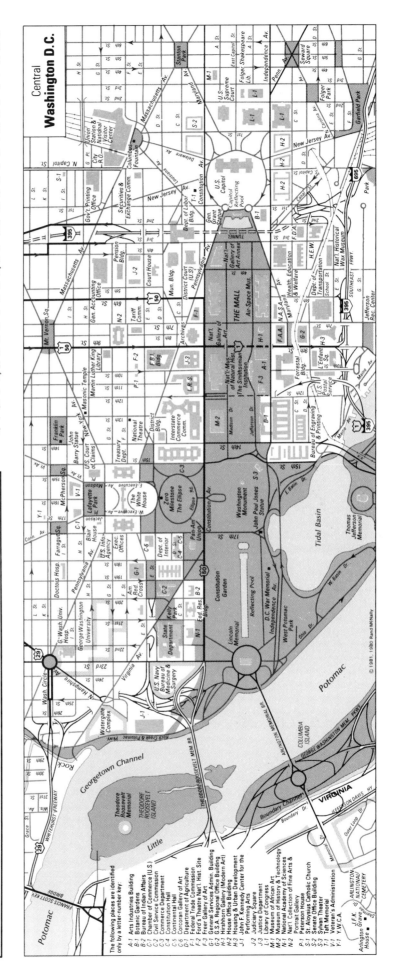

Central **Washington D.C.**

The following places are identified only by a letter-number key:

A-1 Arts Industries Building
B-1 Botanic Gardens
B-2 Bureau of Indian Affairs
C-1 Chamber of Commerce (U.S.)
C-2 Civil Service Commission
C-3 Commerce Department
C-4 Constitution Hall
C-5 Continental Hall
C-6 Corcoran Gallery of Art
D-1 Department of Agriculture
F-1 Federal Trade Commission
F-2 Ford's Theatre Nat'l. Hist. Site
F-3 Freer Gallery of Art
G-1 General Services Admin. Building
G-2 G.S.A. Regional Office Building
H-1 Hirshhorn Gallery (Modern Art)
H-2 House Office Building
H-3 Housing & Urban Development
J-1 John F. Kennedy Center for the Performing Arts
J-2 Judiciary Square
J-3 Justice Department
L-1 Library of Congress
M-1 Museum of African Art
M-2 Museum of History & Technology
N-1 National Academy of Sciences
N-2 Nat'l Collection of Fine Arts & Portrait Gallery
P-1 Peterson House
S-1 St. Aloysius Catholic Church
S-2 Senate Office Building
S-3 Sylvan Theater
T-1 Taft Memorial
V-1 Veteran's Administration
Y-1 Y.W.C.A.

West Virginia

Major Events

See state map, pages 46-47

Alpine Winter Festival, early Mar., Davis, east of Parsons. Canaan Valley Ski Resort hosts this event which features cross-country skiing races, downhill skiing events, lollipop races, and a torchlight parade. Free. 304/259-5315.

W.V. Jazz Festival, late Mar. to early Apr., Charleston. West Virginia groups join nationally known musicians in workshops and concerts at the Cultural Center Theatre. Free. 304/348-0220.

Dogwood Arts & Crafts Festival, mid-Apr., Huntington. This festival is timed with the blooming of the area's dogwood trees, and some of the activities held at the Huntington Civic Center include live entertainment; square-dancing, woodcarving, and furniture-making demonstrations; as well as homemade ice cream, candles, and quilts. Admission. 304/696-5947.

House and Garden Tour, late Apr., Martinsburg, Shepherdstown, Harpers Ferry, and Charles Town. This event offers tours of gardens, buildings, and several homes. The tours are self-guided. Admission. 304/876-6273.

Woodcrafter's Weekend and Spring Nature Walks, early May, Fairmont. Prickett's Fort State Park offers a view of life in 18th-century West Virginia with demonstrations of log hewing and shingle making. Guided tours of the native vegetation and wildlife are also offered. Admission is charged for the fort; the park is free. 304/363-3030.

Three Rivers Coal Festival, mid-May, Fairmont. Exhibits of mining operations and machinery are on display, and there are coal-shoveling contests as well as other forms of competition related to mining work. Additional activities include live entertainment, street dances, arts and crafts, parades, a carnival, and food. Free (except food). 304/366-4256.

Vandalia Gathering, late May, Charleston. The Cultural Center and the Capitol Grounds are the sites for this festival of traditional West Virginia arts. Fiddle and banjo concerts, dancing, many types of food, and quilting competition are some of the activities. Free (except food). 304/348-0220.

W.V. Strawberry Festival, late May, Buckhannon. Strawberries are on display and for sale at this annual event. Other attractions include an arts and crafts show, parades, a coin and stamp show, high school band competition, and the coronation and ball for the Strawberry Queen. Admission is charged for several events. 304/472-4600.

Mountain Heritage Arts and Crafts Festival, mid-June, Charles Town. This event pays homage to West Virginia mountain culture with an arts and crafts show and demonstrations, entertainment by bluegrass music groups, and Appalachian foods. Admission. 304/725-5514.

West Virginia Folk Festival, mid-June, Glenville. Glenville State College hosts this program of early folk music. There is a fiddling contest, and square dances are held along with crafts exhibits and demonstrations. Admission is charged for several events. 304/462-7361.

Wild and Wonderful West Virginia Weekend, mid-June, North Bend State Park, east of Parkersburg. Arts and crafts are on display, and family activities include hayrides, bonfires, marshmallow and hot dog roasts, softball games, and live entertainment. Free. 304/643-2931.

Mountain State Arts and Crafts Fair, early July, Ripley. This large outdoor crafts show exhibits work by more than 100 West Virginia artists and craftsmen. There are demonstrations, where spectators may participate; Appalachian food; and music. Admission. 304/348-2347.

Frontier Fourth Celebration, July 4, Fairmont. Prickett's Fort State Park presents a "salute to independence—18th-century style" at its reconstructed 18th-century log fort. Admission is charged for the fort; the park is free. 304/363-3030.

Old-Time Fiddler and Bluegrass Convention, late July, Bluefield. Different types of music competition, live entertainment, and food are featured at New Glenwood Park. Admission. 304/425-1670.

West Virginia Water Festival, early to mid-Aug., Hinton. Fun on the waterfront includes canoe and kayak races, a street fair with arts and crafts, the Queen Mermaid coronation and ball, parachute and skydiving demonstrations, and majorette competition. Admission is charged for several events. 304/466-3255.

The Ohio River Festival, mid-Aug., Ravenswood. Powerboat racing and a boat parade are highlights of this riverfront celebration that includes arts and crafts exhibits, country and western entertainment, square dancing, fireworks, and a queen's ball. Admission. 304/273-4157.

State Fair of West Virginia, late Aug., Fairlea, west of Lewisburg. This unique state fair, similar to an old-fashioned country fair, features nightly entertainment, a circus, horse shows, a champion livestock parade, a carnival, and fireworks. Admission. 304/645-1090.

West Virginia Oil and Gas Festival, mid-Sept., Sistersville, northeast of Parkersburg. The oil and gas engine show is the highlight of this tribute to local industry. Also featured at this event, which takes place in City Park, are a parade, an antique car show, arts and crafts demonstrations, a photo exhibit, a coin and stamp show, a wrist-wrestling contest, a footrace, and fiddle and banjo contests. Admission is charged for several events. 304/652-7881.

Treasure Mountain Festival, mid-Sept., Franklin. Mountain life is celebrated with exhibits and demonstrations of crafts, an art show, square dancing, music, and traditional foods, including country ham, barbecued beef, and chicken pot pies made in an iron kettle. Free (except food). 304/249-5506.

Preston County Buckwheat Festival, late Sept., Kingwood. Buckwheat cakes and sausage dinners are served during this country-style festival. Activities include a livestock show, a tractor-pulling contest, arts and crafts, an antique car exhibit, live entertainment, and square dancing. Free (except food). 304/329-0021.

Mountain State Forest Festival, late Sept. to early Oct., Elkins. Activities range from woodchopping, archery, fly-casting, and muzzle-loading contests to an art show, forestry crafts, hang-gliding demonstrations, and four-wheel-drive races. Other activities include a carnival, square dancing, and three parades. Admission is charged for several events. 304/636-1824.

The Heritage Arts Harvest Festival, early Oct., Salem. This event celebrates the harvest and recalls 200 years of life in Appalachia. Lectures, demonstrations, and folk games and dances are some of the festivities. Admission. 304/782-5245.

West Virginia Black Walnut Festival, mid-Oct., Spencer. Black walnut products, food, and souvenirs are featured along with a grand parade, a canoe race, footraces, arts and crafts, banjo and fiddle contests, and country cooking. Admission is charged for several events. 304/927-3708.

Apple Butter Festival, mid-Oct., Berkeley Springs. Freshly made apple butter is on hand along with dozens of different types of food specialties made with apples. There is live music, and arts and crafts are on display. Free (except food). 304/258-3738.

W.V. Crafts Weekend, late Oct., North Bend State Park, east of Parkersburg. Traditional arts and crafts are displayed and judged in the lodge of the state park. Live entertainment is also provided. Admission. 304/643-2931.

Old-Tyme Christmas, early Dec., Harpers Ferry. The lighting of the Yule log begins this 18th-century-style holiday celebration. The town is decorated with evergreens, fruits, nuts, and candles, and there are choral concerts, a nativity scene, dramatic presentations, and the "world's largest taffy pull." Free. 304/535-2482.

West Virginia Destinations

ALDERSON, 1,375, E-5. **Pence Springs,** 8 miles west on St. 3, once was a well-known health spa. It was awarded a silver medal at the St. Louis World's Fair for its clear, pure spring water. The resort's hotel is now a women's reformatory operated by the state. Samples of the mineral water may be tasted in the Spring House, which is open to the public. Always open. *See* also **Talcott.**

ANSTED, 1,952, E-4. **Contentment,** on U.S. 60, is a yesteryear museum consisting of an antebellum home, schoolhouse, and museum. Maintained by the Fayette County Historical Society, the buildings contain artifacts from the early days of the county and state. May-Sept., Mon.-Sat., 9 A.M. to 6 P.M.; Sun., 1 to 5 P.M. Adults $1; children under 12, free. 304/465-5617. **Hawks Nest State Park,** on U.S. 60, has an overlook where visitors can view the 60-mile-long New River Canyon. In the park's mountain museum are displays of firearms and items relating to the history of West Virginia. An aerial tramway connects the park's lodge to the marina in the canyon. Park: Always open. Museum: May-Nov., daily, 9 A.M. to 5 P.M. Free. Tram: Memorial Day-Labor Day, Tues.-Sun., 11 A.M. to 7 P.M.; Apr.-Memorial Day, Labor Day-Oct., Sat.-Sun., 11 A.M. to 7 P.M. Adults $1.50, children 75¢. 304/658-5212. (Only lodge open in winter.)

BECKLEY, 20,492, E-4. **Beckley Exhibition Coal Mine,** in New River Park on Paint St. off Valley Dr., is an authentic mine where people ride in remodeled coal cars through 900 feet of underground passageways. The history of mining from the pick and shovel era to mechanization is presented by guides who are former miners. Tours every one-half hour. May-Sept., daily, 10 A.M. to 6 P.M. Adults $3; children under 12, $1.50. 304/257-8671. **Grandview State Park,** south on U.S. 19, then northeast 11 miles on St. 307, is the site of outdoor dramas *Honey in the Rock* and *Hatfields and McCoys.* Mid-June-late Aug., *Hatfields,* Tues., Wed., Thurs., Sat., 8:30 P.M.; *Honey,* Fri., Sun., 8:30 P.M. Admission $3 to $6.50. 304/253-8313.

BERKELEY SPRINGS, 944, B-8. Land where the town now stands was given to the Colony of Virginia by Lord Fairfax in 1776. Because the warm spring water, which has a temperature of 74° F., was believed to have curative powers, the town became a popular health resort. Many well-known people, including George and Martha Washington, came to "Bath," as it was then known, for health and social reasons. In **Berkeley Springs State Park,** near the center of town, are bathhouses which offer a variety of baths, heat and steam treatments, and massages. Main bathhouse:

Year-round, Mon.-Thurs., 8:30 A.M. to noon, 1 to 4 P.M.; Fri., 8:30 A.M. to 8 P.M.; Sat., 8:30 A.M. to 5 P.M.; Sun., 1 to 5 P.M. 304/258-2711. Park: June-Labor Day, daily. Adults $1.25, children 75¢. The **Castle,** northwest on St. 9W, is an English Norman Castle built by 53-year-old Col. Samuel Taylor Suit in 1885 for his young bride; it contains original Victorian furniture. Year-round, daily, 8 A.M. to 8 P.M. Adults $3; persons 65 and over, $2; children $1.50. 304/258-3274.

BETHANY, 1,336, northeast of Wheeling on St. 67, B-5. **Campbell Mansion,** 3/4 mile east on St. 67, was the home of Alexander Campbell, founder of Bethany College. The 27-room mansion, which dates back to 1793, contains furnishings of that period. May-Oct., Tues.-Sun., 10 A.M. to noon, 2 to 4 P.M.; other months, by appointment. Adults $1; students 50¢; under 6, free. 304/829-7341.

BUNKER HILL, 800, south of Martinsburg off U.S. 11, C-8. **Morgan's Cabin,** Runny-Meade Rd., west off U.S. 11 at Bunker Hill, was the home of Col. Morgan ap Morgan, first white settler in what is now West Virginia. Built in 1731-34 with an 1820 addition, it is now reconstructed with part of the original logs. May-Oct., Sat.-Sun., 1 to 6 P.M. Tours by appointment year-round. Free. 304/267-7187. **Morgan's Chapel,** near Morgan's Cabin, was built originally in 1740; the present structure dates to 1851. Site of the first Episcopal congregation in the state, the church was begun by Morgan ap Morgan, Dr. John Briscoe, and Jacob Hite. **Bunker Hill Mill** is one of the oldest mill sites in West Virginia. The present stone building dates to 1800, but the site has been used since 1738. It contains a museum of late 19th- and 20th-century milling equipment. An unusual feature of the mill is that it has two waterwheels. Group tours by appointment. 304/229-8707.

CASS, 173, southeast of Valley Head, D-6. An old logging town off St. 92, it is dominated by **Cass Scenic Railroad,** a steam-powered Shay locomotive which pulls the passenger train through a logging trail in Monongahela National Forest to the top of Bald Knob, second highest point in the state. A four-and-one-half-hour trip goes to the top of Cheat Mountain, Tues.-Sun., noon. A two-hour trip goes to Whittaker Station, Memorial Day-Labor Day, daily, 11 A.M., 1 and 3 P.M. Trains operate same times, Labor Day-Oct., Sat.-Sun. Adults $5; persons 65 and over, $4; 5-11, $3; under 5, free. 304/456-4300. **Snowshoe,** south of Cass off U.S. 219 on top of 4,848-foot-high Cheat Mountain, offers skiing, tennis, hiking, horseback riding, picnicking, boating, and fishing. It has 17 slopes and 10 miles of groomed cross-country trails, a 1,500-foot

vertical drop, and 4 triple chair lifts, one 6,200 feet. Eighty percent of the skiing is on trails 4,000 feet above sea level. Year-round. 304/799-6600.

CEREDO, 2,255, west of Huntington, D-3. **Pilgrim Glass,** adjacent to Huntington's Tri-State Airport, south of Int. 64 off St. 75, has a glass-enclosed gallery where all stages of glassmaking can be viewed. Year-round, Mon.-Fri., 9 A.M. to 4 P.M. Free. 304/453-3553.

CHARLESTON, 63,968, D-4. Chartered in 1794 as Charles Town and changed to its present name in 1819, Charleston was originally the site of Fort Lee, an important frontier post (1788–95) named for Gen. Henry "Light-Horse Harry" Lee (Daniel Boone and his family lived here in the late 1700s). The city has been the state capital since 1885; however, it served in this capacity between 1870 and 1875 when state officers and records were moved here from Wheeling. The present **State Capitol,** on Kanawha Blvd. E, was designed by Cass Gilbert and completed in 1932 at a cost of $10 million; it has a 300-foot dome, once covered with gold, and a 4,000-pound Czechoslovakian crystal chandelier hanging in the Rotunda on a 54-foot, gold-plated chain 180 feet from the floor. Tours leave from the Rotunda every half hour. Year-round, Mon.-Sat., 8:30 A.M. to 4:30 P.M.; Sun., 1 to 4:30 P.M. Free. 304/348-2286. **Governor's Mansion,** 1716 Kanawha Blvd. E, was designed by Walter F. Martens and completed in 1924. Tours start on the half hour from the Capitol Rotunda. Year-round, Thurs.-Fri., 9:30 to 11:30 A.M. Free. 304/348-3588. The **Cultural Center,** Greenbrier and Washington Sts., is a $14 million structure of white Alabama marble containing a museum of West Virginia history, crafts shop, reference library, archives, and theater. Year-round, Mon.-Fri., 9 A.M. to 9 P.M.; Sat.-Sun., 1 to 5 P.M. Free. 304/348-0162 or 304/348-0220. **Sunrise,** 746 Myrtle Rd., a restored mansion, is now an art gallery and museum; it also has a planetarium, small zoo, botanical center, nature trails, and gardens. Year-round, Tues.-Sat., 10 A.M. to 5 P.M.; Sun., 2 to 5 P.M. Free. 304/344-8035. **National Track and Field Hall of Fame,** 1524 Kanawha Blvd. E, houses memorabilia of American track and field champions. Year-round, Mon.-Fri., 9 A.M. to 5 P.M.; tours by appointment. Free. 304/345-0087. **Coonskin Park,** Coonskin Dr., a 1,000-acre park 6 miles from downtown Charleston, has a skeet range, nature trails, 18-hole golf course, driving range, tennis courts, playgrounds, and areas for ice-skating, skiing, boating, and fishing. Year-round, daily, 8 A.M. to dusk. Golf $4, pedal boat per half hour $1.75, swimming $2. 304/345-8000. *See* also **South Charleston.**

CHARLES TOWN, 2,857, C-8. Named for Charles Washington, brother of George Washington, who laid the town out in 1786, the town has many streets bearing names of members of the Washington family. Another resident was W. L. Wilson, postmaster-general (1896), who started America's first rural free delivery in Charles Town. **The Courthouse,** George and Washington Sts., was built in 1837 on the site of an 1803 courthouse, which was destroyed by fire. John Brown was tried for treason here in 1859. Year-round, Mon.-Fri., 9 A.M. to 5 P.M.; Sat., 9 A.M. to noon. Free. 304/725-9761. **Old Opera House,** Liberty and George Sts., was built in 1910 and hosted traveling shows and vaudeville; now restored, it is used for summer productions. Year-round, Mon.-Fri., 9 A.M. to 5 P.M. Free. 304/725-4420. **Charles Town Turf Club,** east on U.S. 340, offers thoroughbred horse racing. Year-round, Wed.-Sat., post time 7:15 P.M.; Sun., 1:30 P.M. Grandstand $1.50, clubhouse $3. 304/725-7001. **Jefferson County Museum,** 200 East Washington St., contains artifacts from the John Brown era, including the wagon which carried Brown to his execution site. Apr.-Oct., Tues.-Sat., 10 A.M. to 4 P.M. Free. 304/725-8628.

DAVIS, 979, C-6. **Blackwater Falls State Park,** just off St. 32, is centered around a five-story waterfall plunging into the Blackwater Canyon. A lodge and recreation center, with naturalist programs, are located on the south rim of the canyon. Year-round. 304/259-5216. **Mountain State Museum,** St. 32, relates the history of early lumbering and mining in West Virginia, dating back to 1884. May-Dec., daily, 10:30 A.M. to 5 P.M.; Jan., Sat.-Sun., same hours. Adults $1.50; students 50¢; under 6, free. 304/259-5323.

FAIRMONT, 26,300, B-6. **Pricketts Fort State Park,** 5 miles north off Int. 70, is a reconstructed 18th-century fort. Interpreters present a living history and show visitors how pioneers lived more than 200 years ago. They demonstrate the skills of candle dipping, soapmaking, weaving, cooking, and sewing. May-Sept., Mon.-Sat., 10 A.M. to 5 P.M.; Sun., noon to 6 P.M.; mid-late Apr., Oct.-Dec., Sat. 10 A.M. to 5 P.M.; Sun., noon to 6 P.M. Adults $1.50, children 75¢. 304/363-3030.

FAYETTEVILLE, 2,366, north of Oak Hill, E-4. On U.S. 19 between Hico and Fayetteville, **New River Gorge Bridge** is a four-lane, steel-arch bridge, claimed to be the longest of its kind in the world. Other statistics claimed for the bridge are that it is the highest span east of the Mississippi River (it rises 876 feet above New River) and the third highest span in the United States. Forty-three million pounds of structural steel were used in building the bridge.

FRANKLIN, 780, D-7. **McCoy's Mill,** south of Franklin on U.S. 220, was built in

1754 and has 40-foot-long, handhewn beams held by pegs. Tours by appointment. 304/358-2271.

GERRARDSTOWN, 250, southwest of Martinsburg on St. 9/51, C-8. **Gerard House,** at the first intersection off St. 51, is one of the oldest stone houses in the state. It was built in 1743 by John Hays and later purchased by David Gerard, founder of Gerrardstown (spelled with two r's). Furnishings are of the mid-1800s; a ladder is used to climb through the trap door to the second floor. May-Oct., Sat.-Sun., 10 A.M. to 5 P.M.; tours by appointment year-round. Free. 304/229-8736.

GRAFTON, 6,845, C-6. An old railroad town chartered in 1856, Grafton was the birthplace of Anna Jarvis, founder of Mother's Day. **Andrews Methodist Church,** 11 East Main St., was the scene of the first Mother's Day observance on May 10, 1908. Apr.-Oct., daily, 9:30 A.M. to noon, 1 to 4 P.M. Free. 304/265-1589. **Grafton National Cemetery,** 431 Walnut St., is the state's only national cemetery. The first Union soldier killed by Confederate forces is buried here. Year-round, daily, 8 A.M. to 5 P.M. Free. 304/265-2044. **Tygart Dam,** Tygart Lake, south of Grafton, controls flooding on the Monongahela River. Tours through the interior of the dam show the machinery which operates it. June-Aug., Wed., 1 P.M. Free. 304/265-1760.

GREEN BANK, 120, D-6. **National Radio Astronomy Observatory,** St. 92, is a national research center for radio astronomers. Tours begin on the hour with a 15-minute movie on radio astronomy, followed by a narrated bus tour and a demonstration of how a radio telescope works. Mid-June-Labor Day, daily, 9 A.M. to 4 P.M.; Memorial Day-June, Sept.-Oct., Sat.-Sun., 9 A.M. to 4 P.M. Free. 304/456-2224.

HARMAN, 181, C-6. The **Old Mill,** north on St. 32, is a gristmill which was built on the Dry Fork River in 1877. The three-story building housed the two water turbines which are still used today in place of a conventional waterwheel. Corn, wheat, rye, and buckwheat are ground into flours, which are available. There are also traditional West Virginia crafts and demonstrations of wool being spun into yarn and woven into cloth. Memorial Day-Labor Day, Mon.-Sat., 10 A.M. to 5 P.M. Free. 304/227-4545.

HARPERS FERRY, 361, C-9. This historic town is in the Eastern Panhandle at the confluence of the Potomac and Shenandoah rivers; in the 19th century, it was a major arms-producing center where the first breech-loading flintlock rifle with interchangeable parts was manufactured. It was here that the militant abolitionist John Brown seized the United States arsenal on October 16, 1859, in an attempt to free the slaves. Brown and his small band of men were taken by the U.S. Marines under Col.

Robert E. Lee, tried for treason, convicted, and hanged. Now under the National Park Service, Harpers Ferry has been restored to its 1859 appearance and is the **Harper's Ferry National Historical Park.** A walking tour of the park area is recommended. *John Brown's Fort,* Old Arsenal Sq., was the armory fire engine house where Brown and his group were captured. Year-round, daily, 8 A.M. to 5 P.M. Free. *Harper House* was built in 1782 by Robert Harper, a millwright. The restored house is the town's oldest surviving structure. Steps from High St., handhewn into the natural stone, lead to the house. Year-round, daily, 8 A.M. to 5 P.M. Free. *Master Armorer's House,* Shenandoah St., was built in 1859 by the armory's chief gunsmith. It is now a museum that traces the history of gun making. Year-round, daily, 8 A.M. to 5 P.M. Free. *Jefferson Rock,* a scenic overlook that Jefferson described in 1783 as "worth a trip across the Atlantic" to view, is above the town. Harpers Ferry National Historical Park Visitors Center, Shenandoah and High Sts., houses exhibits and an audiovisual program. Daily, June-Aug., 8 A.M. to 6 P.M.; other months, 8 A.M. to 5 P.M. Free. 304/535-6371. **John Brown Wax Museum,** High St., depicts scenes from Brown's life through special lighting effects, sound, and animation. Apr.-Nov., daily, 9 A.M. to 5 P.M.; Feb.-Mar., Sat.-Sun., 10 A.M. to 5 P.M. Adults $1.50; high school students $1; elementary school students 75¢; under 6, free. 304/535-6342.

HELVETIA, 50, northwest of Valley Head, D-6. Midway between St. 92 at Mill Creek and St. 20 at French Creek, this is a Swiss community where people still make cheeses in the old-country way. A museum of Swiss artifacts, gift shop, and restaurant are here. 304/924-5467.

HILLSBORO, 276, E-6. **Pearl S. Buck Birthplace, Museum,** north on U.S. 219, is the restored home of the Pulitzer and Nobel Prize winner Pearl Buck, author of *The Good Earth* and many other books. Called the "Stulting House," it was built in 1892 and was the home of the author's grandparents. In the house are some of its original furnishings and memorabilia of the author. Guided tours: Year-round, Mon.-Sat., 9 A.M. to 5 P.M.; Sun., 1 to 5 P.M. Adults $1.50; children 75¢; under 6, free. 304/653-4430. **Droop Mountain Battlefield,** U.S. 219, was the site of a major Civil War battle on November 6, 1863. Part of the battlefield is restored and open to visitors; a small museum contains Civil War artifacts. The 288-acre park also has hiking trails, a playground, and picnic areas. Year-round, daily, 6 A.M. to 10 P.M. 304/653-4254.

HUNTINGTON, 63,684, D-3. Incorporated in 1871, Huntington was named for Chesapeake and Ohio Railroad president Collis P. Huntington, who had designed the city. During the westward expansion of rail transportation, Huntington became the hub of commerce in the West Virginia, Ohio, and Kentucky region. **Huntington Galleries,** 8th St. Rd., Park Hills, is a complete cultural complex with paintings, films, plays, lectures, concerts, library, museum, studio workshops, observatory, bird sanctuary, outdoor amphitheater, and a nature trail. Year-round, Tues.-Sat., 10 A.M. to 4 P.M.; Sun., 1 to 5 P.M. Free. 304/529-2701. **Heritage Village,** 11th St. and Veterans Memorial Blvd., is a restored B & O Railroad yard. It features Victorian architecture, boutiques, and a restaurant which was the old passenger station, circa 1880. Year-round. Most shops: Year-round, Mon.-Sat., 10 A.M. to 5 P.M. Free. 304/696-5954. **Camden Park,** 17th St. exit off Int. 64 to U.S. 60W, is a family amusement park with 26 rides, air-conditioned cafeteria, picnic area, and year-round roller rink. Early May-Labor Day, Tues.-Sun., 10 A.M. to 10 P.M. Park: Admission 25¢, rides extra. All-day pass: $6.50 plus park entrance fee. 304/429-4231. *Camden Queen,* 77-foot replica of an 1890 stern-wheeler, 60-passenger packet boat, leaves Camden Park's landing for one-hour excursions. May-Labor Day, Tues.-Sun., 11 A.M. to 8 P.M. Adults $2.50; children under 13, $1.25. 304/523-9936. **Ritter Rose Garden,** 8th St. Hill, Ritter Park, features four species of roses, including climbers, floribundas, grandifloras, and hybrid teas, with 87 varieties. Always open. Free. 304/696-5954 **Appalachian Craftsmen,** 1209 Third Ave., is a home-industry outlet where patchwork, quilted fashions, and home furnishings produced by more than 100 area craftsmen may be purchased. Year-round, Mon.-Fri., 10 A.M. to 5 P.M.; Sat., 10 A.M. to 3 P.M. 304/525-5189.

See also **Ceredo.**

JACKSON'S MILL, 100, off Int. 79 north of Weston, C-5. Boyhood home of Gen. Thomas J. "Stonewall" Jackson, the first mill was built about 1808 by his grandfather, Col. Edward Jackson. The property is now the site of the West Virginia 4-H Camp. Artifacts of the era are displayed in a museum on the grounds. June-Labor Day, Mon.-Sat., 10:30 A.M. to 5 P.M.; Sun., 1:30 to 5 P.M. Free. 304/269-5100.

LEETOWN, 100, southwest of Shepherdstown, B-8. **Leetown National Fish Hatchery,** north on Co. 1, is a trout and warm-water hatchery. Experimental studies also are conducted here. Grounds open year-round, daily. Visitors Center: May-Sept., daily, 8 A.M. to 4 P.M. Free. 304/725-8461.

LEWISBURG, 3,065, E-5. The town is the site of Fort Savannah, built in 1755. Here at Camp Union, Gen. Andrew Lewis mustered troops which participated in the Battle of Point Pleasant in 1774. **Old Stone Church,** Church St., is one of the oldest churches in continuous use west of the Allegheny Mountains. Built in 1796 by Presbyterian settlers, the church has an adjoining cemetery where many Civil War

Harpers Ferry can trace its origins back to 1733 when a trader by the name of Peter Stephens arrived and started a primitive ferry service at the junction of the Potomac and Shenandoah rivers. But the town takes its name from Robert Harper, a millright who arrived 14 years later. Harper took over the ferry, built a mill, and the town grew steadily for more than a century. The major boosts to its growth occurred in 1790 when President Washington convinced Congress to establish a national armory here, and again in the 1830s when the town benefitted from the construction of the Chesapeake and Ohio Canal and the Baltimore and Ohio Railroad. The decline of Harpers Ferry began on October 16, 1859, with the legendary raid of John Brown, the militant abolitionist. Brown was captured, tried, convicted, and hanged. Sixteen months later the Civil War broke out. Because of its strategic location, Harpers Ferry was often the scene of battles and troop movements. Any hopes of recovery after the war were dashed by a series of destructive floods in the late 1800s. Today Harpers Ferry is a National Historic Park, and many of the buildings, including Brown's Fort, have been restored to their original appearance.

soldiers are buried. Year-round, daily, 9 A.M. to 4 P.M. Free.

LOGAN, 3,029, E-3. **Chief Logan State Park,** U.S. 119, is the site of the outdoor drama *The Aracoma Story,* which portrays the tragic love of Chief Cornstalk's daughter, Aracoma, and a white man. Two weeks, middle of Aug., Thurs.-Sun., 8:45 P.M. Adults $4.50, children $2. 304/752-0253. Members of the Hatfield family, remembered for the infamous Hatfield-McCoy feud, are buried in the **Hatfield Family Cemetery,** just south of Logan. A life-size statue of Devil Anse Hatfield watches over the cemetery. Year-round. Free.

LOST RIVER STATE PARK, C-7. The park was named for nearby Lost River, a stream whose waters vanish beneath the earth, only mysteriously to reappear a few miles beyond as the headwaters of the Cacapon River. The land where the park now stands was the property of the Lee family, who used it as a summer retreat in the 1800s. **Lee Cabin,** which belonged to Revo-

lutionary Gen. Henry "Light-Horse Harry" Lee, has been restored as a museum. Park: Late Mar.-early Dec., daily, 24 hours. Lee Cabin: Memorial Day-Labor Day, daily, 10 A.M. to 6 P.M. Free. 304/897-5372.

MARLINTON, 1,352, E-6. **Edray Trout Hatchery,** Williams River Rd., off U.S. 219, produces rainbow, golden, brook, and brown trout; fish also can be viewed in their natural habitat. Tours: Year-round, daily, 8 A.M. to 5 P.M. Free. 304/799-6461. **Pocahontas County Historical Museum,** 810 2nd Ave., is operated by the Pocahontas County Historical Society and includes displays on all facets of the county's history and its people from the days of the Indians to the present. A Confederate cemetery is on the grounds. June-Labor Day, Mon.-Sat., 11 A.M. to 5 P.M.; Sun., 1 to 5 P.M.; Labor Day-Oct., Sat., 11 A.M. to 5 P.M.; Sun., 1 to 5 P.M. Adults 50¢; persons 12-17, 25¢; children under 12, free. 304/799-6501 or 304/799-4973.

MARTINSBURG, 13,063, C-8. Here was the home of Belle Boyd, Confederate spy. When her house was occupied by Union officers, she listened to their plans and relayed to Gen. Stonewall Jackson information which enabled him to defeat the Union forces. **Adam Stephen's House,** 309 East John St., was the home of the founder of Martinsburg, a leader in the French and Indian War and a major general in the American Revolution. The house, which overlooks the Tuscarora Creek, was constructed in 1773-89. Built of native limestone, it contains fine period furniture. Mid-May-mid-Oct., Sat.-Sun., 2 to 5 P.M.; tours by appointment year-round. Free. 304/267-4796. **Van Meter Ford Bridge,** east of Martinsburg, crosses Opequon Creek. The three-arched bridge, built in 1832, is the oldest known bridge in the state. **Tuscarora Church,** West King St., was established by Scotch-Irish Presbyterians between 1740 and 1790. Wooden pegs on which pioneers hung their guns during services are in the vestibule. Year-round, daily, 8 A.M. to 7 P.M., by appointment. Free. 304/263-4579.

See also **Bunker Hill** and **Gerrardstown.**

MILTON, 1,597, D-3. **Blenko Glass Co.,** Mud River Rd., south of U.S. 60 (Exit 28 from Int. 64), features hand-blown glass created by artisans who use the earliest techniques and tools. There is a gift shop, observation deck, and Designers' Corner where artists from nine leading American stained-glass studios have contributed exhibits of their work. Display room: Mon.-Sat., 8 A.M. to 4 P.M.; Sun., noon to 4 P.M. Craftsmen at work: Mon.-Fri., 8 A.M. to noon, 12:30 to 3:15 P.M. Closed first two weeks in July. Free. 304/743-9081. **Mountaineer Opry House,** 1347 Hillview Dr., has top country and bluegrass music performances, featuring new stars from West Virginia and Nashville, every Saturday

---

Whitewater Rafting Popular on West Virginia Rivers

If you crave high adventure, you'll find it aplenty on a whitewater raft trip down one of West Virginia's untamed rivers. Some 40 professional outfitters operate guided trips in the state and account for about 98 percent of all rafting activity. Most trips begin and end the same day, but some last two days or more. Safety is a high priority among the outfitters, and the state requires that life jackets be worn at all times while on the water. The three most popular rivers are the New River, the Cheat, and the Gauley. For a list of outfitters, write to the Eastern Professional River Outfitters (EPRO), Central Division, Box 55, Thurmond, West Virginia 25936. If you have your own raft and prefer to float on your own, you can push off from numerous "put-ins" along the state's riverbanks. For a list of these places, write to the West Virginia Department of Natural Resources. (See Information Sources, page 198.)

---

night. Year-round, Sat., 8 and 11 P.M. Adults $4.50, children $1. 304/743-6760.

MONONGAHELA NATL. FOREST, D-6. In the Allegheny Mountains, this national forest has many natural attractions. **Cranberry Glades,** on St. 39 near Mill Point, is a natural botanical garden where rare plants grow. Among them are the lowbush cranberry, in primitive conditions. Bog vegetation and flowers are found far south of their normal range. Nearby is the **Cranberry Mountain Visitors Center,** which provides an introduction to Monongahela National Forest and Cranberry Glades; a boardwalk stretches through the fragile glades. Center: Memorial Day-Labor Day, 9 A.M. to 6 P.M.; May, Sept., Oct., Sat.-Sun., 9 A.M. to 6 P.M. Free. 304/846-6558 or 304/653-4826. **Dolly Sods Wilderness,** 10,-215 acres in Tucker and Randolph counties, has rhododendron, second growth hardwood and spruce stands, bogs, streams, beaver ponds, more than 25 miles of hiking trails, hunting, fishing, and camping. 304/636-1800.

MORGANTOWN, 27,605, B-6. Incorporated in 1785, Morgantown is the seat of West Virginia University. An experiment in automated, computer-controlled mass transportation is being conducted on the campus through the use of the Personal Rapid Transit System which connects the university's downtown and Evansdale campuses and the WVU Medical Center. PRT operates year-round, Mon.-Fri., 6:30 A.M. to midnight; Sat.-Sun., 9:30 A.M. to midnight. Fare 25¢. 304/293-3702. **Seneca Glass Co.,** 709 Beechurst Ave., is more than 80 years old. Craftsmen make hand-blown glassware in lead crystal as well as in colors and specialize in decorative cutting. Tours: Year-round, Mon.-Fri., 10 A.M., noon, 1 and 2 P.M. Showroom: Mon.-Fri., 9 A.M. to 4 P.M.; Sat., 9 A.M. to noon. (Closed July 1-15.) Free. 304/201-5035.

MOUNDSVILLE, 12,419, B-5. The city's name is derived from the **Mammoth Grave Creek Indian Mound,** which is located here. Believed to be one of the world's largest Indian mounds, it is 69 feet high and 900 feet in circumference at the base. Numerous Adena relics were discovered in the mound burial chambers when it was excavated in 1838. Year-round, daily, 11 A.M. to 6 P.M. Admission 50¢. 304/843-1410. **Delf Norona Museum,** 801 Jefferson Ave., has exhibits of the Adena culture. Year-round, Mon.-Fri., 10 A.M. to 4:30 P.M.; Sat., 10 A.M. to 4 P.M.; Sun., 1 to 4 P.M. Free. 304/843-1410 or 304/843-1440. **Fostoria Glass Co.,** 1200 1st St., produces hand-blown glass recognized for its clarity and classic styling. Tours: Mon.-Thurs., 8:30 A.M. to 11 A.M., 11:30 A.M. to 3:30 P.M.; Fri., 8:30 to 11 A.M. Free. 304/845-1050.

NEW MARTINSVILLE, 7,109, B-5. **Viking Glass Co.,** 802 Parkway Dr., produces hand-blown and handcrafted glass in

---

various finishes just as it was produced in the first glasshouse in Jamestown, Va., in 1608. Observation area: Year-round, Mon.-Fri., 8 A.M. to 3 P.M. Retail store: Year-round, Mon.-Sat., 8 A.M. to 5 P.M.; Sun. (in summer), noon to 5 P.M. Free. 304/429-1321.

OAK HILL, E-4. *See* **Fayetteville.**

PARKERSBURG, 39,976, C-4. **Blennerhassett Island,** located in the Ohio River just downstream from Parkersburg, was the site of the plantation home of Harman and Margaret Blennerhassett. It was here that Aaron Burr and Blennerhassett allegedly plotted to overthrow the U.S. government in the early 1800s. Archaeological digs are now being undertaken at the mansion and Indian village sites. A self-guided historical map is provided. The stern-wheeler, *Centennial,* transports passengers to the island from The Point, just off St. 68 in downtown Parkersburg, at the confluence of the Ohio and Little Kanawha rivers. June-Aug., Fri.-Sun., 1 to 5 P.M.; Apr.-May, Sept.-Oct., Sat.-Sun., 1 to 5 P.M. Adults $2; children under 12, $1.50. 304/428-3000.

PETERSBURG, 2,084, C-7. **Smoke Hole Cavern,** 8 miles west on St. 28, contains the *Room of a Million Stalactites,* second highest room of any known cavern. It was used during the Civil War to store ammunition. Mar.-Nov., daily, 8 A.M. to 7 P.M. Adults $3.75, children $1.75. 304/257-4442 or 304/257-1705. **Country Store Museum,** north of St. 42, is housed in a reconstructed 100-year-old building; it contains authentic country store furnishings and products. July-Labor Day, Tues.-Sat., 10 A.M. to 4:30 P.M.; Sun., 11:30 A.M. to 4:30 P.M. Adults $1; persons 65 and over, 75¢; children 50¢; under 6, free. 304/257-4026 or 304/257-4811. **Petersburg Trout Hatchery,** 3 miles southwest on Airport Rd., has golden trout, which were discovered and bred here. Year-round, daily, 8 A.M. to 4:30 P.M. Free. 304/257-4014.

PHILIPPI, 3,194, C-6. First land battle of the Civil War was fought in Philippi on June 3, 1861. The covered bridge, jct. U.S. 250 and U.S. 119, was built across the Tygart Valley River in 1852 and used by armies of the North and South in the Civil War; it is still in use.

PIPESTEM RESORT STATE PARK, 14 miles north of Princeton and 12 miles south of Hinton on St. 20, F-4. The park is named for the hollow-stemmed shrub which grows in the area and was used by Indians and early settlers as stems for their pipes. An aerial tram takes visitors to the park's lodge in the Bluestone Canyon. Always open. 304/466-1800.

POINT PLEASANT, 5,682, C-3. **Tu-Endie-Wei State Park,** at the junction of the Ohio and Kanawha rivers, has an 85-foot-high monument commemorating the battle in which Gen. Andrew Lewis and his forces defeated the Shawnee Indians led by

Geology may not have captured your imagination in school, but if you're driving through West Virginia you'll find yourself studying the subject with renewed interest. Outdoor geological laboratories exist wherever roads have been cut through mountains and hillsides, and in mountainous West Virginia that's almost everywhere. The cuts reveal millions of years of earth history at a glance. Even a cursory examination of the strata can tell you things. For example, if one layer is especially thick, you know immediately that the period represented by that layer lasted much longer than the others. Gray layers of limestone reveal the presence of long-vanished oceans; tawny layers of sandstone indicate the existence of a prehistoric beach. And if there's a sandstone on top of limestone, you know that beaches and shallow water replaced an ocean, either because the ocean receded or because the sea floor raised. The angle of the strata discloses even more fascinating information. Sharply slanted layers tell a story of violent forces within the earth, forces so powerful they can raise up mountain ranges or send them toppling.

Chief Cornstalk in 1774. *Mansion House*, erected as a tavern in 1796, is now a museum containing colonial furniture, heirlooms, and relics from the Battle of Point Pleasant. Apr.-mid-Nov., Mon.-Fri., 9 A.M. to 4:30 P.M.; Sat., 9:30 A.M. to 4:30 P.M.; Sun., 1 to 5 P.M. Donations. 304/675-3330. **Mason County Farm Museum,** north of Point Pleasant, east off St. 62, adjacent to the Mason County Fairgrounds, is a living-farm museum containing farm implements, antiques, reconstructed log cabins and church, country store, blacksmith shop, and schoolhouse. Apr.-Oct., Sat., 9 A.M. to 5 P.M.; Sun., 1 to 5 P.M.; Mon.-Fri., by appointment. Free. 304/675-2834 or 304/675-5737.

PRINCETON, F-4. *See* **Pipestem Resort State Park.**

RIVERTON, 150, D-6. **Seneca Caverns,** east of U.S. 33, are interwoven with the legend of the Indian Princess Snow Bird, who was supposed to have lived in this land. In the *Great Ballroom,* according to legend, the Snow Princess married the young brave who proved his love for her by climbing to the peak of the treacherous Seneca Rocks. The *Council Room* was supposed to have been used by Seneca Chief Bald Eagle,

father of Princess Snow Bird, for meeting with his tribe. Memorial Day-Labor Day, daily, 8 A.M. to 7:30 P.M.; Apr.-May, Labor Day-Oct., daily, 9 A.M. to 5 P.M.; Nov., Sat.-Sun., 9 A.M. to 5 P.M. Adults $3, children $1.50. 304/567-2691 or 304/567-2619.

SHEPHERDSTOWN, 1,791, B-8. Claimed to be the oldest town in the state, it was presumably settled between 1730 and 1734, although the first settlers probably arrived as early as 1719. Chartered originally in 1762 as Mecklenburg, the name was changed to Shepherd's Town in 1798 and to Shepherdstown in 1867. The first newspaper in the state, the *Potowmak Guardian and Berkeley Advertiser,* was published here in November, 1790. **James Rumsey Monument,** north end of Mill St., overlooks the Potomac River where James Rumsey gave the first public demonstration of the steamboat in 1787.

See also **Leetown.**

SOUTH CHARLESTON, 15,968, west of Charleston, D-4. **Adena Indian Burial Mound,** U.S. 60, is the second largest mound in West Virginia; it was opened in 1883 by the Smithsonian Institution. Always open. Free. 304/744-0051.

SPRUCE KNOB-SENECA ROCKS NATIONAL RECREATION AREA, C-7. More than 100,000 acres in the Monongahela National Forest have been set aside as a national recreation area. In the area are 4,862-foot-high Spruce Knob, highest point in West Virginia, and Seneca Rocks, a 900-foot-high strata of Tuscarora sandstone of the Silurian Age. Visitors Center: Memorial Day-Labor Day, Mon.-Fri., 9 A.M. to 5 P.M.; year-round, Sat.-Sun., 9 A.M. to 4 P.M. 304/567-2827.

SUMMERSVILLE, 2,429, D-5. **Carnifex Ferry Battlefield State Park,** southwest off St. 39, was the site of the 1861 Civil War battle. *Patteson House,* which marked the division of the Union and Confederate lines during the skirmish, contains Civil War relics. Park: Memorial Day-Labor Day, daily, 24 hours. Museum: May-Sept., daily, 8 A.M. to 10 P.M. Free. 304/872-3773.

TALCOTT, 450, southwest of Alderson, E-5. **Big Bend Tunnels,** St. 3, 6,500-foot-long twin railroad tunnels, have been immortalized by John Henry, the "steel-driving" man. According to legend, Henry worked on the tunnels in 1873 and died after winning a race with a hand drill against a steam-powered drill during the construction of the Chesapeake and Ohio Railroad. A statue of Henry stands in a small overlook on the highway.

TRIADELPHIA, A-5. *See* **Bethany.**

VALLEY HEAD, D-6. *See* **Cass** and **Helvetia.**

WESTON, 6,250, C-5. **West Virginia Glass Specialty Co.,** Exit 96, Int. 79, U.S. 19N, features hand-blown crystal tableware and fired-in ceramic decorated glassware. Tours: Year-round, except July 1-14, Mon.-Fri., 9:30 A.M., 10 A.M., 2 P.M. Children under 12 not admitted. Free. 304/269-2842. *See also* **Jackson's Mill.**

WHEELING, 43,070, A-5. **Jamboree, U.S.A.,** 1015 Main St., is a long-running Saturday evening country-western show heard live on WWVA in the U.S. and Canada. Superstars appear at the Capitol Music Hall regularly. Year-round, Sat., 7:30 and 10 P.M. Admission $6-$8. 304/233-5511. **Oglebay Park,** north of Int. 70, Oglebay Park exit on St. 88N, is a 1,500-acre municipal resort park with facilities for golfing, boating, fishing, swimming, tennis, riding, and skiing. Year-round. 304/242-3000. Also in the park are *Good Zoo,* which features wildlife native to North America and *Benedum Natural Science Theater,* which uses lasers and planetarium projectors and other special equipment to teach science and make the "student" feel a part of what's happening. Zoo and theater: Jan.-Apr., Sept.-Dec., daily, 11 A.M. to 5 P.M.; other months, Mon.-Fri., 10 A.M. to 6 P.M.; Sat., 10 A.M. to 7 P.M.; Sun., 10 A.M. to 8 P.M. Adults $2.75; persons 12-18, $1.50; 2-12, $1.25; under 2, free. 304/242-3000. *Mansion Museum,* summer home of Earl W. Oglebay, who gave the property to the city of Wheeling, contains a large collection of glass produced in and around Wheeling. Year-round, Mon.-Sat., 9:30 A.M. to 5 P.M.; Sun., 1:30 P.M. to 5 P.M. Adults $2, students $1, children free. **West Virginia Independence Hall-Custom House,** 16th and Market Sts., is the site of the meeting in which Virginia's secession from the Union was declared unlawful and the stage was set for the birth of West Virginia. Year-round, Tues.-Fri., 10 A.M. to 4 P.M.; Sat., 1 to 4 P.M. Free. 304/233-1333. **Wheeling Downs,** Wheeling Island, offers greyhound racing. Year-round, Mon.-Sat., 7:30 P.M.; matinees Wed., Sat., 2 P.M. Admission $1. 304/232-5050.

WHITE SULPHUR SPRINGS, 3,371, E-5. **Coal House,** east on U.S. 60, is a private residence and shop built entirely of cannel coal. The blocks were shaped with hatchets and connected with black mortar, and the exterior was glazed to make it waterproof. A shop features coal-crafted items. Apr.-Dec., Mon.-Sat., 8 A.M. to 6 P.M.; Jan.-Mar., Mon.-Sat., 9 A.M. to 5 P.M. 304/536-1598. On U.S. 60 on a lake-dotted plateau is the resort **White Sulphur Springs** and its world-famous hotel, **The Greenbrier.** The springs have been nationally famous since colonial days; fashionable people from the Old South came here as early as 1778, believing the spring waters had curative powers. The first unit of the present Greenbrier Hotel was built in 1913; from 1941 to 1942, it was used for the internment of foreign diplomats. In 1942 the U.S. government converted the hotel into a hospital for wounded soldiers; it reverted to its former owner, the Chesapeake and Ohio Railway Company, in 1946 and reopened in 1948. Always open. 304/536-1110. **Federal Fish Hatchery,** U.S. 60, was established in 1902 and produces several thousand fish annually. Brook, rainbow, brown trout, and bass are raised here. Visitors Center: Year-round, daily, 8 A.M. to 5 P.M. Free. 304/536-1361.

WILLIAMSON, 5,219, E-3. Located in the "Heart of the Billion-Dollar Coal Field," **Coal House Building,** Courthouse Sq., was constructed in 1933 from 65 tons of locally mined bituminous coal. It now houses Tug Valley Chamber of Commerce. Year-round, Mon.-Fri., 9 A.M. to 5 P.M. Free. 304/235-5240.

WILLIAMSTOWN, 3,095, C-4. At **Fenton Art Glass Co.,** Carolina Ave., centuries-old tools and techniques are used in the making of glass, with each glass object being individually molded and blown. Tours: June-Aug., Mon.-Fri., 8:40 to 10 A.M., 11:20 A.M. to 2:20 P.M., 4:20 to 7:20 P.M.; Sept.-Dec., Mar.-May, Tues. and Thurs., also 5:20 to 7:20 P.M. Free. 304/375-7772.

West Virginia Campgrounds

FEES REFLECT MINIMUM RATE FOR 2 ADULTS AND ARE SUBJECT TO INCREASE OR SEASONAL CHANGES

- • – at the campground
- ○ – within one mile of campground
- $ – extra charge
- ** – limited facilities during winter months
- A – adults only
- B – 10,000 acres or more
- C – contribution

- E – tents rented
- F – entrance fee or premit required
- N – no specific number, limited by size of area only
- P – primitive
- R – reservation required
- S – self-contained units only

- U – unlimited
- V – trailers rented
- Z – reservations accepted
- LD – Labor Day
- MD – Memorial Day
- UC – under construction
- d – boat dock

- g – public golf course within 5 miles
- h – horseback riding
- j – whitewater running craft only
- k – snow skiing within 25 miles
- l – boat launch
- m – area north of map
- n – no drinking water

- p – motor bikes prohibited
- r – boat rental
- s – stream, lake or creek water only
- t – tennis
- u – snowmobile trails
- w – open certain off-season weekends
- y – drinking water must be boiled

Map Reference	Park Name	Access	Acres	Tent Spaces	Trailer Spaces	Approximate Fee	Season	Other Swimming Swimming Pool	Fishing	Boating	Playground	Other	Telephone Number	Mail Address
	STATE PARKS													
E5	Babcock	Fr Rainelle, 11 mi W on US 60, 3 mi S on Hwy 41	3227	40	40	4.00	4/1-11/1	$ •	•	r	•	gt		Clifftop 25822
C6	Blackwater Falls	Fr Thomas, 2 mi S on Hwy 32, 2 mi SW	1679	65	65	4.00	5/1-10/15	○	○	r	•	ght		Davis 26260
F5	Bluestone	Fr Hinton, 9 mi S on Hwy 20	1346	79	79	4.00	5/1-10/30	$	○	l	•	g		Bx 3, Athens, Sr.Hinton 25951
D5	Holly River	Fr Webster Sprgs., 24 mi N on Hwy 20	7677	88	88	5.00	5/1-10/15	$		•	•	t		Hacker Valley 26222
C4	North Bend	Fr Ellenboro, 8 mi S on Hwy 16, 6 mi W	1405	55	55	4.00	5/1-10/30	$	○		•	gt		Cairo 26337
C6	Tygart Lake	Fr Grafton, 5 mi S on US 119/250	1803	40	17	4.00	5/1-10/15		○	r	•	g		Rt 1, Grafton 26354
E6	Watoga	Fr Marlinton, 6 mi S on Hwy 39, 10 mi SW	B	88	88	5.00	5/1-10/15	$	○ ○	r	•	ght		Marlinton 24948
C6	Audra	Fr Philippi, 9 mi SW on US 119, 6 mi SE on Co	335	65	65	4.00	5/1-10/30		○ ○		•	g		RFD 5, Buckhannon 26223
C5	Cedar Creek	Fr Glenville, 3 mi SW on US 33, 6 mi S	2034	22	22	4.00	4/30-11/1	$		•	•	t		Glenville 26351
C6	Canaan Valley	Fr Davis, 10 mi S on Hwy 32	6250	34	34	6.00	All year	$	$		•	gkt		Davis 26260
F4	Pipestem	Fr Hinton, 17 mi S on Hwy 20	4800	50	30	6.00	All year	$	$		•	ghkt		Pipestem 25979
D3	Beech Fork-Bowen Branch	Fr Huntington, 8 mi SE on Hwy 10	2000	276	276	6.00	All year			l	•			Rt2 Bx 591,Barboursville25504
F4	Twin Falls	Fr Beckley, SW on Hwy 16, N on Hwy 54, W on Hwy 97	3776	50	50	4.00	5/1-10/15	$			•	gt		P O Box 1023, Mullens 25882
	STATE HUNTING - FISHING AREAS													
E3	Fork Creek	Fr Marmet, 8 mi S on US 119, 10 mi SW to Nellis	B	P20	P20	3.00	All year		•					Nellis 25142
E3	Laurel Lake	Fr US 52, 7 mi E on Hwy 65, NE on Co 3/5	B	P15	P15	4.00	All year	$	•					Lenore 25676
D3	Chief Cornstalk	US 35 to Southside; Nine-Mile Rd nr Pine Grove Church	2	P25	P25	3.00	All year		•					Southside 25187
E6	Handley	On Williams River Rd, 8 mi beyond Edray Fish Hatchery		P14	P14	3.00	All year		•					Rt 1, Marlinton 24954
F5	Bluestone	Fr Hinton, S on Hwy 12	B	P400	P400	2.50	All year		○ $					Indian Mills 24949

Map Reference	Park Name	Access	Acres	Tent Spaces	Trailer Spaces	Approximate Fee	Season	Other Swimming	Swimming Pool	Fishing	Boating	Playground	Other	Telephone Number	Mail Address
E4	Plum Orchard Lake	Fr Charleston, S on I-77 to Mossy Interchange (Ext 4)	2625	P25		3.00	All year			•	•		dlr		Scarbro 25917
F5	Moncove Lake	Fr Union, 10 mi E on Hwy 3, 6 mi N on Hwy 8	300	30	30	4.00	All year			•	•	p	dlr		Gap Mills 24941
C7	Short Mtn	Fr Romney, 8 mi E on US 50, 8 mi S on Hwy 7; fol signs	8800	P30		2.50	All year			•		p			Kirby 26729
C7	Nathaniel Mtn	Fr Romney, 4 mi E on US 50, S on Hwy 10; fol signs	9000	P35		2.50	All year			•		p			Kirby 26729
B8	Sleepy Creek	Fr Berkeley Sprg, 6 mi SE on Hwy 9	B	P75	P75	2.50	All year			•		p	dl		Jones Springs 24901
E3	Big Ugly	Fr Ranger, 9 mi S on Hwy 10	7500	P18	P18	3.00	All year			•					Harts 24901
C6	Pleasants Cr	Fr Grafton, 5 mi S on US 250/119	2500	P35	P35	2.50	5/30-LD			•	•	p	dl		Rt 3, Philippi 26416
C3	McClintic	Fr Pt Pleasant, 7 mi N on Hwy 62		9	9	3.00	All year			o	o	g	r		Rt 1,Bx 125,Pt Pleasant 25500
C5	Conaway Run	Fr Alma, on Hwy 18, fol signs		15	15	3.00	All year			•		g	r		Box 98, Alma 26320
C6	Teter Creek	Fr Belington, 4 mi N on Hwy 92, 3 mi E		20	20	3.00	All year			•		g	r		Rt 1, Montrose 26283
B5	Lewis Wetzel	Fr Jacksonburg, 2 mi S on Hwy 20		12	12	2.50	All year			•		g			Rt 1, Jacksonburg 26377
	STATE FORESTS														
B6	Coopers Rock	Fr Morgantown, 10 mi E on Hwy 73, 1 mi S	B	24	24	4.00	5/1-11/1	o	o		•	gk			Rt 1, Bruceton Mills 26525
E5	Greenbrier	Fr White Sulphur Sprgs, 4 mi W on US 60, 1 mi S	5001	16	16	4.00	5/1-10/15	•	•	o		gh	r •		Caldwell 24925
D4	Kanawha	Fr Charleston, 10 mi S on US 119 & Louden Hts Rd	6597	20	43	5.00	5/1-10/30	•	•			•			Rt 2, Box 285,Charlstn 25314
D6	Kumbrabow	Fr Elkins, 22 mi S on US 219, W on access rd	9431	7	7	3.00	4/1-10/15	•	•			•			Box 10, Huttonsville 26273
F3	Panther	Fr Iaeger, 1 mi N on US 52, 12 mi W	7810	6	6	4.00	4/1-10/15	•	•			•			Panther 24872
E6	Seneca	Fr Bartow, 15 mi S on Hwy 28 to Dunmore, 5 mi SW	B	10	10	4.00	4/1-12/10	o	o			•	r		Rt 1, Dunmore 24934
E3	Cabwaylingo	Fr Ferguson, 5 mi S on US 52, E on access rd	8036	34	34	3.00	5/1-11/1	•	•	•		•			Rt 1, Dunlow 25511
F4	Camp Creek	Fr Camp Creek PO, W on access rd	5897	12	12	3.00	4/1-10/31	•	•			•			Camp Creek 25820
	NATIONAL FORESTS Monongahela NF														
E6	Lake Sherwood West Shore	Fr Neola, 11 mi NE on Hwy 14	10	25	25	3.00	3/1-12/31			•			dlr		Neola
E6	Blue Bend CG	Fr W Sulphur SP, 9 mi N on Hwy 92, 2.6 mi W on Hwy 16, 1.2 mi W on Hwy 21.	12	22	22	2.00	3/1-12/31	1		•					W Sulphur SP
E6	Lake Sherwood Pine Run	Fr Neola, 11 mi NE on Hwy 14.	15	35	35	3.00	5/24-9/1	1		•			dlr		Neola
E6	Blue Meadow	Fr W Sulphur, 9 mi N on Hwy 92, 2.6 mi W on Hwy 16, 1 mi W on Hwy 21	10	18	14	3.00	5/24-9/1	1	1						W Sulphur
C6	Bear Heaven	Fr Bowden, 2.3 mi E on US 33, 2.9 mi NW on FR 91	2	7	7	None	4/1-11/30	5					n		Bowden
C6	Stuart	Fr Bowden, 3.9 mi W on US 33, .5 mi NW on Hwy 6, .2 mi NW on FR 391.	9	27	27	2.00	5/30-9/10	1	1						Bowden
C6	Seneca	Fr Onego, 2 mi NW on US 33, .7 mi SW on Hwy 7	3	6	6	None	4/1-11/15			•					Onego
C7	Smoke Hole	Fr Upper Tract, 1.5 mi on US 220, 4 mi N on Hwy 2	3	12	12	2.00	4/1-10/15			•					Upper Tract
C7	Big Bend Upper	Fr Upper Tract, 1.5 mi on US 220, 8.5 mi N on Hwy 2.	18	29	29	2.00	5/1-9/30			•					Upper Tract
C7	Big Bend Lower	Fr Upper Tract, 1.5 mi on US 220, 8.5 mi N on Hwy 2.	7	12	12	2.00	3/15-12/15			•					Upper Tract
D6	Judy Springs	Fr Riverton, .2 mi S on US 33, 2.6 mi W on CO 4, 10.2 mi S on FR 112, 3 mi N on FR 515.	2	6		None	5/1-10/15			•					Riverton
D6	Spruce Knob Lake	Fr Cherry Grove, 2.5 mi SW on Hwy 28, 9 mi NW on Co 10, .7 mi NE on FR 112, .5 mi SW on FR 1.	10	43	30	2.00	4/1-11/1	1					dl		Cherry Grove
C6	Horseshoe	Fr St. George, 3 mi E on Hwy 1, 4 mi NE on Hwy 7	3	10	10	2.00	5/30-9/10	1		•					St. George
E6	Pocahontas	Fr Minnehaha Springs, 3 mi SE on Hwy 39, 2.5 mi S on Hwy 92	6	9	9	2.00	3/1-12/1			•					Minnehaha Springs
D5	Big Rock	Fr Richwood, 6.2 mi N on FR 76	1	5	5	None	3/15-12/1			•					Richwood
D5	Summit Lake	Fr Richwood, 9.9 mi E on Hwy 39	15	33	33	2.00	3/15-12/1			•			d		Richwood
D5	Cranberry	Fr Richwood, 13.4 mi NE on FR 76	17	30	23	2.00	3/15-12/1			•					Richwood
D6	Laurel Fork	Fr Bartow, 3 mi NE on US 250, 1.9 mi NE on Hwy 28, 18.4 mi N on FR 14, 1.6 mi SE on FR 423	4	6	6	None	4/15-11/30			•					Bartow
	Bird Run	Fr Frost, 1.5 mi E on Hwy 84	7	10	10	2.00	3/1-12/1			•					Frost
D6	Tea Creek	Fr Marlinton, 4 mi N on Hwy 219, 12 mi W on Hwy 17, 3 mi NW on FR 86	5	8	8	2.00	3/1-12/1			•					Marlinton
D6	Day Run	Fr Marlinton, 4 mi N on US 219, 12 mi W on Hwy 17, 1 mi S on FR 216	8	10	10	2.00	3/1-12/1			•					Marlinton
C7	Red Creek	Fr Cabins, 4.5 mi S on Hwy 28, 1 mi N on Hwy 4, 6 mi W on FR 19, 5 mi N on FR 75	2	12	12	2.00	5/1-11/15						n		Cabins
	George Washington NF														
D7	Camp Run	Fr Brandywine, 4 mi N on US 33, 10 mi N on Hwy 3, 2 mi E on Co 3	3	9		None	4/1-12/1	1					d		Brandywine
D7	Brandywine Lake	Fr Brandywine, 2 mi E on US 33	10	31	31	2.00	5/15-12/1	•	•				d		Brandywine
D7	Wolf Gap	Fr Edinburg, Virginia, 12.1 mi NW on Hwy 675	5	10		None	All year	4				h	n		Edinburg, Virginia
D7	Trout Pond	Fr Lost River, 3.5 mi E on Hwy 259-5, 1 mi S on FR 500	21	10	40	3.00	4/15-12/1					h	dl		Lost River
C8	Hawk	Fr Wardensville, 5.6 mi NE on Hwy 55, 2.9 mi NE on FR 502, 1.1 mi W on FR 347	6	15	15	None	All year					h	n		Wardensville
	CORPS OF ENGINEERS Sutton Lake		B											304/765-7192	Box 426, Sutton 26601
D5	Kanawha Run	Fr Sutton, 3 mi N on US 19, 11 mi E on Hwy 15	45		151	4.00	LD-MD	•	•			•	l		Sutton 26601
D5	Bakers Run-Mill Creek	Fr Sutton, 3 mi N on US 19, 11 mi E on Hwy 17	40		130	4.00	LD-MD	•	•			•	l		Sutton 26601
D5	Brocks Run	Fr Sutton, 3 mi N on US 19, 6 mi E on Hwy 15, 2 mi S on Hwy 22/12 & 22/11	12		22	None	All year	•	•				l		Sutton 26601
	Bee Run Trailer Pk	Fr Sutton, 3 mi N on US 19, 1 mi E on Hwy 15, 1 mi S on Hwy 15/1	2		12	None	All year	o	o				lr		Sutton 26601
E5	Summersville Lake Battle Run	Fr Summersville, 7 mi S on US 19, 4 mi W on Hwy 129	10		100	4.00	MD-LD	•	•			•	l	304/872-3459	Bx 250 R 2,Summersville 26651
E3	East Lynn Lake East Fork Camping Area	Fr Wayne, 17 mi E on Hwy 37, 2 mi S on access rd	13	N	100	4.00	5/1-11/1	•	•			•	l p		East Lynn

ACKNOWLEDGMENTS

The Travel Editors of *Southern Living* magazine and of Rand McNally take a great deal of satisfaction in bringing you this edition of *Travel South*.

We think ours is a natural collaboration. No group has more personal knowledge of vacation destinations, events, historical sites, museums, and just interesting locations in the American South than the travel staff of *Southern Living*. And no one has more experience and expertise in creating readable maps than Rand McNally. Its cartographers have a sophisticated system for keeping maps up-to-date, while the Rand McNally editors have insight into travel in the South.

We have made every effort to include the type of maps and the kind of information to help you and your family plan your next trip, whether it is an extended vacation or an overnight excursion. We hope the beautiful photography in the book will move you to visit new places your family has never seen.

All the sites and events in the book have been checked by editors of our combined staffs. We have presented them as we found them, but because circumstances occasionally force changes, we recommend you check with local sponsors before driving long distances.

Please use the maps and the information in this book in the coming year and write us with any suggestions you have to improve the contents of the book or the form in which it is presented.

Southern Living® Travel South

Southern Living®

Travel Editor: Karen Lingo

Southwest Travel Editor: Les Thomas

Assistant Travel Editor: Gary D. Ford

Assistant Travel Editor: Dianne Young

Outdoor Living Editor: Glenn Morris

Director of Photography: Bruce Roberts

Senior Photographer: Geoffrey Gilbert

Senior Photographer: Mike Clemmer

Staff Photographer: Beth Maynor

Oxmoor House, Inc.

Editor: Karen Phillips Irons

Rand McNally & Company

Editor: Dorothy Millikan

Associate Editor: Mike Urban

Art Director: Gordon Hartshorne

Designer: Linda Kolarich

Photographs: Cover, Gulf Coast, Florida; page 1, Atlantic Coast, Florida; pages 2 and 3, left to right and top to bottom, Guadalupe Mountains, Texas; yellow-crowned night heron, Pascagoula Area, Mississippi; Greer's Ferry Lake, Arkansas; shells, Sanibel Island, Florida; Bayou Lafourche, Louisiana; Cranberry Glades, West Virginia; boots, Fort Worth Stockyards, Texas; pages 4 and 5, St. Marks Lighthouse, near Tallahassee, Florida.